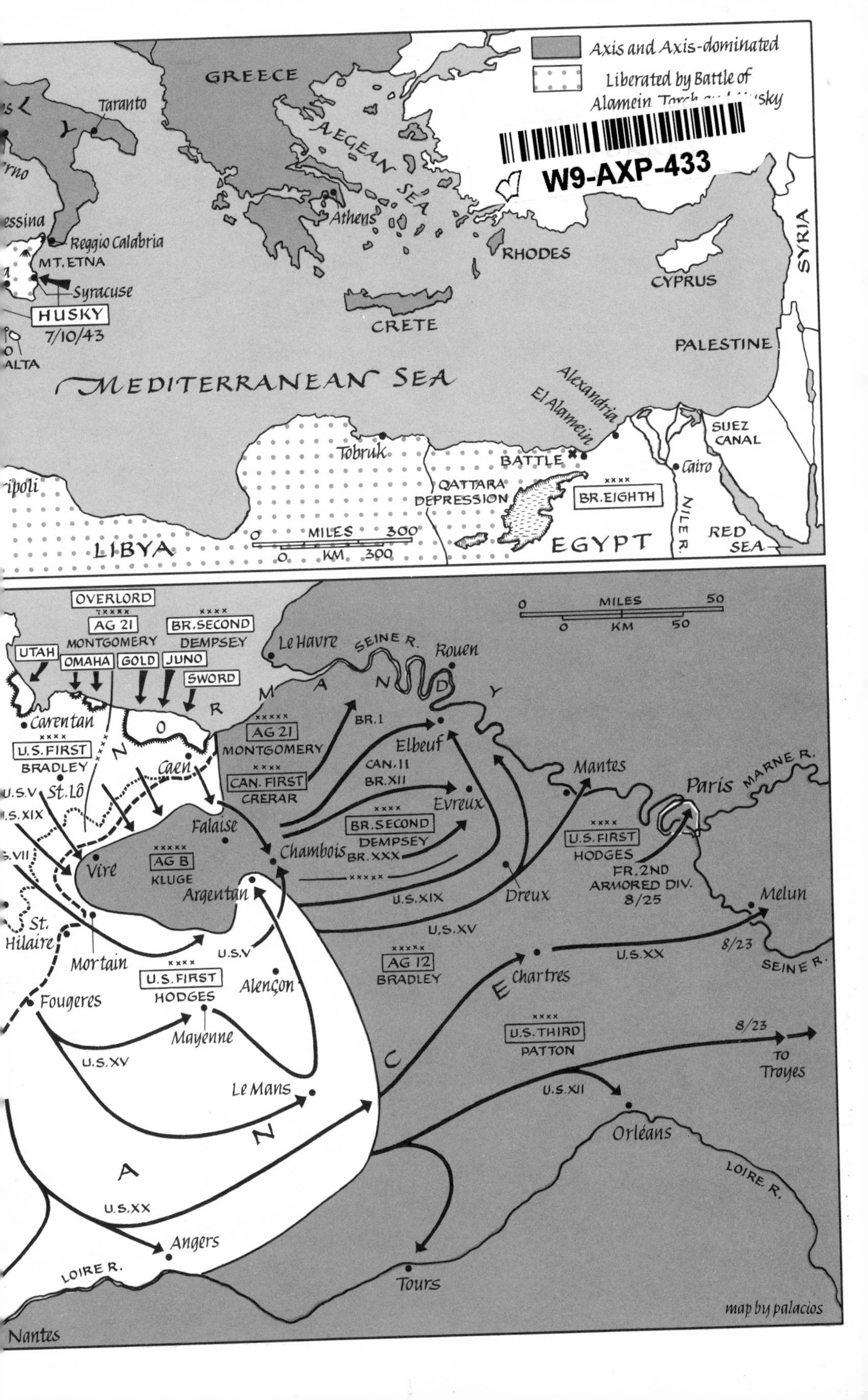
Axis and Axis-dominated
Liberated by Battle of Alamein, Torch and Husky
W9-AXP-433
GREECE
Taranto
AEGEAN SEA
Athens
Messina
Reggio Calabria
MT. ETNA
Syracuse
HUSKY
7/10/43
RHODES
CYPRUS
SYRIA
CRETE
PALESTINE
MEDITERRANEAN SEA
Alexandria
El Alamein
SUEZ CANAL
Tobruk
BATTLE
Cairo
QATTARA DEPRESSION
BR. EIGHTH
NILE R.
RED SEA
LIBYA
EGYPT
0 MILES 300
0 KM 300
OVERLORD
AG 21
MONTGOMERY
BR. SECOND
DEMPSEY
UTAH
OMAHA
GOLD
JUNO
SWORD
0 MILES 50
0 KM 50
Le Havre
SEINE R.
Rouen
NORMANDY
Carentan
U.S. FIRST
BRADLEY
AG 21
MONTGOMERY
BR. 1
Elbeuf
CAN. FIRST
CRERAR
CAN. II
BR. XII
Caen
Mantes
Paris
MARNE R.
U.S. V
St. Lô
U.S. XIX
Evreux
Falaise
BR. SECOND
DEMPSEY
BR. XXX
U.S. FIRST
HODGES
U.S. VII
Vire
AG B
KLUGE
Chambois
Argentan
FR. 2ND ARMORED DIV. 8/25
Dreux
U.S. XIX
Melun
St. Hilaire
Mortain
U.S. XV
U.S. V
AG 12
BRADLEY
U.S. XX
8/23
SEINE R.
U.S. FIRST
HODGES
Alençon
Chartres
Fougeres
Mayenne
FRANCE
U.S. THIRD
PATTON
8/23
TO Troyes
U.S. XV
Le Mans
U.S. XII
Orléans
LOIRE R.
U.S. XX
Angers
LOIRE R.
Tours
Nantes
map by palacios

Also by Stephen E. Ambrose

Ike's Spies:
Eisenhower and the Espionage Establishment

Rise to Globalism:
American Foreign Policy 1938–1970

Crazy Horse and Custer:
The Parallel Lives of Two American Warriors

Eisenhower and Berlin, 1945

Duty, Honor, Country:
A History of West Point

The Supreme Commander:
The War Years of General Dwight D. Eisenhower

EISENHOWER

Volume One

Soldier
General of the Army
President-Elect
1890-1952

STEPHEN E. AMBROSE

SIMON AND SCHUSTER
NEW YORK

Published by Simon and Schuster
A Division of Simon & Schuster, Inc.
Simon & Schuster Building
Rockefeller Center
1230 Avenue of the Americas
New York, New York 10020
SIMON AND SCHUSTER *and colophon*
are registered trademarks of Simon & Schuster, Inc.
Designed by Edith Fowler
Manufactured in the United States of America

10 9 8 7 6 5 4 3 2 1

Library of Congress Cataloging in Publication Data

Ambrose, Stephen E.
Eisenhower

Includes bibliographical references and indexes.
Contents: v. 1. Soldier, general of the army, President-elect, 1890–1952.
1. Eisenhower, Dwight D. (Dwight David), 1890–1969.
2. Presidents—United States—Biography. I. Title.
E836.A828 1983 973.921'092'4 [B] 83-9892
ISBN 0-671-44069-1 (v. 1)

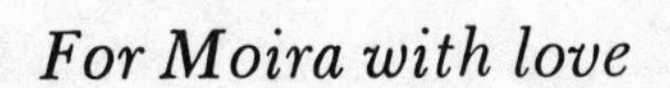

For Moira with love

CONTENTS

FOREWORD

DWIGHT EISENHOWER was a great and good man. He was one of the outstanding leaders of the Western world of this century. As a soldier he was, as George C. Marshall said at the end of the war, everything that the U.S. Army hoped for in its finest products—professionally competent, well versed in the history of war, decisive, well disciplined, courageous, dedicated, and popular with his men, his subordinates, and his superiors. His leadership qualities also included a high degree of intelligence, integrity, commitment to basic principles, dignity, organizational genius, tremendous energy, and diplomatic ability. As a man, he was good-looking, considerate of and concerned about others, loyal to his friends and family, given to terrible rages (which he learned to control), ambitious, thin-skinned and sensitive to criticism, stubborn and inflexible about his habits, an avid sportsman and sports fan, modest (but never falsely so), almost embarrassingly unsophisticated in his musical, artistic, and literary tastes, intensely curious about people and places, often refreshingly naïve, fun-loving—in short, a wonderful man to know or be around. Nearly everyone who knew him liked him immensely, many—including some of the most powerful men in the world—to the point of adulation.

This is a biography of that man. It is not a study of his "life and times." The distinction between the two types of books is, I think, clear. A biography concentrates on the man, his achievements, triumphs, disappointments, failures, and concerns. It is more interested in what he felt and experienced and thought than it is with the events of his lifetime. Biography takes its cue from the man himself; what was important to him is what is important to his biographer. What follows, then, is less a study of the Supreme Commander, or the Chief of Staff, or the president of Columbia University, or the presidential candidate, than it is a study of Dwight Eisenhower.

To be specific, in an earlier study of Eisenhower during the war,* I was concerned with the role of the Supreme Commander—what he did, and why, with what results, within the context of the vast organization he commanded. In that work, there is a great deal of detail about his staff, his plans, his operations, his superiors, his decisions as Supreme Commander, and almost nothing about his personal life. For example, his wife's name appeared but four times in that book's 732 pages, his son's name only six times, and Kay Summersby's name but once. These people were of almost no importance to his actions as the Supreme Commander. But they were of central importance to Dwight Eisenhower the man—he thought about them, worried about them, corresponded with them at length, and looked to them as the sustaining force that made it possible for him to bear his great burdens. Thus their names, their activities, and their relationship with Eisenhower are one of the main features of this book.

The point of view throughout is Eisenhower's; the concentration is on the issues, people, events, and developments that he concentrated upon. I limit the perspective to what he knew, about his enemies, his friends, his superiors, and his subordinates. I am greatly concerned with what his appreciation was of Hitler's, Rundstedt's, and Rommel's situation and intentions from 1942 to May 1945; I seldom undertake an analysis of what their actual situation and intentions were. In the same way, I attempt to understand and describe his appreciation of Stalin's situation and intentions in the period May 1945–November 1952, without attempting any deep analysis of how right or wrong he was about the scope and nature of the Communist threat.

In a previous work,† I have argued that Eisenhower—like Truman and indeed nearly every American politician of the early Cold War—exaggerated Russian strength and misread Stalin's intentions, that what Americans saw as a drive to world conquest by the Communists was in

* *The Supreme Commander: The War Years of General Dwight D. Eisenhower* (Garden City, N.Y.: Doubleday & Co., 1970).
† *Rise to Globalism: American Foreign Policy Since 1938* (London and New York: Penguin, 1972).

fact a defensive policy designed to protect the security of the Soviet Union. But such speculative analysis does not, in my view, belong in a biography. What Eisenhower thought, and why he thought it, does belong.

The vast majority of citations in this book are from Eisenhower's own words—his personal letters, his directives, his memorandums, his diary entries, his telegrams and cables, his speeches, his memoirs, and his statements in dozens of interviews from 1962 to 1969. Only occasionally do I yield to the temptation to second-guess his decisions, and even then I almost always do so within the context of his own, later, self-criticism.

It is not my primary task, as I see it, to judge the man, but rather to explain and describe him. In the process, I hope that I convey some sense of what a truly extraordinary person he was, and—to indulge in one additional judgment—of how much all of us who live in freedom today owe to him.

CHAPTER ONE

Pennsylvania, Texas, Kansas

1741–1900

HIS HERITAGE was ordinary, his parents were humble folk, his childhood was typical of thousands of other youngsters growing up around the turn of the century, and most of his career was humdrum and unrewarded. On the surface, everything about him appeared to be average. Had he died in 1941, on the verge of retirement on his fifty-first birthday, he would not today be even a footnote to history.

Yet Dwight Eisenhower was born to command and became one of the great captains of military history. He was also born to lead, and although he was sixty-one years old before he stood for public office, he became one of the most successful Presidents of the twentieth century.

Eisenhower was born in the year the American frontier came to an end. He died in the year that man walked on the moon. In his lifetime, the pace of technological change was breathtaking, but hardly more so than the changes in American and world politics. Only a handful of men—Lenin, Stalin, Hitler, Mao, Churchill, Wilson, Franklin Roosevelt, and perhaps one or two more—had a greater role than he did in shaping the world of the mid-twentieth century. For the two decades from 1941 to 1961, Eisenhower played a central and crucial role in world events. He was the victorious general who, after the greatest war in history, led his people on the path of peace.

During his period of preparation, however, he showed little evidence of those qualities that would make him one of the most famous and popular men of the century. Yet the qualities of greatness were there, in the boy, in the young man, in the junior officer, and in the major (a rank he held for sixteen years) serving as an obscure staff officer. A discerning few among his friends, his contemporaries, and his superiors saw those qualities. Eisenhower himself made certain that when his opportunity came, an opportunity his parents had told him was his heritage, he was ready to reach out and seize it.

Eisenhower's ancestors were Pennsylvania Dutch. They came from the Rhineland, where the name was originally spelled Eisenhauer—literally iron hewer. They were religious dissenters, followers of Menno Simons, founder of the Mennonites, a persecuted sect in their German homeland. During the Thirty Years' War, the Eisenhauers fled to Switzerland. In 1741 Hans Nicol Eisenhauer, together with his wife, their three sons, and a brother, sailed from Rotterdam on the *Europa,* bound for Philadelphia. The bare genealogical record says nothing about motivation, but the assumption is that Hans left the Old World for the New for the same reasons so many others did, economic opportunity and freedom of worship.

Hans acquired a farm of 120 acres and built a home in Lancaster County, west of Philadelphia. After the Revolutionary War, Hans's grandson Frederick moved some fifty miles west, to Elizabethville, north of Harrisburg. There his son Jacob built a large two-story, nine-room red-brick home that still stands, much the most substantial and impressive house any Eisenhower lived in until well into the twentieth century.

In the early nineteenth century, the Eisenhowers (as the name was now spelled) joined the Brethren in Christ sect of the Mennonites, known as the River Brethren because they held river baptisms. Frederick's son Jacob, born in 1826, became the minister of the Lykens Valley River Brethren. Jacob was an orator, organizer, and leader. He attracted large audiences to his sermons, which he delivered in German, still the only language of the River Brethren. He wore a full beard, which emphasized his stern countenance and flashing eyes. Jacob was in his late thirties when the Civil War was fought; he did not join the Union cause because like most Mennonites he was an uncompromising pacifist. His wife, Rebecca Matter, was pregnant during the tense summer of 1863, when Lee's Army of Northern Virginia passed within twenty miles of the Eisenhower home, on its way to Gettysburg. Just twelve weeks after the great battle, Rebecca gave birth to a son, David, who would become Dwight's father. Jacob named his next son, born in 1865, after Abraham Lincoln. Altogether, Jacob and Rebecca had fourteen children.[1]

After the Civil War, as the railroads pushed onto the Great Plains, the West beckoned. The River Brethren, with their large families and their commitment to farming as a way of life, were looking for a location where land for their children was cheaper than in Pennsylvania. They responded enthusiastically to the inducements of the railroad promoters, who in their pamphlets described Kansas as another Eden.[2] Jacob organized the move, in which some three hundred River Brethren participated. They took the train from Harrisburg, filling fifteen carloads with their freight. Jacob sold his farm and home for $8,500 to pay for the journey and to buy a new place in Kansas. The colony, according to an early history of Kansas, was "one of the most complete and perfectly organized . . . that ever entered a new country."[3]

They settled in Dickinson County, just north of the Smoky Hill River, almost exactly in the middle of Kansas, twenty miles east of the geographic center of the lower forty-eight states, at the point where the Flint Hills of eastern Kansas give way to the flat, arid, treeless Great Plains of western Kansas. Jacob purchased a 160-acre farm, built a house, a barn, and a windmill. He prospered in Kansas; to each of his children, daughters as well as sons, he was able to give as a wedding present a 160-acre farm and $2,000 cash.

One of his sons, David, was fourteen years old when the family moved to Kansas. He had to work from dawn to dusk to make the farm a success, but he hated the endless hours of following the plow or gathering in the hay. The only part of farm life David enjoyed was tinkering with the machinery; he was, according to neighbors, a "natural-born" mechanic.[4] He decided to escape the farm by becoming a full-time engineer. To do so, he told his father, he wanted to go to college. Jacob protested. Farming was God's work, he said, and he put considerable pressure on David to stay on the farm.[5]

Eventually, Jacob yielded. He agreed to finance David's education at a small River Brethren school, then known rather grandly as Lane University, now defunct, in Lecompton, Kansas. It provided a mixture of classical and vocational training. In the fall of 1883, when he was twenty years old, David enrolled in Lane. There he studied mechanics, mathematics, Greek, rhetoric, and penmanship. He became proficient in basic mathematics, excellent in Greek (for the remainder of his life his nighttime reading was his Greek Bible), and got a start on engineering.[6]

At the beginning of the next school year, 1884, twenty-two-year-old Ida Stover enrolled at Lane. Her background was similar to David's. She was a member of the River Brethren and her people had come to

America from the Rhineland in 1730. They had settled on the Pennsylvania frontier, then moved south down the Shenandoah Valley to Mount Sidney, Virginia, where Ida had been born in 1862. Ida's father, Simon P. Stover, was a farmer; her mother, Elizabeth Link Stover, died when Ida was very young. Although she had no personal memory of the ravages of the Civil War, Ida grew up listening to numerous stories about the horrors of war, which reinforced the pacifism that went with her religion. Her father died when she was twelve years old; for the next nine years she lived with her uncle, Billy Link. Highly intelligent and religious, she spent hours reading and memorizing the Bible. According to family tradition, she once won a prize in Mount Sidney for memorizing 1,325 Biblical verses. All her life she prided herself on never having to look up a reference in the Bible.[7]

When Ida was twenty-one years old, Link handed over to her a small inheritance from her father. She used some of the money to pay for a train trip to Kansas, where two of her older brothers had already joined a River Brethren colony. "Kansas was still wild and wooly when Mother went out there," one of Ida's sons later explained. "They didn't care if a woman went to college or not."[8] So Ida used most of the remainder of her inheritance to pay her tuition at Lane. There she met David Eisenhower and fell in love. Youthful passion overrode youthful ambition. On September 23, 1885, in the chapel at Lane, they married. "Maybe the tragedy, as far as Mother's part is concerned," one of her sons later commented, "is that she met Dad before she finished school, got married and started raising a family."[9]

They made a good-looking couple. David was tall, muscular, broad-shouldered. He had a thin, hard-set mouth, thick black hair, dark eyebrows, deep-set, penetrating eyes, and a large, rounded chin. His legs were long, his hands large and powerful. For all his size and strength, however, he was quiet, shy, and retiring. Ida was much more outgoing. She had a beautiful head of brown hair, full lips, a ready grin that spread across her whole face, a grin as big as the Kansas prairie and as bright as Kansas sunshine, a hearty laugh, and a gay disposition. Music and religion were her great outlets; shortly after her marriage she spent the last of her inheritance on an ebony piano, which she kept for the rest of her life. She loved playing the piano and singing hymns.[10] Her most notable physical feature, after her grin, was the twinkle in her eyes, a twinkle that was nearly always there and signified a spontaneity and a liveliness that complemented David's quietness and seriousness. All her sons inherited Ida's twinkle and her ever-ready grin.

As a wedding present, Jacob gave David his standard gift, a 160-

acre farm and $2,000 in cash. David mortgaged the farm to Chris Musser, who had married his sister Amanda. With the capital, David bought a general store in Hope, Kansas, a tiny village twenty-eight miles south of Abilene that the young couple believed had a future befitting its name. With no business experience himself, David took in a partner, Milton Good, who had been a salesman in a clothing store in Abilene and who thus knew something about the retail trade. The Eisenhowers and the Goods had adjoining apartments on the second floor above the store, where they frequently entertained and, in that strict River Brethren community, gained a reputation for living above their means. In November 1886, Ida gave birth to her first son, named Arthur.

Two years later, in 1888, financial disaster struck. David awoke one morning to discover Good gone, most of the inventory with him, and a stack of unpaid bills left behind. According to family tradition, Good had absconded, leaving the innocent David to face the creditors.[11] For a number of years after Good left "for parts unknown," Ida studied law textbooks, hoping someday to bring Good to court, but no suit was ever pressed, for the truth seems to be that the business just collapsed. Kansas was in the midst of the worst agricultural depression in its history. With wheat down to fifteen cents a bushel, the farmers could not pay their bills. David and Good had been carrying them on credit, in the time-honored manner of American general stores. Their failure was a consequence of economic conditions beyond their control.[12]

The failure was total. David turned everything over to a local lawyer, telling the attorney to collect all the outstanding bills owed, pay the debts, and give what money was left to him. The lawyer sold the store; the mortgage on the farm was foreclosed; David's remaining assets, save only for Ida's piano, were converted into cash that was used to pay off the creditors. The lawyer kept the small amount of money that remained as his fee.[13] David never trusted a lawyer again and was most unhappy when his second son, Edgar, decided to enter the legal profession.

Ida too was furious. "Throughout the years that her sons continued to live under the same roof," Dwight Eisenhower recalled years later, "this warm, pleasant, mild-mannered woman never ceased to warn them against thieves, embezzlers, chiselers, and all kinds of crooks."[14]

At the time the business collapsed, Ida was pregnant again. She stayed with friends in Hope as her husband sought employment. He found it in Texas, at $10 a week, working for a railroad. Shortly after Edgar's birth, in January 1889, Ida and her two sons joined David in Denison, Texas, where they lived in a small rented frame house, not much more than a shack, set beside the railroad tracks. There, on October 14, 1890, Ida gave birth to her third son, named David Dwight Eisenhower. Later, she reversed the names, partly because she did not like nicknames and thought that Dwight could never be shortened, partly because it was confusing to have two Davids in the family.

At the time of his birth, Dwight Eisenhower's parents owned their clothes, a few household possessions, and one ebony piano, which Ida had been forced to leave behind in Hope. They had squandered a substantial inheritance. They had three sons and precious few prospects. But they had their health, strong family ties, and determination.

The family rallied around the young couple to give David and Ida a fresh start. Chris Musser had become the foreman at the Belle Springs Creamery, at the company's new plant in Abilene. The River Brethren owned the plant. Musser offered David a job as a mechanic in the creamery, at $50 per month. David quickly accepted. In 1891, when Dwight was not yet one year old, the family returned to Abilene. When the Eisenhowers stepped onto the train platform in Abilene, David had in his pocket the sum total of his capital—$24.[15]

The Eisenhowers rented a frame house on South East Second Street. The house and the yard were small, much too small to contain the energies of growing boys. Ida complained that she spent too much of her time keeping her sons out of other people's yards, which put a severe strain on both the boys and on Ida. Her problems multiplied as she continued to have children: Roy, born in 1892, Paul in 1894 (he died in infancy), and Earl in 1898. Five healthy boys in one tiny house made life difficult and, as they grew, nearly impossible. Again, the family came to the rescue. David's brother Abraham owned a two-story white frame house at 201 South East Fourth Street, set on a three-acre plot. Abraham was moving west. His father, Jacob, had been living with him and needed someone to care for him; his older brother David needed a larger home. Abraham offered to rent the house, at a minimal price, with an option to buy, to David, if David would agree to keep Jacob on in his own room and take care of the old man. David and Ida readily agreed, and in 1898 they moved into the more spacious quarters.[16]

To seven-year-old Dwight, and his brothers and parents, the new house must have seemed palatial. It had a basement, two stories, and an attic. The front parlor provided room for Ida's piano, which finally found a permanent home. There was a large barn behind the house, with a hayloft and stalls for animals. The Eisenhowers acquired a horse for plowing and drawing the buggy, two cows to provide milk, chickens, ducks, pigs, and rabbits to provide eggs and meat, and a smokehouse for curing the meat. The three acres provided land to grow forage for the stock, with enough left over for a large vegetable garden. There was an orchard of cherries, apples, and pears, and a grapevine. Each boy, including the youngest, Milton, born in 1899, had a small piece of garden for himself, where he could raise vegetables to sell door to door. Ida ran the farm and canned fruits, vegetables, and meat, so that except for such basics as salt and flour, no money had to be spent at the grocery store. David's work at the creamery, from six in the morning to six at night, six days a week, provided a bit of cash, never more than $100 a month.

The Eisenhowers were respected around town, because they were self-sufficient, because David paid all his debts promptly (after his experience with the store in Hope, he had a lifelong dread of debt), because Ida was such a good mother, and because the boys were well brought up, hardworking, fun-loving, and honest. The family was in no way prominent. David held no elective office, provided no community leadership. His role in the local economy was a minor one. The name Eisenhower appeared in the local newspaper only when one of his sons graduated, or got married, or upon his own retirement. But the Eisenhowers were content. The parents were frugal out of necessity, but they were proud and ambitious, if not for themselves, then for their sons. "I have found out in later years we were very poor," Dwight said on June 4, 1952, on the occasion of laying the cornerstone of the Eisenhower Museum in Abilene, across the street from his home, "but the glory of America is that we didn't know it then. All that we knew was that our parents—of great courage—could say to us: Opportunity is all about you. Reach out and take it."[17]

By most standards, after the disaster with the general store, David and Ida never reached out to take that opportunity themselves. Instead they invested the hopes they once had in their sons. They taught the simple virtues of honesty, self-reliance, integrity, fear of God, and ambition. They wanted their sons to succeed in a wider setting than Abilene, or even Kansas. They gave the boys the feeling, as one of them later put it, that "if you stay home you will always be looked upon as a boy."[18]

Breaking with the past did not mean abandoning religion or the strong family ties of the Pennsylvania Dutch. The Eisenhower home life revolved around worship. Every day, morning and night, the family members got down on their knees to pray. David read from the Bible before meals, then asked a blessing. After dinner, he brought out the Bible again. When the boys grew old enough, they took turns reading. Ida organized meetings of the Bible Students of the Watchtower Society, which met on Sundays in her parlor. She played her piano and led the singing. Neither David nor Ida ever smoked or drank, or played cards, or swore, or gambled. But they did not impose their prejudices on their sons, all of whom indulged in all those activities. Dwight especially became proficient in his use of Anglo-Saxon curse words and passionate in his card playing and gambling. He was also a heavy smoker. David and Ida did not object.[19]

The boys got more from their parents than simple virtues and pieties. David was a classic German father, the unquestioned head of the household, tough, stern, with a quick and fearful temper. All the boys later recalled that they never heard their father and mother shout at each other, or even raise their voices, and that they never heard them disagree. Dwight said he never heard a dispute between them on a value judgment in family, social, or economic affairs.[20] The reason was simple—Ida accepted all David's decisions and did as he wished in everything. She boosted his ego and bowed to his whims. The household revolved around his needs. As soon as they were old enough, the boys took turns getting up at 5 A.M. to build a fire in the cookstove and prepare his breakfast. They carried his hot lunch to him at the creamery. When he got home in the evening, Ida had his supper ready. After the boys did the dishes, the family gathered around him for the Bible reading. "Finally there was bedtime," Earl recalled, "when Dad got up and wound the clock on the wall. You could hear the ticking no matter where you were. When Dad started winding, you might as well get ready for bed, for that was the bedtime signal."[21]

David was something of a stranger and a terror to his children. He was aloof, paying little attention to their youthful successes or disappointments, seldom discussing with them their activities, hopes or dreams. He was precise in everything he did; his desk was always clean; he would not tolerate messiness of any kind in the children's rooms, much less anywhere else in the house. When the children skipped a chore, or did one poorly, or otherwise misbehaved, Ida would give them a spanking on the spot, unless the offense was of a more serious nature, in which case she would warn them, "I will report this to your father when he comes home tonight." As a result, Edgar recalled, "Dad was held as a bugaboo . . . he went about whipping us in a very businesslike manner. He got himself a maple switch, and really tanned us. As we grew older and began to resist, Dad was more energetic in his application of the switch than he had been."[22]

One of Dwight's sharpest memories about his father concerned the day that David came home unexpectedly for lunch and discovered that Edgar had been skipping school to work at a part-time job. "I never . . . saw him so angry," Dwight recorded. "His face was black as thunder. With no pause for argument, he reached for a piece of harness . . . at the same time grabbing Ed by the collar. He started in." Dwight, twelve years old, began shouting at his father to stop. When that failed to deter David, Dwight cried as loudly as he could, hoping that Ida would come out to the barn. Finally, Dwight came up behind his father and tried to catch hold of his arms. David turned on him, furious, and exclaimed, "Oh, do you want some of the same? What's the matter with you, anyway?"

"I don't think anyone ought to be whipped like that," Dwight sobbed, "not even a dog." David dropped the leather strap, turned away, and stormed off.[23]

Fortunately for the boys, they saw relatively little of their father. "Mother was by far the greatest personal influence in our lives," Dwight remembered.[24] She supervised their chores, made their meals, selected and mended their clothes, soothed their hurts, praised their accomplishments, and lightened the atmosphere in that authoritarian home. Milton, the youngest, said that "Father and Mother complemented one another. Mother had the personality. She had the joy. She had a song in her heart. Dad had the authority."[25]

David hardly ever smiled; Ida smiled as easily as she breathed. She was quick to laugh, quick to give sympathy. Like David, she demanded much of her sons; unlike him, she gave much. She was a born organizer. She assigned her boys to various rooms in such a way as to minimize nightly bedtime fights. She rotated the chores, so that each boy learned to cook, to clean both the house and the stable, to care for the chickens, to do the laundry, to plant, tend, and harvest the vegetable garden. She dealt with the innumerable crises of childhood calmly and efficiently. Edgar recalled, "We all learned a degree of the spirit of service . . . from Mother."[26]

Both David and Ida were open-minded about their sons' development. They imposed a rigid discipline, obviously, but as Earl recalled, "There was no pressure put on us by our parents to choose this career or that. Of course, there were a few hints. . . . I never heard Dad tell anybody that he *had* to be something." All the boys agreed that this was because David had resented his own father's attempts to force him to be a farmer.[27]

In a family of six boys, competition was the natural order of things. Who could do the best job at this or that task? Who could run the fastest? Jump the highest? Lift the heaviest weight? Read the Bible aloud most accurately? Daily, in countless ways, the boys tested themselves against one another. David and Ida encouraged this competition, encouraged them to be ambitious to do the best. Most of all, each of the boys wanted to be the toughest and they fought among themselves to find out who was the best scrapper.

One day when relatives were visiting, Dwight and Edgar began scuffling in the yard. The relatives called Ida's attention to the fight. She smiled and did nothing. "But aren't you going to stop it?" one of the visitors asked. "They have got to get it out of their system," Ida replied. "You can't keep healthy boys from scrapping. It isn't good to interfere too much." Another time Ida was baking in the kitchen. Dwight and Edgar began a fight on the kitchen floor. Soon the older and heavier Edgar was sitting astride the prostrate Dwight, giving him a pounding. "Give up?" Edgar shouted. "No!" Dwight gasped. Edgar grabbed Dwight's hair and began to thump his head against the floor. Earl rushed in to help Dwight. Ida, without turning away from the stove, said sharply to Earl, "Let them alone."[28]

David encouraged his sons to stand up for themselves, among one another and in their relations with boys outside the family. Dwight recalled that his father never wanted to see his sons beaten by their playmates in anything, least of all in a fight. One evening David returned from work to see Dwight being chased by a boy about his own size. "Why do you let that boy run you around like that?" he demanded. "Because if I fight him," Dwight replied, "you'll give me a whipping, whether I win or lose!" Instantly, David replied, "Chase that boy out of here." Dwight did.[29]

It is easy, and tempting, to romanticize Eisenhower's family background. Living in the Norman Rockwell setting of turn-of-the-century Abilene, David and Ida Eisenhower instilled in their sons the time-honored virtues. They could serve as a definition of what most Americans think good parents should be. And the success of each of their six sons in their six different careers seems to provide proof that they were as ideal as they appear to be at first glance.

Certainly their sons regarded them as ideal. After Dwight became famous, he and his brothers were frequently interviewed on the subject of their parents. Not one of the boys could think of a single significant criticism of David or Ida. Arthur did regret his father's lack of a sense of humor, but all the others disagreed with him even on this point.[30] They excused their father's failure in Hope by blaming it on his partner; they ignored his flight to Texas, leaving a pregnant Ida behind him with a baby in her arms; and they never complained about his low income and status. They emphasized instead his steadiness, his hard work, and his strong conviction of right and wrong. As adults, they even managed to remember with a certain fondness the beatings that had so frightened them as children, and they insisted that the punishment was both deserved and beneficial. "I don't believe any of the brothers can honestly say that they were punished when they didn't deserve it," Earl told one interviewer. "I certainly deserved whatever punishment I got."[31]

Thus Dwight, after telling the story of the terrible beating David gave Edgar when Edgar skipped school, stressed that Edgar deserved it because of his truancy and that it did him good because it changed his attitude toward school. "Had it not been for the application of leather, prolonged and unforgettable, my brother might well have become an unhappy handyman in Kansas," rather than a prominent lawyer, Dwight said. As Dwight saw it, "Undoubtedly fear that his boy would seriously damage all the years of life ahead provoked my father to a violent display of temper and temporary damage."[32]

For all their praise of their parents, the Eisenhower boys did not think that David and Ida were in any way exceptional. "There are many David and Ida Eisenhowers in this great country of ours," Edgar said, speaking for all the boys.[33]

Typical parents, in short, raising typical kids in a typical small town in the heart of America, with the success of the boys providing proof that there is a latent greatness within the average American family. So Dwight, in 1952, could tell his audience in Abilene that although the world was far more complex than in his youth, if every American would dwell more on individual initiative, fear of God, and self-reliance, many of the problems would solve themselves. "I think it is possible that a contemplation, a study, a belief of those simple virtues would help us mightily."[34] Most of his audience, and millions of Americans, heartily agreed.

But it is almost as easy to be critical of Eisenhower's upbringing as it is to be romantic, to sneer rather than to praise. David and Ida's outlook was narrow, their vision limited. They lived unquestioning lives, and they taught their sons to do the same. They emphasized accomplishment, rather than intellectual contemplation or a wondering about why things were the way they were and what could be done differently. The counterpoint to their openness about their sons' career choices was a closed mind to anything out of the ordinary. Similarly, the counterpoint to David's steadiness was his caution. The only debt he ever incurred in Abilene was the long-term mortgage on his house. He took no financial risks, made no investments. He was, as Edgar said, a plodder and "a plugger."[35]

The Eisenhowers had no spark of originality or genuine creativity, nor did they encourage these qualities in the boys. The nightly Bible readings provide an example. They were, Milton said, "a good way to get us to read the Bible mechanically." But, he admitted, "I am not sure it was a good way to help us understand it."[36] They never discussed what they had read, never asked "Why?," never explored the deep subtlety or rich symbolism of the Bible. It was the word of God, sufficient unto itself. The duty of mortals was not to explore it, investigate it, question it, think about it, but rather to accept it.

Such a family could, and did, produce great men who could accomplish much, men who were remarkably effective doers with a strong sense of duty and responsibility toward themselves, their own families, the wider community, and their fellow man. It could not, and did not, produce any great artists, or poets, or musicians, or scholars, or—more to the point—any political thinkers. All the Eisenhower boys were highly efficient, and in the cases of Milton and most of all Dwight, remarkably successful managers. They accepted the world as they found it and worked with the tools at hand to make it run better, not differently—which was just the way David and Ida wanted it.

The Abilene Eisenhower grew up in had a lurid reputation. "Sweet Abilene, prettiest town I've ever seen," the old-time cowboys called it. Only someone who had spent six months on the Chisholm Trail, driving cattle through Texas, Oklahoma, and southern Kansas to reach the western terminus of the Kansas-Pacific Railroad, could have thought of Abilene as "pretty." It was hot, dry, dusty in the summer, cold, windswept, and forlorn in the winter. Its buildings were clapboard houses and cheap saloons; its people were a mixture of cattle buyers, prostitutes, railroad men, cardsharps, saloonkeepers, and cowboys. It has since become famous, in large part because "Wild Bill" Hickok spent a short period there as town marshal, but its moment of glory was brief. When the railroad pushed on west, the terminus of the Chisholm Trail went with it, and Abilene changed from a wide-open cow town into a settled community that served the surrounding farmers. When the cowboys left, the prostitutes and saloonkeepers went with them. By 1878, when Jacob Eisenhower arrived, there was nothing distinctive about Abilene.

By 1891, when Dwight Eisenhower was one year old, most people would have regarded Abilene as a dull, dispiriting place. It is doubtful that Dwight ever saw a trail herd in his youth, and certainly he never saw a shoot-out, but like every other youngster in town he grew up with stories—much embellished—about the old, wild days, and he spent countless hours playing "shoot 'em up" on the streets, in imitation of "Wild Bill." His only lasting legacy from Abilene's early days, however, was a lifelong love of cheap Western novels, which he read by the score.

The chief characteristic of Abilene in the 1890s was that it was typical of small-town Midwestern America, which meant, for young Dwight, that it reinforced everything he learned from his parents. There was, first of all, the emphasis on self-sufficiency. Contact with the outside world was minimal, primarily consisting of the daily arrival and departure of the train, which carried in manufactured products from the East and carried out wheat. There were few taxes to pay to, and almost no services provided by, government, save on the local level. The city paid for and ran the school system. Families took care of their own sick, insane, crippled, elderly, or just down-on-their-luck members. There was no police force because in a town small enough (less than four thousand population) for everyone to know, and trust, everyone else, there was no need for one.

There was a strong emphasis on hard work, on getting things done. Little or no time was wasted on reflection or introspection. Everyone in Abilene worked, most of them at hard physical labor. Unemployment was virtually unknown, even among children. The youngest worked around the house; eight-to-twelve-year-olds held odd jobs; teen-agers found regular employment.

Abilene was cautious and conservative in its social outlook, religion, politics, and composition. Everyone was Christian, of European descent, and nearly all voted Republican. There was a strong sense of community, a feeling that the world was divided into "us" (the residents of Abilene, Dickinson County, and to some extent the state of Kansas) and "them" (the rest of the world). Abilene was like a large extended family, giving to its residents a feeling of security. Threats to that security came not from within, but from without, primarily in the form of adverse weather or falling commodity prices.

Abilene's conservatism and sense of security, that is to say, existed within the context of the tremendous risk-taking inherent in growing wheat for a living. Wheat farmers, and the small towns that serve them, are gamblers whose success depends on two factors entirely out of their control, weather and prices. Hailstorms, drought, and grasshoppers are only their most dramatic enemies—a year's hard work can leave them flat broke if their luck goes bad, and all they can do is shrug, mumble "God's will be done," and start over. Even if they bring in a bumper crop, they can end up losing money because of a drop in prices. As soon as he was old enough to know a little about the broader scene beyond his immediate family circle, Dwight learned about the crucial importance of weather and of the world economic situation, even in isolated Abilene.

The conservatism was also tempered by an eager reception of the latest in modern technology. Residents regarded the town as quite up to date. During Dwight's youth, "everyone was putting something in."[37] As Dwight grew, Abilene paved its streets, added board and later cement sidewalks, built a generator to provide electricity, added running water and a sewer system, acquired a telephone system, and welcomed the automobile. Cultural life, however, was limited to church "socials" and an occasional visit from the Chautauqua.

Extremes of wealth and poverty were unknown, but there were marked differences in income, social standing, and prestige. The railroad tracks divided the town. The merchants, lawyers, doctors, and bankers lived on the north side in newly built, large Victorian houses with grand porches, huge cottonwood trees, and sweeping lawns. The railroad workers, carpenters, bricklayers, and mechanics lived on the south side, like the Eisenhowers in small homes with few trees. The adults tended to regard such a division as entirely the normal order of things and hardly ever thought about or commented upon it, but the children, sensing the difference instinctively, tended to think of themselves as "North Siders" or "South Siders." As a result, in school, there was a definite and lively rivalry between the two groups.

In general, however, few people thought in terms of class rank or standing. A man was judged by how hard he worked and whether he paid his bills on time, a woman by how well she ran her household. It was assumed that a man's success depended solely upon his output and that the unsuccessful had no one to blame but themselves. "The isolation was political and economic," Milton Eisenhower recalled, "as well as just a prevailing state of mind. Self-sufficiency was the watchword; personal initiative and responsibility were prized; radicalism was unheard of."[38]

To a friendly observer, Abilene in the 1890s was peaceful, serene, progressive, prosperous, God-fearing, hardworking, and quite capable of taking care of itself through its own exertions, just as it had achieved its success on its own. To a critic, it was dull, backward, narrow, prejudiced, and hostile to culture, outsiders, and new ideas. Moreover, the critic would have pointed out that Abilene's self-image was self-serving. The government that seemed so remote and unnecessary was in fact crucial to its very existence. Had not the U.S. Army driven out the Indians who possessed the country only a decade before Jacob Eisenhower arrived, there would have been no Abilene. Had not the federal government given generous land grants to the Kansas-Pacific Railroad, it would not have been built, and there would have been no Abilene. Had it not been for government tariff policies, designed to encourage agricultural exports, Abilene would have found it difficult to sell its only important product.

To children growing up there, Abilene was simply home. To the Eisenhower boys it seemed then, and always remained in their memories, an ideal place. However rigid and limited it was, it provided more than sufficient scope for a growing boy to discover himself and develop his physical capacity in an atmosphere of security, friendliness, and tolerance of boyish pranks.

In 1947, Dwight Eisenhower spoke from his heart about the town that he loved. He said that Abilene "provided both a healthy outdoor existence and a need to work. These same conditions were responsible for the existence of a society which, more nearly than any other I have encountered, eliminated prejudices based upon wealth, race or creed, and maintained a standard of values that placed a premium upon integrity, decency, and consideration for others. The democracy of our schools . . . helped likewise to emphasize the dignity of work and of accomplishment . . . Any youngster who has the opportunity to spend his early youth in an enlightened rural area has been favored by fortune."[39]

CHAPTER TWO

Abilene

1900–1911

IMAGINE HIM, on the Fourth of July, at the turn of the century, when he was nine and a half years old, standing on a street corner in Abilene, watching the high-school band march past. At first glance, an ordinary Kansas boy, barefoot, wearing hand-me-down clothes that were clean but frequently darned, mended, and patched. He was of normal size for his age, with a full head of light-brown hair and a suntan that highlighted his blue eyes. He had a large, broad mouth, a ready grin, and a friendly disposition. He knew every youngster in the band, indeed nearly everyone in town, and gave a big smile and a vigorous nod of his head to all those who caught his eye. They smiled and waved in return, for he was popular, as evidenced by his nickname, used by all the residents of Abilene save for his mother—"Little Ike." The "Little" was used to distinguish him from his older brother Edgar, who was known as "Big Ike"; the "Ike" was a natural transformation of the first syllable of his last name.

A discerning observer might have noticed some slight differences between Little Ike and his companions. There was, first of all, the great energy. The band had caught his attention and brought a momentary pause in his incessant activity, but it was the first time that day he stood still. He was always on the go, investigating, exploring, playing, working, fighting. It was not his nature to daydream, to lie under the shade of a cottonwood and idly wonder about what his life might be like; rather it was his practice to go out and live it.

Even watching him, as he watched the band, one could see evidence of that energy. His eyes were seldom still. They moved rapidly, taking in everything. Two additional traits grew out of and complemented that energy, an intense curiosity and a remarkable ability to concentrate. He wanted to know all that he could about the world around him, and he would pursue his curiosity with a single-minded concentration until he found the answer. In later years, Edgar said of Little Ike, "If I were to say those flowers out there were Dutch iris, and he thought they were Japanese iris, he'd go out and examine them. If he couldn't tell by that, he'd get out the books and look them up."[1]

Much of his curiosity and concentration centered on his age-mates, as a natural outgrowth of his belligerence and competitiveness. He was a scrapper, getting into fights on an almost daily basis, usually against a boy slightly older and slightly bigger than himself. Most of all, he fought Big Ike. "The occasion for a fight could be the simplest kind of a little thing," Edgar explained years later. "We might be walking with one another and he would try to trip me. Well, I would immediately slug him and then a fight was on. . . . He might take something away from me that I didn't think he was entitled to; then another fight was on." These fights were more wrestling contests than slugging matches, and usually ended with Big Ike on top. "There was no animosity in our fights," Edgar recalled. "We fought for the sheer joy of slugging one another. We had to get rid of our energy, and I think that when a fight was over we probably thought more of one another than we did before it began."[2]

Fights with other boys were a different matter—as Dwight later recalled, "in those cases you stood up and slugged until one gave way." There were many such brawls, with the Eisenhower boys fighting side by side rather than against each other.[3] There was a tradition in Abilene High School for the entering freshman class to have a contest between the champion fighter of the South Side and the champion of the North Side. The year he was a freshman, Big Ike won, giving the South Side boys bragging rights all year. When Little Ike's turn came, in 1904, Wesley Merrifield represented the North Side. Wesley was bigger, stronger, faster. The fight lasted more than an hour. After Dwight became famous, nearly every resident of Abilene claimed to have been there for the "toughest kid fight" they had ever seen. Wesley and Little Ike both had bloody noses, cut lips, and battered ears. Their eyes were swollen nearly shut. Finally Wesley gasped, "Ike, I can't lick you." Ike gasped back, "And I can't lick you."

Little Ike went home and stumbled into bed. Ida tried to soothe his swollen face with warm towels. David suppressed a smile. Arthur summed it up: "That was Father in Dwight. Beaten to a pulp. But never licked. . . . He had Father's stubbornness. He could take it . . . and never whimper."[4]

Dwight also inherited David's terrible temper. Anger would possess him, take complete control, make him oblivious to anything else. The adrenaline rushed through his body, raising the hair on the back of his neck, turning his face a bright beet-red. Only some act of unrestrained violence would release the tension. On Halloween night, 1900, his parents gave Arthur and Edgar permission to go "trick or treating." Little Ike begged, pleaded, and argued to be allowed to go along, but his parents insisted that he was too young. Anger overwhelmed him. He rushed outside and began pounding the trunk of an apple tree with his bare fists. He sobbed and pounded until his fists were a raw bleeding mass of torn flesh. Finally his father grabbed him by the shoulders and shook him until he gained some control over himself.

Dwight went to his bed and cried into his pillow for an hour, out of resentment and rage. His mother came into the room and sat beside him. She took up his hands, putting salve on them and then bandages. After what seemed to him to be a long time, she said, " 'He that conquereth his own soul is greater than he who taketh a city.' " She went on to tell him how futile and self-destructive anger was, and how he, of all her boys, had much the worst temper and the farthest to go in conquering it. When he was seventy-six years old, Eisenhower wrote, "I have always looked back on that conversation as one of the most valuable moments of my life."[5]

Getting control of his temper, however, did not come easily or quickly. Two years after the apple-tree incident, when Dwight was twelve and Arthur sixteen, Arthur incurred his little brother's wrath over some trifling matter. Raging, but frustrated because Arthur was much too big for him to attack with his fists, Dwight looked around. Seeing a brick at his feet, he grabbed it and flung it with all his might at Arthur's head. Arthur just did manage to duck out of the way—Dwight had fully intended to hit him.[6]

Another characteristic that Dwight had difficulty learning to control was his impetuousness. In 1898, heavy spring rains put the Smoky Hill River over its banks. Shortly before noon on the first day of the flood, Ida gave Big and Little Ike a hot lunch to carry to David at the creamery. They made a detour to go to the railroad embankment to look at the flood. On the bank they spotted an old leaky boat, without paddle or visible owner. Never hesitating, they found a board to use as a paddle and jumped in. As they paddled around the brown, swirling floodwaters, other boys joined them. After a couple of hours or so, there were too many boys and not enough boat. The boat sank. Dripping wet, covered with mud, the two Ikes and their companions climbed up onto dry land. Mr. Volkman, one of the Eisenhower neighbors, was standing on the bank. Ominously he said to the Eisenhower boys, "Your mother is looking for you. Do you know that it is now the middle of the afternoon, and you haven't brought your father his lunch?"

The boys had lost the lunch when they lost the boat. Slowly, they dragged their way home. Ida met them at the front door. "Go to the back porch," she said. "Take off your clothes." As they did so, she went out in the yard and cut a maple switch. Then, as Edgar recalled, "She laid on us with all the vigor of a good pioneer arm. I'll never forget that flood as long as I live!"[7]

Four activities that young Dwight concentrated on and became proficient in were exploration, hunting and fishing, cooking, and card playing. All four became passions that he enjoyed the rest of his life. Man and boy, nothing delighted him more than going into a new area, getting a feel for the lay of the land, shooting some quail or catching some trout, cooking them over an open fire, and ending the day with a marathon session of poker or bridge.

His instructor was an illiterate fifty-year-old man, Bob Davis, who made his living from the Smoky Hill River, shooting ducks, catching fish, and trapping muskrat and mink. Davis enjoyed Little Ike's company and always welcomed him to his camp. He taught the boy how to paddle a flatboat, how to find north on a rainy day, how to read the folds in the surrounding countryside and figure out the drainage, how to hunt, fish, and trap, how to cook what they had shot or caught, and how to play poker. Davis played poker strictly by the percentages. His game was five-card draw, and he had no patience for those who chased inside straights. For the next thirty years, Eisenhower played poker on army bases around the world. He never played carelessly. He was such a regular winner that eventually, finding that he was creating resentment among his fellow officers, he quit altogether.[8] Then he took up contract bridge. He became almost a fanatic, and certainly a successful, bridge player.

Dwight attended Lincoln elementary school, directly across the street from his home. The curriculum emphasized rote learning. "The darkness of the classrooms on a winter day and the monotonous hum of recitations," Eisenhower wrote in his memoirs, ". . . are my sole surviving memories. I was either a lackluster student or involved in a lackluster program." He came to life for the spelling bee and arithmetic. Spelling contests aroused in him his competitive drive and his hatred of careless mistakes—he became a self-confessed martinet on the subject of orthography. Arithmetic appealed to him because it was logical and straightforward—an answer was either right or it was wrong.[9]

The subject that really excited him, however, was one that he pursued on his own, military history. He became so engrossed in it, in fact, that he neglected his chores and his schoolwork. His concentrated persistence in following his curiosity, the time and energy he put into reading military history, alarmed his mother (her commitment to pacifism may also have been involved). She took his history books away from him and locked them in a closet. But he found the key to the closet, and "whenever Mother went to town to shop or was out working in her flower garden I would sneak out the books."[10] They were long, detailed accounts of Greek and Roman battles, and they fascinated him. Not that he made a decision there and then that someday he would walk in the footsteps of Alexander or Caesar. He was twenty years old before he gave the slightest serious, conscious thought to a military career. But he had a passion for battle histories. Who attacked? Where? When? On what flank? Who were the heroes that day, and what did they do? Neither the books nor his own curiosity led him to wonder much about why the battles were fought. He memorized dates, to the point that he became a pedant on the subject; "I have a sort of fixation," he wrote in his memoirs, "that causes me to interrupt a conversation when the speaker is one year off . . . in dating an event like Arbela."[11]

Later, in high school, he expanded his reading to include recent European and American military history, and eventually some political history. He did so well in his history classes that his teachers began giving him special assignments to keep him from being bored in class.[12] Still his concentration was, in his words, on "the peaks and promontories—the dramatic features—of the historical terrain. . . . The reading of history was an end in itself, not a source of lessons to guide us in the present or to prepare me for the future."[13]

His first hero was Hannibal. Then he became a student of the American Revolution, and George Washington excited his admiration. He became deeply involved, to such a degree that "I conceived almost a violent hatred of Conway and his cabal" for trying to remove Washington from his command.[14] He talked history to his classmates so frequently that his senior yearbook predicted that he would become a professor of history at Yale (it also predicted that Edgar would become a two-term President of the United States).[15]

• •

During Dwight's freshman year, 1904, Abilene built a new high school on the north side of town. A solid two-story brick building, it seemed quite magnificent to the fourteen-year-old. The new building, and the commitment to education it represented, attracted new and better teachers. The faculty expanded. Most of the teachers were spinsters, whether young or old, dedicated to their pupils, determined to make certain that all their charges learned their basic studies—English, history, mathematics, Latin, and general science. If it was rote learning that encouraged the acceptance of the world as it was, it was superb training, providing those students who took advantage of it with a solid base for later accomplishment. In the year 1950, three pre–World War I graduates of Abilene High School were presidents of three famous eastern universities (Dwight Eisenhower at Columbia, Milton at Penn State, and Deane Malott at Cornell). The school was preponderantly female, with girls outnumbering boys by more than two to one. A majority of the boys dropped out to go to work long before graduation and in Dwight's graduating class there were twenty-five girls and nine boys.[16] Dwight's brother Arthur left school two years before graduation to find work in a bank in Kansas City (he lived in a boardinghouse with Harry S. Truman), and Edgar also dropped out of school for two years, but finally returned and graduated with Dwight in 1909.

During Dwight's high-school years his interests were, in order of importance, sports, work, studies, and girls. He was shy around the girls and in any case wanted to impress his male classmates as a regular fellow, just one of the gang. Paying too much attention to the girls was considered somewhat sissy. He was careless of his dress, his hair was usually uncombed, and he was a terrible dancer on the few occasions he tried the dance floor.[17]

Studies came easily to him and he made good to excellent grades without extending himself. He got all Bs in his freshman year, when the subjects were English, physical geography, algebra, and German. He did a bit better the next year, and as a junior and senior he was an A or A-plus student in English, history, and geometry. His sole B was in Latin.[18]

Throughout his high-school years, he worked, at odd jobs during the school year, more regular ones in the summer. Sometimes he worked at the creamery, sometimes at nearby farms. Joe Howe, who edited a weekly newspaper, and whose office served as a hangout for Dwight and his friends, said that Dwight "would take any job he could do and seldom complained about the work being too hard. He took [hard work] for granted."[19] He used the money he earned to buy clothes, shotgun shells, ice cream sodas, and, most of all, sports equipment.

Sports, especially football and baseball, were the center of his life. He put more time into the games than into anything else, save work, and expended far more energy on sports than he put into his studies. He was a good, but not outstanding, athlete. He was well coordinated, but slow of foot. He weighed only 150 pounds. His chief asset was his will to win. He loved the challenge of the games themselves, enjoyed the competition with older and bigger boys, bubbled over with pleasure at hitting a single to drive in the winning run or at throwing the other team's star halfback for a loss.

The more he played, the more he appreciated the importance of teamwork. His concern was with winning the game. He was the rah-rah type, constantly shouting encouragement to his teammates. He was a self-confident and assured player who knew his own capabilities. Like all serious athletes, he was also highly self-critical, keenly aware of his own shortcomings, blaming himself when his team lost, praising the team as a whole when it won. The first extant piece of his correspondence exhibits his attitude. The postcard, dated May 27, 1908, was written to Orin Snider, an older boy who had gone on to Kansas State College in Manhattan. The subject was a baseball game Abilene High School had just played against the freshman team from the University of Kansas. The card read: "We will probably play the college again next Mon. They beat us in a five inning game the other day, 7–3. I made a rank error. Young Ike."[20]

Editor Howe, who attended most of the games, recalled that Dwight "had self-assurance but never in all my contact with him did he ever show any conceit. He resented this in other boys more than anything else. In fact, he would dislike a boy for being conceited much more than for something he had done."[21]

Dwight, besides being modest, insisted on fair play. In the time-honored tradition of sports in small-town America, most of the games were self-regulated. Even in high-school games against teams from nearby towns, there would be only one umpire or referee at most. There were numerous opportunities to play "dirty," to clip an opponent, to trip him, or to throw a punch at his face during a pileup. Eisenhower would experience a surge of anger when he detected someone, even one of his own teammates, violating the rules. If it were an opponent who was cheating, he would block or tackle him just a bit harder; if one of his side was guilty, he would sharply reprimand the player.

One Saturday afternoon, the Abilene players discovered that the opposition had a Negro on the team. Each Abilene player refused to play across the line from the Negro, who was a center. Dwight stepped forward to say that he would play center that day, although his usual position was end and he had never played center. Both before and after the game, Dwight shook hands with the Negro. "Rest of the team was a bit ashamed [of themselves]," he reported years later.[22]

It was in sports that he first discovered his talents as a leader and an organizer. As a boy, he provided the energy and leadership that led to a Saturday-afternoon game of football or baseball. Later, he was one of the organizers of the Abilene High School Athletic Association, which operated independently of the school system. Dues were twenty-five cents per month and the AHSAA used the money to buy bats, balls, uniforms, and other equipment. Most of the equipment was homemade, with sweat pads taken from livery stables as shoulder pads and old stocking caps for headgear. Dwight wrote to schools in the area to make up a schedule, and solved the problem of transportation by hustling his team onto freight trains for a free ride from Abilene to the site of the contest. In his senior year, he was elected president of the AHSAA. In his year-end report for the yearbook, he wrote: "We improved the condition of the Association itself by drawing up the constitution, which makes the organization a permanent one, and each year it will be simply a question of electing new officers." It was typical of Dwight that he wrote "we" rather than "I," and that the constitution he wrote was good enough to still be in force forty years later.[23]

He was also the team's chief booster. A second extant postcard, written on October 21, 1908, reads: "Dear Orin: We play at J.C. [Junction City] Sat. for sure and I want to see you, Bob and Vet there. I will run some bluff to get you in the game free. Ike."[24]

Dwight also organized camping and hunting trips. He got the boys together, collected the money, hired the livery rig to take them to Lyons Creek, twenty miles south of Abilene, bought the food, and did the cooking. He also participated in winter wolf hunts, for which occasions a score or more adults and boys would turn out, some driving the wolves, coyotes, and jackrabbits in front of them, others shooting. Dwight was one of the shooters, partly because of his skill, partly because he had saved his money and was the proud owner of a Winchester Model 1897 pump-action 16-gauge shotgun.[25]

The central importance of sports, hunting, and fishing to young Eisenhower cannot be overemphasized. He literally could not imagine life without them, as shown by the most dramatic incident of his childhood.

During his freshman year, he fell and scraped his knee. This was a common enough experience, and his only thought was for his ruined brand-new pants, which he had bought with his own earnings. Since there was no bleeding, he went to school the next day. Infection set in, however, and that evening he fell into a delirium on the sofa in the front room. His parents called in Dr. Conklin, but despite his treatment, the infection began spreading. For the next two weeks, Dwight slipped into and out of a coma. Conklin called two or three times a day; Ida stayed at his bedside; they painted a belt of carbolic acid around his leg; still the poison spread and crept up his leg toward his abdomen. Conklin called in a specialist from Topeka. The two doctors agreed that only amputation would save his life.

During one of his conscious moments, Dwight heard his parents discussing amputation. They distrusted surgery, but the doctors insisted on it. Fourteen-year-old Dwight listened, then said, quietly but firmly, "You are never going to cut that leg off." When his parents told Conklin of his decision, the doctor warned, "If the poisoning ever hits his stomach he will die."

By this time the infection had reached his groin and his periods of consciousness were few and short. He called in Edgar and said, "Look, Ed, they are talking about taking my leg off. I want you to see that they do not do it, because I would rather die than to lose my leg." Edgar understood. He made the promise, and from then on stayed at his brother's bedside to make certain that no amputation took place. Conklin grew angry, began mumbling about "murder," but he could not persuade Edgar, or David and Ida, to allow him to amputate. Edgar even slept at night on the floor across the threshold of the door, so that Conklin could not get into the room while Edgar was sleeping.[26]

At the end of the second week, the poison began to recede, the fever left Dwight's body, consciousness returned. After a two-month convalescence, which caused him to have to repeat his freshman year, Dwight recovered completely. It was miraculous enough, but became much embellished decades later. Sunday-school tracts and inspirational literature described the whole family as down on its knees, night and day, praying for his recovery. The Eisenhower boys hated such talk, with its implication that their parents believed in faith healing. They insisted that they prayed no more, and no less, than at other times. "We always prayed," Edgar recalled. "It was just as natural for us to pray, to call upon God for help as it was for us to get up and eat breakfast."[27] And Dwight dismissed the night-and-day-praying stories as "ridiculous."[28]

In May 1909, Dwight and Edgar graduated. Edgar wanted to go to the University of Michigan to study law. His father, still not convinced that a lawyer could be an honest man, told him that if he went to the University of Kansas to study medicine, "I'll help you through, but, if you go to Michigan and take up law, you go on your own." Edgar decided to go to Michigan anyway. His uncle, Chris Musser, now came to Edgar's aid, guaranteeing a $200 loan for him. That was a start. "And then Dwight and I got our heads together," Edgar related, "and we agreed that I would go to college for the first year and he would work and send me his money, and then I would stay out and work and he would go to college and I would give him my money."[29]

Through the summer of 1909, both boys worked and saved their money, Edgar in the creamery, Dwight loading galvanized sheet metal. In September, Edgar went off to Ann Arbor. Dwight took his place at the creamery, first as the iceman, then feeding the furnace. Eventually he became night manager, working from 6 P.M to 6 A.M., seven days a week, for which he made $90 per month, almost as much as his father was earning.[30] The work was not demanding, especially after having tossed around huge cakes of ice or shoveled coal into a furnace, and his friends would often drop in for a game of poker.

Most of the money he earned or won at cards went to Edgar; Dwight kept only enough for shotgun shells or other sports equipment or some item of clothing. Although his working hours severely limited his social life, he was becoming more clothes- and appearance-conscious as he grew out of his boyish shyness around girls. He began a half-serious romance with red-haired Ruby Norman. But his main physical recreation, aside from the inevitable baseball and football games, was hunting.

During the winter, or whenever the weather was bad, he spent his afternoons in Joe Howe's office, reading newspapers. Howe had the dailies from New York, Chicago, St. Louis, and Kansas City. Dwight began to read them regularly, explaining to Howe, "I like to read about what is going on outside of Kansas." As his horizons broadened, so did his interests. He began borrowing books from Howe's library, books on subjects other than military history, the Wild West, or sports. He began to debate current issues with Howe and with some of the other youngsters who gathered in the office. He had an ability to absorb facts and he had a logical mind; during the debates, he would listen awhile, then jump in with an obscure fact that contradicted his opponent, or ask a series of rapid-fire controversial questions that would lead his opponent to contradict himself. But if, Howe noted, "he was being cornered he would come forth with some witticism and put on his best smile. . . . I think his grin saved Ike a lot of trouble."[31]

By this time, too, he had lost much of his chip-on-the-shoulder belligerence. "I never knew of his going out to hunt up the town bully just to lick him," Howe remembered. "He was not revengeful. He never went out looking for trouble, but at the same time, if he became unexpectedly involved, he never ran away from it."[32] He was a serious young man, working hard, saving money, his goals set.

For some unexplained reason, however, his deal with Edgar was pushed back a year. Edgar spent the summer of 1910 in Ann Arbor, and remained there in the fall, while Dwight continued to work. Dwight never complained about it, except during his retirement, when he would grin and say that Edgar still owed him a year's hard labor.[33]

During the summer of 1910, Dwight got to know Everett "Swede" Hazlett, son of one of the town's physicians. He had known Swede only casually before, because Swede had gone to a military school in Wisconsin. Swede had obtained an appointment to the Naval Academy at Annapolis, but in June 1910 had failed the mathematics section of the entrance examination. He had come home to study for a year, in order to repeat the examination the following June. He struck up a friendship with Dwight that became intimate and lasted for the remainder of their lives.

Swede was the first friend young Eisenhower had who did not share his passion for sports. Indeed, Swede actively disliked fighting and other contact sports so much that other boys bullied him and Dwight had to tell the tormentors to leave him alone.[34] But Swede was intelligent, ambitious, witty, and thoughtful. He had been places and seen things, and he was a great talker. He was drawn to Dwight. "I liked him most for his sterling qualities," he later explained. "He was calm, frank, laconic and sensible, and not in the least affected by being the school hero." Swede began dropping in at the creamery at night. The two young men would fry eggs on a brightly polished shovel in the boiler room, then top off the meal with ice cream from the company's freezer. While they ate, they talked. Dwight listened, entranced, to Swede's stories about Wisconsin, about the Eastern Seaboard, and most of all about Annapolis.[35]

Dwight's intentions at this time were to save money, hold Edgar to his bargain, and go to the University of Michigan in the fall of 1911. Unlike Edgar, he did not have law or any other specific profession in mind, but he did know that he wanted a college education and, more specifically, an opportunity to play college football and baseball. Michigan had one of the best football teams in the country. Swede pointed out to him that the Naval Academy played football too, that it had at least as much prestige as Michigan, that it guaranteed an interesting and useful career to its graduates, and best of all that it was free. He wanted Dwight to seek an appointment and become his classmate. Dwight agreed to try. Swede had obtained his Annapolis appointment from a local congressman who was a friend of his father. Dwight approached the same congressman, only to learn that he had already filled all his vacancies. The congressman advised Dwight to turn to Senator Joseph Bristow, who came from nearby Salina. Dwight was not optimistic—he felt he did not have a chance if appointments depended on political influence because his family had none. Swede convinced him it would not hurt to try.[36]

Dwight went after it with characteristic directness. He approached the leading citizens of Abilene, the bankers, newspaper editors, merchants, and the postmaster, asking them to write letters of recommendation to Bristow. All agreed. On August 20, 1910, Dwight wrote his own letter to Bristow: "I would very much like to enter either the school at Annapolis, or the one at West Point." He had decided to put in the Military Academy in the event that Bristow had already made his appointment to Annapolis. "In order to do this, I must have an appointment to one of these places and so I am writing you in order to secure the same.

"I have graduated from high school and will be nineteen years of age this fall.

"If you find it possible to appoint me to one of these schools, your kindness will certainly be appreciated by me.

"Trusting to hear from you, concerning this matter, at your earliest convenience, I am respectfully yours,

Dwight Eisenhower."[37]

His letter, and all his supporting letters, went unanswered. Like most other U.S. senators, Bristow had many more applicants than he had places to fill. Appointing one boy to a position that ten wanted would make him one friend and nine enemies. Bristow solved this problem by using the same method most of his colleagues used, an open, competitive examination.

In September 1910, Dwight read in the local paper an announcement from Bristow's office: on October 4 and 5, in the office of the state superintendent of public instruction in Topeka, there would be a competitive examination for applicants for the service academies. Dwight wrote Bristow a second letter: "Some time ago, I wrote you applying for an appointment to West Point or Annapolis. As yet, I have heard nothing definite from you about the matter but I noticed in the daily papers that you would soon give a competitive examination for these appointments.

"Now, if you find it impossible to give me an appointment outright to one of those places, would I have the right to enter this competitive examination?"[38]

This time, Bristow responded immediately—of course Dwight had the right. Dwight began a cram course. Swede was his tutor. "Ike's God-given brain had sped him along," Hazlett later said, "until he was 'way ahead of his . . . teacher."[39]

Eight candidates gathered in Topeka in early October for the two-day examination. Dwight was outstanding in grammar (99), algebra (94), and arithmetic (96), did well in geography and spelling (90 in each), but somewhat to his surprise not so well in geometry (77), U.S. history (73), and general history (79). He had thought that history would be his strongest subject, but the questions were more about politics and economics than about generals and battles. His overall score was 87½, good enough for second place among the eight contestants. The first-place finisher had indicated that he would accept an appointment only to Annapolis, while Dwight had checked "either" of the academies on the forms.[40]

Early in November, Bristow informed Dwight that he had appointed him to West Point. The entrance examination would be held in St. Louis in January 1911. Swede was disappointed. "This was a cruel blow," Hazlett said years later, "and Ike didn't like it any better than I did. All his hopes had been aimed at Annapolis and he felt that, through me, he knew a good deal about it." Swede urged Dwight to write to Bristow, to ask the senator if he could not reconsider and send him to Annapolis instead. But Dwight had reread the entrance requirements for the Naval Academy and learned that at twenty years of age he was too old to enter. Swede said he could take a year off his age and no one could prove different. Dwight shook his head and mumbled that he could not "look a gift horse in the mouth." He would accept the West Point appointment.[41]

Despite Hazlett's opinion, Dwight was delighted. So were his brothers. His father, typically, showed no emotion whatsoever. His mother, in Dwight's words "the most honest and sincere pacifist I ever knew," was unhappy at the thought of her boy being a soldier, but she made no attempt to stop him.[42] Decades later, people were fascinated by the idea that the world's most famous soldier came from a pacifist family. In July 1954, President Eisenhower was asked about it in a press conference. He responded that it would be "enough to say about his father's religion that he was Pennsylvania Dutch and he had all the temper of a Pennsylvania Dutchman, and there was nothing pacifist about him." And although his mother was a "passionate pacifist," stories that she objected strenuously to his going to West Point were all wrong. "She never said one single word to me."[43]

In the fall of 1910, Swede continued to cram for his second try at Annapolis, while Dwight prepared for the West Point entrance examination. Joe Howe recalled that "he came into the office one evening . . . and wanted to know if he could borrow my *Century Book of Facts.* He said he guessed he would have to do some real studying now."[44] He also returned to Abilene High School for review courses in chemistry, mathematics, and physics, and not incidentally to play another year of football (eligibility limitations were unknown at that time). He did well at both endeavors, becoming the star of the Abilene team and a better student. The train trip to St. Louis in January for the examination took him the farthest he had ever been away from Abilene. The examination itself was similar to the one he had taken for Senator Bristow, and he passed it easily. In June 1911, he was off for West Point.

The goodbyes were calm and dignified. David said his farewell before leaving for work at 6 A.M. Arthur was in Kansas City, Edgar in Ann Arbor. Dwight shook hands with Roy, Earl, and Milton. He left his shotgun and his dog, Flip, in their keeping, sternly telling them to take good care of both. His mother went to the front porch with him, gave him a hug, then waved as he walked toward the train station, suitcase in hand. After he was gone, she went back to her room. Milton later told Dwight that for the first time in his life he heard their mother cry.[45]

Standing outside the station, waiting for the train, he made a striking picture. He had filled out in the past two years, putting on twenty pounds, none of which was fat. At nearly six feet tall, and weighing 170 pounds, with strong, broad shoulders and rock-hard muscles, he was the embodiment of an athlete. He was rawboned, with big hands. He walked on the balls of his feet and carried himself gracefully, as good athletes do.

Most people thought him extremely good-looking. He had light-brown hair, large eyes, and an oversize nose and mouth that fit nicely with his large head. His face was full, round, and symmetrical. His blue eyes sparkled, danced, and looked intently at whatever he saw. His lips were heavy and thick; young women found them sensuous.[46] The lips were seldom at rest, because he grinned as easily as he breathed, a big, lopsided grin that most people found irresistible. He laughed easily too, and loudly, with great gusto, usually slapping his knee in exclamation at the same time. He had a marvelously expressive face that still turned beet-red when he was angry, scowled furiously when he was disapproving, lit up when he was pleased.

He was the most popular young man in town, but carefully avoided anything that might indicate a swelled head. Young women found him charming because of his polite manner, honesty, and mature bearing. Young men liked him because he was such a good organizer, because of his enthusiasm for games and fun, and because he was a straight shooter, a fearsome competitor who nevertheless always played clean. Most of his contemporaries admired him for his earnestness, toward work and sports and, increasingly of late, toward knowledge. They also admired his ambition, his determination to get out of Abilene and make something of himself.[47]

For a twenty-year-old, he had remarkable self-confidence. It showed in his movements and gestures, in his talk, and in his actions. He knew he could provide for himself, that he was good at poker, hunting, fishing, and competitive sports; he knew that he was a good student. He realized that the school he was about to enter was one of the most difficult engineering schools in the country, with a heavy emphasis on mathematics and the physical sciences, but he was confident he could handle it.

He had an active curious mind. He wanted to know about history, about sports, about mathematics, about opportunities, about how things worked and what people had done. His curiosity, however, was neither creative nor original. He had no interest in music, or painting, or any of the fine arts, or literature, or political theory. He directed his great energy and powers of concentration on making things work better, not differently. Internally his goal was self-improvement, whether in sports or studies, not self-change.

Most of all he knew himself and his capabilities, and as he swung himself up on the train and headed east, away from Abilene, his family, and his friends, he broke into one of his biggest grins. He had no doubts about himself. There was not, for him, the self-searching or identity crisis so often associated with young men. Dwight Eisenhower knew who he was and where he was going.

CHAPTER THREE

West Point

1911–1915

IT WAS a full half continent from Abilene to West Point, a three-day train ride. Dwight stopped off at Ann Arbor, where he visited with Edgar, who was taking his final exams. One evening the brothers rented a canoe and paddled down the Huron River with two college girls, passing canoeloads of other students as they went. This was, Dwight recalled, "the most romantic evening I had ever known," and as he resumed his journey, he had the dismaying feeling that he had made a mistake in not joining Edgar at Michigan. "It looked to me as if he were leading the right life."[1]

That feeling must have been strengthened when he arrived on the banks of the Hudson. Most entering cadets were, like Eisenhower, the best athletes or the best students, or both, in their home towns, and they tended to think a great deal of themselves. West Point undertook to shrink their swelled heads. The process began with their arrival at the Point, where they were deliberately given a rude, hard shock.

"Get your shoulders back! Suck in that stomach! More yet! More yet! Hold your head up! Drag in your chin! Hurry up! Hurry up!" They were double-timed from building to building as they turned in their money, collected their bedding, received their uniforms, and moved into their rooms on the fourth floor of Beast Barracks. They discovered they had even left their names behind when they said farewell to civilian life; now they were "Mr. Dumbjohn" or "Mr. Ducrot" or "Mr. Dumgard." They learned that they could not respond quickly enough to any command, that for all their athletic skills they were incredibly clumsy, totally unable to keep step while marching. They learned that they were not cadets, but plebes, not exalted, but degraded, not intelligent, but stupid.

When Eisenhower arrived at West Point, in 1911, hazing was more widely practiced than at any other time in the Academy's history. The techniques, most of which Eisenhower endured on his first day, included bracing (standing at exaggerated attention), picking up all the ants in a hill, one by one, reciting nonsensical stories and poems, holding Indian clubs at arm's length for long periods, "Swimming to Newburgh" (balancing on the stomach on a pole and pretending to swim), and sitting at meals with the feet raised to the bottom of the table. For general nuisance value Yearlings made idle plebes do push-ups and other exercises.[2]

Some boys could not take it. Eisenhower's first roommate, a seventeen-year-old from Kansas, had been escorted to the train by a band when he left home. The contrast of Beast Barracks was too much for him. The first night, and every night thereafter, he wept. When Eisenhower pointed out the obvious, that hundreds of others had gone through the same trials successfully, and that he could do the same, his roommate would sob, "It's easy for you . . ." He shortly left the Academy.[3]

Eisenhower accepted the hazing. He never lost his temper with a red-faced Yearling barking commands; whenever he was tempted to do so, he reminded himself, "Where else can you get a free college education?" Nearly twenty-one years old, he was one or two years older than many of his tormentors, tough enough to do the physical exercises with ease, detached enough to regard hazing and the Yearlings as a bit absurd.[4]

What impressed him was the other side of West Point, the ceremony, the tradition, the idea of joining the Long Gray Line, the sense of duty and service. He felt it at the end of that first day, June 14, 1911, when—together with 264 other appointees—he stood in a line on the parade ground to watch the Corps of Cadets march past. In full-dress uniform, moving as an organic unit in perfect rhythm, the cadets marched by as the band played. It was, and always is, a stirring sight. When he took the oath of allegiance and became a part of the U.S. Army, Eisenhower felt that the words "United States of America" had taken on a new meaning, that from then on he would be serving his country, not himself. It was a precious moment for him, one he always cherished.[5]

West Point regarded its own past with veneration and concentrated on instilling that concept in the plebes, filling them with the feeling that the past was a living thing, all around them. Here was Grant's room, there Lee's, there Sherman's. Over there Winfield Scott lived. Here Custer learned to ride. Eisenhower, with his sense of military history, responded enthusiastically. In his free time, of which there was precious little, he liked to wander about the Plain, climb the cliffs, look down on the Hudson, reflect on the Point's crucial role in the American Revolution, wonder at what might have happened had Benedict Arnold's attempt to betray the post to the British been successful. Years later he told his son he never tired of such speculation.[6]

Hazing, the uglier side of West Point, had little appeal to him, obviously not as a recipient, but not as a Yearling either. Only once, at the beginning of his own third-class year, did he yield to the temptation to haze. A plebe, dashing down the street to carry out an order, ran into him and tumbled to the ground. Reacting with a "bellow of astonishment and mock indignation," Eisenhower scornfully demanded, "Mr. Dumgard, what is your P.C.S. [Previous Condition of Servitude]?" adding sarcastically, "You look like a barber." The plebe pulled himself together and replied softly, "I was a barber, sir." Eisenhower turned red with embarrassment. Without a word, he returned to his room, where he told his roommate, P. A. Hodgson, "I'm never going to crawl [haze] another plebe as long as I live. As a matter of fact, they'll have to run over and knock me out of the company street before I'll make any attempt again. I've just done something that was stupid and unforgivable. I managed to make a man ashamed of the work he did to earn a living."[7] Eisenhower's reaction to the incident typified his four years at the Academy. He took from West Point what was positive and rejected that which was negative.

The Academy made his life as Spartan as possible. Cold rooms in winter, hot ones in summer, plain, unappetizing food, and constant drill in the summer, recitations the remainder of the year, were only the beginning of the discomforts. West Point's first goal was character building, and to that end it pushed, pulled, shaped, and hammered its cadets into the accepted mold of a Christian gentleman and officer. Regulations covered every conceivable act. From the moment Eisenhower woke in the morning to the moment he finally closed his eyes, his life was prescribed. At a time when civilian colleges were shedding themselves of their nineteenth-century regulations, West Point held firm to its traditions. While the country as a whole was undergoing rapid and drastic changes in politics, economics, fashions, and technology, West Point deliberately cultivated a sense of timelessness. Superintendent Hugh Scott explained, "West Point is not a subject for reform. . . . It goes forward on its majestic course . . . moving serenely . . . without need of radical alteration." And Henry H. Arnold, who graduated shortly before Eisenhower entered, remembered of his cadet days, "We lived . . . in conformance with a code, and with daily routines which had not changed . . . since Grant was a cadet."[8]

West Point was even more cut off and isolated from the rest of the world than Abilene had been. Like Abilene, its self-satisfaction was complete; like Abilene, it had a revealed truth and felt no need to examine it. And that truth reinforced much of what Eisenhower had absorbed in his upbringing. At Michigan, Edgar was in the middle of intellectual ferment—everything was questioned, nothing was accepted. At West Point, Dwight was ordered to accept what he was taught and memorize it.

Eisenhower's studies were overwhelmingly narrow and technical, with the emphasis on civil and military engineering. His teachers were, to a man, recent graduates of the USMA. The method of teaching had not changed since the War of 1812. Every day, in every class, every cadet was expected to recite, to give an approved answer to a standard question and to receive a carefully recorded grade on each response.

Often the instructors knew little more than their students. In integral calculus one day, the teacher ordered Eisenhower to do a long, complicated problem on the blackboard. The instructor had previously explained the problem and supplied the answer, but since it had been obvious to Eisenhower that the instructor was doing it entirely by rote he had paid no attention. Thus, when called upon, he had "not the foggiest notion of how to begin." After struggling for almost a full hour, he finally tried a solution that, to his amazement, worked. He was asked to explain his solution; it was shorter and simpler than the rote answer. But the instructor interrupted him to charge that he had merely memorized the answer and then put down a lot of figures and steps that had no meaning.

Eisenhower could not abide being called a cheat. He began to protest so vehemently that he was soon in imminent danger of being expelled on a charge of insubordination. Just then, a senior officer from the Mathematics Department walked in. He inquired about the trouble, had Eisenhower go through the solution again, then pronounced it superior to the one being used in the department and ordered it incorporated into the Mathematics Department's teaching.[9]

Eisenhower was saved, but just barely, for a flexible and sympathetic response from the authorities was unusual at West Point. In most cases, there was no room for discussion or exploration of new answers to old problems. English was composition, never literature; history was fact, never inquiry. It was all rote learning, and Eisenhower was good enough at it that he could stay comfortably in the top half of his class without undue exertion. He was especially good in English; while others struggled for days over a theme, he could produce a high-scoring essay a half hour before class. The chief requirement of a good essay at West Point was a logical presentation of fact. At the end of his plebe year, when his class had shrunk from 265 to 212, he stood tenth in English.[10]

In other subjects, Eisenhower was content to stay in the middle. He preferred enjoying his classmates to competing with them. These classmates were, generally, like him—white (between the Civil War and World War I, West Point admitted only thirteen black cadets, of whom three graduated), Protestant (almost no Jews, and few Catholics), rural or small town in origin, middle class, intelligent, and athletic. Eisenhower's own class later became the most famous in West Point's history, "the class the stars fell on." In 1915, 164 of them graduated. Of the 164, 59 rose to the rank of brigadier general or higher, three to the rank of full general, and two to the rank of general of the army. Members included Vernon Prichard, George Stratemeyer, Charles Ryder, Stafford Irwin, Joseph McNarney, James Van Fleet, Hubert Harmon, and Omar Bradley.[11] Eisenhower knew and liked them all, especially Bradley, who became a close friend, and of whom he wrote, in the 1915 yearbook, the *Howitzer,* "Brad's most important characteristic is 'getting there,' and if he keeps up the clip he's started some of us will someday be bragging that, 'Sure, General Bradley was a classmate of mine.' "[12]

The West Point system is designed to find and break the nonconformist, and is usually successful—Edgar Allan Poe, a cadet in 1830, hated the "God-forsaken place" and, after less than a year, simply walked away.[13] Others, less extreme than Poe, enjoyed testing or bending the regulations, finding out what they could get away with, more or less cheerfully paying the price when they got caught. Eisenhower was one of these. His cadet pranks, which he told with great relish in his old age, as if they were originals, were in fact part of a traditional pattern followed by generations of cadets who managed to adjust to West Point without losing their individuality.

Cigarette smoking was strictly forbidden. "So," Eisenhower recorded laconically, "I started smoking cigarettes." He smoked roll-your-own Bull Durhams. His roommate did not approve; other plebes were worried; Eisenhower smoked anyway. When caught by an officer, he walked punishment tours or served room confinement for a number of hours. He continued to smoke.[14]

This was only one of his small acts of rebellion. He could not or would not keep his room as neat as the regulations required, was frequently late for formation or guard mounting, often failed in his attempts to dress according to the regulations. For all these, and other, sins, he paid a price in demerits, which counted against him in his final class standing. Of the 164 men in his class who graduated, he stood 125th in discipline. It hardly bothered him; he later admitted that he "looked with distaste on classmates whose days and nights were haunted by fear of demerits and low grades."[15] During World War II, he expressed astonishment at the news that one of his classmates had made general officer rank; "Christ," he said, "he's always been afraid to break a regulation."[16]

His own favorite story about a cadet prank centered on the sometimes absurd literalness of the regulations and orders. Eisenhower and another plebe, named Atkins, were guilty of an infraction. The cadet corporal who caught them, named Adler, ordered them to report to his room after tattoo in "full-dress coats," meaning a complete dress uniform. The two plebes decided to do exactly as ordered, and that night reported to Adler wearing their coats and not another stitch of clothing. It was one of West Point's oldest stunts—Edgar Allan Poe had pulled it—but Eisenhower and Atkins nevertheless got the reaction they wanted. Adler roared in anger. He ordered them to return after taps "in complete uniform including rifles and crossbelts and if you miss a single item I'll have you down here every night for a week." They did as ordered and suffered through a long session of bracing and lecturing, but the laughs they and their fellow plebes got from Adler's discomfort made it worthwhile.[17]

Eisenhower's major escape from the grind was not in petty pranks, but in athletics. Sports remained the center of his life. He said later that he had "a lack of motivation in almost everything other than athletics, except for the simple and stark resolve to get a college education."[18] In his plebe year, he played football for the Cullum Hall team, or junior varsity. Over the winter, he ran on the indoor track, practicing fast starts and improving his speed, and worked at gymnastics to strengthen his leg and arm muscles. To build up his weight, he ate until he thought he would burst. In the spring, he played baseball—Omar Bradley was a teammate. By the fall of 1912, he was faster, stronger, and bigger—at 174 pounds—than he had ever been. He was determined to make the varsity. In the first practice game, he did well. After the scrimmage, Coach Ernest Graves told him to get a new, better-fitting uniform, a not-too-subtle way of saying that he was varsity material and, for Eisenhower, a dream come true. He was, in his words, "as high as a kite."[19]

With his improved speed, Eisenhower shifted from the line to the backfield. He got his chance when Army's star ballcarrier, first-classman Geoffrey Keyes, was injured before the first game. Eisenhower led Army to a victory in that game, against Stevens Institute, and was again the star the next week in a win over Rutgers. *The New York Times* described him as "one of the most promising backs in Eastern football" and carried a two-column photograph of him punting a football. Swede Hazlett, then in his second year at the Naval Academy, clipped it out and tacked it on his wall. He recalled "the consternation at Annapolis when the sports pages brought news of a great new Army halfback who could do everything and was running wild against all opponents."[20] In a victory over Colgate, the West Point yearbook reported that "Eisenhower in the fourth quarter could not be stopped."[21]

On November 9, 1912, Army played the Carlisle Indian School, whose star was Jim Thorpe, winner of both the decathlon and the pentathlon at the 1912 Olympic Games. Despite an intense Army buildup to "get Thorpe," Thorpe went wild. He ran for two touchdowns, one for ninety-five yards, passed for another, kicked three field goals and three extra points. Late in the game, Eisenhower arranged with a teammate to "high-low" Thorpe—Eisenhower would hit him high on one side while the other halfback would hit him around the ankles. The technique worked, and the Army backs congratulated themselves on their success. They were sure that their crushing tackle had laid up Thorpe for the remainder of the afternoon. "But," as Eisenhower later told his wide-eyed younger brothers, relating the story with great gusto and grinning broadly, "do you know what that Indian did? He picked himself up, went back to the huddle, took the ball on the next play, and ran for another first down!" Eisenhower, not Thorpe, limped from the field. The final score was Carlisle 27, Army 6.[22]

The following week against Tufts, Eisenhower twisted his knee. There was some swelling and he spent a few days in the hospital, hoping that he would recuperate soon enough to play in the final game of the season against Navy. But that week, while participating in the "monkey drill" in the riding hall—leaping off and back onto a galloping horse—his knee crumbled when he hit the ground. The cartilages and tendons were badly torn. The doctors put his leg in a plaster cast; the pain was so intense that for days he could hardly sleep.[23] His spirits sank even lower when Navy won the game. "Seems like I'm never cheerful any more," he wrote to Ruby Norman. "The fellows that used to call me 'Sunny Jim' call me 'Gloomy Face' now. The chief cause is this game pin of mine—I sure hate to be so helpless and worthless. Anyway I'm getting to be such a confirmed grouch you'd hardly know me."[24]

He hit bottom when the doctors took off the cast and informed him that he would never play football again. So great was his depression that several times his roommate had to talk him out of resigning from the Academy. "Life seemed to have little meaning," he later recalled. "A need to excel was almost gone."[25]

His studies suffered. As a plebe, he had stood fifty-seventh in a class of 212; in his Yearling year, when he hurt his knee, he slipped to eighty-first in a class of 177. P. A. Hodgson wrote of him, "Poor Dwight merely consents to exist until graduation shall set him free. At one time he threatened to get interested in life and won his 'A' by being the most promising back in Eastern football—but the Tufts game broke his knee and the promise."[26]

A ten-week visit to Abilene in the summer of 1913, his only leave in four years, helped revive his spirits. His cadet uniform, erect bearing, confident manner, and stories about the Academy and playing against Jim Thorpe impressed everyone. He was, Earl remembered, the "town hero, and he acted the part. [He] lost no opportunity to impress us with what he knew and had done." Wesley Merrifield thought "he looked like a million dollars."[27]

That fall, back at the Point, he tried to repair the damaged knee by distance running. But for the remainder of his life, the knee would become dislocated under strain. Although his playing days were ended, his interest in football was not. He became a cheerleader, which gave him his first experience as a public speaker—he would address the entire Corps of Cadets the night before a big game, exhorting the members to make an all-out effort as fans the next afternoon.

Like all true fans, his mood ebbed and flowed with the fortunes of his team. "Everything has gone wrong," he wrote Ruby Norman in the fall of 1913. "The football team . . . got beaten most gloriously by Notre Dame last Saturday. The only bright spot is, just now, that trouble with Mexico seems imminent. We may stir up a little excitement yet. Let's hope so—at least." Two weeks later he had forgotten Pancho Villa and the possibility of active duty in Mexico because of the excitement of a victory over Navy. He wrote Ruby, "Back from N.Y.! and we surely turned the trick—22–9. Oh you beautiful doll! Some game, some game! Just a small crowd saw us do it, you know. Just 45,000 people. Sure was sad! . . . You should have seen us after the game. Oh! Oh! Oh! Believe me, girl, I *enjoyed* myself. Course I couldn't raise a riot for I was in uniform—but I went down to Murray's in a crowd of four—and we danced and ate—and oh say—the joy of the thing is too much—I feel my reason toppling."[28]

His enthusiasm was matched by his intense study of the intricacies of the game, to the point that the football coach suggested that he coach the junior varsity. He did so eagerly, and with success, sending a number of players on to the varsity and winning most of his games.

His experiences as a coach—and there were to be many more—strengthened his love for the game. Like many other fans, he made football into something more than just an athletic contest. The act of coaching brought out his best traits—his organizational ability, his energy and competitiveness, his enthusiasm and optimism, his willingness to work hard at a task that intrigued him, his powers of concentration, his talent for working with the material he had instead of hoping for what he did not have, and his gift for drawing the best out of his players. During World War II, a number of his associates compared his techniques as a general with those of a good football coach, pacing up and down the line, urging his team forward. In his private talks with his corps and division commanders, and in his Orders of the Day, Supreme Commander Eisenhower used football slang extensively, urging his men to "pull an end run" and "hit the line" and "break through" and "get that ball across the goal line."

Most of all, as a general and as President, he urged teamwork. At the end of his life, he wrote, "I believe that football, perhaps more than any other sport, tends to instill in men the feeling that victory comes through hard—almost slavish—work, team play, self-confidence, and an enthusiasm that amounts to dedication."[29] Millions of Americans would agree that the act of playing or coaching football built successful men who could go out and get a job done.

His activities as a cheerleader and a coach increased his popularity. Swede Hazlett, who graduated from Annapolis two weeks before West Point's June Week in 1915, came up to the Point to pay Eisenhower a visit. "It was no surprise to find him . . . generally liked and admired," Swede recalled. "Had he not indulged in so many extracurricular activities he could easily have led his class scholastically. Everyone was his friend—but with no loss in dignity or respect."[30] Not pressing anyone for class standing also helped his popularity—he was sixty-first out of 164.

One official judgment was not so flattering as Swede's. "We saw in Eisenhower a not uncommon type," a tactical officer recorded, "a man who would thoroughly enjoy his army life, giving both to duty and recreation their fair values, [but] we did not see in him a man who would throw himself into his job so completely that nothing else would matter."[31] But another officer, perhaps more interested in football, wrote that Eisenhower "was born to command."[32]

• •

What did he learn, other than football, in his four years at West Point? These were the years in which he had his most intensive schooling and adopted or had reinforced his attitudes and assumptions. What he learned as a cadet affected his thoughts and actions as a general and as a President, so it is inherently important.

He learned, first, his profession. West Point gave him a solid base on which to build a career as an officer. He knew Army customs, jargon, traditions, organization. He knew how to march, how to handle a rifle and small artillery pieces, how to ride, how to build a simple bridge or fortification. He knew a great deal about mathematics and geography, some physics and chemistry. He knew how to write an operational order. He knew a multitude of facts about military history.

He had a clear idea of what an Army officer should be. His course on the history of the military art emphasized the Great Captains and their personal attributes, carefully drawing for the cadets the image of the ideal military leader. The good officer, Eisenhower learned, is highly motivated, a man who has dedicated his life to his country, a leader who is able to examine a situation, come to a quick decision, and stick by it. He is a well-dressed, well-behaved gentleman who enthusiastically performs the duties required of him and regards lethargy or indifference as a sign of weakness. He is an unselfish team player whose sense of honor impels him to strive for truthfulness and sincerity while abhorring deceit, quibbling, or evasiveness. He is physically and morally courageous. He respects the privileges and responsibilities of rank and takes pride in his profession.[33]

Beyond his formal schooling, Cadet Eisenhower lived in a climate of opinion, surrounded by a set of ideas that, although unspoken and unacknowledged, nearly every cadet absorbed and embraced as his own. Some of these assumptions Eisenhower held to for the whole of his life, others he gradually rejected, but they were all part of his education. Many of his strengths and weaknesses as President can be traced back to the intellectual milieu at West Point and in the U.S. Army, circa 1915.

The first point to note is how fiercely the Academy resisted the trends in higher education and American society. The climate of opinion at West Point differed markedly, for example, from that at the University of Michigan. Ann Arbor was liberal and progressive; the Academy was conservative and hidebound. At Ann Arbor, the individual was supreme; at West Point, the group was paramount. Ann Arbor encouraged questioning and doubt; West Point demanded obedience and acceptance. Ann Arbor concentrated on the future, West Point on the past. Ann Arbor was optimistic, West Point pessimistic. Ann Arbor believed that mankind was perfectible, a notion the Academy rejected.

When they looked inward, officers saw themselves as part of a well-functioning machine. Individual genius was held to be superfluous, if not dangerous. Teamwork was the key. War had become rationalized and routinized, and the German General Staff, in which any officer could do the duties of any other officer, was the model. It was the corporate ideal, almost diametrically opposed to the popular American faith in rugged individualism, but held to firmly by the officer corps. West Pointers saw themselves as different from, and superior to, civilians. It was difficult for them to suppress feelings of contempt for civilians in general, although of course they regarded their own civilian friends as exceptions. The money-grubbing, the extreme individualism of the marketplace, filled them with distaste, and they wanted no part of it. Nor did they want any part of the politics that went with it.

It was both circumspect and necessary for Army officers to think of themselves as apolitical. Their view was that the military existed to take orders, to carry out policy decided upon by the President, never to set policy itself. Several important corollaries flowed from that premise. The one that would affect Eisenhower most directly was the firmly held belief that politics and officership did not mix. In 1915, it was estimated that not one officer in five hundred had ever cast a ballot.[34] It was unthinkable that an officer should ever present himself as a candidate for political office. This was not merely theory—General Grant's unhappy experience in politics was taken to be a practical lesson in the wisdom of soldiers staying aloof from party politics. Sherman, not Grant, was the model.

Another corollary was the preeminence of the President. Army officers ignored the President's role as head of a political party and instead concentrated on his role as Commander in Chief, the head of the sacrosanct chain of command that stretched from him to the lowest enlisted man. By contrast, Congress was the arena of party politics. "If any convictions . . . were acquired by the cadet," one of Eisenhower's instructors declared, "they were generally of contempt for mere politicians and their dishonest principles of action."[35] All his life, almost twenty years of which was spent in Washington working with congressmen on a daily basis, Eisenhower would heatedly and repeatedly express his scorn for "politicians." To him, as to most officers, noise and clamor came from Capitol Hill, while the White House gave clear orders.

These attitudes led to an exaltation of the office of the President, based on the disingenuous notion that the President was above politics. Of course they knew better, were aware that the President is the supreme politician, but they made the proposition believable, at least to themselves, by putting the emphasis on the office rather than the man himself.

As a cadet and a young officer, Dwight Eisenhower absorbed most of the military prejudices, assumptions, and traditions. Many of the general ideals fit in perfectly with what he had learned from his parents and from Abilene. They were also part of his sports orientation. Inherent in the whole of Eisenhower's education was the concept of dedication, and its corollary, duty. He got it from David and Ida, from Abilene, from his sports activities, most of all from West Point. Robert E. Lee once said duty was the most beautiful word in the English language. Eisenhower felt the same way.

CHAPTER FOUR

San Antonio, Gettysburg

1915–1918

EISENHOWER GRADUATED in June 1915. He had drifted into West Point and, as a student, drifted through it. He had obtained the free education he wanted, but although the Academy had sharpened his sense of duty, it had not given him an intense desire to meet that duty by being an officer. When the doctor at West Point told him that he might not be given a commission in the Army because of his knee, he shrugged, made no protest, and instead sent off for literature on Argentina. He had a vague notion that he might try life on the frontier in South America. The doctor said that he could have a commission in the Coast Artillery, which would have meant a sedentary life and thus no strain on his knee. Eisenhower refused it. Finally the doctor said that if he applied for service in the Infantry, rather than the Cavalry, he could have his commission. Eisenhower did so, primarily on the grounds that he could think of nothing better to do.

For his preferred duty station, he put down the Philippines, the only man in his class to do so. The Philippines appealed to him because they were exotic, not because he could expect rapid advancement there (no assignment could provide that, as promotion was based strictly on seniority). Going to the Far East would give him a chance to see the world. He purchased a set of tropical uniforms, then went to Abilene for his graduation leave. In mid-September 1915, he got his orders. Instead of the Philippines, he was told to report to the 19th Infantry Regiment at Fort Sam Houston, outside San Antonio, Texas.[1] As he set off for Texas, he was determined that so long as he was an officer in the Army, he would do his best to be a good one. It was a resolve rather than an ambition, and sprang from a sense of obligation and responsibility rather than from a competitive drive, for he felt that with the end of his sports career, his competitive days were over.

Fort Sam Houston was one of the Army's most desirable posts, as life there in 1915 was slow-paced, leisurely, meant to be enjoyed. Any competent officer could complete his duties by noon, or earlier, and spend the remainder of the day enjoying the excellent dove and deer hunting, unlimited horseback riding, and gay social life. There were dances, parades, formal and informal calls, bachelor parties, and poker games. It all appealed to Eisenhower's gregarious nature; he found he enjoyed living in the South and being an officer in the U.S. Army.

Eisenhower's reputation as a football coach preceded him, and shortly after he arrived one of the local military academies asked him to coach its football team, at a salary of $150 for the season. Second Lieutenant Eisenhower, assuming that his duties as an officer would require afternoon as well as morning work, politely declined, saying that he had no time for football. A few days later the commander at Fort Sam, General Frederick Funston, told him, "It would please me and it would be good for the Army if you would accept this offer." Eisenhower said, "Yes, sir," and thus he coached that fall, compiling a winning record. The next season, 1916, he moved up to the college ranks, taking over St. Louis College, a Catholic school that had not won a game in five years. Under Eisenhower's direction, the team tied its first game, won five straight, and then lost a close game for the championship of the league.[2]

In the winter of 1915–1916 there was action on the U.S.-Mexican border. Not much action, to be sure—it involved Pancho Villa and his irregulars, who conducted a raid against Columbus, New Mexico—but the first the Army had seen since the Philippine Insurrection. Like most recent West Point graduates, Eisenhower applied for service with General John J. Pershing's Punitive Expedition. His application was rejected. Instead the War Department, which he soon came to regard as "that nebulous region" where incomprehensible decisions were made, assigned him to training duty with a National Guard regiment mobilizing along the border.[3]

Scarcely had the Punitive Expedition returned—without catching Villa—than the 1916 Preparedness campaign got under way. Eisenhower was assigned to the 57th Infantry, a new Regular Army regiment, as supply officer. He was given three days to prepare for the arrival of three thousand recruits at Camp Wilson, on the edge of Fort Sam. Eisenhower, learning one of the most basic lessons of soldiery, made friends with the quartermaster, then pleaded successfully for more tents, rifles, shoes, uniforms, everything. He learned another basic lesson, that any junior officer who complains about the food becomes the mess officer. Eisenhower became the mess officer. He and the regimental adjutant, Captain Walton Walker, already knew enough to realize that a happy CO makes for happy junior officers. Their CO, Colonel D. J. Baker, was fussy about his meals. To please him, and to have a bit of fun themselves, Eisenhower and Walker got up at 4 A.M., rode their horses to the edge of camp, shot enough doves for the colonel's breakfast, and had them on his plate by 8 A.M.[4]

Doing his duties, hunting, and coaching football hardly took up all his time. He played poker with the other junior officers, winning consistently, went drinking with them, and generally got along easily with the gang. He made some lifelong friendships, including Walker, Leonard Gerow, and Wade Haislip (each of these lieutenants became four-star generals).[5]

And he fell in love. The romance began on a Sunday afternoon in October 1915, one of those perfect autumn days in South Texas. Eisenhower was Officer of the Day. Putting on his newly cleaned and pressed uniform, his boots, brightly polished by his orderly, and his service revolver, he walked out of the Bachelor Officers' Quarters to make an inspection of the guard posts. Across the street, on the lawn of the Officers' Club, sitting on canvas chairs enjoying the sunshine, a small group of women was gathered. One of them, Mrs. Lulu Harris, the wife of Major Hunter Harris, saw Eisenhower and called out, "Ike, won't you come over here? I have some people I'd like you to meet."

"Sorry," Eisenhower responded. "I'm on guard and have to start an inspection trip." Turning to her companion, Mrs. Harris muttered, "Humph! The woman-hater of the post." Looking back at Eisenhower, she called again: "We didn't ask you to come over to *stay*. Just come over here and meet these friends of mine."

Eisenhower walked across the street to say a polite hello to the ladies. "The one who attracted my eye instantly," he later recalled, "was a vivacious and attractive girl, smaller than average, saucy in the look about her face and in her whole attitude."[6] She was wearing a starched white linen dress and a big, floppy black hat. She had just arrived in Texas for the season—she lived in Denver during the hot months—and was renewing her many friendships at Fort Sam. She had two younger sisters, she was eighteen years old, and she was intrigued by Mrs. Harris' comment about the woman-hater of the post. Her name was Mary Geneva Doud, but she was known as Mamie.

Mamie's first thought on seeing Eisenhower walk out of the BOQ, resplendent in his brass buttons, determined in his stride, big in his shoulders, had been, "He's a bruiser." As he came closer, her next thought was, "He's just about the handsomest male I have ever seen."[7] When he asked her to accompany him as he walked his rounds, she accepted.

The following day, when Mamie returned home from a fishing expedition, her maid informed her that a "Mr. I-something" had been calling every fifteen minutes all afternoon. The phone rang. It was "Mr. I-something." Very formally, Eisenhower asked "Miss Doud" to go dancing that night. She said she had a date. The next night? Another date. And so on until finally he made a date for a dance four weeks away. Having established her popularity, before hanging up Mamie also established her feelings—"I'm usually home about five," she said. "You might call some afternoon." Eisenhower said he would be there the next day.[8]

A whirlwind courtship ensued. Eisenhower was drawn to the whole Doud family, which pleased Mamie, who was close to her sisters and mother and adored her father. John Doud, in turn, was drawn to Eisenhower, soon treating him like the son he never had. Eisenhower liked Mrs. Doud so much he would call on her even when he knew Mamie was not at home. All the Douds responded to his contagious enthusiasm. Except for the father, the family had no interest in sports, but Eisenhower talked about the team he coached so often that the whole family began attending the games. Soon even the girls were cheering madly for "Ike's boys."

But Mamie, of course, was the real attraction. Eisenhower persuaded her to cancel her dates; they went out together every evening. His $141.67-per-month pay, even though supplemented by poker winnings and his coach's salary, limited them to dollar-per-couple meals at a Mexican restaurant and a once-a-week show at the vaudeville house. To save money, he gave up store-bought cigarettes and returned to rolling his own.[9] On Valentine's Day 1916, he proposed and she accepted. They sealed the engagement with his West Point ring. When he formally asked Mr. Doud for his daughter's hand in marriage, Doud consented, but only if he would agree to wait until November, when Mamie would be twenty years old. Doud told Eisenhower that the couple would be on their own financially, and warned him that Mamie might not be able to adjust from her carefree life to that of an Army wife. She was accustomed to having her own maid and a generous allowance. He made a similar speech to his daughter, in addition pointing out to her that she was agreeing to a life in which she would be constantly on the move, frequently separated from her husband, and often worried about him. She said that she understood and looked forward to the challenge.[10]

That spring of 1916, with the Preparedness campaign putting the Army almost on a war footing, and with American entry into the Great War an increasing possibility, Eisenhower and Mamie decided to push forward the date of their wedding. The Douds agreed. Eisenhower got ten days' leave, and on July 1, 1916, in the Douds' spacious home in Denver, they were married. Eisenhower wore his tropical dress uniform, stiffly starched and dazzlingly white, the crease so sharp he would not sit down; Mamie wore a white Chantilly lace dress, her hair in bangs over her forehead. Doud's chauffeur drove them to Eldorado Springs, Colorado, for a two-day honeymoon.[11] Then they took the train for Abilene, so that Mamie could meet the Eisenhower family.

They arrived at 4 A.M. David and Ida were up, waiting for them. They liked Mamie at once, and she them, especially after they told her they were so glad to finally have a daughter (Dwight was the first of their sons to marry). When Earl and Milton came downstairs, Mamie charmed them by saying, "At last I have some brothers." Ida served a huge fried chicken breakfast.

As to what happened next, the Eisenhowers had divergent memories. He recalled spending only eight hours in Abilene, catching the noon train south for San Antonio. Mamie remembered staying a few days. She said it was sharply etched in her memory because it was the occasion of their first fight. One afternoon, Mamie related, Eisenhower went downtown to play a little poker with his pals. When he had not returned by suppertime, she called him on the telephone—against Ida's advice—and told him to get home immediately. He replied calmly that he never left a poker game when he was behind. She told him to come home now or not at all. He hung up. When he finally came home, at 2 A.M., a winner, Mamie was waiting, furious. They went to their upstairs room, closed the door, and quarreled until dawn.[12]

Back at Fort Sam, they settled into Eisenhower's three-room quarters in the BOQ. He concentrated on his work; she concentrated on him. Eisenhower had firm expectations about his wife's role, which was to center her life around his. That suited Mamie. She was six years his junior; she had been trained for such a role in her Denver finishing school; she had watched her mother devote herself to pleasing her father. As an Army wife, she was ideal. She loved to entertain, as did he, and in a society in which everyone knew exactly how much everyone else earned, there was no need for pretense. Beans, rice, and beer more than satisfied the junior officers and their wives who were their guests. They sang popular songs at the top of their lungs, Mamie playing a rented piano. Eisenhower's favorite was "Abdul the Bulbul Amir," to which he knew some fifty verses. Their apartment came to be known as "Club Eisenhower." Mamie taught her man some of the social graces. "She takes full credit for smoothing the edges off the rough-and-ready Kansan," her son John told an interviewer, "and for teaching him some of the polish that later put him in good stead."[13]

She did not share his love of the out-of-doors, nor of athletics or physical exercise of any kind. But they both enjoyed talking, to each other and to other people, and playing cards together, and music and entertaining. Best of all, for Eisenhower, she never complained, although she had much she might have complained about. In the first thirty-five years of their marriage, they moved thirty-five times. Not until 1953 did they have a home they could call their own. Until World War II, with one exception, in 1918, he was never the CO, so she always had to defer to someone else's wife. His progress in the Army, after World War I, was excruciatingly slow. She had to manage the money to the penny, and watched as he turned down numerous offers for civilian employment at substantially higher salaries. But she never nagged him to leave the Army, never told him that the time had come for him to make something of himself.

Her father provided some help. Although Doud never made life easy for them, he was not as stern in practice as he had been in warning them that they were on their own financially. Shortly after their wedding, he gave them an automobile, a Pullman, and after the birth of their first child, he began giving Mamie a $100-per-month allowance.[14]

In April 1917, the United States entered the war. Eisenhower stayed at San Antonio, training the 57th Infantry. He did well at it, using the same skills he had developed as a football coach, and earned the high praise his superiors gave him in his 201 file, the official record of an officer's career. He was promoted to captain. But he was impatient to get to France. Training troops was like coaching football all week without ever being able to play a game on Saturdays. He had more than the normal American male's mystique about combat; he had been trained, at considerable expense, to fight; his place was on the fighting line, not on the sidelines. He was dismayed, therefore, when in mid-September his orders finally came, and he learned that the War Department was sending him to Fort Oglethorpe, Georgia, to train officer candidates.

In Georgia, he helped construct a miniature World War I battlefield, complete with trenches and dugouts, in which he and the trainees lived while they practiced assaults across no-man's-land. It was not very realistic training, because neither Eisenhower nor his superiors knew much about the actual battlefield conditions; what they did know, they learned from an avid reading of the newspapers. Oglethorpe had none of the advantages of active service, but many of the disadvantages, the chief being that Mamie could not be with him and was thus in San Antonio when, on September 24, 1917, their first son was born. She named him Doud Dwight and called him "Icky."

Eisenhower pestered the War Department with requests for overseas duty. All were turned down. Instead, in mid-December, he was sent to Fort Leavenworth, Kansas, to instruct provisional second lieutenants. The only bright spot was that he got to spend a few days with Mamie and Icky in San Antonio, where they were living for the winter with the Douds. Before reporting at Leavenworth, Eisenhower had made repeated requests to be sent to France. The post commandant called him in to read him a letter from the Adjutant General in the War Department, reprimanding Eisenhower for his frequent requests for a transfer. The commandant began adding reprimands of his own.

Eisenhower cut him off. "Sir," he said through tight lips, "I have only asked to be allowed to go into battle, and this offense—if it is an offense—was committed before I came under your jurisdiction. If there is punishment to be given out, I think that it should be given by the War Department and not added to by yourself, with all due respect." The commandant thought about it, decided Eisenhower was right, and sent him off to do his duty.

That duty, to Eisenhower's dismay, turned out to be supervising the physical training of the unit—bayonet drills, calisthenics, and exercises. It was not even as challenging or as much fun as coaching football. But he did it and again managed to impress his superiors and his trainees. One of the latter wrote, "Our new Captain, Eisenhower by name, is, I believe, one of the most efficient and best Army officers in the country . . . He has given us wonderful bayonet drills. He gets the fellows' imaginations worked up and hollers and yells and makes us shout and stomp until we go tearing into the air as if we meant business."[15]

At Leavenworth, he found time to take a course himself, in the Army's first tank school. In February 1918, he received orders to report to Camp Meade, Maryland, to join the 65th Engineers, the parent group of the 301st Tank Battalion, Heavy, which was slated to go to the battlefield in the spring. Elated, he threw himself into the job. The men were all volunteers, morale was high, expectations even higher. Although none of the men had actually seen a tank, they were convinced that with the new weapon they would break through the German lines and drive straight to Berlin. Insofar as he could do so from newspaper accounts, Eisenhower studied the Battle of Cambrai (November 1917), where the British for the first time used tanks to achieve a breakthrough. They had not gathered together enough tanks to exploit the victory, but they had shown what could be done. In mid-March, he was informed that the 301st would soon be embarking for France from New York, and that he was to be its commander. Exuberant, he rushed to New York to make certain that the port authorities were prepared for the 301st; "Too much depended on our walking up that gangplank," he wrote, "for me to take a chance on a slip anywhere."[16]

Back at Meade, elation gave way to more despair. The War Department had changed his orders. His superior's praise of his "organizational ability" had been so lavish that the authorities had decided to send him to Camp Colt, in Gettysburg, Pennsylvania. It was an old, abandoned camp, on the site of the great Civil War battle. The War Department had decided to reorganize its armored units, take them away from the 65th Engineers and give them an organization of their own, the Tank Corps. The tankers were to be trained at Camp Colt, with Eisenhower in command.

It was, on the face of it, a choice assignment. At twenty-seven years of age, Eisenhower was to be in command of thousands of men, all of them volunteers. He would be working with the weapon of the future (although he was given no actual tanks, nor training manuals, nor experienced armored officers to work with). He could expect a promotion. He was able to rent a house in town, so his wife and son could live with him. Nevertheless, he later confessed, "my mood was black." He completed the preparations for the 301st to embark, then watched the unit sail with a sinking heart.[17]

Eisenhower was certain that the War Department had made a terrible mistake, but in fact, in its wisdom, it had made an excellent selection for the commander at Camp Colt. Working with whatever materials he could find, he transformed the historic ground of Pickett's charge from an open wheat field into a first-class Army camp. He obtained tents, food, and fuel for his men. He taught them to drill, got them into shape, kept up their morale by establishing a telegraph school, then a motor school. By mid-July, he had ten thousand men and six hundred officers under his command, but still no tanks. He went to Washington, badgered the War Department into giving him some old Navy cannons, and drilled his men in their use until they were proficient. He managed to obtain some machine guns; soon his men could take them apart and put them back together again while blindfolded. He mounted the machine guns on flatbed trucks and taught the men to fire the weapons from a moving platform. He used Big Round Top as a backstop and soon the firing there was heavier than it had been during the battle fifty-five years earlier.[18]

He was always trying to improve the training and lift the morale. To that end, he wanted suggestions and ideas from his subordinates, not praise. One of his young lieutenants, anxious to please, nevertheless praised every aspect of his administration. "For God's sake," Eisenhower cut him off one day, "get out and find something wrong with the camp! It can't be as good as you say it is. Either you're not being frank, or you're as big a fool as I am."[19]

The men responded to his leadership. "Eisenhower was a strict disciplinarian," his sergeant major, Claude J. Harris, declared, "an inborn soldier, but most human, considerate, and his decisions affecting the welfare of his officers and men were always well tempered. Despite his youth, he possessed a high understanding of organization, the ability to place an estimate on a man and fit him into a position where he would 'click.' In the event his judgment proved erroneous the man would be called in, his errors pointed out, and adjustments made to suit the situation. This principle built for him high admiration and loyalty from his officers perhaps unequaled by few commanding officers."

That ability to get the best out of an officer, and to find the right officer for the job, was to be one of his hallmarks in World War II. So too were other traits Sergeant Harris observed—Eisenhower's penchant for detail and his concern for his officers. "He was always available to confer with his officers on either military or personal problems," Harris noted.[20]

Like every CO, Eisenhower had a problem with enlisted men and their liquor. He discovered that one hotelkeeper in town, against his orders, was selling liquor surreptitiously to soldiers. The owner promised not to do it again; Eisenhower gave him another chance. The offense was repeated, so Eisenhower surrounded the hotel with a guard, which kept not only the soldiers out but most civilians too. The hotel owner appeared the next day in Eisenhower's office, accompanied by his congressman. Eisenhower refused to remove the guard. The congressman threatened: "We have means," he said. "We can go to the War Department. If you're going to be so stubborn, I'll have to take up the question of replacing you."

"You do just exactly that," Eisenhower shot back. When the congressman looked startled, Eisenhower explained, "Nothing would please me better than to be taken out of this job. I want to go overseas. If they take me out of here, maybe I can get there." The congressman did go to the War Department, but the results were not what either he or Eisenhower wanted—Eisenhower received a letter from the Assistant Secretary of War, praising him for his diligence in looking after the welfare of his men.[21]

The experience reinforced Eisenhower's West Point prejudice against politicians, and strengthened his contempt for civilians who would not put their duty to the nation above their own immediate gain. He had the good feeling of being able to act on principle against the cutters and trimmers. He had no sympathy for the congressman, no feeling for his need to placate, to find a compromise, a way of working things out. He was in a position to take the high ground and stick to it, and he did.

His domestic life helped ease the frustration of not getting to France. Eisenhower enjoyed holding and playing with his infant son, occasionally feeding him and once or twice changing him. Mamie was learning that if she wanted some time with her husband, she would have to share some of his interests. For relaxation, he liked to roam around the Gettysburg battlefield, examining the historic ground. Mamie's indifference to the movement of this Confederate regiment or that Union brigade was complete, but she went along and managed to keep from yawning as he explained the details of the battle. "[He] knew every rock on that battlefield," she later said. It was partly a boast, partly a complaint.[22]

Far more enjoyable were her duties as the CO's wife. Because the tank was a new weapon and the Tank Corps an experiment, Camp Colt attracted various important people, including congressmen, high-ranking Army officers, and industrialists. In their large rented house, a former fraternity house on the Gettysburg College campus, the Eisenhowers entertained them. The food was basic; the music, led by Mamie's piano playing, consisted of popular songs; the conversation, led by Eisenhower, centered on tanks and the war.[23] When the first actual tanks, three Renaults, arrived, two British officers came with them, as advisers. Tank enthusiasts themselves, they told Eisenhower about a British politician named Winston Churchill, who had played a key role in producing the first tanks.[24]

On October 14, 1918, his twenty-eighth birthday, Eisenhower was promoted to lieutenant colonel (temporary). Even more welcome were his orders—he was to embark for France on November 18, there to take command of an armored unit. The Allies, for the first time under a unified command, with Marshal Foch as Supreme Commander, were preparing for a gigantic offensive in the spring of 1919. Tanks would lead the way. Eisenhower saw himself at the head of those tanks. He put Mamie and Icky on a train for Denver and went to New York to make certain that the port authorities were ready for his men and that nothing would go wrong with the embarkation. Then, on November 11, the Germans signed the Armistice. Captain Norman Randolph was sitting in Eisenhower's office when the news arrived. "I suppose we'll spend the rest of our lives explaining why we didn't get into this war," Eisenhower moaned. "By God," he added, "from now on I am cutting myself a swath and will make up for this." But whatever his determination, glittering combat possibilities had turned into demobilization realities. Eisenhower supervised the discharge of thousands of men, the tearing down of Camp Colt, the movement of the remnants of the Tank Corps—including the three Renaults—to Fort Benning, Georgia.[25]

Eisenhower was deflated and depressed. He could hardly believe it had happened to him—he was a professional soldier who had missed action in the greatest war in history. He had never heard a shot fired in anger and now did not expect to in his lifetime. He worried about what he would tell Icky when his son asked him what he did during the war. He envisioned having to sit silent at class reunions when his fellow officers talked about their experiences and exploits in combat. When he met a young officer at Benning who had been in France and who complained that there had been no promotions over there, he snapped back, "Well, you got overseas—that should be promotion enough!"[26]

In 1919, Colonel Ira C. Welborn recommended him for the Distinguished Service Medal. The award finally came through in 1922. It praised Eisenhower for his "unusual zeal, foresight, and marked administrative ability." To Eisenhower, it was more a bitter reminder than a welcome award.[27]

Although it was obviously no fault of his, Eisenhower was nevertheless embarrassed by his lack of participation in the war. During World War II his detractors, led by General Bernard Montgomery, who did have extensive experience in the trenches, began their criticism of Eisenhower by pointing out that he had never commanded men in combat. That was true, but the supposed conclusion, that this fact somehow disqualified him for high command, was not. Eisenhower did not hear the zing of bullets over his head, did not lead men or tanks on charges across no-man's-land. But he did have firsthand experience at setting up and running a camp of thousands of men, for creating and supervising their training schedule, for preparing them for combat. It might even be argued that his not being in the trenches was an advantage in conducting the next war, which was to be so different from 1917–1918-style combat, most of all in its mobility. The caution that was to characterize so many of the veterans of the First World War, especially British officers who had been in the Somme and Flanders battles, was not Eisenhower's. He went into the Second World War with a clear mind, not one burdened by the memory of futile slaughter. And, obviously, it was an advantage for Eisenhower to have been associated with tanks from the beginning.

So too was Eisenhower's contact with civilians. Had he gone overseas in 1917 with a Regular Army regiment, his acquaintances would have remained limited to other professional officers. Dealing on a daily basis with civilians trying to become officers and soldiers was a broadening experience for him. In the same way, entertaining visitors to Camp Colt, working with hotel owners in Gettysburg, and arguing with congressmen gave him a broader perspective on the way in which the American democracy made war than he could have gained on the Western Front. He did not see it that way himself until the end of his career, but in many respects his World War I experience was an excellent preparation for high command in World War II.

CHAPTER FIVE

Camp Meade, Panama, Leavenworth, Washington

1919–1928

EISENHOWER WAS twenty-eight years old when the war ended. His ambitions had been thwarted, his attempts to guide his own career rebuffed. He was a member of an organization that was being practically dismantled. Soldiers shed their uniforms in a rush that dwarfed the Civil War demobilization—within six months, 2,608,218 enlisted men and 128,436 officers had received their discharges, and by January 1, 1920, the Army had only 130,000 men on active duty. Through the 1920s and 1930s it would continue to shrink. By 1935, the Army did not have a single combat-ready unit of any size. It ranked sixteenth among the world's armies. "As anything more than a small school for soldiers," Russell Weigley has written, "the Army scarcely existed."[1]

As the Army shrank, so did Eisenhower's rank. On July 30, 1920, he reverted to his permanent rank of captain. Three days later he was promoted to major. He would remain a major for sixteen years. As the American economy boomed, as fortunes were made, as his own brothers forged ahead in their varied careers, Eisenhower stayed in place. During the war, although he had not been where he wanted to be, he at least had important responsibilities; in the 1920s and 1930s, save as a football coach, he had none. He made almost no decisions between his twenty-eighth and fifty-first birthdays, except to stay in the minuscule Army and do his best. He was getting nowhere, had no realistic prospects of personal advancement, but he was content. He accepted his role, concentrated on doing his assigned tasks to the best of his ability, and for the rest indulged his fun-loving nature.

Inevitably, he had job offers, as would any man with his good looks, winning personality, and obvious abilities. The first offer came even before the war ended—an Indiana businessman who was serving as a junior officer at Camp Colt asked him to join his firm after the war, at a salary considerably higher than he was making as a lieutenant colonel.[2] He turned it down, as he would other offers for civilian employment that came to him through the next twenty years.

Why did he stay in the Army? He had a well-developed sense of patriotism and service, to be sure, but he did not need to remain in the Army to satisfy them, especially an Army that was generally scorned by the few people—mainly congressmen at appropriation time—who bothered to think about it at all. He knew that after the Mexican War some of the best officers in the Army, including Grant, Sherman, George B. McClellan, Philip Henry Sheridan, and Henry Halleck—West Pointers all—had resigned their commissions. Some of them were successful in civilian life, most notably McClellan; some were failures, most notably Grant; all had found life in the pre-Civil War peacetime Army too dull to abide. But Army life in the 1920s and 1930s was much easier, more interesting and challenging, and just plain more fun than in the 1850s. Army officers after the Mexican War served in destitute frontier posts, with no recreational facilities, few if any creature comforts, almost no companionship—they were usually without their wives—and no intellectual challenges. They stayed in the same place year after year, doing the same job, working with the same people, weapons, and doctrine. Army officers after World War I, by way of contrast, were pampered, not with promotions or pay, but nevertheless in meaningful ways. Their Stateside posts had well-run officers' clubs, golf courses, and various types of interesting entertainment. They rotated every year or two. If they could never expect to get rich, they had complete financial security for themselves and their families. They had the challenge of new weapons, especially the tank and the airplane, for which they had to devise new doctrines. For Grant and Sherman and their contemporaries, the Army offered nothing in the way of postgraduate education; for Eisenhower and his contemporaries, the Army offered an extensive system of advanced schooling.

In addition, America after World War I, despite the prevailing isolationist mood, had worldwide interests, which meant that Army officers got to live and serve in various exotic foreign posts. It was a man's world. Officers spent much of their time out of doors, working with soldiers, riding horseback, firing weapons, participating in athletic games. The social life was male-oriented, with the emphasis on poker or singing

Army ballads and popular songs at get-togethers. If the Army of Eisenhower's day was a monastery, as Samuel Huntington insists—and it certainly was narrow and introspective and small and protected from the risks of civilian life—being an officer was a lot more fun than being a monk.

For Eisenhower, it was a satisfactory life, in many ways an exciting one. In 1919, after a short stint at Camp Meade doing demobilization paper work, he accompanied an Army truck convoy on a cross-continent journey. The official reasons for the trip were to test Army vehicles, to show the people samples of equipment used during the war, and to dramatize the need for better roads. Eisenhower later confessed, however, that for him the trip was a lark. He camped out for the entire summer, got to see the country, went hunting and fishing, played practical jokes and poker, and thoroughly enjoyed himself. He also learned firsthand just how miserable the American road network was—the convoy hardly averaged five miles per hour between Washington, D.C., and San Francisco.[3]

In the two decades following the journey, Eisenhower enjoyed a varied life. He attended three postgraduate schools. Among other places, he lived in Panama, Washington, D.C., Paris, and Manila. His family was usually with him. He did not have the satisfaction of having a home of his own, but hardly a year passed, except when he was out of the country, that he did not manage to visit Abilene at least once.

In 1926, there was a grand reunion of all the brothers. Each one was making more money than Dwight—Arthur as a vice-president of a leading Kansas City bank; Edgar as a prominent lawyer in Tacoma, Washington; Roy as a pharmacist in Kansas; Earl as an engineer in Pennsylvania; Milton as a high-ranking official in the Agriculture Department—and each one had brighter prospects than Major Eisenhower. David and Ida, justly proud of them all, may have wondered when Dwight would get going.

But Dwight was not concerned. Various photographs were taken during the reunion—they all show a healthy, suntanned, self-confident Major Eisenhower, much the best-looking of all the boys, and quite obviously the one in the best physical condition. Although he was not jealous of his brothers' successes, the old physical competitiveness was still there. He was anxious to get Edgar into a boxing match, to pay him back for all the beatings he had suffered from Ed when they were children, but Edgar wisely managed to avoid all Dwight's challenges.[4] Dwight had the further satisfaction of learning that although he had not enjoyed the financial rewards of his brothers, he had traveled more than any of them, or all of them put together. And he had had more schooling, grappled with more challenging problems, and dealt with more interesting men.

The schooling was almost continuous, the problems were the nature of the next war and the role of the tank in it, and one of the fascinating men was George S. Patton, Jr. Eisenhower first met Patton in the fall of 1919, at Camp Meade, Maryland. It was an ideal assignment for Eisenhower. He had Mamie and Icky with him and he was working with tanks. The War Department had transferred the Tank Corps out of the Engineers and into the Infantry; Eisenhower and Patton were to help create, and be both students and instructors at, the Infantry Tank School. Each man also commanded a battalion of tanks. Best of all, they had some actual tanks to work with, British heavies, French Renaults, German Marks, and even some American-built tanks.[5]

Eisenhower and Patton immediately became and remained fast friends, despite their much different personalities and backgrounds. Patton came from a wealthy, aristocratic family. He was an avid polo player, well able to afford his own string of ponies. He was extreme in his mannerisms, his dress, and his talk. Eisenhower could swear as eloquently as most sergeants, but he went easy on the curse words in mixed company; Patton, who could outswear a mule skinner, swore at all times as if he were in a stag poker game. Eisenhower's voice was deep and resonant, Patton's high-pitched and squeaky. Eisenhower enjoyed being one of the gang, wanted to be well liked and popular. Patton was more of a loner, did not much care what his associates thought of him. Where Eisenhower tended to qualify all his observations and statements, Patton was dogmatic. Where Eisenhower had no particularly strong views on race or politics, Patton was viciously anti-Semitic and loudly right wing. Where Eisenhower was patient and let things happen to him, Patton was impatient and took charge of his own career. Patton had been in combat, with tanks, and Eisenhower had not. And to hear Patton tell it, as he loved to do, he had ridden into battle on one of his tanks as if it were a polo pony and then single-handedly (well, almost) breached the Hindenburg Line.

But Eisenhower and Patton had enough in common to overcome these differences. Both were West Pointers (Patton graduated in 1909). Both had been athletes—Patton played football as well as polo for the Army—and remained interested in athletics. Both were married, and their wives got along well together. Both had a deep interest in military history, both were serious students of war. Most of all, they were both enthusiastic about tanks, sharing a belief that the weapon would dominate the next war.[6]

It would, that is, if properly understood and utilized. Eisenhower and Patton directed much of their effort toward seeing that it would be. The role of the tank in the next war was, along with air power, the most important challenge all the world's armies faced in the 1920s, and Patton and Eisenhower were in the middle of the discussion from the beginning.

In Europe, British officers Basil H. Liddell Hart and J. F. C. Fuller were the leading theorists of tank warfare. They advocated speed, concentration, and independence for tanks. The Germans translated their writings, read them avidly, and used their teaching to great advantage in the opening stages of the next war. The British and French armies ignored Liddell Hart and Fuller, keeping their tanks small and slow and using them only in support of infantry, to their great disadvantage in 1940–1941. The U.S. Army, with its strong tradition that infantry was the queen of battles, also operated on a doctrine that subordinated armor to infantry. Official doctrine held that the mission of tanks was to precede attacking infantry by fifty yards, destroying machine-gun nests as they crept along at three miles per hour. Tanks therefore did not need speed, nor did they need heavy armor or cannon.

Eisenhower and Patton, testing the various tanks available to them, were convinced that new tactics and bigger, faster tanks were needed. They believed that the tank was "a weapon that could change completely the strategy and tactics of land warfare." By using tanks in mass instead of spread out among the infantry units, Eisenhower and Patton argued, "they could break into the enemy's defensive positions, cause confusion, and by taking the enemy front line in reverse, make possible not only an advance by infantry, but envelopments of, or actual breakthroughs in, whole defensive positions."[7]

In 1920, both officers published articles summarizing their conclusions, Patton for the *Cavalry Journal,* Eisenhower for the *Infantry Journal.* Eisenhower called for a tank "of sufficient length to cross a 9-foot trench, a maximum weight of 15 tons, a firepower of one 6-pounder and two Browning machine guns, sufficient power to run cross-country at a speed of 12 miles per hour, and on good roads, with treads dismounted, at a rate of 20 miles per hour." Eisenhower concluded, "The clumsy, awkward and snail-like progress of the old tanks must be forgotten, and in their place we must picture this speedy, reliable and efficient engine of destruction."[8]

As World War II would prove, the two young officers had it exactly right, so right in fact that their conclusions seem commonplace today. But in 1920 they were two decades ahead of most military theorists, except for Fuller and Liddell Hart, whom they seem to have been unaware of, and whose works were just beginning to appear in any case. Eisenhower and Patton were true pioneers, original and creative in their thought.

But the Army was not pleased. The Great War had been won by infantry, charging in mass. Future wars would be won the same way. The Army's postgraduate schools all taught that basic lesson, all scorned maneuvering and outflanking attempts and concentrated on the problem of how to get the infantry across no-man's-land. The proper role of the tank was to help solve that problem. The head of the Army War College wrote in 1922, "I wish to stress this point; that warfare means fighting and that war is never won by maneuvering," and the American author of a 1928 book on strategy maintained, "Maneuvering in itself will not gain victories."[9]

There was, in short, as in Abilene and at West Point, a revealed truth. For the first time in his life, Eisenhower had rejected it, striking out on a bold, creative, and original course of his own. With what results? He was summoned before the Chief of Infantry. "I was told that my ideas were not only wrong but dangerous and that henceforth I would keep them to myself. Particularly, I was not to publish anything incompatible with solid infantry doctrine. If I did, I would be hauled before a court-martial."[10]

Fuller and Liddell Hart had roughly similar experiences in the British Army. Their reaction was to resign their commissions and continue to express and expand their theories in books and articles. Patton, also slapped down, reacted by getting angry, muttering to hell with it, and transferring out of the Infantry Tank School into the Cavalry, which he said lamely "might display more imagination and receptiveness to ideas." That was hardly likely, but at least in the Cavalry he would have more opportunities to play polo while waiting for the War Department to move into the twentieth century.

And Eisenhower? He reacted by doing exactly as ordered. He published no more articles on the role of tanks, made no lectures on the subject, kept his views to himself, and stayed in the Infantry, hoping for another assignment, away from tanks.[11] Hardly convinced that his superiors knew best, he nevertheless accepted their orders, if not their conclusions. It was not his style to engage in a hopelessly unequal struggle against the full weight of the U.S. Army. It would be a very long time before he again attempted to strike out on his own course.

Instead, he put himself into the hands of others. Already, with Patton, he had revealed a tendency to do his best work under the direction of a strong-willed man. Patton was five years older than Eisenhower, a combat veteran, and a dominating personality. If he and Eisenhower had formed a partnership at Camp Meade, Patton tended to be the senior partner. From 1920 onward, Eisenhower served under a series of domineering generals, men who had a tremendous influence on his life, his thoughts, even his character. They were, in chronological order, Generals Fox Conner, John J. Pershing, Douglas MacArthur, and George C. Marshall.

In 1964, in his retirement, after a career that had put him in intimate working contact with scores of brilliant and talented men, including most of the great statesmen and military leaders of World War II and the Cold War, Eisenhower could still say, "Fox Conner was the ablest man I ever knew."[12]

He first met Conner at a Sunday-afternoon dinner in the fall of 1920 in Patton's quarters at Camp Meade. Patton had known Conner in France; Eisenhower knew him by reputation as one of the smartest men in the Army. A wealthy Mississippian who had graduated from West Point in 1898, Conner had served as Pershing's operations officer in France, where he was generally acknowledged to have been the brains of the AEF. He was currently Pershing's chief of staff in Washington, where Pershing commanded what remained of the AEF, which had been kept alive as an independent entity so that Pershing would not have to serve under Army Chief of Staff Peyton March (Pershing and March were not on speaking terms). Both the General and Mrs. Conner—herself an heiress—were charming, soft-spoken southerners, formal and polite in their manners, but genuinely interested in younger officers and their wives. Eisenhower and Mamie felt drawn to them at once. The Patton dinner was a great success, highlighted by wide-ranging conversations.

After dinner, Conner asked Patton and Eisenhower to show him their tanks and explain to him their ideas about the future of the weapon. This was the first—and was to be the only—encouragement they had from a superior officer, and they spent a long afternoon with him, showing him around Camp Meade, explaining to him their ideas. To their delight, Conner asked penetrating questions, indicating that he was not just trying to kill yet another sleepy Sunday at yet another Army post. When the time came for him to return to Washington, Conner praised them for their work and encouraged them to keep at it.[13]

Shortly thereafter, Eisenhower published his article on tank warfare in *Infantry Journal.* Conner, as a Pershing man, was not an insider in the upper echelons of the War Department, and was unable to protect Eisenhower from the bitterly negative reaction of the Chief of Infantry. He did, however, inform Eisenhower that he had been assigned to Panama to command an infantry brigade, and asked if Eisenhower would like to join him as executive officer. It was a splendid opportunity for an officer whose ideas were so out of joint with his superiors in the Infantry Tank School, and Eisenhower told Conner that he would be delighted to serve under him. Eisenhower went to his commanding general, Samuel Rockenbach, to request what he thought would be a routine transfer. To his dismay, Rockenbach replied that he could not spare him, explaining that he had few experienced field officers. The truth was that Rockenbach was one of those COs who wanted his command to have a winning football team. Eisenhower had done his usual good job as coach in 1919 and 1920, and Rockenbach intended to keep him at that post in 1921. Eisenhower argued the point, saying that he was so much out of sympathy with official tank doctrine that he could not serve usefully at Camp Meade. Rockenbach finally agreed to send Eisenhower's application on to the War Department, but warned him that it would surely be disapproved. It was.[14]

If Eisenhower was getting nowhere in his career, at least his family life was a warm, happy one. He and Mamie thoroughly enjoyed each other and the Army social scene, but most of all they delighted in their son. Icky, three years old in the fall of 1920, was an active, energetic boy, his father's delight and his mother's joy. The soldiers adopted him as a mascot. They bought him a tank uniform, complete with overcoat and overseas cap, and took him along on field maneuvers. He was enthralled by his tank rides. His father took him in the afternoon to football practice, where he would stand on the sidelines, cheering madly at every play in the scrimmage. He would put on his uniform and stand at stiff attention as the band and the colors passed during parades.

The Eisenhowers made plans for a glorious Christmas. Mamie went to Washington to buy presents; Eisenhower put up a tree in their quarters and bought a toy wagon for Icky. But, a week or so before Christmas, Icky contracted scarlet fever. He evidently got it from the maid, a young local girl who had, unknown to the Eisenhowers, just recovered from an attack of the disease. Eisenhower called in a specialist from Johns Hopkins; the doctor could only advise prayer. Icky had to go into quarantine; Eisenhower was not allowed to enter his room. He could only sit outside it and wave to his son through the window. Mamie was also ill and confined to bed. Eisenhower spent every free minute at the hospital, desperate with worry, remembering his younger brother Milton's own struggle with the dreaded scourge of scarlet fever seventeen years earlier, hoping that Icky, like Milton, would somehow pull through.

He did not. On the second of January, Icky died. "This was the greatest disappointment and disaster in my life," Eisenhower wrote in his old age, "the one I have never been able to forget completely."[15] For the next half century, every year on Icky's birthday he sent flowers to Mamie. The Eisenhowers arranged to have Icky's remains laid beside them in their own burial plot.

Inevitably, they blamed themselves. If only they had not hired that maid, if only they had checked on her more carefully, if only . . . These feelings had to be suppressed if the marriage was to survive the disaster, but suppression did not eliminate the unwanted thoughts, only made them harder to live with. Both the inner-directed guilt and the projected feelings of blame placed a strain on their marriage. So did the equally inevitable sense of loss, the grief that could not be comforted, the feeling that all the joy had gone out of life. "For a long time, it was as if a shining light had gone out in Ike's life," Mamie said later. "Throughout all the years that followed, the memory of those bleak days was a deep inner pain that never seemed to diminish much."[16]

Eisenhower did not even have the escape of throwing himself into his work, as his work consisted of going through the motions in a training program in which he had neither faith nor belief. He coached football again in the fall of 1921; Mamie kept up her various activities at the post. But they did little entertaining. They were increasingly polite and formal, rather than close and warm, in their relationship. Eisenhower, desperate to get away from Camp Meade, with its boring duty and heartbreaking reminders of Icky, applied for the Infantry School at Fort Leavenworth, but Rockenbach saw to it that the request was denied.

At the end of the football season, Eisenhower got his break. General Pershing became Chief of Staff of the Army. He would do anything he could for Conner, one of his favorite officers. Conner was commanding the 20th Infantry Brigade at Camp Gaillard in the Panama Canal Zone, and had asked for Eisenhower as his executive officer. Pershing ordered Eisenhower to Panama for his first tour of foreign military service.[17]

The Eisenhowers arrived in January 1922. The accommodations were miserable. Mamie described their house as "a double-decked shanty, only twice as disreputable." Built on stilts, it had been abandoned for a decade and stank of mildew. She had household help, which cost practically nothing in Panama and was worth about as much; she had to do the shopping herself and provide minute supervision of the cooking and housework.[18]

The Conners lived next door; Mamie and Mrs. Conner became close friends. Mamie called on her daily—Virginia Conner became her confidante and adviser. When Mamie complained about some of her difficulties with her husband, Mrs. Conner was forthright in her advice. She told Mamie to cut her hair, change her clothes, brighten herself up. "You mean I should vamp him?" Mamie asked. "That's just what I mean," Mrs. Conner replied. "Vamp him!"[19]

Eisenhower and General Conner, meanwhile, developed a teacher-student relationship. Their duties were light. Their work consisted of little more than housekeeping functions, with the emphasis on keeping up the network of jungle trails for the use of troops and their pack animals. Their responsibility was to defend Culebra Cut in the event of hostile action. They both enjoyed riding horseback through the jungle, spreading their bedrolls on the ground at night, chatting around a campfire. On weekends, they went on fishing expeditions together.

Conner pulled Eisenhower out of the lethargy that had threatened to engulf him after his tank ideas had been so coldly rejected and after Icky's death. He insisted that Eisenhower read serious military literature, rather than Western novels and pulp magazines or training manuals, and forced the younger man to think about what he was reading by asking probing questions. Eisenhower read memoirs of Civil War generals, then discussed with Conner the decisions Grant and Sherman and the others had made. What would have happened had they done this or that differently? Conner would ask. What were the alternatives? Eisenhower was anxious to please, so anxious that he read Clausewitz' *On War* three times through—a difficult enough task to complete even once, made more difficult by Conner's insistent questioning about the implications of Clausewitz' ideas.

They also discussed the future. Conner insisted that because of the deficiencies of the Treaty of Versailles there would be another war in twenty years or less, that it would be a world war, that America would fight with allies, and that Eisenhower had better prepare himself for it. He advised Eisenhower to try for an assignment under Colonel George C. Marshall, who had been with Conner on Pershing's staff. Marshall, Conner insisted, "knows more about the techniques of arranging allied commands than any man I know. He is nothing short of a genius." Indeed, Conner's highest praise was "Eisenhower, you handled that just the way Marshall would have done." Conner had witnessed at first hand the price the Allies had paid for divided leadership in the war, knew the cost of not giving Marshal Foch sufficient powers to go with his grand title. He told Eisenhower that in the next war, "We must insist on individual and single responsibility—leaders will have to learn how to overcome nationalistic considerations in the conduct of campaigns . . ." Prophetic words for Foch's successor.[20]

Eisenhower almost worshiped Conner. His three years in Panama, he later said, were "a sort of graduate school in military affairs . . . In a lifetime of association with great and good men, he is the one figure to whom I owe an incalculable debt."[21] Virginia Conner noted, "I never saw two men more congenial than Ike Eisenhower and my husband. They spent hours discussing wars, past and future. . . . Ike has often said that my husband had more influence on him than any officer he served under."[22] Conner, in his 1924 efficiency report on Eisenhower, wrote that he was "one of the most capable, efficient, and loyal officers I have ever met."[23]

From Conner, Eisenhower first heard two clichés that struck him so forcibly that over the years he quoted them ad nauseam. They were "All generalities are false, including this one" and "Always take your job seriously, never yourself."

Swede Hazlett, who visited the Eisenhowers in Panama, testified to Eisenhower's good spirits and positive reaction to Conner and Panama. Swede found his friend working and studying hard, even though "this was particularly unusual at a torrid, isolated post where most officers spent their off hours trying to keep cool and amused." Swede reported that Eisenhower "had fitted up the second-story screened porch of his quarters as a rough study, and here, with drawing boards and texts, he put in his spare time re-fighting the campaigns of the old masters." But, he added, "[Ike] missed none of the fun. He never did." Swede and Eisenhower went horseback riding, played poker together, and talked. Eisenhower passed on what he was learning from Conner; Swede was impressed, saying that Eisenhower made his explanations with the "enthusiasm of genius."

Swede was in Panama because the submarine he commanded was laid up for repairs. When the work was finished, Swede took Eisenhower for a dive. "I never had a passenger who was more avid for information," he recalled in 1944. "Whenever I was otherwise engaged he wandered through the ship, chatting informally with the crew—and they responded readily. I really believe that by the time he left the ship he knew almost as much about submarines as I did."[24]

Adding to Eisenhower's happiness was the birth of a second son. In the early summer of 1922, Mamie went to Denver to escape the heat and have her child in a modern hospital. In July, Eisenhower took a leave and was present on August 3 when John Sheldon Doud Eisenhower was born. John's presence was a great help in getting over Icky's death; as parents the Eisenhowers tended to be protective of him. Mamie, John later remarked, "was exceedingly affectionate, almost smothering me with concern," and Mamie told an interviewer, "It took me years, many years, to get over my 'smother love'—it wasn't until Johnnie had children of his own that I finally stopped all worry." His father, while stern ("Dad . . . was a terrifying figure") and rigid in his discipline, recalled his own father's beatings only too clearly, and was afraid enough of his own temper, that he never laid a hand on his son. Instead, he gave John sharp verbal dressing downs for transgressions, which, given Eisenhower's standards, were frequent.[25] But overall they got on fine, and as soon as John was old enough Eisenhower included his son in as many of his activities as possible, a practice that grew as the years went by and continued to the father's death.

In the fall of 1924, Eisenhower learned that he was to be transferred. He was pleased with the news—much as he admired and learned from Conner, and much as Mamie liked Mrs. Conner, the Eisenhowers were ready to get out of the sweltering Canal Zone. But his heart sank as he opened the orders and discovered that the War Department was sending him back to Meade to coach football. Someone in Washington had decided that the Army needed to beat the Marines, so the best coaches in the service were being assembled at Meade to produce a winning team. Eisenhower was to be backfield coach. Unfortunately, the attitude in the War Department was that superior coaches meant superior teams; Eisenhower and his colleagues could recruit players only from among the painfully limited talent among enlisted men already stationed at Meade. The result was a disastrous season.

Eisenhower's assignment was temporary—after the last game he was ordered to take command of a battalion of tanks. He went to Washington to protest to the Chief of Infantry, saying that he wished to broaden himself. Instead of resuming the old command he had held before going to Panama, he wanted his orders changed—his wish was to attend the Infantry School. The Chief turned him down without discussion.

Then a cryptic telegram arrived from General Conner: "No matter what orders you receive from the War Department make no protest accept them without question Signed Conner."

A few days later, the perplexed Eisenhower received orders relieving him from duty with the Infantry, putting him on a temporary basis under the Adjutant General's office, and assigning him to Colorado on recruiting duty. Such an assignment was close to an insult, but with Conner's telegram as a guide, Eisenhower held his temper and made no protest. The Eisenhowers spent the winter, spring, and early summer of 1925 in Colorado, which of course delighted Mamie, as her husband's post, Fort Logan, was practically a suburb of Denver. Conner, meanwhile, had used his connections in the War Department to persuade the Adjutant General to assign Major Eisenhower to the Command and General Staff School at Leavenworth, something the Chief of Infantry had consistently refused to do.[26]

When he learned of his appointment, Eisenhower, in his words, "was ready to fly—and needed no airplane!" Then second thoughts set in. He had not attended the Infantry School, assumed to be a prerequisite for C&GS, a competitive school where each student was ranked. Those who did well could expect to advance in the Army; those who did poorly would not. An aide to the Chief of Infantry wrote advising him to stay away from C&GS, because "you will probably fail," and the failure would make him useless as an infantry officer, condemning him forever to a life of coaching inferior football players.

Eisenhower wrote Conner, expressing some of his self-doubts and asking what he should study to prepare himself. In his reply Conner wrote, "You may not know it, but because of your three years' work in Panama, you are far better trained and ready for Leavenworth than anybody I know." He reminded Eisenhower that in Panama he had written a field order for the post every day; in the process, "you became so well acquainted with the technics and routine of preparing plans and orders for operations that included their logistics, that they will be second nature to you. You will feel no sense of inferiority."[27]

Reassured somewhat, Eisenhower, whose duties as a recruiter took practically no time, asked Patton for his notes from his year at C&GS and pored over them. He obtained copies of the Leavenworth problems from previous years, worked through them, and checked his answers against the approved solutions. He discovered that Conner was right; the work came easily and he enjoyed it. In August 1925, he reported at Leavenworth, confident and ready.

In the year that followed, Eisenhower worked as he had never worked before. Given a challenge, any hint of mental laziness disappeared. He was in direct competition with 275 of the best officers in the Army, every one of them handpicked by his superiors to reflect credit on their particular arm or branch of the service. The work load, like the competition, was nearly overwhelming. The students looked on an assignment to C&GS as a reward as well as a challenge, at least before they got there, but the Army regarded it as a test. The school was designed to discover not only who had brains, but who could take the strain. The military differs from all other professions in any number of ways, but the most important is this: field officers get to practice their profession only on rare occasions. For most of their careers, their country is at peace. But their entire *raison d'être* is to fight, and what the Army wants to know about its officers is, Who will meet the ultimate test of combat successfully? C&GS did all it could to approximate the real thing, forcing exhausted men to think and react under extreme pressure, with their careers dependent on the outcome.

The method was war gaming by case studies. Students were given problems. A hostile force of such and such strength was either attacking or defending a position. Students, commanding the Blue Force, had to decide what actions should be taken. After the student had handed in his answer, he was given the approved solution. He then had to work out the movements of the combat units and the supply services to support that solution—in short, the basic staff work that would be required in time of war.

The school did not encourage imagination, independent thought, or genius. There was a correct solution and all others were wrong, with no second-guessing or discussion allowed. C&GS was not trying to turn out Napoleons, but rather competent staff officers; it was not looking for men who would argue with their commanders in the middle of a battle, but men who could be relied upon to implement their commanders' decisions.

Eisenhower did not believe in the doctrine taught at C&GS. The official manual stated flatly, "So let it be understood that, when war comes, there should be only one question that will ever be asked of a commander as to a battle, and that one is, not what flank did he attack, not how did he use his reserves, not how did he protect his flanks, but did he fight?"[28] This ran directly counter to Eisenhower's ideas, which emphasized using the mobility of the tank to outflank the enemy, but he understood that he was not at C&GS to criticize but to prove himself as someone who could be counted on to implement his superiors' ideas.

C&GS was notorious for its pressure. Students would stay up half the night studying. Most joined committees, ranging from four to eight members, in order to share the work load and discuss the problems. The tension was such that nervous breakdowns were fairly common, and there was an occasional suicide. Eisenhower found this atmosphere "exhilarating." He decided that a fresh mind was more important than one crammed full of details, so he limited himself to two and one-half hours of study per night, always going to bed at nine-thirty. He refused an invitation to join a committee because he did not want to waste time in conversation and argument. He did get together with one old friend from Fort Sam, Leonard Gerow. They set up a command post on the third floor of Eisenhower's quarters, covered the walls with maps, filled the shelves with reference works.[29] No sound reached them there; it was off limits to his family. One of John Eisenhower's earliest memories was of the night he invaded this sanctuary. He saw his father and "Gee" bending over a large table, eyeshades protecting them from the glare of the lamp. "I was too small to see what was on the table but stared in wonderment at the huge maps tacked on the wall. The two young officers were going over the next day's tactical problem. Dad and Gee welcomed me with a laugh and shoved me out the door in the course of perhaps half a minute."[30]

The course brought out the best in Eisenhower, his ability to master detail without getting bogged down in it, his talent for translating ideas (even if not his own) into action, his positive (almost eager) reaction to pressure, his mastery of his profession, and his sense of being a team player (the emphasis of the course was on the smooth functioning of the machine). When the final rankings were posted, he stood first in his class (Gerow was second, two-tenths of a point behind), a breathtaking accomplishment for a cadet who had graduated in the middle of his West Point class and for an officer who had not attended his service school.

Eisenhower, elated, informed all his friends and relatives. Messages of congratulations poured in. Fox Conner was delighted with his protégé. Mrs. Doud wired, "Oh boy what a thrill hurrah I am broadcasting the news love and kisses Mother."[31] Arthur Eisenhower organized a victory celebration in the Muehlbach Hotel in Kansas City, complete with a bountiful supply of bootleg gin and whiskey.[32] Patton wrote Eisenhower a letter of congratulations on graduating from C&GS, then learned that Eisenhower was first in his class and wrote again. "That certainly is fine," Patton wrote. "It shows that leavenworth is a good school if a HE man can come out one." He added that Eisenhower's record proved that "if a man thinks war long enough it is bound to effect him in a good way."

Then Patton, more individualistic and independent than Eisenhower, put in a cautionary note. "Good as leavenworth is," he said, "it is still only a means not an end." Since his own graduation two years earlier he had continued to work through all the C&GS problems, but he warned Eisenhower, "I dont try for approved solutions any more but rather to do what I will do in war." Warming to his subject, Patton added, "You know that we talk a hell of a lot about tactics and such and we never get to brass tacks. Namely what is it that makes the Poor S.O.B. who constitutes the casualtie lists fight and in what formation is he going to fight. The answer to the first is Leadership that to the second—I don't know." But he did know that any doctrine based on "super trained heroes is bull. The solitary son of a bitch alone with God is going to skulk as he always has and our advancing waves will not advance unless we have such superior artillery that all they have to do is to walk." He recommended that Eisenhower read Ardant du Picq's *Battle Studies* (du Picq, a French officer, had anticipated the work of S. L. A. Marshall in the American Army by interviewing veterans of the Franco-Prussian War in order to determine what actually happened in battle. His was a truly pathbreaking work on the age-old problem of how to make men fight). Patton told Eisenhower that now that he had graduated from C&GS, he should stop thinking about drafting orders and moving supplies and start thinking about "some means of making the infantry move under fire." He prophesied that "victory in the next war will depend on EXECUTION not PLANS."[33]

Graduating first at Leavenworth did not mean an immediate promotion, not in an Army that was already top-heavy with senior officers. Major Eisenhower, now back in the Infantry, was given a choice: he could go to a northwestern university as ROTC instructor, the duty to include coaching the university's football team at an additional salary of $3,500 per year, or he could take command of a battalion at Fort Benning, Georgia. He chose Benning. When he arrived, the CO informed him that he was to coach the Benning football team. "With an enormous effort of will," Eisenhower said later, he kept his temper and pointed out that he had just turned down $3,500 to coach and certainly did not want to do it for free. He coached anyway.[34]

After the season, Conner came to his rescue. On his recommendation, Pershing, now head of the Battle Monuments Commission, called Eisenhower to Washington and set him to writing a guide to the American battlefields in Europe. It was not a challenging assignment, more a scissors-and-paste job, using unit histories, war maps, battle reports, chronologies, and pictures. There was some pressure, however, as Eisenhower had to have a typescript ready in six months.

Fortunately, he had his youngest brother, Milton, to help him. Dwight and Mamie lived in the Wyoming Apartments, on Connecticut Avenue near Rock Creek Park. Milton and his wife, the former Helen Eakin of Manhattan, Kansas, were neighbors. Milton was the number-two man in the Department of Agriculture, well known around town as a rising star. His special talent was journalism, and he helped his brother put the guidebook together. It was Dwight's initial tour of duty in Washington, and thus his introduction to a world in which American politics was the almost exclusive subject of conversation. Milton was an excellent guide to that world. Dwight found himself drawn into serious political discussion for the first time in his life, and discovered in the process that he was more conservative than Milton. His brother, although he had advanced steadily through the ranks of the bureaucracy during the Republican Administrations of the twenties, nevertheless was chiefly concerned with what the government could do for the people (in his own case, especially farmers), while Dwight, in both their theoretical and practical discussions, found that he put the emphasis on the duty of citizens toward the government. In general, Milton saw a positive role for government and wanted it to grow, while Dwight saw a negative role and wanted it to shrink (except, obviously, in the military).[35]

These were differences of degree, not kind. The brothers, although nine years apart in age, were similar in many ways. Both loved a good game of bridge, as did their wives, and they frequently played together. They looked alike, with the same big grin and hearty laugh, although Dwight was leaner in the face, tougher in the body. Their voices were so similar that, practical jokers both, they would call the other man's wife on the telephone and carry on a conversation, pretending to be each other. The wives never caught on.[36]

Milton, who like his brother had married a wealthy girl, but who unlike Dwight had a generous father-in-law, could afford to entertain frequently. Cabinet members, other bureaucrats, Washington lawyers, and the Washington press club were his usual guests. Dwight and Mamie joined in the fun; to Milton's secret delight, Dwight became known in Washington as "Milton's brother." At one party, as a reporter was leaving, Milton stopped him and said, "Please don't go until you've met my brother; he's a major in the Army and I know he's going places." Shaking hands with thirty-seven-year-old Major Eisenhower, the reporter thought, "If he's going far he had better start soon." But the firm handshake, the lopsided grin, and the complete concentration of Eisenhower's blue eyes on his all impressed the reporter. He decided Milton might be right.[37]

Pershing thought so too. He was delighted when Eisenhower

handed in the guidebook, on time, and sent a lavish letter of commendation: Eisenhower, he said, "has shown superior ability not only in visualizing his work as a whole but in executing its many details in an efficient and timely manner. What he has done was accomplished only by the exercise of unusual intelligence and constant devotion to duty."[38]

As the tone of the letter indicated, Pershing was a coldly formal man—Eisenhower described him as "reserved and even remote." Eisenhower's office was near Pershing's, but despite the general's approval of the guidebook, the two men developed nothing like the intimate relationship that existed between Eisenhower and Conner. Still, Eisenhower had great respect for the commander of the AEF. Until Pershing's death in 1948, Eisenhower sent him birthday greetings and chatty letters, and he was a frequent visitor at Pershing's hospital rooms at Walter Reed during the general's last years. For his part, Pershing respected Eisenhower, enough so that one day in 1928 he called Eisenhower into his office, said he was having difficulty with the writing of his memoirs, especially the sections covering the great battles of St. Mihiel and the Argonne, and asked Eisenhower to read over his manuscript and make suggestions. The memoirs were, in fact, little more than an expanded version of Pershing's daily diary, which made it impossible to tell the stories of the long battles (the Argonne lasted six weeks) in a consecutive, chronological fashion.

Eisenhower recommended that Pershing abandon the diary format in the accounts of the battles, suggesting that they be done in a narrative style. Pershing thought that was a good idea and, being a general, responded by ordering Eisenhower to write a draft of the chapters as he thought they should be written. Eisenhower did so, Pershing read them, said he liked them, but added that in such matters he always looked to Colonel George C. Marshall for final advice. Pershing gave Eisenhower's chapters to Marshall to read; a few days later Marshall came into Eisenhower's office for the first meeting between the two men. Marshall, as stiff and formal as Pershing himself, refused an invitation to sit down. He said he thought Eisenhower's chapters were interesting, but nevertheless he had advised Pershing to stay with the diary format. Eisenhower argued the point. Marshall brought the discussion to an end by remarking that he felt Pershing would be happier if he stuck to his diary. The result was a set of memoirs which, because of their choppy style, were nearly incomprehensible to most readers.[39] Because of Pershing's experience, Marshall refused after World War II to write his own memoirs.

Eisenhower's reward for his work for Pershing was a posting to the

Army War College, at Fort McNair, also in Washington. The college, in theory, was the capstone of an officer's postgraduate education. Its mission was to prepare men for high command. In practice, it was a reward rather than a challenge, a relaxing year (students were neither examined nor ranked), spent mainly in listening to lectures on world affairs by government officials and Army generals. The idea was to broaden the outlook of officers tapped for future high command; the reality was more a pleasant sabbatical.

The Eisenhowers continued to live in the Wyoming Apartments, where many of his fellow students and some General Staff officers lived. Gerow was there, and Wade Haislip, another old hand from prewar Fort Sam, and Jimmy Ord, a West Point classmate and currently an instructor at the War College, and Everett Hughes, an old friend from Leavenworth. Symbolic of their freedom from the pressures of Leavenworth, Eisenhower and Gerow and the others wore mufti. Mamie established another "Club Eisenhower." Kate Hughes described the scene: "Most of the time people were at their house. We'd gather there after the men had played their golf, or when they'd finished for the day at the War College. The men would stop at the Eisenhowers' for a drink and get to talking and then call their wives and we'd all go over. . . . Sometimes we'd go out to a Chinese or Italian restaurant, but mostly we'd stay at the Eisenhowers'. Mamie would have food for us, or sometimes each of us would bring something."[40]

These Army officers, all captains and majors, kept to themselves. They had neither social standing nor prestige in rank-conscious Washington. They wore mufti on orders from the Chief of Staff, who wanted to reduce their visibility in a capital given over to isolationism. Thanks to Milton, Eisenhower had reached out into the general Washington social scene, but his real friends were all Army officers. The prejudices against them made them even more tight-knit than they would have been anyway. They knew one another intimately; everyone knew everyone else's habits, salaries, preferences in food and drink, hobbies (generally golf for the men, bridge for the women), and prospects. They exchanged birthday greetings, sent formal messages of congratulations on appropriate occasions, showed one another their children's report cards, and gossiped incessantly. Being part of that scene was like being part of a large, happy, close family.

In their birthday greetings, the officers usually tried to fit in a pun about the passing of time. Since most of them were rapidly approaching their fortieth birthday and had not had a promotion in years, the puns had a poignant quality.

• •

In June 1928, Eisenhower graduated from the War College. At almost thirty-eight years old, he had completed his formal education. The government had invested a large sum of money in his training; he had responded by investing a large portion of himself in preparing for war. The Army had trained him to the best of its ability; now he, like the Army, would have to wait for an opportunity to use that training.

CHAPTER SIX

Paris, Washington

1928–1935

FOLLOWING HIS graduation from the War College, Eisenhower was given a choice by the War Department. He could either join the General Staff or go to France as a member of the Battle Monuments Commission, to do a revision of his guidebook. He wanted to choose the General Staff, as service in that body was a major plus in an officer's career. And, as he told Mamie, he had not gone to West Point and C&GS and the War College in order to write guidebooks for American tourists. But Mamie, who had so often suffered in silence, insisted on Paris—she was not about to let a chance to live there for a year pass her by. Eisenhower yielded.[1]

In August 1928, the Eisenhowers sailed for France. Mamie found a furnished apartment at 68 Quai d'Auteuil, near Pont Mirabeau, on the left bank of the Seine. Eisenhower's office was close enough for him to walk home for lunch. Six-year-old John entered the McJanet School for American children. Mamie, of course, shopped avidly in Paris, and the family took a tour of southern Europe. Eisenhower spent much of his working time on the road, examining on the spot the American battlefields. But for the rest, the Eisenhowers were isolated in Paris from the culture and the people. Their friends were Army officers, those stationed in Paris and those passing through. They kept "Club Eisenhower" open, featuring card parties, dinners, and music. Even the songs they sang were American ballads and jazz.[2] It was, in short, a restful, pleasant fifteen months, spent pretty much doing nothing of any importance in a charming setting.

• •

In November 1929, the Eisenhowers returned to Washington and the Wyoming Apartments. Eisenhower was assigned to the office of the Assistant Secretary of War. The office was responsible for preparing plans for the mobilization of American industry and manpower in the next war. A job more out of joint with the times could hardly be imagined. Over the next three years, the worst years of the Great Depression, Eisenhower's task was to plan for plant expansion, at a time when factories all across the land were closing their doors; to prepare for material shortages, at a time when no buyers could be found anywhere for enormous quantities of goods already stockpiled; to anticipate a manpower crisis, at a time when one-third of the American work force was unemployed; to draft legislation for an explosion in government expenditures and deficit financing, at a time when the Hoover Administration was trying to reduce government costs and activities in order to balance the budget. Eisenhower spent much of his time conferring with big businessmen, attempting to ascertain what they could do to convert their factories from peacetime to wartime production. These industrialists hardly took Major Eisenhower seriously. They had a crisis on their hands that required their full attention, and anyway few of them believed there would be another war in their lifetimes. Besides, they resented the charges of war profiteering so commonly made in Congress. To most of the industrialists, Eisenhower's talk about cooperation between America's factories and the War Department in a program of unlimited production for war seemed unreal.

Eisenhower's personal life too had more than a touch of unreality to it. Eisenhower's job, and those of his friends in the Army, was secure. He did suffer a slight pay cut, but falling prices more than made up the difference. He lived in Washington, a town in which the only major employer was the federal government. After January 1933, under the new Roosevelt Administration, Washington became the only boomtown in America. All around him, Eisenhower saw new construction going on, to house and entertain the New Deal bureaucrats.

His attitude toward the New Deal was hopeful. A month after the 1932 election he wrote in his diary, "While I have no definite leanings toward any political party I believe it is a good thing the Democrats won—and particularly that one party will have such overwhelming superiority in Congress." A week before FDR's inauguration he explained his reasoning: "Things are not going to take an upturn until more power is centered in one man's hands. Only in that way will confidence be inspired; will it be possible to do some of the obvious things for speeding recovery, and will we be freed from the pernicious influence of noisy and selfish minorities.

"For two years I have been called 'Dictator Ike' because I believe that virtual dictatorship must be exercised by our President, so now I keep still—but I still believe it!"[3]

In contrast to the turbulent excitement of the early New Deal, life in the Wyoming Apartments was pleasant, uneventful. Club Eisenhower flourished. John was doing well in school. On Sundays, the Eisenhowers would climb into their 1927 Buick and drive from one apartment house to another, paying courtesy calls on Eisenhower's superiors, Eisenhower wearing a derby hat and striped pants. John recalled that "this was a chore that Dad detested and he made little secret of it." After the calls, Eisenhower would play golf with his friends. The Pattons were in town—Lieutenant Colonel Patton was stationed at Fort Myer—and the Eisenhowers called on them frequently. Young John held them in considerable awe, partly because Patton outranked his father, but also because of Patton's obvious wealth and the silver horsemanship trophies that covered the walls. John was astonished not only at Patton's ability to swear but at the way he encouraged his three children to do the same.

Although they were parents of an only child, the Eisenhowers could hardly be accused of spoiling John. As he passed his tenth year in 1932, Mamie gradually lost her terror of any cold, cut, or bruise he suffered. John's father, meanwhile, "continually pounded into me that we were not wealthy people." Mamie managed the money, and "every penny counted." When John lost a ten-dollar coat, she was "literally shattered." Although the parents had their quarrels, sometimes severe, they made it a point never to argue in front of their son. He was nonetheless aware of the fights and noted that "the Old Man's views nearly always prevailed."[4]

Dwight and Mamie spent a good deal of their time with Milton and Helen. Even after the change from Republican to Democratic Administrations, Milton remained at the top of the civil service, and his social life flourished. Helen's father had invested heavily in real estate across the Potomac River in Falls Church, Virginia; soon Milton, with help from his father-in-law, moved his family to a handsome residence in Falls Church. Through Milton and Helen, Dwight and Mamie met Harry and Ruth Butcher, and the three couples became close. Butcher had moved from print journalism to become head of the new Washington office of the Columbia Broadcasting System—he got the job thanks to connections he made at Milton's parties in Falls Church. Radio, like government, was that rare anomaly in the thirties, a growth industry. Butcher, in on the boom from the beginning, commanded a large and ever-increasing salary. As handsome as a movie star, charming and breezy, popular around town, Butcher was both fun to be with and a good man to know.[5]

Major General George Van Horn Moseley, who had been Pershing's chief of supply, was Eisenhower's immediate superior in the office of the Assistant Secretary of War. Moseley was a man of extreme right-wing and anti-Semitic views. Much concerned with the specter of Communism, in the fall of 1930 he recommended that the War Department round up all radicals and ship them off to Russia.[6] After his retirement in the mid-thirties, he strongly criticized the New Deal and associated himself with Gerald L. K. Smith, among others.[7] Eisenhower, who was accustomed to hearing Army officers curse radicals and other undesirables, reacted as he usually did to such frothing—he would listen, nod, and change the subject. He did not necessarily disagree with the analysis, such as it was, but he was too much a middle-of-the-road American to accept such solutions as Moseley's recommended deportation. Mostly, he regarded such talk as none of his business and paid little attention. Politics had no interest for him, and he shrank instinctively from extremism.

He thought Moseley, in his professional capacity, an outstanding officer, "dynamic . . . always delving into new ideas . . . an inspiration." Eisenhower was aware that Moseley created the "impression" that he was "a reactionary or a militarist," but said that was a distortion; Moseley, to Eisenhower, "was a patriotic American unafraid to disagree with a consensus."[8] In 1940, Eisenhower told a friend that Moseley, "in spite of his retired activities, was a shrewd judge of officers." For his part, Moseley called Eisenhower "my brainy assistant," and in his efficiency report wrote that "no limit should be placed on this officer." Moseley predicted that "he will go far in the Army."[9]

The two men had a difficult task because the Chief of Staff, General Charles Summerall, was "contemptuous" of their work. Summerall issued orders forbidding any officer on the General Staff to enter the offices of anyone assigned to the Assistant Secretary of War, which meant specifically Moseley and Eisenhower.[10] The problems cut across service lines too. There was an interservice agency, the Army and Navy Munitions Board, that was supposed to engage in joint planning for industrial mobilization, but it hardly ever met and did no significant work, primarily because the Navy was not interested. This was because the

Navy expected to fight the next war with the fleet in being, while the Army anticipated a vast expansion. In a lecture to the students at the Army Industrial College in Washington, Eisenhower put it politely when he noted, "Neither the Army-Navy Munitions Board nor its subsidiary committees have been particularly active during the last nine years, nor have they always been able to settle controversial questions placed before them."[11] Thus Eisenhower and Moseley were isolated from their sister service as well as from the industrialists, the government, and their own General Staff. Under the circumstances, they could do little more than study the experience of the World War, when America had mobilized under the direction of a series of special, civilian-run superagencies, capped by Bernard Baruch's War Industries Board.[12]

In the fall of 1930, Douglas MacArthur replaced Summerall as Chief of Staff. With that change at the top, the office of the Assistant Secretary of War came to life. MacArthur was a close friend of Moseley's, and Eisenhower was delighted by the new Chief of Staff's "enthusiasm" and "encouragement and advice."[13] That same year, Congress created the War Policies Commission to study "policies to be pursued in the event of war" and how "to equalize the burdens and to minimize the profits of war." The resolution creating the commission directed it "to study and consider amending the Constitution" in order to make war unprofitable and require everyone to bear its burdens equally. Supporters talked in terms of conscripting private property as well as men in any mobilization. The general hope was that if the government took the profit out of war through seizure of property, it would eliminate well-financed campaigns agitating for American entry into war. The commission was a high-powered body—Secretary of War Patrick J. Hurley was the chairman, while five other Cabinet officers, four senators, and four congressmen made up the membership. The War Department's plans for mobilization were obviously central to the committee's concerns, and MacArthur was told that he would have the job of presenting the hitherto "secret" (in fact, nonexistent) industrial mobilization plan.[14]

MacArthur told Moseley and Eisenhower to get to work, and by the end of 1930 they had produced a plan. It covered a host of topics, such as price controls, priorities, foreign trade, commandeering industrial plants, and, most important, the creation of special government superagencies to maintain centralized direction over industry, manpower, selective service, and public relations. All these agencies, the plan made clear, would be under civilian control.[15]

In the spring of 1931, the commission held open hearings. Industrialists came to the War Department to discuss their testimony in advance. MacArthur sent them to talk to Eisenhower. It was Eisenhower's introduction to the leaders of what he himself would later call the "military-industrial complex"—which, obviously, hardly existed in 1931, not even in embryonic form. Nevertheless it was an important experience for Eisenhower. Up to 1930, he knew little about American industry, its problems, capacities, or organization. Now he was in daily working contact with some of its great captains. Not surprisingly, Eisenhower found that these men "directly opposed the idea of actual seizure of all property" in time of war.[16] Eisenhower attended the hearings, and although he did not testify himself—MacArthur was the spokesman for the Army—he did confer before and after the sessions with the commission members and those giving testimony.[17]

But in truth, all this activity went on in a vacuum. Despite the prominence of the members of the commission and of the people who testified before it, few people paid much attention. The Hoover Administration had other, more pressing concerns; the Roosevelt Administration ignored the War Department plan. The agencies created in 1941 to supervise mobilization bore only a superficial resemblance to Eisenhower's blueprints.[18] For Eisenhower personally, the work was a valuable introduction to some of the responsibilities and concerns he would deal with as President, although it gave him a one-sided view of labor-management-government relations.

In immediate terms, the best thing about the planning job for Eisenhower was his contact with MacArthur. The Chief of Staff was impressed by Eisenhower's work, his smooth cooperation with the industrialists, his mastery of detail, his writing style, his ability to reflect the attitudes and opinions of his superiors. He began to utilize Eisenhower's talents, asking the major to draft some of his speeches, letters, and reports. The Chief of Staff was generous in his praise; in a handwritten note in 1932 he scribbled on a draft of a report: "Dear Eisenhower; A magnificent effort on your part. Much better than I could have done myself. I am grateful. MacArthur."[19] He also placed more official and formal praise in Eisenhower's 201 file; a typical letter thanked Eisenhower for his willing acceptance of a special assignment (drafting the Chief of Staff's Annual Report) and his fine performance. "I write you this special commendation," MacArthur concluded, "so that you may fully realize that your outstanding talents and your ability to perform these highly important missions are fully appreciated." In his efficiency report on Eisenhower, MacArthur stated flatly that "this officer has no superior of his time in the Army . . . Distinguished by force, judgment and willingness to accept responsibility." MacArthur added that Eisenhower was "well qualified for civilian contacts."[20]

Douglas MacArthur was one of the two most important men in Eisenhower's life. The other was George C. Marshall. It was Eisenhower's luck to know and work for these outstanding generals, each one a powerful personality and a historic figure. They were vastly different in their leadership techniques. MacArthur was bombastic, flamboyant in dress, egotistical, outrageous in his flattery, intensely partisan, keen to enter the political fray. Marshall was soft-spoken, reserved in dress, modest, slow to praise, staunchly nonpartisan, reluctant to enter the political fray. Both served Franklin Roosevelt as Chief of Staff, but their conceptions of the relationship of the head of the Army to the President were sharply different. MacArthur's was one of antagonism, Marshall's of complete support. They also differed on a fundamental strategic question, the relative importance of Europe and Asia to America. One result was to divide the U.S. Army and its General Staff into two groups, the "MacArthur clique" and the "Marshall clique," or the "Asia-firsters" and the "Europe-firsters."

Eisenhower spent eleven of his thirty-seven years in the Army working directly under these two men, seven with MacArthur, four with Marshall. Each general liked and respected Eisenhower. They had good reason to do so. Eisenhower did his work brilliantly. It was always done on time. He loyally supported his chief's decisions. He adjusted himself to his chief's time schedules and to other whims. He was able to think from the point of view of his chief, a quality that both MacArthur and Marshall often singled out for praise. He had an instinctive sense of when to make a decision himself, when to pass it up to the boss. MacArthur said of Eisenhower in a fitness report in the early 1930s, "This is the best officer in the Army. When the next war comes, he should go right to the top."[21] In 1942 Marshall showed that he agreed with that assessment by implementing the recommendation.

Because of his frequent disagreements with MacArthur, a conviction developed that Eisenhower hated working for MacArthur and tried desperately to obtain a transfer. Reportedly, too, MacArthur was bitter toward Eisenhower and deliberately held him back, which supposedly explains why Eisenhower was still a lieutenant colonel in 1940, on his fiftieth birthday. But an account of the Eisenhower-MacArthur relationship that concentrates on bitterness, hatred, and jealousy, with the emphasis on their fights, is much too simple. Their relationship was rich and complex, with many subtle nuances, and was highly profitable to each man. Eisenhower touched on this in an interview during his retirement, when he told MacArthur's ablest biographer, D. Clayton James, that he had always been "deeply grateful for the administrative experience he had gained under General MacArthur," without which he confessed he would not "have been ready for the great responsibilities of the war period." Eisenhower also pointed out the obvious: "Hostility between us has been exaggerated. After all, there must be a strong tie for two men to work so closely for seven years."[22]

In his memoirs, Eisenhower described MacArthur as "decisive, personable, amazingly comprehensive in his knowledge . . . possessed of a phenomenal memory." MacArthur was a "peculiar fellow," Eisenhower said, who had a habit of referring to himself in the third person. Of MacArthur's well-known egotism, Eisenhower commented, "[He] could never see another sun . . . in the heavens." But MacArthur's idiosyncrasies, little and great, were not matters of substance. Eisenhower singled out MacArthur's most important quality in an interview with Peter Lyon: "He did have a hell of an intellect! My God, but he was smart. He had a *brain*." So did Marshall, of course, and Eisenhower too for that matter, although of the three, only MacArthur could read through a speech or a paper once, then repeat it verbatim.[23]

Eisenhower was much closer to MacArthur personally than he ever was to Marshall. Eisenhower and MacArthur frequently exchanged jokes; Eisenhower and Marshall seldom did. Marshall, a graduate of the Virginia Military Institute, did not much care who won the Army-Navy game, while Eisenhower and MacArthur were fanatic followers of West Point's football fortunes. Each fall they engaged in lively discussions about the prospects for and the results of the Army-Navy game. Eisenhower and Mamie had almost no social contact with the Marshalls, while they frequently attended parties and dinners with MacArthur and his wife, Jean.

Eisenhower learned a great deal from MacArthur, far more than simply administrative skills. When he took a position on an issue, MacArthur was very stubborn in maintaining it, especially when the Army was concerned. He mastered the details of an issue and spoke with authority on them. He matched the persistence of his argument with a logical presentation of the facts. Whether consciously or not, during the war and as President, Eisenhower copied MacArthur in debate.

Nevertheless, many of the lessons Eisenhower learned from MacArthur were negative ones, a reflection of the markedly different styles of the two men. MacArthur did not attempt to teach or instruct, to make Eisenhower a protégé, as Marshall tended to do; instead, Eisenhower learned from MacArthur by observing him in action. And MacArthur was certainly a fascinating man to observe. Reporters accompanied him wherever he went, and his pronouncements or activities often made headlines. He was deliberately outspoken on some of the most volatile emotional issues of the day. He lambasted the Communists, the New Dealers, the pacifists, the Socialists, any and all groups that did not meet his definition of 100 percent Americans. He never refused a challenge; he loved to charge into the battle.

MacArthur made no secret of his political ambitions; everyone knew that unlike Pershing he would welcome a presidential nomination. During the Roosevelt years and on into Truman's Fair Deal, rightwing Republicans tried again and again to organize a MacArthur-for-President boom, even in 1944. Such activities always excited the general but never got far. One reason for the failure was obviously MacArthur's extremism, but another was his inability to understand the American people. Eisenhower had a much better intuitive understanding of his fellow citizens' political preferences.

During the 1936 presidential campaign, for example, when Eisenhower and MacArthur were in Manila, MacArthur convinced himself that Republican nominee Alf Landon was sure to win, probably by a landslide. Eisenhower protested that he was wrong. MacArthur insisted that he was correct, and cited a *Literary Digest* poll to prove it. He even bet several thousand pesos on Landon's election and advised the Philippine government to prepare for a change of Administrations in Washington. Eisenhower predicted that Landon could not even carry his home state, Kansas. MacArthur indulged himself in an "almost hysterical condemnation" of Eisenhower's "stupidity." When another of MacArthur's aides, T. J. Davis, supported Eisenhower's position, MacArthur loudly denounced them both as "fearful and small-minded people who are afraid to express judgments that are obvious from the evidence at hand." Eisenhower's comment in a diary that he was beginning to keep on a sporadic basis was "Oh hell." After the election, in which Landon carried only two states, MacArthur accused the *Literary Digest* of "crookedness," but Eisenhower noted, "he's never expressed to TJ or to me any regret for his awful bawling out . . ."[24]

In his first years of working for MacArthur, Eisenhower was often astonished at the way in which the Chief of Staff brushed aside the usual "clean-cut line between the military and the political. If General MacArthur ever recognized the existence of that line, he usually chose to ignore it." To Eisenhower's dismay he found that "my duties were beginning to verge on the political, even to the edge of partisan politics."[25]

The tradition in the Army was to deny that it was ever involved in any way in politics. The Army refused to see itself as a vast bureaucracy, even while it lobbied among congressmen for appropriations (which was a task on which Major Eisenhower spent much of his time). The Army and Army officers were supposed to be above politics. But, as Eisenhower confessed to Merriman Smith in a 1962 off-the-record interview, when Smith said it was his impression that Eisenhower did not like the role of politician, "What the hell are you talking about? I have been in politics, the most active sort of politics, most of my adult life. There's no more active political organization in the world than the armed services of the U.S. As a matter of fact, I think I am a better politician than most so-called politicians." When Smith asked why, Eisenhower explained, "Because I don't get emotionally involved. I can accept a fact for what it is, and I can also accept the fact that when you're hopelessly outgunned and outmanned, you don't go out and pick a fight."[26]

MacArthur embraced controversial issues; Eisenhower avoided them. When Eisenhower became President, the nation paid a price for his avoidance of controversy, as in the desegregation crisis or in dealing with Senator Joseph R. McCarthy. But the avoidance clearly helped Eisenhower's career, as he well knew. MacArthur was famous, but he was never popular enough to win a nomination, much less an election. Watching MacArthur in the thirties, and observing the results of his political activity, reinforced Eisenhower's determination to keep himself above politics. That attitude was crucial to his success as a general and a politician.

MacArthur operated differently, and MacArthur never became President, although he wanted the job much more than Eisenhower ever did. There is an irony here. MacArthur, the most political of generals, never succeeded in politics, while three of the most apolitical generals in American history, Washington, Grant, and Eisenhower, did. They were the true American Caesars, the only American soldiers to hold both supreme military and political power.

Eisenhower's most vivid lesson in the dangers of involvement in partisan politics came as he watched MacArthur deal with the Bonus March. The Bonus Marchers, who descended on Washington some twenty thousand strong in the summer of 1932, were mainly unemployed veterans who wanted an early payment on the "bonus" promised them for their wartime services, a bonus that was not due until 1945. The average bonus was about $1,000. In 1931 Congress, overriding

President Hoover's veto, provided for payment of half the bonus. In the summer of 1932 it was considering a bill to pay the other half. The Bonus Marchers had come to camp in Washington in order to put direct pressure on Congress to pass the legislation.

The veterans camped in abandoned Treasury Department buildings on Pennsylvania Avenue, and on the Anacostia Flats in "miserable little shacks"—this was Eisenhower's description—"built out of cast-off materials, tin cans and old lumber." To the Hoover Administration, already beleaguered, the Bonus Marchers seemed "the menace of Bolshevism attacking the government at its very Capitol."[27] MacArthur was certain that "the movement was actually far deeper and more dangerous than an effort to secure funds from a nearly depleted federal treasury. . . . Red organizers infiltrated the veteran groups and presently took command from their unwitting leaders." The Army Chief of Staff believed that through the Bonus March "the Communists hoped to incite revolutionary action."[28] Eisenhower saw the marchers differently. "In fact," he wrote, "most of them . . . however misled they may have been by a few agitators, were quiet and orderly." As to MacArthur's beliefs, Eisenhower commented, "I just can't understand how such a damn fool could have gotten to be a general."[29]

In June, MacArthur tried to prove the Communist link. He asked his senior officers around the country to provide him with the names of known Communists traveling with the Bonus Marchers. The replies came back—no one knew of any. Despite the lack of evidence, the Chief of Staff and the Hoover Administration assumed the worst. Hoover decided that the 1,100 or so veterans camping in the Treasury Department buildings had to be driven out. On July 27 the Administration ordered the Washington chief of police to evict them. The next morning, at 9 A.M., the police began the eviction process. Everything that happened from that moment on was controversial, each side blaming the other for the violence that occurred and disagreeing over how extensive that violence was. In any event, bricks flew, shots were fired, two veterans were killed, three policemen were injured. Hoover called Secretary of War Hurley and asked for the Army's aid. At 2:55 P.M., Hurley ordered MacArthur to send U.S. troops "immediately to the scene of disorder. . . . Surround the affected area and clear it without delay."[30]

By 4 P.M. MacArthur had Army units ready to move, including the 12th Infantry Regiment and elements of the 3d Cavalry, altogether a total of 793 officers and men. MacArthur decided to accompany the troops himself, explaining that he was going "not with a view of commanding the troops but to be on hand as things progressed, so that he could issue necessary instructions on the ground." Eisenhower had been acting as a liaison between MacArthur and the Washington police. When he heard from MacArthur that the Chief of Staff intended to go to Pennsylvania Avenue himself, he exploded in protest. Recalling the incident three decades later Eisenhower explained, "I told that dumb son-of-a-bitch he had no business going down there. I told him it was no place for the Chief of Staff." MacArthur insisted that revolution was in the air, that the Republic was in danger, and that he had to be there. He ordered Eisenhower to go home, put on his uniform, and report back for duty. Meanwhile MacArthur sent an aide to his quarters to pick up his uniform.[31]

When the general, the major, and Captain T. J. Davis showed up on Pennsylvania Avenue, they made a striking picture and dozens of photographers seized the opportunity. Neither Eisenhower nor Davis had any campaign ribbons or medals on his jacket; MacArthur, his chest covered with medals, shone by comparison. He wore his dress coat, complete with Sam Browne belt, riding breeches, and knee-high polished boots, complete with spurs. All the photos taken show an obviously unhappy Eisenhower, a quite delighted MacArthur.

The cavalry, sabers drawn, cleared the avenue, while the infantry threw tear-gas grenades into the disputed buildings. The troops herded the retreating veterans toward the Anacostia River and the bridge over it to the encampment on the Anacostia Flats. As the troops neared the bridge, Hurley twice sent messengers to tell MacArthur that the President did not want the Army to pursue the veterans across the Anacostia River.[32] Although one of these messages was carried by Moseley personally, MacArthur claimed never to have heard the order. In his memoirs, Eisenhower was loyal to his boss, if more than a bit disingenuous. "In neither instance did General MacArthur hear these instructions," Eisenhower wrote, referring to the orders to halt at the bridge. Contradicting himself, he continued, "[MacArthur] said he was too busy and did not want either himself or his staff bothered by people coming down and pretending to bring orders."[33] Obviously, MacArthur and Eisenhower heard what Moseley had to say; just as obviously, MacArthur decided to ignore Hoover's order.

At 10:30 P.M., MacArthur ordered the troops to move across the bridge in forty-five minutes. He then prepared to leave the scene personally, leaving Eisenhower behind. Eisenhower cautioned him that when he got to the War Department, "there would probably be newspaper reporters trying to see him. I suggested it would be the better part of wisdom, if not of valor, to avoid meeting them. The troop movement had not been a military idea really, but a political order and I thought that the political officials only should talk to the press."[34] MacArthur ignored him. He held an 11 P.M. press conference and told reporters, "That mob down there was a bad-looking mob. It was animated by the essence of revolution."[35]

As MacArthur talked to the reporters, the troops moved in on Anacostia Flats. Suddenly fires broke out. The Army claimed that the veterans had set their own shacks on fire "to show their displeasure"; the Bonus Marchers said the soldiers started the fires. Whatever happened, Eisenhower was heartsick. The veterans, he said, "were ragged, ill-fed, and felt themselves badly abused. To suddenly see the whole encampment going up in flames just added to the pity one had to feel for them."[36]

The entire episode made MacArthur look like an ogre. The assumption was that he had personally made the decision to drive the veterans out of Pennsylvania Avenue and to burn down the Anacostia Flats encampment. The press overwhelmingly agreed that MacArthur had misjudged the situation and bungled the eviction. D. Clayton James concluded that MacArthur "acted with overzealous determination and reckless impulsiveness."[37] MacArthur blamed the bad publicity on the Communists and refused to admit that he had made a mistake. Eisenhower observed that MacArthur "had an obsession that a high commander must protect his public image at all costs and must never admit his wrongs."[38] The event reinforced Eisenhower's horror of extremism and his instinctive drawing back from controversy, while revealing his common sense in a crisis—MacArthur would have done better had he accepted Major Eisenhower's advice.

Seven months later, in February 1933, MacArthur made Eisenhower his personal assistant. Eisenhower drafted speeches and letters for MacArthur, lobbied with Congress, and helped prepare the Chief of Staff's annual reports. These reports were dreary documents. Even after the New Deal began in March 1933, the Army operated on an impossibly restricted budget—$304 million in fiscal 1933; $277 million in 1934; $284 million in 1935. The annual reports bemoaned the Army's almost complete lack of preparedness in a world that was rapidly rearming, with the enemies of democracy taking the lead in building up their armed forces. Eisenhower catalogued the Army's shortcomings for the reports: equipment left over from the World War, with which it was expected to fight the next war, was not only obsolescent but literally wearing out; the Army could not place orders for recently developed semiautomatic Garand rifles because of lack of funds, so the troops still used the Model 1903 Springfield, of which large quantities were on hand; in 1934, the Army had only twelve post-World War tanks in service.[39] MacArthur begged for more, he pleaded, he cajoled, he threatened, he had momentous fights with Roosevelt, but he got nowhere. The Army was the one place where the Roosevelt Administration was determined to economize. For Eisenhower, MacArthur's persistent and vigorous advocacy of what he knew was right was an object lesson, a lesson that was driven home six years later when the U.S. Army paid in lives the cost of the neglect of the mid-thirties, as it went into World War II with inferior equipment, inadequate training, and severe manpower shortages.

The mid-thirties were a difficult time for MacArthur, his assistant, and the Army generally. Army officers did not approve of the New Deal, with its welfare-state implications and its deficit financing (there was plenty of money, it seemed, for every activity of the government, except the Army). Nor did most officers approve of Roosevelt's foreign policy, which included recognition of the Soviet Union, the Good Neighbor policy for Latin America, and independence for the Philippines. The situation of Army officers in Washington had been bad enough under Hoover; the brash young New Dealers seemed to regard the officers with contempt.

In self-defense, the officers tightened their already small circle. MacArthur, Eisenhower said later, discussing the early New Deal days, "lost himself in his work . . . most of his friends whose companionship he really enjoyed were the officers with whom he worked in the War Department. Except for his mother, General MacArthur's life in Washington was almost entirely centered around the Army, which he loved."[40]

Eisenhower too loved the Army, but thanks in large part to Milton and Harry Butcher he was not so completely isolated from life in the capital as were most officers. He at least heard differing points of view. In 1934, Earl and Edgar came to Washington on business. The four brothers had a reunion at Milton's house in Falls Church. They soon set to arguing about the New Deal. Edgar lambasted Roosevelt, as did Dwight, while Milton and Earl defended him. The argument lasted through the night.[41]

In 1935, Swede Hazlett came to town for a tour of duty at the Navy Department. Swede and Eisenhower renewed their friendship. "I saw him frequently," Hazlett said. "He was still the same old Ike." Not quite, however; his usual good humor was turning to depression. "He was still a major with no immediate prospects," Hazlett noted, and he would "gripe about the Army promotion system, and how much better the Navy system was." Hazlett tried to console him with the thought that in the event of war the Army "would expand so much more rapidly that it would eventually pull way ahead in promotion of the Navy." Eisenhower grunted, unconvinced.[42]

If Eisenhower's name was unknown to the general public, he was highly regarded by the press corps covering the War Department. A newspaper chain offered him a job as its military editor. He was sorely tempted. The position would keep him in Washington—and Mamie loved her life in the Wyoming Apartments—and close to his Army friends. He could write balanced and honest assessments of the American military and the overseas threat. Best of all, the salary would be between $15,000 and $20,000 a year, a fortune for a man currently making $3,000 per year. He thought about it, talked to Mamie and Milton about it, almost resigned his commission, but finally decided to stay in the Army. He recalled Fox Conner's prediction that there would be another war, bigger than the last one, and the mad pace of German, Italian, and Japanese rearmament convinced him that war was not far off. He did not want to report on that war—he wanted to fight it.[43]

He also wanted to get some service with troops, as a line officer, away from Washington and the staff, but MacArthur would not let him go. In 1935, MacArthur's tour as Chief of Staff came to an end (Roosevelt had extended it by one year already), and Eisenhower looked forward to a field assignment. But then MacArthur "lowered the boom on me." Congress had voted "commonwealth" status for the Philippines, with complete independence to come in 1946. The new Philippine Commonwealth government, led by Manuel Quezon and the Nacionalista party, would need an army. Quezon asked MacArthur to come to Manila as his military adviser, to take charge of the creation of an army. MacArthur accepted and insisted that Eisenhower accompany him as his assistant.

Mamie was distraught, Eisenhower hardly less so. Mamie felt that her three years in Panama was more than enough time in the tropics for any one person, and indeed for a year she refused to join her husband in Manila, with the excuse that John had to finish elementary school. Eisenhower groaned at the thought of more years of staff work, but "I was in no position to argue with the Chief of Staff." He did try to get MacArthur to fix a terminal date for his duties in Manila, but MacArthur was vague about how long his services would be required.

There were compensations. It was flattering to know that MacArthur felt he could not get along without Eisenhower. He gave Eisenhower the privilege of picking any officer he wanted from the Regular Army to be a part of the mission; Eisenhower chose his West Point classmate Major James B. Ord, then working in the Chief of Staff's office and a close friend. Ord was known for "his quickness of mind and ability as a staff officer," and he spoke Spanish fluently. MacArthur promised Eisenhower quarters in the Manila Hotel, where he himself would be living. Building an army from scratch promised to be an interesting job. And there would be extra money in it for Eisenhower. The members of the mission, although on detached duty from the U.S. Army, would continue to draw their salaries plus an additional salary from the Philippine Commonwealth government—in MacArthur's case, $3,000 per month; for Eisenhower, $980 per month plus expenses.[44] With that kind of income plus the low cost of servants, the Eisenhowers could live a life of comparative luxury in Manila. (That a soft life was the lot of the American officer in the Philippines was well known; when Eisenhower finally returned from Manila, he met General Marshall for the second and last time before Pearl Harbor. Marshall's first remark was "Have you learned to tie your own shoes again since coming back, Eisenhower?" Eisenhower grinned and replied, "Yes, sir, I am capable of that chore anyhow.")

In late September 1935, Eisenhower joined MacArthur on a train headed west for San Francisco, where they would board a ship for Manila. Eisenhower had been in Washington for six years. He had precious little to show for it. No promotions had come to him; neither he nor any other Army officer had been able to persuade the government to begin rebuilding the nation's defenses; he had had no service with troops and seemed fated to be forever a staff officer.

He could, however, take pride in MacArthur's assessment of his service and abilities. On September 30, 1935, the Chief of Staff wrote him a letter, praising him for his "success in performing difficult tasks whose accomplishment required a comprehensive grasp of the military profession in all its principal phases, as well as analytical thought and forceful expression." MacArthur thanked Eisenhower for his "cheerful and efficient devotion . . . to confining, difficult, and often strenuous duties, in spite of the fact that your own personal desires involved a return to troops command and other physically active phases of Army life, for which your characteristics so well qualify you." He assured Eisenhower that his experiences would be valuable to him as a commander in the future, "since all problems presented to you were necessarily solved from the viewpoint of the High Command."

All that praise, so typical of MacArthur (and so well deserved), was welcome, but MacArthur's concluding paragraph must have seemed to Eisenhower just a bit painful. MacArthur wrote, "The numbers of personal requests for your services brought to me by heads of many of the Army's principal activities during the past few years furnish convincing proof of the reputation you have established as an outstanding soldier. I can say no more than that this reputation coincides exactly with my own judgment."[45] Eisenhower wished that MacArthur would have met one of those requests and let him go. But the Chief did not, and now Eisenhower was off for Manila.

CHAPTER SEVEN

Manila

1936–1939

IN JANUARY 1939, shortly after his forty-eighth birthday, Eisenhower wrote his personal definition of happiness. His brother Milton had asked his advice about a job offer. Eisenhower wrote that "only a man that is happy in his work can be happy in his home and with his friends." He continued, "Happiness in work means that its performer must know it to be worthwhile; suited to his temperament, and, finally, suited to his age, experience, and capacity for performance of a high order."[1]

Eisenhower served in the Philippines from late 1935 to the end of 1939. Nothing that he did there met any of the criteria he himself had set down for a happy life. His work was neither rewarding nor suited to his age or abilities. It was also terribly frustrating and, when the test came, proved to be worthless, as the Japanese in 1941 easily conquered the Philippine Army he had labored to help create. His close and warm relationship with MacArthur became distant and cold. His best friend died in an accident. Mamie was ill and bedridden much of the time. John was the only member of the family who enjoyed the Philippines and prospered there. The best that can be said for Eisenhower's years with the Philippine Army was that he gained some experience in juggling and cutting national budgets.

That process began even before he sailed for Manila. When MacArthur was negotiating with Quezon about the creation of an American Advisory Group to guide the building of an army for the Philippines,

Quezon had asked the Chief of Staff, "General, do you think that the Philippines, once independent, can defend itself?" MacArthur had replied with supreme confidence, "I don't *think* that the Philippines can defend themselves, I *know* they can." He explained that the United States would help, because "We cannot just turn around and leave you alone." He did not explain to Quezon that the General Staff's war plans called for abandoning the Philippines altogether in the event of a Japanese attack,[2] but he did put Major Ord, under Eisenhower's supervision, to work on a plan for the Philippine Army.

Ord prepared a plan based on military, not financial, considerations. After Eisenhower reviewed it, the two majors presented it to MacArthur. The general protested that it was too costly (the budget was about 50 million pesos, or $25 million) and instructed Ord and Eisenhower to reduce the costs by 50 percent. They made various cuts, such as assuming that the Filipinos could forgo new weapons and get along with obsolete American Army rifles (and practically no artillery), reducing the pay of the Philippine conscript "to little more than cigarette money," and cutting the contingent of officers "to the point where this would be dangerously close to an army of recruits only. We thought that such a makeshift force would be rejected out of hand as worthless for defense."

Instead, MacArthur told them that Quezon's defense budget could not go above $8 million, and they should try again. Eisenhower and Ord reduced the regular force to 930 officers and 7,000 enlisted men, cut training time for the conscripts from a year to six months, eliminated the artillery altogether, and stretched the munitions procurement program from ten to twenty years. With that plan in hand and accepted, Eisenhower, Ord, and MacArthur arrived in Manila in October 1935. For the first six months, they met in seemingly endless conferences with the Philippine Chief of Staff, General José de los Reyes, his deputies, and leading Philippine politicians. They discussed sites and cost of training camps, size of divisions, ranks and privileges for officers in the Philippine Scouts (a part of the U.S. Army) who were transferring to the new Philippine Army, and the myriad of other problems inherent in building an army from scratch.[3]

There was much discussion, little action. In his diary, Eisenhower remarked that "we—at least Jimmy [Ord] and myself—have learned to expect from the Filipinos with whom we deal a minimum of performance from a maximum of promise. Among individuals there is no lack of intelligence, but to us they seem . . . unaccustomed to the requirements of administrative and executive procedure." In conference, they seemed to understand well enough what was required and promised to deliver shortly, "but thereafter it is quite likely that nothing whatsoever will be done." It then often developed that the Philippine officers had not agreed at all, and the whole matter had to be discussed again. "These peculiar traits we are learning to take into account," Eisenhower wrote, "but obviously they impede progress."[4]

MacArthur, nonetheless, was enthusiastic and optimistic in his first formal report to Quezon, submitted in late April 1936, after MacArthur had rejected a pessimistic draft from Eisenhower and ordered his assistant to prepare a new, more cheerful one. The final report, edited by MacArthur, was bombastic. ". . . progress . . . has exceeded original anticipation," MacArthur claimed. ". . . in the world today there is no other defensive system that provides an equal security at remotely comparable cost to the people maintaining it." When fully developed, MacArthur said his defense system "will present to any potential invader such difficult problems as to give pause even to the most ruthless and powerful." Eisenhower's comment on this extraordinary document—not a single conscript had yet reported for duty, indeed registration had barely begun, and none of the training camps had been built—was restrained. MacArthur's report, Eisenhower said, was "far too optimistic."[5]

Eisenhower was finding it increasingly difficult to work with not only the Filipinos but also with MacArthur. In late May 1936, he and Ord told MacArthur that he would have to modify the order to call twenty thousand conscripts for duty in January 1937. They pointed out that there was not enough money, that the camp sites had not yet been selected, much less prepared (and there were some 130 of them to be scattered around the thousands of tiny islands that make up the Philippines), that there was no officer corps to supervise the training, and that there was no comprehensive supply system for the widely dispersed camps. In response, Eisenhower wrote in his diary, MacArthur "gave us one of his regular shouting tirades. . . . I argue these points with more heat and persistency than does Jim—consequently I came in for the more severe criticism." Eisenhower felt that the endless frustration of attempting to deal with the Filipinos on a staff level might improve if his boss would see their boss. He urged MacArthur to see Quezon at least once a week, but MacArthur refused—"he apparently thinks it would not be in keeping with his rank and position for him to do so."[6]

As a result, Eisenhower spent a great deal of time himself with Quezon, so much that Quezon gave him a private office in the Malacañan

Palace, next to the president's office. Eisenhower spent two or three hours a day there, the rest of his time in his regular office, next to MacArthur's, in the Manila Hotel. One day in 1936 MacArthur strode in, beaming. He said Quezon was going to make him a field marshal in the Philippine Army. At the same time, Quezon wanted to make Eisenhower and Ord general officers. Eisenhower turned pale. He said he could never accept such an appointment. Ord agreed with Eisenhower, "though in somewhat less positive fashion." Eisenhower explained in his diary that he felt that because "so many American officers [stationed in the Philippines] believe that the attempt to create a Philippine army is somewhat ridiculous, the acceptance by us of high rank in an army which is not yet formed would serve to belittle our effort."[7] To MacArthur directly, Eisenhower said, "General, you have been a four-star general [in the U.S. Army]. This is a *proud* thing. There's only been a few who had it. Why in the *hell* do you want a *banana* country giving you a field-marshalship? This . . . this looks like you're trying for some kind of . . ." MacArthur stopped him. "Oh, Jesus!" Eisenhower later remembered. "He just gave me hell!"[8]

MacArthur, obviously, did not share Eisenhower's sensibilities. He believed, and often said, that Asians were peculiarly impressed by rank and title. Since that suited his own tastes, he accepted the field-marshal rank, explaining to Eisenhower that "he could not decline it without offense to the president." Eisenhower noted that MacArthur "is tickled pink."[9]

MacArthur designed his own uniform for the ceremony, which took place on August 24, 1936, at Malacañan Palace. Resplendent in a sharkskin uniform consisting of black trousers and a white coat covered with braid, stars, and unique lapel designs, MacArthur graciously accepted his gold baton from Mrs. Quezon. MacArthur gave a typically grandiloquent speech, which one of his officers, Captain Bonner Fellers, later a close associate, told him was "a Sermon on the Mount clothed in grim, present-day reality. I shall never forget it." To Eisenhower, however, the whole affair was "rather fantastic." Five years later, in 1941, it became even more fantastic to Eisenhower, when Quezon told him "that he had not initiated the idea at all; rather, Quezon said that MacArthur himself came up with the high-sounding title."[10]

In 1936, following John's graduation from the eighth grade, Mamie and John sailed for Manila. Mamie did so with some trepidation. She had health problems, a stomach disorder that the doctors could not diagnose. She later said, "I built myself up for a let-down. I wasn't counting on finding anything delightful or delicious in such a hot place." The reality turned out to be worse than her fears. Her first shock came at the end of the gangplank. Her husband, dressed in a white civilian suit, embraced her. As he did so, he swept off his hat. He was completely bald. As Mamie gasped, he explained that he had shaved his head to help keep cool. Their apartment was not air-conditioned. Eisenhower had arranged for a full complement of servants. They kept the mahogany floor shining like a tabletop, filled the rooms with fresh cut flowers, sprayed the bedroom at sundown with a flit-gun before arranging the mosquito netting over the bed, prepared the meals, and tried to keep the bugs and lizards out. Nevertheless, Mamie found it depressing. She suffered from claustrophobia and hated having to sleep inside a net and having to keep the shutters closed all day against the sun. The heat and humidity caused her stomach to flare up. She spent most of her days in bed, did almost no entertaining, played little bridge. The Philippines, for her, were a terrible experience.[11]

Her son loved the islands. "My years in the Philippines," he wrote, "I look back on as among the happiest of my life." Eisenhower arranged for John to attend the Bishop Brent School for Americans in Baguio, on the island of Luzon, 175 miles north of Manila, at an altitude of five thousand feet, which gave it a climate as appealing as Mexico City's. Brent was small enough so that John could be the star of the tennis team and have what amounted to private tutors in his academic subjects.[12] His father took him along on inspection trips around the islands and tried to play tennis with him, but John always won.

In April 1937, Mamie went to Baguio to visit John. Whether as a result of the jolting ride on jungle and mountain roads, or because of the altitude change, she suffered a stomach hemorrhage and went into a coma. She almost died, spent a month on her back in the hospital, then remained in Baguio until October, recuperating.[13] Her weight fell to less than a hundred pounds. When she returned to Manila, she was delighted to find that there had been a vast improvement in her living conditions. A new wing of the Manila Hotel had been completed, and the Eisenhowers had one of the choicest apartments. Best of all, it was air-conditioned, which not only meant cool air but also that the shutters could be kept open, the windows closed, and the mosquito netting eliminated.[14] The new quarters were a special blessing, as Mamie was still bedridden much of the time.[15]

In June 1938, the Eisenhowers made a trip to the States, Eisenhower to beg equipment for the Philippine Army from the War Department, Mamie to have her gallbladder removed at a hospital in Denver. When they returned in August, Mamie felt well enough to go on early-morning shopping expeditions with Jean MacArthur and play bridge in the afternoons. Her favorite partner was Anne Nevins, wife of Major Arthur Nevins. The two couples had been friends since 1915, when they met at Fort Sam Houston. Nevins' brother Allan was then in the process of becoming one of America's leading historians; Nevins himself remained close to Eisenhower throughout his career. Thanks to Anne Nevins, Marge Clay (wife of Captain Lucius Clay, later head of the American military government in Germany), and Mildred Hodges (wife of Lieutenant Colonel Courtney Hodges, later commander of the First Army during World War II), and thanks to the new apartment and her improved health, Mamie's last year and a half in Manila was more pleasant than her introduction to the city had been. Nevertheless, she never learned to like the place.[16]

Eisenhower too was more or less miserable. His relations with MacArthur became steadily more difficult. This deterioration was the result of two factors, their respective positions vis-à-vis each other and to the Philippine government, and their temperaments. Eisenhower dealt in details, MacArthur in generalities. Eisenhower worked with Quezon on a daily basis, while MacArthur stayed aloof from the Philippine government and his own staff—he would come down from his penthouse to the offices at 11 A.M., work at his desk until a late lunch, then return to the penthouse. He attended only the most formal state functions.[17]

Where the practical Eisenhower saw problems, the visionary MacArthur saw possibilities. To Eisenhower, the Philippine General Staff was beset by rank-consciousness, backbiting, inefficiency, and corruption. To MacArthur, it was composed of loyal, intelligent men who were well on their way to learning how to run an army. To Eisenhower, the Philippine conscripts were generally illiterate and so ignorant of rudimentary sanitarian precautions that much of the training time had to be given over to elementary public-health instruction. To MacArthur, they were men determined to be free and to be able to protect that freedom. Eisenhower agonized over the communications problems—one company of conscripts might speak a half-dozen different native dialects, each unintelligible to the other. MacArthur thought this diversity a source of strength, as it reflected the close ties between the troops and the people.[18]

When MacArthur returned from his trip to the States, in 1936, he was full of optimism. He had talked to the President and the War Department in general terms about the needs of the Philippine Army; in equally vague and general terms, they had promised to do all they could to help. When Eisenhower returned from a similar trip, in 1938, he was depressed. He had been specific about what equipment was needed, and had been consistently turned down. To be sure, the War Department had precious little to give, but even knowing that obvious truth, Eisenhower was upset. He thought that at least the Army could have given the Filipinos some of its old Enfield rifles, which were being replaced by the Garand.

Eisenhower realized that one reason for the War Department's resistance to giving (or selling at a cut rate) the rifles was a general belief among American officers that the attempt to create a Philippine Army was ridiculous. He thought another reason was politics. "The pacifists and other misguided elements of the American electorate," he wrote in his diary, would protest vigorously if President Roosevelt announced that he was arming the Philippines, and "we must never forget that every question is settled in Washington today on the basis of getting votes . . ."[19]

In a series of long letters to MacArthur, written from Washington, Eisenhower gave the details of his problems. In his short replies, MacArthur urged him to keep trying and suggested alternative routes he might explore.[20] On his return, Eisenhower continued to point up problems. After an inspection trip to southern Luzon, Eisenhower reported that "the cadres . . . [are] disappointing, conditions . . . very unsatisfactory." He continued, "The constant rains are, of course, partially responsible for this but many other defects were traceable to neglect on the part of cadre officers and in some instances to distinct failures on the part of our Army Headquarters."[21]

The outstanding problem was money. In 1937, Eisenhower and Ord prepared a new budget. It called for expenditures of $12.5 million in 1938, a figure they thought had been agreed to by Quezon. But, as Eisenhower wrote Ord on September 1, when Ord was on an inspection trip, "It was quite a shock to hear, the other day, that the President [Quezon] is dismayed and astonished by the size of our Budget. He was . . . nonplussed . . ." So was Eisenhower.[22] But MacArthur chose to stress his success in persuading Quezon to maintain a budget of $8 million.

Eisenhower's and Ord's constant complaining began to irritate MacArthur. In July 1937, he called T. J. Davis into his office and treated him to one of his tirades, knowing that T. J. would give a word-by-word account to Eisenhower and Ord. MacArthur said he was fed up with the "conceit and self-centered" attitudes of his staff. Too many of them, he said, were acting as if they were indispensable and each one was selfishly "looking out only for himself." Eisenhower commented in his diary, "It begins to look as if we were resented simply because we labor under the conviction, and act on it, that someone ought to know what is going on in this army and help them over the rough spots." He continued, "However, from the beginning of this venture I've personally announced myself as ready and willing to go back to an assignment in the United States Army at any moment. The general knows this if he knows anything, so I guess I don't have to make an issue of the matter by busting in and announcing it again."[23]

Eisenhower wanted to go back on duty with the U.S. Army for the sake of his own career, and because he was coming to agree with the judgment that the whole venture was hopeless. But defeatist attitudes made MacArthur furious. He saw himself as the leading actor in a great drama, the birth of a new nation. His emphasis was on the unique and historic aspects of that task. No other Western nation had ever done anything significant to prepare one of its colonies for independence, much less set a specific date for that event and participate in building a native army for self-defense (Eisenhower had discovered that one of the objections in Washington to giving weapons to the Filipinos was that the natives might later use them against the United States). As the gateway to the Orient, and as an exporter of raw materials, the Philippines had a bright economic future. The Filipinos were building a genuine democracy, unique in Asia; they formed the only Christian nation on the continent; they were going to be independent, a status currently enjoyed in Asia only by Japan, Thailand, and—to some extent—China. MacArthur liked to dwell on these glittering prospects, hated to hear Eisenhower and Ord talking about the problems.

But that was their job, and it had to be done. "General MacArthur's amazing determination and optimism," Eisenhower said later, "made us forget [our] questions at times, but they kept coming back in our minds."[24] Fifteen years later, in 1954, Eisenhower would be somewhat in MacArthur's position in the Philippines with regard to another infant Asian nation, South Vietnam. Like MacArthur, Eisenhower as President discovered that his position forced him to be optimistic, to emphasize the possibilities and to overlook the shortcomings, to stress the historic aspect of building a democracy from a former European colony, meanwhile remaining aloof from any contact with actual South Vietnamese and leaving all the difficult details to his staff and the Army officers in the field—each of whom despaired of ever accomplishing the mission of creating an army and a democracy in South Vietnam, and each of whom regarded their boss as hopelessly out of touch with reality.

• •

In early January 1938, MacArthur conceived the idea, according to Eisenhower, that "the morale of the whole population would be enhanced if the people could see something of their emerging army in the capital city, Manila." He ordered his assistants to arrange to bring units from all over the islands to a field near Manila, where they could camp for three or four days, winding up the whole affair with a big parade through the city. Eisenhower and Ord did a quick cost estimate, then protested to MacArthur "that it was impossible to do the thing within our budget." MacArthur waved aside their objections and told them to do as ordered.

They did. Soon Quezon learned about the preparations. He called Eisenhower into his office to ask what was going on. Eisenhower was astonished—he had assumed that MacArthur had discussed the project with the president. When he learned that such was not the case, he told Quezon that they should discuss the matter no further until he had had a chance to confer with MacArthur. But when Eisenhower returned to his office in the Manila Hotel, he found a furious MacArthur. Quezon had called him on the telephone, said he was horrified at the thought of what the parade would cost, and wanted it canceled immediately. MacArthur then told his staff that "he had never meant for us to proceed with preparations for the parade. He had only wanted us to investigate it quietly."[25] Eisenhower, "flabbergasted, didn't know what to say. And finally I said to him, I said, 'General, all you're saying is that I'm a liar, and I am *not* a liar, and so I'd like to go back to the United States right away.' Well, he came back . . . and he said, 'Ike, it's just fun to see that damn Dutch temper'—he put his arm right over my shoulder—he said, 'It's just fun to see that Dutch temper take you over,' and he was just sweetness and light. He said, 'It's just a misunderstanding, and let's let it go at that.'"[26] But Eisenhower could never let it go at that; thirty years later he still grew incensed when describing the scene. He commented, "Probably no one has had more, tougher fights with a senior than I had with MacArthur. I told him time and again, 'Why in *hell* don't you *fire* me?' I said, 'Goddammit, you do things I don't agree with and you know damn well I don't.'"[27]

MacArthur did not fire Eisenhower for the best of reasons—he needed him. Eisenhower was his liaison with Quezon, his "eyes and ears" for reports on developments in the various camps, the manager of his office, the man who drafted his speeches, letters, and reports. MacArthur knew that Eisenhower was close to indispensable, and as often as he shouted at his assistant, he found cause to praise him lavishly. In a typical handwritten note, praising Eisenhower for a policy paper,

MacArthur said, "Ike—This is excellent in every respect. I do not see how it could be improved upon. It accomplishes the purpose in language so simple and direct as to preclude confusion and is flexible enough for complete administration."[28] Quezon too was grateful to Eisenhower for his efforts. When Eisenhower drafted a speech for Quezon, the president wrote him a note saying, "It is excellent. You have completely absorbed my thought and expressed it better than I ever could do it."[29]

So despite his own intense desire for service with American troops, despite his unhappy wife, despite his fights with his boss, Eisenhower had no chance of getting out of the Philippines. MacArthur would never consider his requests for a transfer, in fact would not even allow him to make such a request on a formal basis or enter it on his record. There were compensations. The extra pay was welcome, the new apartment was luxurious, John was in a good school, and—in July 1936—Eisenhower was finally promoted, along with the rest of his class, to lieutenant colonel.

The biggest compensation, however, was his friendship with Ord. Eisenhower respected him, enjoyed working with him. He later said he regarded Ord as "the most brilliant officer, of his time, in the American Army," and that he "felt as close to him as even to my own brothers."[30] With U.S. Army Air Corps pilots as instructors, both men learned to fly. They needed the skill to carry out their inspection trips to the various camps around the islands, but they both regarded flying as more fun than work, and took off at any excuse. Eisenhower had more than 350 hours in his flight log when he left the Philippines.

The flying led to a disaster, the worst Eisenhower had to face since Icky's death. On January 30, 1938, Ord's plane crashed. Within a few hours, Ord was dead. "From then on," Eisenhower wrote, "more of the planning work fell on my shoulders, but without my friend, all the zest was gone."[31]

That same year, 1938, Eisenhower had an unusual job offer. At social functions in Manila, the Spanish community (and some of the American businessmen) expressed their admiration for Hitler. Eisenhower thought this a "strange" attitude and said so. The resulting arguments were loud and long. Eisenhower had friends among the small Jewish community in Manila, and his anti-Nazi feelings were well known to them. They were also aware of his abilities. They formed a committee that asked Eisenhower to take on the job of finding a haven for Jewish refugees from Nazi Germany in China, Indochina, Indonesia, or anywhere else in Asia. The committee guaranteed him a salary of

$60,000 a year plus expenses, and promised to place the first five years' salary in escrow to be paid to him in full if for any reason he had to leave the job. Tempting though it was, Eisenhower turned down the offer, saying he thought it best to stay in the Army.[32]

He did so because he could see that war was coming and he felt that America would not be able to stay out of it. He also knew that within a year MacArthur would have to allow him to return to the States, as the law said that any officer who was on detached duty for more than four years either had to resign his commission or return to active duty, and even MacArthur could not force him to resign his commission.

About this time, Troy Middleton asked Eisenhower for some career advice. In World War I, Middleton had risen from the ranks to become a regimental commander and the youngest colonel in the AEF. George Marshall had called him "the outstanding infantry regimental commander on the battlefield in France." In the late thirties Middleton was head of the ROTC unit at Louisiana State University in Baton Rouge. On a trip to the Philippines, he came to see Eisenhower, an old friend. "Ike," Middleton said, "I've been offered the job of comptroller at LSU. To take it, I'll have to resign from the Army. What do you think?"

"Don't do it, Troy," Eisenhower replied. "Don't do it." He explained that "there is going to be a war, and we are going to be in it, and you are sure to be a division commander at least. It's your great opportunity, and if you quit us now, you'll miss it." Middleton nevertheless resigned his commission and took the position at LSU. In 1941, he returned to the Army, eventually taking command of a corps in Normandy in 1944 and compiling an outstanding combat record. So outstanding, in fact, that after World War II General Marshall wanted to make him a permanent two-star general in the Regular Army. Marshall asked Eisenhower's opinion; Eisenhower would not agree. "He left us when the going was tough," Eisenhower growled.*[33]

Shortly after the conversation with Middleton, Eisenhower had another request for career advice, this time from his younger brother Milton, who had been offered a position as dean at Penn State College. Eisenhower typed out a three-page, single-spaced reply. He thought Milton should take the job; the reason he stressed was security. As a dean, Milton would have tenure, and the security it brought "is vastly

* For Middleton, it turned out well, as he returned to LSU, where he soon became president, one of the best in the school's long history.

important to a salaried man that has to think of a wife and two young children." Eisenhower himself had enjoyed security throughout his adult life; indeed, it was perhaps the single best feature of being an Army officer.

In the bulk of his letter, however, Eisenhower almost seemed to be convincing himself that he should leave the Army and take up more rewarding civilian employment. As Henry Wallace's chief assistant in the Department of Agriculture, Milton was one of the top bureaucrats in Washington. He had listed the pros and cons of the Penn State offer in his letter to Dwight, concluding, "Finally, I am not certain that I would be entirely happy in work that lacked the rigorous demands on many fronts that I encounter here." That sentence set Dwight off on a long discussion of happiness, in life and in work, partly quoted at the beginning of this chapter. Dwight said he felt competent to comment "because of similar feelings of my own in the past, and some reflection on the results of my own decisions, that were based upon those feelings."

A major drawback to working for the government, Eisenhower wrote, was the *"driving, continuous mental endeavor"* involved. "Men of ability in the government service see so much to be done, they create . . . so many jobs that lazier men like to shunt from their own shoulders . . . that gradually the victim . . . loses his sense of values, and with this needful governor failing him, he applies his mind, consciously and unconsciously, day and night, to important and intricate problems that march up ceaselessly, one after the other, for consideration." The result of years of such activity, much of which was not much more than shuffling paper, "will be a steady, swift grind until you've definitely damaged your own capacity for enjoying life."

A major advantage to the Penn State offer, Dwight felt, was "freedom in self-expression. The prohibitions, legal and ethical, surrounding the public servant might be largely removed" if Milton became a dean. To be able to speak and write "what you *believe,* not what administration policy supports," struck Dwight as "a tremendous advantage." But Milton rejected the advice, just as Dwight himself, having made an excellent case for his own resignation and a start on a new career, never seriously considered actually doing it.[34]

In September 1939, war began with Hitler's invasion of Poland and the English-French declaration of war on Germany. To Eisenhower, although war would mean advancement in his own career and although he had dedicated his life to preparing for the challenge, the coming of the conflict was a disaster. On the day war was declared, September 3, he wrote Milton, "After months and months of feverish effort to appease and placate the mad man that is governing Germany, the British and French seem to be driven into a corner out of which they can work their way only by fighting. It's a sad day for Europe and for the whole civilized world—though for a long time it has seemed ridiculous to refer to the world as civilized. If the war . . . is . . . long-drawn-out and . . . bloody . . . then I believe that the remnants of nations emerging from it will be scarcely recognizable as the ones that entered it." He feared that Communism, anarchy, crime and disorder, loss of personal liberties, and abject poverty "will curse the areas that witness any amount of fighting." He said it scarcely seemed possible "that people that proudly refer to themselves as intelligent could let the situation come about." He blamed Hitler, a "power-drunk egocentric . . . one of the criminally insane . . . the absolute ruler of eighty-nine million people." And he made a prophecy: "Unless [Hitler] is successful in overcoming the whole world by brute force, the final result will be that Germany will have to be dismembered."[35]

Eisenhower's attitude contrasted sharply with that of his friend Patton, who signed off a 1940 letter to Eisenhower, "Again thanking you and hoping we are together in a long and BLOODY war."[36]

After the Germans overran Poland, stagnation set in as the Wehrmacht and the Western Allies stared at each other across the Maginot Line. In October 1939, Eisenhower confessed to Gerow that "the war has me completely bewildered . . . It seems obvious that neither side desires to undertake attacks against heavily fortified lines. If fortification, with modern weapons, has given to the defensive form of combat such a terrific advantage over the offensive, we've swung back to the late middle ages, when any army in a fortified camp was perfectly safe from molestation. What," Eisenhower wondered, "is the answer?"[37]

By this time, Eisenhower had a fixed date for his return to the States—December 13, 1939. MacArthur had tried to talk him into staying, as had Quezon, who offered him a blank contract for his services and said, "We'll tear up the old contract. I've already signed this one and it is filled in—except what you want as your emoluments for remaining. You will write that in." Eisenhower thanked him but declined, explaining "no amount of money can make me change my mind. My entire life has been given to this one thing, my country and my profession. I want to be there if what I fear is going to come about actually happens."[38]

He was anxious to get going. To Gerow, he wrote wistfully about the rumors he had been hearing "about the rejuvenation and building up of the American Army." He asked Gerow for information about an expansion of the officer corps, and possible promotions, and—fearfully—about the War Department's policy on age-in-grade retirement. He said he realized that Gerow, as chief of staff to the 2d Division at Fort Sam, was too busy to answer all his questions immediately, "but after a while, maybe you'll find time to undertake the education of a poor, ignorant, farmer boy, and when you do, I want you to have some idea of the gigantic size of the job." He also reported that "Mamie is counting the days until December 13. She really wants to come home . . . and as the time draws near, I must say I begin to share her impatience."[39]

Before Eisenhower left, Quezon asked him to prepare a personal report on the Philippine Army and the state of the defense of the islands. Eisenhower wrote a realistic document, stressing the problems but not in a defeatist way. He thought that the most logical enemy, Japan, was so tied down by its war in China that it would be able to commit only a small portion of its forces to the Philippines, so there was at least a chance for a successful defense. But he made a prophecy: If the Filipinos could not stop the Japanese at the beach, the Philippine Islands would be conquered quickly. Over the next five years, Eisenhower would command four amphibious assaults; he therefore often had occasion to recall his words, designed to be encouraging, to Quezon: "Successful penetration of a defended beach is the most difficult operation in warfare."[40]

On December 9, MacArthur wrote a warm letter to Eisenhower. "I cannot tell you how deeply I regret your leaving," he began, after four years of "distinguished and invaluable service" which had been characterized at all times by "superior professional ability, unswerving loyalty and unselfish devotion to duty . . . sound judgment and unflagging enthusiasm." He said he would miss Eisenhower, but would "follow with keen interest the brilliant career which unquestionably lies ahead for you."[41]

On December 12, at a farewell luncheon in the Malacañan Palace, Quezon awarded Eisenhower the Philippine Distinguished Service Star, the citation lauding his "exceptional talents . . . his professional attainments, his breadth of understanding, his zeal and magnetic leadership." After presenting the citation, Quezon made a speech. "Whenever I asked Ike for an opinion I got an answer," Quezon said. "It may not have been what I wanted to hear, it may have displeased me, but it was always a straightforward and honest answer."[42]

The following day, General and Mrs. MacArthur came down to the docks to say their goodbyes to the Eisenhowers. MacArthur gave Eisenhower a bottle of whiskey. "We talked of the gloominess of world prospects," Eisenhower recalled. Theirs had been a tempestuous relationship, one that ended there on the docks. Over the next few years they occasionally exchanged letters, but as Eisenhower's star rose, MacArthur became exceedingly jealous. He made disparaging remarks about Eisenhower, reportedly once calling him a "clerk, nothing more." Eisenhower, as he came under Marshall's influence, and as his strategic perceptions led him to assign a secondary role to the Asian theater in World War II, made his own disparaging remarks about MacArthur, reportedly once saying, "Oh, yes, I studied dramatics under MacArthur for seven years." Not until 1946, when Eisenhower was Chief of Staff, did they meet again. It was a cold, stiff, formal occasion, each man uncomfortable in the unaccustomed relationship. In 1939 MacArthur had predicted a brilliant future for Eisenhower, but as he waved goodbye, he had never thought it would go so far.

The liner pulled out of its dock at noon. By Christmas, 1939, the Eisenhowers were in Hawaii; they celebrated New Year's Eve in San Francisco. The ordeal of their four years in the Philippines was over.

During the voyage, and after they arrived in California, John talked to his father about his future. John, then seventeen years old, was considering going to West Point. Eisenhower had tried not to push John in that direction (although it was clear to John that his father would be delighted if he became a cadet), and before John committed himself, his father wanted to make certain that the young man was fully aware of what he was getting into. Eisenhower began the discussion by contrasting his own experiences as a cadet with those of Edgar at the University of Michigan, stressing the relatively relaxed life at Ann Arbor compared to the rigid discipline at the Academy.

In terms of a career, Eisenhower pointed out that if John became a lawyer, doctor, or businessman, "he could probably go just as far as his character, abilities, and honorable ambitions could carry him." In a grand understatement, he added that "in the Army . . . things are ordered somewhat differently." No matter how good an officer was, no matter how well he did his duty, his promotion was governed strictly by the rules of seniority. Using himself as an example, Eisenhower pointed out that he had been in the Army since 1911. During the past twenty-nine years, he had consistently been praised by his superiors and classed in the top category for his age and rank. He had attended the Army's leading postgraduate schools and graduated first at C&GS. But nothing that he had done had had the slightest influence in pushing him ahead. Seniority governed all promotions until a man became a colonel, when he was eligible for selection to a one-star rank, regardless of seniority. But Eisenhower's class would not reach the grade of colonel until 1950, at which time he would be sixty years old, and the War Department would not promote colonels to general officer grade when they had only a short time remaining before compulsory retirement. Thus, Eisenhower told his son, his own chances of ever obtaining a star in the Army "were nil."

At this point in the discussion, Eisenhower wrote later, "John must have wondered why I stayed in the Army at all." Indeed he must have. Eisenhower explained that he had found his life in the Army "wonderfully interesting . . . it had brought me into contact with men of ability, honor, and a sense of high dedication to their country." He claimed that he had refused to bother himself about promotion. "I said the real satisfaction was for a man who did the best he could. My ambition in the Army was to make everybody I worked for regretful when I was ordered to other duty."

Shortly after the Eisenhowers arrived in the States, Edgar made John an offer. He would finance John's college education if John would take up law and later join him in his flourishing law practice in Tacoma, promising to pay him at least double what an Army officer earned. John considered the offer, thanked his Uncle Edgar, but said no. He had decided to attend West Point. John explained to his father that he made his decision on the basis of "what you told me the other evening. When you talked about the satisfaction you had in an Army career, and the pride you had in being associated with men of character, my mind was made up right then."[43]

For Eisenhower, John's decision was not only pleasing, but a vindication of his own career choice. Not that he needed one. Despite the realism of his remarks to Milton, despite his knowledge (even if subconscious) that everything negative he had said about government service to Milton applied equally to him, despite the frustrations of working for MacArthur, he was satisfied with his life's work. And, as he had told Middleton, for the first time in two decades the future offered opportunity for an ambitious Army officer. The year 1939 was hardly the time to quit the Army, not after all that Eisenhower had invested in it, and that it had invested in him.

When Eisenhower told John that he expected to be retired as a colonel, he had added, "Of course, in an emergency, anything can happen—but we're talking about a career, John, not miracles." By 1940, the emergency was there. Perhaps the miracle would follow.

CHAPTER EIGHT

Fort Lewis, Fort Sam Houston

1940–1941

IN 1940 EISENHOWER had the best year of his career to that date. He was regimental executive to the 15th Infantry of the 3d Division, and commander of the 1st Battalion of the 15th. He did not just enjoy being with troops, he relished it, reveled in it, filled his letters with his enthusiasm. To Omar Bradley, for example, he wrote on July 1, 1940, "I'm having the time of my life. Like everyone else in the army, we're up to our necks in work and in problems, big and little. But this work is fun! . . . I could not conceive of a better job."[1] The relatively leisurely life he had led in Manila gave way to one of constant physical activity, which suited him perfectly. After field maneuvers in Washington State in August—through country that he said "would have made a good stage setting for a play in Hades—Stumps, slashings, fallen logs, tangled brush, holes, and hills!"—he commented to Gerow: "I froze at night, never had, in any one stretch, more than 1¾ hours sleep, and at times was really fagged out—but I had a swell time."[2] His experience strengthened his conviction that "I belonged with troops; with them I was always happy."[3]

His domestic life was also happy. Mamie was delighted to be back in the States, her health was much improved, and she was entertaining again. The Eisenhowers held one big party on the evening of November 5, 1940, to listen to the presidential election returns. Eisenhower anticipated a close race, although he feared that Republican nominee Wendell Willkie's chances of beating Roosevelt were poor. Still he was not prepared for another Roosevelt landslide, nor were his guests, Army officers themselves. The Democratic victory caused the party to "fall flat." Eisenhower expressed the hope that "the Democrats and Republicans will soon get on friendly terms because if this country needs anything at all at this time it is unification."[4]

Eisenhower was pleased when John got an appointment to West Point. There had been considerable difficulty in obtaining the prize. "The tragedy of the whole thing," Eisenhower had written to Milton when he was attempting to secure an appointment for John, "is that six years ago there were at least half a dozen people on the Hill that would have been delighted to give me such an appointment. In fact, I obtained such appointments for other boys, merely on a personal request. All those men . . . have disappeared from the rolls of Congress. In any event, politicians have such short memories that any direct request of mine would now be simply tossed into the wastebasket."[5] Eventually Senator Arthur Capper of Kansas allowed John to take a competitive examination. John scored 92 and finished first. Capper made the appointment.[6] "This accomplishment of John's," Eisenhower wrote Everett Hughes, "has added two inches to my chest and volumes to Mamie's daily conversations about 'her son.' "[7]

Eisenhower hardly needed to add inches to his chest. At age fifty, he was in excellent physical condition. When he returned from the Philippines, a friend told him that he appeared to be thin and worn-out. Eisenhower insisted that he felt fine, that Mamie was the one who had been sick in the tropics, that although the heat had worn him down a bit, he expected to gain some weight and bounce back quickly.[8] He did. By the fall of 1940, he was robust again. Most people thought he looked ten years younger than his actual age. The outdoor life and service with troops restored him to his full strength. Broad of chest and shoulder, he still had the physical grace of the natural athlete. His whole body was animated. He walked with a bounce to his step, swinging his arms, his eyes darting, missing nothing. His voice was deep and resonant. When he talked, his hands flashed through the air, as he enumerated his points on his fingers, one by one. His powers of concentration were greater than ever. He would fix his blue eyes on a listener, compelling attention and respect. He was almost completely bald by now, with only a few strands of light-brown hair on the back and sides of his head, but the exposed pate somehow added to his good looks, perhaps because it balanced his broad, mobile mouth. He retained his infectious grin and hearty laugh. He was mentally alert, ideas coming into his head so rapidly that his words tumbled out. Most of all, he exuded self-confidence. He was good at his job, he knew it, and he knew that his superiors realized it. He expected to be called to challenging posts, and to make a major contribution to the Army and to the nation.

His job was to help prepare the U.S. Army to fight the Wehrmacht. He was part of a vast process, just getting under way, directed by Chief of Staff George C. Marshall, of expanding the Army, equipping it for modern war, and training it for combat. Between 1939 and 1942, the Army grew from 190,000 officers and men to more than 5,000,000. It adopted almost a whole new weapons system and underwent a radical transformation of its organization, doctrines, and tactics. It then fought and defeated a German Army that in 1940–1941 had appeared to be invincible. As Russell Weigley correctly states, "The American army's capacity to transform itself . . . was as impressive an achievement as any in military history." Weigley is also correct in giving the major credit to "the 12,000–13,000 officers of the old army [who] had succeeded in preparing themselves mentally for the transition."[9]

Certainly Eisenhower was eager to do his part in the creation of a citizens' army. He was at his post up to eighteen hours a day, seven days a week. He set up training schedules, made inspections, lectured his newly commissioned junior officers, supervised field exercises, studied the war in Europe and applied the lessons to his own unit. He was concerned with morale, did all he could to build it up and keep it high. He was convinced that "Americans either will not or cannot fight at maximum efficiency unless they understand the why and wherefore of their orders," so wherever he went he talked, asked questions, listened, observed. He was patient, clear and logical in his explanations to his officers and men about why things had to be done this way or that. He mingled with the men on an informal basis, got to know them, listened to their gripes, and, when appropriate, did something about them. He believed that "morale is at one and the same time the strongest, and the most delicate of growths. It withstands shocks, even disasters of the battlefield, but can be destroyed utterly by favoritism, neglect, or injustice." Eisenhower would not abide favoritism or neglect, and tried to be just in his dealings with his men. But he also knew that "the Army should not be coddled or babied, for that does not produce morale, it merely condones and encourages inefficiency."[10] Consequently, he drove his men hard, all day, every day, without letup, just as he did himself.

He was popular with the men of the 15th Infantry. They responded to the efforts he was so obviously making in their behalf; they responded to his enthusiasm; they responded to his powerful personality. His favorite marching song was "Beer Barrel Polka." Soon it was the only piece of music to which the regiment would march.[11] As is usually the case with a popular commander, friendly stories about him circulated among the ranks. One favorite concerned the time he was inspecting the kitchens. Walking past a huge pile of ground beef, he scooped up a handful, grabbed an onion, and continued the inspection, alternately biting on the raw meat and the raw onion. The cook was impressed—"By God," he thought, "*there's* a tough guy!"[12]

Eisenhower strove for realism in his training, a part of which was forcing men who were dead tired to keep going. He was sharply critical of mistakes, but anxious to have them exposed in training rather than in combat, and managed to make most of his officers and men adopt the same attitude. He was always looking for lessons; after one set of field maneuvers, he concluded that the infantry regiment needed more transportation, that better traffic control was required, and that radio communications had to be improved.[13]

Most of all, Eisenhower felt, the Army needed strong, tough, efficient, hardworking officers to meet the demands that he was sure would be placed upon it. By the early winter of 1940, many officers had recovered from the shock of the French defeat in June and, encouraged by England's victory in the Battle of Britain, had fallen back into the lazy habits of peacetime. There was a general assumption that the threat was not so great as it had seemed six months earlier, and that America might not enter the war after all. Eisenhower's anger at such talk, and his vigorous insistence that the threat was greater than ever and that America could not possibly stay out, was such that he gained the nickname "Alarmist Ike."

Eisenhower hated any sign of lassitude, most especially when a Regular Army officer displayed it. He would grow furious when he saw one of his Regulars scanning the training programs "carefully and fearfully to see whether they demand more hours; whether their execution is going to cause us some inconvenience!" He told his old friend Everett Hughes, "I was never more serious in my life than I am about the need for each of us, particularly in the Regular Army, to do his whole chore intelligently and energetically. If ever we are to prove that we're worth the salaries the government has been paying us all these years—now is the time!"

In his letter to Hughes, written at Thanksgiving, 1940, he struck two themes that would be important throughout the remainder of his career. The first was getting rid of the inefficient. "The sooner the weaklings in the officers' corps fall out and disappear, the better." Too many officers who had done their jobs well, even brilliantly, in peacetime, did not measure up under wartime conditions. They could not take the physical or mental strain of combat. One reason Eisenhower drove his unit so hard was to find out which of his officers could still make sound, logical decisions and see to it that their orders were carried out when the officers had gone for days with little sleep, no hot food, no relief from the constant stress of making and enforcing decisions.

The second theme, which would become a principal focus of his Presidency, was the cost of defense. How long, he wondered with regard to the Germans in 1940, as he would wonder with regard to the Russians in the 1950s, could America continue to afford "such great expenditures in money, time, resources and effort" just to be prepared to meet a threat? How long would it be, he wondered, before "public opinion decides that it will eventually be cheaper . . . to *remove* the threat?" For that reason, he told Hughes, "we're going to fight, and no one is going to 'lead' us into it." He believed that "the American population, once it gets truly irritated, is a self-confident, reckless, fast-moving avalanche . . . and it is *our* job to speed up the preparatory forces!"

As for himself, Eisenhower worried about the things lieutenant colonels were supposed to worry about—training schedules, new equipment and when it would arrive, whether or not his cadres would be ready for the recruits that were already pouring into the training camps, and of course his own future. "I want to be considered *fit* and qualified to command a unit," he told Hughes, "and under our system, that means that one must have so many months of troop duty on the official record." Well and good. He was "delighted" to stay with troops for two reasons; first, "I like it," and second, "I want to convince the most ritualistic-minded guy in the whole d—— Army that I get along with John Soldier." He expressed confidence that "long and bitter wars . . . send to the bone pile those that . . . indulge in petty jealousies, personal animosities and the like; they bring to the top the fellow who thinks more of his job than of his own promotion prospects."[14]

Eisenhower was delighted in September 1940 when Colonel Patton, commanding the 2d Armored Brigade in Fort Benning, wrote to say that two armored divisions would soon be formed, the first in the Army's history and the fulfillment of their hopes as young officers back at Fort Meade in 1920. Patton said he expected to command one of the armored divisions. He wondered if Eisenhower would want to serve under him. "That would be great," Eisenhower responded immediately. "I suppose it's too much to hope that I could have a regiment in your division, because I'm still almost three years away from my colonelcy, but *I think* I could do a damn good job of commanding a regiment."[15] Patton wrote back, "I shall ask for you either as Chief of Staff which I should prefer or as a regimental commander you can tell me which you want for no matter how we get together we will go PLACES."[16]

Eisenhower was sure Patton would go places, but he was beginning to feel acute anxiety about his own future. He knew that his reputation throughout the Army was that of an outstanding staff officer (as even Patton's preferences indicated); his many friends at posts around the country reported to him that this or that general had requested his services as chief of staff to a division or even a corps. The thought that he might miss combat again, as in 1918, was almost too painful to bear. He wrote to every friend he had in the War Department, asking that he please, please be left alone with the 15th Infantry, not jerked away to some staff job. At the end of October he confided to Mark Clark, who was stationed in Washington, D.C., that his ambition was to command an armored regiment under Patton. He realized that the people in the War Department "will probably think me a conceited individual, but I see no objection to setting your sights high." He asked Clark to see the Chief of Infantry and tell him to "let me alone." His immediate fear was that if he became a chief of staff to a division, he would not be available for transfer to the Armored Corps when the new regiments were formed.[17]

The anxiety became well-nigh unbearable when Patton wrote, on November 1, 1940, advising him to hurry his application for a transfer. "If you have any pull," Patton said, "use it, for there will be 10 new generals in this Corps pretty damned soon."[18] Ten generals! How could a mere lieutenant colonel compete with a general? Eisenhower put in for the transfer, but he was almost certain that he would be turned down because he was so junior in rank. In mid-November he wrote T. J. Davis (who had left the Philippines and was serving in the Adjutant General's office), explaining the situation and expressing his frustrations over his junior rank. "It strikes me that this business of being so particular about the details of rank is, to say the least, somewhat amusing," he began. "When a man has reached the age of fifty years, has been graduated more than twenty-five, and is some two and one-half years away from his eagles, it seems that the matter of rank could be so adjusted that the War Department could put a man wherever they want to."[19]

Worry about his rank, which he feared would preclude a combat command, and about his reputation, which he feared would insure a staff job, now became an obsession. Shortly after mid-November his fears became a reality when he received a telegram from Gerow, now a brigadier general and chief of the War Plans Division (WPD) in the War Department. The telegram read: "I need you in War Plans Division do you seriously object to being detailed on the War Department General Staff and assigned here please reply immediately."

Eisenhower's first reaction was physical. He had a severe, painful attack of shingles, a skin disease often associated with extreme nervousness or anxiety. From his bed, he wrote a three-page, single-spaced letter to Gerow. "Your telegram," he confessed, "sent me into a tailspin." He said he was tremendously flattered by Gerow's use of the word "need" in his telegram and that there was no officer in the Army he would rather have as a superior than Gerow. But if given a choice, he told Gerow, he would rather stay with troops. His lack of extended troop duty "has been thrown in my teeth" too many times, he said, and he knew that when "ritualistic-minded" officers looked at his record, with only six months of duty with troops since 1922, they reacted automatically, saying that Eisenhower could not possibly be given command of a regiment. For himself, his tour with the 15th had "completely reassured" him that "I am capable of handling command jobs," but he knew he still had to prove it to others.

If Gerow nevertheless insisted, Eisenhower assured him that he would serve in WPD gladly, if only because one of his most basic principles was that an officer's preferences should carry little weight when superior authority decided that he could make his best contribution elsewhere. But if Gerow did insist, Eisenhower wanted a favor; he asked Gerow to make certain that "those in authority" were fully aware that he, Eisenhower, had "earnestly tried for many years to get an assignment to troops." He said he realized that "General Marshall, in person, is not concerned with the assignment of such small fry as myself," but MacArthur had never allowed him to make a request for troop duty for the record, and he wanted the War Department to be made aware of the facts.[20]

While Eisenhower waited for Gerow's decision, he continued to suffer from shingles. He asked Mamie what her wishes were, but Mamie, keenly aware of what was at stake, and good Army wife that she was, refused to express a preference between Washington State and Washington, D.C.

Gerow and Patton were not the only officers who wanted Eisenhower's services. General Thompson, commanding the 3d Division at Fort Lewis, requested that Eisenhower be assigned to him as chief of staff. Gerow talked with Marshall, who was in fact well aware of Eisenhower's reputation, and the Chief decided to leave Eisenhower at Fort Lewis, working for Thompson. Thus Eisenhower escaped staff duty in Washington, D.C., only to be put on a staff in Washington State. But at least his designation was "General Staff *with* troops," and to that extent he felt lucky. The shingles disappeared. Then "on top of everything else," as he explained to Gerow, "it now turns out that Mamie, who wouldn't even give me a hint at what she wanted to do, is broken hearted over not going to Washington!"[21]

Through the winter of 1940–1941, Eisenhower had more than enough work to help him forget his personal problems. As the Army expanded, so did Fort Lewis. As at every other Army post, construction crews were everywhere, while recruits came in by the thousands. Eisenhower did his usual efficient job, and his responsibilities grew as a result. In March 1941, General Kenyon Joyce, commanding the IX Army Corps, which covered the entire Northwest, asked for Eisenhower as his chief of staff. That same month, on the eleventh, he was promoted to the rank of full colonel (temporary). No promotion he ever received delighted him more. Being made a colonel fulfilled his highest ambitions. Mamie and John arranged a celebration. His fellow officers, congratulating him, said it would not be long before he had a star on each shoulder. "Damn it," he complained to John, "as soon as you get a promotion they start talking about another one. Why can't they let a guy be happy with what he has? They take all the joy out of it."[22]

Three months later, he got new orders. On June 11, 1941, Lieutenant General Walter Krueger wrote General Marshall saying he needed a chief of staff for his Third Army, and he knew just the sort of man he wanted: "A man possessing broad vision, progressive ideas, a thorough grasp of the magnitude of the problems involved in handling an army, and lots of initiative and resourcefulness." Krueger also knew just the man for the job, Colonel Dwight Eisenhower. Two days later, Marshall agreed to the assignment.[23] In late June 1941, the Eisenhowers set off for Fort Sam Houston, where Third Army Headquarters were located. They arrived on July 1, their twenty-fifth wedding anniversary. For a present, Eisenhower gave Mamie a platinum watch, with diamonds around a tiny dial. He used some of the money he had saved in the Philippines to pay for it. Mamie wore it the rest of her life. And she was pleased to be back at such a familiar place, with all its happy memories, especially since her husband was now a colonel, which entitled them to one of Fort Sam's fine old brick houses, with shady verandas all around and a large lawn.[24]

A colonel rated a striker and an executive officer. Mamie put up a notice on the bulletin board for a striker. A few days later, Pfc. Michael J. McKeogh volunteered. "Mickey," whose parents had immigrated to the United States from Ireland, had been a bellhop at the Plaza Hotel in New York before he was drafted. He liked Eisenhower "straight off," he later said, because the colonel was "absolutely straight" and "you always knew exactly where you stood with him." He thought Mamie "a very gracious lady." Mickey soon became Eisenhower's most fervent admirer and remained with him for the next five years. As his executive, Eisenhower selected Lieutenant Ernest R. Lee (everyone called him "Tex"), a native of San Antonio, who had been an insurance and a car salesman. Bright, breezy, cheerful, anxious to please, Lee had all the qualities of a good salesman. Eisenhower enjoyed his company, came to rely on him to handle office details. Lee, like Mickey, stayed with Eisenhower to the end of the war. Together, they formed the nucleus of what would become Eisenhower's "family," a close-knit group of enlisted men and women and junior officers who were devoted to Eisenhower and who served him well.[25]

The great experience of Eisenhower's tour as chief of staff to the Third Army was the Louisiana maneuvers, held in August and September 1941. These were the largest maneuvers held by the U.S. Army before America entered the war. They pitted Krueger's Third Army against General Ben Lear's Second Army. Krueger, with 240,000 men, was "invading" Louisiana, while Lear, with 180,000 men, was "defending" the United States. Marshall had insisted on such a large-scale war game because he wanted to uncover deficiencies in training and equipment, and because he needed to uncover hidden talent in the officer corps.

Eisenhower was eager for the test. On August 5, he wrote Gerow, "Next Monday I go to Louisiana . . . All the old-timers here say that we are going into a God-awful spot, to live with mud, malaria, mosquitoes and misery. But I like to go to the field, so I'm not much concerned about it."[26]

Assembling the Third Army was indeed a test. It was much the largest single army the United States had put into the field since 1918, twice the size of Grant's largest army. "The nervous energy, technical competence, and drive required" of every officer involved, Eisenhower wrote from his headquarters in Eunice, "were tremendous." Actually launching a flanking attack against Second Army was even more difficult. Eisenhower hardly slept. He was distressed to discover that company and platoon leadership was inadequate, and he spent much of his time moving from unit to unit, giving advice here, orders there, encouraging the young lieutenants and captains by praising them when he could, passing on criticism when necessary. He was concerned by their "stupid disregard of the danger of air attacks," their neglect of proper camouflage, their poor traffic-handling abilities. Each morning he brought together the principal officers for a critique. He was well aware that they were physically tired and needed to be encouraged, but he also knew that actual combat would be even tougher. "We had to uncover and highlight every mistake," he wrote, "every failure, every foulup that in war could be death to a unit or an army."

When the attack began, Eisenhower moved into the field, living in a tent in a bivouac near Lake Charles. During the war game, his tent "turned into something of a cracker-barrel corner where everyone in our army seemed to come for a serious discussion, a laugh, or a gripe." Eisenhower always welcomed them, even though the talk cut into his limited sleeping time. The officers responded to his personality, his encouragement, his good humor, his seriousness about his job and theirs, his professional competence, most of all to his leadership. "I was often astonished to see how much better they worked after they had unloaded their woes," he later wrote, but astonished or not, he realized full well what a positive effect he was having. He made a sympathetic ear an essential part of his leadership technique.[27]

Not only his officers, but also newsmen gathered around his tent for bull sessions. These reporters, mostly young men, were—like the Army—learning about war and what their jobs would be after America entered the conflict. They responded to Eisenhower as warmly as his officers did, and for the same reasons—his frankness, his facility for explaining things, no matter how technical, so that they could understand them, his easy informality, his jokes, and his honesty.

The honesty was a special surprise to the cynical reporters, accustomed to writing about public figures who inflated their own importance while covering up any shortcomings in their organizations. Eisenhower was self-effacing and made no attempt to hide deficiencies. Instead, he took the reporters into his confidence. Without preaching or complaining, he told them frankly about what was going wrong, and made it possible for them to see the problems with their own eyes. He then counted on them to make the country aware of what was needed. He made jokes about the Army's inadequacies, about the papier-mâché tanks or the ordinary civilian trucks carrying labels on their sides that read "Tank." The reporters covering the Louisiana maneuvers were the first to learn what the rest of the world would soon know—Eisenhower, just by being himself, was an absolute genius at public relations.[28]

He got his first publicity almost immediately. Krueger's Third Army, operating under plans Eisenhower had helped draw up, outflanked Lear's Second Army, forcing it to retreat. "Had it been real war," young reporter Hanson Baldwin wrote for *The New York Times,* "Lear's force would have been annihilated."[29] In their syndicated column, "Washington Merry-Go-Round," Drew Pearson and Robert S. Allen reported that it was "Colonel Eisenhower . . . who conceived and directed the strategy that routed the Second Army." They said that Eisenhower "has a steel-trap mind plus unusual physical vigor [and] to him the military profession is a science . . ."[30]

Eisenhower professed to be unaware of why he received the credit, which he said should have gone to General Krueger. His modesty was genuine and typical. It was also one of his most endearing traits, an essential part of his popularity with the press and the public. His "Aw shucks, who me?" look, his embarrassment at being singled out, his insistence that others, not he, really deserved the praise, became one of his best-known characteristics, something millions of people found irresistibly appealing. In late September, on Krueger's recommendation, he was promoted to brigadier general (temporary). Congratulations came pouring in. Eisenhower responded by writing, "When they get clear down to my place on the list, they are passing out stars with considerable abandon."[31]

Thanks to the promotion, Eisenhower's photograph, stern-faced and saluting the flag, went out over the wire services. The American people—and press corps—began to discover something Mamie had always known, that Eisenhower was one of the most photogenic men in the country, even in the world. A Denver friend, Aksel Nielsen, whom he had met through the Douds, wrote Eisenhower to ask for an autographed print of the photograph. Eisenhower replied, "I'm so tremendously flattered by the thought of anyone asking for my photo that I'm hurrying it off at once—it would be tragic to have you change your mind. Wouldn't you like three or four???"[32]

When they got back to Fort Sam Houston, the officers of the 3d Division said they wanted to hold a parade in Eisenhower's honor. He demurred. They insisted. He told Mark Clark, "I'm completely overcome . . . I've always been on the other end of such things, and I hope to hek I don't fall over my own feet! But durned if the prospect doesn't scare me more than would an order to go charge Hitler's legions!"[33]

In drawing the lessons learned from the maneuvers, Eisenhower concentrated on training, equipment, communications, and junior officer problems, but he did not neglect the high command. "There is a tremendous job facing every senior commander in this Army," he wrote Gerow. "The nervous energy and drive that are required in bringing a large unit along toward high training standards is tremendous; only people who are highly trained professionally and who have an inexhaustible supply of determination can get away with it." Unfortunately, those traits were rarely combined in one person. Some of the officers had plenty of drive but not enough competence, while with others the situation was reversed. He said the senior commander must have "iron in his soul" to fire the incompetent, many of whom were old friends, "but it is a job that has got to be done." He said it was a "hard thing to do," but in fact he would not recognize until he became the senior commander himself just how difficult it was. Throughout the war, some of his most painful moments came when he had to relieve classmates and friends from combat commands.[34]

On Sunday morning, December 7, 1941, Eisenhower went to his office—over Mamie's protests—to catch up on his paper work. About noon, he told Tex Lee that he was "dead tired" and said he "guessed he'd go home and take a nap." He told Mamie he did not want to be "bothered by anyone wanting to play bridge" and went to sleep. An hour or so later, Lee called him with the news from Pearl Harbor.[35]

Five hectic days later he was at his desk with more of the inevitable paper work when he got a call from the War Department. "Is that you, Ike?" Colonel Walter Bedell Smith, secretary of the General Staff, asked. "Yes," Eisenhower replied. "The Chief says for you to hop a plane and get up here right away," Smith ordered. "Tell your boss that formal orders will come through later."[36] Eisenhower assumed that Marshall wanted to talk to him about the state of the defenses in the Philippines, and that he would not be gone long. He told Mickey to pack only one bag for him, assured Mamie that he would be back soon, and got an afternoon plane leaving San Antonio for Washington.

Bad weather forced the aircraft down in Dallas. Eisenhower switched to a train. After the train passed Kansas City and headed east, Eisenhower was riding over the same tracks he had traveled on thirty years earlier, on his trip from Abilene to West Point. As he rode along, he tried to prepare himself for the conference with Marshall. He knew it was not only a great responsibility but also a great opportunity. Perhaps his thoughts strayed, once or twice, to his parents' injunction, which had been in his mind in 1911: "Opportunity is all about you. Reach out and take it." By most standards, he had failed to take the advice. He had passed up the University of Michigan and the Argentine frontier; he had passed up a promising business opportunity in late 1918; he had passed up a chance at fame and influence when he turned down an opportunity to write a column on military affairs for a chain of newspapers in the thirties; he had certainly turned down fortune in 1938 when he declined the offer to work for the Jewish community in Manila. Instead of taking opportunity, he had given his life and his talents to the Army.

As the train sped across Missouri and Illinois, he may have dared to hope that at last the Army was going to give him an opportunity in return.

CHAPTER NINE

Washington

December 14, 1941–June 23, 1942

ON SUNDAY MORNING, December 14, 1941, Eisenhower arrived at Union Station in Washington. He went immediately to the War Department offices in the Munitions Building on Constitution Avenue (the Pentagon was then under construction) for his initial conference with the Chief of Staff. After a brief, formal greeting, Marshall quickly outlined the situation in the Pacific—the ships lost at Pearl Harbor, the planes lost at Clark Field outside Manila, the size and strength of Japanese attacks elsewhere, troop strength in the Philippines, reinforcement possibilities, intelligence estimates, the capabilities of America's Dutch and British allies in Asia, and other details. Then Marshall leaned forward across his desk, fixed his eyes on Eisenhower's, and demanded, "What should be our general line of action?"

Eisenhower was startled. He had just arrived, knew little more than what he had read in the newspapers and what Marshall had just told him, was not up to date on the war plans for the Pacific, and had no staff to help him prepare an answer. After a second or two of hesitation, Eisenhower requested, "Give me a few hours." "All right," Marshall replied. He had dozens of problems to deal with that afternoon, hundreds in the days to follow. He needed help and he needed to know immediately which of his officers could give it to him. He had heard great things about Eisenhower, from men whose judgment he trusted, but he needed to see for himself how Eisenhower operated under the pressures of war. His question was the first test.

Eisenhower went to a desk that had been assigned to him in the War Plans Division of the General Staff. Sticking a sheet of yellow tissue paper into his typewriter, he tapped out with one finger, "Steps to Be Taken," then sat back and started thinking. He knew that the Philippines could not be saved, that the better part of military wisdom would be to retreat to Australia, there to build a base for a counterattack. But the honor of the Army was at stake, and the prestige of the United States in the Far East, and these political factors outweighed the purely military considerations. An effort had to be made. Eisenhower's first recommendation was to build a base in Australia from which attempts could be made to reinforce the Philippines. "Speed is essential," he noted. He urged that shipments of planes, pilots, ammunition, and other equipment be started from the West Coast and Hawaii to Australia immediately.

It was already dusk when Eisenhower returned to Marshall's office. As he handed over his written recommendation, he said he realized that it would be impossible to get reinforcements to the Philippines in time to save the islands from the Japanese. Still, he added, the United States had to do everything it could to bolster MacArthur's forces, because "the people of China, of the Philippines, of the Dutch East Indies will be watching us. They may excuse failure but they will not excuse abandonment." He urged the advantages of Australia as a base of operations—English speaking, a strong ally, modern port facilities, beyond the range of the Japanese offensive—and advised Marshall to begin a program of expanding the facilities there and to secure the line of communications from the West Coast to Hawaii and then on to New Zealand and Australia. "In this," Eisenhower said, ". . . we dare not fail. We must take great risks and spend any amount of money required." Marshall studied Eisenhower for a minute, then said softly, "I agree with you. Do your best to save them." He thereupon placed Eisenhower in charge of the Philippines and Far Eastern Section of the War Plans Division. Then Marshall leaned forward—Eisenhower recalled years later that he had "an eye that seemed to me awfully cold"—and declared, "Eisenhower, the Department is filled with able men who analyze their problems well but feel compelled always to bring them to me for final solution. I must have assistants who will solve their own problems and tell me later what they have done."[1]

Over the next two months Eisenhower labored to save the Philippines. His efforts were worse than fruitless, as MacArthur came to lump Eisenhower together with Marshall and Roosevelt as the men responsible for the debacle on the islands. But throughout that period, and in the months that followed, Eisenhower impressed Marshall deeply, so deeply that Marshall came to agree with MacArthur's earlier judgment that Eisenhower was the best officer in the Army.

Marshall was not an easy man to impress. He was a cold, aloof person—"remote and austere," Eisenhower called him—a man who forced everyone to keep his distance. Franklin Roosevelt had tried at their first meeting to slap him on the back and call him "George," but Marshall drew back and let the President know that the name was "General Marshall," and "General Marshall" it remained. He had few intimate friends. When he relaxed he did it alone, watching movies or puttering in his garden. He kept a tight grip on his emotions and seldom displayed any sign of a sense of humor. His sense of duty was highly developed. He made small allowance for failings in others, but to those who could do the work, Marshall was intensely loyal. He also felt deep affection toward them, though he seldom showed it. Hardly anyone, for example, could resist Eisenhower's infectious grin and he was known throughout the Army by his catchy nickname, but Marshall did resist. In all their years together, Marshall almost always called him "Eisenhower" (except after November 4, 1952, when he called him "Mr. President"). Marshall slipped only once, at the victory parade in New York City in 1945, and called him "Ike." "To make up for it," Eisenhower recalled with a smile, "he used the word 'Eisenhower' five times in the next sentence."[2] For his part, Eisenhower always called Marshall "General." After the years with MacArthur, he found Marshall to be the ideal boss, both as a man to work for and as a teacher. In October 1942, he told an assistant, "I wouldn't trade one Marshall for fifty MacArthurs." He thought a second, then blurted out, "My God! That would be a lousy deal. What would I do with fifty MacArthurs?"[3] As he later wrote more formally, Eisenhower conceived "unlimited admiration and respect" for Marshall, and came to have feelings of "affection" for him. Marshall came to have the dominant role not only in Eisenhower's career, but also in his thinking and in his leadership techniques. He was the model that Eisenhower tried to emulate; he set the standards Eisenhower tried to meet.

The two men, although ten years apart in age, had much in common. Marshall had the build and grace of an athlete, was about Eisenhower's height (six feet), and was equally well proportioned. He had been a football player in college. He was a great fan of Fox Conner and a student of military history. Like Eisenhower, he loved exploring the Civil War battlefields and habitually illustrated his points or strengthened his arguments by drawing on examples from past battles and campaigns. The way he exercised leadership coincided nicely with Eisenhower's temperament. He never yelled, never shouted, almost never lost his temper. He built an atmosphere of friendly cooperation and teamwork around him, without losing the distinction between the commander and his staff—there was never any doubt as to who was the boss.

Marshall headed a stupendous organization. To do so effectively he needed assistants he could trust. In picking them, he took professional competence for granted and concentrated on personality traits. Certain types were, in his view, unsuited for high command. Foremost among these were those who were self-seeking in the matter of promotion. Next came those who always tried to "pass the buck," while officers who tried to do everything themselves and consequently got bogged down in detail were equally unsatisfactory. Men who shouted or pounded on the desk were as unacceptable to Marshall as men who had too great a love of the limelight. Nor could he abide the pessimist. He surrounded himself with men who were offensive-minded and who concentrated on the possibilities rather than the difficulties. In every respect, Eisenhower was exactly the sort of officer Marshall was looking for. Eisenhower himself, as Supreme Commander and later as President, used Marshall's criteria in picking his subordinates.[4]

Within the limits of their abilities, Marshall gave his subordinates a free hand and his own unstinting support. One of the things he liked best about Eisenhower was the way Eisenhower accepted responsibility. Marshall complained that WPD officers would not make decisions and send out orders. The fault, Eisenhower believed, was Marshall's own, because everyone in WPD was afraid of Marshall. Brigadier General Robert Crawford, for example, was in Eisenhower's view a "brilliant man with an unlimited future," but he got tongue-tied in Marshall's presence, because Marshall terrified him, and consequently his talents were never sufficiently utilized.[5]

Eisenhower's immediate superior, the head of WPD, was his old friend "Gee" Gerow. Gerow was not terrified of Marshall, but he was unwilling to make decisions. Marshall had told Gerow, as he had told Eisenhower, that he wanted WPD to make and execute decisions without bothering him about it. Eisenhower did so one day and sent the result to Gerow. Gerow changed the decision to a recommendation and passed it on to Marshall for final action. Eisenhower confronted his superior and declared, "Gee, you have got to quit bothering the Chief with this stuff." "I can't help it, Ike," Gerow replied. "These decisions are too important. He's got to make them himself."[6] Marshall did not agree, and shortly moved Gerow out of WPD, replacing him with Eisenhower.

• •

Eisenhower's first responsibility, getting reinforcements to the Philippines, put him in a difficult and painful position. Due to the lack of American preparedness, there was not much to send; due to superb Japanese planning and execution in the first months of the war, it was almost impossible to get any men or guns or ammunition through. Eisenhower, therefore, was not trying to stave off defeat, but only to stretch it out, in order to provide more time to build a base in Australia. In effect, he had to preside over the defeat and capture of an American garrison that contained many close personal friends, and of a Philippine force that he had helped build. Hardest of all to bear were MacArthur's accusations that the War Department was deliberately sacrificing the islands, and what hurt most about that charge was that it was basically true.

Eisenhower's first actions were to start two transports from San Francisco to Brisbane, to arrange for further shipments, to order two Pan American clippers to fly to Australia with ammunition, and to divert fifteen heavy bombers from Hawaii to Brisbane. After a career of working with tightly restricted budgets, he discovered that when America went to war, money was no object—he was able to send $10 million in cash to Australia to hire blockade-runners from private shippers ("pirates," Marshall called them) to make the run from Australia to the Philippines.[7] On December 22 the Japanese made their major landings at Lingayen Gulf, north of Manila. MacArthur's attempts to stop the enemy at the beaches failed, and by December 26 MacArthur had been forced to declare Manila an open city and to transfer his headquarters to Corregidor, while pulling his forces back to the Bataan Peninsula. The Japanese had aerial and naval supremacy and had cut the line between the Philippines and Australia. "I still think he [MacArthur] might have made a better showing at the beaches and passes," Eisenhower noted in his diary on January 13, "and certainly he should have saved his planes on Dec. 8, but he's still the hero."[8]

Marshall and the War Department, having decided that the Philippines could not be defended, were facing the realities of global war, and although public attention was centered on MacArthur and the Japanese, most WPD planners were concentrating their attention on the German enemy. Eisenhower, as head of the Far Eastern desk at WPD, took a parochial view. "I've been insisting Far East is critical," he noted on January 1, 1942, "and no other sideshows should be undertaken." He was handicapped by the lack of shipping: "Ships! Ships! All we need is ships!" he wrote on January 12. As an afterthought, he added, "Also ammunition, anti-aircraft guns, tanks, airplanes, what a headache!" On January 17 he declared, "My own plan is to drop everything else . . . and make the British retire in Libya. Then scrape up everything everywhere and get it" to the Dutch East Indies, Singapore, and Burma.[9]

He did not advocate attempting to break through to the beleaguered garrison on Bataan. All previous attempts to do so had failed. Despite the lure of $10 million cash, few private shippers could be found willing to try, and of the six that did, only three got through. Two fast ships, loaded with a field artillery brigade, had gotten only as far as Darwin, on the Australian north coast. Pursuit planes that Eisenhower had hoped to fly from Darwin to Bataan arrived in Australia without vital combat parts; by the time these arrived from Hawaii it was too late. Only an occasional submarine, loaded with ammunition and medicine, got through to Corregidor. MacArthur, furious and desperate, sent a series of angry messages to Washington, demanding that the Navy be forced to sally forth from Hawaii and break the blockade. Eisenhower explained to him that because the Japanese had seized the islands of Guam, Wake, the Marshalls, and the Gilberts, and because their land-based airplanes gave them air superiority, the Navy was helpless. MacArthur would have to fight with what he had for as long as possible; he could expect neither reinforcements nor supplies.[10]

That response only added to MacArthur's fury. His forces were being beaten back, suffering heavy losses, fighting with insufficient ammunition, food, and transport, obsolete weapons, and no air cover. To MacArthur, and to the tired, dirty, hungry, unhealthy men of Bataan, the thought of well-dressed, comfortably housed, well-fed staff officers in Washington was infuriating. MacArthur charged that "faceless staff officers" (read "Eisenhower") in Washington were deliberately deceiving him. He believed that had there been sufficient determination in the War Department, reinforcements could have reached Bataan. The charge appeared in a book published two years later, Frazier Hunt's *MacArthur and the War Against Japan.* Eisenhower read it shortly after the liberation of Paris and recommended it to Marshall, with the caveat that "the book practically gave me indigestion." Eisenhower warned that "you will be quite astonished to learn that back in the Winter of '41/'42, you and your assistants in the War Department had no real concern for the Philippines and for the forces fighting there."[11]

That charge of indifference rankled. Through January and February, Eisenhower stayed at the War Department until 10 P.M., and often midnight, seven days a week, trying to scrape up something and find a way to get it through to Bataan. Like MacArthur, he allowed his frustrations to turn to anger; unlike MacArthur, he kept his anger to himself, but he did fill his diary with carping criticism. On January 19, Eisenhower complained, "In many ways MacArthur is as big a baby as ever. But we've just got to keep him fighting."[12] When MacArthur, in what Eisenhower called a "most flamboyant radio message," recommended General Richard Sutherland of his staff as his successor "in the event of my death," Eisenhower's comment was, "[MacArthur] still likes his boot lickers."[13] On January 29, noting that MacArthur had sent a "flood of communications" about breaking the blockade, Eisenhower said that they indicated "a refusal on his part to look facts in the face, an old trait of his . . . He's jittery!"[14] Five days later, Eisenhower accused MacArthur of "losing his nerve. I'm hoping that his yelps are just his way of spurring us on, but he is always an uncertain factor." When MacArthur pointed out that a Navy attempt to break through to Bataan would also constitute an attack on the flank of Japan's southern offensive, and extolled the virtues of a flank offensive, Eisenhower wrote scornfully, "Wonder what he thinks we've been studying for all these years. His lecture would have been good for plebes."[15]

Eisenhower never softened these scathing judgments of his old boss. Nor did Eisenhower show any appreciation for the awful position MacArthur and his men had been put in, which was in many ways similar to that of the Germans at Stalingrad a year later—to stand and fight with what they had for as long as possible, in order to allow other troops in other areas to build their strength, reinforced only by words of encouragement, words that soon became a bitter joke. If Eisenhower or Marshall ever had any guilt feelings about these "stand and fight" orders, they never showed them.

Nor did they show any sympathy for Quezon, who also blamed Washington for the trauma of the Philippines. In February, a desperate Quezon told Roosevelt that if the United States did not intend to defend the islands, then the islands should be neutralized, with both the United States and Japan being told to withdraw their troops. Quezon probably sent the message for its shock effect, as he knew that the Japanese would never voluntarily give up the magnificent port of Manila, or the islands they had overrun, and he could anticipate Roosevelt's reaction (which was, "We can't do this at all"). But what really shocked the high command in Washington was MacArthur's endorsement of Quezon's proposal. MacArthur said it "might offer the best possible solution of what is about to be a disastrous debacle."[16] Eisenhower, to whom Marshall gave the task of drafting a reply for the President, commented in his diary that both MacArthur and Quezon "are babies."[17] In the message to MacArthur, Eisenhower said that if Quezon wanted to surrender the Philippine Army, he could do so, but MacArthur should keep the U.S. troops fighting "so long as there remains any possibility of resistance." Eisenhower, writing for the President, expressed his concern for the plight of those on Bataan, then declared that the service the troops could render by delaying the Japanese advance "is beyond all possibility of appraisement."[18]

The message was so Hitler-like in its exhortation to stand and fight in a hopeless cause for the greater good that MacArthur found it insulting. He replied with some heat that he would not surrender the Philippine units and that he planned to fight in Bataan until his forces were destroyed, then continue the struggle on the island of Corregidor. Roosevelt and Marshall, however, then decided that it would not do at all to have MacArthur go down with his troops, and they directed Eisenhower to draft orders telling MacArthur to leave the Philippines and proceed to Melbourne, there to take command of the Southwest Pacific Theater. It was a delicate process, because there was justifiable fear that MacArthur would refuse to leave his troops in the lurch. Eisenhower noted, "Bataan is made to order for him. It's in the public eye; it has made him a public hero; it has all the essentials of drama; and he is the acknowledged king on the spot."[19] But after some hesitation, MacArthur did obey the orders, and in mid-March, accompanied by his wife, son, and immediate staff, made his dramatic escape on a PT boat from the Philippines. Eisenhower, still bitter over what he regarded as MacArthur's lack of appreciation for all his efforts, and still unwilling or unable to see the debacle from MacArthur's point of view, noted MacArthur's escape and subsequent publicity in his diary, and said disgustedly that now MacArthur was a bigger hero than ever.[20]

Meanwhile MacArthur's successor, Lieutenant General Jonathan Wainwright, continued the fight. Eisenhower, despite increasing feelings of helplessness, kept trying to send aid. "For many weeks—it seems years—I've been searching everywhere to find any feasible way of giving real help to the P.I. We've literally squandered money; we wrestled with the Navy, we've tried to think of anything that might promise even a modicum of help. I'll go on trying, but daily the situation grows more desperate."[21] When Corregidor finally surrendered, on May 6, Eisenhower expressed pity for Wainwright, who did the fighting while MacArthur got the glory. Eisenhower frequently expressed contempt of one form or another of MacArthur's fame, but his anger at the publicity MacArthur received for the flight to Australia sat ill with the man who had written MacArthur's orders in the first place. Resistance in the Philippines had lasted five months, which, compared to the British debacle in Malaya and Singapore, was not a bad record. Still Eisenhower could find nothing praiseworthy in MacArthur's actions; his final comment was, "General Mac's tirades to which TJ and I so often listened in Manila, would now sound as silly to the public as they then did to us. But he's a real hero! Yah."[22] MacArthur, like Montgomery later, was one of the few people to touch the adult Eisenhower deeply enough to call forth buried feelings of jealousy and bitterness, like those of his childhood.

MacArthur was not the only cause of Eisenhower's irritation; the U.S. Navy made him equally furious. Partly this was due to the Navy's flat refusal to even consider running the blockade, but Eisenhower's real anger rose over the Navy's more general refusal to cooperate with the Army in making long-term war plans. The Navy obviously intended to fight its own war in the Pacific, which Eisenhower regarded as obviously impossible. "What a gang to work with," he wrote disparagingly of the Navy.[23] Noting that the Navy would not sail its ships into waters controlled by land-based Japanese aircraft, Eisenhower wondered in mid-February "why it does not quit building battleships and start on carriers, and more carriers."[24] Eisenhower also realized that the Japanese could not be driven back from their advance bases without a series of amphibious assaults, and he was the first officer to insist that the United States would need more, bigger, and better landing craft. Shortage of landing craft was a problem that would plague him until the last months of 1944; he first anticipated the problem in January 1942, when he tried to talk to Admiral Ernest J. King, the Chief of Naval Operations, about it. But the Navy was more concerned with rebuilding its capital ship fleet, and King could not be bothered.[25]

Eisenhower hated having to work with King. The admiral seemed to him to be petty in his rank-consciousness, stubborn and misguided in his views on strategy and weapons, and much too full of the traditional interwar rivalry between the Army and the Navy.[26] Eisenhower thought King "the antithesis of cooperation, a deliberately rude person, which means he's a mental bully," and commented, "One thing that might help win this war is to get someone to shoot King."[27]

In King's presence, Eisenhower could suppress such feelings. Once Marshall sent him to King to discuss an important problem. Eisenhower made his request. King, scarcely looking up from his desk, responded with one word, "No." Eisenhower quietly but firmly said that King was not giving Marshall's request proper consideration and added that King's attitude could not do much to assure cooperation between the two services. Startled, King looked at Eisenhower for a moment, invited him to sit down, and admitted, "Look, I sometimes wonder whether in making decisions I depend too much on old naval customs, disciplines, prejudices—or whether I'm really thinking my problems through. Now just state that question again." Eisenhower did so and King said he thought it could be done. Later, King proved to be one of Eisenhower's strongest supporters.[28]

The first three months of 1942 were terribly trying on Eisenhower. Until February 7, he lived with Milton and Helen in Falls Church, but he never saw the house in daylight. His driver would pick him up before dawn to take him to his office on Constitution Avenue, and bring him back at 10:30 P.M. or later. He wolfed down his meals, often no more than a hot dog and coffee, at his desk. When he got to Falls Church, Helen would have a snack for him, and he would wake up his nephew and niece for a chat before going to bed himself. Always thoughtful, he arranged to send flowers to Helen for a big dinner party he could not attend, and had an aide purchase Christmas presents for the children.[29] But he missed Mamie and was delighted when she came up to Washington in February and found a small apartment at the Wardman Park Hotel. Mickey, who drove the family Chrysler east from Texas, was shocked when he first saw Eisenhower: "He was more tired-looking than I'd ever seen him; all of his face was tired. . . . His voice was tired, like his face."[30] Small wonder; on February 22 Eisenhower noted that he had gone to a Sunday dinner in honor of two visiting Chinese and that this was the "longest I've been out of the office in daytime since coming here ten weeks ago today."[31]

Part of the strain was due to the nature of his job. He wanted to be in the field, with troops, not behind a desk. "My God, how I hate to work by any method that forces me to depend on someone else," he complained.[32] Considering the whole Washington-in-wartime scene, he remarked, "There's a lot of big talk and desk hammering around this place, but very few doers. They announce results in advance in a flashy way and make big impressions, but the results often don't materialize, and then the workers get the grief."[33]

On March 10, David Eisenhower died. His son could barely take the time to record the fact in his diary. The following day, Eisenhower wrote that "war is not soft, it has no time to indulge even the deepest and most sacred emotions." That night he quit work at 7:30 P.M., noting, "I haven't the heart to go on tonight." On March 12, the day of the funeral in Abilene, he closed his office door for a half hour, to think about his father and to compose a eulogy. He praised his father for his "sterling honesty, his pride in his independence, his exemplary habits . . ." and for his "undemonstrative, quiet, modest" manner. "I'm proud he was my father," Eisenhower wrote, and then expressed his only regret—"It was always so difficult to let him know the great depth of my affection for him."[34]

Worn-out, angry at his country for not having prepared for the war, angry at MacArthur and King for the way they were fighting it, angry at being stuck in Washington, one day Eisenhower almost lost his temper completely with Marshall. It happened on March 20, in Marshall's office. Marshall and Eisenhower had settled a detail about an officer's promotion. Marshall then leaned forward to say that in the last war, staff officers had gotten the promotions, not the field officers who did the fighting, and that he intended to reverse the process in this war. "Take your case," he added. "I know that you were recommended by one general for division command and by another for corps command. That's all very well. I'm glad they have that opinion of you, but you are going to stay right here and fill your position, and that's that!" Preparing to turn to other business, Marshall muttered, "While this may seem a sacrifice to you, that's the way it must be."

Eisenhower, red-faced and resentful, shot back, "General, I'm interested in what you say, but I want you to know that I don't give a damn about your promotion plans as far as I'm concerned. I came into this office from the field and I am trying to do my duty. I expect to do so as long as you want me here. If that locks me to a desk for the rest of the war, so be it!" He pushed back his chair and strode toward the door, nearly ten paces away. By the time he got there he decided to take the edge off the outburst, turned, and grinned. He thought he could see a tiny smile at the corners of Marshall's mouth.[35]

Whether Marshall smiled or not, Eisenhower's anger returned full force after he left the office. He went to his desk and filled his diary with his feelings. The thought of spending the war in Washington, missing combat again, was maddening. It seemed so unfair. Marshall's cold, impersonal attitude just added to the anger. He cursed Marshall for toying with him; he cursed the war and his own bad luck. The next morning, Eisenhower read what he had written, shook his head, and tore the page out of his diary, destroying it. Then he wrote a new entry. "Anger cannot win, it cannot even think clearly. In this respect," he continued, "Marshall puzzles me a bit." Marshall got angrier at stupidity than anyone Eisenhower had ever seen, "yet the outburst is so fleeting, he returns so quickly to complete 'normalcy,' that I'm certain he does it for effect." Eisenhower envied Marshall that trait and confessed, "I blaze for an hour! So, for many years I've made it a religion never to indulge myself, but yesterday I failed."[36]

A week later Marshall recommended Eisenhower for promotion to major general (temporary). In his recommendation to the President, Marshall explained that Eisenhower was not really a staff officer, but was his operations officer, a sort of subordinate commander. Surprised and delighted, Eisenhower's first reaction was "This should assure that when I finally get back to troops, I'll get a division."[37] Decades later, in his memoirs, he wrote that he "often wondered" if his outburst—and the way in which he had been able to control his emotions and end the session with one of his big lopsided grins—had led Marshall to take a greater interest in him.[38]

Perhaps, but unlikely. Marshall had already been pushing Eisenhower ahead, increasing his responsibilities, at a rapid pace. In January, he had taken Eisenhower along as his chief assistant to the first wartime conference with the British, and had given Eisenhower the task of preparing the basic American position on organization and strategy for global war. In mid-February, when he sent Gerow back to the field, to take command of a division, he made Eisenhower the head of WPD, and thus his principal plans and operations officer. On March 9, as a part of a general reorganization of the War Department, WPD was renamed the Operations Division (OPD) and given expanded functions, with Eisenhower as its commanding officer. This steady progress surely indicated that Marshall, with or without that display of what MacArthur called "Ike's damn Dutch temper," thought Eisenhower's potential unlimited.

By the beginning of April, Eisenhower had 107 officers working directly under him in OPD. As its responsibilities included both plans and operations, OPD was in effect Marshall's command post, and it was concerned with all Army activities around the world, which gave Eisenhower a breadth of vision he could not have obtained in any other post.

His office was the scene of constant activity, with a stream of officers and messages coming in, decisions made, and orders and plans sent out. Lucian K. Truscott, Jr., who was on his way to London as a military observer, spent a day in Eisenhower's office that spring and remembered "listening to the discussions of problems and studies brought to him by officers of the Operations Division, by other sections of the War Department, by naval officers, Congressmen, committees, and by the endless chain of visitors that passed through his office during his long days." Truscott was impressed by Eisenhower's calm, steady manner. "Every view was considered. Each problem was carefully analyzed." Eisenhower had an "extraordinary ability to place his finger at once upon the crucial fact in any problem or the weak point in any proposition . . .

[and] to arrive at quick and confident decisions." Equally impressive was Eisenhower's "charming manner and unfailing good temper."[39]

Keeping track of decisions made, messages to be sent, orders given, and all the other details was itself a challenging task. Eisenhower, who later in the war and again as President would show that he was an eager recipient of the latest gadgets and technology, solved the problem by wiring his office with Dictaphones that picked up and recorded every word uttered in the room. Secretaries transcribed the recordings into notes and memoranda for the officers of OPD, which made it possible for them to be aware of all decisions reached and to get out the appropriate orders without further reference to Eisenhower. Eisenhower did inform all his visitors of the system, explaining that it saved him hours of work.[40]

Crucial to all his work was intelligence. To make realistic decisions and to prepare realistic plans, he needed to know the strength of the enemy, his dispositions, and—if possible—his intentions. But intelligence was one area that Marshall and his predecessors had badly neglected. Eisenhower found a "shocking deficiency" in the field of intelligence. The Intelligence Division (G-2) in the War Department was staffed by "estimable, socially acceptable gentlemen" who had been assigned to their overseas posts on the basis of their finances—unless they were independently wealthy, they could not afford the expense of living in foreign capitals. As a consequence, "results were almost completely negative." Fortunately, Eisenhower had his own common sense to draw on, one of the most important traits of the consumer of intelligence, because the providers can sometimes get carried away. Thus when the U.S. military attaché in Rumania was finally released from internment in early 1942 and reported to the War Department, Eisenhower and his staff immediately debriefed him. The attaché was convinced that Germany could not be beaten. He cited, as one proof, the existence of forty thousand combat aircraft that the Luftwaffe was holding in reserve. Eisenhower scoffed at this; it just did not seem to him to be possible that Hitler would have held forty thousand airplanes out of the battle of Moscow, which had just been concluded and which the Germans had lost. Eisenhower, of course, was right, his agent wrong.[41]

Working in daily contact with the units in the field, as well as preparing plans on grand strategy, gave Eisenhower a realistic sense of the scope of modern war. In late February, he had been complaining in his diary about both MacArthur and King. (King was "an arbitrary, stubborn type, with not too much brains and a tendency toward bullying his juniors.") The outburst led him to write a sentence that described the essence of Eisenhower's leadership style, both as a general and as

President. "In a war such as this, when high command invariably involves a president, a prime minister, six chiefs of staff, and a horde of lesser 'planners,' there has got to be a lot of patience—no one person can be a Napoleon or a Caesar."[42] Eleven years later he made the same point more vividly, when as President-elect he wrote in his diary, "Winston [Churchill] is trying to relive the days of World War II. In those days he had the enjoyable feeling that he and our president were sitting on some . . . Olympian platform . . . and directing world affairs from that point of vantage. But . . . many of us who, in various corners of the world, had to work out the solutions for . . . problems knew better."[43] Of all the generals, Eisenhower himself came closest to a Napoleonic role, but he would never make such a comparison. Having been a staff officer for so long himself, he was acutely aware of the importance of his staff to him; he was just as acutely aware of the indispensability of the subordinates in the field commands who carried out his orders. He had no false modesty, was conscious of the crucial nature of the role he played, but he never thought of himself as a Napoleon. Always, his emphasis was on the team. The only difference in his Presidency was that he applied the principle on an even wider scale. He was not self-effacing, but realistic, aware that there were definite limits on his powers and keeping his self-image in perspective.

Throughout the winter and early spring of 1942, Eisenhower continued to move up in Marshall's esteem. Marshall had been impressed by the smooth relations Eisenhower had established with the British at the Arcadia conference, held in Washington from late December to mid-January. Eisenhower attended the meetings as Gerow's deputy, and it was apparent that the British liked him. This in itself was unusual. Many American officers found their British opposite numbers to be insufferable not only in their arrogance but in their timidity about striking the enemy. Such officers could not hide their feelings. Nor could most of the British officers, whose ingrained sense of superiority led them to an ill-concealed dislike for their partners, whom they regarded as amateurs. What impressed Marshall was that Eisenhower, to a large extent, was able to rise above the national rivalries and concentrate on the positive aspects of the Alliance. Eisenhower's ability to remain calm and reasonable at Allied conferences was the more remarkable because he himself shared many of the anti-British prejudices of his colleagues. Thus on January 5 he wrote in his diary, "The conversations with the British grow wearisome. They're difficult to talk to, apparently afraid someone is trying to tell them what to do and how to do it. Their practice of war is dilatory."[44] A few days later the topic was aid to China:

"British, as usual, are scared someone will take advantage of them even when we furnish everything."[45] On February 5, he remarked that the British "are certainly stiff-necked."[46] But he kept these feelings to himself—Fox Conner had told him that working with allies would be difficult, but that it had to be done—and the British officers in Washington thought him fair-minded and objective.

The main concern of Arcadia was to agree on a plan for an offensive in the European theater in 1942. That Europe would be the main theater was taken for granted, despite MacArthur's plea that Asia generally and the Philippines particularly should come first. Sitting behind Marshall at the conference, listening daily to discussions of global strategy, Eisenhower's own views broadened. At first, he had protested against sending American troops to Northern Ireland, and by implication against the concentration of resources against the European enemy. He managed to stop part of one convoy destined for Ireland and sent it to Australia instead, but that did not satisfy him. "Damn 'em, I tried," he scribbled in his diary, "but I don't wear 45s. We're going to regret every damn boat we sent to Ireland."[47] On January 17 he had wanted to "drop everything else" and go all out in the Far East. By January 22, however, a dramatic switch had occurred. "We've got to go to Europe and fight," he wrote, "and we've got to quit wasting resources all over the world, and still worse, wasting time." Arcadia, Marshall's persuasive abilities, hard military facts, and broadened responsibilities had caused him to change his mind. He criticized the British, the American General Staff (and himself), when he wrote, "Everybody is too much engaged with small things of his own," adding, five days later, "We can't win by . . . giving our stuff in driblets all over the world." Piecemeal reinforcement should give way to concentrated counterattacks. Eisenhower now advocated a program of keeping Russia in the war, holding a defensive line in the Far East, and then "slugging with air at West Europe, to be followed by a land attack as soon as possible."[48]

It was a bold program, too bold for the British, who regarded Eisenhower's proposal of a direct assault on the French coast as wildly impractical. Rejecting American impetuousness, they advocated instead hitting the Germans with a series of blows against their periphery—Norway, North Africa, Greece—and waiting for Germany to wear itself down in the war against Russia before attempting a cross-Channel invasion. No final decision was reached at Arcadia, except to agree to continue the shipment of American troops to Northern Ireland.

Marshall then put Eisenhower to work drafting a plan for the first offensive. Eisenhower spent most of February on it. His overview was simple: "We've got to keep Russia in the war and hold India. Then we can get ready to crack Germany through England."[49] There was a need for haste, as the Germans would certainly launch another offensive in Russia in the spring of 1942, and the Red Army's chances of survival seemed poor. "We've got to . . . build up air and land forces in England," Eisenhower wrote, "and, when we're strong enough, go after Germany's vitals, and we've got to do it while Russia is still in the war, in fact, only by doing it soon can we keep Russia in."[50]

If soon, then where? Eisenhower recommended "an attack through Western Europe." In support of his proposal, he pointed out that the major Allied problem was shortage of ships; an attack through Western Europe used the shortest possible sea routes. The sea-lanes to Britain had to be maintained in any event, so there need be no dispersal of warships escorting convoys. Building a base in Britain for the U.S. Army would, by itself, constitute a threat to the French coast and thus force the Germans to maintain and increase their defenses. The railroad and highway networks in Western Europe were superior to those available "in any other area from which either enemy can be attacked." Britain already had airfields from which a large air force could operate to secure air superiority, a *sine qua non* of a successful assault. "Nowhere else is there such a base, so favorably situated with respect to either of our enemies." Speed was essential, both to relieve pressure on Russia and to take advantage of the fact that Germany was heavily involved in desperate battles hundreds of miles inside Russia.

Eisenhower's plan had the ring of Horace Greeley's "Forward to Richmond" cry in the summer of 1861—gear up, hit the enemy a concentrated blow in one big battle, and then on to his capital. The United States had been in the war for only three months, had no combat-ready divisions in England, could expect to get few there before 1943, had an untrained, inadequately equipped air force that had no combat experience, a Navy whose principal fighting ships rested at the bottom of the sea and which had hardly any assault landing craft (and few building), and a General Staff that had no real intelligence arm. Yet Eisenhower was proposing that this nation come to grips with the mighty Wehrmacht and Luftwaffe in an all-out campaign on the plains of northwestern Europe.[51] But despite its overly ambitious nature, Marshall approved, and set Eisenhower to drawing up a detailed proposal.

By late March, Eisenhower and his staff had a specific plan ready. The code name was Roundup. It called for a force of 5,800 combat airplanes and an eventual total of forty-eight infantry and armored divisions, half of them British, assaulting the French coast between Le Havre and Boulogne, northeast of the mouth of the Seine River, with a target date of April 1, 1943. Meanwhile raids and forays along the coast should be mounted to harass the Germans, and if necessary, Sledgehammer, a suicide operation designed to take the pressure off the Russians in the event a Russian surrender appeared imminent, could be mounted in September 1942. The emphasis, however, was on Roundup, the 1943 cross-Channel assault.[52]

Marshall took Eisenhower's plan to Roosevelt, who approved and told Marshall to fly to London to obtain British agreement. Marshall left on April 7 for six days of conferences. The British finally agreed to Roundup, although as Marshall told Eisenhower when he returned, many British officers "hold reservations." Eisenhower noted in his diary, "I hope that, at long last, and after months of struggle by this division, we are all definitely committed to one concept of fighting. If we can agree on major purposes and objectives, our efforts will begin to fall in line and we won't be just thrashing around in the dark."[53]

The buildup phase of American power in Britain, which was code named Bolero and which was to begin immediately, ran into trouble at the outset. The President, responding to pressure from the Australian government, the U.S. Navy, and MacArthur, decided to increase the U.S. ground forces in Australia by twenty-five thousand men. Eisenhower drafted a memorandum for Marshall to present to the President, pointing out that such action would jeopardize Bolero.[54] Admiral King entered the fray, writing Roosevelt that "important as the mounting of Bolero may be, the Pacific problem is no less so, and is certainly more urgent." Marshall, for his part, told Roosevelt flatly that he would have to choose between Bolero and Australia. In his own adroit fashion, Roosevelt said he had never meant to send the men to Australia, that he had only wanted the possibilities studied. Now that he knew the cost, he declared bluntly, "I do not want Bolero slowed down."[55] The incident was settled, Bolero saved, but Eisenhower was apprehensive. Such meddling by the President destroyed the value of staff planning. "Bolero is supposed to have the approval of the president and prime minister," he wrote. "But the struggle to get everyone behind it and to keep the highest authority from wrecking it . . . is never ending." Turning to a more general theme, he added, "The actual fact is that not one man in twenty in the Govt (including W. and N. Depts) realizes what a grisly, dirty, tough business we are in!"[56]

Eisenhower continued to worry about landing craft, so essential a part of any amphibious invasion. He did not quarrel with the Navy's program of giving top priority to building escort vessels for convoys, as there could be no Bolero if the convoys could not get to England. But the Navy was also rebuilding its capital ship fleet, at the expense of landing craft. On the morning of May 6, Eisenhower met with Navy officers to ask who was responsible for building landing craft, what type were being built, how many were under way, etc. He could not get clear answers, and commented disgustedly, "How in hell can we win this war unelss we can crack some heads?"[57]

Marshall too was disturbed at the lack of progress, not only on specific equipment but on Bolero in general. He was concerned about the senior U.S. Army officer currently in London, Major General James E. Chaney, who had been in England for more than a year, originally as military observer. Marshall doubted that Chaney had the qualities required to command what Marshall expected would become the major U.S. Army base overseas, and he was concerned by the poor communications between Chaney and OPD; as Eisenhower put it, "either we do not understand" Chaney and his staff, "or they don't understand us." Marshall decided to send Eisenhower to London to see what could be done about improving the situation (and to give the British an opportunity to see Eisenhower on his own and get their reaction to him, as he already had it in mind to replace Chaney with Eisenhower).[58]

On May 23, Eisenhower flew to Montreal, then on to Goose Bay, Labrador. Bad weather forced him to spend a night and a day at Gander, Newfoundland, where he shot skeet while taking his first day off in half a year. On May 25 he made it to Prestwick, Scotland, where a British driver, Mrs. Kay Summersby (a divorcée), a young and attractive Irishwoman with sparkling eyes and a pert smile, extremely chatty but a bit awed by being in the presence of a general, met him. She drove him to an exercise involving landing craft, and they visited the birthplace of Robert Burns and scenes associated with Robert Bruce.[59] That evening Eisenhower took the train to London, arriving the next morning and spending the day in conference with Chaney and his staff. He was appalled by what he saw. Chaney and his assistants "were completely at a loss," stuck in a "back eddy,"[60] still wearing civilian clothes, working an eight-hour day, and taking weekends off. They knew none of the British high command and had no contacts with the British government.

On May 27 Eisenhower observed a field exercise in Kent, under the direction of Lieutenant General Bernard Law Montgomery. Later Eisenhower attended a lecture at which Montgomery explained the exercise. Montgomery wore a field greatcoat which emphasized his own small physical stature and tiny steps. He had a permanent scowl that gave him a crabbed look. He was, by nature, condescending, especially toward Americans, most of whom regarded him with extreme distaste. While he lectured, Eisenhower calmly lit a cigarette. He had taken about two puffs when Montgomery broke off in midsentence, sniffed the air with his nose held high, and demanded, "Who's smoking?" "I am," Eisenhower replied. "I don't permit smoking in my office," Montgomery said sternly. Eisenhower did not permit the bad start to color his view of Montgomery; when he got back to the States he reported that Montgomery was "a decisive type who appears to be extremely energetic and professionally able." [61]

During his ten days in Britain, Eisenhower met two other officers with whom he was destined to spend a great deal of time. One was General Alan Brooke, the Chief of the Imperial General Staff. Brooke, a fiery Irishman with impressive credentials, carried throughout the war the handicap of a deep-seated prejudice against the Americans. After his first meeting with Marshall, Brooke had commented that Marshall was "rather overfilled with his own importance," a unique judgment. Brooke admitted that Marshall was "a pleasant and easy man to get on with [a conclusion he would later change]. But I should not put him down as a great man." [62] Brooke's comments on Eisenhower, from beginning to end, were similar but more scathing. He put Eisenhower down as an affable type with no strategic sense or command ability. Eisenhower's own practice was to either say something nice about an associate or not mention him at all, and he seldom mentioned Brooke.

With Vice-Admiral Lord Louis Mountbatten, however, Eisenhower struck up an immediate and lifelong friendship. Mountbatten, young, titled, handsome, wealthy, already had a distinguished record in the Royal Navy, but unlike men like Montgomery and Brooke, he rather liked Americans and responded with special warmth to Eisenhower. The two men got on famously from their first meeting. What drew them together, aside from personality, was that both were offensive-minded, committed to the earliest possible attack against the French coast, and thus keenly interested in the development of landing craft. They agreed that the bigger those craft, the better, and they wanted as many as possible. Eisenhower was also much impressed by the way Mountbatten had created a joint staff of British Army, Navy, and Air officers at Combined Operations, an organization that was planning amphibious assault techniques.[63]

On June 3, Eisenhower returned to Washington, dissatisfied with what he had seen. Except for Mountbatten, it was clear that none of the British high command really believed in Roundup, much less Sledgehammer; it was equally clear that Chaney would have to be replaced. Eisenhower noted in his diary, "It is necessary to get a punch behind the job or we'll never be ready by spring, 1943, to attack. We must get going." [64] He recommended that Marshall appoint Major General Mark Clark to the command of the American ground forces in England and send him over to London at once; Marshall did so. Marshall rejected, however, Eisenhower's recommendation for a replacement for Chaney. Eisenhower wanted the post of theater commander to go to Major General Joseph McNarney, an Army Air Force officer who had been one of the first to urge a cross-Channel attack. Because most of the early strength in Bolero would take the form of air power, Eisenhower thought an Army Air Force officer should be in command. But Marshall wanted McNarney as his Deputy Chief of Staff and said no to the recommendation.[65]

Marshall in fact already had Eisenhower in mind for the job. Churchill had reported to Marshall that the British high command liked Eisenhower personally and were impressed by his dedication to the Alliance. The day before Eisenhower returned from England, Mountbatten had arrived in Washington for a conference; to both Roosevelt and Marshall, Mountbatten praised Eisenhower and said the British were quite ready to work with him as the senior American officer in Britain. Army Air Forces Chief of Staff Henry Arnold, who had accompanied Eisenhower to Britain, and Mark Clark, who had also been on the trip, had agreed among themselves that Chaney's successor "should be Ike." Arnold had passed this recommendation on to Marshall. (As Eisenhower had recommended Clark for the post of ground forces commander in Britain, Marshall later told Clark, "It looks to me as if you boys got together.")[66]

Not that Marshall needed any urging. For six months he had been in daily, often hourly, contact with Eisenhower. He had given Eisenhower broad responsibilities and a wide scope. Not once had Eisenhower let him down. Eisenhower had become his protégé, showing a remarkable ability to think like Marshall, to anticipate his chief's wishes, to accept his views and translate them into action. Marshall appreciated the manner in which Eisenhower accepted responsibility and, even more, Eisenhower's offensive-mindedness, his calm confidence that if the Allies made an all-out effort, they could successfully invade France in 1943. Marshall also felt that Eisenhower could get along with the British better than any other officer in the U.S. Army.

On June 8, Eisenhower took to Marshall a draft directive for the commander of the European Theater of Operations (ETO), a name Eisenhower himself had given the London command. Eisenhower urged "that absolute unity of command should be exercised by the Theater Commander," who should organize, train, and command the American ground, naval, and air forces assigned to the theater. As Eisenhower handed the draft to Marshall, he asked the Chief to study it carefully because it could be an important document in the further waging of the war. Marshall replied, "I certainly do want to read it. You may be the man who executes it. If that's the case, when can you leave?"[67] Three days later Marshall appointed Eisenhower to the command of ETO.

Marshall's decision appeared more momentous in retrospect than it did at the time. Eisenhower had noted in his diary, "It's a big job; if the U.S.-U.K. stay squarely behind Bolero and go after it tooth and nail, it will be the biggest American job of the war." But he realized that "command now does not necessarily mean command in the operation."[68] The general assumption in June 1942 was that Roundup would be launched in the spring of 1943 with Marshall himself in command, and Eisenhower as his chief of staff. Marshall's association with Eisenhower had convinced him that Eisenhower would work perfectly in that assignment, and that in the meantime Eisenhower could put some energy into the Bolero program. The major factor in Marshall's thinking, however, was simple and direct. After the war, speaking of Eisenhower's promotion, Marshall commented, "If he hadn't delivered he wouldn't have moved up."[69]

Eisenhower spent the next two weeks preparing for his departure, conferring with various government officials and his OPD associates. He paid a call on Admiral King, and was delighted when King promised him the full support of the Navy in this unique venture of creating a genuinely unified field command for all three services. King said he would see to it that Eisenhower was in fact as well as in name the "commander" of U.S. Navy forces in the British Isles and added that if any naval officer questioned Eisenhower's single authority, Eisenhower should report it to him at once.[70]

Another vote of confidence came from an unexpected source and caused Eisenhower considerable embarrassment. Manuel Quezon had arrived from the Pacific to plead the cause of the now-occupied Philippines. He called on Eisenhower in the War Department. After catching up with the news about the fate of individual friends in the Philippines, Eisenhower was startled when Quezon offered him an honorarium for his services to the Commonwealth in the late thirties. Eisenhower did not record the amount offered, but it was probably more than $100,000. Eisenhower would not accept the money. He explained to Quezon that for him to do so might well lead to a misimpression and thus "destroy whatever usefulness I may have to the allied cause in the present war." Eisenhower's attitude contrasted sharply with MacArthur's, who in early 1942 accepted $500,000 in cash from Quezon, while his chief of staff received $75,000, with somewhat smaller amounts going to lesser officers.[71]

The Eisenhowers could have used the money. With her husband

leaving Washington, Mamie had to move out of their just acquired quarters at Fort Myer. Luckily, she found a small apartment at the Wardman; to save money, she asked Ruth Butcher to share the apartment and the expenses. Harry Butcher, who had joined the Navy and been commissioned as a lieutenant commander, was going along to London with Eisenhower as his "naval aide"—King had made special arrangements at Eisenhower's request after Eisenhower explained that he wanted one old, close friend with him.

The weekend before Eisenhower left, John got a leave and took the train from West Point to spend two days with his parents. Father and son discussed life at the Academy, some of the conversations taking place in Eisenhower's bedroom, as he was flat on his back as a result of taking his typhus, tetanus, smallpox, and typhoid injections all on the same day. When John had to leave, on Sunday afternoon, he hugged his mother, shook hands with his father, and marched down the gravel path to a waiting taxi. At the door he stopped, did an about-face, and—wearing his full cadet uniform—snapped his hand up to his visor in a formal salute. It was more than Mamie could bear; she burst into tears. It was the last family get-together until after the war.[72]

On June 19, just before leaving, Eisenhower wrote a friend, Brigadier General Spencer Akin, who was on MacArthur's staff, a summary of his six months' experience in WPD-OPD. It had been a "tough, intensive grind," Eisenhower said, "but now I'm getting a swell command." It meant the world to him that he had gained Marshall's confidence, because he felt "the Chief is a great soldier." Eisenhower described Marshall as "quick, tough, tireless, decisive and a real leader. He accepts responsibility automatically and never goes back on a subordinate." The last point was particularly important; Eisenhower felt that his greatest asset in London would be the knowledge that as long as he did his job, Marshall would stand behind him.[73] Marshall had almost as high an opinion of Eisenhower, but all of Eisenhower's achievements, to date, had been as a staff officer serving under strong-willed superiors. All his superiors, including MacArthur, thought he would be a success as an independent commander, but that was only prediction. No one really knew how he would react when commanding on his own, away from the daily influence of a decisive superior. But Eisenhower himself was confident.

UNLESS OTHERWISE NOTED, ALL PHOTOS ARE COURTESY OF THE EISENHOWER LIBRARY.

Earliest known photograph of Dwight Eisenhower, at age three, taken in 1893 shortly after the family moved back to Abilene. Arthur is holding Roy, while Edgar is standing behind Dwight.

In 1901, Dwight entered fifth grade at Lincoln Elementary School, just across the street from his home. Emma Wolfe, in the upper left corner, was his teacher. Dwight is second from the left in the front row.

A family snapshot, taken in 1907 when Dwight was 17. Dwight is in the middle, Milton on the left, Earl on the right. The dog, Flip, was Dwight's; when he left for West Point he told Milton and Earl to take good care of Flip.

Two family portraits, a quarter of a century apart. The first was taken in 1902, the second during a family reunion in 1926. David, Milton, and Ida in the front row; Dwight, Edgar, Earl, Arthur, and Roy in the back row. At the 1926 reunion, Dwight asked Edgar if he wanted to box. Edgar hastily declined. But in 1902, he was beating up Little Ike on a regular basis.

A camping trip on the Smoky Hill River, circa 1907. Dwight is second from the left, seated. He organized such trips on a regular basis. Here, and with the Abilene High School football and baseball teams, he first showed his talents for organization and leadership.

Dwight, aged 20, en route to West Point, stopped in Chicago to visit his high school friend Ruby Norman. She took this snapshot on June 9, 1911, on South Michigan Avenue. By fall 1911, Eisenhower was a full-fledged plebe, a member of the Corps of Cadets. He had learned to stand straight, get his shoulders back, his chest out, and hold his head up. He was to learn much more.

Following graduation from West Point, Eisenhower went home to Abilene before reporting for duty at Fort Sam Houston. Here he is with Jake Kruger of Abilene, on their way to a baseball game.

Wedding portrait, Denver, July 1, 1916. Mamie took one look and decided he was the handsomest man she had ever seen. He took one look at her and lost his heart. They married within the year.

Camp Meade, Maryland, 1919. Eisenhower poses beside one of the small tanks with which he and George Patton were experimenting. Each man advocated faster tanks that would operate en masse, independently; each was reprimanded for advancing views that went counter to current doctrine.

Eisenhower on the U.S. Army's first transcontinental convoy. On July 13, 1919, he had his snapshot taken at the Firestone Homestead in Ohio.

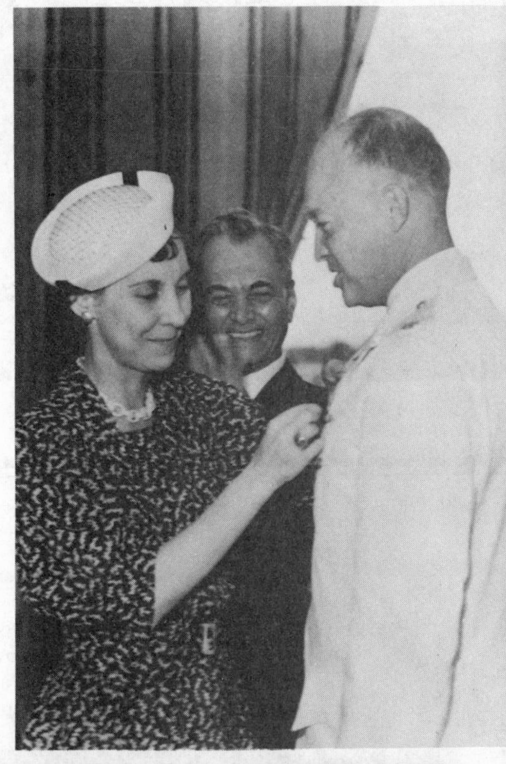

Captain T. J. Davis and Lt. Colonel Eisenhower with General MacArthur, Manila, 1935.

Mamie pins the Distinguished Service Star of the Philippines on Lt. Colonel Eisenhower, December 12, 1939, Manila. President Quezon of the Philippines looks on. This was Mamie's favorite picture of herself and her husband together.

Christmas in the Philippines, 1938. *Left to right,* Eisenhower, Mrs. Jean MacArthur, Paul V. McNutt, the U.S. High Commissioner, Mamie, and General MacArthur.

An obscure colonel in 1941, two years later Eisenhower was working on an intimate basis with the most powerful men in the Allied world. Below left, he is with George Marshall at a press conference in Algiers, June 2, 1943; with Franklin Roosevelt en route to Malta, December 8, 1943; with Winston

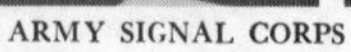

ARMY SIGNAL CORPS

Far left, in 1938, the Eisenhowers returned to the States for a visit. They stopped off in Abilene, where Eisenhower and his mother posed for John Eisenhower's camera. Ida was then 76 years old, Dwight 47.

Left, the Eisenhowers at Fort Lewis, Washington, preparing a picnic for a group of Army friends, 1941.

Right, November 14, 1941, during the Louisiana maneuvers. This photo went out over the wire services and gave Eisenhower his first national publicity. He sent a print to his parents.

Churchill, leaving a pre-Overlord briefing in May 1944; and below, with his British colleagues at Villa dar el Ouard, June 3, 1943—Eden, Brooke, Tedder, Cunningham, Alexander, Marshall, Montgomery, and Eisenhower surround Churchill.

ARMY SIGNAL CORPS

The two most important women in the Supreme Commander's life were Kay Summersby and Mamie. In Algiers, he posed for a snapshot by Harry Butcher with Kay. In his office in the St. George Hotel, he is reading a letter from Mamie. His hundreds of letters to Mamie during the war were full of his love and concern for his wife, but they also reveal a sometimes testy husband who felt his wife did not understand him. Like millions of others, he found that the long wartime separation put a strain on his marriage.

Eisenhower with his troops. Throughout the war, he got information and inspiration by visiting with the men. His first question, invariably, was, "Where are you from?" His easy rapport with the men, exemplified by his eye contact, was a part of his magic as a commander.

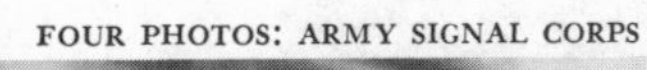

FOUR PHOTOS: ARMY SIGNAL CORPS

Eisenhower, Tedder, and Montgomery observe armored maneuvers at Gillingham, England, March 1, 1944.

THREE PHOTOS: ARMY SIGNAL CORPS

Eisenhower on board the British mine layer *Apollo,* June 7, 1944, off the Norman coast, studying the invasion beach.

Eisenhower and Charles de Gaulle in Granville, Normandy, outside the Supreme Allied Commander's headquarters, August 21, 1944. De Gaulle was urging on Eisenhower the military benefits of liberating Paris immediately; Eisenhower wanted to bypass the city.

Eisenhower and his lieutenants, Bradley and Patton, in Bastogne, February 5, 1945.

Eisenhower, Bradley, and Patton examine art treasures looted by the Germans and stored in a salt mine.

TWO PHOTOS: ARMY SIGNAL CORPS

Eisenhower and an interpreter question an inmate at the Ohrdruf Nord concentration camp, April 13, 1945. Patton, who was there, thought the man "was such a well-fed-looking person that I had an idea he might have been one of the executioners." Two days later, the man was torn limb from limb by his inmate victims. Eisenhower's face seems to sum up the world's reaction to the revelation of the full extent of the Nazi horror.

AP

ARMY SIGNAL CORPS

CRAIG CANNON

Opposite, top left, Eisenhower arriving at Washington National Airport, June 18, 1945. "Oh God," he said as he stepped on American soil, "it's swell to be back."

Opposite, top right, Eisenhower and Marshal Georgi K. Zhukov, Leningrad, August 1945. Eisenhower was determined to get along with the Russians; his excellent personal relations with Zhukov encouraged him to believe that postwar cooperation was possible.

Opposite, in May 1946, Chief of Staff Eisenhower took an extended inspection trip to the Pacific; he relaxed in Hawaii before going on to Japan.

Above, Eisenhower and his son leaving a banquet in Washington, D.C., June 19, 1945.

Right top, the successful fisherman does not have to lie about his catch. Minoqua, Wisconsin, July 27, 1946.

Right, Mamie's birthday party, November 14, 1947; Eisenhower had just given her the mink coat—her first—as a birthday present.

Right bottom, Eisenhower with two of his grandchildren, Anne and David, November 3, 1951.

ARMY SIGNAL CORPS

STARS AND STRIPES

April 1951. Eisenhower has just been told that Truman has fired MacArthur.

Eisenhower and Dean Acheson, June 2, 1952. Although Eisenhower had been closely involved in the creation of the Truman-Acheson foreign policy, as a candidate for the presidency, Eisenhower was a vigorous critic of that policy; the Democrats, for their part, were furious with Eisenhower because of what they considered his hypocrisy.

As President of Columbia University. He did a better job than he was given credit for, and he enjoyed the job more than most people suspected.

UP

INS

EISENHOWER AND TRUMAN. Their relationship was cordial in 1945, close in 1946–48, and intimate in 1951. But in 1952 it disintegrated to one of complete hostility. At Potsdam, July 21, 1945, with Patton. On the White House lawn, June 1, 1952, with Robert Lovett, Secretary of Defense, and Frank Pace, Secretary of the Army. In the Oval Office, November 18, 1952, at the transition meeting.

ARMY SIGNAL CORPS

UP

Eisenhower and Taft, Chicago, July 1952, immediately after Eisenhower's nomination. The candidate's first impulse was to reach out to Taft and get him on the team.

AP

Following the nomination, Eisenhower went to Fraser, Colorado, for a brief vacation. Nixon came to spend an afternoon. It was only their second meeting. Eisenhower is attempting to introduce Nixon to the art of casting a fly rod; in casting, as in politics, Eisenhower was terribly earnest in his attempts to educate Nixon, with frustrating results in both cases.

CHAPTER TEN

London

June 24–September 15, 1942

ON JUNE 24, Eisenhower arrived in England. There were no bands to greet him, no speeches at the airport, no ceremonies. It was almost the last time in his life he would have such a quiet arrival anywhere. On June 24, he was still unknown to the general public, in America as well as in Britain. In Washington, he was often referred to by those who did know him as "Milton's brother" or as "Marshall's assistant." But the day following his arrival in London, he held a press conference. An announcement was passed out identifying him as the commander of the American forces in Britain. From that moment forth, his life was dramatically and unalterably changed. He suddenly became a world figure, in the jargon of World War II, a Very Important Person, or VIP. It hardly mattered that his role was more that of an administrator than a commander, or that the numbers of men under him were relatively small (55,390 officers and men). Precisely because there were so few American forces in Britain, in fact, and because they were not involved in combat, Eisenhower received more coverage. His appointment was a front-page story. Every reporter in London, whether British or American, who could do so attended Eisenhower's first-ever press conference.

Eisenhower was destined to be a world figure from June 1942 until January 1961. In those two decades, virtually his every move, decision, habit, friendship, and action were observed and reported. No other public figure in America of his century, not even Franklin Roosevelt, spent so long a time under such close scrutiny; no other public figure, save only Roosevelt, was so popular with the working press; no other public figure, save the two Roosevelts, enjoyed such widespread and deep popularity with the American people. In his twenty years at the pinnacle, Eisenhower made countless decisions, engaged in innumerable actions; in almost every instance, with the glaring exceptions of the Darlan Deal of 1942, his handling of McCarthyism between 1952 and 1954, and his policies on civil rights, 1954 to 1961, he enjoyed an overwhelmingly favorable press coverage. It might be argued that Eisenhower was more successful at public relations than any other VIP of the twentieth century.

Eisenhower's talent for public relations set him apart from his two chiefs, MacArthur and Marshall, neither of whom ever established anything like the good relations with the press that Eisenhower did. Reporters enjoyed picking on MacArthur, with his bombastic ways and haughty manner; they had much more respect for Marshall, but never loved him as they did Eisenhower. And although MacArthur and Marshall differed in their styles—MacArthur craved the headlines while Marshall shunned them—they were alike in that neither man ever had much time for the press. Eisenhower always did. Eisenhower was fifty-one years old when he had his first encounter with a press conference. As in the five hundred or more that followed in the next twenty years, he was a great personal success. He immediately proved to be a genius, not only in the way he dealt with the reporters but also in the content of what he said. Eisenhower had a distinctive and unerring sense, as good as Roosevelt's, of what the public wanted to hear and how it would respond.

Eisenhower was so good at public relations, and his success in this area was so important to his career, that some analysis of how he did it is required. There was, first and foremost, the man himself. He *looked* like a soldier (and later, like a President). He dressed with care, in solid conservative taste, neither flamboyant like Patton nor carelessly like Grant. He stood erect, with his square, broad shoulders held back, his head high. His face and hands were always active, his face reddening with anger when he spoke of the Nazis, lighting up as he spoke of the immense forces gathering around the world to crush them. To cameramen, he was pure gold—for them a good photo of Eisenhower, whether tight-lipped and grim or laughing heartily, was usually worth at least two columns on the front page. His relaxed, casual manner was appealing, as was the nickname "Ike," which seemed to fit so perfectly. His good humor and good looks attracted people. Most reporters found it impossible to be in Eisenhower's presence and not like him. His mannerisms complemented his good looks. Recording before a newsreel camera for the movie-theater audience back in the States, he spoke with great earnestness directly into the camera, his eyes riveted on the invisible audience. It was a perfect expression of a devotion to duty that he felt deeply, and it electrified viewers. So too did his manner of speaking bluntly about the difficulties ahead, the problems that had to be met and overcome, all followed by that big grin and a verbal expression of Eisenhower's bouncy enthusiasm. He habitually used expressions that immediately identified him as just plain folks. He would speak of someone who "knows the score," someone else as a "big operator," or he would say, "I told him to go peddle his papers somewhere else." He called his superiors the "Big Shots." He made innumerable references to "my old home town, Abilene," and described himself as a "simple country boy," sighing and responding sadly to a question, "That's just too complicated for a dumb bunny like me."[1]

The more the public heard from and about Eisenhower, the more it liked him, and the more coverage he got in the Sunday supplements. Stories about his simple tastes were widely circulated. When he arrived in London, there was a suite waiting for him at Claridge's, then London's best and most expensive hotel. Its great advantage was that it was only three blocks from his office, at 20 Grosvenor Square, the heart of the American section of London, as it was the site of the embassy and most of the office buildings around the square were taken over by either U.S. State Department or Army and Navy personnel. There were so many Americans in the square, in fact, that the British took to calling it "Eisenhowerplatz." But, as the world soon learned, Eisenhower did not like his fancy quarters. The liveried footmen were not to his taste, nor was the ornate lobby, and he found his suite, with its black-and-gold sitting room and pink bedroom, appalling. He complained to Mickey that the sitting room "looks exactly like a funeral parlor," and to Butcher that the bedroom made him "feel as though I were living in sin."[2] After a week he moved to the more modern but less ostentatious Dorchester Hotel, also within easy walking distance of his office and across Park Lane from Hyde Park, which at that time was filled with anti-aircraft guns. At the Dorchester, his three-room suite had a functional living room and two simple bedrooms, one for Eisenhower and the other for Butcher. Eisenhower had only two complaints—the British plumbing, and living in the center of the West End, where he felt both cramped and overly conspicuous. He wanted a quiet place in the country where he could relax on an occasional weekend and escape the fishbowl existence he was subjected to in London. In August, Butcher found what was wanted, a small seven-room house in Kingston, Surrey, called Telegraph Cottage, forty minutes by car from Grosvenor Square. It was secluded, and was located on the edge of a golf course, so Eisenhower could play a few holes without being seen, shoot a pistol for sport, and settle down with his Wild West magazines in the evening. All this was widely reported; it was exactly the sort of thing the average American could and did identify with.

So too did the public respond positively to the stories about Eisenhower's "family." Tex Lee, Mickey McKeogh, and Harry Butcher were the first to be written about, but the others soon followed, including Kay Summersby and Mary Alice Jaqua, a secretary. The fact that Mickey wrote letters regularly to Eisenhower's wife and mother about his health and his doings was soon common knowledge. So was Eisenhower's acquisition of a dog—he had told Tex Lee to find one for him and Lee had picked up a pedigreed Scottie pup. Eisenhower named him Telek, a shortened form of Telegraph Cottage, and the newspapers described Telek as a symbol of Anglo-American friendship. That this powerful general liked dogs and needed to surround himself with his "family" was widely appreciated by the American public. So too were the anecdotes that illustrated his dislike of formality.[3]

Eisenhower's real family, and his background, also made ideal copy for feature writers. Reporters descended on Abilene to interview Ida and Ike's childhood friends. They were delighted by what they found, as were their readers—the classic American theme of a poor boy who made it big. If Eisenhower was not born in a log cabin, the shack in Denison, Texas, was close enough; if his family was not poverty-stricken, it was poor enough. Soon every literate American knew about the little white house in which Ida lived and Ike grew up. Small town, baseball, and motherhood—what American could resist such themes? Mamie too was besieged by reporters. She sought and followed Milton's advice; Milton said that the American people were entitled to know about the man who would lead their sons into battle, and it was Mamie's responsibility to cooperate with the reporters. Mamie tried to keep the interviews she granted on the subject of her husband, but enough was found out about her, and her photograph was taken often enough, for her to become a public figure too, her bangs and her smile known around the country. Mamie did manage to avoid most of the Washington social scene and to do some volunteer work, incognito, at servicemen's canteens in Washington.[4]

Eisenhower, in short, was an extremely likable person with a very attractive background and wife who came to the public's attention at exactly the right moment in the war. Nothing was happening in the European Theater to write about, but London was overrun with reporters looking for copy. As for personalities, the five most prominent Allied leaders in the early summer of 1942 were Churchill, Roosevelt, Marshall, Brooke, and MacArthur, none of whom could inspire in the general public feelings of identification as Eisenhower could. Much of Eisenhower's good press coverage came by his just being himself, and by coincidence.

But there was much more to his success than a fetching smile and the coincidence of timing. Eisenhower manipulated the press, for his own purposes and for the good of the Allied cause. Again with only Roosevelt as an exception, Eisenhower was more aware of the importance of the press, and better at using it, than any other public figure of his day. Partly this recognition was a result of his instincts and his common sense, but he had excellent teachers. His closest civilian friend, Harry Butcher, and Milton Eisenhower were media experts. Milton had been a working reporter in his youth, was in charge of public relations for the huge Department of Agriculture in the thirties, and was in 1942 serving as the number-two man in the Office of War Information, a position that made it possible for him to do his brother's image and reputation much good. Milton not only taught his brother about the importance of the press; he also supplied reporters with anecdotes about General Eisenhower and suggested stories and angles. On one important occasion—during the Darlan Deal—Milton went himself to the scene to protect his brother's reputation.

As to Butcher, Eisenhower said he wanted "Butch" along in London because "I've got to have someone I can relax with," but he was not unaware of Butcher's other assets. He set Butcher to keeping an office diary with at least one eye on posterity, but Butcher's main job was to serve as a full-time, if unofficial, public relations officer. In that capacity, Butcher was ideal. He had been a journalist, a magazine editor, and a CBS radio official. He knew many of the reporters personally, and he knew how to cultivate all of them. A reporter could always count on Butcher to find him a hotel room or a bottle of booze, to cut the red tape and get a story past the censor, or—with luck—to arrange an interview with the general. Most of all, Butcher provided good material—he was the one who made certain the press knew about Eisenhower's penchant for Wild West stories, about Telek, about the "family," about the general's simple tastes in living arrangements.

Good as Milton and Butcher were, they could have done little without the active cooperation of the subject himself. Eisenhower enjoyed meeting with the press, liked reporters as individuals, knew some of them himself from his long years in Washington, called them by their first names, posed for their photographs, flattered them not only by the attention he paid to them but by telling them that they had a crucial role to play in the war. Eisenhower believed that a democracy could not wage war without popular, widespread support for and understanding of the war effort, which only the press could supply. At his first press conference, he told the reporters that he considered them "quasi members of my staff," part of the "team," a thought that delighted the reporters no end, and he promised to be open and honest with them always. Only the most cynical of reporters could fail to respond to such blandishments. After the conference, Butcher remarked, "Watching Ike deal with the press, I don't think he needs a public relations adviser. He is tops." With the photographers, "no one but a Sunday school teacher with a class of nice girls could have been as obliging as Ike."[5] Thor Smith, a British officer who later became Eisenhower's public relations head at SHAEF, recalled that "the press idolized him" and at the same time liked him personally, because "he was their kind of a guy."[6] In fact, as Milton, Butcher, Smith, and later Jim Hagerty, could and did testify, being Eisenhower's press secretary was about as easy and rewarding a job for a public relations man as could be imagined.

Eisenhower's sense of public relations extended far beyond himself. He used the press to sell the idea of Allied unity. He believed that Anglo-American friendship was a *sine qua non* of final victory, and did all he could to make that friendship genuine and lasting. In the summer of 1942, his major effort was to smooth relations between the British public and the American soldiers, airmen, and sailors who were coming to the British Isles in ever-increasing numbers—eventually, more than two million young American men came to the United Kingdom. On an island only slightly larger than Colorado these men had to be sheltered, fed, trained, and equipped, all in the midst of a local population that was itself crowded and underfed. Adding to the problem, the GI came viewing himself as a warrior who had arrived to pull Britain out of a hole, while the British saw themselves as the ones who had held the fort while waiting for the Americans to make up their minds. The GIs were the best-paid soldiers in the world; most of them were unmarried; they had no compunction about blowing their pay. It bothered the British to see young men throwing so much money around and their own girls so eager to catch some for themselves. They could accept the fact that the Americans got more and better food, but were appalled at the waste. Everyone in London, it seemed, saw something about the Yanks they did not like. To Charles de Gaulle the GIs seemed "good-natured, bad-mannered."

Harold Nicolson expressed the reaction of many British aristocrats when he said the GIs were "conscious of their inferiority in training, equipment, breeding, culture, experience and history."[7] A popular London saying expressed a more general attitude: "The trouble with the Yanks is that they are overpaid, oversexed, overfed, and over here."

Eisenhower set out to improve the image. He ordered his commanders to conduct vigorous campaigns to persuade the soldiers to put some of their pay into war bonds, so as to cut down on the spending spree. He wanted the GIs informed about the current and past sacrifices of the British people. He instituted a program to instruct the troops in British customs, and he ordered that bus tours of London be organized, with the emphasis on the tours placed on the bombed-out sections of the city. He told his commanders to be personally responsible for the appearance of the GIs on the street in order to "convince the British that we are here not as muddling amateurs but as earnest, competent soldiers who know what we are about." He put special emphasis on the importance of saluting.[8]

Eisenhower worried more about reality than appearance, more about the fighting abilities than the military bearing of the young men sent to him. His major concerns were discipline and morale. Most of the GIs were well educated, independently minded youngsters who had been conscripted into the service and who were contemptuous of the ways of the old Army. They had certain obvious strengths, such as their mechanical ability, good health, and cocky optimism, and certain obvious weaknesses, chief of which was a tendency to be soft and to grouse, not only at the big things like the bad luck that had sent them instead of their neighbors to a war zone, but at any meal that was not hot. Worst of all, they were relatively untrained. Eisenhower insisted on intensive training and intensive discipline. He spent much of his time on the road, visiting units in the field, overseeing their training, explaining the purpose of the exercises to the officers and men. Eisenhower believed such explanations, and broader ones about the nature of the war, were critical for a citizen army in a democracy, so critical that he ordered the immediate relief of any commander who neglected "this important phase of training intelligent, patriotic Americans."[9]

Eisenhower told his commanders that he wanted to form, in Britain, "the best army that the United States has ever put into the field." To that end, one of Eisenhower's responsibilities was to choose the best commanders. In the summer of 1942, when he was still forming judgments, he wrote a West Point classmate explaining his criteria for selection. Eisenhower said he had "developed almost an obsession as to the certainty with which you can judge a division . . . merely by knowing its commander intimately." He was struck by "how infallibly the commander and unit are almost one and the same thing." Looking ahead, Eisenhower wrote, "This is a long tough road we have to travel. The men that can do things are going to be sought out just as surely as the sun rises in the morning. Fake reputations, habits of glib and clever speech, and glittering surface performance are going to be discovered and kicked overboard." For a man to make it in this war, he had to be a leader with "inexhaustible nervous energy . . . and iron-clad determination." He would also need imagination—Eisenhower confessed that he was "continuously astounded by the utter lack of imaginative thinking . . ."[10]

Eisenhower, the man at the top, was the most important individual in molding the British attitude toward the U.S. Army. He was aware of it, accepted the responsibility, and met it magnificently. London took him to her heart. He was so big, so generous, so optimistic, so intelligent, so outspoken, so energetic—so American. Besides being good copy personally, he represented the American military machine that was coming to win the war, so inevitably he was a center of attention. His relations with the London press were as good as with the American. The British appreciated reports that he took them as they were, neither trying to ape their mannerisms nor make fun of their ways. They laughed at an item that related Eisenhower's practice of levying on the spot a fine of twopence on any American who used a British phrase such as "cheerio." Another favorite London story concerned Eisenhower's heavy smoking—he consumed four packs of Camels a day. The American ambassador, deeply embarrassed, had told Eisenhower after a dinner party that it was the custom in England not to smoke at the dinner table before the toast to the King had been drunk. Eisenhower's response was that he would attend no more formal dinners. When Mountbatten nevertheless invited him to a dinner. Eisenhower said no. When Mountbatten pressed the point and assured Eisenhower he would not have to curtail his smoking, Eisenhower reluctantly agreed to go. After the sherry, the party sat down to soup. As soon as it was consumed, Mountbatten jumped to his feet and snapped, "Gentlemen, the King!" After the toast, he turned to Eisenhower and said, "Now, General, smoke all you want."[11] With such stories making the rounds, and with his picture in the papers frequently, Eisenhower became a great favorite in London. Taxi drivers would wave; people on the street would wish him good luck.

Beyond the rapport he established with the British public, he got on well with British leaders, best of all with Churchill himself. He soon became a regular weekend visitor at Churchill's country home, Chequers. Eisenhower's informality appealed to Churchill, and the

Prime Minister responded in kind. On the evening of July 5, for example, Eisenhower recorded in his diary, "We spent the early part of the evening on the lawn in front of the house, and . . . took a walk . . . into the neighboring woods, discussing matters of general interest in connection with the war." After dinner, they saw a movie, then talked until 2:30 A.M. Eisenhower slept that night in a bed Cromwell had slept in.[12] Mountbatten frequently accompanied Eisenhower on field exercises; when they went south of London they stayed overnight at Mountbatten's spacious country estate, Broadlands; when they went north, to Scotland, they stayed on his yacht.[13]

Admiral Sir Andrew B. Cunningham was another member of the British elite who, although he had little in common with the self-described "simple Kansas farmboy," became one of Eisenhower's close friends. Cunningham was the embodiment of the Royal Navy, a man of dignity and grace, striking in appearance, cool, competent, and aggressive in action. Eisenhower came to admire, almost to the point of adulation, many of his British associates, but none ever made quite the impression upon him that Cunningham did. Eisenhower described him as "vigorous, hardy, intelligent, and straightforward. . . . a real sea dog,"[14] and used him as a standard; thus so-and-so would be "almost as good as Cunningham."

For his part, Cunningham, in a postwar tribute, described how he—and most Britons—reacted to Eisenhower: "I liked him at once. He struck me as being completely sincere, straightforward and very modest. In those early days I rather had the impression that he was not very sure of himself; but who could wonder at that? He was in supreme command of one of the greatest amphibious operations of all time, and was working in a strange country . . . But . . . it was not long before one recognized him as the really great man he is—forceful, able, direct and far-seeing, with great charm of manner, and always with a rather naïve wonder at attaining the high position in which he found himself."[15]

Throughout the war, Eisenhower's good relations with the British leadership would be one of his great strengths. The friendships included the leading politicians, the RAF generals, the admirals, and the various British staff officers who worked at his headquarters. The only exceptions were the British Army generals, especially their two leaders, Montgomery and Brooke. Otherwise, Eisenhower's relations with the British could not have been better, or done more good for the cause of Anglo-American unity.

While Eisenhower was trying to sell the idea of Anglo-American unity in July 1942, on the strategic front little unity in fact existed. The absence of agreement made Eisenhower's job more complicated. In addition to setting up ETO, Eisenhower—promoted to lieutenant general in July—was directing planning for Sledgehammer, the 1942 suicide operation, and Roundup, the main invasion scheduled for April 1943. But the British would not support Sledgehammer. Instead they proposed, for the fall of 1942, an invasion of North Africa. In mid-July, Roosevelt sent Marshall, King, his adviser Harry Hopkins, and various aides to London with instructions to reach an agreement with the British. Brooke noted in his diary, "It will be a queer party, as Harry Hopkins is for operating in Africa, Marshall wants to operate in Europe, and King is determined to stick to the Pacific."[16] When he arrived, Marshall asked Eisenhower to prepare a specific plan for Sledgehammer. Eisenhower returned with a recommendation that the landing take place near Le Havre, that it be under British command with two U.S. divisions participating, and that the target date be September 15, 1942. He estimated that the chances of getting the lead division ashore were about one in two, while the chances of establishing a six-division beachhead were about one in five. In short, Sledgehammer had a 20 percent chance of success. That was far too great a risk to run, under almost any circumstances, but as Eisenhower wrote and then underscored, *"But we should not forget that the prize we seek is to keep 8,000,000 Russians in the war."* To allow the Red Army to collapse, Eisenhower argued, without making any effort to relieve the pressure on it, would make the Western Allies "guilty of one of the grossest military blunders of all history."[17] So he was willing to accept the risk and go ahead with Sledgehammer.

It was a dramatic recommendation, and a remarkable reflection of Eisenhower's "can do" attitude. But he was not only speaking for himself—he was also speaking for millions of Americans and a deeply rooted American tradition. Marshall felt it too, and he agreed with Eisenhower's conclusions. On July 20 he presented the plan to the British. For two days they argued. Brooke pounded away at Marshall, ridiculed Sledgehammer, noting scornfully that a failure would do the Russians no good, while even a success on a six-division scale would not draw German troops away from the Eastern Front. Marshall insisted that something had to be done to help the Russians, and Sledgehammer was the only operation that could do so. Eisenhower, who did not attend the meetings, fussed and fumed as he waited for the outcome. "The decisions to be made are not only highly secret but momentous," he wrote in his diary. "There is an atmosphere of tension that will disappear once the decisions are completed and we actually know what we are to do."[18]

Eisenhower and his staff "sat up nights . . . and tried to open our eyes clearly to see all the difficulties and not be blinded by a mere passion for doing something." Still, that word "something" stuck out. Something to show the Russians that the Western Allies really were on their side; something to give the British and American people "the feeling that they are attempting something positive."[19] Increasingly, in the CCS (Combined Chiefs of Staff) debates, Brooke used that last point against Marshall. Something had to be done in 1942. Sledgehammer was too risky with not enough payoff. The logical target, therefore, Brooke argued, was French North Africa.

Marshall and Eisenhower thought the idea absurd. Why go chasing nearly a thousand miles south of London to find an enemy to fight, when there were plenty of Wehrmacht troops stationed less than twenty-five miles from Dover? Going into North Africa, Marshall declared, would divert so many resources that it would put Roundup back from 1943 to 1944. The British, who were committed to a 1943 Roundup, at least on paper, argued that a North African operation would not force a postponement of Roundup, and stood firmly against Sledgehammer. On July 22, Marshall sent a cable to Roosevelt, admitting that he and the British were deadlocked. Roosevelt cabled back that as the British would not participate in Sledgehammer, the Americans would have to cooperate with them in an invasion of North Africa. Churchill, delighted, gave the new operation its code name, Torch. It would be the first joint Anglo-American offensive since the French and Indian War.

Eisenhower was darkly depressed by the decision. At breakfast on July 23 he told his ground commander, Mark Clark, "Well, I hardly know where to start the day." He thought that Wednesday, July 22, 1942, could well go down as the "blackest day in history."[20] He felt so strongly and took such an extreme view because he believed that the decision for Torch "rejects the thought that the allies can do anything to help the Russians," and that going to North Africa represented passive and defensive thinking. He was sure that Torch would preclude Roundup.[21] He was right, of course, but controversy will forever rage around the more general question, Was a 1943 invasion of the Continent possible? Each advantage for either side in 1943 is balanced by a disadvantage. German production of tanks, aircraft, and other weapons did not reach its peak until 1944, when the Wehrmacht was at its greatest strength, but the Luftwaffe was weaker in the West in 1944 than in 1943, primarily because of shortages of fuel. German defenses in the West, in troop strength, beach obstacles, and fixed gun emplacements, were more than twice as strong in June 1944 than in the spring of 1943.[22] In 1943 the Germans were fighting well inside Russia, making it more difficult for them to shift reinforcements from the East to the West. But Allied strength, in all categories, especially in the five critical areas of proved leadership, intelligence, aircraft, landing craft, and trained American divisions, was much less in 1943 than it would be in 1944. Marshall nevertheless believed that "if a great businessman were faced with pulling off [a] *coup* or going bankrupt he would strain every nerve to pull off the *coup* and would probably succeed," and Eisenhower agreed with him.[23] Most military historians do not.

One thing seems clear: the only chance the British and Americans had of winning the war sooner was to mount the cross-Channel attack earlier. The risks would have been greater, but so too would be the rewards. A successful Roundup might have concluded with British and American troops liberating Eastern Europe. The implications of that possibility are enough to justify Butcher's comment on July 16: "Upon the discussions to take place in the next few days may rest the future history of the world."[24] To indulge in one speculation: If Roundup had gone forward, and if it had worked, Eisenhower's armies might have gotten to Berlin in 1944, with incalculable consequences, not least for Eisenhower himself. As President in the 1950s, his foreign policy was in large part a reaction to two of the major results of the decision made on "the blackest day in history." The first result was Russian mistrust of the West, a mistrust based on the failure to open a promised Second Front in 1942 or even 1943, and a mistrust that became a paranoia and played a central role in the Cold War. The second result caused Eisenhower some of his most anxious moments in the White House—it was the Red Army occupation of Eastern Europe, which might have been prevented had the Western Allies gotten to Central Europe sooner. Roundup was the only way to do it, but it was never tried so never proved, nor disproved.

For Eisenhower personally, the decision for Torch was a godsend, as it eventually gave him his first field command. On July 25, the CCS met to discuss Torch. Someone needed to take charge of the planning. "Well, you've got him right here," Admiral King remarked. "Why not put it under Eisenhower?"[25] The British agreed, their idea being that Eisenhower could make the plans for Marshall, or someone else, who would take command later. The commander had to be an American, it was agreed, because Torch was aimed at French North Africa (Morocco, Algeria, and Tunisia), and the French, although neutral since June 1940, were furious at the British, first for deserting them at Dunkerque and leaving them to fight alone, then for British attacks on their fleet.

Marshall was pleased with Eisenhower's appointment; indeed, it was the only decision in the series of July conferences that did please him. He asked Eisenhower to come to his suite at Claridge's. When Eisenhower arrived, Marshall was in the washroom. Through the closed door he called out that Eisenhower was now in charge of planning for Torch and that he and King favored him for eventual command of the expedition.[26]

Eisenhower went immediately to work, and immediately another serious Anglo-American disagreement arose. This time roles were reversed. In planning the grand strategy of 1942 the Americans had been bold, the British cautious; but in working out the details of Torch, it was the British who were prepared to take great risks while it was the Americans—although not Eisenhower—who were cautious. The aim of Torch was to drive the Axis out of North Africa. Torch's role was to take Morocco, Algeria, and Tunisia while the British Eighth Army drove west from Egypt in what would be a gigantic pincers movement against Field Marshal Erwin Rommel's Afrika Korps. Enormous distances were involved; it was nearly eight hundred miles from Casablanca on the Atlantic coast of Morocco to Algiers, another four hundred from Algiers to Tunis. The Allies could reduce the distances they had to advance by landing as far to the east inside the Mediterranean as possible, thus putting them closer to Tunis—the main prize—and giving them a chance to get troops into Tunis before the Germans could occupy the city with troops sent through Italy and Sicily. The Allied problem was Spain. If Franco decided to join the war on Hitler's side, the Spanish might overrun Gibraltar, close off the Mediterranean, and thus cut the supply line of the Torch forces operating inside the Mediterranean. By taking Casablanca, on the African Atlantic coast, the Allies could insure their communications, as Casablanca was a good port and a railroad ran from it to Algiers.

Marshall's major objection to Torch was that North Africa was an awfully long way from Germany, but when Roosevelt ordered him to go ahead with the operation, he then advocated landings at Casablanca, which was an awfully long way from Tunis. Marshall wanted to hold down the commitment of resources to Torch, and at the same time he was concerned with the success of the initial landings and with the security of the supply lines. Casablanca was an easier target, and as Marshall explained, "A failure in Sledgehammer, for which the public has been adequately prepared, could have been accepted, but failure in Torch would only bring ridicule and loss of confidence."[27] The British could see no point to Torch if half its strength were directed against Morocco. There were sufficient ships and divisions for only two landings, and the British wanted both inside the Mediterranean, extending as far as Tunis itself, while Marshall would agree to only one "inside" landing, at Oran, with the other "outside," at Casablanca. The British said the heavy surf at Casablanca constituted a greater risk than the possibility of Spanish intervention at Gibraltar. Marshall disagreed.

Eisenhower wanted to go inside. The nearest Axis troops to Casablanca were fifteen hundred miles away. A glance at the map would show the Germans that Tunis was the ultimate target; from Sicily, only slightly more than one hundred miles away, they could rush troops into Tunis, and the French colonial forces there would probably not resist. Like the British, Eisenhower did not believe Franco would take Gibraltar, nor that Hitler had the surplus strength to overrun Spain and thus threaten Gibraltar. Eisenhower could see no good reason to terminate the seaborne phase of the amphibious assault one thousand miles away from the objective, which itself was on the coast and could be reached much quicker on ship than on foot. Opposed to Torch anyway, he reasoned that if it was going to be mounted, especially with himself in command, it should produce the maximum result at the cheapest price. Events were to show that he was right about Spain, right about a German take-over of Tunis before the Allies could get there, right about the time and manpower wasted on maintaining a line of communications on a single-track railroad from Casablanca to Algiers, and right about the probable French reaction (he doubted that the French would fight; Marshall supposed that they would). Still, Marshall insisted on following the safe course. He always hated being drawn into the Mediterranean and throughout the war he held back on commitments to the theater. This was not out of spite at not getting his way, but a result of his strongly held conviction that no matter how many resources the Allies put into the Mediterranean, no matter what risks they took and what great victories they won, nothing significant would ever come of it. The Mediterranean did not lead anywhere; the Germans were not going to lose the war by losing the Mediterranean. They would have to be beaten in northwest Europe.

As an adviser, Eisenhower had agreed with Marshall. But now he was in command himself (on August 14, the CCS issued the orders appointing him to command of Torch, with all naval, air, and ground forces of both countries committed to the operation taking their orders from him). He wanted to get the most out of Torch that he could. With his remarkable ability to shake a depression and bounce back, Eisenhower had assumed that attitude shortly after his gloomy July 23 breakfast with Clark. "From the instant that I was authorized to assume executive charge of the proposition," he wrote Marshall, "I laid down a specific charge to all subordinates that the time for analysing the wisdom of the original decision had passed—that we were going to . . . make the best possible plan within the framework of visible assets . . ."[28] Throughout August, Eisenhower insisted that the best possible plan was to take everything inside the Mediterranean, go as far east as possible (Eisenhower advocated Bône, a little more than a hundred miles west of Tunis), and accept the risk at Gibraltar. Marshall sent an aide to tell Eisenhower that even Algiers was too far east to land. With more ships, landings could be made both inside, at Algiers and Oran, and outside, but there were not sufficient warships to protect three convoys. Now it was Eisenhower's turn, like MacArthur before him, to demand a greater effort by the U.S. Navy. But Admiral King said No, there was nothing available, he was stretched too thin already.

The CCS inside-outside debate continued; it began to wear Eisenhower down. "For the past . . . weeks we have been living under conditions of strain, uncertainty, and tension," he noted in his diary.[29] He told Butcher he felt as if he were engaged in a "transatlantic essay contest."[30] Casablanca was out as far as the British were concerned, unless King could be forced to free up some warships; Marshall would not allow Eisenhower to go even to Algiers, much less Bône or Tunis, unless there was a simultaneous landing at Casablanca; unless the Allies went at least as far east as Algiers, the British saw no point to the operation. On August 15, Butcher remarked that, as far as he could tell, Marshall wanted to call the whole thing off. Eisenhower thought that was a real possibility.[31]

Time was pressing. If there was to be any operation before winter, detailed planning had to begin at once; detailed planning required a fixed target. Stalin was clamoring for help; Churchill had undertaken the task of going to Moscow to explain why there would be no Second Front in France and to emphasize the advantages of Torch. Churchill was sending daily cables from Moscow saying he wanted "superhuman efforts" behind Torch, and that he wanted it mounted soon. Meanwhile the British Chiefs of Staff sent a formal note to Eisenhower, saying that they were aware of his difficulties and did not want to embarrass him, but that they were "extremely anxious to get the plan settled."[32] So was Eisenhower, but he and Marshall, like London and Washington, remained deadlocked on the target selection.

• •

Although the debate on targets was unresolved, Eisenhower spent much of his time in August putting together a staff at Allied Force Headquarters (AFHQ). He put great stress on this project, which in his mind shared top priority with the transatlantic essay contest. As Butcher noted, "Ike is most worried when he is uncertain about an organizational pattern. Once the pattern clarifies in his mind, his brow unwrinkles."[33]

At AFHQ, Eisenhower had the unique challenge of creating a mixed staff of British and American officers who would work together on a daily, intimate, equal basis. His success in meeting the challenge played a major role in his victories in World War II and became one of his hallmarks. From the start, Eisenhower was aware of the importance of getting it done right. "There was no historical precedent" for the combined staff at AFHQ, he noted, and he considered his decisions in creating it "as among the most important and far-reaching" of the war.[34] Eisenhower insisted upon complete integration, across service lines as well as national lines. Thus at AFHQ, British Army officers worked beside American Navy officers, RAF personnel beside U.S. Army officers. Initially, Eisenhower recalled, they came together like a bulldog meeting a cat, but all realized that the job had to be done and they made valiant efforts to understand each other's accents, slang usages, and administrative practices. In large part, the integration was due to Eisenhower's driving example and insistence; he was, in his own words, a fanatic on the subject of Allied unity.[35]

Eisenhower's commitment to the Alliance became legendary. Many stories circulated to illustrate it; one concerned the time General Hastings Ismay, Churchill's chief staff officer, reported to Eisenhower that he had heard of an American officer who, when drinking at Claridge's, boasted that the Americans would show the British how to fight. Eisenhower "went white with rage." He summoned an aide and told him to arrange for the officer to report the next morning. As the aide left the office, Eisenhower hissed to Ismay, "I'll make the son of a bitch swim back to America." The officer was sent home—by boat. A week later, Eisenhower heard of a fracas between an American and a British officer on the AFHQ staff. He investigated, decided that the American was at fault, ordered him reduced in rank, and sent back to the States. The British officer involved called on Eisenhower to protest. "He only called me the son of a bitch, sir, and all of us have now learnt that this is a colloquial expression which is sometimes used almost as a term of endearment." To which Eisenhower replied, "I am informed that he called you a *British* son of a bitch. That is quite different. My ruling stands."[36]

AFHQ was located at Norfolk House on St. James's Square. Eisenhower's deputy was Mark Clark. The naval commander was Admiral Cunningham, an appointment that delighted Eisenhower. The British ground troops—organized as the British First Army—would be commanded by Lieutenant General Sir Kenneth Anderson.[37] One part of the American contingent would combat-load in Norfolk, Virginia, and sail across the Atlantic directly to its assault beaches. Eisenhower told Marshall he wanted Patton to command that force, and Marshall complied. The American troops coming out of Britain, organized as II Corps, would be led by Major General Lloyd Fredendall. Marshall had made the selection—Eisenhower hardly knew Fredendall—but the Chief assured Eisenhower that Fredendall was one of the best.

On the basis of his own experience, Eisenhower believed that the most crucial appointment was his chief of staff. He knew the man he wanted, Brigadier General Walter Bedell Smith, currently serving in the War Department as the secretary of the General Staff. Eisenhower sent numerous requests for Smith to Marshall, but Marshall would not let Smith go. The tug-of-war lasted until the end of August, when Marshall finally relented and allowed Smith to go to London.

Smith remained with Eisenhower to the end of the war. He was indispensable. His square jaw and Prussian appearance dominated Eisenhower's headquarters. He decided who would see the boss and who could not, handled most of the administrative duties, was the "No" man in the office, and frequently represented Eisenhower at meetings, always confident that he was speaking for his boss and represented his thinking. Eisenhower trusted Smith completely and regarded him as a "godsend—a master of detail with clear comprehension of the main issues." Years later Eisenhower said Smith was like a crutch to a one-legged man, "the perfect chief of staff."[38] Smith was also, as Eisenhower politely put it, "strong in character and abrupt by instinct." Or, as Eisenhower explained to a British officer, "Remember Beetle [Smith's nickname] is a Prussian and one must make allowances for it."[39] Smith suffered from an ulcer, and looked it, his face pinched together in constant pain, while his nervous energy kept him in constant motion. Although he could be suave and conciliatory when on a diplomatic mission, he was a terror in his own office, reducing his subordinates to a bundle of shaking nerves. He yelled, bellowed, threatened, and insulted them. Once when he was holding a conference in his own office his secretary, Ruth Briggs, a gracious lady who later ran for governor of Rhode Island, stuck her head in the door. Smith shouted, "Get the hell out of here." Without pausing for breath, and before the startled Miss Briggs could withdraw,

Smith turned to the officers around the table and declared, "You'll have to excuse her, gentlemen. She's an idiot." * [40]

Smith's most important duty was to be the channel through which the various assistant chiefs of staff at AFHQ communicated with Eisenhower. This duty he handled without strain or fuss. Smith "takes charge of things in a big way," Eisenhower told a friend shortly after Smith arrived. "I wish I had a dozen like him. If I did, I would simply buy a fishing rod and write home every week about my wonderful accomplishments in winning the war."[42] Smith had two deputies, General Alfred Gruenther, an old friend of Eisenhower's and one of his favorite bridge partners, and the British Brigadier John F. M. Whiteley; both Gruenther and Whiteley stayed with Eisenhower through the war.

Eisenhower's life was an unending series of conferences, meetings, debates, trips, and inspections. He was constantly surrounded by people. Yet he complained to Mamie, "This is a lonely existence," precisely because "I live in a gold fish bowl."[43] He had "no home to go to . . . no exercise, either." When he was in his hotel room, he found himself constantly wondering, "Why isn't Mamie here?" He told her he missed her, because "You're good for me—even for my official efficiency. And please be good to yourself."

Like millions of other Americans in World War II, Eisenhower had to face the problem of communicating with his wife for the period of an indefinite separation, with no phone calls allowed for security reasons, when he could not discuss his work and had long since run out of new ways to say "I love you." Or, as Eisenhower himself put it, "I take my pen in hand with a feeling of 'what can I say except to tell her I'm well and just as much in love with her as ever?' "[44] Eventually, Eisenhower wrote 319 letters to Mamie during the course of the war (he hated writing by hand, and did so only to Mamie; during one extremely busy period, he dictated a letter, but Mamie's objections were such that he never did it again). They are love letters of a high quality, not in any literary sense, but in the sense that they provided the reassurance so necessary in a wartime husband-to-wife letter. "It's impossible for me to tell you how tremendously I miss you," he would write, and then assure her that he had her photograph on his office desk, "right in front of my

* After the war, Smith served for a time as the U.S. ambassador to Russia. Eisenhower said he did not approve of professional soldiers serving as diplomats, but then, thinking about the men in the Kremlin having to put up with Smith and his ulcer, he grinned and remarked, "It served those bastards right."[41]

eyes." He said he thought of her always and wished he could write more often so that she would know "you're the only person I'm in love with." On her forty-sixth birthday, he told her, "I've loved you for 26 years," and "Your love and our son have been my greatest gifts from life." He worried about her health, and said again and again that he wished she could be with him. He fantasized about a three-day leave in Miami for the two of them—"I can get all excited just thinking about it"—and about their future. He looked forward to retiring to a rural setting, where "with a few pigs and chickens we can be as happy as a pair of Georgia crackers with a good still! . . . I know that no matter how I fumble the pen . . . you'll read between the lines that I'm thinking of you, and wishing again that we could have, together, a life in a home of our own."[45]

Many of his themes were common to men at war. He worried that Mamie was buying too many clothes, and expressed concern about having enough money to pay the income tax. He told her to get the oil changed in the car and to make sure to run it every other day. He noted the passing of time—"Tomorrow, Sept. 24, Icky would have been 25 years old. Seems rather unbelievable doesn't it? We could well have been grandparents by this time. I'm sorry we're not! Lord knows that at times I feel old enough to tack a 'great, great' on to it." John and his progress at West Point were standard features of the letters. "I'm so tied up in him it hurts," Eisenhower wrote on August 9. Like every parent, he wondered why John could not write more often. "After all," Eisenhower wrote, speaking for all fathers, "suppose he'd have had to start at 13 or 14 getting up at 4 or 5 in the morning working through a hot summer day to 9:00 at night—day after day—or doing his winter work with cold chapped hands and not even gloves—maybe he'd think writing a letter wasn't so terribly difficult!"[46]

The doings of mutual friends helped fill many a paragraph. Eisenhower usually managed to get in a story about Mickey, or Butch or Tex Lee. In a typical middle-aged man's inept way, he had enthusiastically described Kay Summersby to Mamie when he returned from his trip to London in May. Mamie responded to the news that this good-looking, lively younger woman was suddenly a part of her husband's life with a predictable coldness. In his first letter, Eisenhower reassured her: "This time they have assigned me an old time Britisher as a chauffeur. He is safe and sane, and seems to know every nook and cranny of the country." He never mentioned Kay or her new duties as one of his secretaries. Eisenhower's special problem was that his every move was reported on, so Mamie nevertheless knew all about Kay, who was one of the featured members of the "Eisenhower family." Gossip about the general and his former chauffeur was inevitable. In the summer of 1942, it was also baseless; Kay was engaged to be married, and Eisenhower and Kay never had a moment alone together. But to those who knew them both, it was obvious that they enjoyed each other's company—telling stories and sharing observations and a laugh—enough so to start the rumors. The gossip may have been on Eisenhower's mind when he wrote on October 27, "I've liked some—been somewhat intrigued by others—but haven't been in love with anyone else and don't want any other wife."[47]

Although he could not discuss his work, Eisenhower was able to use his letters to Mamie as an outlet for the kind of complaints only she would understand. He was not getting enough sleep; he was smoking too much; British food was awful; he never got a chance to see a movie. And she was the person to whom he could describe the complexities and demands of his job without seeming to brag: "In a place like this the C.G. . . . must be a bit of a diplomat—lawyer—promoter—salesman—social hound—*liar* (at least to get out of social affairs)—mountebank—actor—Simon Legree—humanitarian—orator—and incidentally . . . a soldier!" Becoming a bit wistful, he wrote, "Soldiering is no longer a simple thing of shouting 'Turn boys turn!'"[48] To Mamie, he could confess that he was delighted to have "no *conferences*" on his schedule that day. "I'm getting to hate the sound of that word."

Most of all, Eisenhower used his wartime letters to Mamie to clear his mind and spend a half hour thinking only of her, and John, and their life together, and not about the war. "When I see the unhappiness here," he wrote, "I thank the Lord that somewhere, some people, can have their minds relatively free . . . I want you to be happy as you can—and how I wish you were living here! You cannot imagine how much you added to my efficiency in the hard months at Washington. Even I didn't realize it then; at least not fully—but I do now, and I'm grateful to you."[49]

By the end of August, the AFHQ organization was settled, most of the forces for Torch assigned, the commanders selected. But the debate on landing sites continued. On August 25, Churchill returned from Moscow. Eisenhower and Clark dined with him that night; after the meal, the Prime Minister talked until almost dawn. Eisenhower reported to Marshall that Churchill was "completely committed to launching Torch at the earliest possible date, on as grand a scale as possible and with ambitious objectives."[50] Churchill was about to put his tremendous energies and great determination into breaking the deadlock.

When Churchill felt strongly about something, few could resist him. His jutting chin, round shoulders, and fat cigar all bespoke determination. With his cherubic face and bulldog head he was capable of portraying grumpiness incarnate. He was a great talker, stubborn, sure of himself. When the "Prime" got an idea into his head, he would argue for it until everyone was exhausted. He considered himself to be a military expert, especially strong on strategy, and he meddled in every plan and operation of the war. He was the individual most responsible for the Mediterranean campaign, which many critics regard as the greatest strategic blunder of the war, as it required a far greater allocation of resources by the Allies to clear North Africa and drive through Sicily and Italy than it did by the Germans to defend the area. And even when the Allies did finally occupy most of Italy, in the spring of 1945, the immense barrier of the Alps still stood between them and the Reich. But for Churchill the Mediterranean was a magnet—American officers accused him of putting Britain's postwar position in the Middle East ahead of the task of defeating Germany—and throughout the war he urged a greater commitment to the area. Eisenhower and Churchill had a number of violent disagreements during the war, especially over Mediterranean strategy, but Eisenhower had great respect and admiration for Churchill, and their friendship was never affected by their quarrels. Eisenhower later paid tribute to Churchill's ability to forget the arguments once a decision had been reached: "In countless ways he could have made my task a harder one had he been anything less than big, and I shall always owe him an immeasurable debt of gratitude for his . . . zealous support."[51]

Upon Churchill's return from Moscow, where he had promised Stalin that Torch would be a major operation, he fired off messages to Roosevelt, to his own chiefs, to Eisenhower. He had Eisenhower and Clark spend the weekend of August 28–30 with him at Chequers and kept them up most of the night, discussing landing sites. Churchill snorted that it was ridiculous to think that Franco would enter the war and said Marshall was making too much of the Spanish threat, and overestimated the French colonial army's willingness and ability to fight. Eisenhower agreed with Churchill, but neither man was able to sway Marshall. Marshall insisted on Oran and Casablanca; Churchill and Eisenhower favored Oran and Algiers. As the debate proceeded, Eisenhower confessed to Patton, "I feel like the lady in the circus that has to ride three horses with no very good idea of exactly where any one of the three is going to go." He was in an irritable mood, he said, "because last night when I hit the bed, I started thinking about some of these things all over again and at two-thirty I was still thinking."[52]

On the morning of September 3, Butcher woke Eisenhower to hand him a message from Marshall. Eisenhower grabbed the cable and grumbled, "There'll be something impossible in it." But there was not; it proved to be the breakthrough. Admiral King, it seemed, had finally yielded to the pressure and found that he could, after all, spare a few ships, enough to protect and support the troop convoys going from Virginia to Casablanca. That freed up the U.S. Navy vessels already in the British Isles, which meant there was now enough naval support for three simultaneous landings. Marshall said that if Churchill would accept Casablanca, he would accept Algiers and Oran. Eisenhower took the proposal to the British. Churchill cabled Roosevelt, "We agree to the military layout as you propose it." Roosevelt replied with one word, "Hurrah!" Churchill responded, "O.K., full blast."[53]

The targets were, at last, fixed. Still Eisenhower was not happy with Torch. He would be invading at three widely separate points, with inferior numbers if he encountered determined resistance. Torch was based on two hopes, that neither France nor Spain would resist. Eisenhower compared it to Napoleon's return to France from Elba, an operation based on psychological prediction rather than military reality. "If the guess . . . is correct," Eisenhower wrote in his diary, "we may gain a tremendous advantage in this war; if the guess is wrong, it would be almost as certain that we will gain nothing and will lose a lot." If he had more troops he would feel better, but as it was, "we are simply sailing a dangerous political sea, and this particular sea is one in which military skill and ability can do little in charting a safe course."[54]

But whatever his private forebodings, in the company of others he was cheerful, positive, and optimistic. On September 14, Eisenhower called together his principal American officers. He told them that "success or failure in [Torch] will be . . . the measure of the individual's value," and that for officers who were successful in carrying out their mission, "there would be no limit to the representations I would make to the War Department" in their behalf. If they failed, their "usefulness was ended" and they would be sent home. He stressed that "this [is] not an ordinary task in which reasonable effort and reasonable measures had any application. On the contrary, it must be considered as a major crisis." There would be, Eisenhower warned, "no excuses for failure." Then he spoke at length on the need to improve discipline and training among the American divisions, and to relieve commanders whose "units . . . are not coming up to standard."[55]

With the targets selected, Eisenhower's immediate problem was setting a date for Torch. Churchill wanted the earliest possible D-Day, as did Roosevelt; when Marshall told Roosevelt that Eisenhower was making the decision on the date, Roosevelt "held up his hands in an attitude of prayer and said, 'Please make it before Election Day'"—U.S. congressional midterm elections were to be held on November 3.[56] In mid-September, Eisenhower spent a weekend at Chequers. Churchill pressed Eisenhower for the date of D-Day; Eisenhower said that the earliest Torch could take place was November 4, but that his own guess was November 8.[57] That was less than two months away. As Eisenhower told his subordinates on September 14, "The time has passed for dilly-dallying."[58]

CHAPTER ELEVEN

London, Gibraltar, Algiers

September 16–December 31, 1942

PERHAPS THE STRONGEST argument that can be made against a 1943 cross-Channel attack is that the Allied high command was too inexperienced to successfully direct such a complex operation. The record in North Africa in the fall of 1942 makes the argument almost irrefutable. The heads of government, the foreign offices, the CCS, the generals in the field, the intelligence services, and the logistical experts made a series of mistakes, big and little, that had a negative impact through to the end of the war and on into the postwar period. The legacy of the campaign, in foreign affairs, was one of profound mistrust of the Americans and the British by the French and the Russians. On the military side, a powerful force—about 500,000 well-armed troops, with supporting aircraft and naval vessels—was eventually gathered in the Mediterranean, but it nevertheless took more than half a year to clear the African coast of Axis troops, another three months to clear Sicily of two German divisions, and yet another three months to establish Allied forces in southern Italy. Not until June 1944, more than a year and a half after the Allies launched the Mediterranean campaign, did Anglo-American forces get to Rome. And when they got to Rome, they had nowhere to go, except up against the Alps. The campaign brought minimal military rewards, and diplomatic disaster, at a high cost. The best that could be said about it is that the campaign gave the high command in general, and Eisenhower particularly, badly needed experience. Considering just how often and how seriously Eisenhower botched things in North Africa, that is perhaps sufficient justification for Torch.

In his first combat experience, Eisenhower was unsure of himself, hesitant, often depressed, irritable, liable to make snap judgments on insufficient information, defensive in both his mood and his tactics. Nineteen months later, he had improved dramatically. So had his superiors and subordinates. The team that invaded France in June 1944 was vastly superior to the team that invaded French North Africa in November 1942. In that respect, the payoff for Torch was worth the price.

From the beginning, the weakness and confusion in the French army was Eisenhower's most vexing problem. On September 16, shortly after the landing sites had been agreed upon, Eisenhower met secretly with Robert Murphy, to hear Murphy's description of the state of affairs in French North Africa. Murphy had been serving in Algeria for the State Department since the Franco-German armistice, had arranged an economic accord between the United States and Algeria, and had long advocated that the Allies launch an offensive there. He had some contacts with possible collaborators in the French army, had created some poorly organized, and almost completely unarmed, underground resistance movements in Algiers and Oran, had some information of French coastal defenses, and claimed to understand the French mentality. Marshall had flown him to London to brief Eisenhower, with instructions that Murphy would be Eisenhower's contact with North Africa and his chief civil affairs adviser.

Murphy was a tall, dark, heavyset, good-looking man who exuded charm and talk. He was an insider's insider, sure of himself, even cocky. He was the sort of man who appealed to Eisenhower—as conservative in his politics as in his dress, personable, optimistic, knowledgeable, self-confident. The problem, which Eisenhower did not see, was the narrowness of Murphy's vision; Charles de Gaulle, who did see it, described that narrowness best when he said that Murphy thought that France consisted of the people he dined with in town at night.

Murphy described, with gusto and in great detail, the complexities of French politics, to which Eisenhower listened with "horrified intentness." Murphy said Eisenhower could cut straight through the struggle among de Gaulle's Free French, Marshal Pétain's Vichy French, and the various factions in the French colonial forces by turning to an outsider, General Henri Giraud. Giraud was a retired officer who had lost a leg to the Germans in World War I and escaped from a POW camp in 1940. He was living in the unoccupied south of France. Murphy told

Eisenhower that he had been assured by General Charles Mast, chief of staff to the corps commander in Algiers, that all the French colonial troops would rally to Giraud if he were to appear in Algiers, and that Giraud's presence could thus lead to an unopposed landing. How Murphy could have believed such a story is a mystery; so is Eisenhower's acceptance of it. Except for Mast's word, there was no reason to believe that professional French soldiers, who had already rejected de Gaulle's invitation to join the Free French, would disobey the orders of their commanders and legal superiors, especially Marshal Pétain (whose orders they had followed without question since June 1940), and throw in with Henri Giraud, who had no place in the hierarchy of the French army, and to do so while their territory was being invaded, with Giraud on the side of the invaders.

Sensing some of the facts, Eisenhower did not put his entire faith in Giraud. He told Murphy that he intended to come ashore with sufficient strength to overcome the French defenses if the French did fight, and he refused to take seriously Murphy's underground organization. When Murphy asked for arms for his resistance groups, Eisenhower waved the request aside. When Murphy asked for the date of the operation, so that he could coordinate underground activities with the landings, Eisenhower refused to give it to him—tell the French, Eisenhower said, that we will be coming sometime in February. When Murphy indicated that Giraud would expect to take command of Torch, on the grounds that he outranked Eisenhower and that the campaign would be fought on French soil, Eisenhower dismissed the idea as sheer nonsense. Long discussions on the personalities of the various French commanders ensued, Murphy indicating which ones would be likely to collaborate with the Allies, which not. Algiers seethed with conspiracy and intrigue. Murphy said that among other possibilities, Admiral Jean Darlan, commander in chief of the Vichy armed forces, had indicated that he might be interested in cooperating with the Allies. But mainly Murphy insisted, time and again, that Giraud was the man. Eisenhower, much pleased with the conference, told Marshall that he was "very much impressed" by Murphy and had the "utmost confidence" in him.[1]

In the days following the meeting with Murphy, Eisenhower and his staff worked fourteen hours a day on loading schedules, tide data and weather information, air cover, and a myriad of other details, all presenting new problems to officers who had never before participated in, or even studied, an amphibious operation. Progress seemed, at times, to be so slow that Eisenhower confessed to Marshall that "impatience . . . irritation and irascibility" sometimes set in. Still, he was fairly well satisfied. He told Marshall that he expected the plan to develop "almost perfectly up to the point of departure." After that, who knew what the French might do?[2]

Churchill had high expectations. He hoped that by the end of November—by D-Day plus twenty—the Allies "will be masters of French North Africa" and Eisenhower's forces would be striking at Tripoli, in Libya, while the British Eighth Army in Egypt hit Rommel's Afrika Korps from the east. "If all goes well," Churchill predicted, ". . . we might control the whole North African shore by the end of the year."[3] With such sanguine visions, Churchill was terribly upset one weekend evening at Chequers when Eisenhower casually remarked that because of Torch it would be impossible to mount Roundup. Churchill said he was "very much astonished" at this news, and he kept coming back to the subject, jutting out his chin and declaring that it simply could not be so. "Torch is no substitute for Roundup," Churchill declared, and added that he had been convinced by Marshall that only in northwest Europe could the Allies bring their main forces to bear on Germany. He complained that "this will be another tremendous blow for Stalin," who was already "asking questions about the spring offensive [Roundup]." Eisenhower in his turn was astonished that Churchill could be astonished. All of Marshall's arguments against Torch had revolved around its cost to Roundup, but evidently they had made no impression on the Prime Minister. Eisenhower was dismayed by Churchill's ignorance.[4]

In the fall of 1942, Churchill was at the height of his powers. He reveled in being the senior partner in the coalition, the leader of the nation that had been at war with Germany the longest. Almost single-handedly, he had shifted the first offensive of the Western Allies away from France and into North Africa. He was exceptionally active, hurling thunderbolts here, there, everywhere. When he learned, or was finally forced to admit, that Torch did make Roundup impossible, he immediately set his staff to work on plans for such projects as a 1943 invasion of Norway. But he did not, unfortunately, provide Eisenhower with any realistic guidance, at a time when Eisenhower was about to immerse himself in the intense rivalries and the deep complexities of French politics.

Eisenhower badly needed a guide. On October 16, he received two messages from Murphy, who had returned to Algiers. The first concerned personalities. General Mast reported again that Giraud would not participate unless he was the supreme commander. Murphy said there was an alternative to Giraud; Admiral Darlan's son had sought

Murphy out to assure him that the admiral was willing to cooperate with the Allies. As Darlan was commander in chief of the Vichy forces, while Giraud commanded nothing, it was tempting to contemplate abandoning Giraud for Darlan. But Mast had told Murphy that neither he nor Giraud nor the French army would have anything to do with Darlan. Murphy wanted a directive on how to proceed. The second message said that Mast insisted that Eisenhower send a delegation from his staff to Algeria to meet with Mast and his fellow conspirators for an exchange of information.[5]

Eisenhower tentatively decided that he would handle "the delicate command situation" by making Giraud the governor general of all French North Africa, then "request" that he make "proper contacts" with Darlan and appoint Darlan the commander in chief of the armed forces. Eisenhower knew that the Allies would have to decide, sooner or later, whether they wanted to make Darlan or Giraud "our chief collaborator," but he was anxious to "secure the advantages accruing to us" if both would cooperate.[6] Such matters were, however, not military affairs but political and foreign policy problems. Before acting, Eisenhower needed authoritative direction from his superiors. It being the weekend, Churchill was at Chequers. Eisenhower got him on the telephone and asked him to return to London immediately for a conference. Churchill reluctantly agreed.

When Eisenhower, accompanied by his deputy, Clark, arrived at the Prime Minister's residence, Clark recorded, "There was about as dazzling an array of Britain's diplomatic, military and naval brains as I had yet seen." Clement Attlee was there, along with Mountbatten, Admiral of the Fleet Sir Dudley Pound, Field Marshal Brooke, and Foreign Secretary Anthony Eden, plus Churchill. Eisenhower asked for guidance on two subjects—Mast's demand that some members of the AFHQ staff come to Algeria for a secret rendezvous, and what to do about Darlan.[7]

The Darlan question was much the most serious. The admiral's record was odious. He was a fascist, an eager collaborator with the Nazis, author of Vichy's anti-Semitic decrees, and violently anti-British. Darlan represented, almost perfectly, the reactionary forces in Europe that Roosevelt and Churchill said they were fighting against. And he was a sworn personal enemy of de Gaulle, whom he accused of treason in June 1940, when de Gaulle had fled France for London. Momentous questions about the nature of the war were tied up in the problem of how to respond to Darlan's overture.

But the Darlan problem was hardly discussed during that Saturday-afternoon conference at 10 Downing Street. Churchill casually remarked, "Kiss Darlan's stern if you have to, but get the French navy." He then turned to the proposed rendezvous with Mast. The idea appealed to the Prime Minister's keen sense of high adventure. (As it had to Eisenhower and Clark. When Clark saw Murphy's message, he had blurted out, "When do I go?" Eisenhower replied, "Probably right away." Butcher recorded, "Clark was as happy as a boy with a new knife.") Consequently, the conference concentrated on trivia, Churchill advising Clark on what clothes to wear, how much bribe money to take, how to carry the money (in gold coins, carried in a money belt), and so on. He ordered Admiral Pound to have a submarine waiting that night in Gibraltar for Clark, to take him to Algeria. "The entire resources of the British Commonwealth are at your disposal," Churchill said solemnly to Clark, shaking hands.[7] The results of this extraordinary conference, in short, were that Eisenhower had no guidance on the crucial political question, except to deal with whoever seemed able to deliver, but he did get enthusiastic encouragement for a highly questionable, childishly romantic, secret rendezvous with obscure French officers on the very shores the Allies were going to invade in less than a month. Clark knew all the details of Torch; to risk his capture was to risk all. Nevertheless Churchill, Clark recorded, "was as enthusiastic as a boy with a new electric train."[8]

Clark left that evening for Gibraltar. While he was gone and out of contact, Eisenhower fretted. He inspected some field exercises in Scotland. Back in London, he closed up the office early one afternoon and announced that he was going to drive himself out to Telegraph Cottage for a quiet night. He was not sure of the way, had never driven in England before, and had no driver's license, but he started the car and zoomed off. "When last seen," Butcher reported, "he was going down the middle of the road, veering a little bit to the right and a bit uncertain."[9] On Sunday, October 25, Clark returned to London; Eisenhower and Smith met with him at Telegraph Cottage. Clark reported various misadventures, including having to spend a day submerged off the coast when the initial rendezvous was missed, losing the gold he had brought along while going ashore in a rubber boat, and almost getting captured (along with Murphy and Mast) by the Vichy police. Safely home, he was jubilant. Mast had given him details on the location of troops, batteries, and installations at Oran and Algiers, assured him of French cooperation, and emphasized the importance of moving on Tunis before the Germans could get there. The military intelligence was welcome (but, it turned out, neither complete nor new); there had been no progress, however, on the command problem. Mast continued to insist that Giraud had to have the supreme command, and that Darlan be excluded from any share of the power. No practical arrangements were made to either arm or cooperate with Murphy's underground forces. Clark refused to tell Mast the date of the attack and shamefully exaggerated the size of the assault force, saying that 500,000 American troops would be coming ashore, when the actual figure was more like 100,000, of whom more than half were British.[10]

A great risk had been successfully run. Clark was a hero. Churchill insisted on hearing the story of his adventure in full detail. Later, Eisenhower took Clark to Buckingham Palace to meet King George, who said to Clark, "I know all about you. You're the one who took that fabulous trip."[11] In truth, however, there were no practical results. Eisenhower generously declared in his memoirs, "This expedition was valuable in gathering more details of information," but admitted, "These did not compel any material change in our planned operation."[12] None of the real problems—cooperation with the French resistance, the command arrangements, Darlan's role—had been settled.

Clark's brief visit with Mast was the only contact anyone at AFHQ had had with the French, and it illustrated what a chancy undertaking Torch was. The only Frenchman in any position of authority to whom the Allies had talked was Mast, who was a staff officer in command of nothing—and they had lied to him. As Eisenhower wrote Marshall, "If a man permitted himself to do so, he could get absolutely frantic about questions of weather, politics, personalities in France and Morocco, and so on." He refused to panic, he said, and instead would trust "in his luck and figure that a certain amount of good fortune will bless us when the critical day arrives."[13]

That Eisenhower, on the eve of the invasion, had to put his trust in his luck, rather than in his firepower, illustrated just how unprepared the United States had been for the war, and how poorly it had done in the eleven months since Hitler declared war on the country. Eleven months—and the first offensive was against a demoralized, dissension-ridden, inadequately equipped French army, and even that was a chancy operation. Eleven months—and neither the United States nor the British had a settled, coherent policy toward the French. Eleven months—and the largest force the United States could throw into battle was two divisions, at a time when Germany and Russia were hurling hundreds of divisions at each other on the Eastern Front.

Eisenhower, as he prepared to leave London for his command post, told Marshall that the most worrisome problem was Giraud's demand for the supreme command. It was "going to be a delicate" situation, Eisenhower feared, and he expected that he would "have to ride a rather slippery rail on this matter."[14]

When he left London, Eisenhower went into a war zone for the first time in his life. He obviously would not be leading troops in the front lines, but he did expect to go well forward on inspection trips and his headquarters would be a prime target for air attack. The personal danger was not a subject he brooded over, or mentioned to anyone, or regarded as anything other than a part of his job. But he did look at the situation from Mamie's point of view—she would be reading in the papers about every air raid within fifty miles of his headquarters. And of course, he might indeed get killed in a raid, leaving Mamie to face widowhood. Knowing these things, he wrote her, just before he flew out of London, to share his thoughts on the risks and do what he could to ease her mind. "I hope you won't be disturbed or worried," he wrote. "War inevitably carries its risks to life and limb—but the chances, in my case, are all in my favor—a fact which you must always remember. Moreover—even if the worst should ever happen to me, *please* don't be too upset." He pointed out that he had been in the Army for thirty-one years and so far had avoided the risk that soldiers expected to encounter, and reminded her that he might well have gotten to France in 1918 only to get killed. And he added, "I truly feel that what the United States and the world are facing today is so much bigger than anyone of us can even comprehend, that personal sacrifice and loss must not be allowed to overwhelm any of us."[15]

Eisenhower planned to go to Gibraltar on November 2, to take command of the Rock, the best communications center in the area, and direct the invasion from there. Bad weather prevented the flight on November 2 and again on the third; on the fourth Eisenhower ordered his reluctant pilot, Major Paul Tibbets (by reputation the best flier in the Army Air Forces; he later flew the *Enola Gay* on the first atomic-bomb mission), to ignore the weather and take off. Six B-17 Flying Fortresses, carrying Eisenhower and most of his staff, got through safely, but only after engine trouble, weather problems, and an attack by a German fighter airplane had been overcome. After a bumpy landing, Eisenhower went to his headquarters, which were in the subterranean passages. Offices were caves where the cold, damp air stagnated and stank.[16] Despite the inconveniences, Eisenhower got a great kick out of being in actual command of the Rock of Gibraltar, one of the symbols of the British Empire. "I simply must have a grandchild," he scribbled in his diary, "or I'll never have the fun of telling this when I'm fishing, gray-bearded, on the banks of a quiet bayou in the deep South."[17]

He might as well have gone fishing in Gibraltar. His fleet had sailed and was already carrying the troops to their destination. All the ships were maintaining radio silence, which meant there was nothing Eisenhower could do to influence events. He spent his time talking with his subordinates, writing long letters to Mamie and to Marshall, scribbling in his diary, but mainly just worrying, mostly about Giraud. The evening of November 6, Eisenhower, Clark, and Butcher sat around in Eisenhower's office for a bull session. It would not be long, Clark said, before they were either lions or lice. Eisenhower mused that he would rather be leading an invasion directly into France. Clark cursed all the politics in Torch. Eisenhower declared that he would be happier commanding a division but added that he was thankful he had an opportunity to make some mark in history. Admiral Cunningham came in with the news that Giraud had been spirited out of southern France by a submarine and, after some mishaps, was on his way to Gibraltar. Cunningham suggested that now that the Allies had Giraud in hand, they should simply issue statements, pamphlets, and proclamations in his name. That made sense, but Eisenhower rejected it as being too "double-crossy."[18]

A message arrived from Murphy. He had just learned that Giraud was going to Gibraltar to meet with Eisenhower, not to Algiers to take command. Murphy said that without Giraud "the success of the operation could not be assured," and urged that the assault be put off for two weeks, or that the target be changed to either Norway or southern France. As Eisenhower told Marshall, Murphy had developed "a bit of hysteria" and was suffering from a "bad case of jitters." As for himself, Eisenhower said he was satisfied that everything that could be done had been done to insure a successful landing, and in any event "we are standing . . . on the brink and must take the jump—whether the bottom contains a nice feather bed or a pile of brickbats!"[19]

On the afternoon of November 7, with the invasion less than fourteen hours away, Giraud arrived at Gibraltar. He insisted on seeing Eisenhower immediately. More than six feet tall, Giraud was a stiffly erect figure despite his more than sixty years, abrupt and nervous in speech and mannerism. He demanded to be flown to Algiers, where he proposed to take command of Torch. Eisenhower, speaking through an interpreter, asked him instead to issue a statement that could be broadcast that night to Morocco and Algiers, urging the French army to co-operate with the invaders. Giraud flatly refused, unless given the command, and added that he wished to change the target from North Africa to the southern coast of France. Eisenhower kept returning to the subject of a radio broadcast or statement, and promised that as soon as the Allies had moved eastward to Tunisia, Giraud could have command of the French-controlled rear areas. Giraud kept saying *Non.* Eisenhower promised him "the governorship, virtually the kingship, of North Africa," along with unlimited American aid in providing the French with modern equipment. Giraud spurned all the bribes—without the command, and unless the target was changed, he would not participate. The argument went on for eight hours.

It was a preposterous situation. Eisenhower's troops were on the verge of going ashore, and he was putting all his energy and time into an argument that had no point to it. Giraud had no position in the French army, no infantry, no artillery, no airplanes, no navy, no following, nothing, yet he was demanding the supreme command of American and British soldiers. Only because Murphy continued to insist that Giraud's name was "something to conjure with" did Eisenhower so completely waste his time. When the meeting finally broke up, Giraud's last statement was "Giraud will be a spectator in this affair."[20]

By then, the assault forces were on their way in. Butcher jubilantly reported that the surf was down at Casablanca and Patton was going ashore. A garbled radio message from Oran indicated that so far the landings there were going well. There was no news from Algiers. Satisfied and exhausted, at 4:30 A.M. Eisenhower unfolded a cot in his office and went to sleep. He was up at seven, reading reports and talking about what to do with Giraud. Butcher reported that Eisenhower and his staff "felt something had to be done with [Giraud], even a little airplane accident." The British governor of Gibraltar told Eisenhower that "he had a good body disposal squad if needed." Instead of such drastic measures, Eisenhower decided to exaggerate the size and success of the landings to Giraud and then tell him flatly that he either got aboard now or, as Clark told Giraud, "Old gentleman, . . . your ass is out in the snow."[21] The pressure brought Giraud around. He told Eisenhower he would accept the original offer—Giraud to be commander in chief of all French forces in North Africa, and governor general of the area, in return for urging French troops to cooperate. Happy, the Americans then began to broadcast Giraud's proclamation (written for him by Eisenhower) to Algiers, Oran, and Casablanca. Then what certainly should have been predictable happened—nothing. No French soldier paid the slightest attention. Giraud's name rallied no one, meant nothing. On every front the French were resisting, Americans dying. All the time, money, and energy spent on Giraud had been a complete waste.

In Casablanca, the French were fighting Patton. In Oran, the resistance was heavy and effective. In Algiers, Murphy's underground forces had tried to arrest General Alphonse Juin, the French army commander in the city, only to be arrested themselves. Both Murphy and Darlan hurried to Juin's residence. By the time Darlan arrived, Murphy had convinced Juin that his best interests, and those of France, lay with the Allies. Juin had thereupon issued orders to his troops to cease firing in Algiers. He urged Darlan, in his capacity as Vichy commander in chief, to send out similar cease-fire orders to Oran and Casablanca. Darlan refused to do so until he had met with Eisenhower. He added that he would not cooperate with Giraud. For his part, Giraud had told Eisenhower that under no circumstances would he work with Darlan. Disgusted, Eisenhower exclaimed, "All of these Frogs have a single thought—'ME.'" Butcher reported that Darlan would talk only to Eisenhower. "Ike spluttered" at the news and muttered, "What I need around here is a damned good assassin!"[22] By cable Eisenhower explained to Smith, who was still in London, that Giraud "wants to be a big shot, a bright and shining light, and the acclaimed saviour of France," and so did Darlan. He told Smith he was tired, but not because of the operation—"it's the petty intrigue and the necessity of dealing with little, selfish, conceited worms that call themselves men." He was sending Clark to Algiers to confer with Darlan.[23] Meanwhile Pétain had issued orders from Vichy to the French in North Africa to resist the invasion, and in Casablanca and Oran the fighting continued.

Incoming reports indicated that the American troops were fighting well, but it infuriated Eisenhower that the French were making them do so. Every bullet that was expended against the French was "that much less in the pot with which to operate against the Axis." Worse, every minute lost meant time lost in the race for Tunis. "I am so impatient to get eastward . . . that I find myself getting absolutely furious with these stupid Frogs," Eisenhower exclaimed.[24]

That day, November 9, Clark flew to Algiers to meet with Darlan in the Hotel St. Georges and demand that he issue cease-fire orders. A tall man, Clark towered over the tiny Admiral Darlan. Enraged, he said he would force Darlan to cooperate, shouting that the admiral's alternatives were to play ball or go to prison. Darlan insisted that he had to wait for Pétain's orders. Clark flew into another rage. Juin pulled Darlan aside and lectured him on the senselessness of resistance. Darlan finally agreed to order a cease-fire in Casablanca and Oran, but he still refused to instruct the French in Tunisia to resist the Germans there (and Eisenhower had already learned, through Ultra, the British system of reading German radio messages, that the Germans were sending troops to Tunis to occupy the city).

On November 11, Hitler also began moving troops into southern, previously unoccupied, France. Darlan then announced that this meant that Pétain was now a prisoner, no longer free to act, and then claimed that he, Darlan, had secret orders from Pétain (which he never produced) that gave him authority to act under such circumstances. For many French officers, Darlan's claim was the crucial factor, as it allowed them to follow his instructions and cooperate with the Allies while maintaining the fiction that they were obeying legal orders. Therein lay Darlan's power, and constituted the chief reason Eisenhower was eager to conclude a deal with him. Eisenhower believed that Darlan could convince the French in Tunisia to resist the Germans, and that he could deliver the French fleet into Allied hands. Speed was essential, as the Germans were reacting with impressive efficiency. They had recovered quickly from their initial surprise and were flying first-rate troops, and shipping tanks, into Tunis.

By November 11, Eisenhower had a sinking feeling that the chances of Torch achieving a strategic success had already vanished. Everything depended on the French in Tunis. Eisenhower declared that if they "would only see reason at this moment, we could avoid many weeks of later fighting and have exactly what we will then gain at the cost of many lives and resources," but he realized—one of the few times he saw events from the French officers' point of view—that they had "been brow-beaten too long" to act against Germany. Still, if Darlan could persuade them to act, they could "cut the throat of every German and Italian" in Tunisia. "A situation such as this creates in me so much fury," he told Smith, "that I sometimes wish I could do a little throat-cutting myself."[25]

Instead of throat-cutting, he instructed Clark to make a deal with Darlan. Clark should make Darlan the High Commissioner in North Africa, and insist that Giraud be made commander in chief of the French armed forces (which showed a rather astonishing loyalty to Giraud in view of his lack of effectiveness), with Juin as his deputy in charge of ground troops. Eisenhower was most concerned with getting on to Tunisia; to that end, he wanted a secure rear area; to get it, he was ready to work with the existing French administration, no matter how bad its fascist reputation. He warned Clark not to allow any dissension to arise among the Arab tribes "or encourage them to break away from existing methods of control," because Eisenhower did not want "any internal unrest or trouble."[26]

On November 13, Eisenhower flew to Algiers to meet with Darlan and complete the deal. The tiny, moonfaced, fidgety French admiral was more than happy to shake hands and sign an agreement, promising to respect it "scrupulously" and to turn the "full fury" of the French colonial army and the fleet against the Germans. It was a momentous moment that was to have far-reaching repercussions.[27]

The irony was that by following the seemingly more cautious path of completing arrangements with Darlan and securing his rear area, Eisenhower took a much greater political risk, one that almost cost him his job.

When the Darlan Deal was announced, there was a tremendous storm of criticism. In their first offensive of the war, the first thing the Allies had done was to make a deal with one of Europe's leading fascists. Press and radio commentators were uniformly hostile, some passionately so. The intense reaction took Eisenhower by surprise; his usual good sense of public relations had deserted him. He was hurt by it, not so much at the criticism of the deal itself, which in some measure he had anticipated, but by the intensity of the criticism and, even more, at the charge that he was a simpleminded general who had gotten himself into political waters well over his depth. He grew to be defensive about the Darlan Deal, and refused to admit that he had been surprised by the reaction. Three months later he wrote his brother Edgar, "The only thing that made me a little peeved about the matter was that anyone should think I was so incredibly stupid as to fail to realize I was doing an unpopular thing." And in his 1948 memoirs, he claimed, "I well knew that any dealing with a Vichyite would create great revulsion . . ."[28] But the truth was that he never anticipated the depth of feeling the Darlan Deal aroused, had no real sense of what the political reaction would be. He assumed there would be some complaints but thought that so long as Darlan cooperated the deal would be accepted on the grounds of military expediency.

Despite the charges of the critics, Eisenhower was no fascist. To his son, John, he wrote, "I have been called a Fascist and almost a Hitlerite," when the fact was that he had "one earnest conviction" about the war: "It is that no other war in history has so definitely lined up the forces of arbitrary oppression and dictatorship against those of human rights and individual liberty." His single goal was to do his full duty in helping "to smash the disciples of Hitler."[29] Indeed, Eisenhower thought of himself as an idealist; "I can't understand why these long-haired, starry-eyed guys keep gunning for me," he declared. "I'm no reactionary. Christ on the Mountain! I'm as idealistic as Hell."[30] And he could be eloquent in describing and defending democracy. He said that the Allied cause was an inspiring one, because it was "completely bound up with the rights and welfare of the common man." He ordered his commanders to make sure that every GI was made to realize that "the privileged life he has led . . . is under direct threat. His right to speak his own mind, to engage in any profession of his own choosing, to belong to any religious denomination, to live in any locality where he can support himself and his family, and to be sure of fair treatment when he might be accused of any crime—all of these would disappear" if the Germans won the war.[31]

But his passion for democracy was essentially conservative, a defense of the basic principles of Anglo-American liberties. It was not offensive, a vigorous attempt to spread either democracy or its meaning. He had not come to North Africa to improve the condition of the Arabs, or relieve the persecution of the Jews. As he wrote Mamie, "Arabs are a very uncertain quantity, explosive and full of prejudices. Many things done here that look queer are just to keep the Arabs from blazing up into revolt. We sit on a boiling kettle!!"[32] Deeply fearful of a revolt, Eisenhower never went beyond mildly urging Darlan to make some small reforms in the anti-Semitic legislation. Darlan asked for time, arguing that if "sensational steps to improve the lot of the Jews" were taken, there would be a violent Moslem reaction which the French could not control. Eisenhower agreed that governing the tribes was a "tricky business" that had best be left to the French. There were no changes in the anti-Semitic laws.[33] Eisenhower had seen, in the Philippines, how to deal with natives—work through the local elite, don't ask questions about local conditions, don't interfere. Given Eisenhower's beliefs and experiences, it never occurred to him not to deal with Darlan. It was because he could see no alternative that he was so surprised at the criticism.

Still in London, Smith was the first to inform him of the intensely hostile British response. Churchill claimed to be thunderstruck by the deal, and the British Foreign Office said that Darlan's record was so odious that he could not be considered for the permanent head of North Africa. "There is above all our own moral position," the British declared. "We are fighting for international decency and Darlan is the antithesis of this."[34] Roosevelt too was indicating that he was anxious to repudiate the deal and in the process, perhaps, repudiate the general who had made it. Eisenhower's military campaign, to date, had been marked by hesitation and lost opportunities. Torch was already a strategic failure, and Eisenhower's political activities had unleashed a barrage of criticism. He was vulnerable.

Realizing this, he reacted quickly and decisively. On the morning of November 14 he sent a long cable to the CCS, written to defend his actions. "Can well understand some bewilderment in London and Washington with the turn that negotiations with French North Africans have taken," he began. In explanation, he said that "the actual state of existing sentiment here does not repeat not agree even remotely with some of prior calculations," which was a damning indictment of Murphy. The first fact about life in North Africa was that "the name of Marshal Pétain is something to conjure with." All French officers tried to create the impression that they lived and acted "under the shadow of the Marshal's figure." Frenchmen agreed that only one man had a right "to assume the Marshal's mantle," and "That man is Darlan." They would follow Darlan "but they are absolutely not repeat not willing to follow someone else." Eisenhower realized that "there may be a feeling at home that we have been sold a bill of goods," but he insisted that without Darlan, he would have to undertake a complete military occupation of North Africa. The cost in time and resources "would be tremendous." In a separate message, Eisenhower told Churchill, "Please be assured that I have too often listened to your sage advice to be completely handcuffed and blindfolded by all of the slickers with which this part of the world is so thickly populated."[35]

The message made a strong impression on Roosevelt. So did Secretary of War Henry L. Stimson, who barged into the President's office and insisted that Roosevelt absolutely had to support Eisenhower. Marshall told him the same thing. In addition, Marshall held a press conference, where he lambasted American reporters. He said that planning estimates had declared American losses might go as high as 18,000 in the Torch landings; since they were in fact only 1,800, the Darlan Deal had saved 16,200 American casualties.* Press reports from Morocco and Algeria had continued to emphasize that under Darlan the natives had no political rights, that the Jews were still persecuted, that Communists, Jews, Spanish Republicans, and anti-Vichy Frenchmen filled the prisons, while fascist organizations continued to bully the population and Vichy officials were still in office. Marshall denied none of this, but told the reporters their criticism of Eisenhower and the Darlan Deal was "incredibly stupid." It would play into the hands of the British, who would demand Eisenhower's replacement by a Britisher. So, Marshall concluded, the press was criticizing American leadership,

* Put the other way around, Murphy's failure to coordinate with the French had cost 1,800 American casualties.

which, if successful, would put the United States into a position of world prestige beyond anything the country had previously experienced. One of Marshall's aides said, "I have never seen him so concerned as he was on this occasion." As a result of his press conference, a number of American newspapers refused to print critical stories about the North African situation.[36]

Milton Eisenhower, too, helped his brother. Roosevelt had met Eisenhower only once or twice, but he knew Milton well. The President called Milton in, discussed the problem with him, then asked Milton to draft a statement endorsing the Darlan Deal. To Milton's disgust, Roosevelt changed the draft extensively, using the word "temporary" to the point of redundancy and insisting that this piece of "military expediency" did not prejudge the eventual government of French North Africa.[37] The President issued the statement on November 18; the most immediate result was a protest from Darlan, who complained to Clark that "I am but a lemon which the Americans will drop after it is crushed."[38]

But neither Marshall nor Roosevelt was able to halt the flow of criticism, which grew in volume as reporters made their way to Algiers and found they had little battlefield news to write about. Eisenhower then made another blunder—he imposed a strict censorship on political news. There was another howl of protest. Milton, the number-two man in the Office of War Information, flew to Algiers. There, Murphy recorded, he flew into a rage because some radio commentators were still calling his brother a fascist. Milton said that "unless drastic action were taken immediately," the general's career might be irreparably damaged. "Heads must roll, Murphy!" Milton exclaimed. "Heads must roll!"[39]

Unfortunately for Eisenhower, and despite Marshall's assertions, proof of the wisdom of dealing with Darlan was hard to find. The admiral had convinced the French at Dakar, on the African west coast, to join in with the Allies, and Eisenhower could claim that the fighting ceased in Oran and Casablanca because of Darlan's orders. But Darlan's efforts to convince the French in Tunis to resist the Germans, and his attempts to persuade the French fleet to come over to the Allied side—the two things Eisenhower wanted most out of Darlan—had failed miserably. On November 25, as the Germans prepared to board the warships in the French port of Toulon, the French admirals ordered their captains to scuttle. Three battleships, 7 cruisers, and 167 other ships went to the bottom.[40] In Tunis, the French army withdrew rather than resist the Germans. The Allies, in short, had paid a high political price for a minor material gain. The Darlan Deal had little to recommend it, but Eisenhower did not see, then or later, what he could have done differently. He did not have enough troops to impose a military occupation, and Roosevelt would not allow him to work with de Gaulle and the Free French. Giraud was hopeless. During all the talks about French politics before the invasion, no one—not Churchill, not Roosevelt, not Murphy—had warned him of the possible political complications of dealing with Darlan. He had not been well served by his political advisers.

The price paid for the Darlan Deal went far beyond Eisenhower's personal discomfort and the damage it did to his reputation. The deal had long-term repercussions. Stalin naturally wondered if the agreement made with the Vichy officials indicated that the Allies would make a deal with the German generals or even Hitler himself when the time came. This was a factor in Roosevelt's announcement of a policy of unconditional surrender, made two months later; it amounted to an assurance to Stalin that there would be no more Darlan deals. Another result was the adverse effect on resistance movements in the occupied countries, especially France. If the Allies were going to deal with the existing collaborationist officials when they came to "liberate" a country, what point to resistance? The deal hurt resistance members and morale badly; it took more than a year to recover. In addition, the deal was one of the most important events in de Gaulle's long association with the United States, and the one that most influenced his thoughts and actions. Given the importance of de Gaulle in American foreign policy in the fifties and sixties, the mistrust that he took from the Darlan Deal may have been its chief result.

For Eisenhower, the main result was that he had survived the crisis. He would have survived much more easily if he had had any progress on the battlefront to show as a result of the deal, but he did not. That was partly Darlan's fault, partly Eisenhower's. As early as the fourth day of Torch, Eisenhower was showing that as a field commander he would not take chances. He had a floating reserve, part of the British 78th Division; because it was at sea it had outstanding mobility. He could have sent it into Bizerte, but on November 11 he decided that Bizerte was too risky and instead put the men ashore in Bougie, only one hundred miles east of Algiers. Meanwhile, the Germans, taking much larger risks, continued to build their strength in Tunis.

The CCS had hoped for more from the employment of the floating reserve. The Chiefs proposed that Eisenhower broaden his operations in the Mediterranean by invading Sardinia. It would have to be a shoestring operation, the Chiefs recognized, but Sardinia was garrisoned by poorly equipped, dispirited Italian troops who would not put up much resistance. The Chiefs said that Eisenhower could divert the Torch follow-up troops from Algiers to Sardinia. The potential gain, for such a small investment, was great—possession of Sardinia would give the Allies airfields from which to attack Tunis, Sicily, and Italy, and it would threaten the southern French coast. Best of all, the entire Italian peninsula would be outflanked.

But to Eisenhower's orderly, staff-oriented mind, now burdened in addition by the responsibility of command, it was a shocking proposal. He had no maps, no plans, no intelligence, no preparations, and was by no means satisfied with the situation in North Africa. "I am unalterably opposed to any suggestion at this time for reducing contemplated Torch strength," he told the Chiefs. Like them, he said, he wanted to take advantage of any opportunity, but he insisted on moving ahead in an orderly fashion; "For God's sake," he said, "let's get one job done at a time." The first requirement was to create a stable rear area. "I am not crying wolf nor am I growing fearful of shadows," he declared defensively, but as he told Smith later in the day, "Don't let anybody get any screwy ideas that we've got the job done already."[41] In retrospect, it was one of the great missed opportunities of the war. Had the Allies captured Sardinia by a *coup de main* in November 1942, the entire campaign in the Mediterranean would have been drastically changed. But it involved a degree of risk that Eisenhower was unwilling to accept.

In Tunisia, meanwhile, Anderson's attempt to take Tunis by storm had failed. On November 28, the British First Army was on the Tunisian border, but by that time the Germans had flown in fifteen thousand combat infantry, with supporting armor, while Anderson was leading only a few thousand men in a reconnaissance in force. The Germans had all-weather airfields; Anderson did not. The Germans could supply Tunis by sea; Anderson was dependent on unimproved dirt roads and a poorly maintained single-track railroad. These proved to be insurmountable difficulties, although Eisenhower would not admit that fact until a month later, nor would he admit that the fault was his—that his only real chance had been to send the floating reserve ashore in Bizerte. Instead, he blamed Anderson and declared that the only thing to do was to "take the British by the horns."[42] But he did not follow up on his strong words. Instead of going to the front to galvanize Anderson, he stayed in Algiers, where he devoted nearly all his time to politics; instead of rushing reinforcements, by whatever means, to Tunis, he concentrated on securing his rear. By the middle of December he had nearly 150,000 men under his command, but only 31,000 of them were at the front. His own estimate was that the Germans had 30,000 troops in and around Tunis, of whom 25,000 were combat troops.[43] The Allies had been too slow getting there, and too weak when they arrived; the man most responsible was, obviously, Eisenhower himself.

Eisenhower nevertheless, then and later, bristled at charges that he was too cautious. In his memoirs, he emphasized the "great gamble" he had taken in rushing Anderson toward Tunis, and claimed that "we abandoned caution" in the attempt. At the time, he stressed that the inadequate supply line made it difficult to support even those few thousand troops fighting the Germans outside Tunis. The logistical situation, he told Marshall, was so bad it would "make a ritualist in warfare go just a bit hysterical." He complained that he had no motor transport to speak of, "in spite of impressing every kind of scrawny vehicle that can run," while shipping by sea was impractical because of German command of the air. Anderson, he told Marshall, "is apparently imbued with the will to win, but blows hot and cold."[44]

To his successor as head of OPD, General Thomas Handy, Eisenhower wrote, "I think the best way to describe our operations to date is that they have violated every recognized principle of war, are in conflict with all operational and logistic methods laid down in textbooks, and will be condemned, in their entirety, by all Leavenworth and War College classes for the next twenty-five years."[45] Eisenhower might have done better in his first command had he left behind him the emphasis on an orderly, systematic advance that he had imbibed at C&GS, and instead adopted the attitude Patton had expressed back in 1926, when he told Eisenhower always to remember that "victory in the next war will depend on EXECUTION not PLANS."[46] But Eisenhower had been a staff officer for twenty years and could not shake the patterns of thought that had become second nature to him. He concentrated on administrative matters and politics, and insisted on an orderly, rather than a bold and risky, advance, even when his superiors urged him to take more chances.

In mid-December, after Eisenhower had agreed with Anderson that the Allies were not strong enough to attack yet and ordered another delay in mounting the offensive, the CCS reminded Eisenhower that "large initial losses in a determined assault were much preferable to the wastage inherent in a war of attrition." That was tantamount to accusing him of being too cautious, a charge that in Eisenhower's view was completely unfounded.[47] Yet shortly thereafter, when General Lloyd Fredendall, commanding the American troops on the right flank of the

British First Army, proposed to attack in the direction of Sfax or Gabès, Eisenhower strongly disapproved. To make sure there would be "no misunderstanding," he met personally with Fredendall and instructed him to concentrate on securing his position. "Only when . . . the whole region was safe from attack" could Fredendall contemplate any offensive action, and even then he was to make certain that no lead elements got cut off and isolated.[48] In his diary, Eisenhower wrote that he had learned in his first month of combat that "rich organizational experience and an orderly, logical mind are absolutely essential to success," and that "the flashy, publicity-seeking type of adventurer can grab the headlines and be a hero in the eyes of the public, but he simply can't deliver the goods . . ."[49]

Then and later, Eisenhower insisted that he had no choice but to wait for more men and supplies, and he may well have been right. One cannot help but wonder, however, what a bolder commander—Patton, for example, or Rommel—might have accomplished.

Eisenhower was "like a caged tiger," Butcher recorded, "snarling and clawing to get things done."[50] He was snapping at his subordinates, irritated by his superiors. Political problems continued to plague him. He resented the way his staff officers thrust their burdens on to him. He complained that they never seemed to realize that "when they receive orders to do something, they themselves have been relieved of a great load of moral responsibility."[51] To Mamie, he admitted that he had never worked so hard nor been so tired—"London was a picnic compared to this"—and added, "I hope I get home before I'm decrepit with age but since I sometimes think that I live ten years per week, I'm not so sure I'll be any young, gay, darling blade!" He began one letter with the hope that it "won't sound as irritated and mean as I feel this evening. The day has been one of vexatious problems, each requiring hours of dictating, writing, scratching the head and plenty of profanity." He said he missed Mamie and John more than he would have thought possible, reminded her that his "*sole* . . . diversion from constant problems" was her letters, asked her to write more often, and concluded, "I envy my Scottie dog, he has no worries . . ."[52]

The tone at AFHQ, located in the Hotel St. Georges, was bad. Morale was dropping. Smith had come down from London, but his ulcer was acting up and he blistered anyone who came within range; Butcher complained that Smith, whatever his reputation, "is just a neurotic with an aching ulcer." Even more disturbing was Eisenhower's habit at lunch of ending a discussion by saying, "Anyone who wants the job of Allied Commander-in-Chief can have it." The saying began as a joke, but it seemed that he was beginning to mean it.[53] General Ian Jacob, on an inspection tour for Churchill, paid a visit to AFHQ in December and was disturbed by what he saw. "Though a man of decisive mind in immediate issues," Jacob wrote in his diary, "General Eisenhower is far too easily swayed and diverted to be a great commander in chief." Jacob recognized that Eisenhower had been forced to grapple with a baffling political situation and his "downright and honest character has been of great value in this task," but his lack of experience "and his naturally exuberant temperament prevent him from preserving a steady course towards a selected goal."[54] Brooke, meanwhile, was writing in his diary, "Eisenhower . . . was far too much immersed in the political aspects of the situation. . . . I had little confidence in his having the ability to handle the military situation confronting him, and he caused me great anxiety."[55]

Jacob had seen Eisenhower privately; in public, Eisenhower had a remarkable ability to shed his weariness, self-pity, and pessimism. He held weekly press conferences and was consistently cheerful in his assessment of the situation. As he explained to Mamie, when "pressure mounts and strain increases everyone begins to show the weaknesses in his makeup. It is up to the Commander to conceal his; above all to conceal doubt, fear and distrust."[56] How well he was able to do so was indicated by a member of his staff, who wrote at this time, "[Eisenhower] was a living dynamo of energy, good humor, amazing memory for details, and amazing courage for the future."[57]

On December 22, Eisenhower started for the front, where he wanted to see conditions for himself and, he hoped, get an attack started. On Christmas Eve day, he and Anderson visited the units in the field. Steady rain had turned the entire countryside into a quagmire. It was impossible to maneuver any type of vehicle off the roads, and hard enough on them. Eisenhower decided to call off the attack, to wait for better weather and more reinforcements. He told the CCS that "the abandonment for the time being of our plan for a full-out effort has been the severest disappointment I have suffered to date," and called it a "bitter decision."[58] The race to Tunis had been lost. A protracted campaign loomed ahead.

In his first command experience, Eisenhower had shown both strengths and weaknesses. His greatest success had been in welding an Allied team together, especially at AFHQ. His ability to get along with others and to see to it that British and American officers got along with each other was much appreciated. But at the point of attack, he had shown a lack of that ruthless, driving force that would lead him to take control of a tactical situation and, through the power of his personality, extract that extra measure of energy that might have carried the Allies into Tunis or Sardinia. He had not forced himself or his subordinates to the supreme effort; there had been an element of drift in the operations he directed.

As dusk fell on Christmas Eve, Eisenhower sat down at the mess table at Anderson's field headquarters for dinner. As he began eating, a messenger rushed in from the communications tent. Darlan had just been assassinated. Mumbling to himself, Eisenhower got into his car, an armored Packard, for a thirty-hour drive through snow, rain, and sleet back to Algiers. When he arrived, he wrote a sympathy note to Mme. Darlan, then had his staff brief him on what had happened.

A young Frenchman, Bonnier de la Chapelle, who had once been a member of one of Murphy's underground organizations, had shot the admiral. He had almost been forced to stand in line to do so, as Algiers was crawling with men who wanted to kill Darlan; everybody—Germans, Vichy Frenchmen, de Gaulle's people, the Americans, and the British—had good reason to want to remove the admiral. On December 18, Darlan had told Murphy, "You know, there are four plots in existence to assassinate me."[59] The assassin was a part of a conspiracy—he had many helpers, some highly placed—but whether it was a conspiracy to promote de Gaulle, or to punish Darlan, or to restore the French monarchy was unclear. It was never cleared up, as Giraud had the assassin executed within forty-eight hours, without an interrogation, and thereafter destroyed all the records in the case.[60] Eisenhower asked no questions of Giraud; instead, he put Giraud in Darlan's place. Taking it all in all, Darlan's death was the best thing that could have happened; as Clark put it, "Admiral Darlan's death was, to me, an act of Providence. . . . His removal from the scene was like the lancing of a troublesome boil. He had served his purpose."[61]

Eisenhower made no public comment, but to Mamie he expressed his feelings. "Poor old Darlan is gone. He was a weak character—at least nothing more than an opportunist, but so far as I could ever find out, he played square with us here. . . . He was a necessity . . . I don't know what would have happened had he been a really strong person and told us to go to . . . ; but now he's before the highest judge of all, and I guess he'd best be left alone by the rest of us."[62]

On December 22, Marshall had ordered Eisenhower to "delegate your international diplomatic problems to your subordinates and give your complete attention to the battle in Tunisia."[63] With Darlan gone, Eisenhower felt he could now afford to do just that.

CHAPTER TWELVE

Algiers, Casablanca, Constantine

January 1–May 13, 1943

January in Tunisia was cold, windy, and wet. The weather conditions precluded offensive operations on the battlefront. A logistical marathon ensued. In this race, the Germans had certain advantages, including excellent airfields in Sicily and good ones in Tunisia, short shipping lanes, and ports close to the battlefield. They also had experienced commanders (Generaloberst Juergen von Arnim in Tunis and Field Marshal Erwin Rommel at the Marath Line on the border between Tunisia and Libya), veteran troops, and more tanks. Encouraged, Hitler was talking about an advance from Tunis to Casablanca. That, however, was sheer fantasy. Although Eisenhower complained constantly about his logistical problems, the truth was that despite their advantages the Germans could not win the race to get more firepower into Tunisia because the demands of the Eastern Front for men, weapons, and ammunition were so great that the Germans had only driblets to spare for North Africa. The Allied problem, by contrast, was to find enough ships to carry the output of America's factories to their only major battlefront. They did so well that when Rommel first encountered American troops, in February 1943, he commented that they were "fantastically well-equipped" with "far better and more plentiful" weapons than the Germans. He was especially impressed by the "standardisation of their vehicles and spare parts."[1] Rommel would have been even more impressed had he known that Eisenhower's troops had enjoyed turkey and the trimmings for both Thanksgiving and Christmas dinners, shipped frozen from Texas.[2]

Under these circumstances, Eisenhower's real problems were welding these well-equipped Americans into a genuine army, winning the final victory in North Africa as quickly and as decisively as possible, and in the process holding together the Allied team, which now included the French. First, however, he had to save his own position and the concept of unity of command.

Rumors from Washington reached AFHQ that Eisenhower was to be sacrificed. Churchill was unhappy at the Christmas Eve postponement of the attack toward Tunis. Roosevelt reportedly regarded Eisenhower's retention as "politically inexpedient." There had been another storm of criticism when Eisenhower, in early January, appointed Marcel Peyrouton as governor of Algeria, because Peyrouton had been the Vichy minister of the interior and was a notorious fascist. (Eisenhower's comment, in his diary, was, "Peyrouton's appointment . . . has been received with howls of anguish at home. Who'd they want? He is an experienced administrator, and God knows it's hard to find many of them among the French in Africa.")[3] Meanwhile Giraud had arrested de Gaulle's Free French adherents in North Africa, raising yet another storm. The criticism increased Eisenhower's vulnerability to the point that Mamie wrote him a warning that "the big boys [are] preparing to give [you] the boot." Butcher recorded that "I told him his neck is in a noose, and he knows it."[4] The most likely possibility was that when Eisenhower's forces linked up with those of the British Army, coming westward on Rommel's heels, General Harold Alexander, the overall British commander in the desert, would become the Allied commander in chief. Eisenhower would then return to either England or the War Department. Indeed, it seemed virtually inevitable, as Alexander outranked Eisenhower, had won great victories, and had far more experience—and the British would have two armies, the Eighth and the First, fighting in Tunisia, while the Americans would have only one corps, the II.

Added to the strain of insecurity was the strain of an impossible work schedule. Eisenhower, always critical of subordinates who got themselves bogged down in detail, got bogged down in detail himself. He tried to do everything—attend conferences, pacify the French, meet with reporters, make countless tactical decisions, engage in long-range planning, run the theater, get supplies and reinforcements to the front, supervise the air war, deal with the British, and a host of other details. He had contracted the flu on his Christmas Day drive from Tunisia to Algiers, and could not shake it, even after spending the second week of January in bed, where he conducted his business more or less as usual.

Otherwise, he was in his office fourteen hours a day. He got no exercise and took no relaxation. His social life was so nil that he went for weeks without taking a drink, not because he had any thought that a man in his position ought not to touch alcohol, but simply because he was too busy to take the time for a predinner cocktail, ate too fast to have any wine with dinner, and worked too late in the evening for a nightcap. His only vice was his chain-smoking, which made his flu and his nerves worse.[5]

Morale at AFHQ was low, a reflection of the boss's anxiety. Ian Jacob found "a general air of restless confusion . . . quite enough to reduce the overall efficiency by at least a half . . . They find their task harassing and irritating in the extreme." Jacob put most of the blame on Eisenhower's deputy, Clark, whom he described as "a most disturbing factor . . . a most ambitious man, able and active, with a strong personality." But Jacob recognized where the ultimate responsibility lay: "Eisenhower has such an exuberant and emotional temperament that he goes up and down very easily . . ." and lacked self-confidence.[6]

Eisenhower's future would be decided at the Casablanca Conference. Between January 14 and 24, Churchill, Roosevelt, and their staffs met to agree on a strategy for 1943, to make the appropriate command arrangements, and to discuss world politics. Eisenhower went to Casablanca for a day, January 15, to report on the situation in his theater. Initially, he made a poor impression on Roosevelt, who remarked to his adviser Harry Hopkins, "Ike seems jittery." Hopkins explained that it was the result of a harrowing plane ride (over the Atlas Mountains, Eisenhower's B-17 had lost two engines, and he had almost had to bail out), the flu, and the disappointment over losing the race to Tunis. He might have added that concern about his future was upsetting Eisenhower.

That concern was quickly laid to rest, as Churchill and Roosevelt agreed not only to keep Eisenhower in command of the Torch forces, but to put the British Eighth Army under him too, as soon as it reached the Tunisian frontier. There were many reasons for their decision. Marshall remained a steadfast Eisenhower supporter, which weighed heavily with Roosevelt. Both Churchill and Roosevelt knew that they were at least as responsible for the Darlan Deal as was Eisenhower. Both men were impressed by Eisenhower's presentation at Casablanca, and even more impressed by his continuing commitment to the Alliance and his magic touch in getting a mixed staff to work together. And although the British were making the preponderant investment in troop strength in Tunisia, Churchill knew that it would subject the French to intolerable pressure to have to serve under a British commander. It had to be Eisenhower.

On the strategic issue, the CCS decided to invade Sicily after defeating the Axis in Tunisia, with the implication that they would invade Italy after Sicily fell. This decision was another blow to Marshall, who—as Jacob put it—"regarded the Mediterranean as a kind of dark hole."[7] Admiral King, too, wanted to shut down operations in the Mediterranean and get on with the invasion of France; he growled that the invasion of Sicily was "merely doing something just for the sake of doing something."[8]

Eisenhower was disturbed by such attitudes, partly because he tended to agree with the British (although he did not participate in the strategic debate, he let Marshall know that in his view the Allies ought to take advantage of the huge base they were building in Algiers to extend operations in the Mediterranean), but mainly because he feared an anti-British feeling would have a detrimental effect on the prosecution of the war.[9] His concern with the Alliance was greater than ever because of the command arrangements made at Casablanca. The CCS made Alexander the deputy commander in chief of land operations, Admiral Cunningham the deputy in command of the naval forces, while Air Marshal Arthur Tedder took charge of the air forces, with Eisenhower as overall commander.

This solution to the command problem pleased Marshall, as it kept Eisenhower on top; it also pleased Brooke, who took the lead in arranging it, because it put control of day-to-day operations in the hands of Eisenhower's British deputies. Brooke had been impressed by the way Eisenhower built an Allied staff at AFHQ, but distinctly unimpressed by Eisenhower's handling of the campaign—"He had neither the tactical nor strategical experience required for such a task," Brooke said of Eisenhower. Just as bluntly, Brooke admitted his motive in elevating Eisenhower to the supreme command of the combined forces: "We were pushing Eisenhower up into the stratosphere and rarefied atmosphere of a Supreme Commander, where he would be free to devote his time to the political and inter-allied problems, whilst we inserted under him . . . our own commanders to deal with the military situations and to restore the necessary drive and co-ordination which had been so seriously lacking."[10]

All three of the deputies outranked Eisenhower, whose permanent rank was still lieutenant colonel; he wore the three stars of a lieutenant general on a temporary basis, while his deputies all wore four stars. But Eisenhower was never awestruck by rank or title. He intended to work with his deputies, not by imposing his will on them, but through persuasion and cooperation, to draw on their talents by establishing a close personal relationship with them. He already knew, admired, and got on perfectly with Cunningham. At Casablanca, he had a long talk with Alexander and was impressed. What Churchill called Alexander's "easy smiling grace and contagious confidence" charmed Eisenhower, as it did everyone else. With Tedder, he quickly hit it off. When they were introduced, Eisenhower gave his big grin and thrust out his hand. "Well, another Yank," Tedder thought to himself. Once Eisenhower started to talk, however, Tedder decided "he made a good deal of sense." Suave and handsome, Tedder had strong prejudices and concepts which he did not hesitate to express. He usually had a pipe stuck in his mouth and the amount of smoke it gave forth was a good indication of the amount of emotion he was feeling. Like Eisenhower, he preferred to work informally and hated conferences. He was to stay with Eisenhower through to the end of the war and become the British officer who had the greatest influence on Eisenhower's thought and action.

Brooke's hopes that the three deputies would get Eisenhower out of the way were soon dashed, primarily by Eisenhower himself, who resisted all attempts to impose the British system of command by committee on Mediterranean operations. When on January 20 the CCS issued a directive that indicated that actual control of operations would be in the hands of the deputies, Eisenhower—who described himself as "burning inside"—dictated a "hot message challenging such intrusion" into his command setup and insisted on maintaining the principle of unity of command. Smith pleaded with him to moderate the message, but Eisenhower would only allow Smith to tone it down, not change its meaning.[11] As long as he was supposed to be the commander, he was determined to exercise that authority. "Manifestly, responsibility . . . falls directly on me," he told Marshall.[12]

Marshall was equally determined to maintain unity of command; to help Eisenhower, he told him privately that he was recommending him for the rank of full general. The promotion came through on February 10. Eisenhower learned of it from Butcher, who had heard an announcement on the BBC. Always far more sensitive to matters of rank than he ever admitted, Eisenhower was delighted—but also irritated, because he had not been notified by the War Department before hearing of it on the radio. But the irritation quickly gave way to satisfaction, as this was his momentous promotion. The four-star rank was the highest in the U.S. Army at that time (and was fairly recent; even Grant had worn only three stars) and had been reserved for the Chief of Staff.

In 1943, only Marshall and MacArthur were full generals. Two years earlier, Eisenhower had been a temporary colonel, and had told John that he expected to be retired at that rank. With his staff he downplayed the importance of the new rank, while with his wife he was appropriately modest. He confessed to Mamie that he was naturally pleased to have such a stamp of approval of his past actions, but claimed that "anyone worthy of high command is so concerned with the enormity of the tasks, for which his own faculties so frequently seem pitifully inadequate, that what the world calls success or promotion does not loom up as particularly important." He said that most men in positions of responsibility had a superior somewhere to whom the really tough decisions could be referred, but in his case that was impossible, as the CCS were too many and too scattered to provide real direction. "Loneliness is the inescapable lot of a man holding such a job." Subordinates could advise, urge, help, and pray, but only he could decide, "Do we or don't we?" Furthermore, at his level, "the stakes are always highest, and the penalties are expressed in terms of loss of life or major or minor disasters to the nation." In summary, he told Mamie that "I feel damned humble" as a result of the promotion, "but I do not feel that I've 'arrived'—or that my major job is finished. I've just begun." He promised "always to do my duty to the extreme limit of my ability."[13]

But his modesty and sense of responsibility, while genuine, did not preclude a normal vanity. Congratulations poured in from friends around the world (although none came from MacArthur); Eisenhower insisted that each letter and telegram be answered. He was far more concerned, however, with approval from those he loved most, Mamie and John. A telegram of congratulations from Mamie was warmly welcomed, but John never got around to mentioning the subject, which led Eisenhower to remark on four or five occasions to Mamie, "I don't yet know how this latest promotion struck him!"[14] Finally giving up on getting any praise from his son, Eisenhower wrote John, "When I was made a BG, you wrote a full page about it. When I was a Major General, you asked me to defer all future promotions until after you had gotten to be a Yearling. You congratulated me, at least feebly, on being a Lieutenant General; but you paid not the slightest attention to the fact that I finally got my fourth star." Eisenhower claimed that "I really got a laugh out of it," and praised John for being "the only one that had the sense to see that it doesn't amount to a tinker's damn . . ."[15]

The Casablanca Conference produced a promotion in rank for Eisenhower, and an increase in the size and scope of his command, but it also created new problems for him, especially with the French. Following Darlan's assassination, the only link between the French in North Africa and those in Vichy was gone. By putting Giraud in Darlan's place, Eisenhower had made it clear that he was, in fact, the only authority that counted in North Africa. That authority was based solely on the right of conquest, which Eisenhower did not like to admit; he preferred, instead, to maintain the fiction that the North African government, under Giraud, was sovereign and was cooperating with the Allies of its own free will. To keep the fiction alive, Eisenhower allowed Giraud to retain control of all civil affairs. Giraud had used his power to fill the jails with anti-Vichy Frenchmen. Roosevelt, embarrassed by the continuing and near-unanimous press criticism of Vichy methods in North Africa, wanted Eisenhower to take tighter control and liberalize the regime. On New Year's Day, Roosevelt had described his attitude in a cable to Churchill (the War Department sent Eisenhower a copy). "I feel very strongly that we have a military occupation in North Africa and as such our Commanding General has complete charge of all matters civil as well as military," the President said. "We must not let any of our French friends forget this for a moment." If they did not "play ball," Roosevelt warned, "we will have to replace them."[16] Eisenhower, concerned as always first of all with a secure rear area, was horrified. He told Butcher that if Roosevelt forced him to issue orders to Giraud that would provoke French antagonism, he would "of course carry out the order, but would then ask to be relieved." He thought such a course "would no doubt mean reversion to the rank of lieutenant colonel, and retirement," but insisted that he would do it.[17] In a series of notes, he asked Smith, Marshall, Murphy, and Handy to undertake "a course of long-distance education that might make our governments understand . . . actualities," and warned that if anything were done to upset the French, there was a "very definite possibility that we shall have to retreat hastily out of Tunisia."[18]

The main problem with Roosevelt's get-tough policy was that he had no one with whom to replace Giraud. De Gaulle was the obvious candidate, but he had been blistering in his denunciations of the Darlan Deal, and Roosevelt, primarily for personal reasons, mistrusted and even hated de Gaulle. At Casablanca, in his one private conference with Roosevelt, Eisenhower was shocked to hear the President lightheartedly talk about the disposition of France's colonies as if they were a prize to be shared among the victors, and of running a military occupation in France itself as if it were Germany.[19] Roosevelt's ideas ran so completely counter to de Gaulle's policy that a clash seemed inevitable. Eisenhower pleaded with Roosevelt not to precipitate a crisis; so did Churchill. Roosevelt gave in to the extent of allowing Churchill to bring de Gaulle down from London to Casablanca for a "shotgun marriage" with Giraud. The result was a famous photograph of the two tall French generals shaking hands, but nothing more. De Gaulle returned to London without having gained any share of the power in North Africa.

Eisenhower was so concerned about keeping the French happy that he violated his own principle of unity of command to do so. In December the French army, under Juin, had taken its place in the line in Tunisia, between the British to the north and the Americans to the south. Eisenhower wanted Anderson to exercise control over all three nationalities, but Juin and Giraud insisted that the French could not take orders from a British general. In what he later admitted was an egregious error, Eisenhower gave in, allowing the French to fight their own battle (he did establish an advance command post for himself, at Constantine, with the thought that he personally could coordinate the battlefront, but the distance between Constantine and Algiers was so great, and his responsibilities in Algiers so pressing, that he spent little time at the advance command post and in fact did little to effect coordination).[20] Adding to the problem was the miserable shape of French equipment, which was both inadequate and out of date. All through January the Germans took advantage of the situation by launching small probing attacks against the French that kept driving them back and forcing Eisenhower to send reinforcements piecemeal into the line.

On January 24, following the Casablanca Conference, Marshall, Admiral King, and other VIPs came to Algiers to see for themselves America's largest overseas base. Marshall was glad to see and talk with Eisenhower, delighted at getting out of Washington, and anxious to see in action the army he had built. He flew to the front, then returned to Algiers to discuss strategy and command arrangements with Eisenhower. Butcher noted that Marshall's "whole attitude toward Ike was almost that of father to son." Marshall feared that Eisenhower was pushing himself beyond the limits of physical endurance, that he was working too hard and making too many trips to the front. Eisenhower replied that Marshall's headquarters were in Washington and yet here he was in Algeria. Marshall scowled and replied, "I don't come to the field very often." He told Eisenhower, "You ought to have a masseur. They're great for relaxing you before you go to bed." Eisenhower replied that having another man rub his back made him more nervous than relaxed. Marshall said Eisenhower should get some exercise; Eisenhower replied that he had no time. Finally Marshall went to Butcher, and at the Chief's insistence Butcher produced a masseur and told Eisenhower he would have to follow Marshall's orders. Eisenhower, grumbling, submitted to one rubdown, then fired the masseur. He did allow Butcher to acquire a villa for him fifteen miles outside Algiers, a secluded place that overlooked the sea and provided access to a wooded area. A British officer obtained four Arab stallions for Eisenhower, and he did go riding two or three times a week, usually accompanied by Kay Summersby, who had spent her childhood in Ireland and was an outstanding horseback rider.[21]

AFHQ by now consisted of more than one thousand officers and five thousand enlisted personnel. It was reported on intensively and it was big enough to inspire a great deal of gossip. Consequently, Eisenhower's horseback rides with Kay were soon widely known, reported on, and discussed. The other female members of the staff, especially those in the inner circle, were also near-celebrities. Inevitably, Mamie worried about her man, surrounded by all these young, glamorous, unmarried women, and she expressed her worries in her letters. Eisenhower did his best to reassure her. "Don't go bothering your pretty head about WAACS—etc, etc." he told her, and "You must realize that in such a confused life as we lead here all sorts of stories, gossip, lies and etc can get started without the slightest foundation in fact." He was upset that anyone could be "banal and foolish enough to lift an eyebrow at an old duffer such as I am in connection with Waacs—Red Cross workers—nurses and drivers . . ." When Mamie asked about a WAAC from Denver serving in AFHQ, whom she had read about, Eisenhower replied that there were lots of WAACs around, "but where any is from or what is her background I wouldn't know." A bit sarcastically, he added, "If you want me to get you a lot of vital statistics I'll have [Tex] Lee form them up, march them in here, and I'll give each a questionnaire." When Mamie mentioned that she had read in *Life* magazine that her husband's "London driver" (Kay Summersby) had joined him in Algiers, Eisenhower hastened to assure her that the reason was "that she is terribly in love with a young American Colonel [Richard R. Arnold] and is to be married to him come June—assuming both are alive. I doubt that *Life* told that."

Mainly, however, Eisenhower took the offensive, again and again telling his wife such things as "I'm old—my days of romance may be all behind me—but I swear I think I miss you more and love you more than I ever did." He said that if it were not for the bombing threat, "I'd be tempted to initiate a nefarious and unfair scheme to get you here."[22] Such an arrangement would have been unusual, but not unique—Jean

MacArthur was living with her husband at his headquarters in Australia, and Martha Washington had lived with her husband at Valley Forge. But Eisenhower decided he would have to wait until the war was over before attempting to follow their example, primarily because it would be patently unfair to every other officer in AFHQ and throughout the theater.

On the battlefront, the race to get firepower up to the front lines was being won by the Allies. One reason was the sheer output of America's factories—Eisenhower got one hurry-up shipment of five hundred trucks—another was the surge of Allied air power, which with increasing numbers of planes and the use of forward airfields was beginning to take command of the air from the Germans. The immediate result was that the Germans were finding it increasingly difficult to interrupt Allied supply lines, or to defend their own. The German convoys were having trouble getting through to the North African ports, and shipments were falling far below requirements. Eisenhower was aware of the Germans' problems, thanks to Ultra intercepts, and he expected Arnim and Rommel to launch an offensive soon, before the disparity in strength became greater.

Eisenhower worried most about the southern end of his line, partly because that was Rommel's sector, partly because it was at the long end of his precarious supply line, but mainly because it was manned by unblooded American troops. The II Corps consisted of the 1st Armored Division, the 1st Infantry Division, and the 34th Infantry Division, with the 9th Infantry in reserve. None of these divisions had had any combat experience beyond a one- or two-day fire fight with the French back in November, but they had all been brought to strength in a hurry and sent to North Africa before they had time for thorough training in the States. They were complacent, poorly disciplined, unprepared for what they would shortly have to face. On one inspection trip, Eisenhower was dismayed to find a unit that had been in position for two days and still had not laid a minefield. The officers remarked that they intended to get around to it the next day. Eisenhower blistered them, then pointed out that when the Germans took up a defensive position, they had their minefields laid, their machine guns emplaced, and troops located in ready reserve within two hours. Eisenhower was equally upset by the discovery that when troops were out of the line, their officers allowed them to go to the nearest village to relax. The British, he knew, put even their most veteran troops through long and realistic training exercises whenever they were out of the line.

On January 15, Eisenhower sent a circular letter to his principal

American subordinates, telling them that what struck him most forcibly about the American troops were their "deficiencies in training." The chief reason, he felt, was the failure of senior commanders to "impress upon our junior officers, on whom we must depend in great measure, the deadly seriousness of the job, the absolute necessity for thoroughness in every detail." Throughout the theater, Eisenhower charged, officers failed to carry out orders, men failed to construct foxholes or slit trenches, drivers neglected to use vehicle blackout lights and ran their road columns closed up. As a result many men died needlessly. The great need, as Eisenhower saw it, was for stricter discipline. Too many officers, reflecting the widespread American attitude of casualness, were winking at minor infractions. Eisenhower said he would no longer tolerate such an attitude. "Every infraction from a mere failure to salute, a coat unbuttoned, to more serious offenses, must be promptly dealt with, or disciplinary action taken against the officer who condones the offense." On the positive side, Eisenhower ordered more training. He wanted the men exercised more, made capable of marching twenty-five miles a day, with packs and without sleep.

"Perhaps the above may appear elementary," Eisenhower admitted in his conclusion. "It is so intended. The defects in training in elementary subjects are the most outstanding of the lessons learned in this campaign. The mistakes made in maneuvers nearly two years ago are now being repeated on the battlefield—almost without variation—but this time at the cost of human life instead of umpire penalties."[23]

Elementary or not, Eisenhower's instructions were badly needed. The problem was that he was too late, owing to the time he spent on the Darlan deal, and too far away to enforce his orders, owing to the continuing need to be in Algiers. There was little improvement in II Corps.

The confused command situation made matters worse. Anderson was supposed to be coordinating the battle, but he was concentrating on his own front, to the north, and was not well informed on the situation in the south. Eisenhower had serious doubts, meanwhile, about Fredendall's abilities, and had offered command of the II Corps to Clark. But Clark, already commanding the Fifth Army in Morocco, made it clear that it would be beneath him to step down from army to corps command. Eisenhower thought Clark was making a great mistake, but did not insist. He thought about replacing Fredendall with Patton, but again his worries about his rear prevented action; he decided to leave Patton in Morocco "in the event of trouble" with the Arabs.[24] To Fredendall himself, Eisenhower tried to provide firm guidance, but only managed to give him conflicting orders. Thus he wanted Fredendall to so conduct II Corps operations "as to enhance the reputation of the American Army with the British," but he simultaneously cautioned Fredendall to avoid any pitched battles, for fear of a humiliating defeat.

Two things about Fredendall particularly bothered Eisenhower. First, he heard that Fredendall commonly made anti-British remarks. Eisenhower warned Fredendall that "our Allies have got to be partners and not people that we view with suspicion and doubt." Second, Fredendall seemed excessively concerned with the safety of his command post. Fredendall had located it miles to the rear and far up a canyon in a gulch that could be entered only by a narrow, twisting road. Down between towering mountains, Fredendall had two hundred engineers work for three weeks at blasting underground shelters for himself and his staff. "Most American officers who saw this command post for the first time," an observer later wrote, "were somewhat embarrassed, and their comments were usually caustic." Fredendall rarely left it. When Eisenhower paid a visit in early February, he asked an engineer who was working on a tunnel if he had first assisted in preparing front-line defenses. A young II Corps staff officer accompanying Eisenhower spoke up: "Oh, the divisions have their own engineers for that!"[25]

Eisenhower's method was to lead through persuasion and hints, rather than direct action. Although he worried about Fredendall's burying himself in his tunnels, all he did about it was to tell Fredendall that "one of the things that gives me the most concern is the habit of some of our generals in staying too close to their command posts," and asking him to "please watch this very, very carefully among all your subordinates." Eisenhower reminded Fredendall of the advantage of personally knowing the ground and reminded him that "generals are expendable just as is any other item in an army." Fredendall ignored the hints and stayed at his command post.

On February 11 the AFHQ head of intelligence, or G-2, British Brigadier Eric E. Mockler-Ferryman, reported that Arnim was receiving reinforcements from Rommel's Afrika Korps and would shortly be launching a major attack at Fondouk, the northern limit of the II Corps line. Mockler-Ferryman's information came from Ultra intercepts; there was no other confirmation, but the British were so enamored with Ultra that Mockler-Ferryman insisted that he was right. Eisenhower decided to go to the front personally to prepare for Arnim's attack. On the afternoon of February 13, he arrived at Fredendall's headquarters for a conference, followed by an all-night tour of the front lines. He was disturbed by what he saw. The American troops remained complacent, and the command situation was a muddle. Fredendall had divided the

1st Armored Division into two parts, Combat Command A and B (CCA and CCB), and Anderson had placed CCB at Fondouk, to meet the expected attack, while keeping CCA to the south. The two parts of the division were not capable of providing mutual support. The division commander, Major General Orlando Ward, had only his headquarters, with neither troops nor tanks to command. Fredendall had told Brigadier General Paul Robinett of CCB to report directly to him, bypassing Ward. Robinett complained about the situation to Eisenhower, who promised to straighten it out. Eisenhower's meddling in the command structure merely added to the confusion. Robinett alternately thought he was under Eisenhower, Anderson, Fredendall, Ward, or Juin.[26]

Eisenhower made another error when he began interfering in the tactical disposition of these relatively small units. Robinett said he did not expect an attack at Fondouk, whatever Mockler-Ferryman said, because his patrols had penetrated well into the German lines without encountering any major enemy buildup. Robinett said he had reported these facts to Anderson and Fredendall, but they did not believe him. Eisenhower did, and promised to change the dispositions the next day.[27] Eisenhower's willingness to interfere in the affairs of his subordinates ill became a man who often waxed eloquent on the subjects of the sanctity of unity of command and the chain of command; his violation of his own principles was a reflection of his lack of confidence in Fredendall, whom he was either unwilling or afraid to remove, as Fredendall was Marshall's handpicked choice.

After conferring with Robinett, Eisenhower drove down to CCA headquarters, where he went for a stroll in the moonlit desert. Looking eastward, he could just make out the gap in the black mountain mass that was the Faid Pass. Beyond the pass, Rommel and his Afrika Korps were assembling, but in the pass itself, nothing moved. At about 3:30 A.M. Eisenhower drove on to Fredendall's headquarters, where he arrived two hours later to learn that thirty minutes after he had been at Faid Pass, the Germans had launched an attack through it against CCA. Still assuming that the main attack would be in the north, Eisenhower thought it was probably a feint and decided to drive on to his own advance headquarters at Constantine, where he could keep an eye on the whole front. When he reached Constantine, about midafternoon of February 14, he learned that the attack out of Faid was a major one. Rommel's panzers had destroyed an American tank battalion, overrun a battalion of artillery, and isolated the remaining American troops. Eisenhower wanted Anderson to release CCB at Fondouk, but Anderson insisted that Mockler-Ferryman was right and the main German attack would come in the north and refused to do so. Eisenhower spent the day trying to get other reinforcements to the Faid area, but the distances involved, and the poor road network, made it virtually impossible to help the beleaguered CCA. Rommel continued his attack on February 15, in the process knocking out 98 American tanks, 57 half-tracks, and 29 artillery pieces. CCA had, for practical purposes, been destroyed.[28]

On February 16, as the Afrika Korps drove toward the next range of mountains, and the pass through them, called Kasserine, Anderson released one of the CCB battalions, sending it south to counterattack Rommel's flank. That battalion got chewed up, so the next day Anderson sent the remainder of CCB to the south. As Eisenhower noted in his diary, "All of this resulted in piecemeal action, and the enemy's advance succeeded in overwhelming our tank strength—one packet at a time."[29] American troops had performed poorly in their first battle, failing to fortify their positions properly and abandoning them in a panic. Their commanders had provided little leadership. Robinett charged that no one at II Corps was coordinating the units in the field, no one knew what unit boundaries had been assigned, no one knew who was on the flanks or in support, no one was coordinating defensive fire or providing military police in the rear areas, and the piecemeal commitment of small units was causing great confusion.[30] Fredendall blamed Ward. He told Eisenhower, "At present time, 1st Armored in bad state of disorganization. Ward appears tired out, worried and has informed me that to bring new tanks in would be the same as turning them over to the Germans. Under the circumstances do not think he should continue in command. . . . Need someone with two fists immediately."[31]

While the Americans bickered among themselves, Rommel drove on toward Kasserine, beyond which lay open ground and the major Allied supply base, at Le Kef. The situation was intolerable. Eisenhower could try to patch things up by relieving Fredendall, or by relieving all his subordinates. The last alternative was hardly feasible, and Eisenhower did not want to relieve Fredendall in the middle of a battle. He did relieve Mockler-Ferryman, charging that he was "too wedded to one type of information"—the Ultra intercepts.* He refused to relieve Ward, as Fredendall had demanded, or to relieve Fredendall, as the

* Mockler-Ferryman's mistake resulted from a German command situation that was almost as confused as that of the Allies. Arnim and Rommel despised each other and operated independently. The German high command had wanted Rommel to give some of his troops to Arnim for an attack in the north—that was the radio intercept Mockler-Ferryman acted on—but instead of following orders, Rommel had launched his own attack.[32]

situation demanded. He did try to rush reinforcements to the battle. He got the 9th Division artillery started on a 735-mile march for the front, stripped the 2d Armored and 3d Infantry of equipment to send to Fredendall, and cannibalized other units in Algeria and Morocco in order to get trucks, tanks, artillery, and ammunition to the front.[33]

Despite the embarrassing and costly losses, Eisenhower was not disheartened. He realized that all his lectures on the need to eliminate complacency and instill battlefield discipline among the American troops had had little effect, but he also realized that the shock of encountering the Wehrmacht on the offensive was accomplishing his objectives for him. "Our soldiers are learning rapidly," he told Marshall at the height of the battle, "and while I still believe that many of the lessons we are forced to learn at the cost of lives could be learned at home, I assure you that the troops that come out of this campaign are going to be battle wise and tactically efficient."[34] The best news of all was that American soldiers, who had previously shown a marked disinclination to advance under enemy fire, were recovering rapidly from the initial shock of Rommel's attack. The troops did not like being kicked around and were beginning to dig in and fight.

Nevertheless, on February 21, Rommel got through Kasserine Pass. Eisenhower regarded this development as less a threat, more an opportunity, because by then Eisenhower's efforts had produced a preponderance of American firepower at the point of attack, especially in artillery. Now it was Rommel who had a long, single supply line that ran through a narrow pass; now Rommel was vulnerable. "We have enough to stop him," Eisenhower assured Marshall, but he expected to do more than that. He urged Anderson and Fredendall to launch an immediate counterattack on Rommel's flanks, seize the pass, cut off the Afrika Korps, and destroy it. But Anderson and Fredendall disagreed with Eisenhower's conclusion that Rommel had gone as far as he could; they expected him to make one more attack and insisted on staying on the defensive to meet it. Rommel, accepting the inevitable, began his retreat that night. It was successful, and a fleeting opportunity was lost.[35]

In a tactical sense, Rommel had won a victory. At small cost to himself, he had inflicted more than five thousand American casualties, destroyed hundreds of tanks and other equipment. But he had made no strategic gain, and in fact had done Eisenhower a favor. In his pronouncements before Kasserine, Eisenhower had consistently harped on what a tough business war is and on the overwhelming need to impress that fact on the troops. But the man most responsible for American shortcomings was Eisenhower himself, precisely because he was not tough enough. He had allowed Fredendall to retain command, despite his serious and well-founded doubts. He had allowed a confused command situation to continue, even made it worse by his own intervention, and then allowed his subordinates to bicker among themselves. He had accepted intelligence reports based on insufficient sources. And at the crucial moment, when Rommel was at his most vulnerable, he had failed to galvanize his commanders, which allowed Rommel to get away. Kasserine was Eisenhower's first real battle; taking it all in all, his performance was miserable. Only American firepower, and German shortages, had saved him from a humiliating defeat. But Eisenhower and the American troops profited from the experience. The men, he reported to Marshall, "are now mad and ready to fight." So was he. "All our people," he added, "from the very highest to the very lowest have learned that this is not a child's game and are ready and eager to get down to . . . business." He promised Marshall that thereafter no unit under his command "will ever stop training," including units in the front line.[36] And he fired Fredendall, replacing him with Patton.

When Patton arrived, Eisenhower gave him advice that might better have been self-directed. "You must not retain for one instant," Eisenhower warned Patton, "any man in a responsible position where you have become doubtful of his ability to do the job. . . . This matter frequently calls for more courage than any other thing you will have to do, but I expect you to be perfectly cold-blooded about it."[37] To his old friend Gerow, then training an infantry division in Scotland, Eisenhower expanded on the theme. "Officers that fail," Eisenhower said, "must be ruthlessly weeded out. Considerations of friendship, family, kindliness and nice personality have nothing whatsoever to do with the problem . . . You must be tough." He told Gerow to get rid of the "lazy, the slothful, the indifferent or the complacent," even if he had to spend the rest of his life writing letters explaining his actions.[38] Whether Eisenhower could steel himself sufficiently in this regard remained to be seen.

During the last stages of the Kasserine battle, Alexander had reported to take up his duties as deputy commander for the land forces. At about the same time, Montgomery and the Eighth Army reached the Tunisian frontier and the Marath Line. Now the Allies had the Germans encircled, albeit on a vast front, and Rommel's gamble had failed. It was only a question of time. Still there was no overall strategic plan for the final offensive, and Alexander saw the problem immediately. "There is no policy and no plan," he wrote Brooke. "This is the result of no firm direction or centralised control from above." He also expressed disdain for the fighting qualities of the Americans. Like Eisenhower, he thought the solution was more training, and he emphasized that point in a series of instructions. He also insisted that British officers create and run the training program, something that Eisenhower had resisted before Kasserine, on the grounds of national pride, but to which he now agreed.[39]

Patton, meanwhile, was doing for II Corps what Montgomery had done earlier for the Eighth Army. He tightened discipline to a martinet standard, while his whirlwind tours in his open command car, horns blaring and outriders roaring ahead and behind him, impressed his presence on everyone in the Corps. His flamboyant language and barely concealed contempt for the British created pride in everything American. When British officers made slighting remarks about American fighting qualities, Patton thundered, "We'll show 'em," and then demanded to know where in hell the Brits had been during the crisis of Kasserine.

The war of words soon grew serious and began to spread into the newspapers. Eisenhower called a March 9 press conference to give "a rather heated lecture" on the subject of the Alliance, warning that he would order any offending reporter out of the theater. But censorship only covered up and did not solve the problem. On April 1, Patton's operations officer (G-3) issued a situation report (sitrep) in which he protested that "total lack of air cover for our units" permitted the German Air Force to "operate almost at will." The Royal Air Force was responsible for air cover over the II Corps area; Air Marshal Arthur Coningham replied to the sitrep by charging that Patton was using the RAF "as an alibi for lack of success on ground . . . it can only be assumed that II Corps personnel . . . are not battleworthy." Coningham ended by deploring "this false cry of wolf."[40] Both documents were widely circulated. Eisenhower talked over the telephone to Tedder, now his deputy in charge of air operations, and Tedder promised to order Coningham to withdraw his rejoinder. That only made matters worse. Eisenhower was so upset that, according to Tedder, he drafted a message to Marshall saying that since it was obvious he could not control his subordinates he should be relieved. Smith talked him out of sending it.[41] Tedder meanwhile took Coningham to meet with Patton. Everyone shook hands, declared peace, and settled down to a drink. At that moment, three German aircraft flew overhead and strafed the building. Tedder looked at the grinning Patton and said, "I always knew you were a good stage manager, but this takes the cake." Patton replied, "If I could find the sonsabitches who flew those planes I'd mail them each a medal."[42]

• •

Patton did not grin when he got Alexander's orders. He had hoped to attack Rommel's rear and sever German communications, but Alexander held him back, fearful that the Americans would take a pounding, and responding, too, to Montgomery's wishes. Montgomery had written Alexander about the Americans: "Don't let them be too ambitious and ruin the show."[43] Eisenhower agreed with Patton that it would be good for the American troops to strike a blow into Rommel's rear area, and that it made tactical sense, but nevertheless he twice stood aside and said nothing when, at his Constantine headquarters, Alexander told Patton to avoid pitched battles and stay out of trouble.[44]

Not being allowed to attack, forced to stand to one side while Montgomery delivered the final blow to the Afrika Korps, was galling to Patton. He asked Eisenhower to send him back to Morocco, where he could continue his planning for the invasion of Sicily. Eisenhower did so, replacing Patton with the recently arrived II Corps deputy, Major General Omar Bradley. (When Patton took command of II Corps, and discovered that Bradley was at headquarters, serving at Marshall's suggestion as Eisenhower's "eyes and ears," Patton had, quite correctly, exploded that he did not want any "goddam spies running around," and insisted that Bradley be made his deputy and directly subordinate to him, not to Eisenhower.)[45] Eisenhower had known "Brad" well at West Point and was impressed by his calm confidence, professional proficiency, and low-key manner.

While the change in commanders was being made, Alexander issued his orders for the last offensive. They envisioned Montgomery moving up from the south and joining his left to Anderson's right, squeezing the Americans out of the line before the final assault could be made. Bradley was "alarmed" by this directive, Patton "exploded" with indignation, and Eisenhower was shocked, enough so that he began to assert himself. For a month after Kasserine, he had been passive, allowing Alexander to run the battle, even when he did not approve of Alexander's tactics. What Brooke had hoped to achieve at Casablanca had, evidently, come to pass—Eisenhower had the title, but his British deputies were running the show. Marshall expressed alarm at this trend, and also pointed out to Eisenhower that there had been a "marked fall in prestige of American troops." The Chief said he was opposed to Alexander's plan, which relegated the Americans to such a minor role, and added that he was afraid that Eisenhower "in this vital matter . . . might give way too much . . . with unfortunate results as to national prestige."[46] With Marshall's message in hand, and Bradley's and Patton's vehement objections ringing in his ears, Eisenhower on April 14 went to the front to confer with Alexander. He told Alexander that it was essential that the Americans have their own sector in the final phase of the Tunisian campaign. He ordered Alexander to bring the II Corps around to the north coast and give it Bizerte as an objective. Alexander demurred, saying that the terrain was difficult and the logistical problem of bringing the Americans out of the line, marching them across Anderson's supply lines, and establishing a new front was too great. Adding to the insult, he said that the Americans had failed at Kasserine and thus their place was at the rear.

Eisenhower held his temper, but his words were firm. He told Alexander that the United States had given much of its best equipment to the British. If the American people came to feel that their troops would not play a substantial role in the European theater, they would be more inclined to insist on an Asian-first strategy. But most of all, Eisenhower insisted, Alexander had to realize that in the ultimate conquest of the Nazis, the Americans would necessarily provide the bulk of the fighting men and carry most of the load. It was therefore imperative that American soldiers gain confidence in their ability to fight the Germans, and they could not do so while in the rear. Alexander tried to debate the point, but Eisenhower insisted, and eventually Alexander agreed to place II Corps in the line, on the north coast.[47] Not incidentally, the fact that Alexander had to have such rudimentary matters explained so carefully to him shows what a poor choice he would have been for the supreme command.

Having persuaded the reluctant Alexander, Eisenhower turned his attention to Bradley. He told Bradley that he realized the sector assigned to II Corps was poorly suited to offensive action (Anderson had been forced to use mules for transporting supplies in the area), but insisted that Bradley had to overcome the difficulties and prove that the U.S. Army "can perform in a way that will at least do full credit to the material we have." He instructed Bradley to plan every operation "carefully and meticulously, concentrate maximum fire power in support of each attack, keep up a constant pressure and convince everyone that we are doing our full part . . ." He concluded by warning Bradley to be tough. Eisenhower said he had just heard of a battalion of infantry that had suffered a loss of ten men killed and then asked permission to withdraw and reorganize. That sort of thing had to cease. "We have reached the point where troops *must* secure objectives assigned," Eisenhower said, "and we must direct leaders to get out and *lead and to secure the necessary results.*"[48]

• •

"Ike's position just now is something like that of a hen setting on a batch of eggs," Butcher recorded on April 25. "He is waiting for the eggs to hatch, and is in the mental state of wondering if they will ever break the shell."[49] The shell was the German bridgehead at Bizerte-Tunis (now without Rommel, who had returned to Germany on sick leave), and three separate beaks—the British Eighth and First Armies and the U.S. II Corps—were trying to break it. Neither of the British armies was making much progress, despite the enemy's increasingly severe supply shortages. This put it up to the Americans. Eisenhower spent the last week of April touring the front lines, and was pleased by what he saw. Bradley was "doing a great job," he concluded, and he was delighted to hear a British veteran say that the U.S. 1st Infantry was "one of the finest tactical organizations that he had ever seen." The 9th Infantry and 1st Armored were also doing well. The 34th Infantry was another matter—"there is no blinking" that it was open to criticism, Eisenhower said, especially for its poor showing at Kasserine. Its morale was low and it needed to prove itself. Eisenhower told Bradley to give the 34th an important objective and see to it that the position was won. Bradley complied, assigning the 34th the strategically key point of Hill 609, a position protected not only by its own height and artillery but also by fire from nearby high ground, which gave the Germans a cross fire on the slopes leading up to it.

On April 30 the attack went forward. The troops slogged up the hill, falling before the cross fire but advancing relentlessly. "I sincerely hope the 34th takes Hill 609 today," Eisenhower told Alexander. "It would do worlds for the division and for the campaign."[50] By the next morning, the Americans had the hill. The Germans counterattacked furiously, but the 34th, its self-respect restored and its confidence high, repulsed the enemy. Eisenhower's insistence about employing the 34th paid handsome dividends, not only in the Tunisian campaign but through the war, as the 34th went on to compile one of the best combat records in the American Army.

Following the capture of Hill 609, the British armies began to move. By the first week in May, Arnim's bridgehead was reduced to the area immediately around the cities of Bizerte and Tunis. On May 7, Anderson's men moved into Tunis itself; that same day, Bradley sent Eisenhower a two-word message—"Mission accomplished." The II Corps had captured Bizerte. Only mopping-up operations remained to clear the Axis completely out of Tunisia.

Eisenhower spent the last week of the campaign at the front, and it made a deep impression on him. In February, he had told Mamie that whenever he was tempted to feel sorry for himself, he would think of "the boys that are living in the cold and rain and muck, high up in the cold hills of Tunisia," and be cured.[51] In May, he heard about a story in the American press on his mother; the story stressed Ida's pacifism and the irony of her son being a general. Eisenhower wrote his brother Arthur that their mother's "happiness in her religion means more to me than any damn wisecrack that a newspaperman can get publicized," then said of the pacifists generally, "I doubt whether any of these people, with their academic or dogmatic hatred of war, detest it as much as I do." He said that the pacifists "probably have not seen bodies rotting on the ground and smelled the stench of decaying human flesh. They have not visited a field hospital crowded with the desperately wounded." Eisenhower said that what separated him from the pacifists was that he hated the Nazis more than he did war. There was something else. "My hatred of war will never equal my conviction that it is the duty of every one of us . . . to carry out the orders of our government when a war emergency arises." Or, as he put it to his son, "The only unforgivable sin in war is not doing your duty."[52]

On May 13, the last Axis forces in Tunisia surrendered. Eisenhower's forces captured 275,000 enemy troops, more than half of them German, a total bag of prisoners even larger than the Russians had gotten at Stalingrad three and a half months earlier. Congratulations poured in on Eisenhower from all sides—from the President, the Prime Minister, the Russians, the CCS, and soldiers, sailors, and private citizens throughout the world. Eisenhower claimed to be indifferent. He told Marshall he wished he had a disposition that would allow him to relax and enjoy a feeling of self-satisfaction, but he did not. "I always anticipate and discount, in my own mind, accomplishment, and am, therefore, mentally racing ahead into the next campaign. The consequence is that all the shouting about the Tunisian campaign leaves me utterly cold."[53]

There was a bit of dissembling involved in the statement—he instructed his staff to answer, in his name, every congratulatory message—but not about his mind racing ahead to the next campaign. He had learned, from his experience with Fredendall, that one of his major problems would be the high command. Shortly after Arnim surrendered, therefore, he wrote a memorandum to himself with a paragraph on each of his leading commanders, "for reference when I may need them at a later date." Admiral Cunningham was at the top of his list. Tedder was a close second. Alexander had a "winning personality," and was highly energetic, but Eisenhower worried about his ability to control Montgomery, who had a habit of going his own way. Montgomery, Eisenhower thought, was "a very able, dynamic type" who "loves the limelight" and had "a flare for showmanship. . . . I personally think that the only thing he needs is a strong immediate commander." Turning to his American subordinates, Eisenhower began with Clark, "the best organizer, planner and trainer of troops I have yet met." He was concerned by Clark's refusal to take command of II Corps—"a bad mistake"—and by Clark's "desire to push himself." Patton "believes in showmanship to such an extent that he is almost flamboyant." Patton talked too much, which "creates a very bad impression." But he was the best fighting general the Americans had, and Eisenhower intended to keep him, whatever the cost. Bradley never gave Eisenhower any worry. Bradley "is about the best rounded, well balanced senior officer we have . . . I feel that there is no position in the Army that he could not fill with success."[54]

As to the North African campaign, Eisenhower knew that it had taken too long—six months—and cost too much—his forces had lost 10,820 men killed, 39,575 wounded, and 21,415 missing or captured, a total of 71,810 casualties. But it was over, and his men had won. His only great contribution had been not so much directing the Anglo-American victory, but insisting that they won as allies. Thanks in large part to Eisenhower, the Alliance had survived its first test and was stronger than ever. Following a victory parade in Tunis, Eisenhower joined his British political adviser, Harold Macmillan, for the flight back to Algiers. As their Flying Fortress passed over Bizerte, they looked down to see a huge Allied convoy proceeding unmolested toward Egypt. Macmillan touched Eisenhower's arm. "There, General," he said, "are the fruits of your victory." Eisenhower turned to Macmillan, smiling, with tears in his eyes. "Ours, you mean, ours."[55]

CHAPTER THIRTEEN

Algiers, Malta, Sicily

May 14–September 8, 1943

BROOKE HAD THOUGHT that by elevating Eisenhower to the stratosphere of supreme command he was getting the inexperienced American general out of the way. In fact, Brooke had inadvertently made Eisenhower the supreme arbiter of three of the most important decisions the Allies had to make in 1943—how to relate to de Gaulle and the French, whether or not to invade Italy, and how to deal with the post-Mussolini Italian government. This remarkable grant of power to a general in the field came about because unresolvable differences existed between Churchill and Roosevelt over a French and Italian policy, and between the British Chiefs and the JCS over a proper strategy. When the "big shots" reached an impasse, they turned to Eisenhower for resolution. Partly this happened because of the structure of the command system—Eisenhower was the only high-ranking officer or official directly responsible to both governments—but it was also due to Eisenhower's genius at conciliation, his ability to find workable compromises, and his rapidly improving skill as a diplomat.

Roosevelt called the French situation a "horrible mess," as indeed it was. American attempts to weaken de Gaulle had failed. In mid-May, the Resistance inside occupied France had formed a National Council and proclaimed its loyalty to de Gaulle. French troops who supported de Gaulle and who had fought with the British in the desert had filtered into Algiers, where they were proselytizing among Giraud's people with great success. Prominent French residents of Algiers demanded that de Gaulle replace Giraud. In early June, bowing to pressure from his own advisers, Giraud met with de Gaulle. They agreed to form a seven-member French Committee of National Liberation (FCNL), in which they would serve as co-presidents, with Giraud retaining his position as head of the armed forces. Bickering soon broke out. De Gaulle wanted the old Vichy officials replaced by his own people, demanded that the anti-Semitic laws be repealed, and tried to take control of the armed forces from Giraud. At a meeting of the FCNL on June 10, de Gaulle stated his position, failed to carry a majority on the FCNL, and thereupon indulged in a calculated outburst. "Shrouded in sorrow," he declared he could "no longer associate with the Committee" and resigned.[1]

De Gaulle's resignation delighted Roosevelt, who felt he now had the Free French leader out of the way. The President told Eisenhower that "this de Gaulle situation was bound to come to a head sooner or later" and better now than later, because de Gaulle was becoming "well-nigh intolerable."[2] But de Gaulle's following in Algiers had reached the point that it was impossible to govern without him (de Gaulle had counted on that), and in response to his resignation the FCNL expanded to fourteen members, with de Gaulle back as co-president and with control of the armed forces given over to a subcommittee composed of de Gaulle, Giraud, Juin, and two others. De Gaulle had a majority on the new committee and appeared on the verge of taking complete control of French affairs.

Roosevelt was furious. "I am fed up with de Gaulle," he cabled Churchill. "There is no possibility of our working with [him]." He accused de Gaulle of a "double cross" and said "the time has arrived when we must break with him."[3] Churchill demurred. He could not be a part of "sweeping away a Committee on which many hopes are founded" and said the Allies would have to find a way of working with de Gaulle. That way was through Eisenhower, who Churchill felt could be used to control de Gaulle.[4]

Eisenhower, like Churchill, was appalled at the thought of breaking with de Gaulle. All around him in Algiers he could see evidence of de Gaulle's political strength and he feared civil war in North Africa if de Gaulle were forced out of the FCNL. He was preparing to invade Sicily and could not afford chaos in his rear areas. He therefore tried to calm Roosevelt down a bit, telling him that "the local French difficulties . . . have been magnified." Much of the "acrimonious discussion" between de Gaulle and Giraud was more indicative of typical French politics than anything else. He begged the President not to force the issue and promised to meet with Giraud and de Gaulle in order to insist that Giraud retain control of the French armed forces.[5]

The meeting took place on June 19 in Eisenhower's office in the Hotel St. Georges. De Gaulle purposely arrived last and spoke first. He strode into the room in full uniform, his tall frame ramrod stiff, his Roman nose suspiciously sniffing the air. "I am here in my capacity as President of the French government," he announced, a preposterous opening gambit, as there was no French government, only the FCNL, and he was not its president, but co-president. De Gaulle plunged on. "If you wish to address a request to me," he said to Eisenhower, "be assured that I am disposed beforehand to give you satisfaction . . ." Eisenhower then politely asked de Gaulle to leave Giraud in charge of France's armed forces. De Gaulle, feigning outrage, responded that "the organization of the French command is the province of the French government, not yours." Eisenhower repeated his position, whereupon de Gaulle asked, "You who are a soldier, do you think that a leader's authority can subsist if it rests on the favor of a foreign power?" He admitted that Eisenhower was in a strong position, insofar as he was directing the rearming of the French forces with American equipment, but he recalled World War I, when the Americans had fired only French cannons, driven only French trucks, flown only French airplanes. "Did we," he asked, "in return . . . demand of the United States that they appoint this or that leader or institute this or that political system?"[6]

De Gaulle thought Eisenhower was acutely embarrassed to have to demand assurances from a head of government about his army leaders and did so only because of the pressure from Roosevelt. To a large extent, he was right. Eisenhower wanted no part of French politics, but more clearly than Churchill, and much more clearly than Roosevelt, he was aware of de Gaulle's strength. He had developed a grudging admiration for de Gaulle, as de Gaulle had for him. The two men never became close friends, but they did respect each other. De Gaulle admired Eisenhower for his openness and honesty; Eisenhower admired de Gaulle for his abilities and his uncompromising devotion to the cause of French sovereignty. Although there were no immediate results from this, their first meeting, the two generals established a relationship that was destined to last, and strengthen, for nearly two decades.

On June 22 Eisenhower sent a long analysis of the situation to Marshall. He emphasized the importance of a secure rear area after the Sicilian invasion was launched, and begged Marshall to see to it that Roosevelt did not force a crisis. He claimed he could "control" de Gaulle, but did admit that supporting Giraud was difficult, because Giraud's only strength was Roosevelt's support, while "his great weakness is the uneasy feeling . . . that he is reactionary, old-fashioned, and cannot be persuaded to modernize . . . It must be admitted that he moves with ponderous slowness. He has no repeat no political acumen whatsoever."[7]

De Gaulle, meanwhile, began pressing for recognition of the FCNL as the provisional government of France. This issue was far more important than Giraud's position. Recognition would force Eisenhower and the Allies to deal with the FCNL rather than with Giraud, it would open the way for representatives of the FCNL to participate in Allied committees, it would permit the FCNL access to French credits held in the United States (estimated at $1 billion in gold), and most of all it would give the FCNL the inside position when the liberation of France took place. Churchill, Eisenhower, and Eisenhower's political advisers, Murphy and Macmillan, all thought recognition the best solution. Roosevelt's response, however, was to send a blistering cable to Eisenhower demanding to know what was going on. "Under no condition are you to recognize the Committee . . ." Roosevelt warned.[8]

Eisenhower was "astonished" at the suggestion that he intended to recognize the FCNL on his own authority. He assured Marshall, "I am quite well aware of the exclusive authority of the President in such matters, and I am . . . disturbed that any rumor of such a kind can gain such force . . . as to create an impression that I would step out of my own proper sphere to this extent." Still, he added, he continued to feel that "some kind of limited recognition . . . would be helpful."[9] Eventually, in August, Roosevelt agreed to a compromise along the lines Eisenhower had suggested. After roundly declaring that he would not "give de Gaulle a white horse on which he could ride into France and make himself master of a government there," Roosevelt chose to "recognize" the FCNL "as administering those French overseas territories which acknowledge its authority." The British, meanwhile, gave the FCNL a much broader and less circumscribed recognition.[10]

Eisenhower was delighted. He continued to assure the President that he would "watch" de Gaulle and could "control" him, and even suggested that de Gaulle was losing support because of his intransigence. But he knew full well that de Gaulle was regularly outmaneuvering the dim-witted Giraud and gathering all power in his own hands, an outcome that pleased rather than alarmed him, as he had so much higher an opinion of de Gaulle than of Giraud. For his part, de Gaulle never doubted that it was his own skill and determination that brought him to the top, but he also realized that Eisenhower's common-sense approach to the problem, and Eisenhower's ability to handle Roosevelt, were important factors in his success.

• •

In April, as the Tunisian campaign was drawing to an end, Eisenhower looked ahead to Sicily and beyond. He told Marshall that after Sicily was taken, he wanted to invade Sardinia and Corsica, then use them as springboards to invade western Italy. He realized that such an extension of the Mediterranean offensive ran directly counter to Marshall's views, and those of the planners in OPD. Indeed, had he still been in OPD, he undoubtedly would have also wanted to shut down operations in the Mediterranean in order to concentrate on the buildup for the cross-Channel attack. But as a theater commander, he could not take such a broad view. "I personally have never wavered in my belief that the Roundup conception is the correct one," Eisenhower assured Marshall, but meanwhile—and here he sounded exactly like Churchill in July 1942—wasn't it a pity that nothing could be done in the summer of 1943? Especially when it could be done so cheaply. The Mediterranean was a major theater already, Eisenhower pointed out, and the troops had to be maintained anyway, so with a relatively minor additional expenditure the Allies could keep the pressure on Germany and satisfy the public that something was being done.[11] That was precisely the problem, OPD officers replied, it was doing something for the sake of doing something. There was no strategic objective. Knocking Italy out of the war would be more of a burden than a help, as Allied shipping would have to be used to support the population (ten million tons of coal a year alone would be required, and huge stocks of food). Once occupied, Italy would provide airfields for bombing southern Germany, an asset too slight to be worth the effort. As Marshall told Eisenhower, "The decisive effort must be made against the Continent from the United Kingdom sooner or later," and it would come sooner if there were no more offensives after Sicily in the Mediterranean.

In May, the CCS met in Washington to decide the issue. They argued for two weeks. The Chiefs finally agreed to a commitment to a cross-Channel attack in 1944, but made no decision on what to do in the Mediterranean after Sicily. They left that decision up to Eisenhower, directing him "to plan such operations in exploitation of Husky [code name for Sicily] as are best calculated to eliminate Italy from the war and to contain the maximum number of German forces." Eisenhower could decide for himself how to accomplish these vague aims. He could use the forces he already had in the theater, minus seven divisions that would be transferred to the United Kingdom on November 1.

No one was satisfied with the result. Since Eisenhower would decide, Churchill flew to Algiers to persuade the general to go for Italy. Brooke and other staff officers accompanied him, as did Marshall—

Churchill had insisted that he come along, completing the spectacle of the superiors come to woo the subordinate. They stayed a week, Churchill talking constantly. He did not want Eisenhower to invade Sardinia, but Italy; Sardinia would be a "mere convenience," he said, while Italy would be "a glorious campaign." The glory would come from the capture of Rome, which "would be a very great achievement" and a fitting climax to the Eighth Army's odyssey. "The PM recited his story three different times in three different ways last night," Eisenhower complained on May 30. That night, Churchill called after dinner to ask if he could come over. It was nearly 11 P.M. and Eisenhower wanted to sleep. He said he was tired of going over the same ground again and again. Churchill insisted. Eisenhower said all right. Churchill arrived fifteen minutes later, then talked steadily for two hours. Butcher finally had more or less to push him out the door. Brooke saw the "very sleepy Eisenhower" the next day and admitted "I smiled at his distress, having suffered from this type of treatment [from Churchill] repeatedly."[12]

Marshall did not want either Sardinia or Italy. He urged Eisenhower to begin drawing down in the Mediterranean as soon as Sicily was over. He was suspicious of the British, doubted their resolve for the cross-Channel attack. On this point he was right. Brooke came privately to Eisenhower to have his say, which was that the Allies ought to apply their naval and air strength toward blockading Germany and leave the ground fighting to the Russians. He said that in northwest Europe, the Allies would be fighting at "a great disadvantage and would suffer tremendous and useless losses." They should therefore limit themselves to fighting in Italy.[13]

Eisenhower heard them all out and kept his own counsel. Much would depend on how hard the Germans fought for Sicily, and whether or not they moved additional divisions into Italy. Eisenhower was left with the power to decide, based on enemy reactions, what to do after Sicily.

First, Sicily had to be taken. To do that, a plan of attack had to be agreed upon. There were two armies involved, Montgomery's Eighth and Patton's Seventh. Montgomery wanted to strike a concentrated blow against the southeastern coast, with Patton in immediate support on his left. Patton, and Eisenhower's deputies, wanted a series of scattered landings. Tedder felt that Montgomery was afraid to take risks and that his concern about overwhelming firepower at the point of attack was at the expense of a rapid overrunning of the island. Patton wanted his own show. Through April and on into May the generals argued. Eventually, Montgomery had his way—the two armies would go ashore on the southeastern coast, side by side, with Patton in a supporting role. They were landing a long way off from the only strategic spot in Sicily, Messina—and Mount Etna stood between Montgomery's assault beaches and Messina. Nevertheless, when Montgomery outlined the plan for Eisenhower, Churchill, Brooke, and Marshall on the afternoon of June 2, he exuded confidence. His boys would get ashore; there would be ten days of hard fighting; he would then take Messina and cross to the Italian mainland. Even if Montgomery delivered on that promise, his plan offered the "small solution," driving the two German divisions on Sicily back into Italy rather than cutting them off at Messina and capturing them. But Alexander did what Montgomery wanted him to do, and Eisenhower went along. As the official American history concludes, "The whole approach toward Sicily was cautious and conservative."[14] Even at that D-Day was set back to July 10, in order to allow time for more landing craft to come into the Mediterranean, so as to bring more men ashore in the first waves.

Although it is convenient to divide Eisenhower's concerns into separate discussions here, for him they were all going on at once—the debates over a plan for Sicily coincided with the final campaign in Tunisia, while Eisenhower's first meeting with de Gaulle coincided with the Churchill-Brooke-Marshall visit. Eisenhower found it impossible to concentrate on one job at a time and was constantly switching from issue to issue. In addition to all his official responsibilities, only just outlined here, he had some worries about Mamie. By May of 1943 the couple had been separated for almost a full year. Eisenhower had his never-ending work to occupy him, and in addition was surrounded by old and new friends. Except for Ruth Butcher, Mamie was alone, and Ruth was not much help, as she was a heavy drinker and her marriage was in trouble (when the war ended, the Butchers were divorced). Eisenhower, robust as usual, could drive himself right through an occasional cold or touch of diarrhea; Mamie, delicate as always, was ill and bedridden much of the time. She had little interest in food and her weight had slipped to 112 pounds. In her own words, she "lived after sorts, read mystery thrillers through the nights—and waited."[15] She was being plagued to make public appearances, which she detested, and was receiving voluminous mail, which helped her pass the time, as she answered by hand every letter.

Writing letters to her husband was much more satisfying, to her and to him (the first thing he looked for in every incoming mail pouch was a letter from his wife), but no matter how cheerful and chatty she tried to be in her notes, he could read between the lines. "Your letters often give me some hint of your loneliness," Eisenhower wrote in June, "your bewilderment and your worries in carrying on . . . when you're lonely, try to remember that I'd rather be by your side than anywhere else in the world."[16] He was also concerned by reports from Washington that people were "darn near placing you on a royalty basis."

Mamie's biggest problem—aside from living without her husband—was her realization that the price she had to pay for the thrill of being married to a world-famous man was that that man was no longer her "personal property." Eisenhower reassured her: "In spite of all the publicity," he wrote, "you are quite mistaken in saying that I no longer belong to you and Johnny. . . . So far as I, as a person, am concerned—I'm just 1/3 of the family (yours and Johns and mine). So don't fret your head about that phase of the thing. At least no crack-brain has yet started running me for political office."[17]

He indulged himself in fantasies about their getting together. He had hoped to be called to the Washington conference of the CCS in May to testify—he could have then spent a day or two with Mamie—but was not. He thought about meeting her in Bermuda. Because of a slight heart condition and an inner-ear problem, Mamie was not allowed to fly; Eisenhower wrote that if the doctors would agree to her flying, he would arrange to meet her somewhere, perhaps London. "Last night I dreamed you had come over here," he wrote in July. "We were having a lot of fun fixing things up the way you wanted them—particularly my house at my main headquarters. Then you found out that I was leaving at once for quite a trip; and did you give me hail Columbia!"[18]

What she was really giving him hell for was Kay. It seemed to Mamie that Kay was with her husband constantly—Kay appeared frequently in photographs, standing beside or just behind the general. And indeed Eisenhower could hardly deny that he liked Kay, enjoyed being with her, responded to her warmth, charm, good looks, and flirtatious manner, even if he was twenty years her senior. In his high-powered world of generals, admirals, prime ministers, and French politicians, he needed a soft touch, a light laugh, an escape from the constant pressure of war and death, and Kay met those needs. She was driving for Eisenhower again, as well as serving as a secretary at AFHQ. She often joined Eisenhower and his friends for dinner, and served as his partner in an occasional game of bridge. Brigadier General Everett Hughes, an old friend of the Eisenhowers', and Harry Butcher made up the opposition. Hughes kept an extensive, gossipy diary; in it he recorded that his own driver was worried "over Kay and Ike. She foresees a scandal. . . . I tell her . . . Kay will help Ike win the war." After one party, he sat around with Eisenhower and "discussed Kay. I don't know whether Ike is alibiing or not. Says he wants to hold her hand, accompanies her to house, doesn't sleep with her."[19] Eisenhower's obvious enjoyment of her company, and the fact that she was around so much of the time, fueled the gossip, in Algiers and in Washington, about the general and his driver. Mamie grew heartily sick of reading about and being asked about Kay.

In Eisenhower's mind, his relationship with Kay was perfectly innocent and lots of fun. He deeply resented but would not comment upon the gossip, just as having Kay's presence singled out left him furious but helpless. Once he told Patton, "The other day Kay and I were out riding and a soldier yahooed at us." Eisenhower said he could do nothing more than glare at the man and ride on.[20] At first glance, Eisenhower seems particularly inept in carrying on a middle-aged flirtation with a woman young enough to be his daughter, and equally insensitive to his wife's reaction to seeing Kay standing next to him whenever his picture was in the newspapers. But the truth was that if he wanted to see and be with Kay at all—and he certainly did—it had to be in public, as they never had time alone together.

Until June of 1943 there was a limit to how far the gossip could go, because of Kay's impending marriage. But then her fiancé was killed by a land mine. Kay, naturally, took it hard; Eisenhower, naturally, tried to console her. Mamie continued to ask about Kay in her letters; Eisenhower responded, "She is a very popular person in the whole headquarters and everyone is trying to be kind. But I suspect she cannot long continue to drive—she is too sunk!" He thought Kay should go back to London, but she insisted on continuing her work at AFHQ, and he cheerfully agreed.[21] Mamie's anxieties increased, needlessly in Eisenhower's view, inevitably in everyone else's.

"Cunningham commands the naval forces, Tedder commands the air forces, and Alexander commands the ground forces. What in hell does Eisenhower command?" a group of touring American senators demanded to know. The answer was, he commanded Cunningham, Tedder, and Alexander, as the capture of the island of Pantelleria showed. The island, about halfway between Tunisia and Sicily, was heavily garrisoned by Italians. The coastline was rocky, there were no beaches, and the only approach was through a narrow harbor. Eisenhower wanted the island for its airfield. Alexander was thoroughly opposed to any attempt to take Pantelleria. Cunningham initially agreed with Alexander that it was too risky. So did Tedder, but Tedder wanted that airfield and was the first of Eisenhower's deputies to swing around to support the operation. After his air forces had pounded the harbor and defensive installations for three weeks, Cunningham came around, saying that he now agreed with Eisenhower that Italian morale was so low the enemy would not put up a fight. But Alexander continued to object, as did the British general assigned to lead the assault, who protested to Eisenhower that the plan would never work and that the casualties would be awful. Pantelleria, he said, was a miniature Gibraltar bristling with guns, and he and Alexander filled Algiers with their "dismal forebodings." Eisenhower insisted that whatever the cost, he had to have the island, but the protests were so strong that he decided to make a personal reconnaissance immediately prior to the assault. He set out on the morning of June 7, along with Cunningham, on H.M.S. *Aurora,* as a part of a fleet that was going to Pantelleria to bombard the island. The *Aurora* sailed right up to the coast and blasted away, with Cunningham directing some of the fire personally. Only two Italian shore batteries replied, neither with any accuracy. Eisenhower told Cunningham, "Andrew, if you and I got into a small boat, we could capture the place ourselves." Eisenhower returned to Algiers and ordered the assault to go ahead on schedule.

On June 11 the British troops set sail, with H-Hour set for twelve noon. Eisenhower had not slept well the night before; Butcher noted that "he has been going through the same type of jitters and worries which marked the days immediately preceding our landings in North Africa." Eisenhower fretted all morning, but the finale was anticlimax. Shortly after noon, Cunningham reported that Pantelleria had surrendered before a single British soldier set foot ashore. The Italians had cracked. Some eleven thousand men surrendered. There was one casualty; a British Tommy was bitten by a mule.[22]

Eisenhower was elated. "I am afraid this telegram sounds just a bit gloating," he confessed in reporting the success to Marshall. He felt so good that he added, "Today marks the completion of my twenty-eighth year of commissioned service and I believe that I am now legally eligible for promotion to colonel," that is, a permanent colonelcy in the Regular Army.[23] He took justified satisfaction in the results; it had been his plan from the beginning, he was the one who insisted upon it, and despite the numerous and highly placed doubters, some of whom were senior to him in rank and experience, it had worked. It was a command decision that showed that the experts were not always right, and it gave him confidence in his own abilities and judgment. In later years, whenever he was accused of being too cautious as a general, he would immediately mention Pantelleria; to the astonishment of interviewers, many of whom had never heard of the place, he would speak of Pantelleria with as much pride as about Overlord.[24]

Sicily was next. "Everybody is tremendously keyed up," Eisenhower told Marshall on July 1. "Whenever I have a short conference with a staff section, my whole effort is to get the attending individuals to relax a bit." The planners had been working on Sicily since January and they were showing the strain.[25] It was natural enough, considering the complexity of the operation and the size of the force involved. Sicily was the largest amphibious assault ever attempted. At dawn on July 10 seven divisions, preceded by airborne operations involving parts of two parachute divisions, would go ashore simultaneously along a front of one hundred miles. Both the frontage and initial assault forces were larger than those at Normandy eleven months later.[26] Estimates were that some 350,000 Italian troops were stationed on Sicily, but how well they would fight was an open question. There was no doubt that the two German divisions on the island would put up a stiff resistance.

On July 7 Eisenhower flew to Malta, Cunningham's command post, to direct the invasion. Eisenhower said he felt "as if my stomach were a clenched fist."[27] On D-Day minus one—July 9—the weather turned bad. The wind came up from the west and increased in force, piling up whitecaps in the Mediterranean, tossing about the landing craft in which Patton's men were crossing from Tunisia to Sicily. Staff officers suggested to Eisenhower that he postpone the invasion before it was too late. But Cunningham's meteorological experts said that the wind would drop around sundown. Marshall sent a wire asking if the invasion was on or off. As Eisenhower later put it, "My reaction was that I wish I knew!" But as the wind did indeed slacken, he decided to go ahead. After giving the orders, accompanied by Cunningham he climbed to the highest point in Malta to watch the transports of the British 1st Airborne Division fly through the rain toward Sicily. He silently prayed for the safety and success of all the troops under his command.[28]

He returned to his office to wait. He wrote a letter to Mamie. "In circumstances such as these men do almost anything to keep them from going slightly mad," he said. "Walk, talk, try to work, smoke (all the time)—anything to push the minutes along to find out a result that one's own actions can no longer affect in the slightest degree. I stand it better than most, but there is no use denying that I feel the strain."[29]

• •

In the morning, waiting for reports, Eisenhower went for a walk on the beach with Butcher. He had no immediate decisions to make, it was a rare free time, and he took the opportunity to do some reflecting. He said he had 150,000 men going ashore against a mostly undefended coast, with a follow-up force of 350,000, supported by the largest armada assembled to that date, and a correspondingly large air force. It suddenly seemed an awfully big force to be throwing against such a small target, a tremendous expenditure of effort for so slight a return on the investment. Eisenhower thought that the Germans would breathe a sigh of relief when they realized the Allies were only going after Sicily, not something bigger. He anticipated that they would throw up a defensive cordon around Messina and Mount Etna, fight a delaying action, tie up the Allied armies for some weeks, then withdraw to the mainland.[30]

He was exactly right. His troops got ashore without serious opposition, and the Italians surrendered in droves, but the two German divisions fought skillfully and fiercely, so that the campaign that ensued in Sicily followed his prediction and in consequence has been condemned by nearly all military historians. Montgomery did not drive for Messina; he hardly even crawled. He and Patton fought among themselves until Patton, furious at the passive role he had been assigned, struck out on his own, toward Palermo, in western Sicily, away from the Germans but toward the headlines. The Germans were amazed by this development; Field Marshal Albert Kesselring, overall commander in Italy, spoke of the "slowness of the Allied advance" and expressed astonishment that "strong forces had been dispersed to the western part of Sicily which . . . just marched and captured unimportant terrain, instead of fighting at the wing where a major decision had to be reached."[31] Having reached Palermo, Patton turned right and began attacking along the northern coast, toward Messina. The Germans used every feature of the terrain and their expertise at laying minefields to delay him. Patton pushed himself, and his men, to the extreme limit, for by now he was in a race with Montgomery for Messina. Bradley, commanding a corps in Patton's army, directed the bulk of the fighting.

Eisenhower played practically no role; as will be seen, he was deeply involved in other matters, and he left the ground war to Alexander. He was irritated at the slow progress, saying he could not understand why 500,000 Allied troops, supported by air and naval gunfire, could not settle the issue with 60,000 Germans more quickly. He was even more upset when his new G-2, British General Kenneth Strong, reported that in his opinion if Montgomery had been "less conservative and his forces more mobile, he could probably have been to Messina during the first week."[32] Eisenhower agreed with the assessment, but put the blame where it belonged. "I did not sufficiently appreciate the situation," he admitted, and had therefore not gone to Montgomery's headquarters to demand action.[33]

On August 17, Patton's men beat the British to Messina. That, and the excellent showing of the GIs in the rough mountain fighting, was the only bright spot in an otherwise dismal conclusion. The Germans had gotten away, after holding back a half million Allied troops for thirty-eight days and inflicting twenty thousand casualties, at a cost of twelve thousand. Kesselring was delighted with the results; Eisenhower and his commanders were correspondingly deflated.

On the day Patton reached Messina, Eisenhower's surgeon handed him a report from one of his doctors. It said that Patton, a week earlier, had lost his temper while visiting a field hospital when he saw a young GI who had nothing visibly wrong with him. Patton wanted to know why he was a patient. The soldier replied, "It's my nerves. I can't stand the shelling any more," and began sobbing. Patton, cursing and screaming, slapped the man, twice, accused him of cowardice, and ordered the doctors not to admit him.

Eisenhower read the report. He was feeling friendly toward Patton that day, for he was secretly pleased that the Americans had beaten Montgomery to Messina, so his initial reaction was mild. "I guess I'll have to give General Patton a jacking up," he said, then praised Patton for the "swell job" he had done in Sicily. He told the surgeon to go to Sicily and conduct a full investigation, but to keep it quiet. "If this thing ever gets out," he feared, "they'll be howling for Patton's scalp, and that will be the end of Georgie's service in this war. I simply cannot let that happen. Patton is *indispensable* to the war effort—one of the guarantors of our victory."[34]

Eisenhower then wrote, by hand, a long personal letter to Patton. "I clearly understand that firm and drastic measures are at times necessary in order to secure desired objectives," he began, "but this does not excuse brutality, abuse of the sick, nor exhibition of uncontrollable temper in front of subordinates." Eisenhower warned that if the reports were true he would have to "seriously question your good judgment and your self-discipline." This would raise "serious doubts . . . as to your future usefulness." But exasperating as Patton was, Eisenhower would go to almost any length to keep him, and he assured Patton that "there is no record of the attached report or of my letter to you, except in my own secret files." He also promised there would be no official investigation. He did, however, order Patton to make a private report of his own, and to apologize to the soldier he had struck and to the nurses and doctors in the hospital.

Eisenhower found writing the letter painful in the extreme. Since the days at Fort Meade, almost a quarter of a century ago, Eisenhower and Patton had dreamed of fighting together. Now they were actually doing it, side by side in history's greatest war. Patton's temper had jeopardized everything. Eisenhower confessed, "No letter that I have been called upon to write in my military career has caused me the mental anguish of this one, not only because of my long and deep personal friendship for you but because of my admiration for your military qualities." But he concluded, sternly, "I assure you that conduct such as described in the accompanying report will *not* be tolerated in this theater no matter who the offender may be."[35]

Eisenhower hoped that with that the incident would die, but when a general slaps a private the story gets around. The press corps in Sicily got hold of it. On August 19 Demaree Bess of *The Saturday Evening Post*, Merrill Mueller of NBC, and Quentin Reynolds of *Collier's* came to see Smith, to tell him that they had the facts but did not want to embarrass General Eisenhower. They offered a deal—if Patton were removed from command, they would hold the story. When Smith took that offer into Eisenhower's office, Eisenhower commented sadly, "I might have to send Georgie Patton home in disgrace after all." He called Bess, Mueller, and Reynolds into his office, where he nearly begged the reporters to let him keep Patton. Eisenhower told them that Patton's "emotional tenseness and his impulsiveness are the very qualities that make him, in open situations, such a remarkable leader of an army. The more he drives his men the more he will save their lives." Eisenhower made it seem that victory over Germany depended on George Patton; under the circumstances, the reporters felt they could do nothing other than agree to hold the story of the slapping.[36] Patton, meanwhile, had made the apologies Eisenhower had required, then wrote his boss, "I am at a loss to find words with which to express my chagrin and grief at having given you, a man to whom I owe everything and for whom I would gladly lay down my life, cause for displeasure with me."[37]

The incident was closed, or so Eisenhower hoped. He was so anxious to keep it a secret that he did not inform Marshall, even after Marshall asked him for a candid assessment of the generals under his command (at this time, late August of 1943, the assumption was that Marshall would take command of the cross-Channel invasion in the spring of 1944, and Marshall was beginning to assemble a team of commanders). Eisenhower said that Patton's chief characteristics were energy, determination, and unflagging aggressiveness. He kept the troops going when anyone else would have let them stop and rest. Eisenhower did hint at the slapping by adding, "Patton continues to exhibit some of those unfortunate personal traits of which you and I have always known and which during this campaign caused me some most uncomfortable days." His explanation was vague; he said Patton's "habit of . . . bawling out subordinates" had extended to "personal abuse of individuals." Eisenhower said he had taken "the most drastic steps; and if he is not cured now, there is no hope for him." He believed Patton was cured, partly because of his "personal loyalty to you and to me," but mainly because "he is so avid for recognition as a great military commander that he will ruthlessly suppress any habit of his own that will tend to jeopardize it."

In reply to Marshall's question—Who should command the American Army group in the cross-Channel attack?—Eisenhower was direct. "You should take Bradley . . . He has never caused me one moment of worry." Less than a week later, Bradley had his orders, and on September 8 left for England to take command of the American Army assembling there.[38]

On August 10, Eisenhower submitted to a physical exam (a routine requirement before he could be promoted to full colonel). The doctors thought he was hypertensive and found his blood pressure too high. They ordered a week's rest, in bed. Five days later, Eisenhower actually did take two days off, staying in his bedroom, but not in his bed. Butcher found him pacing the room nervously, worrying about his responsibilities, but nevertheless in a reflective mood. With Butcher for an audience, he did a critique of his own generalship. He thought that he had made two serious errors, both the result of overestimating the enemy and therefore advancing too cautiously. He felt he should have gone farther east with the Torch landings, all the way to Tunis. He also wished that he had invaded Sicily at its northeastern tip, landing on both sides of Messina, thus cutting off the Germans and forcing them to attack Allied defensive lines.[39] It was an accurate, if painful, self-criticism, and a mark of the man that he was forthright in engaging in it. But there were many campaigns to go, and he did not want to repeat his mistakes. He was determined to seize whatever opportunities opened up to him, to avoid the small solutions and the resulting long-drawn-out, wasteful battles of attrition that had characterized Tunisia and Sicily.

• •

Italy came next. Eisenhower had decided, on July 17, to follow up the Sicilian campaign with an invasion of the mainland, taking advantage of the immense buildup of men and material in North Africa and Sicily to knock Italy out of the war. The questions were where to invade, and when, and how to take advantage of Italy's war weariness. The farther up the Italian coast the landings took place, the less fighting the troops would have to do to get to Rome; the sooner they could get started, the better; prior arrangements with the Italians, on the rough model of the deal with Darlan, would minimize, even eliminate, the need for hard fighting. In November 1942, during the first days of Torch, Eisenhower had passed up opportunities to take Sardinia or Tunis cheaply, on the run as it were; if such an opportunity opened in Italy, he said he was ready to seize it.

On July 19, the Allies carried out their first bombing raid against Rome, staying well clear of the Vatican and the major historical shrines and concentrating on the railroad yards. The most immediate result was a coup d'état in Rome. Mussolini was arrested and King Victor Emmanuel III, who was a part of the conspiracy, appointed Marshal Pietro Badoglio in his place. The following day Badoglio broadcast the news of Mussolini's fall and stated, "The war continues. Italy . . . keeps faith to its pledged word." But the statement convinced neither the Germans nor the Allies and only bewildered the Italian people.[40] Everyone expected Italy to quit the war. How to take advantage of her defection was now the question. Eisenhower was eager to seize the opportunity to deal, but Roosevelt thought defensively. The President told Churchill he thought the Italians ought to be held to terms "as close as possible to unconditional surrender." If that formula meant anything, it meant there would be no more Darlan deals, and Badoglio was the Italian equivalent of Darlan. Roosevelt, burned once, insisted, "In no event should our officers in the field fix any general terms without your approval or mine." Churchill was inclined to deal more gently and freely with the Italians: "Now Mussolini is gone," he replied to the President, "I would deal with any non-Fascist Italian government which can deliver the goods." But he too insisted on limiting Eisenhower's authority. Roosevelt, meanwhile, in a July 28 radio broadcast, emphatically affirmed that "our terms to Italy are still the same as our terms to Germany and Japan—unconditional surrender. We will have no truck with Fascism in any way, shape, or manner." To the Prime Minister, Roosevelt added privately, "There are some contentious people here who are getting ready to make a row if we seem to recognize the House of Savoy or Badoglio. They are the same element that made such a fuss over [Darlan]."[41]

While Roosevelt and Churchill talked, Hitler acted. The day Mussolini fell, the Germans began rushing troops into northern Italy, including two divisions from France, and Kesselring began planning for an occupation of Italy south of Rome.

Eisenhower too wanted to act immediately. He was eating breakfast in Tunis when he got the news of Mussolini's arrest. He called Macmillan on the telephone and asked him to come right over; when Macmillan arrived he found Eisenhower in a "state of considerable excitement and full of plans and ideas for exploiting the situation created by Mussolini's fall."[42]

Eisenhower's concern was the campaign. He was willing to accept the personal risk of making another deal with yet another European reactionary general if it would help him gain possession of the Italian peninsula quickly and cheaply. Churchill had already complained that the plans for the invasion seemed to him unduly cautious. Avalanche (code name for the assault) was scheduled to go ashore at Salerno, south of Naples; Churchill wanted to go farther north, closer to Rome. Eisenhower had explained to him that it was critical to keep the invasion force under the protection of land-based fighter aircraft, and that Salerno was at the extreme limit of the range of Sicilian-based fighters. Eisenhower had assured Churchill that he wanted to "avoid nibbling and jabbing" so as "to leap straight at the vitals of the enemy," but he had to have those fighters overhead.[43] Now Mussolini's fall opened the possibility of taking Rome on the run, if only the proper approach could be made to Italy to allow Eisenhower's troops into the Eternal City before the Germans got there in force. It would be another race, as in Tunis eight and a half months earlier.

Seizing the moment, Eisenhower wanted to make an immediate proposal to the Italians, via radio, promising them an honorable peace and stressing that the Allies would come to Italy as liberators to "rid you of the Germans and deliver you from the horrors of war."[44] Murphy told Eisenhower that AFHQ had no authority to make such a political offer and he must clear the broadcast with the two governments. Eisenhower sighed and said that he wished he were back in the days of the sailing ships, when generals in the field were free to act. But he knew Murphy was right and submitted the text to the CCS for approval. Much wrangling over the wording ensued; by the time a text had been agreed upon, more than a week later, the whole proposal was out of date. Meanwhile, German troops had continued to stream into Italy, supposedly to bolster the defenses of the Italian ally, actually to be prepared to take control when Italy defected.

Eisenhower also took the initiative in drawing up formal surrender terms, which he had ready by the end of the day on which Mussolini fell. He sent them on to the CCS, expressing the hope that they could serve as a basis for an immediate directive to him from the CCS. Eisenhower said he expected Badoglio to approach him, and he wanted to be ready to reply, and to make things easy for the Italians, so the terms he proposed granted peace to Italy and allowed the House of Savoy and Badoglio to remain in power. The terms were much less than unconditional surrender. All of Eisenhower's superiors, therefore, were displeased. Churchill said the Italians should be forced to disarm the Germans in Italy and spoke of turning the "fury of the Italian population" against the Hun. Eisenhower, much more realistic, replied that "there is no fury left in the population . . . . The people are tired and sick of the war and want nothing but peace." Roosevelt stuck to his demand for unconditional surrender. Marshall cautioned Eisenhower that his authority was limited to concluding local surrenders; so did Churchill. The State Department, the Foreign Office, the CCS, and the heads of government all sent long cables, each saying that Eisenhower must add this or that requirement to the surrender terms. "Poor Eisenhower," Macmillan noted, "is getting pretty harassed."[45] Caught between the two governments, Eisenhower confessed to Mamie, "In my youthful days I used to read about commanders of armies and envied them what I supposed to be a great freedom in action and decision. What a notion!! The demands upon me that must be met make me a slave rather than a master."[46]

While the Allied governments and soldiers debated, the Germans started four more divisions on the road to Italy; they even went to the extreme of withdrawing two SS panzer divisions from the Eastern Front.[47]

The bickering between AFHQ on the one hand, and London and Washington on the other, continued. Eisenhower, frustrated and irritated as he watched the German buildup in Italy in the daily Ultra intercepts, complained to the CCS: "I do not see how war can be conducted successfully if every act of the Allied Commander in Chief must be referred back to the home government for advance approval."[48] By then almost two weeks had passed since Mussolini's fall, and the Allies still did not have an agreed surrender policy, still had made no offer to Badoglio. Because Roosevelt's and Churchill's public announcements had insisted on unconditional surrender, no Italian official had approached AFHQ about making a deal. Eisenhower thought his superiors incredibly shortsighted and hopelessly legalistic in their approach; he had to admire the way Hitler brushed aside all technicalities and continued to rush troops into Italy.

Eisenhower had other complaints. He was being forced to draw down on his strength, required to ship landing craft, men, and aircraft to London for the cross-Channel buildup. He thought this policy, too, shortsighted; he thought it preferable to complete the Italian campaign first. He begged Marshall for more bombers, argued with him, pleaded his case. With more bombers, he could immobilize the German ground forces in Italy, he claimed, which would guarantee success in Avalanche. Without the bombers, the Germans would be free to build their defensive strength south of Rome. He also asked to be allowed to retain landing craft scheduled to go to England, so that he could mount and support a larger Avalanche. But Marshall would do nothing that threatened to reduce the commitment to the cross-Channel invasion, even for his protégé Eisenhower, and refused. Still Eisenhower persisted. When it came to obtaining firepower for AFHQ, he was as vigorous in presenting his case as MacArthur was in his Pacific domain, and a long way from the position he had taken a year earlier, when he promised Marshall that he "would not be adding to your troubles by insistently clamoring for more than you can furnish." Marshall, unmoved by Eisenhower's pleas, and never wanting an invasion of Italy anyway, said no again. Eisenhower's deputies then warned him that without the bombers and additional landing craft, Avalanche was too risky and should be called off.[49]

On August 17—the same day Eisenhower learned of the Patton slapping incident and Messina fell—the Italians finally approached the Allies. General Giuseppe Castellano of the Italian General Staff arrived in Lisbon and talked to the British ambassador there. He proposed a double cross—as soon as the Allies landed in strength in Italy, the Italians would sign an armistice with the Allies and simultaneously declare war on Germany. Eisenhower, hearing this proposal, was enthusiastic. He asked the CCS for permission to send General Strong to Lisbon immediately, to work out details with Castellano. He wanted Strong to avoid all the complications of any formal negotiations, make a simple military agreement with the Italians, and put off the politics until the peninsula was securely in Allied hands. In short, another Darlan deal.[50]

But while Eisenhower thought of the possibilities, his superiors thought of the reaction at home. Churchill and Roosevelt insisted that Eisenhower demand unconditional surrender. He could tell the Italians that they would be allowed to join in the crusade against the Nazis, but first they must submit publicly.[51] The obvious problem with their policy was that it delayed everything; by the time Eisenhower had concluded an agreement that his superiors would accept, the Germans had moved nineteen divisions into Italy. The bill for the delay was paid in blood at Salerno, Anzio, and Cassino.

On August 18, Eisenhower received his directive from the CCS. The Chiefs told him to send Strong and Smith to Lisbon to meet with Castellano. They should demand an unconditional surrender on the basis of the "short terms"; meanwhile Churchill and Roosevelt would work out the "long terms," which would include economic, political, and financial clauses and which the Italians would be required to sign later. Under the short terms, the Italians were to announce the armistice at once, send their fleet and air force to Allied territory, and join in the war against Germany.[52]

The directive was a strange document. Eisenhower was supposed to require Italian collaboration, but he was specifically forbidden to reveal his military plans to Badoglio's representative. How, under such circumstances, could he arrange for Italian collaboration? Eisenhower was supposed to demand "unconditional surrender" on the "conditions" of the short terms, in itself a comment on the logic being used. Eisenhower's bosses were ignoring realities. Italy was caught between the hammer and the anvil. Allied troops in Sicily were poised for invasion, while Allied planes pounded Italian cities from the skies. But the Germans were already in Italy in large numbers, with more coming in every day. If Italy surrendered to the Allies before Eisenhower's divisions got to Rome, the Germans would overthrow the government and occupy the country. The Italians scarcely knew where the greater threat lay. Their key question to Eisenhower, the one on which their decision would have to be based, was: Are you able to occupy Rome and protect us from the Germans? If so, the Italians were ready to cooperate. But the CCS insisted that Eisenhower should under no circumstances answer the question, for the very good reason that the answer was no. The Italians grossly overestimated Allied strength. They thought Eisenhower could bring fifteen divisions into Rome, when in fact he did not have enough resources to land three divisions in the Bay of Salerno.

On August 19, Smith and Strong had a nine-hour meeting with Castellano. The Italian general was shocked at the demand for unconditional surrender; Smith kept telling him that the words were irrelevant and that the terms would be modified in favor of Italy in accordance with the amount of help the Italians gave the Allies. Grasping at that straw, Castellano said he would take the short terms back to Rome for Badoglio's approval. He and the AFHQ representatives arranged to meet again on August 31.

On August 27, the CCS sent Eisenhower the "long terms," or comprehensive surrender document. Eisenhower groaned at the sight of it; the document contained forty-one tightly worded paragraphs covering military, civil, social, economic, and political affairs. Macmillan called the long terms "a planner's dream and a general's nightmare."[53] Eisenhower informed the CCS that on the basis of the long terms, nothing could be accomplished; he begged permission to proceed on the basis of the short terms. The CCS reluctantly agreed, but insisted that the long terms would eventually have to be signed by the Italians.

On August 31 Smith and Strong related this decision to Castellano, who tried to bargain, got nowhere, and then asked for assurances that the Allies would send an airborne division to Rome on the day of the invasion. Smith thought that might be possible, if the Italians could hold an airfield for the Allies to land on. Castellano thought they could. On that note, Castellano returned to Rome, promising to urge Badoglio to accept the short terms, with the proviso that an airborne division would land in Rome. The announcement of the armistice would be made the evening before the Allied landings.[54]

The following day, September 1, Eisenhower sent a full report to the CCS. Italy, he regretted to say, "is in fact an occupied country . . ." The Allies had responded too slowly; the Germans were already there in force. But there was one slim chance left, not to take the whole peninsula, but to take Rome and everything south of the city. That chance was the 82d Airborne Division, which Eisenhower had decided—as Smith had thought he would—to fly into Rome on the eve of Avalanche.[55]

On September 3, Montgomery's Eighth Army slipped across the Strait of Messina and landed on the Italian toe, a pointless military operation but one of some psychological significance, as it kept the pressure on the Italian government. The following day, in Sicily, Smith and Castellano signed the short terms and agreed to announce the armistice simultaneously late in the evening of September 8, a few hours before Avalanche would begin. After the signing, Smith calmly handed Castellano a copy of the long terms. Castellano blanched, tried to back out. Smith finally mollified him by handing him a written promise: "The additional clauses [i.e., the long terms] have only a relative value insofar as Italy collaborates in the war against the Germans."[56]

Eisenhower then made some rapid adjustments in his plans, to take advantage of Italian cooperation. The 82d Airborne had already been assigned to Rome. Castellano had promised that the Italians would open the port of Taranto on the Italian heel to the Allies, so Eisenhower decided to rush the British 1st Airborne Division there. The Allies would thus be entering Italy from four different directions—Montgomery coming north from the toe, Mark Clark's Fifth Army striking at Salerno, the 82d Airborne going to Rome, and the 1st Airborne at Taranto. Best of all was the prospect of taking control of Rome, because that would cut all German communications with the forces south of Rome and make reinforcement on the Salerno front difficult. If everything worked out, Eisenhower's forces would be established north of Rome before the end of the month.

Still, Eisenhower was worried, mostly about Badoglio's resolution. On September 6, he decided to send Major General Maxwell Taylor, commander of the 82d Airborne's artillery, to Rome, secretly, to make last-minute arrangements with Badoglio, to recommend changes as needed, and to keep Badoglio to the mark. Taylor got to Rome safely, only to find the Italians frightened to death. They insisted that the Allied force coming to Rome was too small to hold off the Germans (they were shocked to discover that only one division was involved), that the Italians could not hold the airfield for the 82d, that the landings at Salerno—about which they had just learned, and which were less than one-fifth the size they expected—were too weak and too far south and would do the Italians no good at all. In short, they wanted out of the whole deal. Taylor did not get to see Badoglio himself until midnight, September 7–8. Badoglio too wanted to cancel the landings in Rome, at Salerno, the armistice, everything. He said he would not make an announcement. Taylor argued, threatened, eventually gave up, informed Eisenhower of Badoglio's double cross, and recommended that the flight of the 82d to Rome be called off.[57]

On the morning of September 8, Eisenhower woke early, dictated some messages, then left Algiers for Amilcar, his advance command post near Tunis. Shortly after he left, Taylor's message saying the armistice had been renounced by Badoglio came in and was decoded. It threw Smith off balance. After sending a copy to Eisenhower at Amilcar, Smith sent a message to the CCS asking whether or not to proceed with AFHQ's own armistice announcement.[58]

When Eisenhower arrived at Amilcar and saw the message, he was furious. The blood rushed to his face, his mouth tightened, his eyes flashed, his muscles contracted. His anger with Smith for bucking the problem to the CCS was almost as great as his anger at Badoglio for his double cross. He grabbed a pencil, broke it, took up another, broke it, cursed, took a breath, then began dictating a reply to Badoglio. "I intend to broadcast the existence of the armistice at the hour originally planned," he began. That hour was 6:30 P.M. that day, less than twelve hours away. "If you . . . fail to cooperate as previously agreed I will publish to the world the full record of this affair." Eisenhower's voice rose as he went on. "Failure now on your part to carry out the full obligations to the signed agreement will have the most serious consequences for your country. No future action of yours could then restore any confidence whatever in your good faith and consequently the dissolution of your government and nation would ensue."[59]

Most reluctantly, Eisenhower then decided to cancel the 82d's operation. That decision was in accordance with the cautious tactics Eisenhower had used—and later condemned—in both the North African and the Sicilian landings, but out of phase with his own expressed desire to take more risks in the future, and his insistence on getting the most out of the Italian surrender. But it seemed impossible that the 82d, by itself, without the support of the Italian Army, could hold Rome. And Taylor, the man on the spot, recommended against trying; Taylor was a West Pointer with a reputation for brilliance and courage, and an ability to keep his head in a crisis. Eisenhower felt he had to trust Taylor.

At 6:30 P.M., on schedule, Eisenhower went on the air on Radio Algiers. "This is General Dwight D. Eisenhower, Commander in Chief of the Allied forces," he began. "The Italian government has surrendered its armed forces unconditionally. As Allied Commander in Chief, I have granted a military armistice." That armistice became effective "this instant." He urged the Italian armed forces to "help eject the German aggressor from Italian soil." When he finished, technicians at Amilcar quickly turned their dials to pick up Radio Rome. No announcement came from Badoglio. After waiting ten minutes, Eisenhower had the text of Badoglio's proclamation—written for him by Smith—read out over Radio Algiers. It ordered the Italian armed forces to cease all acts of hostility against the Allies and urged them to fight the Germans.[60] An hour later, Badoglio read the same announcement over Radio Rome. Eisenhower grunted his satisfaction. He had "played a little poker," he said, and he had won.[61]

How much he had won he did not know, as no one could tell what Italian assistance would be worth. Now Eisenhower entered the waiting period before an invasion, that maddening time when he could only pray. He wrote two letters to Mamie. "Here I am once more," he said, "waiting . . . This is the thing that is making an old man of me!" He made up pipe dreams about things they would do together after the war—the "predominant note is laziness, soft climate, and utter contentment."[62]

Clark's men were on their way to the beaches. The Germans were preparing to take control of Rome. They already had a division in Salerno, and with Rome in their hands, they could quickly get more there. "I am frank to state," Eisenhower told Marshall, "that there is more than a faint possibility that we may have some hard going."[63]

CHAPTER FOURTEEN

Algiers, Naples, Cairo

September 9–December 31, 1943

WHEN EISENHOWER awoke on September 9, he learned that Clark's Fifth Army was getting ashore successfully, but that the Germans had taken control of Rome, where the Italian government had panicked. At 5 A.M. the king, Badoglio, and the most important military leaders had fled the capital, headed for the south and safety under Allied protection. No one bothered to send any orders to the Italian ground forces (numbering some 1.7 million men); the Germans disarmed most of them, while the rest threw away their uniforms and merged into the civilian population. Almost overnight, the Italian Army ceased to exist and Italy was an occupied country.[1] Eisenhower cabled Badoglio, who had made it to Brindisi, urging him to take action. "The whole future and honor of Italy depends upon the part which [Italy's] armed forces are now prepared to play," Eisenhower said. He asked Badoglio to issue a clarion call to all patriotic Italians to "seize every German by the throat."[2] It did little good. The Italian fleet did sail from its ports, eventually to join the Allies, which left the ports of Bari, Brindisi, and Taranto open to Cunningham's ships, who took possession and allowed the British 1st Airborne Division to occupy the heel of Italy. But as for the ground forces, asking the Italians to act was like beating a dead horse. Aside from the fleet, all the Allies had gotten out of the armistice was a symbol of leadership in the persons of the king and Badoglio, and those two had fled their capital.

At Salerno by midmorning the initial success was giving way to disturbing developments. There was a twenty-five-mile gap between the British and the American beaches, and efforts to link up were meeting increasingly heavy resistance. Clark wanted Eisenhower to rush the 82d Airborne into the gap; Eisenhower was trying to find the landing craft with which to do the job. "I feel that Avalanche will be a matter of touch and go for the next few days," Eisenhower told the CCS at noon on September 9. If he had sufficient landing craft to put the 82d ashore immediately "the matter would be almost a foregone conclusion," but as it was "we are in for some very tough fighting."[3]

They were indeed. On September 10, Kesselring began a series of counterattacks against the beachhead, concentrating on the gap between the British and the American forces. By the eleventh the Germans had five divisions in the area and seemed on the verge of destroying Clark's Fifth Army. Eisenhower had no landing craft available to reinforce Clark. He did have a part of the 82d drop by parachute into the beachhead. He urged Montgomery to speed up his movement north, from the Italian toe, in order to threaten Kesselring's left flank (the British Eighth Army and advanced only forty-five miles during its first seven days on the mainland, against negligible resistance). Eisenhower rushed fighter aircraft to the small airfield on the constricted beachhead, and prepared another infantry division to go to Salerno as soon as the landing craft were available. He begged the CCS for more B-24s, saying, "I would give my next year's pay for two or three extra heavy groups right this minute."[4]

It was a most dangerous moment. An army of four divisions was on the verge of annihilation. Eisenhower received a message from Clark that indicated that Clark was making plans to put his headquarters on board ship in order to control both sectors and to continue the battle in whichever one offered the greater chance for success. The message made Eisenhower almost frantic. He told Butcher and Smith that the headquarters should leave last, that Clark ought to show the spirit of a naval captain and if necessary go down with his ship. He thundered: "By God!, the Fifth Army ought to emulate the Russians at Stalingrad and stand and fight." He wondered aloud if it had not been a mistake to give Clark the command—he wished he had selected Patton. But neither then nor later, after Clark continued to disappoint him, did he seriously consider removing Clark from command. For one reason, he liked and respected Clark; for another, he blamed the CCS for the situation, not Clark. If his bosses had listened to reason and given him the bombers and landing craft he had asked for, there would be no problem at Salerno. As it was, "we have such a painfully slow buildup and the enemy can constantly bring so much strength against us" that the situation was critical. Eisenhower admitted, in a diary entry of September 14, that his deputies had warned him that there was insufficient landing craft and air cover for the invasion, which they had wanted to call off, and that the decision to go ahead "was solely my own, and if things go wrong there is no one to blame except myself." In a note to Marshall, he said that he thought Clark could hold on, but if he did not, "I would . . . merely announce that one of our landings had been repulsed—due to my error in misjudging the strength of the enemy at that place." But he had "great faith that even in spite of currently grim reports, we'll pull out all right."[5]

All that day, September 14, the Germans attacked. At the critical point, American artillerymen stood to their guns and prevented a German breakthrough. Eisenhower sent words of encouragement to Clark, told Tedder to put "every plane that could fly" over Salerno, including all the bombers, and told Cunningham to bring up close to shore every ship that could fire so that they could pound the Germans. The air forces dropped 3,020 tons of bombs that day, while the naval forces—mostly Royal Navy—delivered more than 11,000 tons of shells in direct support of the ground forces on the beachhead. By nightfall, the crisis was over. Kesselring called off any further counterattacks. The next day, lead elements of the Eighth Army made contact with a Fifth Army patrol. On September 18, Kesselring began a deliberate disengagement and withdrawal.[6]

Within two weeks, Eisenhower's forces had a continuous line across Italy, as Montgomery's right wing met with the left of the British 1st Airborne coming from the heel. Losses had been high but unevenly distributed—Fifth Army had suffered fourteen thousand casualties to Eighth Army's six hundred. The drive for Naples and the airfields at Foggia, on the east coast, then began.

At this point, Marshall sent Eisenhower some criticism of his generalship and a suggestion on how to improve. Marshall said he had been disappointed at Eisenhower's failure to seize Rome with the 82d Airborne, and disappointed too by the landings in the Italian toe, which struck him as unduly conservative. He said he feared that if Eisenhower took time to secure his position around Naples, the Germans would have time to prepare their defenses and thus make the road to Rome long and difficult. He wondered if Eisenhower had considered the possibility of halting Fifth and Eighth Army efforts toward Naples once the city was "under the guns" and making a dash for Rome, perhaps by amphibious means.[7]

Eisenhower replied with some heat that he too wanted to be bold—"I would give my last shirt to be able to push a strong division landing into the Gulf of Gaeta" (north of Naples)—but he simply did not have the landing craft, as Marshall surely knew, since Marshall himself was the man most responsible for the shortage. As Eisenhower dictated his defense of himself, his face set in a deep scowl of concentration. His usual practice while dictating was to pace the room, talking rapidly, or else to shift from chair to chair. This time he became so engrossed that he walked right out the open door into the hallway and kept on dictating. His secretary scurried after him, taking shorthand all the while. Eisenhower reminded Marshall that he did not have sufficient landing craft, and that the Germans had a panzer division in the Gulf of Gaeta, another in Rome, and a reserve division that could reinforce either one. Eisenhower felt that if he landed a small force it would be quickly eliminated, while a force large enough to sustain itself could not be mounted or maintained.

Eisenhower felt unfairly accused, by a man who should have known better and yet one whom he respected more than anyone else in the world. "As a final word," he concluded, "I want to say that we are looking every minute for a chance to utilize our air and naval power to turn the enemy positions . . . I do not see how any individual could possibly be devoting more thought and energy to speeding up operations or to attacking boldly and with admitted risk than I do." As Eisenhower was dictating, a message came in from Churchill. The Prime Minister congratulated Eisenhower on the Salerno landings and commented, "As the Duke of Wellington said of the Battle of Waterloo, 'It was a damned close-run thing.'" Churchill said he was proud of Eisenhower for his policy of "running risks." Eisenhower triumphantly passed the message along to Marshall and commented, "I feel certain that [Churchill] looks upon me as a gambler."[8]

Gambler or not, by September 26 Eisenhower was committed to the slow, direct, expensive overland approach to Rome. He based his decision on Ultra intercepts and his shortages of landing craft and bombers. Ultra revealed that Hitler planned to withdraw to northern Italy, and without landing craft to make wide, sweeping end runs, or the aircraft to block the German retreat, Eisenhower felt there was little he could do beyond staying on the Germans' heels. In late September, after Fifth Army had Naples and Eighth Army had Foggia, he thought about calling a halt, but rejected the idea because of Rome's political prestige, because there were airfields around Rome which AFHQ could use, and because if the Allies ceased their offensive, Kesselring might counterattack. Kesselring, meanwhile, had convinced Hitler that he could fight a successful delaying action south of Rome and received permission to construct a "Winter Line," a series of defensive positions, organized in depth, across the Italian peninsula, well south of Rome. Ultra did not pick up the new decision, so Eisenhower, at the end of September, still expected to take the city before the end of October.[9]

He was badly mistaken. Problems with weather, terrain, and enemy resistance slowed the offensive to a crawl. The Allied air forces could not operate because of the torrential rains, tanks could not maneuver off the roads, artillery got bogged down in the mud, and there were no landing craft to take advantage of control of the sea, so all of Eisenhower's assets were relatively useless, while the Germans took advantage of their more than two-to-one manpower advantage (Eisenhower's eleven divisions were engaging twenty-five German divisions) to make every step forward bloody and costly. All through October and November the Fifth and Eighth Armies tried to attack, but with minimal success. Kesselring had imposed a stalemate in Italy.

Eisenhower decided to move AFHQ forward, closer to the front lines, partly to keep in better contact with Montgomery and Clark, mainly because he did not want the staff digging in at one location, particularly in a large city like Algiers. The staff did not get its required work done when the officers had comfortable billets and social obligations, and the troops resented it when they saw staff officers living in splendor. Eisenhower told Smith to set up an advance headquarters near Naples. It took more than a month to arrange the move, and when it did come it accomplished few of Eisenhower's objectives. Smith had picked a sumptuous villa for himself, Butcher had found another for Eisenhower, Prince Umberto's hunting lodge. It proved to be a poor choice. Butcher bubbled over with accounts of its splendors, but Eisenhower had hardly entered the place when an aide came running downstairs—there was a rat in the general's bathroom. Eisenhower took personal command. Pulling a revolver, he marched into the bathroom and fired four shots. All missed. Butcher finally killed the rat with a stick. They then got onto the elevator, where they became stuck and stood around for half an hour waiting to be freed. The fireplace in Eisenhower's bedroom did not work and there were lice in the beds. Butcher's laconic comment was "It's a tough war."[10]

Eisenhower's new office was in the Caserta Palace north of Naples. He had a room large enough to serve as a railroad station. He protested at the excess space, in vain. His staff had a conqueror's complex, as did his generals. On a cruise around the Isle of Capri, Eisenhower spotted a large villa. "Whose is that?" he asked. "Yours, sir," someone replied—Butcher had arranged it. Nodding at another, even larger villa, Eisenhower asked, "And that?" "That one belongs to General Spaatz." Eisenhower exploded. "Damn it, that's *not* my villa! And that's not General Spaatz' villa! None of those will belong to any general as long as I'm Boss around here. This is supposed to be a rest center—for combat men—not a playground for the Brass!" He meant it. When he returned to shore, he wired Spaatz, "This is directly contrary to my policies and must cease at once."[11]

Such concern with the men under his command was typical of Eisenhower. It enhanced his popularity. The Capri story, and others similar to it, quickly got out to the troops and delighted them. Nothing pleased the footslogger struggling in the mud of Italy more than hearing that Eisenhower had put Spaatz or some other general in his place. The fact that Eisenhower swore like a sergeant was much appreciated by the men. So were his frequent visits to the front lines, especially because he listened to the troops' complaints and, when he could, did something about them. For his part, Eisenhower enjoyed escaping from the VIPs who were coming into his theater in large numbers by going to the front. Chatting with troops restored his energy. "Our soldiers are wonderful," he told Mamie. "It always seems to me that the closer to the front the better the morale and the less the grumbling. No one knows how I like to roam around among them—I'm always cheered up by a day with the actual fighters."[12]

Also cheering was news from Washington that Mamie was doing well; indeed that was the best part about the constant stream of VIP visitors. Many of them had seen Mamie recently and "all report you [Mamie] in tip-top shape . . . [and] fine fettle—and a person of whom the whole army is proud—because of your tact, good sense and modesty." Eisenhower reported that his sister-in-law had written him, asking him to "order" Mamie to San Antonio for the winter; his comment to Mamie was "I give lots of orders, but I'd play —— trying to give you one!"

When the VIPs got back to Washington, they brought their purchases with them, and boasted about how little this or that item had cost in Naples. Mamie wondered why her husband did not buy her a dress, or a leather handbag, a scarf, something. "Possibly it's difficult for you to understand that I cannot get time to go browsing around shops like a lot of others can," Eisenhower replied, and explained that he had not been in a shop in more than a year. He did send aides out looking for good buys, but complained that when they went shopping, "they think first of themselves."

With the front lines stabilized, Italy relegated to the status of a secondary theater, and the buildup for the cross-Channel attack well under way, AFHQ was full of gossip about command changes. The most persistent rumor had Marshall taking command in London, with Eisenhower moving to Washington as his successor. Eisenhower told Mamie he did not know what would happen, but whatever did, "I do hope I can have a visit with you before too long." Reflecting on their eighteen-month separation, and on the events that had transpired and their effect on him, he commented, "I know I'm a changed person—no one could be through what I've seen and not be different from what he was at the beginning."[13]

However great his desire to be with Mamie, the prospect of going to Washington filled Eisenhower with dismay. Chatting one day at breakfast with Butcher and Smith about the possibility of his becoming the Chief of Staff, Eisenhower said that it was a "tremendous mistake" because he was "not temperamentally fitted for the job." He feared it would destroy him, as he had no patience with politicians because he could not bear to continue an argument "after logic had made the opposition's position untenable, yet politicians persist against all logic." Butcher rejoined that in his opinion there was nothing to worry about, as Eisenhower was "the logical and inevitable choice for the European command." Eisenhower liked the idea but thought it impossible. He felt the obvious choice for Overlord—the new code name for the cross-Channel attack—was either Brooke or Marshall. If Marshall took command of Overlord, it would be politically necessary to give the Mediterranean command to a British officer in order to retain balance; a suitable post would then have to be found for Eisenhower. He hoped he would be named ground commander for Overlord—that is, take the role Alexander had in the Mediterranean—but was afraid he would have to go back to Washington. "This uncertainty takes the pep out of everyone," Butcher reported. Eisenhower was "sweating it out in big drops."[14]

At this juncture, with a presidential election a year away, another possibility for Eisenhower's future opened. Republicans were casting about for a candidate to challenge Roosevelt. MacArthur was one obvious choice and a boom began to develop for him. Inevitably, Eisenhower's name also began to pop up. Arthur Eisenhower was bothered by this. He told his younger brother that MacArthur's reputation was suffering because he refused to deny that he had political ambitions, and he urged Eisenhower to make an emphatic denial of his own ambitions. Eisenhower told his brother he had seen some "careless and ill-considered items in the newspapers" about his supposed candidacy, but he felt this would happen to any man whose name "appears with some frequency in the public print." He saw no need to make "any statement whatsoever because to do so would, I think, merely be making myself ridiculous." What he would do was negative—"I will not tolerate the use of my name in connection with any political activity of any kind."[15] Then Walter Winchell, in a radio broadcast, said that if the Republicans ran MacArthur, Roosevelt would take Eisenhower as his running mate on the Democratic ticket. Eisenhower's comment was short: "I can scarcely imagine anyone in the United States less qualified than I for any type of political work."[16] Lacking the slightest encouragement from the prospective candidate, the Eisenhower boom quickly faded from the infinitesimal into total obscurity.

The President himself, meanwhile, came to the Mediterranean, on his way to Cairo for a meeting of the CCS. Eisenhower flew to Oran to meet Roosevelt, then accompanied him to Tunis, where they went on a motor trip to inspect battlefield sites, both recent and ancient, and had a long talk. Roosevelt shifted quickly from subject to subject and Eisenhower found him a fascinating conversationalist. At one point the President touched on Overlord. He said he dreaded the thought of losing Marshall in Washington, but added, "You and I, Ike, know the name of the Chief of Staff in the Civil War, but few Americans outside the professional services do." He thought it only fair that Marshall have an opportunity to make his mark on history as commander of a field army. Later that day Admiral King, who had accompanied Roosevelt, told Eisenhower that he had urgently and persistently advised the President to keep Marshall in Washington, but had lost. "I hate to lose General Marshall as Chief of Staff," King told Eisenhower, "but my loss is consoled by the knowledge that I will have you to work in his job." Eisenhower took King's statement as "almost official notice that I would soon be giving up field command to return to Washington."[17]

On November 21, Roosevelt's party flew to Cairo, where they argued for three days with the British about operations in 1944 and future command arrangements. On November 24, Eisenhower went to Cairo to testify before the CCS on his theater. The Chiefs were impressed by his presentation. He demonstrated a firm grasp of the military situation and showed himself to be realistic about the possibilities.

That night Marshall gave a huge dinner party. The menu included turkey, cranberries, stuffing, and all the trimmings. When one of the guests was leaving he said to Marshall, "Thank you very much for a fine Thanksgiving dinner." Eisenhower, astonished, turned and said, "Well, that shows what war does to a man. I had no idea this was Thanksgiving Day." Marshall decided he had been working too hard and suggested that he take some time off. Eisenhower replied that there was too much work to do. Marshall made the suggestion an order. "Just let someone else run that war up there for a couple of days," he said sternly. "If your subordinates can't do it for you, you haven't organized them properly."[18] So Eisenhower traveled briefly to Luxor in the Valley of the Kings, and to Jerusalem and Bethlehem, but he found he could not relax and enjoy the sights. After a couple of days of fretting, he called the vacation off, returning to Algiers.

Roosevelt, Churchill, and the CCS had meanwhile gone on to Teheran, Iran, for a meeting with Stalin. Stalin's concern continued to be the Second Front. When Roosevelt assured him that it was definitely on for the spring of 1944, Stalin demanded to know who was in command. Roosevelt replied that the appointment had not yet been made. Stalin said in that case he did not believe the Western Allies were serious about the operation. Roosevelt promised to make the selection in three or four days.

Despite his promise, Roosevelt shrank from the distasteful task of making the decision. His preferred solution—Marshall for Overlord, Eisenhower as his replacement in the War Department—had little to recommend it. It would make Eisenhower Marshall's boss, an absurd situation, and—worse—put Eisenhower in a position of giving orders to MacArthur, which MacArthur was certain to resent. Nevertheless, Roosevelt desperately wanted to give Marshall his opportunity. When they got back to Cairo, in early December, he asked Marshall to express his personal preference, and thus, he hoped, make the decision for him, but Marshall replied that while he would gladly serve wherever the President told him to, he would not be the judge in his own case.[19]

Eisenhower, meanwhile, still assumed that he was about to return to Washington. The American officers at AFHQ anxiously asked him who he was going to take home with him to serve on his staff at the War Department. Eisenhower laughed and said he thought he had better leave them all in the Mediterranean, as he would be carried up to Arlington Cemetery six months after assuming his responsibilities anyway. He hated to leave the Mediterranean, especially when his forces were still short of Rome, but there it was. At a meal with his staff on

December 4, he tried to keep his spirits up by concentrating on the bright side and reminding himself of how lucky he had been. He expressed his gratitude to Marshall and Roosevelt for the opportunity he had been given, and said he thought of himself as "a fortunate beneficiary of circumstances." He had a lot to be thankful for, whatever happened next. He was a soldier and he was prepared to do his duty. He expected to depart for Washington in the near future, and thought he would go by a round-the-world route, stopping off to visit MacArthur in Australia and Mountbatten in Burma. Such a trip would give him firsthand information on conditions in their theaters.[20]

While Eisenhower was making these plans, Roosevelt made his decision. As the last meeting at Teheran was breaking up, Roosevelt asked Marshall to write a message to Stalin for him. As Roosevelt dictated, Marshall wrote. "From the President to Marshal Stalin," it began. "The immediate appointment of General Eisenhower to command of Overlord operation has been decided upon." Roosevelt then signed it.

It was the most coveted command in the history of warfare. It gave Eisenhower his great, unique opportunity. Without it, he would have been only one among a number of famous Allied generals rather than *the* Great Captain of World War II and, as a consequence, President of the United States. He got the appointment, it seemed, by default. In explaining his reasoning afterward, Roosevelt said that he just could not sleep at night with Marshall out of the country. Butcher had been right all along—Eisenhower was the logical choice because Marshall was too important to be spared, even for Overlord. Since the commander had to be an American, a process of elimination brought it down to Eisenhower.

There were, nevertheless, manifold positive reasons for Eisenhower's selection. Overlord, like Torch, was going to be a joint operation, and Eisenhower had proved that he could create and run an integrated staff and successfully command combined British-American operations. No other general had done so. Admiral Cunningham, now a member of the CCS (he had assumed the duties of First Sea Lord in mid-October), had said it well when he left the Mediterranean. He told Eisenhower it had been a great experience for him to see the forces of two nations, made up of men with different upbringings, conflicting ideas on staff work, and basic, "apparently irreconcilable ideas," brought together and knitted into a team. "I do not believe," Cunningham said, "that any other man than yourself could have done it."[21]

The key word was "team." Eisenhower's emphasis on teamwork,

his never-flagging insistence on working together, was the single most important reason for his selection, much more important than his generalship, which in truth had been cautious and hesitant. Eisenhower's dedication to teamwork was, of course, a theme that had characterized his whole life, stretching back to the Abilene High School baseball and football games. Gathering the disparate forces for Overlord, welding them into a genuine team, making the plans for the actual engagement, and directing the action once the conflict began were challenges rather like coaching a football team, albeit on an immensely larger scale. The job required an ability to spot and exploit each player's strength, and to force each player—many of them "stars," egotistical and self-centered—to merge his talents with the others in order to fight together in a common cause. Marshall, for all his awesome abilities, did not have the patience required to work smoothly and efficiently with prima donnas, especially British prima donnas. Nor did Marshall have Eisenhower's experience in commanding amphibious operations. Brooke, a man who was consistently and scathingly critical of Eisenhower's professional competence, recognized this truth. "The selection of Eisenhower instead of Marshall," he wrote, "was a good one."[22]

Another, related factor in Roosevelt's choice was Eisenhower's popularity. Everyone liked him, responded positively to his outgoing personality, even when they disagreed with his decisions. His hearty laugh, infectious grin, relaxed manner, and consistent optimism were irresistible. Equally important, he was physically strong enough to withstand the rigors and pressures of a long and arduous campaign. Fifty-three years old, he was tough enough to get along on four or five hours sleep a night, to shake off a cold or the flu, to rouse himself from near-total exhaustion and present a cheerful face to his subordinates. It was not that he did not pay a price for all his activity, but that he did not let it show. In September 1943, a relative told him that he was pleased to see from some snapshots taken in Sicily that Eisenhower looked so healthy. In reply, Eisenhower said, "I must admit that sometimes I feel a thousand years old when I struggle to my bed at night."[23] Nevertheless, the overriding impression he gave was one of vitality. Dwight Eisenhower was an intensely alive human being who enjoyed his job immensely.

That quality showed in his speech, his mannerisms, his physical movements, most of all in his eyes. They were astonishingly expressive. As he listened to his deputies discuss future operations, his eyes moved quickly and inquisitively from face to face. His concentration was intense, almost a physical embrace. The eyes always showed his mood—

they were icy blue when he was angry, warmly blue when he was pleased, sharp and demanding when he was concerned, glazed when he was bored. Most of all, they bespoke his supreme self-confidence, a certainty of belief in himself and his abilities. It was neither a blind nor an egotistical confidence. As has been seen, he was a sharp and insightful critic of his own decisions before both Torch and Husky. Like the successful football coach studying the movies of the preceding week's game, his self-criticism was searching and positive, designed to eliminate errors and improve performance. He had made, and would have to make, countless decisions, decisions that involved the lives of tens of thousands of men, not to speak of the fate of great nations. He did so with the certainty that he had taken everything into account, gathered all relevant information, and considered all possible consequences. Then he acted. This is the essence of command.

His self-confidence inspired confidence in him. When associates described Eisenhower, be they superiors or subordinates, there was one word that almost all of them used. It was trust. People trusted Eisenhower for the most obvious reason—he was trustworthy. Disagree as they might (and often did) with his decisions, they never doubted his motives. Montgomery did not think much of Eisenhower as a soldier, but he did appreciate other qualities. While he thought Eisenhower intelligent, "his real strength lies in his human qualities . . . He has the power of drawing the hearts of men towards him as a magnet attracts the bit of metal. He merely has to smile at you, and you trust him at once."[24]

With his staff and with his troops, with his superiors and with his subordinates, as with foreign governments, Eisenhower did what he said he was going to do. His reward was the trust they placed in him. Because of that trust, and because of the qualities he possessed that brought it about, he was a brilliant choice as Supreme Commander, Allied Expeditionary Force, quite possibly the best appointment Roosevelt ever made.

On December 7, Eisenhower met Roosevelt in Tunis, where the President was stopping on his way back to Washington. Roosevelt was taken off his plane and put in Eisenhower's car. As the automobile began to drive off, the President turned to the general and said, almost casually, "Well, Ike, you are going to command Overlord."[25]

The news electrified Eisenhower and his AFHQ associates. Their morale had declined as they prepared for Eisenhower's imminent departure for Washington. "We now feel," Butcher wrote, "that we have a definite and concrete mission. This adds zest to living and interest in pursuing the objective. It has already made a remarkable difference in Ike. Now he is back to his old system of incessant planning and thinking out loud of qualifications of this or that man for certain jobs."[26]

Personnel selection was crucial, and Eisenhower threw himself into the task. Bradley had already been selected to command the U.S. First Army, which delighted Eisenhower. For his British ground commander, he wanted Alexander, but accepted Montgomery when Churchill insisted on keeping Alexander in Italy. He kept Smith as his chief of staff, although Churchill begged him to leave Smith in Algiers to assist his successor, British General Henry "Jumbo" Wilson. Even Marshall complained that he was stripping AFHQ bare. But Eisenhower took Smith anyway, along with other key members of the Mediterranean command, such as Tedder (as his Overlord deputy), and Spaatz, to command the American bomber forces in Britain, and all the British officers on his AFHQ staff. The most important of these was Kenneth Strong, the G-2. A blunt, hardy Scot, Strong was popular with the Americans because of his unpretentious nature and quiet efficiency and the complete absence of the usual British superciliousness. Strong was, in addition, the best intelligence officer in the Allied camp; for that reason Brooke and Churchill wanted to keep him in the Mediterranean, where, despite Overlord, they hoped to keep the offensive going. Smith and Brooke fought over Strong, to the point that Eisenhower felt obliged to apologize to Brooke for Smith. Eisenhower explained that Smith "fights for what he wants" but meant no disrespect, then made it clear that apology or not, he wanted Strong with him for Overlord—and he got him. He also insisted on bringing his "family" to London with him—Butcher, Tex Lee, Mickey, Kay, two stenographers (WAAC's), two drivers (also WAACs), his cook, and the two black enlisted men who served as his houseboys.[27]

The American general he most wanted, next to Bradley, was Patton (although unwilling to relieve Clark in Italy, he never considered taking Clark to England for an Overlord command). He wanted Patton badly. It cost him something to get Patton, because just as he was making his selections, radio commentator Drew Pearson broke the news of the Patton slapping incident in a garbled and exaggerated broadcast. Eisenhower, the War Department, and the White House all received hundreds of letters, most demanding that any general who would strike a private in a hospital be summarily dismissed from the service. Marshall, who must have known of the incident but who had not been officially informed by Eisenhower, asked for an explanation. Eisenhower's reply ran to four single-spaced pages. He assured Marshall that despite reports that Patton had received no official reprimand (which was true), he had taken "corrective action" that was "adequate and suitable." Eisenhower thought the best thing to do was "to keep still and take the brunt of the affair myself."[28] He refused to make a public defense of his actions, or lack of them, and advised Patton to keep quiet, since "it is my judgment that this storm will blow over."[29] Eventually, it did, and Eisenhower took Patton to England with him, along with almost everyone else he wanted from the Mediterranean.

Through the second half of December, Eisenhower and his staff were anxious to get to London and go to work on Overlord. They were losing interest in the Mediterranean problems. They had to hang on, however, until the new year, when the shift would take place. Their lame-duck status in the Mediterranean, and their eagerness to get started on Overlord, led to anxiety and irritability. "Nothing has been exactly right [lately]," Eisenhower told Mamie on December 26. "Everybody about me is having a tough time. I try to hang on to some shreds of a good disposition, but it does get tough at times."[30]

He made an extended trip to the front, his last in Italy. It rained most of the time and, pepped up though he was after seeing the troops, he became thoroughly miserable during the seven-hour drive through rain and fog on the trip back to Naples. Smith was with him, and as they neared Naples, Eisenhower asked Smith to join him for dinner. Smith was as depressed as his boss and grumbled that he would rather not. Eisenhower had a violent reaction. He snapped that Smith was discourteous, that no subordinate, not even the chief of staff, could abruptly decline his commanding officer's invitation to dinner. Smith cursed, told Eisenhower he wanted to quit. Eisenhower said that would be just fine with him. "By God," he thundered, "I'll do what Churchill wants and leave you in the Mediterranean." "That suits me," Smith growled. The two men then settled into a sullen silence. After a bit, Smith mumbled an apology. Eisenhower did too, and they agreed to forget the whole thing.[31]

That Eisenhower could so completely lose his temper with Smith only illustrated how tired he was and how badly he needed a rest. Marshall had recognized this early in the month, and after he got back to Washington he began urging Eisenhower to come to the States and take a furlough. That suited Eisenhower's repeatedly expressed desire to spend a few days with Mamie, but ran counter to his sense of duty and anxiety to plunge into his new job. He begged off, telling Marshall that there was too much work to be done. Marshall finally made it a direct order. "You will be under terrific strain from now on," Marshall pointed out. "I am not interested in the usual rejoinder that you can take it. It is of vast importance that you be fresh mentally and you certainly will not be if you go straight from one great problem to another. Now come on home and see your wife and trust somebody else for 20 minutes in England."[32]

Eisenhower capitulated. He decided to fly to the United States and take two weeks off. He left at noon on the last day of 1943. Just before departing the Mediterranean, he wrote a friend, "I have put in a hard year here and I guess it is time to go."[33]

CHAPTER FIFTEEN

Washington, London, Bushy Park

January 1–May 15, 1944

EISENHOWER ARRIVED in Washington at 1:30 A.M. on Sunday, January 2. Mamie had learned only a few hours earlier that he was coming; she was still awake when her husband rushed to the Wardman Park Hotel to greet her. The Eisenhowers talked through the night, the words tumbling out—about the doings of old friends, taxes, the car, Eisenhower's assignment, John's progress, and a dozen other subjects. Mamie noticed changes in her husband. He was heavier, noticeably older, more self-assured than he had been eighteen months ago. She thought he was more serious, his voice a shade more decisive than it had been. She was worried about his excessive smoking, pleased by his infectious confidence in himself and in Overlord. After breakfast, he announced that he was off to the War Department to see Marshall, and just that quick he was gone. Time was precious to him now, in a way that it had never been before, and in the two weeks that followed, Mamie learned that it had become habitual for him to terminate a conversation or interview abruptly, not because he had grown rude, but simply because he was accustomed to it and expected everyone around him to understand that he had to get on to the next problem.[1]

At the War Department he made his first major decision as Supreme Commander. Smith had gone on ahead to London, to examine the plans worked up by British Lieutenant General Frederick Morgan. Morgan had used as his starting point the plans Eisenhower had developed in the summer of 1942 for Roundup; he had been forced to keep the size of the initial assault force at three divisions because of the limitations on the number of landing craft the CCS had allowed him for planning purposes. Eisenhower had glanced at Morgan's plan a month or so earlier, when one of Morgan's staff brought a copy to Algiers for criticism; Eisenhower had said at that time that the assault frontage was too narrow and would have to be broadened.[2] Now Smith had come to the same conclusion and wired Eisenhower that it was imperative to widen the assault. Smith said that if it was necessary in order to obtain the landing craft for Overlord, the scheduled simultaneous landing in the south of France, code name Anvil, should be abandoned. Eisenhower, using Marshall's desk, replied that he agreed completely with Smith—the assault had to be in at least five-division strength. But he hoped that by improvising and cutting every other possible corner they could come up with the craft necessary for both Anvil and Overlord. He would abandon Anvil only as a last resort, but whatever happened, Overlord had to be a five-division assault.[3]

On January 6, the Eisenhowers got into Marshall's private railroad car to go to White Sulphur Springs, where the Chief of Staff had arranged for them to stay at a small, private cottage, for two days of complete privacy. It was not an altogether restful and relaxing vacation, because twice Eisenhower slipped and called Mamie "Kay," which made Mamie furious.[4] Eisenhower blushed, explained that Kay really meant nothing to him; it was just that she was practically the only woman he had seen in a year and a half and her name just naturally popped out. Mamie found it a less than satisfactory explanation.

Later in the week, Eisenhower flew to Fort Riley, Kansas, then drove the short distance to Manhattan for a family reunion. Mamie, unable to fly, returned to Washington. Manhattan was the home of Kansas State College, where Milton had just assumed the duties of president. Ida Eisenhower came over from Abilene, while Arthur and his wife drove from Kansas City. Roy had died suddenly in 1942, and Edgar and Earl lived too far away to make the reunion. Milton warned his brother that Ida had lost her memory after David died, so he should not expect too much of her, but the tiny, white-haired Ida surprised them all when Eisenhower embraced her—"Why, it's Dwight!" she cried, laughing and crying at the same time. She was as cheerful and fun-loving as she had always been and joined in the talk and the jokes that filled Milton's house that afternoon. Eisenhower's brothers were impressed by his maturity, self-control, calm confidence, and determination. "Looking at Ike now," Arthur said. "you can't help but feel a little sorry for his enemies."[5]

The next day, Eisenhower flew back to Washington for a series of conferences. He met with Marshall and General Henry Arnold, who commanded the Army Air Forces. Eisenhower was concerned about the organization and command structure of the air forces in Britain. The CCS had assigned the tactical air forces, the fighters, to Overlord; their activities would be controlled by Marshal of the Royal Air Force Trafford Leigh-Mallory, who was directly responsible to Eisenhower (Tedder, although Eisenhower's deputy supreme commander, was without portfolio), but the bombers were not a part of the Overlord structure. General Arthur Harris headed the RAF Bomber Command, while General Carl Spaatz had the U.S. Eighth Air Force. Both Harris and Spaatz had their own strategy, Harris to bring about a German capitulation through terror bombing of German cities, Spaatz to force a German surrender through the selective destruction of certain key industries, especially oil production facilities. Neither man believed Overlord was necessary. Spaatz's subordinates had been heard to say that they wanted only twenty or thirty clear operational days and they would finish the war on their own.[6]

To Eisenhower, this was dangerous nonsense. He believed that Germany would have to be defeated on the ground before she would ever quit. Overlord was therefore the great operation of the war. In the initial stages, the Allies would be outnumbered on the ground ten to one in France; only air superiority made Overlord feasible. Eisenhower wanted to take the bombers away from the campaign inside Germany and use them for purposes that would be immediately helpful to Overlord. To that end, he had to have personal command of RAF Bomber Command and the Eighth Air Force. He discussed the situation with Marshall and indicated that he thought Harris and Spaatz should be placed under his command for a period of at least several weeks before the invasion. Marshall agreed. To Eisenhower's delight and surprise, so did Arnold.[7]

On January 12, Eisenhower went to the White House for a private conference with Roosevelt. He found the President in bed, ill with the flu. They talked for two hours, mainly about French and German affairs. Eisenhower was upset at the attitude toward de Gaulle that he found in Washington. Just before leaving Algiers, Eisenhower had met with de Gaulle, in what Butcher described as a "love fest." "I must have your help," Eisenhower had told de Gaulle, "and I have come to ask you for it." De Gaulle had replied, "Splendid! You are a man! For you know how to say, 'I was wrong.'"[8] What Eisenhower had in mind was the French Resistance; he counted on it for sabotage operations on D-Day, and for information on German dispositions and movements, and he knew that the Resistance would respond only to de Gaulle. Smith and de Gaulle had worked out an agreement whereby the Resistance would obey Eisenhower, in return for which Eisenhower promised that French forces would participate in the liberation of Paris and the FCNL would take control of civil affairs in the liberated areas of France.

But in Washington, to his distress, Eisenhower discovered that no one wanted to deal with de Gaulle. Roosevelt insisted that the French people would not submit to the authority of the FCNL and that any attempt to impose de Gaulle on France could lead to civil war. Eisenhower thought the President's position unrealistic, and politely told the President so, but Roosevelt was adamant. The difficulties that ensued from the Allied attempt to ignore de Gaulle, Eisenhower later said, caused him one of the "most acutely annoying problems" he had to face before D-Day.[9]

Eisenhower then turned to the problem of the occupation of Germany. He told the President that the plan to divide Germany into three zones, one for the Americans, one for the British, and one for the Russians, was a mistake. Germany, he declared, should not be divided into zones; the military government ought to be conducted by a coalition of the Allied forces, under a single commander. This would make administration simpler and make it easier to control the Red Army's behavior in the areas it occupied. Roosevelt, unconvinced, said he could deal with the Russians.[10] Eisenhower's attempts to change policy on the FCNL and on the occupation of Germany failed, and thus for Eisenhower the interview concluded on an unsatisfactory note.

The following day, Eisenhower's furlough ended. Little had been accomplished. Admiral King had refused to release landing craft from the Pacific, so there was no assurance that Overlord could be mounted on a five-division basis; Marshall and Arnold had promised to put Harris and Spaatz under Eisenhower's command, but the issue had not been settled; Eisenhower and Mamie had argued about Kay; Mamie was unhappy at her husband's single-minded concentration on Overlord, his obvious anxiety to get back to London, and the little time he had spent with her. Watching him pack for yet another lengthy, undetermined separation, her heart nearly broke. "Don't come back again till it's over, Ike," she said. "I can't stand losing you again."[11] A week later, Eisenhower wrote her: "I find myself very glad I came home—even though things did seem to be a bit upsetting! I guess it was just because we'd been separated so long, and before we could get really acquainted again, I was on my way." Four days after that, he thanked

Mamie for "the third letter I'd received since coming here and all of them have been wonderful—quite the nicest you've written since I left home in June '42." His conclusion was that, although everything had not gone as well as he had hoped, "My trip home has paid dividends!" [12]

Back in London, Eisenhower set up his headquarters on familiar grounds, at 20 Grosvenor Square. "Right now we are busy getting settled and going through the business of ramming our feet in the stirrups," he wrote a friend shortly after his arrival.[13] The process was much easier than it had been in June 1942. The SHAEF staff came primarily from AFHQ; the commanders of the field forces, with the exception of Leigh-Mallory, had had combat experience in the Mediterranean; Eisenhower now had three amphibious operations behind him; taken together, Eisenhower's team was battle-tested, committed to Allied unity, full of faith in Eisenhower, and eager to get to work. Compared to the team that had started on Torch, it was far superior; as Eisenhower put it, "Order had replaced disorder and certainty and confidence had replaced fear and doubt." [14]

There was also a single-mindedness not present in Torch. As Eisenhower said, at SHAEF there was "a very deep conviction, in all circles, that we are approaching a tremendous crisis with stakes incalculable." [15] Everyone was "working like dogs," he was pleased to note. As always, his emphasis was on the positive. "Our problems are seemingly intricate and difficult beyond belief," he said, but he refused to allow anyone even to hint that they would not be overcome. Privately, he was more worried than anyone else, but he never let his subordinates know it. "As the big day approaches," he wrote in early April, "tension grows and everybody gets more and more on edge. This time, because of the stakes involved, the atmosphere is more electric than ever before." Under the circumstances, "a sense of humor and a great faith . . . are essential to sanity." [16]

Another great difference between the pre-Torch and the pre-Overlord periods was that in 1944 Eisenhower did not have to prove himself to the British. His relations with Churchill were such that he could disagree violently with the Prime Minister over issues without affecting their friendship or mutual respect in any way. Except for Brooke, he got on well with the British Chiefs of Staff. His relations with Montgomery were formal and correct, rather than warm; with Tedder, by way of contrast, he had struck up a close friendship. With Cunningham, Eisenhower had established a mutual admiration society. In February, Cunningham hosted a stag dinner party for Eisenhower; the other guests were British officers who had served under Eisenhower in the Mediterranean. They presented Eisenhower with a silver salver, with their signatures inscribed on it, as a token of their esteem. Eisenhower was quite overcome. Never much interested in money nor a connoisseur of art objects, he nevertheless appreciated expensive gifts, which he accepted with embarrassment but held on to with pride. In this case, he wrote Mamie a long description of the gift "that would grace a king." He had it insured, photographed front and back, and placed in a vault in a bank outside London, away from the bombing area.[17]

In making the presentation, Cunningham began by recalling the days of October 1942, when many of the men present first started to work under Eisenhower. They had all wondered what sort of a man he was. "It was not long before we discovered that our Commander was a man of outstanding integrity," Cunningham declared, "transparent honesty and frank almost to an embarrassing degree . . . No one will dispute it when I say that no one man has done more to advance the Allied cause." Eisenhower, flushing deeply, could only manage to mumble a reply. The next day he apologized to Cunningham for not being more eloquent but said that the gift itself, plus the admiral's remarks, "came so nearly overwhelming me that my only recourse was to keep a very tight hold on myself."[18]

Closer personal relations with the British were possible in 1944, in contrast to 1942, partly because this time the place, time, and date of the assault were all fixed, rather than subjects for dispute. The place would be Normandy, west of the mouth of the Orne River, the time would be shortly after dawn, the date May 1. A complex set of factors had gone into these selections. The state of German defenses was the overriding consideration; they were strongest around the French ports and especially in the Pas de Calais, which otherwise would have been the obvious target as it was on the shortest line between England and Germany. Dawn was the time because it would allow the fleet to cross the Channel under the cover of darkness and give the troops a full day to establish a beachhead. May 1 was the date because of moon and tidal conditions; the AEF had to come ashore shortly after dead low tide due to the German underwater obstacles, and the bombers and paratroopers needed at least a half-moon the night before. The assault had to come late enough in the year to allow for final training of troops in the British Isles, but soon enough to give the Allies at least four months of good campaigning weather in France. These conditions were met only three times in the spring of 1944—during the first days of May and the first and third weeks of June.[19]

The issue that was not settled, and thus the one that would cause Eisenhower a great deal of anguish, was the scope of the commitment in landing craft and air power to Overlord. To Eisenhower, convinced that Overlord was *the* great operation of the war, it was almost inconceivable that there should be any question about a total commitment. "Every obstacle must be overcome," he declared in his initial report to the CCS, "every inconvenience suffered and every risk run to ensure that our blow is decisive. We cannot afford to fail." That meant, above all else, that he had to have sufficient landing craft to mount a five-, rather than a three-, division assault, with enough additional craft for two follow-up divisions to go ashore on D-Day. "Nothing less will give us an adequate margin to ensure success," he warned, and to get it he was willing to make sacrifices elsewhere. He had to have 271 landing craft beyond those already assigned to Overlord, and to have them he had decided, within a week of his arrival in London, to put D-Day back a month, from May 1 to early June, in order to have available an extra month's production of landing craft (amounting to almost one hundred vessels). He was also willing to reduce the simultaneous Anvil to a threat—that is, to postpone the landings in the south of France by a month or more—but "only as a last resort and after all other means and alternatives have failed to provide the necessary strength" for Overlord.[20] As he was making major concessions, he expected the CCS to do no less.

But the CCS could not agree on a strategy; they had bitter disagreements over what to do in the Mediterranean after Rome had fallen. To simplify a complicated debate, the British wanted to throw a right hook, by mounting an amphibious offensive in the Adriatic; the Americans favored a left hook, into the Gulf of Lions, in southern France. In the American view, the left hook would outflank the Alps, allowing troops from the Mediterranean to advance toward Germany through the Rhône Valley, while operations to the east, in the Adriatic, would simply run into more mountains. Anvil would give direct support to Overlord, both by pinning down German forces in southern France and by opening the port of Marseilles, which would give the AEF badly needed logistical support and, as a bonus, open a theater through which additional American and French divisions could participate in the battle for France. Neither Marshall nor Eisenhower could see any advantage whatsoever to the British proposal of a right hook.[21]

The worldwide shortage of landing craft colored the entire situation and made all events related. At one point Churchill growled that "the destinies of two great empires . . . seem to be tied up in some Goddamned things called LSTs."[22] The shortage stemmed from three sources: a failure earlier in the war to heed Eisenhower's advice and put landing craft at the top of the production priority list; the U.S. Navy's (and MacArthur's) insistence on assuming the offensive in the Pacific; and the unexpectedly determined German resistance in Italy, especially at Anzio, where the Allies had tried an end run in January, only to be pinned down at the beachhead, which therefore required landing craft for maintenance.

Eisenhower had never been enthusiastic about Anzio, but the operation had been mounted after he left the Mediterranean and he could do nothing about it. He could, and did, complain about the U.S. Navy. On January 25 he growled that Admiral King was keeping all information as to the number and location of landing craft in the Pacific a secret. Army planners were forever in the dark. No one but King and his immediate subordinates, Eisenhower claimed, knew how many craft there were in the Pacific, which he called "the Navy's private war."[23] Two weeks later Eisenhower wrote in his diary, "The fighting in the Pacific is absorbing far too much of our limited resources in landing craft during this *critical* phase of the European war." He thought this was a major error, because Overlord should have every available resource until the invading force was firmly established on the Continent. "But we are fighting two wars at once—which is wrong—so far as I can see from my own limited viewpoint." Whatever the cause, the landing craft simply were not there for simultaneous landings in the west and the south of France. "It looks like Anvil is doomed," Eisenhower wrote. "I hate this."[24]

When he expressed that view about Anvil to Marshall, however, Marshall was upset. Marshall's major concern was getting all the divisions that had been formed in the States into combat, and that could only be done by opening a front in southern France. He was fearful that Eisenhower's willingness to abandon Anvil reflected British opinion, that Eisenhower had been unduly swayed by Brooke and Churchill. "I merely wish," the Chief declared, "to be certain that localitis is not developing and that pressure on you has not warped your judgment."[25] Eisenhower replied with a ringing defense of himself. "In the various campaigns of this war I have occasionally had to modify slightly my own conceptions of campaign in order to achieve a unity of purpose and effort," he wrote. "I think this is inescapable in Allied operations but I assure you that I have never yet failed to give you my own clear personal convictions about every project and plan in prospect." He was not aware of being "affected by localitis," and protested that his overriding concern was to make sure Overlord worked. He warned Marshall,

"From D day to D plus sixty this thing is going to absorb everything [the Allies] can possibly pour into it."[26] Finally, in April, Marshall agreed to postpone Anvil, thus freeing up the landing craft in the Mediterranean for Overlord and thereby meeting Eisenhower's demands.

Living in London caused constant interruptions, because Churchill, the American ambassador, and other VIPs felt free to call him at any hour, and the staff found the temptations of London night life too much to pass up. In February, Eisenhower sent his British aide, Lieutenant Colonel James Gault, out into the countryside to find him a quieter, remote home and a suitable headquarters site. Gault selected a large mansion in Kingston Hill, near Bushy Park, for Eisenhower's home; the new headquarters would be in Bushy Park itself. Tents went up, camouflage covered them, and the SHAEF staff, some grumbling, moved in. Eisenhower decided that the mansion Gault had picked for him was much too grand; he inquired about Telegraph Cottage, discovered that Tedder and his new wife were living there, and persuaded Tedder to switch residences. The Supreme Commander thus had the least pretentious home of any general officer in England, but Eisenhower was happy, for at Telegraph he could work, think, relax, play a hole or two of golf, and read Westerns without being interrupted. He could even enjoy an occasional moment alone with Kay.

In public, Kay was very much in evidence. She accompanied Eisenhower to meetings with Churchill, King George VI, and others. Although she was a British subject (she had been born in County Cork, Ireland), Eisenhower was arranging to have her commissioned as a WAAC lieutenant. Decades later, in a book published after her death, Kay claimed that they had fallen in love, and that both had realized it when he returned from Washington. "His kisses absolutely unraveled me," she wrote. According to her account, it was a passionate but unconsummated romance, partly because—save for an odd moment or two at Telegraph Cottage—they were seldom alone together, mainly because, on the one evening they did try to make love, Eisenhower was flaccid. This may have been because, as one aide put it in a grand understatement, "Ike had a lot on his mind," or because his stern sense of morality overrode his passion. Or it may be that the incident never happened, that it was merely an old woman's fantasy. No one will ever know. What is important to note is that not even Kay ever claimed that they had a genuine love affair.[27]

Other generals did have affairs, as men at war have done since time out of mind, but no other general was so completely exposed to public scrutiny, or so busy, as Eisenhower. When Mamie wrote to him about the "tales . . . I've heard" about the "night clubs, gayety and loose morals" of the American officers in London, he quickly responded, "So far as I can see . . . 99% of officers and men are too busy to have any time for anything else [but work] . . . the pictures painted by gossips are grossly exaggerated. So far as the group around me is concerned, I know that the principal concern is work—and that their habits are above reproach."[28]

Overlord was a direct frontal assault against a prepared enemy position. The German line, or Atlantic Wall, was continuous, so there was no possibility of outflanking it. The Germans had an overwhelming manpower advantage and the benefit of land lines of communication, so Eisenhower's forces could not hope to overwhelm them. Eisenhower's advantages were control of the air and of the sea, which meant that Allied bombers and ships could pound the enemy emplacements and trenches on a scale even larger than the World War I artillery barrages. In addition, he was on the offensive, which meant that he knew where and when the battle would be fought. Even better, he had no defensive lines to maintain, so he could concentrate all his resources on a relatively narrow front in Normandy, while the Germans had to spread their resources along the coast. Harris' and Spaatz' bombers would play a key role.

There was no dispute about this point; all agreed that on the eve of D-Day every bomber that could fly would participate in the attack on the Normandy coastal defenses. There was, however, intense debate over the role of the bombers in the two months preceding the invasion, a debate that revolved around the question of command of the strategic air forces. Harris and Spaatz, as noted, wanted to retain their virtual independence and continue their air offensives inside Germany; Eisenhower wanted them brought under his command and utilized in a more direct role in support of Overlord. Specifically, Eisenhower proposed that the bombers be used to paralyze the French railroad system. Harris and Spaatz protested vigorously. Harris argued that Bomber Command, built for night raids and area bombing, could not achieve the accuracy required to hit marshaling yards, repair facilities, and other pinpoint railroad targets. Tedder, a strong advocate of the so-called Transportation Plan, indeed the man who had convinced Eisenhower of its necessity, even accused Harris of juggling figures to prove that his airplanes could not hit the proposed targets. Spaatz insisted that the continuing success of operations against German aircraft production facilities and oil refineries would assure the greatest support for Overlord, and he convinced Arnold to change his mind and support him. But Spaatz realized that he would have to convince Eisenhower, so he argued for an Oil Plan, which gave first priority to the German oil industry. This, he announced, would in the long run immobilize the Germans much more effectively than the Transportation Plan.[29]

It would also allow the strategic air forces to retain their independence from SHAEF, a point on which Spaatz insisted, because he objected strenuously to being placed under Leigh-Mallory. Like Harris, he thought Leigh-Mallory's calculations as to the effect of the Transportation Plan quite unrealistic, and he thought Leigh-Mallory—whose experience was exclusively with fighter aircraft—unqualified to command the bombers. Eisenhower was embarrassed by Spaatz' open hostility to Leigh-Mallory and tried to reassure Spaatz that he and Tedder would personally supervise the air campaign. Further, as Spaatz noted in his diary, Eisenhower "tried subtly to sell Leigh-Mallory [to me], saying that . . . he felt that maybe proper credit had not been given to the man's intelligence. I told him that my views had not and would not change."[30]

Eisenhower nevertheless persisted in his demand that the bombers come under SHAEF control, and that they then be used to implement the Transportation Plan. On March 6, Patton came to visit Eisenhower at Bushy Park. He was shown into Eisenhower's office while Eisenhower was on the telephone with Tedder. "Now, listen, Arthur," Eisenhower was saying, "I am tired of dealing with a lot of prima donnas. By God, you tell that bunch that if they can't get together and stop quarreling like children, I will tell the Prime Minister to get someone else to run this damn war. I'll quit." Patton took careful note of the tone of command in his voice; Eisenhower was obviously taking charge, and Patton could not help but be impressed.[31]

Eisenhower believed that the difficulty with the Oil Plan was that it would have no immediate effect. The Germans had accumulated large stocks of oil and gasoline in France and scattered and camouflaged the stocks so that they were comparatively safe. Only when the supplies on hand were used up—only, that is, well after D-Day—would a stoppage of oil production affect German military operations in France. Spaatz shrugged off this point by saying that the Transportation Plan would be only of slight help in isolating the battlefield, while the Oil Plan would be of major help later. This was exactly the attitude to which Eisenhower objected and the crux of the matter; Spaatz assumed that it would be easy to get ashore and stay there, while Eisenhower did not.

Eisenhower wanted any help he could get. The Transportation Plan promised some help for Overlord, while the Oil Plan offered none.

Marshall supported Eisenhower in the dispute; Churchill supported Harris and Spaatz. Eisenhower pressed the Prime Minister; eventually Churchill offered a compromise—the bombers would be "attached" to SHAEF for specific operations, but SHAEF air plans would be subject to CCS approval. Eisenhower objected strongly and "demurred at anything short of complete operational control of the whole of Bomber Command and the American Strategic Forces." If his bosses refused to make anything less than a full commitment to Overlord by holding back the bombers, Eisenhower told Churchill that he would "simply have to go home."[32] This extreme threat brought the British around; they drew up a directive that gave Eisenhower "supervision" of the bombers. Marshall then suggested the word be changed to "command." The British refused, leaving Eisenhower "astonished" at their reluctance to substitute "command" for "supervision." On March 22 he wrote in his diary, "If a satisfactory answer is not reached, I am going to take drastic action and inform the CCS that unless the matter is settled at once I will request relief from this Command." That same morning the British Chiefs were meeting. When Eisenhower heard the results of their deliberations he added a postscript to his diary entry: "I was told the word 'direction' was acceptable to both sides . . . Amen!"[33]

Tedder then prepared a list of more than seventy railroad targets in France and Belgium. On April 3 it went before the War Cabinet for approval. The British had previously forbidden air attacks on occupied countries if there was risk of high civilian casualties, and now they drew back from the Transportation Plan for that reason. "The argument for concentration on these particular targets," Churchill wrote Eisenhower, "is very nicely balanced on military grounds." He added that the Cabinet took "rather a grave and on the whole an adverse view of the proposal." Foreign Secretary Eden was especially adamant. He pointed out that after the war Britain would have to live in a Europe that was already looking to Russia "more than he would wish." He did not want the French people to regard the British and Americans with hatred.[34]

Eisenhower admitted that the weight of the argument brought against the Transportation Plan was "heavy indeed," but stated that he was convinced it would increase the chances for success in Overlord, "and unless this could be proved to be an erroneous conclusion, I do not see how we can fail to proceed with the program." The French people, Eisenhower reminded Churchill, were "slaves." They were the ones who would benefit most from Overlord. "We must never forget," Eisenhower added in his strongest argument, "that one of the fundamental factors leading to the decision for undertaking Overlord was the conviction that our overpowering air force would make feasible an operation which might otherwise be considered extremely hazardous, if not foolhardy." He said it would be "sheer folly" to refuse approval to the Transportation Plan.[35]

Churchill put Eisenhower's views before the War Cabinet. He spoke eloquently of Eisenhower's onerous responsibilities. Care should be taken, he said, not to add unnecessarily to his burdens. Still, he said he had never realized that air power would assume so cruel and remorseless a form. The Transportation Plan, he feared, "will smear the good name of the Royal Air Forces across the world."[36] He thought the French themselves should be consulted. Smith then talked to Major General Pierre Joseph Koenig, de Gaulle's representative in London. "To my surprise," Smith reported, "Koenig takes a much more cold-blooded view than we do. His remark was, 'This is War, and it must be expected that people will be killed. We would take the anticipated loss to be rid of the Germans.'"[37] Churchill, almost but not quite beaten down, decided to take the issue to the President and thus force the Americans to take their share of the responsibility for approval of the plan. He told Roosevelt of the War Cabinet's anxiety about "these French slaughters" and of the British doubts "as to whether almost as good military results could not be produced by other methods." He then left the matter up to the President. Roosevelt replied that the military considerations must dominate, and Eisenhower had his way.[38]

The Transportation Plan had won. Eisenhower and Tedder put the bombers to work on the French railway system. By D-Day the Allies had dropped seventy-six thousand tons of bombs on rail centers, bridges, and open lines. The Seine River bridges west of Paris were virtually destroyed. Based on an index of 100 for January and February 1944, railway traffic dropped from 69 in mid-May to 38 by D-Day. The French people accepted the necessity of the program and there were no serious political repercussions. Casualties were relatively light, much less than the pessimists in the War Cabinet had feared. After the war, the American experts on strategic bombing disagreed on the effectiveness of the Transportation Plan.[39] The men who should have known best, as they were the most directly affected by it, did not. The German generals were "strong in their belief that the various air attacks were ruinous to their counteroffensive plans" against the beachhead.[40] Gordon Harrison, the closest student of Overlord and author of the standard work on the subject, concluded that by D-Day the "transportation system was on the point of total collapse," and this was "to prove critical in the battle for Normandy."[41]

Eisenhower had made everyone amply aware of the strength of his feelings. He had dozens of major and hundreds of minor disagreements with Churchill and the CCS during the war, but the only occasion on which he threatened to resign was over the issue of command of the strategic air forces. He was certain at the time that he was right, and he never saw any reason to question that belief. In 1968, in one of his last interviews, he stated that he felt the greatest single contribution he personally made to the success of Overlord was his insistence on the Transportation Plan.[42]

The point to the Transportation Plan was to isolate Normandy, so that the Germans could not use their manpower and logistical advantages to overwhelm the invading force. Equally important, perhaps more so, in keeping the Germans away from the battle was the deception scheme, Operation Fortitude. It was designed to make the Germans think that there would be a preliminary attack in Norway, followed by the main assault at the Pas de Calais. Eisenhower did not play as personal a role in Fortitude as he did in the Transportation Plan, mainly because there was no disagreement about Fortitude, which meant that it was a problem of implementation rather than policy-making. Eisenhower only had to approve the activities of others, primarily the British Secret Service, which devised and executed Fortitude. The key to Fortitude was to make the Germans believe the AEF was much larger than it in fact was, and that the Allies had unlimited landing craft available. This was done through radio signals, sent in code but with the knowledge that the Germans would decipher and read them. The messages "created" entirely notional armies in Scotland (presumably to attack Norway) and around Dover (to attack the Pas de Calais). Fortitude built on German expectations, such as their fixed belief that the Pas de Calais was the logical target, and that Patton was the logical commander of the invasion. The Germans thought Patton the best general in the Allied camp, a judgment with which Patton heartily agreed, but Eisenhower did not. Eisenhower wanted Bradley to fight the Normandy battle and planned to bring Patton into the fray after the troops had broken out of the beachhead; he meanwhile took advantage of the German preconceptions by placing Patton in command of the notional army around Dover. There is neither space nor need to go into the details of Fortitude here, except to note that it relied heavily on the British Double-Cross System (every German spy in Britain had been "turned" by the British Secret Service and forced to send reports to Germany about the various notional divisions and armies gathering in Scotland and around Dover) and on Ultra intercepts (which let the Allies know that the Germans had fallen for the deception and credited Eisenhower with vastly greater forces than he possessed). By June 1, German intelligence counted a total of eighty-nine Allied divisions in Great Britain, when in fact there were forty-seven. Hitler reinforced his garrison troops in Norway; by late spring he had thirteen divisions there, more than double the total needed for occupation duties. Best of all, the Germans had concentrated their strongest defenses and their best army (the Fifteenth) at the Pas de Calais.[43]

Security was an integral part of Fortitude. The entire deception plan was built on a scaffold so intricate that pulling even one piece out of the structure would have brought the whole tumbling down. Eisenhower would go to any length to maintain security. He forced Churchill, very much against the Prime Minister's wishes, to impose a ban on privileged diplomatic correspondence leaving the United Kingdom. He also asked Churchill to bar the entry of civilians into the southern coastal areas, because the buildup and the training exercises going on there were potential sources of leaks. Churchill objected. Knowing that the reason was political, Smith's deputy, the British General Morgan, warned, "If we fail, there won't be any more politics." Still Churchill refused. Eisenhower then bluntly told Churchill, "It would go hard with our consciences if we were to feel, in later years, that by neglecting any security precaution we had compromised the success of these vital operations or needlessly squandered men's lives." Four days later the War Cabinet imposed the ban.[44]

With the British government cooperating so admirably, Eisenhower could not do less. His orders on security to his commanders were clear, direct, and stern. He insisted on harsh punishment for anyone who violated security, and was as good as his word. In April, Major General Henry J. Miller, a West Point classmate of Eisenhower's and an old friend, went to a cocktail party at Claridge's Hotel. He drank too much and began talking freely about D-Day, even mentioning the date. Eisenhower, informed of the indiscretion, acted immediately. He ordered Miller reduced to his permanent rank of colonel and sent him back to the States in disgrace.[45] Miller pleaded with Eisenhower to send him home at his present rank and protested his innocence. Eisenhower wrote back, "I know of nothing that causes me more real distress than to be faced with the necessity of sitting as a judge in cases involving military offenses by officers of character and of good record, particularly when they are old and warm friends." But he said his decision stood. Miller retired shortly after returning to the States. To Marshall, Eisenhower confessed, "I get so angry at the occurrence of such needless and additional hazards that I could cheerfully shoot the offender myself. This . . . is almost enough to give one the shakes."[46]

There were many aspects to Overlord in which Eisenhower's role was more supervisory than direct, including such items as the artificial harbors, the specially designed tanks, assault techniques, and the logistical problems involved in getting the men and equipment to the southern English ports, transporting them across the Channel, and supplying them in Normandy. Overlord was the greatest amphibious assault in history, with the largest air and sea armadas ever assembled. It required, and got, painstakingly detailed planning, with thousands of men involved. SHAEF alone had a total strength of 16,312, of whom 2,829 were officers (1,600 Americans, 1,229 British). There were in addition the staffs of the U.S. and British armies, corps, and divisions, all devoting their entire energy to Overlord. These vast bureaucracies did very well what they were created to do, but their limitations were obvious. They could suggest, plan, advise, investigate, but they could not act. Nor could any single member of the bureaucracies see the problem whole. Every individual involved had a specific given role to play and could concentrate on one set of problems; each staff officer was an expert struggling with his specialty. The officers could study and analyze a problem and make recommendations, but they could not decide and order.

Someone had to give the bureaucracies direction; someone had to be able to take all the information they gathered, make sense out of it, and impose order on it; someone had to make certain that each part meshed into the whole; someone had to decide; someone had to take the responsibility and act.

It all came down to Eisenhower. He was the funnel through which everything passed. Only his worries were infinite, only he carried the awesome burden of command. This position put enormous pressure on him, pressure that increased geometrically with each day that passed. "Ike looks worn and tired," Butcher noted on May 12. "The strain is telling on him. He looks older now than at any time since I have been with him." It would get worse as D-Day got closer and innumerable problems came up each day, many unsolved and some unsolvable. Still, Butcher felt that all would turn out all right, that Eisenhower could take it. "Fortunately he has the happy faculty of bouncing back after a night of good sleep."[47]

Unfortunately, such nights were rare. Eisenhower's tension and tiredness began to show in his face, especially when he was inspecting training exercises, watching the boys he would be sending against Hitler's Atlantic Wall. The anxieties also showed in his letters to Mamie. Almost without exception, every letter he wrote her in the pre-Overlord period had a fantasy about his retirement plans when the war was over—the emphasis was on loafing in a warm climate.

Writing to Mamie was practically the only time he was free to think about issues that went beyond Overlord. He took the opportunity to express some of his deepest feelings. He loathed war and hated having to send boys to their death. "How I wish this cruel business of war could be completed quickly," he told Mamie. He was the man who had to total up all the casualties, bad enough in the air war, with worse to come when Overlord began. Counting the human costs was "a terribly sad business." It made him heartsick to think about "how many youngsters are gone forever," and although he had developed "a veneer of callousness," he could "never escape a recognition of the fact that back home the news brings anguish and suffering to families all over the country. Mothers, fathers, brothers, sisters, wives and friends must have a difficult time preserving any comforting philosophy and retaining any belief in the eternal rightness of things. War demands real toughness of fiber—not only in the soldiers that must endure, but in the homes that must sacrifice their best."

"I think that all these trials and tribulations must come upon the world because of some great wickedness," he said in another letter, "yet one would feel that man's mere intelligence to say nothing of his spiritual perceptions would find some way of eliminating war. But man has been trying to do so for many hundreds of years, and his failure just adds more reason for pessimism when a man gets really low!"[48]

The contrast between Eisenhower and those generals who gloried in war could not have been greater. Small wonder that millions of Americans in the 1940s felt that if their loved one had to join the fight, Eisenhower was the general they wanted for his commander. Patton, MacArthur, Bradley, Marshall, and the others all had their special qualities, but only Eisenhower had such a keen sense of family, of the way in which each casualty meant a grieving family back home. Eisenhower's concern was of such depth and so genuine that it never left him. In 1964, when he was filming with Walter Cronkite a television special entitled "D-Day Plus 20," Cronkite asked him what he thought about when he returned to Normandy. In reply, he spoke not of the tanks, the guns, the planes, the ships, the personalities of his commanders and their opponents, or the victory. Instead, he spoke of the families of the men buried in the American cemetery in Normandy. He said he could never come to this spot without thinking of how blessed he and Mamie were to have grandchildren, and how much it saddened him to think of all the couples in America who had never had that blessing, because their only son was buried in France.

One reason, more rational than emotional, that Eisenhower was concerned about his troops was his realization that while he, SHAEF, the generals, and the admirals could plan, prepare the ground, provide covering support, ensure adequate supplies, deceive the Germans, and in countless other ways try to ensure victory, in the end success rested with the footslogger carrying a rifle over the beaches of Normandy. If he was willing to drive forward in the face of German fire, Overlord would succeed. If he cowered behind the beached landing craft, it would fail. The operation all came down to that. For that reason, Eisenhower spent much of his pre-D-Day time visiting troops in the field. He wanted to let as many men as possible see him. He made certain that every soldier who was to go ashore on D-Day had the opportunity to at least look at the man who was sending him into battle; he managed to talk to hundreds personally. In the four months from February 1 to June 1 he visited twenty-six divisions, twenty-four airfields, five ships of war, and countless depots, shops, hospitals, and other installations.[49] He would have the men break ranks, gather around him while he made a short speech, then go around shaking hands.

He always managed to talk to the enlisted men as individuals. Other generals did too, of course, but none had Eisenhower's touch. Bradley, Patton, Montgomery, and the rest would ask a man about his military specialty, his training, his unit, his weapons. Eisenhower's first question invariably was "Where are you from?" He wanted to know about their families, what they did in civilian life back in the States, what their postwar plans were. He enjoyed discussing cattle ranching in Texas with them, or dairy farming in Wisconsin, or logging in Montana. To Eisenhower's associates, the men were soldiers; to Eisenhower, they were citizens temporarily caught up in a war none of them wanted, but which they realized was necessary. His face would light up whenever he met a boy from Kansas; he kept hoping to find one from Abilene, but never did. The British and Canadians responded as enthusiastically to Eisenhower's friendliness, informality, curiosity about them as individuals, and sincerity as did the Americans.

To the graduating class at Sandhurst, in the spring of 1944, Eisenhower delivered an impromptu, ad-lib address that ranks as one of his best. He spoke of the great issues involved, and made each individual aware that his own chances for a happy, decent life were directly tied up in the success of Overlord. He reminded them of the great traditions of Sandhurst. He told the newly commissioned officers that they must be like fathers to their men, even when the men were twice their age, that they must keep the enlisted men out of trouble, and stand up for them when they committed a transgression. Their companies, he said, returning to his favorite theme, must be like a big family, and they must be the head of the family, insuring that the unit was cohesive, tough, well trained, well equipped, ready to go. The response of the Sandhurst graduates, according to Thor Smith, a public relations officer at SHAEF, was "electric. They just loved him."[50]

To lead the men, Eisenhower needed more than fifty division commanders. He was not involved in the selection of British or Canadian generals, but he did insist on picking the Americans. He regarded the command of a division as the most important in the war, a position that carried in his view more responsibility, and offered greater rewards, than corps or army command. A division was the largest organization that could fight as a unit, the largest that one man could impose his personality on, the largest that the men could identify with. The GIs seldom spoke of the corps or the army that they were attached to, but they took great pride in their division, its shoulder patch providing an immediate and lasting identification, its leader the "old man." The U.S. infantry division of World War II had as its heart, or fighting core, 5,211 officers and men organized into twenty-seven rifle companies. Total strength was 14,253. It was compact enough and self-sufficient enough for one man to be able to mold it and to be its unquestioned head. Eisenhower always maintained that he could know a division, its strengths and weaknesses, merely by knowing its commander. In a most revealing phrase, he would speak of a division as being "well brought up." Consequently he spent a goodly portion of his time on getting the division leaders he wanted.

Almost all the generals he picked were Regular Army, many of them men he had known at West Point or during his prewar career. Old ties counted heavily. Eisenhower talked with Bradley and Smith about prospective division commanders; in every case one of the three generals knew the man in question well; in many cases all three knew him. In a letter to Marshall about a prospective officer, Eisenhower made a remark that illustrated the way he worked: "This happens to be one man that I don't know personally, but Bradley thinks he is tops. So does Smith."[51]

As far as possible, Eisenhower wanted men with combat experience. Obtaining them was not easy, however, because the bulk of the American Army had not yet been engaged in battle. Most of the generals who had experience were still in the Mediterranean, and Eisenhower wanted almost every one of them. But the senior U.S. Army commander in the Mediterranean, General Jacob Devers, was reluctant to let them go—like Churchill and Brooke, Devers felt that Eisenhower was stripping AFHQ bare. At one point Devers wired to say, "We have tried to meet your requests for personnel to the utmost possible limit. Sorry we could not do it 100 per cent. . . . You may count on me to be in there pitching with one idea, to assist you." Smith sarcastically noted on the bottom of the cable form, "This is just swell. I love this 'One idea to assist you' stuff." Eisenhower called Devers "obstinate."[52] To Marshall, he complained that "Devers has constantly reported it is impossible to let any [more] of his people come up here."[53] Still Eisenhower persisted, and usually had his way. The man he most wanted, however, he did not get—Lucian Truscott.

For his corps commanders for the American forces in Overlord, Eisenhower selected two men he had known for decades. He insisted on Gerow as one; Gerow was one of his oldest and best friends, and Eisenhower felt he knew Gerow well enough to be able to discount Gerow's lack of combat experience. The other corps commander was Major General J. Lawton Collins. Eisenhower had known Collins at West Point and was much impressed by his combat record at Guadalcanal in late 1942, where Collins had won an enviable reputation and the nickname "Lightning Joe." For the first follow-up corps, Eisenhower picked another old friend, Troy Middleton, but only after an exchange of views with Marshall. An objection had been raised to Middleton on physical grounds, which—according to Bradley—led Marshall to remark, "I would rather have a man with arthritis in the knee than one with arthritis in the head." Eisenhower's version was different; he recalled that he asked Marshall for Middleton but Marshall replied, "Fine. I agree with you in his value. But he's in Walter Reed Hospital with his knees." To which Eisenhower replied, "I don't give a damn about his knees; I want his head and his heart. And I'll take him into battle on a litter if we have to."[54]

The commander of the U.S. First Army, Bradley, had already been selected by Marshall, on the basis of Eisenhower's enthusiastic recommendation. Eisenhower had selected Patton to lead the follow-up army, the Third. Until the Third Army was activated, Patton's role was to command the fictitious army group at Dover, which kept him out of the active preparations and made him even more nervous and irritable than usual. To increase his visibility to the Germans, he attended numerous public functions. On April 25, at the opening of a club sponsored by British women for American servicemen, he spoke on Anglo-American unity. He told the audience it was an important subject, "since it is the evident destiny of the British and Americans to rule the world, [and] the better we know each other the better job we will do." A reporter covering the event put the statement out over the wire services; it was widely circulated. A storm of criticism at Patton's indiscretion broke, and Eisenhower had another problem to deal with. Marshall, much upset, wired Eisenhower. The Chief said he had just sent a list of "permanent makes," that is, permanent Regular Army promotions, to the Senate, and Patton's name was on the list. Marshall sadly noted, "This I fear has killed them all." He asked Eisenhower to investigate.

Eisenhower was out observing a training exercise when Marshall's message came in. Smith got Eisenhower on the telephone. Eisenhower dictated his reply over the phone. "Apparently he is unable to use reasonably good sense," Eisenhower said of Patton. "I have grown so weary of the trouble he constantly causes you and the War Department to say nothing of myself, that I am seriously contemplating the most drastic action."[55] Marshall responded the same day. After quoting an extremely hostile editorial from the Washington *Post,* he pointed out that Patton had actual experience in fighting Rommel, who commanded the German defenses in Normandy. Marshall said this advantage had to be kept in mind, but left the decision up to Eisenhower. "You carry the burden of responsibility as to the success of Overlord." If Eisenhower thought the operation could succeed without Patton and wanted to relieve him, "all well and good." If Eisenhower felt that he had to have Patton, "then between us we can bear the burden . . . of keeping him."[56]

Eisenhower sent a stinging letter to Patton. He said that he was not so upset at the press reaction as at "the implication that you simply will not guard your tongue. . . . I have warned you time and again against your impulsiveness in action and speech . . ." The incident forced Eisenhower to doubt Patton's "all-round judgment, so essential in high military position." He concluded by saying he had not decided on what action to take, but if in the meantime Patton did anything that in any way embarrassed the War Department or SHAEF, "I will relieve you instantly."[57]

On April 30, Eisenhower had Smith call Patton to order him to report to SHAEF the following day. He had about decided to relieve his old friend. He told Marshall he intended to do so "unless some new and unforeseen information should be developed in the case." He thought General Courtney Hodges, Bradley's deputy at U.S. First Army, would do as well commanding the Third Army as Patton. For all that he admired Patton's dash and courage, Eisenhower said, he had about given up on him. "After a year and a half of working with him it appears hopeless to expect that he will ever completely overcome his life-long habit of posing and of self-dramatization which causes him to break out in these extraordinary ways."[58] Marshall reiterated his position: "The decision is exclusively yours," he told Eisenhower. "Consider only Overlord and your own heavy burden of responsibility for its success. Everything else is of minor importance."[59]

At 11 A.M. on May 1, Patton was ushered into Eisenhower's office. An old hand at getting out of a fix, Patton let out all the stops. He was plunged into despair, said he felt like death, but he would fight if "they" would let him. He dramatically offered to resign his commission to save his dearest friend from embarrassment. Although wearing his helmet (he was the only officer who ever wore a helmet for an interview with Eisenhower at Bushy Park), he was the picture of remorse, looking like a small boy who had inadvertently committed a big sin and who was deeply ashamed of himself. Eisenhower could not bring himself to send "Georgie" home. He said he had decided to keep him on. Tears streamed down Patton's face. He assured Eisenhower of his gratitude and loyalty. As Eisenhower later described it, "in a gesture of almost little-boy contriteness, he put his head on my shoulder." That caused his helmet to fall off and tumble across the floor. The whole scene struck Eisenhower as "ridiculous," and he terminated the interview. Patton, now smiling and jaunty, returned to Dover, where he noted in his diary that he had pulled one on Ike. He claimed his retention in command "is not the result of an accident," but rather was "the work of God."[60]

Butcher was never as taken in by Patton as Eisenhower was. He noted that Patton "is a master of flattery and succeeds in turning any difference of views with Ike into a deferential acquiescence to the views of the Supreme Commander."[61] But if Butcher saw something that Eisenhower missed, there was a reverse side to the coin. Patton bragged that he was tolerated as an eccentric genius because he was considered indispensable, and he was right. The very qualities that made him a great actor also made him a great commander, and Eisenhower knew it. "You owe us some victories," Eisenhower told Patton when the incident was closed. "Pay off and the world will deem me a wise man."[62]

Eisenhower was willing to take the heat for retaining Patton because, he said, he was personally indifferent to newspaper criticism. In cases like this, he was. He was also willing, indeed eager, to spread favorable publicity among his subordinates; in doing so, he was in direct contrast to MacArthur, who in the Southwest Pacific Theater almost kept the names of his chief subordinates a military secret. MacArthur's headquarters announced the victories; MacArthur's name was the only one known to the general public. Eisenhower's practice was to tell reporters to go interview his division commanders, or to do a feature story on Bradley or Spaatz. For himself, Eisenhower was unconcerned with personal publicity (which, it should be noted, made him even more appealing to reporters), and he claimed that he paid no attention whatsoever to the newspapers.

He did, though; he read them as avidly as anyone else. And on one subject, although he professed supreme indifference to criticism, he was extremely sensitive and deeply resentful. His diary entry of February 7 noted that the London newspapers were full of evaluations of the personalities and abilities of the various Overlord commanders. "Generally speaking," he wrote, "the British columnists . . . try to show that my contributions in the Mediterranean were administrative accomplishments and 'friendliness in welding an allied team.' They dislike to believe that I had anything particularly to do with campaigns. They don't use the words 'initiative' and 'boldness' in talking of me, but often do in speaking of Alex and Monty." It made him furious. In the first place, he wrote, Cunningham and Tedder had been the bold British officers, not Alexander and Montgomery. In the second place it was he, Eisenhower, who had ordered Alexander to use the II Corps in the final campaign in Tunisia; he, Eisenhower, who had ordered the taking of Pantelleria; he, Eisenhower, who had insisted on Salerno. "It wearies me to be thought of as timid," he complained, "when I've had to do things that were so risky as to be almost crazy." Then he professed, again, his supposed indifference. His concluding words were "Oh hum."[63]

On May 15, Eisenhower's commanders met at the ancient St. Paul's School, in West Kensington, for a final review. St. Paul's was Montgomery's 21st Army Group Headquarters (it had also been his boyhood school) and the show was primarily his. It was a distinguished, rather than a large, gathering. SHAEF sent out formal, engraved invitations—the King was there, and the Prime Minister, and Field Marshal Jan Smuts, and other notables. Eisenhower made a brief speech of welcome, then turned the stage over to Montgomery. He had a huge relief map of

Normandy the width of a city street on the floor and—as Bradley recalled—"with rare skill, Monty traced his 21st Group plan of maneuver as he trampled about like a giant through Lilliputian France."[64] In deference to Eisenhower and Churchill, Montgomery even broke his long-standing rule and allowed smoking in his presence. He began by reminding the audience of the problem—the Germans had sixty divisions in France, ten of them armored, commanded by the redoubtable Rommel. Montgomery called his opponent "an energetic and determined commander; he has made a world of difference since he took over [in January]. He is best at the spoiling attack; his forte is disruption; he is too impulsive for the set-piece battle. He will do his level best . . . to prevent our tanks landing, by using his own tanks well forward." German morale was high; the enemy believed that, through a combination of the underwater obstacles, the fixed coastal defenses, and the extensive, well-manned trench system, the Allies could be stopped at the beaches. Then Rommel would call up his reinforcements, and his ability to do so, according to Strong's intelligence, was impressive. Montgomery said Rommel might have nine divisions in the battle for Normandy by the second day, and thirteen by the third. By D-Day plus six, Rommel might counterattack with all ten panzer divisions. The SHAEF buildup, by contrast, would be exceedingly slow; the Germans thus expected to drive the Overlord forces back into the sea.

In spite of these gloomy predictions, when Montgomery turned to the Allied picture, he exuded optimism. As he talked and explained, he grew expansive. Storming the beaches was the least of his problems. He wanted to get well inland on D-Day itself and "*crack about* and force the battle to swing our way." It was possible, he said, that he would get to Falaise, thirty-two miles inland, the first day. He intended to send armored columns quickly toward Caen, for "this will upset the enemy's plans and tend to hold him off while we build up strength. We must gain space rapidly and peg claims well inland." He said he intended to take Caen the first day, break through the German lines on that (left, or eastern) flank, then drive along the coast toward the Seine River.[65]

After Montgomery spoke, the king made a brief address. Then Churchill "let go with a slow-starting but fast-ending stemwinder. He preached bravery, ingenuity and persistence as human qualities of greater value than equipment." The king had to leave early; before he left, Eisenhower thanked him for his attendance and told him not to worry. There would be eleven thousand planes overhead on D-Day, he said. The navies had "marshalled the greatest armada . . . the world had ever seen." All the ground troops had to do was to land and capture some villas for the VIPs, "particularly one to accommodate the King who would be . . . welcome in France."[66]

Spaatz, Harris, Bradley, and the naval commander, Admiral Bertram Ramsay, then spoke on the role of the forces under their command in the great undertaking. Brooke, who was in a sour mood, was unimpressed. Spaatz bored him. In his diary, Brooke complained that [General] Harris told us how well he might have won the war if it had not been for the handicap imposed by the existence of the two other Services." Brooke was especially worried about Eisenhower. "The main impression I gathered was that Eisenhower was no real director of thought, plans, energy or direction." He feared that the Supreme Commander was "just a co-ordinator, a good mixer, a champion of inter-Allied cooperation." He wondered if those abilities were sufficient for the task at hand and doubted it.[67] As the meeting broke up (thus ending, the minutes noted, "the greatest assembly of military leadership the world has ever known"),[68] Brooke was still shaking his head.

But the meeting did help dispel Churchill's long-standing doubts. At the beginning of 1944 the Prime Minister had still wondered about the wisdom of a cross-Channel attack, saying to Eisenhower on one occasion, "When I think of the beaches of Normandy choked with the flower of American and British youth . . . I have my doubts . . . I have my doubts." Early in May, Eisenhower had lunched alone with Churchill. As they were parting, the Prime Minister grew emotional. With tears in his eyes he said, "I am in this thing with you to the end, and if it fails we will go down together." But after the St. Paul's briefing, Churchill told Eisenhower, "I am hardening toward this enterprise."[69]

Eisenhower, for his part, had never doubted that it could be done, not since that day in January 1942, when he had scribbled in his diary, "We've got to go to Europe and fight." Now his confidence was higher than ever. As he put it, "The smell of victory was in the air."[70]

CHAPTER SIXTEEN

Bushy Park, Southwick House, Normandy

May 16–July 21, 1944

"I SEEM TO LIVE on a network of high tension wires," Eisenhower wrote Mamie a week before the invasion.[1] D-Day was set for June 5. As it approached, the pressure increased and the tension mounted. Making last-minute adjustments helped relieve the strain, but for Eisenhower the most complete escape came in a game of bridge, especially when he held good cards. Often he just walked or brooded. On May 24 he reported to Mamie that he had taken a long, solitary horseback ride in Richmond Park. He was alive to the life around him, describing to Mamie the flowers, birds, deer, shrubbery, rabbits, pheasants, partridge, wild ducks, even the crows. Butcher recorded that on Sunday, May 28, after working at the office in the morning, he ate a late lunch, then "enjoyed lolling in the garden at Telegraph Cottage, which is now gloriously alive with . . . flowers . . . We even have cuckoos with echoes." Some nights, Eisenhower pored over seed catalogues and planned a vegetable garden for Telegraph. He also tried sketching, once a pine tree, another time the cottage, but was dissatisfied with the results. "Baloney," he wrote on one sketch.[2]

He needed all the relaxation he could get, for he could not escape last-minute problems and worries. On May 29 Leigh-Mallory wrote him to say that he was disturbed over intelligence information acquired during the past week that indicated the Germans were reinforcing the area where the American paratroopers were going to drop. Leigh-Mallory said that it was probable that "at the most 30 percent of the glider loads will become effective for use against the enemy." He concluded that the airborne operation was likely "to yield results so far short of what [you] expect and require that if the success of the seaborne assault . . . depends on the airborne, it will be seriously prejudiced." He wanted the airborne assault canceled.[3] Thinking the matter over, Leigh-Mallory then decided that his letter alone was not sufficient and on May 30 he called on Eisenhower to present his case personally. He spoke of the "futile slaughter" of two fine divisions (the 82d and 101st Airborne), warning that losses might run as high as 70 percent.

As Eisenhower later put it, "It would be difficult to conceive of a more soul-racking problem." He knew that Bradley counted on the paratroopers. He went to his tent, alone, and thought about the alternatives. He decided that the greater risk was in cancellation, went to the telephone, and told Leigh-Mallory that the operation would go ahead as scheduled. He followed up the call with a letter, telling Leigh-Mallory that there "is nothing for it" but for the commanders to "work out to the last detail every single thing that may diminish the hazards." Eisenhower also ordered him to see to it that the troops involved were not needlessly depressed. "Like all the rest of the soldiers, they must understand that they have a tough job to do but be fired with determination to get it done."[4]

On June 2, Eisenhower drove from London to Southwick House, just north of Portsmouth, a lovely English country estate with broad vistas, site of Admiral Ramsay's headquarters, which Eisenhower now took over for SHAEF, making it his advance command post. There, on June 3, he had to face the vexing problem of Charles de Gaulle.

Following his unsuccessful discussions with Roosevelt in January about de Gaulle, Eisenhower had continued to press for a realistic French policy, meaning a recognition of the FCNL as the provisional government of France, with de Gaulle as its head. Recognition was important because Eisenhower wanted the cooperation of the French Resistance, and because he wanted to turn over to a French government control of the countryside as the front lines moved forward. Roosevelt still refused. Eisenhower wanted to at least enter into a civil affairs agreement with General Koenig, de Gaulle's representative, but Roosevelt opposed that too. On June 1, de Gaulle came to London, at Churchill's request. He immediately began to say *Non* to every Allied request, the most important of which was that he broadcast to the Resistance on the eve of D-Day, ordering it to obey SHAEF. De Gaulle refused until the FCNL was recognized. On June 3, Churchill brought de Gaulle to see Eisenhower at Southwick House. Eisenhower took de Gaulle on a grand tour of the war room, pointing to the map and explaining Overlord. De Gaulle lectured Eisenhower on how it should be done. Eisenhower nodded gravely and said he regretted that he did not have time to make the changes de Gaulle suggested. Churchill then withdrew and Eisenhower and de Gaulle went for a stroll up a shady path "where there was enough elbow room for de Gaulle to wave his arms and talk. Ike did some too."[5]

Eisenhower showed de Gaulle a copy of the speech he was going to make to the French people; in it, he urged Frenchmen to "carry out my orders," told them that local administration would continue (that meant Vichy officials would continue to hold their posts, which made de Gaulle furious), and promised that once France was liberated "the French themselves would choose their representatives and their government." De Gaulle said that the speech would have to be changed. Eisenhower replied that it was too late—it had already been cleared with both governments and recorded. In that case, de Gaulle declared, he would not speak after Eisenhower, for that would give the impression that he approved of the SHAEF program.[6]

Another major issue was currency. SHAEF had printed occupation francs and wanted de Gaulle to issue a statement telling the French people he authorized their use and would guarantee them. De Gaulle refused. He pointed out, with some heat, that France was being treated precisely like Italy and that he alone, as president of the provisional government (Giraud had recently been forced out as co-president), had the right to issue currency. It was, Eisenhower sadly noted, "a rather sorry mess."[7]

The evening of June 5 Smith telephoned Eisenhower—who had other things on his mind—to report that de Gaulle had withstood tremendous pressure from Churchill and still would not speak. Giving in to his impulses, Eisenhower replied, "To hell with him and if he doesn't come through, we'll deal with someone else." There was, however, no one else to deal with and the efforts to convince de Gaulle to make the broadcast and approve the currency continued. Final victory was de Gaulle's. He spoke on the day of the invasion, from his own text. "The orders given by the French government and by the leaders which it has recognized must be followed precisely," he emphasized.[8]

After the June 3 meeting with de Gaulle, Eisenhower went into his tent and, as he had done on the eve of Torch, wrote a memorandum for the diary. It gave him a chance to occupy his time and allowed him to put his worries into perspective. At the top of his list was de Gaulle, and he dictated three paragraphs on the difficulties of dealing with the French. Next came weather. "The weather in this country is practically unpredictable," he complained. If it turned bad, he knew he would be advised by at least some of his associates to call off the invasion. That might mean a delay of some weeks. "Probably no one that does not have to bear the specific and direct responsibility of making the final decision as to what to do," he declared, "can understand the intensity of these burdens." Only the Supreme Commander could sort out conflicting weather reports and decide on which one to act. Only he could make the kind of judgment involved if, for example, the weather were suitable for all other plans, but unsuitable for the airborne operation. In that case should he risk the airborne movement anyway, or defer the whole operation in hopes of getting better weather?

Outside Eisenhower's tent the wind was coming up and the sky darkening. He would soon have to make the final decision. "My tentative thought," he recorded before going to meet with the weathermen again, "is that the desirability for getting started on the next favorable tide is so great and the uncertainty of the weather is such that we could never anticipate really perfect weather coincident with proper tidal conditions, that we must go unless there is a real and very serious deterioration in the weather."[9] Then he found time to think of John. His son was about to graduate from West Point, a great day in John's life, and for his father too. Eisenhower wrote Mamie, who was going to the Academy for the ceremonies, "There's nothing I would not have given to have been with you and John on June 6, but c'est la guerre!"[10]

The AEF was set to go, living on the edge of fearful anticipation. "The mighty host," in Eisenhower's words, "was tense as a coiled spring," ready for "the moment when its energy should be released and it would vault the English Channel."[11]

SHAEF had prepared for everything except the weather. It now became an obsession. It was the one thing for which no one could plan, and the one thing that no one could control. In the end, the most completely planned military operation in history was dependent on the caprice of winds and waves. Tides and moon conditions were predictable, but storms were not. From the beginning, everyone had counted on at least acceptable weather for D-Day. There had been no contingency planning. Eisenhower's inclination, as he noted in his diary, was to go, whatever the weather, but if he held to a rigid timetable and conditions became really bad, the invasion might fail. Wind-tossed landing craft could flounder before reaching the shore, or the waves might throw the troops up on the beaches, seasick and unable to fight effectively. The Allies would not be able to use their air superiority to cover the beaches. If Overlord failed, it would take months to plan and mount another operation, too late for 1944.

The evening of June 3, Eisenhower met in the mess room at Southwick House with his commanders and RAF Group Captain J. M. Stagg, his chief weatherman. Stagg had bad news. A high-pressure system was moving out, and a low was coming in. The weather on June 5 would be overcast and stormy, with a cloud base of five hundred feet to zero and Force 5 winds. Worse, the situation was deteriorating so rapidly that forecasting more than twenty-four hours in advance was highly undependable. It was too early to make a final decision, but word had to go out to the American Navy carrying Bradley's troops to Omaha and Utah beaches, since they had the farthest to travel. Eisenhower decided to let them start the voyage, subject to a possible last-minute cancellation. He would make the final decision at the regular weather conference the next morning.[12]

At 4:30 A.M. on Sunday, June 4, Eisenhower met with his subordinates at Southwick House. Stagg said sea conditions would be slightly better than anticipated, but the overcast would not permit the use of the air forces. Montgomery said he wanted to go ahead anyway. Tedder and Leigh-Mallory wanted a postponement. Ramsay said the Navy could do its part but remained neutral when asked whether or not the whole operation should go. Eisenhower remarked that Overlord was being launched with ground forces that were not overwhelmingly powerful. The operation was feasible only because of Allied air superiority. If he could not have that advantage, the landings were too risky. He asked if anyone present disagreed, and when no one did he declared for a twenty-four-hour postponement.[13] The word went out to the American fleet by prearranged signal. Displaying superb seamanship, the fleet drove through the incoming storm, regained its ports, refueled, and prepared to sail again the next day.

That evening, June 4, Eisenhower ate at Southwick House. After dinner he moved into the mess room. Montgomery, Tedder, Smith, Ramsay, Leigh-Mallory, Strong, and various high-ranking staff officers were already there. The wind and the rain rattled the window frames in the French doors in staccato sounds. The mess room was large, with a heavy table at one end and easy chairs at the other. Two sides of the room were lined with bookcases, most of which were empty and forlorn. A third side consisted of the French doors; the fourth wall was covered with a huge map of southern England and Normandy, filled with pins, arrows, and other symbols of Allied and German units. The officers lounged in easy chairs. Coffee was served and there was desultory conversation. Stagg came in about nine-thirty with the latest weather report. Eisenhower called his associates to order and they all sat up to listen intently.[14]

Stagg reported a break. Kenneth Strong recalled that at Stagg's prediction "a cheer went up. You never heard middle-aged men cheer like that!" The rain that was then pouring down, Stagg continued, would stop in two or three hours, to be followed by thirty-six hours of more or less clear weather. Winds would moderate. The bombers and fighters ought to be able to operate on Monday night, June 5–6, although they would be hampered by clouds. Leigh-Mallory remarked that it seemed to be only a moderately good night for air power. Tedder, his pipe clenched between his teeth and forcibly blowing out smoke, agreed that the operations of heavies and mediums were going to be "chancy." Eisenhower countered by pointing out that the Allies could call on their large force of fighter-bombers.

The temptation to postpone again and meet the following morning for another conference was strong and growing, but Ramsay put a stop to that idea by pointing out that Admiral Alan G. Kirk, commanding the American task force, "must be told in the next half hour if Overlord is to take place on Tuesday [June 6]. If he is told it is on, and his forces sail and are then recalled, they will not be ready again for Wednesday morning. Therefore, a further postponement would be forty-eight hours."[15] A two-day delay would put everything back to June 8, and by that time the tidal conditions would not be right, so in fact postponement now meant postponement until June 19.

Whatever Eisenhower decided would be risky. He began pacing the room, head down, chin on his chest, hands clasped behind his back. Suddenly he shot his chin out at Smith. "It's a helluva gamble but it's the best possible gamble," Smith said. Eisenhower nodded, tucked his chin away, paced some more, then shot it out at Montgomery, huddled in his greatcoat, his face almost hidden. "Do you see any reason for not going Tuesday?" Montgomery straightened up, looked Eisenhower in the eye, and replied, "I would say—Go!" Eisenhower nodded, tucked away his chin, paced, looked abruptly at Tedder. Tedder again indicated he thought it chancy. Finally Eisenhower halted, looked around at his commanders, and said, "The question is just how long can you hang this operation on the end of a limb and let it hang there?"

If there was going to be an invasion before June 19, Eisenhower had to decide now. Smith was struck by the "loneliness and isolation of a commander at a time when such a momentous decision was to be taken by him, with full knowledge that failure or success rests on his individual decision." Looking out at the wind-driven rain, it hardly seemed possible that the operation could go ahead. Eisenhower calmly weighed the alternatives, and at 9:45 P.M. said, "I am quite positive that the order must be given."

Ramsay rushed out and gave the order to the fleets. More than five thousand ships began moving toward France. Eisenhower drove back to his trailer and slept fitfully. He awoke at 3:30 A.M. A wind of almost hurricane proportions was shaking his trailer. The rain seemed to be traveling in horizontal streaks. He dressed and gloomily drove through a mile of mud to Southwick House for the last meeting. It was still not too late to call off the operation. In the now familiar mess room, steaming hot coffee helped shake the gray mood and unsteady feeling. Stagg said that the break he had been looking for was on its way and that the weather would be clear within a matter of hours. The long-range prediction was not good, to be sure, but even as he talked the rain began to stop and the sky started to clear.

A short discussion followed, Eisenhower again pacing, shooting out his chin, asking opinions. Montgomery still wanted to go, as did Smith and Ramsay. Smith was concerned about proper spotting for naval gunfire but thought the risk worth taking. Tedder was ready. Leigh-Mallory still thought air conditions were below the acceptable minimum.

Everyone stated his opinion. Stagg withdrew to let the generals and admirals make the decision. No new weather reports would be available for hours. The ships were sailing into the Channel. If they were to be called back, it had to be done now. The Supreme Commander was the only man who could do it. Eisenhower thought for a moment, then said quietly but clearly, "O.K., let's go." And again, cheers rang through Southwick House.[16]

Then the commanders rushed from their chairs and dashed outside to get to their command posts. Within thirty seconds the mess room was empty, except for Eisenhower. The outflow of the others and his sudden isolation were symbolic. A minute earlier he had been the most powerful man in the world. Upon his word the fate of millions depended. The moment he uttered the word, however, he was powerless. For the next two or three days there was almost nothing he could do that would in any way change anything. The invasion could not be stopped, not by him, not by anyone. A captain leading his company onto Omaha, or a platoon sergeant at Utah, would for the immediate future play a greater role than Eisenhower. He could now only sit and wait.

Eisenhower was improving at killing time. He visited South Parade Pier in Portsmouth to see some British soldiers climb aboard their landing craft, then returned to his trailer. He played a game of checkers on a cracker box with Butcher, who was winning, two kings to one, when Eisenhower jumped one of his kings and got a draw. At lunch they exchanged political yarns. After eating, Eisenhower went into a tent with representatives of the press and announced that the invasion was on. Smith called with more news about de Gaulle. After hanging up, Eisenhower looked out the tent flap, saw a quick flash of sunshine, and grinned.[17]

When the reporters left, Eisenhower sat at his portable table and scrawled a press release on a pad of paper, to be used if necessary. "Our landings . . . have failed . . . and I have withdrawn the troops," he began. "My decision to attack at this time and place was based upon the best information available. The troops, the air and the Navy did all that bravery and devotion to duty could do. If any blame or fault attaches to the attempt it is mine alone."[18] Putting the note in his wallet, Eisenhower went to dinner. Then at 6 P.M. he and a group of aides drove to Newbury, where the 101st Airborne was loading up for the flight to Normandy. The 101st was one of the units Leigh-Mallory feared would suffer 70 percent casualties. Eisenhower wandered around among the men, whose blackened faces gave them a grotesque look, stepping over packs, guns, and other equipment. A group recognized him and gathered around. He chatted with them easily. He told them not to worry, that they had the best equipment and leaders. A sergeant said, "Hell, we ain't worried, General. It's the Krauts that ought to be worrying now." And a private piped up, "Look out, Hitler, here we come." A Texan promised Eisenhower a job after the war on his cattle ranch. Eisenhower stayed until all the big C-47s were off the runway.[19]

As the last plane roared into the sky Eisenhower turned to Kay, who was his driver that night, with a visible sagging in his shoulders. She saw tears in his eyes. He began to walk slowly toward his car. "Well," he said quietly, "it's on." It took nearly two hours to get back to camp on the narrow British country roads. Eisenhower arrived at his trailer at 1:15 A.M., June 6. He sat around and chatted with Butcher for a while, then finally went to bed. Shortly before 7 A.M. Ramsay called to tell him everything was going according to plan. Then Butcher came over to his trailer with good news from Leigh-Mallory—the air drop had been a success and casualties were light. Butcher found the Supreme Commander sitting up in bed, smoking a cigarette and reading a Western novel.[20]

Through the morning, news from the beachhead was spotty and

sometimes contradictory, but it was good enough to spread a smile across Strong's Scottish face, as he told everyone that the Germans had been fooled—Fortitude had worked. Eisenhower sent a brief message to Marshall, informing him that everything seemed to be going well and adding that the British and American troops he had seen the previous day were enthusiastic, tough, and fit. "The light of battle was in their eyes."[21] At noon, a messenger brought a note from Leigh-Mallory; he said that it was sometimes difficult to admit that one was wrong, but he had never had a greater pleasure in doing so than on this occasion. He congratulated Eisenhower on the wisdom of his command decision in sending the airborne troops in and apologized for having added to the Supreme Commander's worries.[22]

For the remainder of the day Eisenhower paced, his mood alternating between joy and worry as he received news of the situation on the British and Canadian beaches, where the opposition was remarkably light; from Utah, where the Americans were well established; and from Omaha, where the troops were pinned down by surprisingly heavy German fire. After eating, Eisenhower retired to get a good night's sleep. At a cost of only 2,500 casualties, mainly at Omaha, his men had gained a striking victory. More than 23,000 airborne troops had dropped into Normandy the night of June 5–6, and 57,500 Americans and 75,215 British and Canadian troops had come ashore during the day. More than 156,000 Allied soldiers had breached Hitler's much-vaunted Atlantic Wall.

After breakfast on June 7, Eisenhower boarded the British minelayer *Apollo* to visit the beachhead. The *Apollo* went in close to Omaha Beach and dropped anchor; Bradley came aboard to discuss the situation. It was generally good—the troops had moved off the beaches and were driving inland—but there was cause for concern. The Germans were fighting hard, but fortunately they were finding it difficult to move reinforcements to the battle because of bombed-out bridges and railroad centers. The French Resistance, now unleashed, was adding seriously to the German problems. The Resistance, in fact, was contributing beyond even Eisenhower's high hopes. Air power had not been effective in neutralizing the coastal fortifications, however, which continued to pour artillery shells into the beachhead, but naval gunfire support here was making an increasingly successful contribution.[23]

After Bradley left, the *Apollo* moved east along the British beaches. Montgomery came aboard, said he was happy, and indicated that the battle was going well. After he left, the *Apollo* began moving east again, with Eisenhower urging the captain to take them in closer so he could see more. He watched the British unloading and saw some of the artificial breakwaters and harbors being towed toward their destinations. Aircraft were overhead the whole time; the air forces had flown 10,500 sorties on June 6 and nearly as many the next day. Wherever Eisenhower looked he saw only Allied ships and Allied planes. The Luftwaffe had not been seen.[24]

The next few days were spent in consolidating gains. Nowhere along the front had initial objectives been fully achieved on D-Day or even D plus one and two, but the Allies held the initiative by putting the pressure on the Germans everywhere. Fortitude remained very much alive; Hitler kept the Fifteenth Army intact at the Pas de Calais waiting for the main landing there. By the end of the first week of the invasion Eisenhower's forces had consolidated a bridgehead eight to twelve miles deep and fifty miles wide.[25] Eisenhower kept busy, holding press conferences, answering messages of congratulations, dealing with de Gaulle, talking to Churchill, gathering incoming information, and urging all his subordinates to redouble their efforts. He removed a division commander who had failed the test of combat.[26]

On June 10, Marshall, Arnold, and King arrived in London, ostensibly for a meeting of the CCS, in reality because they wanted to see the great invasion for themselves. Eisenhower gave them a guided tour of his headquarters, where the maps showed current unit positions. Churchill loved the setup, and even Marshall was impressed. Eisenhower and Marshall discussed promotions, decorations, the need to speed the buildup, and the schedule of shipping divisions into France from the United States.[27] On June 12 Eisenhower, Marshall, King, Arnold, and members of their staffs crossed the Channel in a destroyer and went ashore on Omaha Beach. They lunched at Bradley's headquarters on C rations and discussed recent operations with some of the corps and division commanders. Marshall praised Eisenhower, although characteristically not to his face. "Eisenhower and his staff are cool and confident," the Chief reported to Roosevelt, "carrying out an affair of incredible magnitude and complication with superlative efficiency."[28]

The trip to Omaha symbolized the success of Overlord. If that much brass could safely go ashore in France, the beachhead was clearly secure. More than ten divisions were now engaged on the Allied side, with more coming in every day. The artificial harbors were in place and functioning. There were still problems, but the great invasion had worked.

There had already been enough drama in Eisenhower's decision on the morning of June 5 to launch Overlord to satisfy anyone, but more was to come. On the morning of June 19 a severe storm struck the French coast, ripping up one of the artificial harbors and bringing unloading to a standstill. The Allies in fact suffered more from the storm than they had from the German resistance on D-Day. Stagg wrote to Eisenhower, reminding him that if he had decided on June 5 to delay until June 19 he would have run into the worst weather in twenty years. Eisenhower scribbled at the bottom of the message, "Thanks, and thank the gods of war we went when we did!" and sent it back to Stagg.[29]

Eisenhower's gamble on the weather had paid off. What Churchill rightly called "the most difficult and complicated operation that has ever taken place" had put the Allies back on the Continent.

Eisenhower, typically, was as excited by family news as by the great event. On June 9, he had sent a teletype to Mamie and John, at West Point, saying that "Due to previous plans it was impossible for me to be with you and John [for the graduation exercises] . . . but I thought of you and hope you and he had a nice time . . ." Then Marshall told him that he had made special arrangements for Second Lieutenant Eisenhower to spend his two-week graduation leave with his father. Eisenhower beamed. "How I look forward to seeing Johnny. It will be odd to see him as an *officer of the Army!* I'll burst with pride!" On June 13, expecting his son to arrive in a couple of hours, he told Mamie, "I'm really as excited as a bride."[30]

Tex Lee went up to Scotland to get John and drive him back to Bushy Park. When John arrived at headquarters, late in the afternoon of June 13, he walked into his father's office, threw his arms around him, and kissed him on the cheek. "Ike was just one big grin," Kay reported. She drove them to Telegraph Cottage, where they talked through most of the night.[31] John had not seen his father since 1942, and he was both surprised and a bit amazed at the number of people who surrounded Eisenhower and devoted their energies to translating his wishes into reality. Drivers, cooks, aides, houseboys—John had not sufficiently appreciated his father's importance until he saw them scurrying around whenever Eisenhower indicated that he wanted this or that done. In the days that followed, John was further impressed by his father's easy familiarity with some of the most famous and powerful men in the world, and by the way in which the press reported on his every move.

Eisenhower enjoyed impressing his son, but he did not like the notoriety. He wrote a friend, "When this war is over I am going to find the deepest hole there is in the United States, crawl in and pull it in after me."[32] John had brought with him a letter from Mamie that dealt with publicity—a Hollywood firm had offered Eisenhower a large financial inducement for the right to do a film biography. Eisenhower had responded that he might allow the film to be made, but only if the money were put into an endowment fund for Kansas State. Now Mamie wrote that she felt he ought to accept the money. Eisenhower replied, "I can understand your feelings . . . but my own convictions as to the quality of a man that will make money out of a public position of trust are very strong! I couldn't touch it—and would never allow such a thing to occur. We don't need it anyway—it's fun to be poor!"[33]

During the two weeks that followed, John was constantly at his father's side. Eisenhower assured Mamie that "I love to be with him," that "he and I have talked, every night, well past midnight," and—on the eve of John's departure—"I hate to see him go!" But he also admitted that "it is difficult to tell when he is pleased."[34] In truth, there was a certain awkwardness in their relationship. Eisenhower's position and the never-ending demands on his concentration added to the normal difficulties inherent in a father-son relationship when the son has emerged into manhood. John was a bit stiff and shy to begin with, and very much the recent West Point graduate, shouting out his "Yes, sir!" and "No, sir!" responses, bracing to full attention and snapping out his salutes. Kay felt that although Eisenhower obviously loved his son and was proud of him, he was much too critical. When Second Lieutenant Eisenhower offered textbook advice on military problems to Supreme Commander Eisenhower, the general would snort and exclaim, "Oh, for God's sake!"[35] Concerned about military protocol, one day John asked his father, "If we should meet an officer who ranks above me but below you, how do we handle this? Should I salute first . . . ?" Annoyed, Eisenhower snapped, "John, there isn't an officer in this theater who doesn't rank above you and below me."[36]

John got to know Kay and, as did almost everyone else, liked her immediately. He noted her popularity and how relaxed his father was in her presence. In the evenings, he and Butcher took on Kay and Eisenhower in a few rubbers of bridge. Eisenhower was highly critical—almost embarrassingly so—of John's play.[37]

The games, and the father-son talks, were often interrupted by the "Baby Blitz." Hitler's V-1 vengeance weapons—the pilotless airplanes—were raining down on London. The British Secret Service, as a countermeasure, was inducing the Germans to aim short of London, which brought many of the V-1s down near Bushy Park. Churchill had insisted on building a shelter outside Telegraph Cottage, but at first Eisenhower ignored it. When the siren howled at 1 A.M. during the initial assault, he stayed in bed with his Western novel. "I prefer to stay here," he told Butcher. "I don't want to shuttle back and forth to the shelter all night." But when a bomb exploded a few hundred yards away, he, John, and the members of his household all fled to the shelter, to spend the night camping on the cold concrete floor. On June 19, in one six-hour period, there were twenty-five explosions in the vicinity. "Most of the people I know," wrote Butcher, "are semidazed from loss of sleep and have the jitters, which they show when doors bang or the sounds of motors, from motorcycles to aircraft, are heard." John noted, "Dad is tired."[38]

John wanted to see the battle zone; on June 15 his father took him along on a flight to the British sector. Together with Tedder, they drove to Bayeux, headquarters of the British Second Army and home of William the Conqueror, the only other man—save Eisenhower and Caesar—to have successfully commanded a cross-Channel attack. De Gaulle, who had come to France against Eisenhower's wishes and without his knowledge, had been in Bayeux the day before, where, Eisenhower learned, he had made a speech in which he declared that the French were now, "with the aid of the Allies," reconquering their homeland. Eisenhower nearly choked; John feared for his blood pressure.[39]

Driving around the beachhead area, John was startled to see vehicles moving bumper to bumper, in complete violation of textbook doctrine. "You'd never get away with this if you didn't have air supremacy," he told his father. Eisenhower snorted, "If I didn't have air supremacy, I wouldn't be here."[40]

John, eager to do his part in the war, soon began to argue that he should not be sent home. He said that the course at the Academy had already covered the lessons he would learn at training camp, so he wanted his father to assign him immediately to a unit in France. Eisenhower thought that Marshall would agree, but said he felt such action would make John vulnerable to a charge of favoritism and that it would hurt his career if he was known as a "teacher's pet." His real reason, however, was fear of Mamie's reaction to his putting John into the fight; no one would accuse a junior infantry officer who asked for a combat assignment of seeking special favors.[41] At the end of June, John had to report at Fort Benning, where he began his career as an infantry officer.

The Normandy battle was not going well. The Americans, on the right, or western, flank, found themselves fighting in a country of small fields separated by hedges, banks, and sunken roads. Tanks could not operate, while the infantry had to advance from hedgerow to hedgerow, a painfully slow and expensive process against the skillful and determined German resistance. On the left, Montgomery had promised to take Caen on the first day, but had not done so even by the end of June. Less than two weeks after the exultation over the success of D-Day came the letdown, and with it a severe strain on Anglo-American relations in general, and the relations between Eisenhower and Montgomery specifically.

That the two men would have difficulty in dealing with each other was almost inevitable, given the contrasts between them. Eisenhower was gregarious, while Montgomery lived in isolation. Eisenhower mixed easily with his staff and discussed all decisions with his subordinates; Montgomery set himself up in a lonely camp, where he slept and ate in a wood-paneled trailer he had captured from Rommel in the desert. Montgomery wrote his directives by hand and handed them down from on high, while Eisenhower waited for general agreement among his staff and usually had his operations officer write the final directive. Montgomery shunned the company of women after his wife's death and did not smoke or drink. Eisenhower was modest, Montgomery conceited. "I became completely dedicated to my profession," Montgomery once said of himself. He had indeed made an intensive study of how to command. What he had not studied was how to get his ideas across. He always seemed to be talking down to people, and his condescension became more marked the more intensely he felt about a subject. Montgomery's arrogance offended even British officers, while most Americans found him insufferable. What one American called "his sharp beagle like nose, the small grey eyes that dart about quickly like rabbits in a Thurber cartoon," his self-satisfaction, all irritated.[42]

The personality differences were significant factors in the always strained Eisenhower-Montgomery relationship, but what mattered more was fundamental disagreement over strategy and tactics, and their different structural positions. Eisenhower's military theory was straightforward and aggressive. Like Grant in the Virginia Wilderness in 1864, he favored constant attack, all along the line. He was an advocate of the direct approach and put his faith in the sheer smashing power of great armies. He was once accused of having a mass-production mentality, which was true but beside the point. He came from a mass-production society, and like any good general he wanted to use his nation's strengths on the battlefield. To Montgomery, "it was always very clear . . . that Ike and I were poles apart when it came to the conduct of the war." Montgomery believed in "unbalancing the enemy while keeping well-balanced myself." He wanted to attack on a narrow front, cut through the German lines, and dash on to his objective. Further, Eisenhower was responsible to the CCS, and beyond that body to the two governments. Montgomery was in theory responsible to Eisenhower, but in reality he looked to Brooke, not Eisenhower, for guidance. Montgomery was the senior British officer on the Continent, and as such saw himself as responsible for his nation's interests. The British had neither the manpower nor the material resources to overwhelm the Germans, and they had learned, from 1914 to 1918, that it was near suicidal for them to attempt to do so. The British strength was brains, not brawn. Montgomery proposed to defeat the Germans in France by outthinking and outmaneuvering them; Eisenhower wanted to outfight them.

The initial difficulty centered around the taking of Caen. Montgomery had promised it, did not have it, would not attack it. By mid-June, he was claiming that he had never intended to break out of the beachhead at Caen, on the direct road to Paris; rather, his strategy was to hold on his left while Bradley broke out on the right. His critics charge that he changed his plan because of his failure at Caen; Montgomery himself insisted that he had all along planned to pin the German panzers down in front of Caen while Bradley outflanked them. There is a fierce, continuing, and unresolvable controversy among military experts on this point. Individual reactions depend less on nationality, more on reactions to Montgomery's personality. Thus one British officer at SHAEF who did not like Montgomery maintained vehemently that Montgomery was a "big cheat" in his claims. For Montgomery to say that he was holding the Germans for Bradley's breakout was "absolute rubbish" and "a complete fabrication" that only developed after he was stopped outside Caen.[43] Tedder felt the same way, and in addition was furious because Montgomery had promised to deliver the airfields south of Caen on the first day, but had not and was showing no sense of urgency about getting them. Tedder, indeed, mistrusted Montgomery so much that within two weeks of D-Day he was urging Eisenhower to either get Montgomery to move or get rid of him.

Eisenhower's response was passive. He did not approve of Montgomery's handling of the battle, but he never gave clear and forceful orders in Normandy to insure that it was fought the way he wanted. One of the strongest American military traditions was to give a high degree of independence to tactical commanders, and Eisenhower was a firm believer in that tradition. It was Montgomery's battle, not his; as Supreme Commander, he could only indicate broad policy, not take control of the battle. Through the second half of June, and on into July, he encouraged Montgomery to attack at Caen but, to Tedder's disgust, did not insist. Montgomery, meanwhile, kept promising to "blitz" the Germans; on June 25, for example, he said he was attacking "all out" in the morning and "I will continue battle on eastern flank till one of us cracks and it will not be us."[44] But the brave words were not matched by deeds; his advance was slow and cautious, and after a gain of less than five miles, he called off the offensive. He had kept the Germans off balance, to be sure, and forced them to commit their reinforcements piecemeal, a clear plus, but hardly enough to satisfy Eisenhower. "Ike is considerably less than exuberant these days," Butcher noted.[45] The reason, according to Montgomery, was that Eisenhower never understood the plan. Montgomery blamed Bradley for his problems, saying that the Americans should have attacked both toward Cherbourg to the north (which fell to the Americans on June 27) and toward Coutances to the south, but—said Montgomery—"Bradley didn't want to take the risk." In a typical condescending remark, Montgomery added, "I have to take the Americans along quietly and give them time to get ready."[46]

The Allied generals seemed to be fighting one another more than the Germans. Two factors fed the irritation and backbiting. First, there was the old fear that the stalemate of 1914–1918 would be repeated in Normandy. Second, the V-1s, although more a nuisance than a real military threat, were having a devastating effect on British nerves. In June and July, the V-1s killed more than five thousand people, injured thirty-five thousand more, and destroyed some thirty thousand buildings. Even worse, Allied intelligence anticipated that the Germans would soon have the V-2s—the world's first medium-range ballistic missiles—in operation. Bombing attacks on the launching sites had failed to produce satisfactory results. The sites would have to be overrun on the ground to be put out of action. Churchill was so upset that in early July he proposed using poison gas against the sites. Eisenhower responded that he would refuse to be a party to the use of gas: "Let's, for God's sake, keep our eyes on the ball and use some sense," he said.[47] But something had to be done, soon. The Americans were still stuck in the hedgerow country, the British outside Caen.

On July 1, Eisenhower went to Normandy to see what he could do to galvanize his commanders. He told Bradley he was bringing "nothing but a bedroll, one aide and an orderly" and wanted "nothing but a trench with a piece of canvas over it."[48] He stayed five days, visiting with troops, inspecting the battlefield, talking with Bradley and the American corps and division commanders. None of them liked having Eisenhower around, because their various headquarters were all subject to sporadic German artillery fire. Eisenhower's old friend Wade Haislip, commanding the XV Corps, told him flatly to get out. "Don't think I'm worrying about your possible demise," he added. "I just don't want it said that I allowed the Supreme Commander to get killed in my corps area. Now if you want to get killed, go into some other area."[49] At one point Eisenhower commandeered a jeep and, accompanied by his British aide, James Gault, and an orderly, with no other escort, personally drove around the countryside, and even managed to wander behind the German lines. No startling events occurred, and he did not know he had been in danger until he reached 90th Division headquarters and was told where he had been. The GIs were delighted to see Eisenhower driving the jeep and shouted and whistled as he drove past.

On July 4, Eisenhower went to a fighter airfield; while there, he learned that a mission was about to be flown. Eisenhower said he wanted to go along in order to see the hedgerow country from the air. Bradley, who was with him, demurred, but Eisenhower insisted. His last words, as he climbed into a Mustang, were, "All right, Brad, I am not going to fly to Berlin."[50] He did, however, fly over German lines, which led to a *New York Times* feature article. The headline read, "EISENHOWER FLIES OVER NAZI LINES," and the story featured such items as, "He was in exposed positions most of the time [during the five-day trip] and twice German artillery barrages started just after he had left a certain area. Scorning helmet, the General wore only a cloth cap."[51] Seeing the story and knowing the effect it would have on Mamie, Eisenhower wrote her on July 11, "Pay no attention to such tales. I'm most careful—and I'm not talking for effect. Ask Johnny how promptly I duck to the shelter when the 'buzzers' come around!"[52] And indeed he did not take unnecessary risks during the war, did not feel any need to prove his manhood through bravado. He just had to see for himself what was going on.

When he got back to Bushy Park, disappointed at the lack of progress in the hedgerows, despairing of ever breaking out in that awful country, Tedder and Smith both told him that it was all Montgomery's fault. They insisted that Eisenhower had to force him to act. Tedder complained that Montgomery was unjustly blaming the air forces for his own failure and said that "the Army did not seem prepared to fight its own battles."[53] Eisenhower wrote a letter to Montgomery, but it was too weak—more a statement of desired objectives than a firm order—to impel action. Eisenhower took his complaints to Churchill, telling the Prime Minister that Montgomery was bogged down and appealing to Churchill to "persuade Monty to get on his bicycle and start moving."

Churchill did, and Montgomery responded by promising a "big show" on July 9. He asked for, and got, the all-out support of the bombers. The attack, however, failed. On July 10, Montgomery called it off.

Eisenhower, Butcher said, was "smoldering." So was Tedder. So was Patton, who had come to Normandy as an observer. On July 12, Patton commented in his diary, "Ike is bound hand and foot by the British and does not know it. Poor fool. We actually have no Supreme Commander—no one who can take hold and say that this shall be done and that shall not be done."[54] There was a general uneasy feeling around SHAEF that Eisenhower would never take hold of Montgomery.

But Montgomery kept promising big attacks, with big results. On July 12, he told Eisenhower of yet another offensive, code name Goodwood. "My whole Eastern flank will burst into flames," he said, as he demanded that the full weight of all the air forces be thrown into the battle.[55] He wanted, and got, a truly awe-inspiring bombardment—7,700 tons of bombs delivered by 1,676 heavy bombers and 343 medium and light bombers, in what was "the heaviest and most concentrated air attack in support of ground troops ever attempted."[56] Montgomery later claimed that Eisenhower had completely misunderstood Goodwood's objective, that he never intended to break out on the left, as Eisenhower thought, but merely to hold the German armor on his front so that Bradley could break out on the right. But the Germans could not use tanks in the hedgerow country any more than the Americans could in any event. Further, four days before Goodwood began, Eisenhower promised Montgomery that Bradley would "keep his troops fighting like the very devil" to prevent the Germans from shifting troops from the western to the eastern flank; Eisenhower also said, "I would not be at all surprised to see you gaining a victory that will make some of the 'old classics' look like a skirmish between patrols."[57] Montgomery thus had ample opportunity to tell Eisenhower that he had it backward, that Goodwood's objective was to support Bradley, not vice versa; that he did not do so is sufficient evidence that Montgomery in fact thought Goodwood would be decisive, opening the short route to Paris.

But the main reason Montgomery so egregiously exaggerated the aim of Goodwood was his realization that the pressure on Eisenhower to dismiss him was mounting. Gossips at SHAEF were speculating on "who would succeed Monty if sacked." This simple solution was, to Eisenhower, out of the question, because of Montgomery's popularity with the British troops, Brooke, and the British public. Further, Eisenhower had no right to remove the senior British commander. The Supreme Commander seems to have been the only man at SHAEF to recognize these obvious truths, and they provide the answer to the nagging question, Why did Eisenhower put up with Montgomery? He had no choice. He had to cooperate with the difficult and exasperating British general, for Montgomery's place in the command structure was secure. The real threat to Montgomery's position was Tedder's recommendation that Eisenhower move his headquarters to Normandy and take personal control of the land battle.[58] Montgomery knew that he needed to buy time, not so much to protect his position as to keep Eisenhower in England so that he could run the land battle.

Goodwood began on July 18. In its initial stages, assisted by the tremendous air bombardment, it went well. But after Montgomery lost 401 tanks and suffered 2,600 casualties, he called it off. The British Second Army had taken Caen, gained a few square miles, and inflicted heavy casualties on the Germans, but there had been nothing like a breakthrough. Montgomery announced that he was satisfied with the results.[59]

Eisenhower was livid. He thundered that it had taken more than seven thousand tons of bombs to gain seven miles and that the Allies could hardly hope to go through France paying a price of a thousand tons of bombs per mile.[60] Tedder blamed Montgomery for "the Army's failure," and SHAEF officers wondered aloud whether Montgomery should be made a peer and sent to the House of Lords or given the governorship of Malta.[61]

This was all wild and irresponsible talk. After the war, Eisenhower said he felt the powers of a supreme commander should be greater, that he should have the right to dismiss any subordinate, whatever his nationality. But even had Eisenhower had that power in 1944, he would not have exercised it.[62] Sensitive to the morale factor and keenly aware of Montgomery's great popularity, he would not consider asking for Montgomery's removal. Tedder was so angry he thought of doing it himself. On July 21, the day after Montgomery called off the Goodwood offensive, the Allies learned of the attempt on Hitler's life the previous day by members of the German high command. Tedder said that "Monty's failure to take action earlier had lost us the opportunity offered by the attempt on Hitler's life," and added that he intended "to put my views in writing to the British Chiefs of Staff. I told Eisenhower that his own people would be thinking that he had sold them to the British if he continued to support Montgomery without protest." At Smith's regular morning meeting on July 21, Tedder said it was imperative that the Allies get to the Pas de Calais quickly in order to overrun the Germans' flying-bomb sites. Smith groaned. "We are in fact not going to get there anytime soon," he said. Tedder snapped, "Then we must change our leaders for men who will get us there." [63]

At Smith's and Tedder's urging, Eisenhower then sent a letter to Montgomery. *"Time is vital,"* he said, and he urged Montgomery to resume the attack. Many American officers thought that Montgomery hesitated because of the critical British manpower situation. The United Kingdom could no longer make good the losses in the Second Army, so it could not afford the cost in casualties of an all-out attack. Eisenhower argued that an attack now would save lives in the long run, and turned the British manpower crisis on its head by pointing out that eventually the Americans would have many more troops in Europe than the British, "but while we have equality in size we must go forward shoulder to shoulder, with honors and sacrifices equally shared." [64]

Tedder saw a copy of Eisenhower's letter that afternoon. He was upset because he had not seen it before it was sent, and commented that it was "not strong enough. Monty can evade it. It contains no order." [65] Everyone was depressed, irritable. After seven weeks of fighting, the deepest Allied penetrations were some twenty-five to thirty miles inland, on a front of only eighty miles, hardly enough room to maneuver or to bring in the American forces waiting in England for deployment. The V-1s continued to bombard London. The Americans were still struggling in the hedgerow country, measuring their advance in yards rather than miles. Goodwood had failed and Montgomery refused to mount another attack. The newspapers were full of the ugly word "stalemate."

There were two bright spots. Ultra intercepts revealed that the Germans were stretched to the limit, in large part because Fortitude was still alive and they were therefore retaining large forces in the Pas de Calais; and Bradley was working on a plan, code name Cobra, to break out on the right. As Eisenhower had noted in his letter to Montgomery, "Now we are pinning our hopes on Bradley."

CHAPTER SEVENTEEN

London, Normandy, Paris

July 22–September 1, 1944

By July 23, the Americans had landed a total of 770,000 troops in Normandy. First Army had suffered 73,000 casualties. The British and Canadians had landed 591,000 troops and suffered 49,000 casualties. There was a large, immediately available reserve of American divisions in England waiting to enter the battle. The supply situation was basically good; landing craft continued to bring material in over the beaches, and on July 19 the first supplies were brought in through Cherbourg. The Germans in Normandy, meanwhile, had twenty-six divisions in place, six of them armored, to face the AEF's thirty-four divisions. As the Allies were on the offensive, their superiority on the ground was only marginal; in addition, the German Fifteenth Army was still intact in the Pas de Calais, pinned down by Fortitude, but Fortitude was wearing thin by late July, which meant that the German ability to reinforce was greater than that of the Allies.[1] Eisenhower's great advantage continued to be control of the air. Bradley planned to use it in Operation Cobra to break through the German lines; once he was through, Eisenhower intended to rush divisions over from England, activate Patton's Third Army, and send it racing for Brittany to open the ports there.

The problem with air power was weather; it was a weapon that could be used only under suitable conditions. Cobra was scheduled to begin on July 21, and that day Eisenhower flew over to Normandy to witness the beginning. The sky was overcast and his B-25 was the only plane in the air. By the time he arrived it was raining hard. Bradley told him the attack had been called off and dressed him down for flying in such weather. Eisenhower tossed away his soggy cigarette, smiled, and said his only pleasure in being Supreme Commander was that nobody could ground him. "When I die," he added, looking at the steady rain, "they ought to hold my body for a rainy day and then bury me out in the middle of a storm. This damned weather is going to be the death of me yet."[2] The next day, as the rains continued, he flew back to London; on the twenty-fourth, still waiting for a clear day, he wired Bradley, urging him to an all-out effort when the weather permitted. "A break through at this juncture will minimize the total cost," he said, and added that he wanted First Army to "pursue every advantage with an ardor verging on recklessness." If it broke through, "the results will be incalculable."[3]

Bradley hardly needed urging, but Montgomery did. Eisenhower wanted Second Army to attack when Cobra began—indeed had promised Bradley he would see to it—so after sending his message to Bradley, Eisenhower flew to Montgomery's headquarters. What he wanted, as Smith noted, was "an all-out co-ordinated attack by the entire Allied line, which would at last put our forces in decisive motion. He was up and down the line like a football coach, exhorting everyone to aggressive action."[4] All this was highly irritating to Montgomery and Brooke. "It is quite clear that Ike considers that [General Miles] Dempsey [commanding Second Army] should be doing more than he does," Brooke wrote to Montgomery. "It is equally clear that Ike has the very vaguest conception of war." The British officers agreed that Eisenhower had no notion of balance. If everybody was to attack, Montgomery argued, nobody would have the strength to make a decisive breakthrough or to exploit it. Eisenhower "evidently . . . has some conception of attacking on the whole front," Brooke complained, "which must be an American doctrine."[5]

Tedder too was unhappy with Eisenhower, but as usual he disagreed with Montgomery and Brooke. Cobra got started on the morning of July 25; that day, Tedder called Eisenhower on the telephone, demanding to know why Montgomery was not doing more and what Eisenhower was doing about it. Eisenhower said he had talked with Churchill and that they were satisfied that this time Montgomery's attack would be in earnest. Tedder "rather uh-huned, being not at all satisfied, and implying the PM must have sold Ike a bill of goods." Eisenhower told Butcher of the conversation and said he thought he could work things out satisfactorily, for "there's nothing so wrong a good victory won't cure."[6]

To get away from the carping, and, he hoped, to enjoy seeing the beginning of a "great victory," Eisenhower flew to Normandy. The tremendous air bombardment—almost 2,500 bombers dropped more than four thousand tons of explosives—was impressive, but Eisenhower returned to London that evening glum, even depressed. There had been a series of shortfalls, killing and wounding several hundred GIs. General Lesley McNair, commander of the Army Ground Forces, who had gone to the front lines to observe, had been killed. In addition the ground attack seemed to be going slowly. The only encouraging note came when Bradley said he was convinced that the next day his forces would make extraordinary advances. Eisenhower would not allow his hopes to rise; he had heard the same promises the first day of Goodwood. Worse than the slow progress on the ground were the shortfalls, which convinced Eisenhower that he could not use his air power to help the troops break out. He told Bradley he would no longer employ heavy bombers against tactical targets. "That's a job for artillery," he said. "I gave them a green light this time. But I promise you it's the last."[7]

By the next evening, however, a smile had replaced the frown. Major General J. Lawton Collins' VII Corps was breaking through. Bradley had put Collins at the point because he thought Collins "nervy and ambitious," and Collins held nothing back, committing all his reserves on the second day of the battle. The air attack had stunned the enemy, destroying his communications and rendering many of his weapons ineffective. Before going to bed an elated Eisenhower wrote Bradley, "You have got the stuff piled up and we must give the enemy no rest at all until we have achieved our objective. Then we will crush him."[8] By July 27 Collins had reached Coutances, while the VIII Corps, under Troy Middleton, to Collins' right, had taken Granville and Avranches.

Bradley's forces had achieved a penetration and were on the verge of scoring a complete breakthrough. Brooke continued to complain about Eisenhower's lack of strategic sense, but Eisenhower's insistence on attack everywhere had brought about the crisis of the Battle of France. If the Germans could not restore their line, American troops would pour through the gap and be free in their rear. Eisenhower, fully aware that the crisis had arrived, was rushing Patton's divisions over to the Continent to prepare for the exploitation. He also continued to pressure Montgomery. "Never was time more vital to us," he told Montgomery on July 28, and "we should not wait on weather or on perfection of detail of preparation. . . . I feel very strongly that a three division attack now . . . will be worth more than a six division attack in five days' time." He urged Montgomery not to waste an hour.[9] Montgomery, beginning to share the sense of urgency, ordered Dempsey to throw all caution overboard and "to accept any casualties and to step on the gas." He declared that the enemy "must be worried, and shot up, and attacked, and raided, whenever and wherever possible."[10]

To this point, Smith's comparison of Eisenhower to a football coach was inexact. Eisenhower had not called the plays. He was less a coach, more a cheerleader. But by the end of July, as the AEF swelled, he was beginning to assume control. He decided to activate Patton's Third Army as of August 1; at that time, General Courtney Hodges would take over U.S. First Army and Bradley would move up to command of the 12th Army Group, consisting of First and Third Armies. Until SHAEF could establish a forward command post on the Continent, Bradley would continue to receive his operational instructions from Montgomery, but in fact Eisenhower was assuming command of the land battle.

On August 1 Patton was unleashed and began his race through Brittany. The nightmare of a static front was over. "This is great news," Eisenhower exulted. Just before lunch on August 2, Butcher met Eisenhower in the hall at Bushy Park. The Supreme Commander was all smiles. "If the intercepts are right," he said, "we are to hell and gone in Brittany and slicing 'em up in Normandy."[11] He then made a momentous decision. The pre-Overlord plans had laid great emphasis on Brittany and its ports. Patton was supposed to concentrate all his forces on Brest. But with the German left flank wide open, Eisenhower decided to send only one of the four corps of Patton's army into Brittany, devoting the "great bulk of the forces to the task of completing the destruction of the German Army . . . and exploiting . . . as far as we possibly can."[12] Patton, like Bradley, needed no special urging. Montgomery did. Eisenhower therefore told Montgomery to make certain all commanders were aware "that in an emergency we can drop them supplies by airplane in considerable quantities." Whatever happened, Eisenhower insisted, the momentum should not be lost. "I know that you will keep hammering," he wired Montgomery on August 2, "as long as you have a single shot in the locker."[13]

While the British Second and U.S. First Armies continued to attack, contain, and destroy the Germans in Normandy, Patton's Third Army moved rapidly, taking Rennes on August 3 and getting as far as Le Mans, almost halfway to Paris, five days later. The air forces gave Third Army all possible support, with fighters and fighter-bombers protecting the flanks while the heavy bombers continued to interdict behind the German lines. French Resistance activities added immeasurably to the German woes. The Germans were reduced to moving troops by night; their supply deficiencies were acute. Hitler, nevertheless, saw an opportunity to cut Patton's line of communication, recapture Cherbourg, and possibly even drive the Allies back into the sea. He proposed to do this by counterattacking through Mortain and on to the coast at Avranches. Hitler described the situation as "a unique, never recurring opportunity for a complete reversal of the situation."[14] To strengthen the attack, he sent additional units to Field Marshal Guenther von Kluge, who had replaced Rommel (who was a casualty of an air attack on his staff car); the units came from the Pas de Calais, the Germans finally having seen through Fortitude. Hitler also withdrew units facing Second Army for the Mortain counterattack.

Because Hitler mistrusted his generals, he took control of the battle, which forced him to use the radio, allowing Ultra to pick up both the general plan and most of the specific details. Thus when Kluge struck, late in the evening of August 6, Eisenhower knew his strength and intentions. Six German armored divisions hit one U.S. infantry division, the 30th, and elements of the 30th were quickly surrounded. Without Ultra, an attack of such strength, so weakly resisted, at such a critical spot, would have caused consternation in the Allied high command. Instead, thanks to Ultra, Eisenhower saw the attack as an opportunity; in his view the Germans were sticking their heads into a noose.

On August 7, Eisenhower set up an advance command post in Normandy, a tented headquarters in an apple orchard near Granville, which was less than twenty-five miles from Mortain and almost directly in Kluge's path. He met with Bradley, and they immediately agreed to hold Mortain with minimal forces while rushing every available division south. They bolstered the flanks of the salient with American artillery and called in the fighter-bombers. Eisenhower told Bradley that "if the Germans should temporarily break through from Mortain to Avranches and thus cut off the southward thrust, we would give the advance forces two thousand tons of supply per day by air." The following morning, Eisenhower told Marshall, "The enemy's . . . counter attacks . . . make it appear that we have a good chance to encircle and destroy a lot of his forces."[15]

The gamble at Mortain paid off; in a classic defensive action, the 30th Division held, while the artillery and air forces virtually destroyed the German tanks. On August 9 Kluge discontinued his offensive and refused to renew it despite Hitler's orders. The Canadians and Patton were posing a threat he could not ignore. The Allied offensive was in full swing, all forces meshing, aiming for the destruction of Kluge's Seventh and Fifth Panzer Armies, which were in a huge salient, with the tip at Mortain and the base on the Falaise–Argentan line. "Ike keeps continually after both Montgomery and Bradley," Butcher noted, "to destroy the enemy now rather than to be content with mere gains of territory."[16]

Eisenhower was splitting his time between Normandy and London; in London, he was engaged, on almost a daily basis, in "one of the longest-sustained arguments that I had with Prime Minister Churchill throughout the . . . war."[17] The argument had begun in June, continued through July, and reached its climax in early August. The subject was Anvil, the landing in the south of France. Much earlier in the spring, Eisenhower had agreed to postpone the Anvil operation, in order to have the use of the landing craft, but only on the understanding that the invasion would go forward later. This meant shutting down the offensive in Italy, where Rome had fallen on June 5. In early June, Eisenhower recommended an August 15 landing at Marseilles. Churchill objected; he wanted Anvil called off, in favor of further operations in Italy and the Adriatic. The JCS refused. Churchill went over their heads and appealed directly to Roosevelt. He told the President he was disturbed by the "arbitrary" tone the Americans were adopting and asked Roosevelt to "hear both sides" before making a decision. Churchill claimed that he was willing to help Eisenhower, but not at the expense of the complete ruin "of our great affairs in the Mediterranean and we take it hard that this should be demanded of us." He called Anvil "bleak and sterile" and declared that it would do nothing to help the AEF in Normandy. But Eisenhower insisted that it would, not only by putting additional pressure on the Germans in France, but even more important by opening the port of Marseilles, one of the best in France, and by bringing additional American and French divisions into the battle, which could not be done through the clogged Normandy ports. Roosevelt supported Eisenhower, explaining to Churchill, "For purely political reasons over here, I should never survive even a slight setback in Overlord if it were known that fairly large forces had been diverted to the Balkans."[18]

Churchill then turned again to Eisenhower. On August 4, with Middleton's corps headed toward Brest, he asked Eisenhower to shift Anvil (which he had renamed Dragoon, on the grounds that he had been "dragooned" into it) from Marseilles to Brest. As Churchill saw it, the great advantage was not only that the Dragoon forces could then make their contribution in northwest France, but also that the drain on Alexander's armies in Italy would be relatively small and Alexander still might reach Trieste before winter. But it was an absurd proposal. Dragoon was scheduled to go in eleven days; Churchill was recommending transferring it some 1,600 miles from its base, beyond the reach of air cover, with no plan, no idea of how much shipping would be involved, and no assessment of its effect on current operations or the subsequent campaign. Eisenhower learned of the proposal late in the evening of August 4, after returning to Southwick House from Normandy. Churchill told him about it on the telephone, then said he was driving to Portsmouth the next day for lunch and discussion. That morning, waiting for the Prime Minister, Eisenhower wired Marshall to assure the Chief that "I will not repeat not under any conditions agree at this moment to a cancellation of Dragoon."[19]

At lunch, Churchill grandiloquently declared that history would show that Eisenhower had missed a great opportunity if he did not shift Dragoon from southern France to Brest. Eisenhower mumbled that it was too late to make a change, which was just the sort of argument that made the Prime Minister most impatient. He believed that anything in war was possible if men just put their heads to it. After lunch, Smith, Cunningham, and Ramsay joined Churchill and Eisenhower in the war room at Southwick House. The argument continued for six hours. Eisenhower said no to Churchill, kept saying no all afternoon, and "ended saying no in every form of the English language at his command." Cunningham supported Churchill, as did Smith, much to Eisenhower's surprise. Ramsay sided with Eisenhower. By the end of the session, Eisenhower was limp, but Dragoon was still on. After Churchill left, Eisenhower told Marshall that he feared the Prime Minister "would return to the subject in two or three days and simply regard the issue as unsettled."[20]

Eisenhower was right. On August 9, two days after Eisenhower moved his advance headquarters to near Granville and one day after the Mortain battle had reached its climax, Eisenhower flew to London to meet with Churchill at 10 Downing Street. Eisenhower later described the session that followed as one of the most difficult of the entire war. Churchill pressed his point. He intimated that the United States was taking the role of a "big strong and dominating partner" rather than attempting to understand the British position. The Americans, he complained, were indifferent to British interests. It was painful for Eisenhower to see the Prime Minister so "stirred, upset and even despondent." He did his best to refute Churchill's charges that the

United States was ignoring British interests. "I do not, for one moment, believe that there is any desire . . . to disregard British views," Eisenhower told Churchill, "or cold-bloodedly to leave Britain holding an empty bag." He added that he was always objective in his military decisions "and I am sorry that you seem to feel that we use our great actual or potential strength as a bludgeon."

Eisenhower wondered if Churchill's motives were political, if his aim was to get Allied troops into the Balkans ahead of the Russians. If that were so, he told the Prime Minister, then Churchill should lay the facts and his own conclusions before the President. Eisenhower said he well understood that military campaigns could be affected by political considerations, and if the heads of government should decide that getting into the Balkans was worth prolonging the war, then he would "instantly and loyally adjust plans accordingly." But Eisenhower insisted that so long as Churchill argued the matter on military grounds he was wrong. Churchill, knowing how much Americans disliked admitting to "political" motives (which were somehow construed as tainted) and insisted on making all decisions on "military" grounds (which were thought to be straightforward), insisted that he had no political objectives. The correct military policy, he said, was to avoid the sterile campaign in the south of France, open Brest, and push on in Italy. "In this particular field I alone had to be the judge of my own responsibilities and decisions," Eisenhower later commented. "I refused to consider the change so long as it was urged on military considerations."

The distinction between military and political considerations, which Eisenhower made on a number of occasions when it suited his purpose, was essentially a false one. On the strategic level, with entire armies involved, the two considerations merged into one. Eisenhower himself never hesitated to use "political" arguments to support his "military" decisions. Thus on this occasion he reminded Churchill that the American government had gone to great expense to equip and supply a number of French divisions, that de Gaulle was most anxious to have them fight in France, and that the only way they could be brought into the battle was through Marseilles. Eisenhower also argued that Dragoon must go ahead because Roosevelt had promised Stalin there would be a south of France invasion, which was a purely political point.

Churchill remained unimpressed. When the meeting broke up, he was still unhappy, indeed had tears in his eyes. Eisenhower reported to Marshall, "So far as I can determine he attaches so much importance to the matter that failure in achieving this objective would represent a practical failure of his whole administration." At one point Churchill told Eisenhower that if he did not have his way, "I might have to go to the King and lay down the mantle of my high office."[21]

But Churchill could not move Eisenhower, and Dragoon headed toward Marseilles. On August 10, Churchill left for a visit to Italy. While there, on August 15, he took the opportunity of watching the assault he had hoped would never take place. He wired Eisenhower to say that he had "adopted" Dragoon and was delighted by the unopposed landings. When Eisenhower heard this, and when he thought of "all the fighting and mental anguish I went through in order to preserve that operation, I don't know whether to sit down and laugh or to cry."[22]

The Dragoon forces (6th Army Group, General Jacob Devers commanding, consisting of one French and one American army) advanced northward, up the Rhône Valley, against negligible resistance. They tied down only a relatively small number of German troops, but they did open Marseilles, and its docks made an invaluable contribution to the supply situation. From September through December 1944, Marseilles unloaded more tonnage than any of the other ports available to SHAEF. In the last three months of 1944, more than one-third of the total supplies unloaded in Europe by the Allies came in through the south of France. Not until January 1945, when Antwerp was in full operation, was Marseilles superseded as SHAEF's major port, and even then nearly one-quarter of the weapons and shells used against Germany in the last campaign came into Europe via Marseilles. For that reason, Eisenhower never doubted that he made the right decision.[23]

In Normandy, meanwhile, the Germans were on the verge of debacle. On August 8, the day before his last Dragoon argument with Churchill, Eisenhower drove to Bradley's headquarters to suggest to him that Patton "should swing in closer [that is, to the north from Le Mans, toward Argentan, rather than eastward toward Paris] in an effort to destroy the enemy by attacking him in the rear." He found that Bradley "had already acted on this idea." Then he drove to Montgomery's headquarters "to make certain that Monty would continue to press" the Canadians southward from Caen toward Falaise.[24] If the Canadians could take Falaise, then move on to link up with Patton in Argentan, two German armies would be encircled.

The Canadian attack, however, went slowly. Patton, facing slimmer resistance, made a steady advance. By August 10 Kluge was nearly trapped; Patton's units had cut off all but one of the supply roads for the German Seventh and the Fifth Armies. On August 12, Patton's lead corps reached Argentan. The Canadians were still short of Falaise. Patton, impatient, wanted to cross the army boundary line and close the gap. He called Bradley on the telephone and pleaded, "Let me go on to Falaise and we'll drive the British back into the sea for another Dunkirk." Bradley refused. He did not believe Patton was strong enough to hold the gap once the Germans started the rush to escape. Besides, he thought the Canadians could complete the encirclement. Bradley made the decision on his own, without reference to Montgomery or to Eisenhower (who was at that moment arguing with Churchill over Dragoon).[25]

By August 14 the Allies were on the verge of closing the trap. Eisenhower, Butcher reported, was "sunny, if not almost jubilant."[26] He called for an all-out effort. On the fourteenth, he issued a rare Order of the Day (he sent out only ten in the course of the war), exhorting the Allied soldiers, sailors, and airmen. "The opportunity may be grasped only through the utmost in zeal, determination and speedy action," Eisenhower declared. If everyone did his job, "we can make this week a momentous one in the history of this war—a brilliant and fruitful week for us, a fateful one for the ambitions of the Nazi tyrants." The Order of the Day was broadcast over BBC and the Allied radio network, and distributed to the troops in mimeographed form.[27]

There was the greatest excitement at SHAEF, and indeed throughout the Allied world. Churchill, Roosevelt, Marshall, and Brooke all felt it. In New York, the stock market tumbled in anticipation of peace. Newspaper correspondents who had been overly pessimistic during the Normandy stalemate now asked Eisenhower, at an August 15 press conference, how many weeks it would take to end the war. In the days that followed, he would hear that question again and again. People thought of November 1918, when the German army cracked, and expected a repetition in August or September of 1944. The thought persisted, indeed grew stronger and plagued Eisenhower until October.

The expectation of a German collapse was based on a misreading of the lesson of November 1918, an inaccurate assessment of the situation in August 1944, and a failure to understand the German character. In 1918 the Germans had been pushed behind their last defensive line, while in 1944 they still had the West Wall to fall back to. In 1918 the Germans had fallen behind in the technological race (it was the Allies who had the tanks), while in 1944 the Nazis could legitimately ask the Wehrmacht to hold on just a little longer, because Germany's secret weapons might well win the war for them; many of those weapons, such as the V-1s and V-2s, jet aircraft, and diesel submarines, were already realities. In 1918, it was the dim-witted, indecisive Kaiser and the shattered Ludendorff who had agreed to an armistice; Eisenhower knew that Hitler was made of sterner stuff.

Most of all, Eisenhower knew that the Germans would not quit until they were incapable of resistance. He knew it, in part, because of his own German heritage. Just as "Little Ike" had gotten off the ground time and again after Edgar knocked him down, refusing to quit until he was incapable of standing any longer, so did the mature Eisenhower expect the Germans to fight until it was impossible for them to continue. He knew that they could retreat to the West Wall, and in the process fall back on their supply base, while the AEF supply lines grew longer. He also realized that because of the Transportation Plan, because his ground commanders had called on the heavy bombers so often in Normandy, and because of the bombing effort against the V-1 and V-2 sites, Germany itself was still relatively untouched. He knew that the Germans were producing more tanks, artillery, and other weapons in 1944 than in any previous year; he knew that the AEF was, therefore, in for a tremendous fight.

The theme appears again and again in his letters to his wife. On August 11, he told her, "Don't be misled by the papers. Every victory . . . is sweet—but the end of the war will come only with complete destruction of the Hun forces." In September, when expectations of a German collapse were even higher, he said, "I wonder how the people at home can be so complacent about finishing off the job we have here. There is still a lot of suffering to go through. God, I hate the Germans!"[28]

So, when reporters asked him on August 15 how many weeks to the end, he was furious. Butcher recorded, "Ike vehemently castigated those who think they can measure the end of the war 'in a matter of weeks.' He went on to say 'such people are crazy.'" Eisenhower reminded the press that Hitler knew he would hang when the war ended so he had nothing to lose in continuing it. In 1918, the Kaiser had had reason to hope for a soft peace on the basis of Wilson's Fourteen Points; in 1944, Hitler had only Roosevelt's unconditional surrender demand to contemplate. (Anticipating this problem, in April 1944 Eisenhower had asked Roosevelt to clarify the meaning of unconditional surrender, "by announcing the principles on which the treatment of a defeated Germany would be based." Eisenhower said this was highly desirable "in view of the accumulated evidence that German propaganda is interpreting the words of 'Unconditional Surrender' to strengthen the morale of the German Army and people." He wanted to emphasize law, order, private property, and the undoubted right of the German people to govern themselves. But Roosevelt, fearful of charges of bad faith after the war criminals were put on trial, declined to make any clarification.)[29]

Eisenhower, on August 15, told the reporters that he expected that Hitler would end up hanging himself, but before he did he would "fight to the bitter end," and most of his troops would fight with him.[30] It was a leap into the mind of the enemy, the highest form of the military art, and he was exactly right.

Just how right Eisenhower was the Germans demonstrated in the Falaise pocket. They rejected the easy way out—surrender—and fought to hold open their escape route. Despite Eisenhower's plea in his Order of the Day, it was the Germans, not the Allies, who made the supreme effort at Falaise. The rigidity with which the field commanders held to the boundary lines at Argentan and Falaise helped the Germans, to be sure, but the main factors were German fighting ability and determination. The gap was not closed until August 19; some forty thousand Wehrmacht troops escaped.

Eisenhower was disappointed but not downcast. "Due to the extraordinary defensive measures taken by the enemy," he explained to Marshall, "it is possible that our total bag of prisoners will not be so great as I first anticipated."[31] Falaise left a taste of bitterness and led to recrimination between the British and the Americans as to whose fault it was that any Germans escaped, much less forty thousand. Still, the disappointment should not obscure the fact that Falaise *was* a victory. Some fifty thousand Germans were captured, another ten thousand were killed. Those who escaped left their equipment behind. Later in August, Eisenhower toured the battlefield with Kay, Jimmy Gault, and press representatives. Gault wrote, "We were certainly not disappointed in the results, because the scene was one of masses of destroyed tanks, guns, transports and equipment of all sorts lying around, including many dead Germans and horses. The smell was tremendous."[32] Eisenhower said that the scene "could be described only by Dante. It was literally possible to walk for hundreds of yards at a time, stepping on nothing but dead and decaying flesh."[33] Falaise, in fact, ended the Battle of France. The Germans, those who were left, were retreating pell-mell toward the border. They could not defend the line of the Seine, nor any other in France; their only safety lay in the West Wall. But, as Eisenhower knew, although everyone around him seemed at one time or another to forget, victory in France did not mean the end of the war, and as he told Mamie in early August, "In war there is no substitute for victory."[34]

Following Falaise, the AEF overran France. Montgomery's 21st Army Group drove along the coast toward Belgium, while the First and Third Armies headed east, toward Paris and beyond to the German border. The immediate question was, Should Paris be liberated? Eisenhower wished to avoid it for the present. To attack Paris might involve the Allies in prolonged street fighting and lead to the destruction of some of the most hallowed cultural monuments in the West (and Eisenhower had already issued stern general orders that no fighting should take place in areas containing important historical or religious monuments, explaining that they represented, in large part, what the Allies were fighting for). Once the Allies took Paris, they would be responsible for supplying its two million civilians; planners estimated that four thousand tons of supplies per day would be required, equivalent to the daily needs of seven full divisions. But on August 19 Resistance groups in Paris took control of the city; that evening the German commander agreed to an armistice. On August 21 de Gaulle, accompanied by Koenig, called on Eisenhower. They asked him to rush General Jacques LeClerc's 2d French Armored Division, a part of First Army, brought into France in late July, to Paris. Eisenhower demurred. American divisions were closer to Paris, and in any event he did not want to take control of the city as yet. De Gaulle then withdrew, angry, and sent Eisenhower a note, saying that he might have to order LeClerc to Paris on his own. Eisenhower scribbled on de Gaulle's note, "It looks now as if we'd be compelled to go into Paris."[35] LeClerc started for the city, without orders; meanwhile representatives of the Resistance in Paris came to Granville to beg Eisenhower to send troops into the city before the Germans broke the armistice.

Eisenhower was under pressure from all sides, from de Gaulle, from LeClerc, from the Resistance, even from his own commanders. Paris was a magnet, attracting everyone toward it. Combat soldiers could hardly wait to get into the city and sample its pleasures. Every division, corps, and army commander in Europe wanted the honor of liberating the city. Late on August 22, therefore, Eisenhower decided to send LeClerc, along with the American 4th Division and a British contingent, into Paris. He stressed that he did not "want a severe fight [nor] any bombing or artillery fire on the city . . ."[36]

LeClerc entered the city on August 25. De Gaulle arrived shortly thereafter, appointed Koenig the military governor of the city, and took control of the government buildings. The following day, de Gaulle led a parade down the Champs Elysées. Eisenhower, meanwhile, drove to see Bradley at his command post near Chartres. The lure of Paris had become too much for him to resist, and he suggested to Bradley that they enter the city the next morning. It would be a Sunday, Eisenhower reminded Bradley, and "everyone will be sleeping late. We can do it without any fuss."

Sunday brought a beautiful, sunny morning, adding to the general air of gaiety and the exultant feeling of liberation. No one slept late. Bicycles crowded the roads. Cheering Parisians quickly recognized Eisenhower and Bradley and surrounded them, waving enthusiastically, and occasionally grabbing and kissing the generals. Eisenhower told Mamie he did not have time to visit their old apartment on Pont Mirabeau, but he expected it was unchanged because in Paris "one sees little evidence of physical damage." As for himself, "I prefer camps to cities."[37]

Eisenhower and Bradley called on de Gaulle at the Prefecture of Police. He had surrounded himself with the traditional Republican Guards, but he was nevertheless worried, especially about controlling the Communists in the Resistance. He asked Eisenhower for a show of force. Eisenhower turned to Bradley to ask what could be done. Bradley was already planning to attack eastward out of Paris, and said he could march his men straight through the city instead of around its outskirts. Eisenhower told him to do it, which not only gave de Gaulle his show of force but also reminded the Parisians that the Americans had, after all, played a role in their liberation.[38]

Eisenhower, meanwhile, had approved a civil affairs agreement worked out between Smith and Koenig, an agreement that established a forward zone, where SHAEF's powers were practically complete, and a zone of the interior, which would be administered by the French government. But it was only a military accord, not a formal recognition, and de Gaulle continued to press Eisenhower on the latter point. Eisenhower, in turn, pressed Roosevelt. The general told the President that it was in the Allies' interest to have a strong French government. He also remarked that it would be a long, cold winter and that SHAEF could provide only one-third the amount of coal for civilian consumption that the Germans had allotted; better that a French government than SHAEF be blamed for this. Eisenhower added that there was no opposition leader in sight who had the slightest chance of overthrowing de Gaulle, and if he were by some miracle overthrown, chaos would follow. Eisenhower concluded by pointing out that if France fell into the orbit of "any other country" the remainder of Western Europe would follow. He did not believe that it would be in America's interest to have the Continent dominated by any single power. Such difficulties could be avoided, Eisenhower maintained, by recognizing and working with de Gaulle's government.[39]

On August 30 de Gaulle proclaimed the establishment of the provisional government of the French Republic. Still Roosevelt refused recognition. Meanwhile the armies moved forward, and on October 20 Eisenhower reported that he was turning over control of the zone of the interior to de Gaulle. That announcement undercut Roosevelt, leaving his French policy in shambles. He could no longer ignore the reality of de Gaulle, nor pretend that France was an occupied country to be run by an Allied military government. On October 23 the United States recognized the French provisional government. It had been a long, tortuous struggle for everyone involved, and it left a heritage of bitterness. De Gaulle had triumphed, partly with Churchill's help but mainly on his own, and certainly against the wishes of the Roosevelt Administration. France had been liberated, thanks in large part to the Army and the Navy of the United States, but few Frenchmen, least of all de Gaulle, felt much gratitude.[40]

But if the Franco-American relationship was cold, at least there was a relationship. The two sides talked to each other and could still cooperate on common objectives. French armies fought under Eisenhower's command. That was fitting, for as much as any man on either side, Eisenhower could take the credit for what was positive in the relationship. In part, this was because he was the one in the middle, the man who had to have compromise between those two great egos, Roosevelt's and de Gaulle's; in part, it was due to Eisenhower's diplomatic skills. A man of fierce temper, he had, despite countless provocations, never lost it in de Gaulle's presence. Thanks to Eisenhower, America's French policy in World War II was not a total failure. Through a mixture of patience, common sense, and honesty, Eisenhower had accomplished much. His dealings with the French marked one of his great achievements.

On August 23, the SHAEF G-2 summary declared, "The August battles have done it and the enemy in the West has had it. Two and a half months of bitter fighting have brought the end of the war in Europe within sight, almost within reach." First Army G-2 reflected the same thoughts. The Combined Intelligence Committee, in London, was certain that the German strategic situation had deteriorated to the point "that no recovery is now possible." Patton said that he could cross the German border in ten days,[41] then drive on almost at will to Berlin. And Montgomery told Eisenhower, "I consider we have now reached a stage where one really full-blooded thrust toward Berlin is likely to get there and thus end the German war." Marshall too was euphoric. He sent a message to all his commanders on the subject of redeployment of U.S. Army forces to the Pacific. The Chief of Staff's message began, "While cessation of hostilities in the war against Germany may occur at any time, it is assumed that in fact it will extend over a period commencing . . . between September 1 and November 1, 1944."[42]

It was inevitable that the high command should feel optimistic. The last two weeks of August and first week of September 1944 were among the most dramatic of the war, with great successes following one another in rapid succession. In France, First Army liberated Paris and 21st Army Group swept forward, covering in hours distances that had taken months and cost tens of thousands of lives to cross in World War I. In the last week of August alone, 21st Army Group covered two hundred miles. Rumania surrendered to the Soviets, then declared war on Germany. Finland signed a truce with the Russians. Bulgaria tried to surrender. The Germans pulled out of Greece. The Allies landed in the south of France and drove to Lyons and beyond, and Devers' 6th Army Group joined the AEF. American troops continued to come from England to France, enough for the creation of yet another army, the Ninth, under Lieutenant General William Simpson. It was assigned to 12th Army Group. British and American paratroopers in England were organized into the First Allied Airborne Army and constituted a highly mobile reserve, ready to strike wherever Eisenhower directed. Alexander was attacking in Italy. The Russians' summer offensive carried the Red Army to Yugoslavia, destroying twelve German divisions and inflicting 700,000 casualties. The end of the war did indeed seem at hand.

But not to Eisenhower, who was more realistic than Marshall and the others. One of his major functions was the allocation of supplies to the field armies, which made him acutely aware that every step Montgomery's forces took to the northeast, and that Patton's army took toward the east, carried them farther away from the Normandy ports, adding to an already serious supply problem. On August 20 Eisenhower told reporters that his forces had advanced so rapidly and supply lines were so strained that "further movement in large parts of the front even against very weak opposition is almost impossible."[43]

The supply situation, which soon turned critical, raised the questions of priority and the nature of the advance into Germany. There are two natural invasion routes—north of the Ardennes, through Belgium and Holland into northern Germany, and south of the Ardennes, straight east from Paris past Verdun and Metz to cross the Rhine at Mainz. The pre-Overlord plan called for using both routes, but as Eisenhower told Marshall on August 24, "The decision as to exactly what to do at this moment has taken a lot of anxious thought because . . . [we cannot] do *everything* that we should like to do simultaneously." He decided to give priority to Montgomery's attack on the left because of the importance of the objectives there—the V-weapons' launching sites and the great port of Antwerp. But he also wanted to build Patton's strength "just east of Paris so as to be ready to advance straight eastward to Metz." He would have preferred to move forward on both fronts at once but did not have the supplies. "I cannot tell you how anxious I am to get the forces accumulated for starting the thrust eastward from Paris," he told Marshall. "I have no slightest doubt that we can quickly get to the former French-German boundary [and thus the West Wall] but there is no point in getting there until we are in a position to do something about it."[44] His great hope was that the AEF could outflank the West Wall on the northern end, and get through it east of Metz before the Germans had time to reorganize, sow their minefields, and put adequate manpower into the fortifications, pillboxes, and trenches. *If* the AEF got through or around the West Wall, he too thought there would be a quick end to the war. But already, at the end of August, Montgomery and Patton were demanding more gasoline and other supplies than Eisenhower could provide; already each general was urging Eisenhower to give him all the supplies so that he could drive through to Berlin.

Despite these problems, Eisenhower's hopes were high enough for him to worry about governing Germany after the surrender. He told Marshall, on August 31, that he had a "suspicion that the fanatics . . . may attempt to carry on a long and bitter guerrilla warfare. Such a prospect is a dark one and I think we should do everything possible to prevent its occurrence." He thought Alexander ought to be prepared to rush troops into the Austrian Alps "to defeat any [German] hope . . . for making that country one of guerrilla action." Churchill and Roosevelt were due to meet soon at the Second Quebec Conference, and Eisenhower said he hoped that much good would come out of the conference, "because as signs of victory appear in the air, I note little instances that seem to indicate that the Allies cannot hang together so effectively in prosperity as they can in adversity."[45]

• •

One of the signs of friction among the Allies was a clamoring for the credit for victory. For the first three weeks of August, while Third Army raced through France, Eisenhower withheld Patton's name from the press. Butcher pleaded with Eisenhower to give Patton some publicity, to prove that Eisenhower had been right to retain him in command. But Fortitude still had a spark of life in it, so Eisenhower refused, saying, "Why should I tell the enemy?"[46] When the news finally was released, Patton's name dominated the headlines, to his great delight and Montgomery's discomfort. At the same time, SHAEF announced that 12th Army Group had been activated and that Bradley was now equal to Montgomery. London newspapers thereupon deplored Montgomery's apparent demotion. SHAEF Public Relations made matters worse by announcing that Bradley was not equal to Montgomery, because Montgomery still gave general directives to Bradley. It did not explain that in a week Eisenhower intended to take personal control of the land battle and at that point Bradley would have the same status as Montgomery. Meanwhile, American newspapers demanded an apology from the British for saying that it was a "demotion" for Montgomery to be placed on an equal footing with Bradley, and complained about "British dominance" of the AEF, because the British headed the principal air, sea, and ground commands and Eisenhower was merely a figurehead.[47]

Marshall was upset. On August 17 he told Eisenhower that the Secretary of War, Henry L. Stimson, "and I and apparently all Americans are strongly of the opinion that the time has come for you to assume direct exercise of command of the American Contingent." Eisenhower was at Bradley's headquarters when he received Marshall's message. Both generals were "somewhat taken aback" at the extreme reaction and at the apparent misunderstanding in the War Department of ultimate command arrangements. Eisenhower had no intention of taking command of the "American Contingent," for example. More serious was the bickering over credit. "It seems that so far as the press and the public are concerned," Eisenhower complained, "a resounding victory is not sufficient; the question of 'how' is equally important." But he himself was disturbed by the statements that he was a figurehead, and he responded with a defense of himself and his authority. "In the first place," he explained, "I have always been directly responsible for approving major operational policies and principal features of all plans of every kind." Montgomery coordinated the land battle, true, but he always operated "under plans of campaign approved by me.

There has been no major move made of which I have not been cognizant or which has been contrary to the general purposes I have outlined." He was "exceedingly sorry" if Bradley's reputation had suffered. "As for myself, I am indifferent to what the New York *Times* or any newspaper may say about my conduct of this operation." But he did ask Marshall to have the War Department inform the press that "no major effort takes place in this theater by ground, sea or air except with my approval and that no one in this Allied command presumes to question my supreme authority and responsibility for the whole campaign."[48]

That same day, August 19, Eisenhower told Montgomery and Bradley that it was his intention to take personal control of the land battle as soon as SHAEF could set up in France a forward command post with adequate communication facilities (Granville had almost none, which was why Eisenhower spent so much of his time traveling by road or air to confer with his subordinates). He also outlined a plan of campaign that would send 21st Army Group northeast, toward Antwerp and the Ruhr, with 12th Army Group heading straight east from Paris toward Metz. Now it was Montgomery's turn for anger. On August 22 he sent his chief of staff, Freddie de Guingand, to see Eisenhower and protest against both decisions. Montgomery argued that the quickest way to end the war was to hold Patton in Paris, give control of First Army and all incoming supplies to 21st Army Group, and send it to Antwerp and beyond to the Ruhr. This force had to operate as a single unit under single control, which was "a WHOLE TIME job for one man." Montgomery warned that "to change the system of command now, after having won a great victory, would be to prolong the war."[49] De Guingand pressed these points in a two-hour meeting with Eisenhower, but Eisenhower refused to change his mind. Montgomery then invited Eisenhower to come to his tactical headquarters at Condé for lunch the next day, August 23, to discuss future operations.

Eisenhower drove to Condé for the meeting. Smith was with him, but when they arrived Montgomery abruptly announced that he wanted to see Eisenhower alone and thus Smith would have to stay outside. Eisenhower meekly accepted Montgomery's really quite insulting demand that Smith be locked out, even though de Guingand was with Montgomery. ("It was noticeable," John Eisenhower had observed in June, "whenever Dad met with Montgomery during this period . . . how concerned he was to treat Montgomery with every courtesy, even deference. . . . He was obviously determined that any friction that might occur between the two would never be the result of any personal slight on his own part. Their differences would be based solely on military judgment in a common cause.")[50]

Once inside the trailer, Montgomery tried his best to be tactful, but his idea of tact was to deliver a patronizing lecture on elementary strategy that a Sandhurst or West Point cadet would have found insulting. Standing before his map, his feet spread, hands behind his back, head up, eyes darting about, Montgomery outlined the situation, said the immediate need was for a firm plan, discussed logistics, told Eisenhower what the plan should be (a single thrust to the Ruhr by 21st Army Group, with First Army in support), declared that if Eisenhower's plan were followed the result would be failure, and told Eisenhower that he "should not descend into the land battle and become a ground C-in-C." He said that the Supreme Commander "must sit on a very lofty perch in order to be able to take a detached view of the whole intricate problem" and that someone must run the land battle for him. Eisenhower explained, quietly but firmly, that because of Marshall's insistence and American public opinion, he had to take control of the land battle. Montgomery replied that he felt so strongly about unified command that if American public opinion was the only problem, he would gladly serve under Bradley, an offer that made his point dramatically, but one which he knew perfectly well was politically out of the question. Eisenhower replied that he would not change his mind and intended to take control on September 1.

Unable to move Eisenhower on the question of command, Montgomery shifted to the real issue, the nature of the advance into Germany. He wanted Patton stopped where he was; he wanted the Airborne Army and First Army assigned to him; he wanted all available supplies; he wanted a directive that would send him through the Pas de Calais, on to Antwerp and Brussels, and beyond to the Ruhr. Eisenhower, after an hour's argument, made some concessions, of which the most important were to give Montgomery control of the Airborne Army and the "authority to effect the necessary operational coordination" between the right flank of 21st Army Group and Bradley's left (i.e., First Army). In addition, 21st Army Group would have "priority" in supplies. Still, Eisenhower insisted, to Montgomery's dissatisfaction, "on building up . . . the necessary strength to advance eastward from Paris toward Metz."[51] After the meeting, Montgomery reported to Brooke that "it has been a very exhausting day," but overall he was pleased, as he felt he had won the main points, "operational control" over the Airborne and the First Armies, plus priority in supplies.[52]

Eisenhower's attempt to appease Montgomery made both Bradley and Patton furious. The two American generals met; Patton recorded in his diary that Bradley "feels that Ike won't go against Monty . . . Bradley was madder than I have ever seen him and wondered aloud 'what the Supreme Commander amounted to.'" Patton felt that the southern advance offered much better tank terrain than the waterlogged country to the north, but noted in disgust that Montgomery "has some way of talking Ike into his own way of thinking." He suggested to Bradley that they threaten to resign. "I feel that in such a showdown we would win, as Ike would not dare to relieve us."[53]

Bradley would not go so far, but he did spend two days with Eisenhower, arguing against giving First Army to Montgomery. Tedder agreed with Bradley, as did Eisenhower's operations officer (G-3), Major General Harold Bull, and his G-2, General Strong. Eisenhower yielded to their pressure. When he issued his directive, on August 29, he did not give operational control of First Army to Montgomery; instead, Montgomery was only "authorized to effect"—through Bradley—"any necessary coordination between his own forces" and First Army.[54] That decision, and its sequel, strengthened Montgomery's and Brooke's—and Bradley's and Patton's—conviction that Eisenhower always agreed with the last man he talked to.

It was a most serious charge, but a bit off the mark. Montgomery tended to hear what he wanted to hear, read what he wanted to read; Eisenhower tended to seek out words and phrases that would appease. There was, consequently, a consistent misunderstanding between the two men. Nevertheless, Eisenhower never yielded on the two main points, command and single thrust, not in August and September 1944, nor again when they were raised in January and March 1945. He took—and kept—control of the land battle, just as he said he would. And he never wavered, from the moment he first saw the SHAEF plans for a two-front advance into Germany to the last month of the war, on the question of the so-called "broad front." He did waver, sometimes badly, on some important issues, primarily the relative importance of Arnhem and Antwerp, and the meaning of the word "priority." But he never told Montgomery anything that a reasonable man could have construed as a promise that Patton would be stopped in Paris and 21st Army Group be sent on to Berlin. Nor did he ever encourage Patton to believe that he would be sent to Berlin alone. He always insisted on invading Germany from both north and south of the Ardennes.

His reasons were manifold. His analysis of German morale and geography played a large role. Even after the Allies got through the

West Wall, there was still a major barrier between them and the German heartland, the Rhine River. A single thrust, especially beyond the Rhine, would be subject to counterattacks on the flanks. Eisenhower believed that the counterattacks might be powerful enough to sever the supply lines and then destroy the leading armies. Currently, with the Allies' limited port capacity, the Allies could not bring forward adequate supplies to sustain an army beyond the Rhine. Every mile that the advancing troops moved away from the Normandy ports added to the problems. For example, forward airfields had to be constructed to provide fighter support for the troops. But to construct them it was necessary to move engineers and building materials forward, at the expense of weapons and gasoline. One senior engineer involved pointed out that if Patton had gone across the Rhine in September he would have done so without any logistical or air support at all. "A good task force of Panzerfaust, manned by Hitler Youth, could have finished them off before they reached Kassel."[55]

As for 21st Army Group, de Guingand pointed out that when (and if) it reached the Rhine, bridging material would have to be brought forward, at the expense of other supplies. Like Eisenhower, de Guingand doubted that there would be a collapse of German morale; he expected the enemy to fight to the bitter end. As, of course, the Germans did; it took the combined efforts of 160 Russian divisions *and* the entire AEF *and* Alexander's Italian offensive *and* eight additional months of devastating air attack to force a German capitulation. After the war, de Guingand remarked, a bit dryly, that he had to doubt that Montgomery could have brought about the same result with 21st Army Group alone. "My conclusion, is, therefore," de Guingand wrote, "that Eisenhower was right."[56]

The personality and political factors in Eisenhower's decision are obvious. Patton pulling one way, Montgomery the other; each man insistent; each certain of his own military genius; each accustomed to having his own way. Behind them, there were the adulating publics, who had made Patton and Montgomery into symbols of their nation's military prowess. In Eisenhower's view, to give one or the other the glory would have serious repercussions, not just the howls of agony from the press and public of the nation left behind, but in the very fabric of the Alliance itself. Eisenhower feared it could not survive the resulting uproar. It was too big a chance to take, especially on such a risky operation. Eisenhower never considered taking it.

Montgomery and Patton showed no appreciation of the pressures on Eisenhower when they argued so persistently for their plans, but then Eisenhower's worries were not their responsibility. Montgomery wanted a quick end to the war, he wanted the British to bring it about, and he wanted to lead the charge into Berlin personally. Patton would have given anything to beat him to it. Had Eisenhower been in their positions, he almost surely would have felt as they did, and he wanted his subordinates to be aggressive and to believe in themselves and their troops.

Eisenhower's great weakness in this situation was not that he wavered on the broad-front question, but rather his eagerness to be well liked, coupled with his desire to keep everyone happy. Because of these characteristics, he would not end a meeting until at least verbal agreement had been found. Thus he appeared to be always shifting, "inclining first one way, then the other," according to the views and wishes of the last man with whom he had talked. Eisenhower, as Brooke put it, seemed to be "an arbiter balancing the requirements of competing allies and subordinates rather than a master of the field making a decisive choice."[57] Everyone who talked to him left the meeting feeling that Eisenhower had agreed with him, only to find out later that he had not. Thus Montgomery, Bradley, and Patton filled their diaries and letters and conversations with denunciations of Eisenhower (Bradley less so than the others).

The real price that had to be paid for Eisenhower's desire to be well liked was not, however, animosity toward him from Montgomery and Patton. It was, rather, on the battlefield. In his attempts to appease Montgomery and Patton, Eisenhower gave them great tactical leeway, to the point of allowing them to choose their own objectives. The result was one of the great mistakes of the war, the failure to take and open Antwerp promptly, which represented the only real chance the Allies had to end the war in 1944. The man both immediately and ultimately responsible for that failure was Eisenhower.

CHAPTER EIGHTEEN

London, Normandy, Versailles, Reims

September 2–December 15, 1944

THE GROUND COMMAND issue that Montgomery persisted in raising was essentially phony. It hardly mattered, except for publicity purposes, if Bradley reported to Eisenhower directly or through Montgomery. As Eisenhower emphasized to Montgomery, nothing happened without his approval, whether or not he had direct control of the land battle. What did matter was logistics, the flow of supplies. Eisenhower allocated supplies, and that was his real power. The way in which Eisenhower distributed the available supplies would determine the direction and the nature of the offensive, no matter who had the title of land commander.

So, where Eisenhower could afford to be generous with Montgomery, he was, while retaining the reality of power. Words of praise cost nothing and gained much, and Eisenhower was free with them. On August 31, Eisenhower called a press conference in London. "Now," he told the reporters, "the time has come when we have broken out of that initial beachhead, and General Bradley is taking over his part of the job, reporting directly to SHAEF headquarters, and anyone that interprets this as a demotion for General Montgomery simply won't look facts in the face. He is not only my very close and warm friend, but a man with whom I have worked for two years, and for whom I have a tremendous admiration, one of the great soldiers of this or any other war." He gave Montgomery credit for the victories in France. As to the American criticism that Montgomery had been too cautious before Caen, Eisenhower said he would not hear of it. "Every foot of ground he [the enemy] lost at Caen was like losing ten miles anywhere else. Every piece of dust there was more than a diamond to him."[1]

Churchill, as aware as Eisenhower of the blow to Montgomery's ego from the command changes, also helped soften the blow. On September 1, Churchill announced that Montgomery had been promoted to field marshal (which created a situation in which Montgomery outranked Eisenhower, five stars to four). The field marshal's baton, however, led Montgomery to increase, not slacken, his demand that his plan be implemented. Nor did it impress Patton sufficiently to persuade him to give in to Montgomery.

At the beginning of September, Eisenhower declared that 21st Army Group should have priority in supplies. But he also wanted 12th Army Group to "build up" east of Paris and to "*prepare* to strike rapidly eastwards." Exactly as Montgomery had feared, Bradley allowed Patton to advance to Reims and beyond. On August 30, Patton crossed the Meuse River, which put him more than a hundred miles east of Paris and not much more than that distance from the Rhine. He was, however, out of gas; that day, he received only 32,000 gallons of the 400,000 gallons of gasoline he needed. Still, he wanted to push on. When one of his corps commanders reported that he had stopped because if he went any farther his tanks would be without fuel, Patton told him "to continue until the tanks stop and then get out and walk." Patton realized that when his tanks ran dry Eisenhower would have to give him more gasoline, even at the expense of the 21st Army Group.[2]

On September 2, Eisenhower went to Versailles to see Bradley, Hodges, and Patton to discuss future operations. Before the meeting, Kay noted in the SHAEF office diary that "E. says that he is going to give Patton hell because he is stretching his line too far and therefore making supply difficulties." But Patton seized the offensive; he gleefully told Eisenhower that he had patrols on the Moselle and—stretching the truth—in Metz. "If you let me retain my regular allotment of tonnage, Ike, we could push on to the German frontier and rupture that Goddamn Siegfried Line [the West Wall]. I'm willing to stake my reputation on that."

"Careful, George," Eisenhower responded, thinking of Patton's recent difficulties, "that reputation of yours hasn't been worth very much." Patton, thinking of his recent dash through France, rejoined, "That reputation is pretty good now."[3] Patton then convinced Eisenhower that the opportunities on his front were too good to pass up, and got Eisenhower to agree to allocate additional gasoline to Third Army. Eisenhower also gave Patton permission to attack toward Mannheim and Frankfurt, and agreed to Bradley's demand that First Army stay on Patton's left, south of the Ardennes.

When Montgomery learned that Patton was getting more gasoline and that Hodges had been detached from his right flank, he exploded. There were not enough supplies for two offensives, Montgomery thundered, and Eisenhower had to choose one or the other. The one selected "must have all the maintenance resources it needs without qualifications." Time was vital. "If we attempt a compromise solution and split our maintenance resources so that neither thrust is full-blooded we will prolong the war," he warned. Eisenhower replied that he still gave priority to 21st Army Group and was allocating supplies on that basis.[4]

Two days later, September 7, Montgomery protested that he was *not* getting priority in supplies. He had been forced to cut his intake to 6,000 tons a day, which "is half what I consume and I cannot go on for long like this." He needed an airlift of 1,000 tons a day and was getting only 750. After reciting the facts and figures of more of his shortages, Montgomery added, "It is very difficult to explain things in a message like this." He wondered if it would be possible for Eisenhower to come to see him.[5]

It was typical of Montgomery that he should make such a request. It never seems to have occurred to him that he, not Eisenhower, was the supplicant. Only once during the entire campaign did he visit Eisenhower at SHAEF, even though he was regularly invited to attend conferences. He always insisted that Eisenhower come to him.

Montgomery's request of September 7 was particularly untactful, because Eisenhower had just suffered an accident and movement was painful for him. The accident happened on September 2, when Eisenhower was returning to Granville from his meeting with Bradley and Patton at Versailles. Eisenhower's B-25 broke a muffler and he switched to a small L-5, a one-passenger plane with a limited range, designed for liaison work. A storm came up; the pilot lost his way and could not find the airstrip. The L-5 was about to run out of gasoline, and they made an emergency landing on a beach. Eisenhower hopped out to help the pilot push the plane above the tide line and, in the wet sand, slipped and twisted his knee. The pilot helped him limp across the salt marshes to the road, where a GI passing in a jeep picked them up and drove them to Granville. Wet, exhausted, bedraggled, Eisenhower had two aides carry him up to his bedroom. The knee swelled; the pain was bad; Eisenhower was immobile. A doctor flew over from London and ordered him to stay in bed for a week; a few days later, as the swelling went down, the doctor put Eisenhower's knee in a plaster cast.

From his bed, Eisenhower had a grand view of Mont St. Michel, but it did little to raise his spirits. He had a ringing in his ears, caused—he supposed—by high blood pressure (he would not allow the doctors to check for fear they might send him home); the pain in his knee drained his energy; he was irritated with all his subordinates, American as well as British. Most of all, he hated having to use crutches or a cane just to get around in his bedroom. The pain persisted; two weeks later he told Mamie he was taking daily treatments, one and a half hours of baking and rubbing, but it hardly helped. A bit later, he told Mamie that "my leg is improving, but not as rapidly as if I were 30 instead of almost 54. It is OK except for soreness, and I have to be so d—— careful! Annoying." Until the end of the war, the knee continued to bother him, occasionally forcing him to spend a day or two in bed, often requiring the aid of a cane or crutches (but never in public.)[6]

Montgomery knew about the injury, but still decided it would be better for Eisenhower to come to Brussels than for him to fly to Granville, despite Eisenhower's request that he do so. On the afternoon of September 10, Eisenhower therefore flew to Brussels. Getting aboard the plane was painful, getting off out of the question. So Montgomery came aboard. Pulling Eisenhower's latest directive from his pocket, waving his arms, Montgomery damned the plan in extreme language, accused the Supreme Commander of double-crossing him, implied that Patton, not Eisenhower, was running the war, demanded that control of the land battle be returned to him, and asserted that the double thrust would result in certain failure. As the tirade gathered in fury Eisenhower sat silent. At the first pause for breath, however, he leaned forward, put his hand on Montgomery's knee, and said, "Steady, Monty! You can't speak to me like that. I'm your boss."[7] Montgomery mumbled an apology. He then proposed that 21st Army Group make a single thrust through Arnhem to Berlin. Eisenhower, according to Tedder, who was present, thought "it was fantastic to talk of marching to Berlin with an army which was still drawing the great bulk of its supplies over beaches." Montgomery insisted that it could be done if he got all the supplies, but Eisenhower refused even to consider the possibility. As Eisenhower put it in his office diary later, "Monty's suggestion is simple, give him everything, which is crazy."*[8]

* It was crazy because, in the first place, Paris required 4,000 tons of supply daily, and second, even if Patton were stopped, he needed food, ammunition,

Sitting in Eisenhower's B-25 on the Brussels airfield, the Supreme Commander and the field marshal argued for another hour. Eisenhower finally agreed to a plan, code name Market-Garden, that Montgomery said promised great results. It called for a crossing of the Lower Rhine at Arnhem, in Holland, with the Airborne Army and British Second Army.

Eisenhower agreed to the plan because, like Montgomery, he wanted to get a bridgehead across the Rhine before the momentum of the offensive was lost. He also liked the idea of using the Airborne Army for a major operation. But Market-Garden had some obvious disadvantages. By moving northward from the Belgian-Dutch border, rather than east, Second Army would open a gap between its right flank and First Army's left. Hodges would have to slide his divisions to his left to cover the gap, which meant an even broader front than before, with more stretching by everyone. The direction of the attack would carry 21st Army Group away from the Ruhr and give it another river to cross. Worst of all, it would delay the opening of Antwerp.

Antwerp had always been emphasized in SHAEF's pre-Overlord plan. It was Europe's biggest port, and the one closest to the German heartland. SHAEF had always known that no major operations could be conducted in Germany without Antwerp. Yet Eisenhower allowed Montgomery to ignore Antwerp in favor of a reckless operation, at Arnhem, that promised no great results even if successful.* Similarly,

---

and gasoline for minimum battlefield requirements, and he was not getting enough in any event for more than probing attacks. Patton had a much shorter route to Germany than Montgomery, and the Germans, fearing an invasion in the south more than one in the north, were concentrating their resources against Third Army, which they were preparing to counterattack. Under those circumstances, it was madness to talk about "cutting off" Patton's supplies.

* Market-Garden's defenders argue that a success at Arnhem would have outflanked the West Wall and allowed 21st Army Group to either encircle the Ruhr or go on to Berlin. But the truth is that it was on too narrow a front to do more than create a salient, and at that a salient that would be subjected to heavy counterattacks from both sides, from the bulk of the German Army to the south and the still intact Fifteenth Army to the north. To continue the argument, the ferocity of the attacks on the flanks of the Second Army as it attempted to get to Arnhem speaks for itself. But two additional things need to be noted. First, it was not the unsuspected (and thus "unlucky") presence of two panzer divisions in Arnhem that led to the failure (John Frost of the British "Red Devils" *did* take and hold the bridge there); rather it was the inability of Second Army to get to Arnhem on the ground, and it was unable to get there precisely because of the Fifteenth Army counterattacks on its northern flank. Second, even the small salient that was created was an embarrassment to the Allies, costing more to defend than it was worth.

Eisenhower had said, "There is no point in getting there [to the West Wall] until we are in a position to do something about it." But, because he allowed Patton to advance willy-nilly, and because he failed to insist on Antwerp, that is exactly what happened. It was his worst error of the war.

But Eisenhower felt the potential of Market-Garden was too glittering to pass up. The conference aboard Eisenhower's plane at Brussels ended on a happy note of agreement. Tedder wired his superior in London, "I feel the discussion cleared the air, though Monty will, of course, be dissatisfied in not getting a blank cheque."[9] The more basic problem was that Montgomery, with his eyes on Arnhem, diverted supplies from the Canadians to Second Army. Thus although the Canadians took the city of Antwerp in early September, the Germans still held the Scheldt Estuary, making it impossible for the Allies to use the port, and the Canadians were not strong enough to drive them out. On September 11 Eisenhower wrote in his office diary, "Monty seems unimpressed by necessity for taking Antwerp approaches,"[10] but Eisenhower himself was just as guilty. By agreeing to Market-Garden, the Supreme Commander had in practice agreed to take supplies from Patton (he allotted one thousand additional tons of supply per day to Second Army, and immobilized three 12th Army Group divisions to provide trucks for Montgomery) and to ignore Antwerp in order to achieve a tactical, not a strategic, gain. All the AEF was involved in half measures, or less. It would have been impossible to perceive at this point which the Supreme Commander wanted most, Antwerp, or Arnhem, or a penetration of the West Wall south of the Ardennes.

In his own defense, Eisenhower wrote, long after the war, "I not only approved Market-Garden, I insisted upon it. What we needed was a *bridgehead* over the Rhine. If that could be accomplished, I was quite willing to wait on all other operations. What this action proved was that the idea of 'one full-blooded thrust' to Berlin was silly."[11] But of all the factors that influenced Eisenhower's decisions—to reinforce success, to leap the Rhine, to bring the highly trained but underutilized paratroopers into action—the one that stands out is his desire to appease Montgomery. At no other point in the war did Eisenhower's tendency toward compromise and his desire to keep his subordinates happy exact a higher price.

On September 17, Market-Garden began. The first day went badly for Second Army, but well for the paratroopers. An elated Eisenhower told Marshall that "the Team is working well. Without exception all concerned have now fully accepted my conception of our problem and are carrying it out intelligently and with energy."[12] That was wishful thinking—neither Bradley nor Montgomery approved of Eisenhower's policies; each felt that the other man was getting too much support. By September 21, due to a variety of factors, of which bad weather, German counterattacks, and Montgomery's strange passivity in prodding Second Army were the most important, Market-Garden was on the verge of failure. Montgomery, rather than putting his energy into making Dempsey hurry up, was concentrating on Eisenhower. "I can not agree that our concepts are the same and I am sure you would wish me to be quite frank and open in the matter," he told Eisenhower. He wanted Patton stopped, by binding orders, and urged Eisenhower to "put every single thing into the left hook."[13] But even "every single thing" would not be enough without Antwerp. The entire line was in bad shape, Eisenhower confessed to Marshall, "reminiscent of the early days in Tunisia—but if we can only get to using Antwerp it will have the effect of a blood transfusion."[14]

The previous day, September 20, Eisenhower had moved SHAEF headquarters to Versailles (Eisenhower insisted on avoiding Paris, where there were "too many temptations to go night clubbing"). SHAEF took over the Hotel Trianon at Versailles. Eisenhower's office was too large for his tastes, so he had it partitioned, giving the other half of the room to Kay and the other secretaries. The secretaries lived together in a flat above what had once been the stables of Louis XV, while Eisenhower lived in a handsome mansion that had recently been occupied by Field Marshal Gerd von Rundstedt. Eisenhower had Telek and his by-now numerous offspring with him;[15] he made them live outside, but in the evening he would let them in—a dozen or more—for play. The Scotties usually ended up on Eisenhower's lap. His knee continued to hobble him; the ringing in his ears was still there; he had a cold; a cyst on his back added to his discomfort. But what bothered him most was the German resistance. He told Mamie that people kept asking him what he was going to do when the war was over. "The question makes me angry, because you can be certain this war is not 'won' for the man that is shivering, suffering and dying up on the Siegfried Line. . . . My whole time and thought is tied up in winning the bloody mess." His only thought about his postwar position was "Golly, I'm going to be useless." When he had a rare idle moment, his mind went backward rather than forward. "Yesterday I thought so frequently of Icky," he wrote on September 25. "He would have been 27 years old!"

That thought, plus a letter from Mamie saying that she feared he had changed so much that she would not know him, led to a bit of reflection. "Of course we've changed," he wrote her. "How could two people go through what we have . . . without seeing each other except once in more than two years, and still believe they could be exactly as they were. The rule of nature is constant change. But it seems to me the thing to do is to retain our sense of humor, and try to make an interesting game of getting acquainted again. After all, there is no 'problem' separating us—it is merely distance, and that can some day be eliminated."[16]

To bring that day closer, and to clear the air among his subordinates, Eisenhower called for a conference at Versailles on September 22. It was the largest since D-Day. There were twenty-three generals, admirals, and air marshals there—everyone of importance in the AEF, in fact, except for the man whose name was uppermost in the minds of those present. For Montgomery had decided not to attend, and sent de Guingand to represent him. The field marshal had good reason for not coming. He knew he was not particularly good at persuasion, especially before a hostile audience, and the group at Versailles was almost uniformly hostile toward him. De Guingand, on the other hand, was popular at SHAEF, even with Bradley and Patton.

Eisenhower's purpose in calling the conference was not to seek advice on what to do next, but rather to announce his plans. Before he left his office to go to the conference room, he dictated a letter to Montgomery, handing down that decision. "I insist upon the importance of Antwerp," he said—without noting that this was the first time he was unequivocal on the subject—and said he would give the Canadians whatever was needed to open Antwerp, "including all the air forces and anything else that you can use."[17] He then moved to the conference room, where he began the meeting by asking for "general acceptance of the fact that the possession [of Antwerp is] an indispensable prerequisite for the final drive into Germany." He also asked for an understanding of the clear distinction between logistical requirements for operations to breach or outflank the West Wall and the requirements for a drive to Berlin.

De Guingand then presented Montgomery's views. Although Second Army had not yet made it to Arnhem and a linkup with the paratroopers holding the bridge there, Montgomery still had hopes of achieving that objective, then crossing the Lower Rhine to attack the Ruhr from the north. Eisenhower's determination to insist on Antwerp crumbled in the face of de Guingand's insistence that "the envelopment of the Ruhr from the north . . . is the main effort of the present phase of operations." De Guingand said—and Eisenhower weakly agreed—that opening Antwerp was only "a matter of urgency." Eisenhower then told Bradley to send Hodges farther north, in support of 21st Army Group, while limiting Third Army to local actions. De Guingand, naturally, was much encouraged. He wired Montgomery that his plan had been given "100 percent support." It was a measure of Eisenhower's vagueness, and his penchant for agreeing with whatever one of his generals said, that Patton was just as pleased with the conference. He recorded in his diary that "things look better today. Ike still insists, for the present at least, the main effort must be thrown to the British . . . However, he was more peevish with Montgomery than I have ever seen him. In fact [at a private lunch], he called him a 'clever son of a bitch,' which was very encouraging."[18]

Patton came away from the meeting convinced that it was up to him to make the greatest possible use of any loopholes in SHAEF directives to spur on his own battle. In order to avoid having to stop his offensive, he declared, "It was evident that the Third Army should get deeply involved at once . . ." He explained later, "In order to attack, we had first to pretend to reconnoiter, then reinforce the reconnaissance, and finally put on an attack."[19] Eisenhower expected Patton to do exactly that, which infuriated Montgomery. The Supreme Commander seemed to be constantly agreeing to 21st Army Group plans, then reneging by allowing Patton to go his own way. But Montgomery was just as bad; he continued to attack in Holland, even after it was clear that Second Army would not reach Arnhem in time, to the neglect of Antwerp. Through the last week of September and the first week of October, Patton attacked at Metz, Montgomery in Holland, neither with sufficient strength to break through, while the Canadians struggled, unsuccessfully, because they were inadequately supplied, to gain the approaches to Antwerp.

Everything had turned out badly. The great offensive of August in France had not led to victory in Europe. Market-Garden had failed and Antwerp was not opened in time to do any good in 1944. The ultimate blame for this situation rested with the man who had the ultimate responsibility, the Supreme Commander himself.

On October 9, Eisenhower finally began to give Montgomery a shaking. The immediate provocation was a report from Admiral Ramsay's office that the Canadians would be unable to accomplish anything until November 1 because of ammunition shortages. A furious Eisenhower wired Montgomery, "Unless we have Antwerp producing by the middle of November our entire operations will come to a standstill. I must emphasize that, of all our operations on our entire front from Switzerland to the Channel, I consider Antwerp of first importance, and I believe that the operations designed to clear up the entrance require your personal attention." He took all the sting out of the message, however, by adding, "You know best where the emphasis lies within your Army Group."[20]

Montgomery fired back a cable the same day. "Request you will ask Ramsay from me by what authority he makes wild statements to you concerning my operations about which he can know nothing rpt nothing." The Canadians, Montgomery said, were already attacking. He reminded Eisenhower that there "is *no* rpt *no* shortage of ammunition." He reminded Eisenhower that at the Versailles conference the Supreme Commander had made the attack in Holland the "main effort"; as for Antwerp, he claimed that "the operations [there] are receiving my personal attention."[21] Eisenhower replied that "the possession of the approaches to Antwerp remains . . . an objective of vital importance," and added, "Let me assure you that nothing I may ever say or write with respect to future plans . . . is meant to indicate any lessening of the need for Antwerp."[22]

Shortly thereafter Smith called Montgomery on the telephone and demanded to know when SHAEF could expect some action around Antwerp. Heated words followed. Finally Smith, "purple with rage," turned to his deputy, General Morgan, and thrust the telephone into his hand. "Here," Smith said, "you tell your countryman what to do." Morgan, expecting that Montgomery would be head of the British Army after the war, thought to himself, "Well, that's the end of my career." He then told Montgomery that unless Antwerp was opened soon his supplies would be cut off.*[23]

Montgomery, incensed by this threat, put down the phone and wrote to Smith. He blamed the failure of Market-Garden on a lack of coordination between his forces and Bradley's, and once again demanded that he be given sole control of the land battle. This was too much (even Montgomery's great friend Brooke felt he had gone too far). Eisenhower's patience with the field marshal was almost limitless, but not quite. "The Antwerp operation does not involve the question of command in any slightest degree," Eisenhower told Montgomery. In any event, as far as command went, he would not, ever, turn 12th Army Group over to Montgomery. Then Eisenhower used his ultimate threat; he said that if Montgomery, after reading the SHAEF plan of campaign,

* Morgan was right about his career. Neither he, nor any other British officer who served at SHAEF, nor for that matter de Guingand, prospered in the postwar Montgomery-run British Army. As Eisenhower once told Peter Lyon, speaking of Montgomery, "He's just a little man, he's just as little inside as he is outside."[24]

still characterized that plan as "unsatisfactory, then indeed we have an issue that must be settled soon in the interests of future efficiency." Eisenhower said he was well aware of his own powers and limitations, "and if you, as the senior Commander in this Theater of one of the great Allies, feel that my conceptions and directives are such as to endanger the success of operations, it is our duty to refer the matter to higher authority for any action they may choose to take, however drastic."[25]

Montgomery knew full well that if Eisenhower told the CCS it was "him or me," Eisenhower would win. "I have given you my views and you have given your answer," Montgomery hastened to reply. "I and all of us will weigh in one hundred percent to do what you want and we will pull it through without a doubt." He said he had given Antwerp top priority and would terminate the discussion on command arrangements. "You will hear no more on the subject of command from me," he promised, and signed off, "Your very devoted and loyal subordinate, Monty."[26]

Montgomery could be as abject as Patton when it had to be done, but like Patton, he still insisted on going his own way. Despite this exchange, he continued to emphasize Second Army's attack, at the expense of the Canadians. According to the most careful student of the campaign, Charles B. MacDonald, it was October 16 before Montgomery gave up on operations in Holland and "blessed it [Antwerp] with unequivocal priority."[27] Then, the taking of the approaches to Antwerp proved to be a difficult and time-consuming tactical problem; the Allies did not drive the Germans out of the Scheldt Estuary until November 8; after that, the mines had to be cleared; not until November 28 did the first Allied convoy reach Antwerp's docks.[28]

By then, bad weather had long since set in, and any chance of ending the war in 1944 was gone. As Brooke declared, "I feel that Monty's strategy for once is at fault. Instead of carrying out the advance on Arnhem he ought to have made certain of Antwerp in the first place. Ike nobly took all the blame on himself as he had approved Monty's suggestion to operate on Arnhem."[29]

The Germans had pulled off "the miracle of the West." They had established a firm defensive line from the North Sea to the Swiss border, a defensive line that was based on the West Wall, which was proving to be much more formidable than Allied intelligence had anticipated. The Germans had rebuilt their once-shattered divisions, brought new ones into the fight, and were superior in numbers (although not in tanks or artillery) to the AEF. Worst of all, they were fighting in defense of their homeland just as hard as Eisenhower had feared they would. The rosy Allied expectations of August and September were gone.

Who had failed? Montgomery blamed Eisenhower. In his view, Eisenhower's vacillation had caused the breakdown of the grand offensive. Eisenhower always said he was giving priority to the north, but in practice, Montgomery charged, he let Patton get away with far too much. Eisenhower was a coordinator, not a commander, Montgomery said, and his policy of "Have a go, Joe," instead of bringing victory all across the line, had brought stalemate everywhere. Bradley and Patton, on the other hand, thought that Eisenhower had been much too lenient with Montgomery. They accused Montgomery of refusing to obey direct orders and Eisenhower of refusing to make his orders strong enough. They felt, justifiably, that Eisenhower was lax in issuing final orders and stopping further debate on Antwerp and Arnhem.

Fall was never Eisenhower's best season. In 1942 he had been stuck in the mud of Tunisia, in 1943 bogged down on the Italian peninsula, and in 1944 the rains came again to turn the fields of northwest Europe into quagmires. As Eisenhower told Marshall, "I am getting exceedingly tired of weather."[30] His airplanes could not fly, his tanks were unable to maneuver, and his soldiers marched only with difficulty. He was still short on supplies and was beginning to have replacement problems. Under these circumstances, the fall battles resulted in little beyond heavy casualties on both sides. On October 1 First Army launched an offensive designed to take Cologne, but it ran into German units brought down from the Arnhem front. Not until October 21 did the Germans pull out of Aachen (the first major German city to fall to the Allies), and even then Hodges was still far from Cologne. To the south, Third Army attacked, but without success, the ancient fortress system around Metz. Even farther south, 6th Army Group made some gains, but was unable to drive the Germans out of Colmar.

The temptation at the end of October was to abandon the offensive, create an easily defended line, wait for the supply situation to improve, and prepare to attack when good weather came in the spring. But Eisenhower gave little consideration to such an alternative. There was still a feeling in SHAEF that somewhere the Germans had to crack. The emphasis in Eisenhower's plan was, therefore, not so much on a probe here or a skirmish there as it was on a general attack, designed to make sure the Germans suffered heavy casualties, which in turn would mean a further stretching of their line. "During this period," he wrote after the war, "we took as a general guide the principle that operations . . . were profitable to us only where the daily calculations showed that enemy losses were double our own." It had become a war of attrition. Like Grant in 1864–1865, Eisenhower could afford to adopt it because his overall resources were superior to those available to the Germans. Like Grant, Eisenhower justified what many critics considered a sterile, cold-blooded strategy on the grounds that in the long run "this policy would result in shortening the war and therefore in the saving of thousands of Allied lives."[31] Attrition is always a cautious and unimaginative strategy, but it appeared to Eisenhower that the only way to defeat the Wehrmacht was to destroy it. As he told Roosevelt's press secretary, Steve Early, "People of the strength and war-like tendencies of the Germans do not give in; they must be beaten to the ground."[32]

The campaign that resulted was the least glamorous, and the toughest, of the war. Hodges fought against bitter opposition, especially in the Huertgen Forest, where roads were nothing more than forest trails. Rain and snow added to the difficulties of mines, artillery, and the German infantry. By a supreme effort at the end of October, First Army reached the Roer River, but it was still far from crossing the Rhine. Patton, meanwhile, did little better. Eisenhower eloquently described his difficulties: "Every day we have some report of weather that has broken records existing anywhere from twenty-five to fifty years. The latest case is that of the floods in Patton's area. His attack [launched on November 8] got off exactly as planned. . . . Then the floods came down the river and not only washed out two fixed bridges, but destroyed his principal floating bridge and made others almost unusable." Still, Eisenhower was optimistic. He hoped that "some little spell will come along in which we can have a bit of relief from mud, rain, and fog" so that the tanks, infantry, and air could do their job.[33] But the weather did not improve, and although Patton was able to take Metz on November 23 and, on his right, reach the Saar River, his offensive soon ground to a halt.

Throughout the fall, Eisenhower traveled incessantly. "Weather is so miserable that all my travel is by auto," he told Mamie, "which takes lots of time." He usually traveled with only his driver, Sergeant Dry, and Jimmy Gault (who read the maps), while he sat alone in the back seat. "I have hours to think," he wrote Mamie, "and since the staff is not there to plague me, I think of you a lot. Some of the roads

I travel are the ones we rode over 15 years ago, and I always wish you were along to see them, with me, again."[34]

Eisenhower tried to visit every division in the AEF, talk with as many men as possible, and spend at least some time with their officers. The trips involved a good deal more than simply showing himself to the frontline troops. He was upset to discover that his policies on recreation, rest, and comfort for the men were not being applied. "This applies to such matters as billets for resting of troops," he told his American subordinates, "to conditions of sanitation and convenience while travelling by motor, train or ship, and, *above all, it applies to equality of treatment as between officers and enlisted men."* He pointed out that GIs had complained to him that officers had whiskey rations while enlisted men did not, that unit commanders disapproved leave for enlisted men but granted it freely to officers, that when units were out of the line the men had to stay in their billets while the officers had the use of a jeep, that on the trip over to the Continent the GIs were jammed into the holds while the officers had ample deck space, and that the PX supplies were frequently reserved for officers. He personally saw troops making bivouacs along the roads when "with a bit of care and foresight," shelter could have been found for the night. He had also seen truckloads of men driving in the rain without top covers on the trucks.

Eisenhower wanted all these conditions changed. He laid it down as a rule that "care must be taken that privileges given to officers . . . must be available in proper proportion to enlisted men." Officers should not have the use of a jeep when their units were out of the line unless the enlisted men did too; leave and furlough policies had to be applied with absolute fairness. All captured wine should be issued "on a basis where the enlisted man receives exactly as much as any officers" (he had the forlorn hope that hard liquor could be reserved for medical use). Just in case anyone missed the overriding point, Eisenhower concluded, "Officers must invariably place the care and welfare of their men above their own comfort and convenience."[35]

The response to these orders was, as might be expected, neither instantaneous nor uniform, but there was improvement. In early December, Eisenhower reported with some pride that "the morale and condition of our troops stay remarkably high. It is noticeable that each division, after it has been out of the line three or four days . . . is fit and ready to go back again into the line."[36]

Nevertheless, it was a discouraging period all around. "Well sweet, I'd like to think that this mess would be over soon, so I could come home," Eisenhower wrote his wife on November 22. "But the fighting and the dying go on—and the end is not yet. 'Civilization' is not pretty when it resorts to war. Anyway, some day victory will be ours, and I'll come a running!" "It's all so terrible, so awful," he said in another letter, "that I constantly wonder how 'civilization' can stand war at all." The strain of the long separation on his marriage was getting worse, Mamie's complaints about her loneliness and his indifference harder to bear. "It's true we've now been apart for 2½ years," he wrote in November, and he recognized how "painful" this was for her. "Because you don't have a specific war job that absorbs your time and thoughts I understand also that this distress is harder for you to bear. But you should not forget that I do miss you and do love you, and that the load of responsibility I carry would be intolerable unless I could have the belief that there is someone who wants me to come home—for good." In a heartfelt plea for understanding, he added, "Don't forget that I take a beating, every day." In mid-December, he told her he prayed that this would be their last Christmas apart, and promised her endless hours of talking when the war was over. "We'll have to take a three month vacation on some lonely beach—and oh lordy, lordy, let it be *sunny*!!"[37]

There would be precious little sunshine for Eisenhower in that fall of 1944. Adding to his woes, Montgomery and Brooke were on the rampage again, almost frantic about the way Eisenhower was conducting the war. "Ike has never commanded anything before in his whole career," Montgomery complained to Brooke on November 17. "Now, for the first time, he has elected to take direct command of very large-scale operations and he does not know how to do it." On November 24 Brooke wrote in his diary that he was upset about "the very unsatisfactory state of affairs, with no one running the land battle. Eisenhower, though supposed to be doing so, *is on the golf links at Rheims*—entirely detached and taking practically no part in the running of the war."* Three days later Brooke added, "Ike is incapable of running a land battle, and it is all dependent on how well Monty can handle him." Eisenhower, Brooke believed, "has no strategic vision."[39]

On November 28, at Montgomery's request, Eisenhower went to

* Where Brooke got this idea is a puzzle. Eisenhower had just written Mamie, "The war seems to have lasted forever. I can't remember the time when I had an occasional chance to take out a golf club . . . I regret the times I missed when I might have gone."[38] He had established an advance headquarters in Reims, in a red-brick schoolhouse, with the tents and trailers set up on the grounds of the Athletic Club of Reims. He was near a golf course, but what with the weather, his trips, and his schedule, he never played it.

21st Army Group headquarters to discuss future operations. The atmosphere was unpleasant, because Montgomery could barely conceal his contempt for Eisenhower. The field marshal did most of the talking. Eisenhower, patient as always, let him speak on without interruption, which unfortunately created the impression that Eisenhower agreed with what Montgomery was advocating, which was not at all the case. Montgomery later reported to Brooke that Eisenhower had agreed that the SHAEF plan had failed and that "we had, in fact, suffered a strategic reverse." Montgomery also thought he had convinced Eisenhower of the need to assign the First Army to 21st Army Group. Two days later, Montgomery wrote Eisenhower, "to confirm the main points that were agreed on during the conversations . . ." He opened by saying, "We have failed: and we have suffered a strategic reverse. We require a new plan. And this time *we must not fail*." He said he and Bradley made a "good team," and that things had not gone well "since you separated us. I believe to be certain of success you want to bring us together again; and one of us should have the full operational control . . . and if you decide that I should do that work—that is O.K. by me."[40]

Eisenhower, after taking a few hours to let his temper cool down, told Montgomery in reply that he did *not* at all concur. The only thing Montgomery's letter contained was "your conception and opinions as presented to me the other evening." Eisenhower said he did not know what Montgomery meant by strategic reverse. "We gained a great victory in Normandy," he pointed out, and "Bradley's brilliant break through made possible the great exploitation by all forces, which blasted France and Belgium and almost carried us across the Rhine." Had the AEF not gone forward on a broad front "we would now have the spectacle of a long narrow line of communication, constantly threatened on the right flank and weakened by detachments of large fighting formations." Eisenhower said he would not give Montgomery control of the First Army, and that he had "no intention" of stopping Devers' and Patton's operations. Eisenhower concluded, "I most definitely appreciate the frankness of your statements, and usual friendly way in which they are stated [*sic*], but I beg of you not to continue to look upon the past performances of this great fighting force as a failure merely because we have not achieved all that we could have hoped. I am quite sure that you, Bradley, and I can remain masters of the situation and the victory we want will certainly be achieved."[41]

A week later, Montgomery asked for another meeting. Eisenhower drove to Maastricht, where Bradley, Tedder, and Smith also gathered for the conference. Eisenhower reviewed operations since September, outlined his plans for further offensives all along the front, then asked Montgomery for his views. Montgomery said there were two requirements for the immediate future. First, the Allies had to cut off the Ruhr; second, they had to force the Germans into mobile warfare. The only place where that could be done was north of the Ruhr. It was therefore necessary, Montgomery said, to put everything into a concentrated attack across the Rhine north of the Ruhr, with First Army participating, under his command. He covered, in short, the same old ground, with the same result—Eisenhower said no. Tedder, Bradley, and Smith said little, but it was clear where their support lay. After the meeting Montgomery blamed them for his inability to persuade Eisenhower. "It is . . . clear that any points I made which caused Eisenhower to wobble will have been put right by Bradley and Tedder on the three-hour drive back to headquarters," he complained. He told Brooke that Eisenhower "has obviously been 'got at'" by the two officers and added, "I personally regard the whole thing as quite dreadful."[42]

Montgomery decided that he had done all that he could do, so now it was up to Brooke. Brooke invited Eisenhower to London, and on December 12 Eisenhower and Tedder had dinner with Churchill and Brooke. At Brooke's urging, Eisenhower presented his plan. "I disagreed flatly with it," Brooke recorded in his diary later, "accused Ike of violating principles of concentration of force, which had resulted in his present failures." Brooke became highly critical, and extremely loud, until Churchill interrupted to say that he agreed with Eisenhower. Brooke sadly realized that he had failed "in getting either Winston or Ike to see that their strategy is fundamentally wrong."[43]

Almost as vexing to Eisenhower as his problems with the British field marshals were his problems with Second Lieutenant John Eisenhower, or, more precisely, with John's mother. John had been assigned to the 71st Division, which was scheduled to leave Fort Benning for France in the near future. Mamie found out about this development before Eisenhower did and complained, "You didn't tell me what you had cooked up." Eisenhower protested, "I've cooked up nothing, and I don't know where he is or what he is going to do. I did make sure that *if he wanted* to go to a division coming to this theater, the W.D. would not object merely because I was in command here." Five days later he learned of John's assignment to the 71st, and commented, "I will have a hard time keeping from 'interfering.' I'm so wrapped up in that boy—but I keep reminding myself that he is a man, with a man's job to do and his own career to make. How I wish I dared go and stay with him."[44]

To John, Eisenhower offered an old infantryman's advice on how to train his platoon. "Go around and see every man, see that he gets into warm, dry clothing . . . that he gets a good hot meal and that his weapons are in tiptop shape. Shoes, socks and feet are of tremendous importance, and you should try to wear exactly the same kind of materials as your men do when in field training or in combat. By pursuing these methods you will not only have a splendidly trained platoon, but one that will follow you anywhere."

When the moment for John's departure came, Mamie felt hurt, angry, deserted. Despite her husband's disclaimers, she was sure he had arranged the assignment. "I fully understand your distress . . ." Eisenhower reassured her, "but it always depresses me when you talk about 'dirty tricks' I've played and what a beating you've taken, apparently because of me. You've always put your own interpretation on every act, look or word of mine, and when you've made yourself unhappy, that has, in turn, made me the same. . . .

"So far as John is concerned," he continued, "we can do nothing but pray. If I interfered even slightly or indirectly he would be so resentful for the remainder of his life that neither I (nor you, if he thought you had anything to do with it) could be comfortable with him. . . . But, God, how I do hope and pray that all will be well with him." Eisenhower assured Mamie, "I'm not 'fussing' at you. But please try to see me in something besides a despicable light and at least let me be *certain* of my welcome home when this mess is finished.

"I truly love you and I do know that when you blow off steam you don't really think of me as such a black hearted creature as your language implies. I'd rather you didn't mention any of this again."[45]

Another item Eisenhower did not want to think about was politics. In October, with a presidential election coming in November, a reporter asked Mamie what party General Eisenhower belonged to. She replied that she could not say. Eisenhower read the statement in the newspaper, laughed, and wrote Mamie, "Neither could I!!!" He said that politics was far from his mind, and added, "All soldiers have one Commander-in-Chief; the President. Duty and loyalty and unity—all absolutely essential now to our future as a nation, demand that soldiers tend to their own jobs—exclusively!"[46]

Through the fall, the great offensive continued. The only place the Allies were not on the attack was in the Ardennes itself, which was thinly held by Troy Middleton's corps. On his way to Maastricht on December 7 Eisenhower had noted how spread out the troops in the

Ardennes were, and he questioned Bradley about the vulnerability of this sector of the front. Bradley said he could not strengthen the Ardennes area without weakening Patton's and Hodges' offensives, and that if the Germans counterattacked in the Ardennes they could be hit on either flank and stopped long before they reached the Meuse River. Although he did not expect a German counterattack, he said he had taken the precaution of not placing any major supply installations in the Ardennes. Eisenhower was satisfied by Bradley's explanation.[47]

On December 15 Montgomery wrote Eisenhower to say he would "like to hop over to England" for Christmas in order to spend the holiday with his son. Eisenhower said he had no objection and added, "I envy you."[48] Eisenhower, too, began to anticipate the holiday, and the really crushing blow his armies would deliver in the new year.

CHAPTER NINETEEN

Versailles, Verdun, Reims

December 16, 1944–March 6, 1945

DECEMBER 16 WAS A DAY of celebration at SHAEF Main in Versailles, featuring a wedding, a promotion, and a medal. In the morning, Mickey McKeogh married one of the WAC sergeants. Eisenhower hosted a champagne reception in his house in Saint-Germain. He had something else to celebrate; the Senate had just announced his promotion to the newly created rank of General of the Army, which made him equal in rank to Marshall, MacArthur—and Montgomery. Adding to Eisenhower's pleasure, he was able to tell Second Lieutenant Kay Summersby (in October he had arranged for her commission as a WAC) that he had been talking to Churchill about her—the Prime Minister was very fond of Kay—and that Churchill had said he was going to award her the British Empire Medal.[1]

Late in the afternoon, Bradley arrived, to complain about the replacement situation. The United States now had all but one of its divisions committed, the flow of replacements was not keeping pace with the casualty rate, and because of the general offensive that Eisenhower insisted on conducting, SHAEF had few men in reserve. While they talked in Eisenhower's office, Strong interrupted to inform them that a German attack had been launched that morning in the Ardennes. Bradley's initial reaction was to dismiss it as a mere spoiling attack, designed to draw Patton's forces out of the Saar offensive. But Eisenhower immediately sensed something bigger. "That's no spoiling attack," he said, explaining that since the Ardennes itself offered no worthwhile objective, the Germans must be after some strategic gain. "I think you had better send Middleton some help," he told Bradley. Studying the operations map with Strong, Eisenhower noticed that the 7th Armored Division was out of the line, in First Army sector, and that the 10th Armored Division, a part of Third Army, was currently uncommitted. He told Bradley to send the two divisions to Middleton, in the Ardennes. Bradley hesitated; he knew that both Hodges and Patton would be upset at losing the divisions, Patton especially, as the 10th Armored was one of his favorites. With a touch of impatience, Eisenhower overruled Bradley, and orders went out that night, sending the 10th to the southern flank of the penetration, while the 7th occupied a road junction named St. Vith, on the northern flank.

Having made these arrangements, Eisenhower and Bradley, joined by Everett Hughes, settled down to enjoy what was left of the champagne, open a bottle of Highland Piper Scotch that Hughes had brought, and play five rubbers of bridge. They would make another assessment of the situation in the morning, when Strong would have more information for them.[2]

The news Strong brought, based on identification of German divisions in the Ardennes and on captured documents, was about as bad as it could have been. Eisenhower's rapid and intuitive judgment had been right—the Germans were engaged in a counteroffensive, not just a counterattack. Two German panzer armies of twenty-four divisions had struck Middleton's corps of three divisions. The Germans had managed to achieve both complete surprise and overwhelming local superiority, an eight-to-one advantage in infantrymen and a four-to-one advantage in tanks.[3] This was due to a variety of complex factors, of which the most important were Allied complacency—everyone at SHAEF was thinking offensively, about what they could do to the enemy, and never about what the enemy might do to them—and German professionalism. Using the same type of deception tricks the Allies had utilized in Fortitude, plus some of their own, the Germans had completely fooled an intelligence service that liked to think of itself as the best in the world. No one saw the buildup in the Eifel; no one expected anything more than local German counterattacks; no one anticipated that the Germans would be capable of attacking in even greater strength than they had done against the French in May 1940, and over the same ground at that.

Eisenhower accepted the blame for the surprise, and he was right to do so, as he had failed to read correctly the mind of the enemy.

Eisenhower failed to see that Hitler would take desperate chances, and Eisenhower was the man responsible for the weakness of Middleton's line in the Ardennes, because he was the one who had insisted on maintaining a general offensive.

But despite his mistakes, Eisenhower was the first to grasp the full import of the offensive, the first to be able to readjust his thinking, the first to realize that, although the surprise and the initial Allied losses were painful, in fact Hitler had given the Allies a great opportunity. On the morning of December 17, Eisenhower showed that he saw the opportunity immediately, when he wrote the War Department that "if things go well we should not only stop the thrust but should be able to profit from it."[4]

After dictating that letter, Eisenhower held a conference with Smith, Strong, and Whiteley. SHAEF now had only two divisions in reserve, the 82d and 101st Airborne, which were refitting from the battles around Arnhem. The SHAEF generals anticipated that the Germans would attempt to cross the Meuse River, thus splitting 21st and 12th Army Groups, and take the huge Allied supply dumps at Liége. The dumps were crucial to the Germans, as they contained the fuel Hitler counted on to sustain a drive to Antwerp. Whiteley put his finger on the small Belgian town of Bastogne and declared that the crossroads there was the key to the battle. Bastogne was surrounded by rolling countryside, unusually gentle in the rough Ardennes country, and had an excellent road net. Without it the Germans would not be able to cross the Ardennes to the Meuse. Eisenhower agreed with Whiteley's analysis. He decided to concentrate his reserves at Bastogne. He ordered a combat command of the 10th Armored to proceed immediately to the town, and told the 101st to get there as soon as possible. He also sent the 82d to the northern edge of the penetration, where it could lead a counterattack against the German right flank. Finally, the Supreme Commander ordered the cessation of all offensives by the AEF "and the gathering up of every possible reserve to strike the penetration in both flanks."[5]

By December 18, these movements were under way. By that date too Strong had better information on the German formations and plans. Rundstedt had hoped to be across the Meuse by then, but his forces were nowhere close to achieving that objective. Middleton's corps, although badly battered and overrun, had not been destroyed. Small units continued to fight, often without any direction from above or any idea at all about what was happening around them. Individual acts of heroism abounded; as a result the German timetable was badly off schedule. One reason Eisenhower had agreed to hold the line so thinly in the Ardennes was that the limited road network there made it difficult country for tanks. In 1940, the Germans had blown right through the French, but in 1944, American resistance was slowing the Germans and thereby causing terrific traffic jams. Still, the Fifth Panzer Army was making progress at the point of the penetration, although it was delayed on its left by the Allied forces in Bastogne and on its right by the 7th Armored at St. Vith. But if they could not hold, there was nothing between Fifth Panzer Army and the Meuse. Eisenhower reviewed the situation, then called Bradley, Patton, and Devers to a conference the next morning, December 19, at Verdun.

The generals met in a cold, damp squad room in a Verdun barracks, on the site of the greatest battle ever fought. There was only one lone potbellied stove to ease the bitter cold. Eisenhower's subordinates entered the room glum, depressed, embarrassed. Noting this, he opened by saying, "The present situation is to be regarded as one of opportunity for us and not of disaster. There will be only cheerful faces at this conference table." Patton quickly picked up on the theme. "Hell, let's have the guts to let the —— —— —— go all the way to Paris," he said. "Then we'll really cut 'em off and chew 'em up."[6]

Eisenhower said he was not *that* optimistic; the line of the Meuse had to be held. But he was not thinking defensively. He informed his commanders that he was not going to let the Germans get away with emerging from the West Wall without punishing them. He asked Patton how long it would take him to change the direction of his offensive, from east to north, to counterattack the Germans' left, or southern, flank. Patton replied, "Two days." The others chuckled at this typical Patton bravado; Eisenhower advised him to take an extra day and make the attack stronger. He told Patton to cancel his offensive in the Saar, change directions, and organize a major counterblow toward Bastogne by December 23. He told Devers to prepare to retreat, in order to shorten his line and thus release units for Patton's attack, and said he was going to have Montgomery organize an attack in the north, against the German right flank.[7] In short, by December 19, on the fourth day of the Bulge, well before the issue was settled at Bastogne or on the Meuse, Eisenhower had already put in motion a counterattack designed to destroy the German panzer armies in the Ardennes.

While Eisenhower was driving from Verdun back to Versailles, the SHAEF staff was preparing a recommendation for him. Strong had told Whiteley that the Germans would soon have a wedge driven between Bradley's forces, making it difficult for Bradley to communicate with First Army. Strong thought that under the circumstances, Eisenhower should give Montgomery command of all forces north of the Ardennes. This would mean that Bradley would keep Third Army, while Montgomery got First and Ninth Armies (Bradley had put Ninth Army into the line on First Army's left, so that the next time Eisenhower gave one of the American armies to the British, it would be the inexperienced Ninth, not the veteran First). Such a command arrangement was what Montgomery had all along been proposing and Eisenhower refusing, and a transfer of command at this point would look as if the Americans had to turn to the British to rescue them from the crisis. But Strong and Whiteley agreed that the communications problem was so serious that the step had to be taken. They took the proposal to Smith. He exploded, shouted at them to get the hell out, got control of himself, thought it over, and decided to call Bradley on the telephone. Bradley insisted that it was not necessary, but Smith—by now convinced of the need for it*—told Bradley, "It seems the logical thing to do. Monty can take care of everything north of the Bulge and you'll have everything south." Bradley did not disagree, but did protest that such a shift would discredit the American command. "Bedell," he added, "it's hard for me to object. Certainly if Monty's were an American command, I would agree with you entirely."[8]

No decision was made that night. The next morning, December 20, Eisenhower held his regular 8 A.M. meeting with his staff in the Trianon Palace. Smith brought up Whiteley's proposal. It was obvious that giving Montgomery command of two American armies at the height of the battle would be a blow to American pride, but Eisenhower decided that national pride would have to suffer and declared that he would make the command shift.

He called Bradley on the telephone to inform him. By now, Bradley was set against any such change. Strong could hear him shouting at Eisenhower: "By God, Ike, I cannot be responsible to the American people if you do this. I resign." Eisenhower, flushed with shock and anger, drew a deep breath, then said, "Brad, I—not you—am responsible to the American people. Your resignation therefore means absolutely nothing." There was a pause, then another protest from Bradley, but this time without any threats. Eisenhower declared, "Well, Brad, those are my orders." He then turned the conversation to Patton's counterattack, which he declared he wanted mounted in the greatest possible strength.[9]

* Smith later apologized to Whiteley and Strong. "What made me really mad," he said, "was that I knew you were right."

After hanging up, Eisenhower placed a call to Montgomery to inform him of the command switch. The telephone connection was unfortunately indistinct. Eisenhower could not tell if Montgomery could hear him or not; giving up, he sent the orders by wireless. Montgomery, however, anxious to step forward and take control, heard what he wanted to hear and attached his own meaning to the garbled conversation. He told Brooke that Eisenhower had called. "He was very excited," Montgomery said, "and it was difficult to understand what he was talking about; he roared into the telephone, speaking very fast." The only thing Montgomery understood was that Eisenhower was giving him command of First and Ninth Armies. "This was all I wanted to know. He then went on talking wildly about other things."[10]

Within two hours of his conversation with Eisenhower, Montgomery had visited with Hodges and General William Simpson, commander of the Ninth Army. A British officer who accompanied him said he strode into Hodges' headquarters "like Christ come to cleanse the temple." Montgomery reported to Brooke that Simpson and Hodges "seemed delighted to have someone to give them firm orders."[11]

While Montgomery made matters worse, Eisenhower tried to make them better. To cheer Bradley, and to ward off criticism that interpreted the command shift as a judgment on Bradley's abilities, Eisenhower cabled Marshall, asking the Chief of Staff to promote Bradley to four-star rank. "While there was undoubtedly a failure, in the current operations to evaluate correctly the power that the enemy could thrust through the Ardennes," he said, Bradley was by no means solely responsible; Eisenhower admitted that "all of us, without exception, were astonished at the ability of the [Germans] to act offensively." Bradley had "kept his head magnificently" and proceeded "methodically and energetically."[12] The Senate, however, had adjourned, so no immediate action on Bradley's promotion was possible.

Bradley's problem was ego; Simpson and Hodges had the problem of working under Montgomery. To encourage them, Eisenhower sent each man a cable, congratulating them for what they had done so far and asking them to remain calm, determined, and optimistic. Getting to the point, he added, "Now that you have been placed under the field marshal's operational command I know that you will respond cheerfully and efficiently to every instruction he gives."[13] Eisenhower then informed the CCS of his command changes and added that he had ordered Montgomery and Bradley "to hold their flanks securely but with minimum forces, to gather all available reserves and to thrust with great force against the flanks of the penetration."[14]

• •

What Eisenhower needed most desperately to insure the success of his plans was men, especially rifle-carrying infantrymen. To obtain them, he made an offer to the thousands of GIs inside the Army's prison stockades in England and Europe—any man who would pick up a rifle and go into the battle could have a pardon and a clean slate. Results were disappointing; only those who had a fifteen-year or longer sentence at hard labor volunteered.[15] Another untapped potential source of infantry was the Negro servicemen, nearly all of them in the Services of Supply, driving trucks or unloading ships. In contrast with the criminals, they were eager to fight, if given the chance, especially if they could join a veteran outfit. Eisenhower therefore issued a circular offering the Negroes an opportunity to serve in infantry units and promising that they would be assigned "without regard to color or race." When Smith saw the circular, he blew up. In a stern note to Eisenhower he pointed out that integration ran directly counter to War Department policy, and added, "Two years ago I would have considered the . . . statement the most dangerous thing that I had ever seen in regard to Negro relations." Eisenhower, no more ready than Smith to promote a social revolution, gave in. Saying he did not want to "run counter to regulations in a time like this," he rewrote the circular. The upshot was that the Negroes who did volunteer—and noncoms had to give up their stripes to do so—were segregated into all-Negro platoons, with white noncoms and officers. Nevertheless, thousands did volunteer; they fought well. So well, in fact, that many senior officers began to question the wisdom of regulations that kept more than 10 percent of the Army's enlisted men out of the front lines.[16]

In his efforts to find infantry replacements, Eisenhower ordered the entire Services of Supply combed out for men who could fight. He also ordered service units organized for the defense of the Meuse bridges, stressing "the vital importance of insuring that no repeat no Meuse bridges fall into enemy hands intact."[17] To Bradley, the order seemed to indicate that Eisenhower was getting "an acute case of the shakes," while Bradley's chief of staff, after reading the message, asked, "What the devil do they think we're doing, starting back for the beaches?"[18]

Adding to the impression of panic at SHAEF were the elaborate security precautions instituted at Versailles. SHAEF intelligence had learned that the Germans had organized a special group of English-speaking German soldiers, dressed them in American uniforms, given them captured American jeeps to drive, and spread them behind the

American lines. Their mission was to issue false orders, spread defeatism, and capture bridges and road junctions. Rumor quickly spread, however, that their main intention was to assassinate the Supreme Commander. Thus everyone at SHAEF became super security conscious. Eisenhower was sealed into the Trianon Palace. Guards with machine guns were placed all around the palace, and when Eisenhower went to Verdun or elsewhere for a meeting, he was led and followed by armed guards in jeeps. Butcher noted that "he is a prisoner of our security police and is thoroughly but helplessly irritated by the restriction on his moves." After two days of being so confined, he came out of his office and grumbled, "Hell's fire, I'm going out for a walk. If anyone wants to shoot me, he can go right ahead. I've got to get out!" Slipping out a back door, he walked around the yard in the deep snow.[19]

He resented the constant presence of guards, but accepted it as necessary, even when the security remained in place into the new year. On January 7 he complained to Mamie that he never got any exercise, never was alone, because "there are always guards, snoopers, etc. There is even a guard in my upstairs hall. (For Lord's sake—don't tell anyone that! They'd think I was scared.)" In the middle of February, he wrote, "I'd like to get out for a short walk today, and really hope to make it before dark. The only trouble is that the area in which they will let me walk . . . is very constricted, so there's nothing but a small circle to tramp around. Rather boring."[20]

Security was tightened throughout the theater, not just at SHAEF. Understandably nervous at the idea of thousands of German soldiers running around in American uniforms, MPs stopped every passing jeep and, ignoring rank and credentials, quizzed the occupants on American slang or customs. This added to the general nervousness. Perhaps most serious of all, SHAEF Public Relations ordered a news blackout, without Eisenhower's knowledge, which gave the impression in the United States that the Allies were taking a terrific beating.[21] Viewed from the outside, the combination of actions—Eisenhower's offer to the criminals, his proposal to integrate Negro troops, his "back to the wall" order to hold the Meuse bridges, the ultimately absurd security measures, the news blackout, turning First and Third Armies over to Montgomery, and most of all the German gains on the map—indicated that SHAEF had fallen into a panic and felt beleaguered and hopeless.

In fact, Eisenhower and SHAEF were quietly confident, and eagerly anticipating the AEF counterattack. On December 22, while waiting for the skies to clear, so that the air forces could get into action, and for

Patton to shift directions, so that he could attack toward Bastogne, Eisenhower issued an Order of the Day. "We cannot be content with his mere repulse," he said of the enemy. "By rushing out from his fixed defenses the enemy may give us the chance to turn his great gamble into his worst defeat. . . . Let everyone hold before him a single thought—to destroy the enemy on the ground, in the air, everywhere—destroy him!"[22] Inside the Bulge, at Bastogne, the encircled 101st Airborne was doing just that. At noon on December 22, the Germans paused in their attacks to demand a surrender; Brigadier General Anthony McAuliffe made his famous "Nuts" reply. The Germans attacked again; again the 101st beat them back with heavy losses. The next day, St. Vith fell to the Germans, but the 7th Armored had stalled an entire corps that had been flushed with earlier easy victories, choked one of the main German lines of communications, forced days of delay on the westward movement of troops and supplies, and given the Allies time to organize both their defenses at the tip of the Bulge and their counterblow. As Tedder commented, "The fact that the Hun has stuck his neck out is, from the point of view of shortening the whole business, the best thing that could happen. It may make months of difference."[23]

The best news came on December 23, when day broke clear and cold, with virtually unlimited visibility. From the first, Hitler had counted on a sustained period of bad weather to neutralize the Allied air forces. With the sunrise on the twenty-third, every Allied plane that could fly got into the air. Lumbering C-47s dropped tons of supplies to the 101st inside Bastogne; fighter planes strafed the Germans in the Bastogne ring; P-47s hit them with fragmentation bombs, napalm, and machine-gun fire. Patton began his thrust, which by the day after Christmas carried him into Bastogne and lifted the siege. To the north, meanwhile, Montgomery was tidying up the battlefront. He told Eisenhower he had reorganized First Army and it was "in good trim. We will fight a good fight up here." Actually First Army had not been reorganized so much as it had re-established communications with its units, many of which had been cut off. Through great effort, Hodges had been able to direct a coherent defense that, at least as much as the more publicized struggle at Bastogne, had been responsible for stopping the Germans.

For Eisenhower, victory in the defensive phase of the battle brought with it more problems from his two chief subordinates. Montgomery made no effort to conceal his pleasure and delight at the Americans' discomfort, nor any attempt to soothe Bradley's injured pride. At a

Christmas Day meeting, he told Bradley that the Americans deserved the German counteroffensive, saying that if there had been a single thrust none of this would have happened. "Now we are in a proper muddle." Montgomery reported that Bradley "looked thin, and worn and ill at ease" and claimed that the American general agreed with everything he said. Montgomery noted of Bradley: "Poor chap; he is such a decent fellow and the whole thing is a bitter pill for him."[24] Then the field marshal expressed his view that Patton's attack would not be strong enough to "do what is needed [and] I will have to deal unaided with both Fifth and Sixth Panzer Armies." He therefore demanded that Eisenhower give him more American troops, which he wanted taken from 6th Army Group and rushed north to him. Bradley, meanwhile, came away from his meeting with Montgomery in a furious state of mind. He demanded that Eisenhower return First and Ninth Armies to his command.[25]

Eisenhower resisted the pushing and pulling on him from both sides and rejected both Montgomery's and Bradley's demands. He did agree that troops should be taken from the southern end of his line, but not that they should then be assigned to 21st Army Group. Instead he started to build a strategic reserve. Nor would he restore First and Ninth Armies to Bradley, not yet anyway, because he felt it was still logical for Montgomery to control the forces on the northern flank of the Bulge.

On December 26, Eisenhower met with his staff in the Trianon. Standing before a huge operations map, he told his G-3, General Harold "Pinky" Bull, "'Pink,' you'd better go and see Devers today. I think the best line is this." Eisenhower outlined a withdrawal in the Strasbourg area. "I'll tell you, boys," he continued, "what should be done. See Devers and give him this line. It will be a disappointment giving up ground, but this area is not where I told Devers to put his weight."[26]

Eisenhower's confidence in himself had grown tremendously during the crisis. His initial intuitive judgment had been proved right; his decision to rush the 7th and 10th Armored, and the 82d and the 101st Airborne, into the battle had been proved right; he still felt that his handing over the northern flank to Montgomery was right; his decision to have Patton attack toward Bastogne was right. Now he was laying down the line, telling the boys how it should be done. Whatever Brooke and Montgomery might say about his lack of experience, he had taken control of this battle and made it his. But Eisenhower still had the supreme test to face. Giving firm orders to Bradley, Patton, and Devers was one thing, giving them to Field Marshal Montgomery quite another.

Eisenhower was beginning to worry that, as at Kasserine, the Allies would be too late in their counterattack. Montgomery, it appeared, was going to insist that every condition was optimum before he moved forward. Two days after Christmas, at the regular SHAEF 8 A.M. meeting, the discussion centered upon the need to begin soon. Tedder emphasized that the good weather would not last much longer and that it was important to hit the Germans while the airplanes could still fly. At this point word arrived that Montgomery had a new plan for attack, one that involved two corps. "Praise God from whom all blessings flow," Eisenhower remarked.[27]

The tension that had characterized the Eisenhower-Montgomery relationship since mid-June 1944 now reached its height. As before Caen, it centered around differing perceptions of the Germans' intentions and the timing and strength of the Allied attack. Eisenhower believed the German divisions in the Bulge were understrength and badly battered, with their supply lines in poor shape. He wanted to hit them, hard and quickly. Montgomery hesitated. He told Eisenhower, at a December 28 meeting at his headquarters, that the Germans would make one last big attack on the northern shoulder of the Bulge. He thought the best thing to do would be to receive that attack, then launch his counterattack with First Army after the Germans had been stopped. To add to Eisenhower's dismay, Montgomery wanted to strike against the tip of the Bulge, driving the Germans back to the West Wall, rather than attacking on the flank in an attempt to cut them off. Eisenhower told him that if he waited, Rundstedt would either withdraw from the Bulge or put infantry divisions into the line, pulling out his tanks and putting them in reserve. The latter, Eisenhower said, "we must not allow to happen," and he again urged Montgomery to attack quickly. Montgomery repeated that first he had to receive and stop the expected German attack. Eisenhower grumbled that there would be no attack, and finally got Montgomery to agree that if one did not come that day or the next, First Army would counterattack against the German flank on January 1. Or at least Eisenhower thought Montgomery agreed.[28]

When Eisenhower got back to Versailles he felt he had things well in hand. Tedder was going to Moscow to confer with Red Army leaders in an attempt to coordinate future operations and to find out when the Russian winter offensive would begin. Eisenhower told Tedder to inform Stalin that his intentions were to eliminate the Bulge, pin down the panzers committed to the battle and destroy them, and then start a drive toward the Rhine. "The basic thing," Eisenhower said, "is to defeat the German armies west of the Rhine."[29]

On December 30, however, de Guingand came to SHAEF with the bad news that Montgomery would not attack until January 3 or later. The blow to their hopes was more than any of the SHAEF officers could take. "What makes me so Goddam mad," Smith exploded, "is that Monty won't talk in the presence of anyone else." Speaking for Montgomery, de Guingand claimed that Eisenhower had misunderstood—there had been no agreement on a January 1 attack. "Damn it, there was!" Eisenhower responded. He felt that he had been lied to, that Montgomery was trying to lead him by the nose, that a great opportunity was about to be lost, and that therefore the time had come to make a break with Montgomery. Eisenhower dictated a blistering letter to Montgomery, demanding that Montgomery live up to his promises. If he did not, Eisenhower continued, he would be sacked. De Guingand, shown a copy of the letter, begged Eisenhower to hold it. He said he would talk to Montgomery and straighten things out. Eisenhower liked de Guingand, as did everyone at SHAEF; his affable personality, common sense, and reasonableness stood in sharp contrast to his boss and made him the perfect broker between Montgomery and SHAEF. Eisenhower agreed to hold the letter until de Guingand could consult with Montgomery.[30]

On New Year's Eve, after some difficulties caused by weather, de Guingand managed to fly from Versailles to Brussels. He conferred with Montgomery, then flew back to Versailles, where he reported that Montgomery held firm to his view that the proper strategy was to let the Germans exhaust themselves with one last attack before taking up the offensive. Eisenhower, livid, said that Montgomery had definitely promised him an attack on January 1. De Guingand repeated that Eisenhower must have misunderstood. Eisenhower sent some staff officers to the files to see if they could find a message from Montgomery confirming the January 1 date. De Guingand warned him that the search would be fruitless. "Knowing Monty," he said, "the last thing he would do is to commit himself on paper."[31] Bradley, meanwhile, was already attacking, believing that Montgomery would begin his offensive on January 1. But Montgomery did not, and the Germans switched panzer divisions from the north to the south to stop Bradley.

Eisenhower thought Montgomery's sense of timing in military operations was seriously deficient. That point may be open to question, but there can be none about Montgomery's total lack of a sense of timing in personal relations, or his complete inability to see things from someone else's point of view. At the height of the debate over what Montgomery had or had not promised, Montgomery sent a letter to Eisenhower, damning the Supreme Commander's policies and demanding that he, Montgomery, be given full control of the land battle. And, of course, there must be a single thrust, in the north, with Patton held where he was. Montgomery even wrote out a directive to those ends for Eisenhower's signature.[32]

Instead of doing as told, Eisenhower issued his own directive, which ran counter to Montgomery's draft on every point. He returned First Army to Bradley's control and insisted on a double thrust into Germany. "The one thing that must now be prevented," he emphasized, "is the stabilization of the enemy salient with infantry, permitting him opportunity to use his Panzers at will on any part of the front. We must regain the initiative, and speed and energy are essential."[33]

In a covering note to Montgomery accompanying the directive, Eisenhower was simple, direct, and forceful. "I do not agree," Eisenhower said, referring to Montgomery's contention that there should be a single ground commander. He said he had done all he could for Montgomery and did not want to hear again about placing Bradley under Montgomery's command. "I assure you that in this matter I can go no further." He added, "I have planned an advance" to the Rhine on a broad front, and ordered Montgomery to read his directive carefully. All the vagueness of earlier letters and directives to Montgomery was now gone.

In conclusion, Eisenhower told Montgomery that he would no longer tolerate any debate on these subjects. "I would deplore the development of such an unbridgeable gulf of convictions between us that we would have to present our differences to the CCS," he said, but if Montgomery went any further that was exactly what he would do. "The confusion and debate that would follow would certainly damage the good will and devotion to a common cause that have made this Allied Force unique in history," Eisenhower admitted, but he could do nothing else if Montgomery persisted.[34]

De Guingand, meanwhile, was working on Montgomery. He told his boss that the depth of feeling against him at SHAEF was very great. Smith "was more worried than I had ever seen him." The general sentiment was that Montgomery had to go. Montgomery scoffed at this. "Who would replace me?" he demanded. "That's already been worked out," de Guingand replied. "They want Alex." Montgomery paled. He had forgotten about Alexander. He began pacing his trailer, finally turned to de Guingand to ask, "What shall I do, Freddie? What shall I do?" De Guingand pulled out the draft of a message he had already prepared for Montgomery's signature. "Sign this," he said. Montgomery read it, and did.[35] The cable said that Montgomery knew there were many factors Eisenhower had to consider "beyond anything I realize." It asked Eisenhower to tear up the letter demanding sole command of the ground forces.[36]

Montgomery followed up the cable with a handwritten letter. "Dear Ike," he began, "You can rely on me and all under my command to go all out one hundred percent to implement your plan."[37] On January 3 he began his attack. It was not all that Eisenhower wanted, but much better than Montgomery had originally proposed. For the next month the Allies battered away at the Bulge. The Germans, schooled in winter warfare from the Russian front, waged a fighting retreat, and not until February 7 had the original line been restored. Eisenhower had hoped for better results, but these were satisfactory, for most of the German armor was destroyed in the process. The enemy had practically no mobility left, and once Eisenhower's forces broke through the West Wall they would be able to dash through Germany almost at will. In that dash, in fact as well as in name, their commanding general would be Eisenhower.

"You will understand," Eisenhower wrote Mamie at this time, explaining why he had not written more letters, "that we're preoccupied right now."[38] It was a grand understatement. Simultaneously with his showdown with Montgomery, he had to deal with another of his allies, a man equally difficult to work with, Charles de Gaulle. The French leader was unhappy with Eisenhower's plan to pull back around Strasbourg. "The French government," de Gaulle said, "obviously cannot let Strasbourg fall into enemy hands again without first doing everything possible to prevent it." He declared he was ready to "push all French forces that were being mustered in this direction." Eisenhower responded that he too was concerned about the fate of French citizens in Alsace if the Germans returned to the area, but added that he was grateful to de Gaulle "for indicating that you share my views from the military point of view."[39] De Gaulle shot back, "Nothing of what you have been told from me and nothing I have written can make you think that from the military point of view I approve of your views. I should tell you frankly that the truth is just the opposite."

A confrontation was obviously necessary. It came after lunch on January 3. Churchill was present, having flown over to Versailles to confer with Eisenhower on the Montgomery problem. De Gaulle stormed into Eisenhower's office, where he informed the Supreme Commander that it would be fatal to withdraw from Strasbourg, especially without a fight. French public opinion would not stand for it. Eisenhower began to show de Gaulle on the map why it was necessary. De Gaulle cut in, "If we were at Kriegspiel I should say you were right, but I must consider the matter from another point of view. Retreat in Alsace would be a national disaster." The two men then threatened each other. De Gaulle said he would have to remove the French army from Eisenhower's command. Eisenhower countered that if he did so, SHAEF would stop the flow of supplies to the French. De Gaulle threatened right back. If Eisenhower did that, he said, the AEF's lines of communications, all of which ran through France, would be in jeopardy. Eisenhower then yielded. In de Gaulle's presence, he telephoned Devers to cancel the order to withdraw from Strasbourg. When de Gaulle left, pleased with himself, Churchill told Eisenhower, "I think you've done the wise and proper thing."[40] Eisenhower hated having to give in, hated—as always—having to base his strategy on "political" rather than straightforward "military" considerations. "The French continue to be difficult," he complained to Marshall. "I must say that next to the weather I think they have caused me more trouble in this war than any other single factor." Thinking all the way back to Torch and putting the French in perspective, he added, "They even rank above landing craft."[41] But Strasbourg was held; indeed, later in January the French went on the offensive in Alsace, and by February 9 the 6th Army Group as a whole had closed to the upper Rhine.

After his meeting with de Gaulle, Eisenhower found time to scribble a short note to Mamie. He apologized for not writing more often, explaining that "we have been under some stress, and you'll understand that it has been hard to sit down and to compose thoughts applicable to a letter to one's best and only girl." His heart was heavy, he said, because "yesterday my . . . great friend, Admiral Ramsay, was killed in an accident." Ramsay's small plane had gone into a stall on the takeoff. "War is truly a brutal business!" Eisenhower commented. John was about to leave Fort Benning for Europe; Eisenhower realized that his presence in the war zone would add immeasurably to Mamie's anxiety, and he knew that "it's hard to just sit and pray." The only advice he could offer was to "be of good courage—we must hang on to the faith and hope—and we must believe in the ultimate purposes of a merciful God." On the battlefront, he assured her, "We are hammering away. Regardless of setbacks, disappointments, and everything else, we are on the road to victory! What a boon peace will be to this poor old world!"[42]

Four days later, on January 7, he received a letter from Mamie full of complaints about his failure to write. "It always distresses me when I get a message from you indicating anxiety or impatience because I have failed to write," he hastened to reply. "Please, please understand that I do go through periods when I simply cannot sit down and write a note. To hold a pen is sometimes sheer mental, almost physical, agony." He explained that he had become so accustomed to dictating his thoughts "that when I pick up a pen I get completely uncoordinated." The next time he went to war, he added, "I'm going to take you along!" which would solve the problem of letter writing. "These are trying days," he concluded, ". . . and I really have a few things on my mind."[43]

As was so often the case, what was uppermost on his mind was Montgomery. On the day Eisenhower wrote Mamie, January 7, Montgomery held a press conference to explain how he had won the Battle of the Bulge. It was a quite incredible manifestation of Montgomery's insensitivity. He told the press that on the very first day, "as soon as I saw what was happening I took certain steps myself to ensure that if the Germans got to the Meuse they would certainly not get over the river. And I carried out certain movements so as to provide balanced dispositions to meet the threatened danger; . . . i.e., I was thinking ahead." Soon Eisenhower put him in command of the northern flank, and he then brought the British into the fight, and thus saved the Americans. "You have thus the picture of British troops fighting on both sides of American forces who have suffered a hard blow. This is a fine Allied picture." It had been an "interesting" battle, he said, rather like El Alamein; indeed, "I think possibly one of the most interesting and tricky battles I have ever handled." What came next nearly destroyed Allied unity. Montgomery said the GIs made great fighting men, when given proper leadership.[44]

Bradley, Patton, and nearly every American officer in Europe were furious. As they saw the battle, they had stopped the Germans before Montgomery came onto the scene. Almost no British forces were even engaged in the Bulge. Far from directing the victory, Montgomery had gotten in everyone's way and botched the counterattack. But what was especially galling about Montgomery's version of the Battle of the Bulge was his immense satisfaction with the outcome. Patton ranted and raved to every reporter who would listen, telling them publicly what he had already written privately in his diary—that had it not been for Montgomery, "we [could have bagged] the whole German army. I wish Ike were more of a gambler, but he is certainly a lion compared to Montgomery, and Bradley is better than Ike as far as nerve is concerned. . . . Monty is a tired little fart. War requires the taking of risks and he won't take them."[45] Bradley also talked to reporters. He could not bring himself to comment on Montgomery's assertion about what good soldiers the GIs made when given proper leadership, but he did say that the Germans had been stopped before Montgomery took control of the northern flank. The result was a debate in the British and American press over who had really won the battle.

From Eisenhower's perspective, 12th Army Group was getting as difficult to deal with as 21st Army Group. On January 24, Whiteley called Bradley on the telephone; Bradley was at Patton's headquarters at the time. Whiteley said that Eisenhower wanted Bradley to loan several divisions to Devers for an attack against the Germans in Alsace. Patton wanted the divisions for his own offensive against the Germans in the Eifel. "We would be giving up a sure thing for a side show," Bradley roared at Whiteley, his hand gripping the telephone so tightly that his knuckles were turning white. "Go ahead and take all the corps and divisions!" he shouted. "There is more at stake than the mere moving of divisions and corps. . . . If you feel that way about it, then as far as I am concerned, you can take any goddam division and/or corps in the 12th Army Group, do with them as you see fit, and those of us that you leave back will sit on our ass until hell freezes." His final words were "I trust you do not think I am angry. But I want to impress upon you that I am *goddam well incensed*." Patton, in the background, said in a voice loud enough to be heard over the telephone, "Tell them to go to hell and all . . . of us will resign. I will lead the procession." As Bradley slammed down the receiver, every officer on Patton's staff rose to his feet and applauded.[46] Under this barrage, Eisenhower relented, and 6th Army Group had to make do with the troops it had.

In the middle of January, Eisenhower reminded Mamie that more than three years had passed since he left San Antonio for Washington. In some ways, he said, it felt like only yesterday, "but on the other hand I cannot remember the time when I was free of these continuing problems involving staggering expense, destruction of lives and wealth, and fates of whole peoples." The Russians had just begun their winter offensive; Eisenhower commented, "How I hope this new Russian offensive keeps right on going into the heart of Germany. In any event its initial successes must be a shock to the d—— Germans."[47]

That same day, Eisenhower responded to an inquiry from Marshall, who wanted Eisenhower's broad estimate on the resources the AEF would require and the steps that needed to be taken "to bring this war in Europe to a quick conclusion." Eisenhower said the key to the situation was what happened on the Eastern Front. If the Red Army offensive was weak and ineffective, the Germans could safely maintain a numerical superiority on the AEF front; if the Russian offensive "really gets to rolling," the Germans would have to withdraw troops from the West, to the great benefit of the AEF. "I do not even mention a lack of Russian offensive," Eisenhower added, "for without this a quick decision cannot be obtained."[48]

One reason for Eisenhower's pessimism was the fighting quality of the German troops, supported by a steady flow of new and excellent equipment to the front. He told Marshall that "there is a noticeable and fanatical zeal on the part of nearly all his fighting men as well as the whole nation of 85,000,000 people, successfully united by terror from within and fear of consequences from without. The Germans are convinced they are fighting for their very existence and their battle action reflects this spirit." In late 1944, the Germans were attaining record monthly levels of production of tanks and airplanes; only Spaatz' oil campaign stood between them and control of the air. And, contrary to the popular impression, the enemy was stronger on the Western Front than on the Eastern. In the last two months of 1944 the Germans sent 2,299 new or refitted tanks to the Western Front, only 921 to the East; the Luftwaffe deployed 2,998 fighters in the West, only 567 in the East. As Russell Weigley points out, in January 1945, "on the 1,000-kilometer section of the Eastern Front from the Baltic to the Carpathians . . . the Germans had only some seventy-five divisions, a smaller number than on the similar length of the Western Front, and with no fixed defenses equivalent to the West Wall."[49] As against this strength, Eisenhower had seventy-one divisions, but many of the U.S. divisions were badly undermanned in infantry, no replacements were in sight, and the French divisions in the AEF were poorly equipped and consequently had a low combat value. Small wonder that Eisenhower could write to Mamie, "The Russians are still making good progress after their early spectacular successes. Lord knows they can't go too fast and too well for me. More power to them."[50] The Russian offensive, which began on January 12, was truly massive—the Red Army achieved a six-to-one manpower superiority—and did force Hitler to begin withdrawing troops from all his secondary theaters, and even some from the West Wall.

• •

Nevertheless, Eisenhower was seriously deficient in that most basic of fighting resources, combat infantrymen. It was on that basis that he had to plan for the final offensive, and it was that factor, above all others, that shaped his strategy. With the crisis of the Bulge behind them, the Allies resumed the debate that had taken up so much of their time since August. The British wanted Third Army and 6th Army Group stopped where they were, First and Ninth Armies assigned to 21st Army Group, and a single crossing of the Rhine, north of the Ruhr, led by Montgomery. The American generals insisted on bringing their armies up to and then across the Rhine.

Eisenhower opted for the double thrust, with crossings of both the upper and the lower Rhine. It was consistent with what he had all along planned to do, and in any event he felt that it was forced upon him by the relative equality in infantry between the AEF and the Germans in the West. He felt it was imperative to close to the Rhine everywhere before crossing it anywhere. *"Unless we get a good natural line for the defensive portions of our long front,"* Eisenhower emphasized by underscoring, *"we will use up a lot of divisions in defense."* Once all the American and French divisions reached the Rhine, he would need to keep only twenty-five divisions on defense. Brooke and Montgomery were most unhappy at the thought of fighting *any* battles west of the Rhine—just give 21st Army Group all that you have, they told Eisenhower, and let it drive to Berlin—but Eisenhower replied that as Hitler would surely attempt to hold German territory west of the Rhine, the Allies could seize the opportunity to kill or capture large numbers of German infantry, destroy the remaining German armored units, and thus make the crossings of the Rhine easier. "We must substantially defeat the German forces west of the Rhine if we are to make a truly successful invasion with all forces available," Eisenhower explained to Marshall.

Once his forces had closed to the Rhine, Eisenhower could pull twenty divisions out of the line. This reserve force would then be capable of exploiting any opportunity that came along, thereby giving the AEF great flexibility. Eisenhower stressed this point again and again. "If we jam our head up against a concentrated defense at a selected spot," he declared, "we must be able to go forward elsewhere. Flexibility requires reserves." By this stage of the war, flexibility was Eisenhower's outstanding tactical quality. He never made plans that were set and rigid; he strove to create tactical situations that gave him alternatives. Flexibility was what set him apart from most planners, including his own SHAEF staff. One never knew what to expect in war, except that the unexpected was likely. Only those who were ready could take advantage of the breaks, and to be ready it was imperative to have reserves.

So, in mid-January 1945, Eisenhower envisioned a campaign in which all his armies would fight their way forward to the Rhine, in the process inflicting great damage on the Wehrmacht. Montgomery would make the major crossing north of the Ruhr, with Hodges and Patton making secondary crossings to the south. Eisenhower could then use his reserve to support whatever opportunities presented themselves. Eisenhower expected that with Montgomery coming down from the north, and Bradley coming up from the south, the two army groups could encircle the Ruhr, Germany's industrial heart. In preparing this plan, Eisenhower went back to his childhood reading and his first hero, Hannibal—he and Smith discussed in some detail Hannibal's encirclement of the Romans at Cannae.[51]

Once the Ruhr was encircled, Eisenhower intended to fan out and overrun Germany. Again Montgomery and Brooke disagreed with his plan; they thought 21st Army Group ought to get all the supplies for a thrust to Berlin. But Eisenhower already had in mind using Bradley for the main campaign east of the Rhine. This was based in part on his faith in Bradley, and in part on his lack of confidence in Montgomery. As Whiteley put it after the war, "the feeling [at SHAEF] was that if anything was to be done quickly, don't give it to Monty. . . . Monty was the last person Ike would have chosen for a drive on Berlin—Monty would have needed at least six months to prepare."[52] Or, to use the football jargon Eisenhower was so fond of using, when the Allies got down near the goal line, the back Eisenhower relied upon was Bradley and he wanted Bradley to carry the ball.

That was the plan. Marshall agreed with it, but Brooke and Eisenhower's field subordinates had objections. Patton wanted a larger role; Bradley thought there was too much emphasis on Montgomery's crossing; Montgomery thought there was not enough. But Eisenhower held firm and saw to it that it was his plan that was implemented. Smith, in an April press conference, when the operation had been successfully completed, said, "Of all the campaigns I have known this one has followed most exactly the pattern of the commander who planned it. With but one small exception, it proceeded exactly as General Eisenhower originally worked it out."[53] John Eisenhower, who visited his father around this time, noted, "Probably at no time in his life did I ever see the Old Man enjoying such peace of mind . . . He was . . . exercising the professional skills and knowledge that he had been developing for thirty years. And he was doing so at the highest levels." It was this period Eisenhower had in mind some years later, when he told a reporter that war brought on an "exhilaration that you can feel everywhere you go." It came from the "matching of wits . . . in the intellectual and spiritual contest." But he was no war lover; he immediately went on to quote Robert E. Lee that it was well that war was so horrible, or else "we would grow too fond of it."[54]

John's assignment to the European Theater was, naturally, a major concern for Eisenhower. It was unthinkable that John should be sent into the front lines, because of the possibility that he might become a POW (not to speak of Mamie's reaction). Bradley solved the problem by detaching John from the 71st Division and assigning him to a special communications unit. On January 30, a week before John arrived, Eisenhower confessed to Mamie, "I'm so anxious to see him that I feel like a June bride ten days before her wedding." In another letter, he reassured her about John's job and commented, "It will be one to broaden and instruct him, and at the same time will be one where I can see him reasonably often." When John got to Europe, Bradley gave him four days off to spend with his father at Versailles. "John and I sat up until very late last evening," Eisenhower reported to Mamie. They discussed John's girl friends, his new job, his training, and his career prospects. Eisenhower gave his son a fur-lined coat, a new combat jacket, and gloves, but when John left to take up his duties, he forgot them. "He has a habit of vagueness," Eisenhower told Mamie, "out of which I hope he will grow. . . . He's lots of fun and we have a thoroughly good time when he is here. But I can't quite figure him out when he gets just sort of roaming about in his mind."[55]

During John's visit, Eisenhower's knee was bothering him again, and he was submitting to daily rubdowns. He had a cold he could not shake; the cyst on his back was getting worse. He kept this information from Mamie, telling her only that he had had a medical checkup and "except for a stinging lecture [the doctor] gave me on the number of cigarettes I smoke, he seemed pleased with my condition. BP was 138/82. Then, of course, I'm eight pounds overweight." But John noted his physical discomfort immediately, and Kay commented that "Ike complained that there was not one part of his body that did not pain him." When he was in public, "he pulled himself together by sheer willpower and looked healthy and vigorous and exuded his usual charm. But the moment he got back to the office . . . he slumped."[56]

But whatever physical toll the war had taken on him, Eisenhower's spirits were buoyant. On February 20 he told Marshall, "If the weather improves with the advancing spring, I feel that matters will work out almost exactly as projected." He admitted that the weather made him "terribly impatient . . . but I never . . . lose my basic optimism."[57] As the AEF took up the attack all along the line, Eisenhower spent much of his time at SHAEF Forward at Reims, where he could keep a closer watch on the battle. He spent the first week in March visiting his commanders in the field. He did not interfere with their conduct of operations but he was anxious to see how things were proceeding and wanted to be where the action was. He usually contented himself with giving Simpson or Hodges or Patton a pat on the back and telling them to keep up the good work.

Simpson got across the Roer on February 23; by March 2 he had reached the Rhine, in the process achieving one of Eisenhower's basic purposes in the Rhineland campaign—Ninth Army killed six thousand Germans and took thirty thousand prisoners. Farther north, the British Second and Canadian First Armies closed to the Rhine and Montgomery began his preparations for crossing the river. To the south, Hodges reached the Rhine on March 5 at Cologne; Patton got to the river three days later.

Just as Eisenhower had expected, the Germans insisted on fighting west of the Rhine. At the conclusion of the campaign, Eisenhower held a press conference. A reporter asked him if he thought it was Hitler or the German General Staff that made the decision. Eisenhower replied, "I think it was Hitler. I am guessing because I must confess that many times in this war I have been wrong in trying to evaluate that German mind, if it is a mind. When it looks logical for him to do something he does something else. . . . When we once demonstrated . . . that we could break through the defense west of the Rhine, any sensible soldier would have gone back to the Rhine . . . and stood there and said, 'Now try to come across.' . . . If they had gotten out the bulk of their force they would have been better off."[58]

As a result of Hitler's decision, the Germans had taken a fearful beating. In the Rhineland campaign they lost 250,000 prisoners and untold killed and wounded. More than twenty divisions had been effectively destroyed. The Germans had only thirty or so divisions to defend the Rhine. Spaatz' oil campaign, now going full blast, had virtually eliminated the German fuel reserves. The Allied air forces took full advantage of the lengthening days and better weather, blasting every German who moved during daylight hours, flying as many as eleven thousand sorties in one day.[59]

Eisenhower's plan had worked. Late in March he met Brooke on the banks of the Rhine. Brooke had come to observe Montgomery's crossing. "He was gracious enough," Eisenhower reported to Marshall, "to say that I was right." Eisenhower added that he did not want to sound boastful, "but I must admit to a great satisfaction that the things that . . . I have believed in from the beginning and have carried out in face of some opposition from within and without, have matured so splendidly."[60] Best of all, however, was the creation of a large and powerful reserve, which was now available to Eisenhower to exploit any opportunity that might arise.

CHAPTER TWENTY

Reims

March 7–May 7, 1945

ON MARCH 7, Eisenhower returned to Reims from a week of travel along the front. After reviewing all the reports and attending a conference in the war room, he dictated some personal letters. That evening he planned to relax and asked a few of his corps commanders to dinner. They had just sat down to eat when the telephone rang. It was Bradley, who wanted to talk to Eisenhower. When the Supreme Commander got on the line, Bradley said that one of Hodges' divisions had taken intact the Ludendorff railroad bridge at Remagen. "Brad, that's wonderful," Eisenhower boomed. Bradley said he wanted to push all the force he had in the vicinity over to the east bank. "Sure," Eisenhower responded, "get right on across with everything you've got. It's the best break we've had." Eisenhower's G-3, Pinky Bull, was with Bradley, and Bradley said that Bull objected to establishing a bridgehead at Remagen, because the terrain on the east bank was unsuitable to offensive exploitation and in any case a crossing at Remagen was not part of the SHAEF plan. Eisenhower dismissed Bull's objections out of hand. "To hell with the planners," Eisenhower said. "Sure, go on, Brad, and I'll give you everything we got to hold that bridgehead. We'll make good use of it even if the terrain isn't too good."[1]

The next morning, Eisenhower informed the CCS that he was rushing troops to Remagen "with the idea that this will constitute greatest possible threat" to the Germans.[2] Because he had insisted on closing to the Rhine, SHAEF had sufficient divisions in reserve for

Eisenhower to exercise flexibility and exploit the opportunity. Over the following two weeks, he sent troops to Hodges, who used them to extend the bridgehead. The Germans made determined efforts to wreck the bridge, using air attacks, constant artillery fire, V-2 missiles, floating mines, and frogmen, but Hodges' defenses thwarted their efforts. By the time the big railroad bridge finally collapsed, the bridgehead was twenty miles long and eight miles deep, with six pontoon bridges across the river. It constituted a threat to the entire German defense of the Rhine. To the north, meanwhile, Montgomery was preparing his crossing, as was Patton to the south. Eisenhower told Mamie, "Our attacks have been going well . . . The enemy becomes more and more stretched . . ." Unfortunately, "he shows no signs of quitting. He is fighting hard. . . . I never count my Germans until they're in our cages, or are buried!"

Eisenhower spent the evening of March 16 with Patton and his staff. Patton was in a fine mood and set out to kid and flatter Eisenhower. He said that some of the Third Army units were disappointed because they had not had an opportunity to see the Supreme Commander. "Hell, George," Eisenhower replied, "I didn't think the American GI would give a damn even if the Lord Himself came to inspect them." Patton smiled. "Well," he said, "I hesitate to say which of you would rank, sir!" The banter went on through the evening. Patton noted in his diary, "General E stated that not only was I a good general but also a lucky general, and Napoleon preferred luck to greatness. I told him this was the first time he had ever complimented me in the 2½ years we had served together." Eisenhower wrote Mamie the next day, saying he had spent the evening "with Georgie P. He's always the same—and a good time." [3]

General Arnold paid a visit to Eisenhower's headquarters at Reims. Eisenhower confided that he was feeling the pressure. The war, Arnold noted, "had taken a whole lot out of him but he forced himself to go on and would until [the] whole mess was cleaned up." [4] His physical condition worried those closest to him. He had a touch of the flu. The cyst on his back had been cut out, leaving a deep and painful wound that required a number of stitches. His knee was swollen. Smith told him frankly that he was pushing himself too hard and that he would have a breakdown if he did not take some time off. Eisenhower started to get angry; Smith cut him off by saying, "Look at you. You've got bags under your eyes. Your blood pressure is higher than it's ever been, and you can hardly walk across the room." A wealthy American had offered Eisenhower and his staff the use of his luxurious villa on the French

Riviera, Sous le Vent, in Cannes. Smith insisted that Eisenhower accept and take a leave. Eisenhower finally said he would do so if Bradley came along.

On March 19 Eisenhower, accompanied by Bradley, Smith, Tex Lee, and four WACs, including Kay, took the train to Cannes. They stayed four days. Eisenhower was so run-down that he spent the first two days sleeping. He would wake for lunch, have two or three glasses of wine, and shuffle back to bed. One afternoon Kay suggested a game of bridge. Eisenhower shook his head. "I can't keep my mind on cards," he said. "All I want to do is sit here and not think."[5]

Other generals came to Cannes, among them Everett Hughes. Hughes had a talk with Tex Lee about the Eisenhower-Summersby relationship. Lee shared an office with Kay and told Hughes that in his opinion they were not sleeping together. Hughes was not convinced, but remarked, "There is nothing we can do about it." By this stage of the war there was, in fact, a noticeable cooling in Eisenhower's relationship with Kay. He still thought she was great fun to be with, still the only woman he saw on a regular basis, still someone he could talk to privately and frankly. But the intimacy that had prevailed in North Africa and in England was gone. Partly this was due to Eisenhower's almost constant travels, partly to the imminent end of the war. Eisenhower's early 1945 letters to Mamie were filled more than ever with references to their getting together as quickly as the war ended. When that time came Eisenhower knew there would be no place for Kay in his life.

Shortly after returning to Reims from Cannes, Eisenhower wrote Mamie that he had been thinking about "the problem of devising a 'policy' once the Germans stop fighting, under which I could get you over here quickly. It is difficult, of course, to do anything like that arbitrarily. I must not give others the chance to say 'The Boss doesn't care how long he stays here, he has his family, while we . . . are still separated from ours.' About such things it is impossible to 'reason'—we have to be most careful. But when the shooting stops I'm going to figure out something—you can bet on that! We've been far too long apart."[6]

They needed to get together for many reasons, not the least of which was John. "Mamie gives me hell," Eisenhower told Hughes. Rumors about the supposedly loose morals and high living of the American Army in Europe had reached her, and she told Eisenhower she was worried about exposing John to such influences. Eisenhower was aghast at such charges. "It's amazing to read what you have to say about the 'pitfalls' of last summer," he wrote Mamie. "[John] scarcely left my side, going, I think to only one party—and that attended by a large number of people. So where he could have been in jeopardy is beyond me." His own worries about John, in fact, were the opposite of Mamie's. "I must say I find him conservative and rather sedate," Eisenhower wrote. "I wish he'd have a bit more fun, or get more laughs out of life." One major complaint was that "he's the champion non-letter writer!" Eisenhower kept reminding himself that "[John] is a man now with his own problems—daily life, etc. It is exceedingly hard for him to realize how important he is to us. But it is difficult to be philosophical."

Mainly, however, Eisenhower's letters to his wife during the last months of the war were filled with the hope that they would soon be together. "Just when this mess is to be over," he wrote her in early April, ". . . I cannot even guess. But, thereafter, if I have to stay here indefinitely, you must come as soon as I can get a permanent abode."[7]

Even at Cannes, Eisenhower could not enjoy the luxury of not thinking. After catching up on his sleep, he spent hours discussing the options in the final campaign with Bradley. The result of their talks was a SHAEF directive that instructed Bradley to send Third Army over the Rhine in the Mainz-Frankfurt area, then make "an advance in strength" toward Kassel. Hodges should meanwhile push east from Remagen. This would lead to a linkup between First and Third Army, to be followed by an encirclement of the Ruhr. It would also make 12th Army Group's offensive greater in size and scope than that of 21st Army Group. Since January, and especially after Remagen, Eisenhower's inclination had been to keep increasing the strength of the attack on Bradley's front. At first it had been intended as a diversion, then as a secondary effort to help Montgomery, then as an alternative major thrust if Montgomery had difficulties. By the third week in March, Bradley's operations had become, in Eisenhower's mind, the main thrust.[8]

On March 22, the day after he received the SHAEF directive, Patton made a surprise crossing of the Rhine. The following day Eisenhower flew from Cannes to Wesel, on the lower Rhine, where he watched Simpson's Ninth Army (attached to 21st Army Group) make its practically unopposed crossing of the Rhine. To the north, meanwhile, Second Army made an assault crossing following preparations that nearly equaled those for Overlord. Simultaneously, Hodges and Patton extended their bridgeheads. The final offensive was rolling.

On March 25 Eisenhower went to Montgomery's headquarters for a quick visit. Churchill and Brooke were already there. The Prime Minister showed Eisenhower a note he had received from Soviet Foreign Minister Molotov. Molotov accused the West of dealing "behind the backs of the Soviet Union, which is bearing the brunt of the war against Germany," by conducting surrender negotiations with the German military command in Italy. Eisenhower, Churchill later recorded, "was much upset, and seemed deeply stirred with anger at what he considered most unjust and unfounded charges about our good faith." Eisenhower told Churchill he would accept surrenders in the field whenever offered; if political matters arose he would consult the heads of governments. Churchill responded that he thought the AEF ought to make a definite effort to beat the Russians to Berlin and hold as much of eastern Germany as possible "until my doubts about Russia's intention have been cleared away."[9]

Thus was raised what would be the last great controversy of World War II. Once the AEF was over the Rhine, and given the Red Army position on the Oder-Neisse line, the fate of Germany was sealed. For almost three and one-half years, the Wehrmacht had been at the center of Eisenhower's thoughts. Now Churchill wanted him to think rather less about the Germans, more about the Russians. Eisenhower resisted such a switch. There were political reasons for his resistance, which will be discussed later, but there were also some immediate military factors, of which the most important was the simplest—Eisenhower would not believe the Wehrmacht was finished until it had surrendered unconditionally.

Aside from his general analysis of the German character, Eisenhower had a specific fear—that the Nazis intended to set up a mountain retreat in the Austrian Alps, from which Hitler would direct guerrilla warfare. The Alps were easily defended, and from his mountain stronghold Hitler could—Eisenhower feared—combine what remained of the fighting forces in Germany and Italy and hold out indefinitely. SHAEF intelligence reported that Germany's best SS divisions were moving toward Berchtesgaden, southwest of Salzburg, and stories were circulating about prepared positions. "This area is, by the very nature of the terrain, practically impenetrable," SHAEF G-2 declared. "Here, defended by nature and by the most efficient secret weapons yet invented, the powers that have hitherto guided Germany will survive to reorganize her resurrection; here armaments will be manufactured in bomb-proof factories, food and equipment will be stored in vast underground caverns and a specially selected corps of young men will be trained in guerrilla warfare, so that a whole underground army can be fitted and directed to liberate Germany from the occupying forces."[10]

There was an element of gross exaggeration in that report, but it was true that the Germans were attempting to stockpile food and ammunition around Innsbruck and Salzburg, and the Alps were like a magnet to German forces retreating before 12th Army Group's advance. Eisenhower wanted a quick, sharp, definitive end to the war; to get it, he believed, the AEF had to occupy the Alps. They were, to him, a more important objective than Berlin. He thus rejected Churchill's argument that he should race the Russians to the German capital.

That decision represented a change in plan and was a bitter blow to British pride. It has been much criticized since, and not just by the British. Eisenhower's detractors, on both sides of the Atlantic, regard it as his worst mistake of the war.

The capture of Berlin was the obvious culmination of the offensive that began in 1942 in North Africa. The Western press, and the British and American people, assumed that SHAEF was directing its armies toward Berlin. The SHAEF planning staff had in fact planned for it. In September 1944, when it seemed that the AEF would soon be advancing into Germany, the planners drew up a proposal for the final offensive. "Our main object must be the early capture of Berlin," it began, "the most important objective in Germany." The way to accomplish this was to make the major advance north of the Ruhr with 21st Army Group; 12th Army Group would operate in a supporting role. Eisenhower accepted this plan; on a number of occasions he told Montgomery, "Clearly Berlin is the main prize."[11]

Why then did he change his mind? The main reason was that the military situation in March 1945 was far different from that prevailing in September 1944. In September, the Red Army was still outside Warsaw, more than three hundred miles from Berlin; the AEF was about the same distance away. In March 1945, the AEF remained more than two hundred miles from Berlin, while the Red Army was only thirty-five miles away. At a March 27 press conference, a reporter asked Eisenhower, "Who do you think will be into Berlin first, the Russians or us?" "Well," Eisenhower replied, "I think mileage alone ought to make them do it. After all they are thirty-three miles [away]. They have a shorter race to run."[12]

A second factor in Eisenhower's decision was Bradley's advice. His influence on Eisenhower's thinking was always great, and in the last months of the war it grew even stronger. At Cannes, the two generals had a long talk about Berlin. Bradley pointed out that even if Montgomery reached the Elbe River before the Red Army reached the Oder, fifty miles of lowlands separated the Elbe from Berlin. To get to the capital, Montgomery would have to advance through an area studded with lakes, crisscrossed with streams, and interlaced with canals. Eisenhower asked Bradley for an estimate on the cost of taking Berlin.

About 100,000 casualties, Bradley replied. "A pretty stiff price to pay for a prestige objective, especially when we've got to fall back and let the other fellow take over" (Berlin was well within the occupation zone already assigned to the Russians at the Yalta Conference).[13]

Personality, as always, played a role. "Monty wanted to ride into Berlin on a white charger," as Whiteley put it. By this stage of the war, however, Eisenhower was barely on speaking terms with Montgomery. As Eisenhower later told Cornelius Ryan, "Montgomery had become so personal in his efforts to make sure that the Americans—and me, in particular—got no credit, that, in fact, we hardly had anything to do with the war, that I finally stopped talking to him."[14] Eisenhower wanted Bradley to lead the last campaign. Had Bradley been on the northern flank, Eisenhower might well have sent him to Berlin. But 12th Army Group was in the center, so Eisenhower decided to make the main thrust there, with Dresden as the objective. This line offered the shortest route to the Red Army and would divide the remaining German forces roughly in half. To provide Bradley with sufficient force, Eisenhower took Ninth Army away from 21st Army Group and gave it to Bradley. To ensure cooperation with the Russians, he wired Stalin to inform him of his intentions, to suggest that the Red Army meet the AEF around Dresden, and to ask for information as to Russian intentions.[15]

Eisenhower's cable to Stalin, dated March 28, set off a flurry of activity in the capitals of the Big Three. The Russians acted first. Stalin agreed that Dresden was the best area for a meeting between the AEF and the Red Army, and added that Berlin had lost its former strategic significance. Stalin said that the Red Army planned to allot only secondary forces to the capture of the German capital. In fact, however, the Red Army had already begun a major redeployment, carried out "in almost frantic haste," designed to make Berlin its primary objective, assigning to that objective 1.25 million soldiers, supported by twenty-two thousand pieces of artillery.[16]

The British agreed with the Russians about the importance of Berlin; consequently they were decidedly unhappy with Eisenhower's plan to aim toward Dresden instead, and unhappy too with Eisenhower for opening direct communications with Stalin. They feared that Stalin would make a dupe of Eisenhower. "I consider we are about to make a terrible mistake," Montgomery wired Brooke. The British Chiefs sent their own strong protest directly to Marshall.[17]

In the United States, where Roosevelt was sick and Marshall had taken charge of the conduct of the war, the Americans in their turn were upset by the British protests. They resented the way their British allies called into question the strategy of the most successful field commander of the war, and they thought it unseemly for the British—of all people—to object to Eisenhower's direct approach to Stalin, as Churchill had always felt free to bypass the CCS and deal directly with Eisenhower. Most important, the JCS—especially Marshall—thought Eisenhower was right. The line from Kassel to Dresden offered the shortest distance to the Russians and thus to the division of Germany. The route avoided the waterways of the northern plains and it provided a central axis from which the AEF could turn north or south as required. It led directly to Germany's second-largest industrial area, the Silesian basin. Finally, after Eisenhower's success in the Rhineland campaign, Marshall thought that for the British to display such a lack of trust in Eisenhower was incredible, and he told them so.[18]

Unaware of Marshall's response to the British, Eisenhower sent a justification of his own to the Chief of Staff. He denied that he had made any change in plans—which was simply not true—and then turned British criticism of his strategy on its head. "Merely following the principle that Field Marshal Brooke has always shouted to me," he said, "I am determined to concentrate on one major thrust and all that my plan does is to place the Ninth U.S. Army back under Bradley" for that thrust. He showed some of his long-suppressed irritation with the British in his concluding paragraph: "The Prime Minister and his Chiefs of Staff opposed 'Anvil'; they opposed my idea that the German should be destroyed west of the Rhine . . . ; and they insisted that the route leading northeastward from Frankfurt would involve us merely in slow, rough-country fighting. Now they apparently want me to turn aside on operations in which would be involved many thousands of troops before the German forces are fully defeated. I submit that these things are studied daily and hourly by me and my advisors and that we are animated by one single thought which is the early winning of this war."[19]

The next day, March 31, Churchill tried again. He wired Eisenhower, "Why should we not cross the Elbe and advance as far eastward as possible? This has an important political bearing, as the Russian Army of the south seems certain to enter Vienna . . . If we deliberately leave Berlin to them, even if it should be in our grasp, the double event may strengthen their conviction, already apparent, that they have done everything." He wanted the British to get to Berlin first, and he wanted Ninth Army given to 21st Army Group to make it possible. Such a solution, Churchill said, "avoids the relegation of His Majesty's Forces to an unexpected restricted sphere."[20]

Churchill's plea, according to the SHAEF office diary, "upset E quite a bit." He immediately dictated a reply. He repeated that he had not changed his plan. He said he still intended to send Montgomery over the Elbe River, but toward Lübeck, not Berlin. By going to Lübeck, 21st Army Group would seal off the Danish Peninsula and keep the Russians out of Denmark. This was an important objective, Eisenhower insisted, and confessed that "I am disturbed, if not hurt, that you should suggest any thought on my part to 'relegate His Majesty's Forces to an unexpected restricted sphere.' Nothing is further from my mind and I think my record over two and a half years of commanding Allied forces should eliminate any such idea."[21]

The British, realizing that nothing they could say or do would change Eisenhower's mind, made the best of it. The storm began to subside, as neither side wanted a split. The British agreed in practice to the relegation of Montgomery to a secondary role. Churchill, keenly aware of the need for Anglo-American solidarity in the postwar world, took the lead in calming the waters. In a message to Roosevelt he said, "I wish to place on record the complete confidence felt by His Majesty's Government in General Eisenhower, our pleasure that our armies are serving under his command and our admiration of his great and shining quality, character and personality."[22] Churchill sent a copy to Eisenhower, saying in addition that it would "be a grief to me" if anything he had said "pains you." The Prime Minister could not resist the opportunity, however, to add that he still felt the AEF should take Berlin. "I deem it highly important that we should shake hands with the Russians as far to the east as possible."[23]

Thus, although the British had accepted the transfer of Ninth Army from Montgomery to Bradley, and resigned themselves to seeing the major thrust in central Germany, they still wanted the question of Berlin left open. Montgomery pushed that position on April 6, when he told Eisenhower that although he realized Eisenhower did not feel Berlin had much value, "I personally would not agree with this; I consider that Berlin has definite value as an objective and I have no doubt whatever that the Russians think the same; but they may well pretend that this is not the case!!"[24]

Meanwhile, however, Marshall was telling the British Chiefs, "Only Eisenhower is in a position to know how to fight his battle, and to exploit to the full the changing situation." As to Berlin, the JCS felt that such "psychological and political advantages as would result from the possible capture of Berlin ahead of the Russians should not override the imperative military consideration, which in our opinion is the destruction and dismemberment of the German armed forces."[25]

The next day, Eisenhower set the controversy in perspective while making his own position in the structure of the high command clear. He said he was making his decisions on military grounds and that he would require a new directive from his superiors on the CCS if the CCS wished him to operate on political grounds. He said a drive to Berlin was militarily unsound, then added, "I am the first to admit that a war is waged in pursuance of political aims, and if the Combined Chiefs of Staff should decide that the Allied effort to take Berlin outweighs purely military considerations in this theater, I would cheerfully readjust my plans and my thinking so as to carry out such an operation."[26] The British, knowing that they could not change Marshall's mind, did not even try. The CCS made no change in Eisenhower's directive. He therefore continued to operate under orders that required him to aim at the destruction of the German armed forces.

Through the first weeks of April the AEF rolled forward. Superiority in quality of troops, mobility, air power, material, and morale was enormous. Regiments, companies, squads, sometimes even three men in a jeep dashed on ahead, leaving their supply bases far behind, ignoring wide gaps on the flanks and enemy units in their rear, roaming far and wide with only sketchy knowledge of the enemy's positions, all the time certain that there was little or nothing the Germans could do about it. The German high command was, for all practical purposes, nonexistent; most German units were immobilized because of lack of fuel. There was no coherent defense.[27]

Eisenhower played a small role in the direction of the battle. He intervened only when army group shifts were required, or where a major change in the direction of an army was called for, or when a command question with political overtones was involved. While spearheads of 12th and 6th Army Groups moved into central and southern Germany, Bradley undertook the systematic reduction of the Ruhr pocket. By April 18 resistance there came to an end as 317,000 German soldiers surrendered, the largest mass surrender of German troops in the war.

On April 11, the leading units of Simpson's Ninth Army reached the Elbe River at Magdeburg. Simpson got two bridgeheads over the river, one north of Magdeburg on April 12, another to the south on April 13. The one to the north was destroyed by a German counterattack on April 14, but the one to the south held.

Suddenly it seemed that the Americans had an opportunity to take Berlin. The Russian drive for the capital had not yet begun and Simpson was within fifty miles of the city. He felt he could get to Berlin before the Red Army and asked Bradley's permission to try. Bradley checked with Eisenhower. Eisenhower said no. Simpson was stopped where he was. Patton was appalled. His romanticism, his strong sense of the dramatic, and his deep knowledge of military history all led him to believe that Eisenhower was passing up a historic opportunity. "Ike, I don't see how you figure that one," Patton told his boss. "We had better take Berlin and quick."[28]

Eisenhower disagreed. He felt that taking Lübeck in the north and occupying the Alpine redoubt area to the south were tasks "vastly more important than the capture of Berlin." He also thought that Simpson could not get to the capital before the Russians and so it was foolish to try. "We'd get all coiled up for something that in all probability would never come off." While it was true that Simpson had a bridgehead over the Elbe, "it must be remembered that only our spearheads are up to that river; our center of gravity is well back of there."[29]

The British nevertheless urged Eisenhower to send Simpson to Berlin. On April 17, Eisenhower flew to London to confer with Churchill on the subject. He convinced the Prime Minister of the soundness of his views; Churchill admitted that the immense strength of the Red Army on the eastern edges of Berlin, in comparison with Simpson's force (Simpson had fewer than fifty thousand men over the Elbe, and had gone beyond the range of fighter support), inevitably meant that it would be the Russians who first battered their way into the ruins. Eisenhower also convinced Churchill of the significance of Lübeck. As Churchill told his Foreign Secretary, "Our arrival at Lübeck before our Russian friends . . . would save a lot of argument later on. There is no reason why the Russians should occupy Denmark, which is a country to be liberated and to have its sovereignty restored. Our position at Lübeck, if we get it, would be decisive in this matter." As indeed it was. Churchill also agreed with Eisenhower's decision to push on south of Stuttgart to capture the German atomic research facilities in the area before the French got there.[30]

There was one last controversy with the British. By April 25 (the day Germany was split in half by an American-Russian linkup at Torgau, northwest of Dresden), Patton's Third Army reached the Czech border. There was open ground between his tanks and Prague. The British felt there would be "remarkable political advantages derived from liberation of Prague and as much as possible of Czechoslovakia by U.S.-U.K. forces." The British Chiefs thought Eisenhower should be directed "to take advantage of any improvement in his logistical situation or any weakening of enemy resistance to advance into Czechoslovakia provided such action does not hamper or delay final German defeat." In passing this message on to Eisenhower, Marshall commented, "Personally and aside from all logistic, tactical or strategical implications I would be loath to hazard American lives for purely political purposes."[31]

Eisenhower agreed. He told Marshall that his priorities remained Lübeck and the Alpine redoubt. These operations were "straining our resources" and were all that could be currently undertaken. The Red Army was in position to clean out Czechoslovakia and it appeared to Eisenhower that it could certainly reach Prague before Patton could. In conclusion, Eisenhower assured Marshall, "I shall *not* attempt any move I deem militarily unwise merely to gain a political prize unless I receive specific orders from the Combined Chiefs of Staff."[32]

The decision was not as firm as it sounded. Eisenhower wavered under countervailing pressure before he finally refused to move toward Prague. On April 30, he told the Russians of his intention to hold AEF forces approximately along the 1937 Czech border, while in the south advancing to Linz in Austria. The Red Army leaders quickly indicated their agreement with these proposals. But on May 4, events and arguments changed Eisenhower's position. Lübeck had been taken and the Alpine redoubt no longer posed a threat, and Patton was straining to go forward to Prague. Czechoslovakia, after all, was like Denmark; neither country had been assigned to the Russians and each was due to have its sovereignty restored. Eisenhower therefore reversed his decision and decided to go for Prague, but before doing so he decided to clear the operation with the Russians. When he told them of his change in plans, General Antonov of the Red Army replied immediately, expressing strong dissent. To avoid "a possible confusion of forces," Antonov asked Eisenhower "not to move the Allied forces in Czechoslovakia east of the originally intended line." Antonov pointed out that the Soviet forces had stopped their advance north of Berlin well short of the Elbe, leaving Lübeck to Montgomery, and said he hoped Eisenhower would comply with Russian wishes in Czechoslovakia. Eisenhower thereupon assured Antonov that he would not allow Patton to go farther east. He thus left Prague and most of Czechoslovakia to the Soviet forces. He finally held to this position even when the Czechs in Prague rose up against the Germans and, over captured radios, specifically asked the AEF for help.[33]

Lübeck contrasted strangely with Prague. Eisenhower's policy was inconsistent, even taking into account that the Russians had said nothing about Lübeck, but specifically requested that he stay out of Prague. The inconsistency may have been caused by general exhaustion, or the confusion at headquarters in the rush of events, or the failure of the CCS to provide clear objectives. It may have been a consequence of Roosevelt's illness and death, or—more broadly—the difference in outlook between Eisenhower's masters in Washington and those in London. American policy was to attempt to get along with the Russians; the British were anxious to take a firm line with them. Eisenhower could never satisfy both governments. This obvious fact was in its turn only a reflection of the complexity and contradictions inherent in the Grand Alliance; these complexities and contradictions were the main elements shaping Eisenhower's own thinking about the Russians.

Because he became a two-term President of the United States at the height of the Cold War, what Eisenhower personally thought about the Russians was of fundamental, worldwide significance. Some account of the evolution of his thinking about the U.S.S.R. up to mid-1945 is therefore in order. It properly belongs at this point in the narrative, because it was in early May of 1945, even before the German surrender, that the Russians replaced the Germans as the central focus of his concern. And from that moment to the end of his life, they stayed there.

Before the war Eisenhower had thought very little about the U.S.S.R. He made no attempt to study either Russia or Communism, and he accepted unquestioningly the strongly anti-Communist diatribes he heard so often from MacArthur and Moseley in the thirties. He had neither any responsibility for policy toward Russia nor any concern with it. When, in early 1942, Marshall set him to thinking about worldwide strategy, he did have responsibility and concern, but nevertheless he thought of Russia mainly in terms of the Red Army. Like Roosevelt, Eisenhower concentrated on winning the war; he put off any consideration of the shape of postwar Europe and the world. At Yalta, in early February 1945, Roosevelt could delay discussion about the settlement no longer. It was at Yalta that the zones of occupation in Germany were settled. Eisenhower opposed this division of Germany, urging Roosevelt instead to create a supreme commander for all three of the Allies and run Germany as a unit. As will be seen, this general approach was an integral part of his thoughts on how to get along with the Russians after the war.

Eisenhower had no personal contact with any Russians, and SHAEF had none until January 1945, when Eisenhower sent Tedder to

Moscow to ascertain Stalin's plans. Eisenhower knew, better than any other individual, just how crucial the Red Army was to the final defeat of Germany. Unconditional surrender could not possibly have been achieved without it. Eisenhower was angered by Russian charges of Allied bad faith in the Italian surrender negotiations, but after cooling down he could see the Russian point of view on the matter, and he took it into consideration when conducting his own surrender negotiations.

Churchill wanted to get tough with the Russians; Montgomery wanted to (and did) stack the arms of the Germans surrendering to him in such a way that the Wehrmacht could be quickly rearmed if it came to a fight between the West and Russia; Patton was talking wildly about using the great American army in Europe, while it was still there, to drive the Red Army back to Moscow, in cooperation with the Wehrmacht. Herein lay the seeds of NATO, dominated by a German-American military alliance, which replaced the prewar *cordon sanitaire* to contain the Russians. Eisenhower, in 1945, regarded such an alliance as irresponsible and self-defeating. He advocated, instead, making every effort to cooperate with the Russians to build a better world.

His reasons were manifold. There was, most immediately, his hatred for the Germans. It was deeply felt, a subject he returned to time and again in his most private letters. He blamed the Germans for starting the war, for the immense destruction he saw all around him, and for continuing the conflict long after any reasonable people would have quit. The hatred deepened as a result of the sights he saw inside Germany itself. "The other day I visited a German internment camp," he wrote Mamie on April 15. "I never dreamed that such cruelty, bestiality, and savagery could really exist in this world! It was horrible."[34] To Marshall, he confessed, "The things I saw beggar description." In one room he saw naked men piled to the ceiling, dead by starvation. "I made the visit deliberately," Eisenhower added, "in order to be in a position to give *first-hand* evidence of these things if ever, in the future, there develops a tendency to charge these allegations merely to 'propaganda.'" He saw to it that reporters, British MPs, and American congressmen visited the concentration camps to see for themselves, and sent photographs of the camps to Churchill.[35]

Having never visited or studied the Soviet Union, he could not imagine in his wildest dreams that anything remotely like the Nazi concentration camps could exist there. He felt, in the spring of 1945, as so many people in the West felt, that while the Nazis (and quite possibly the German people as a whole) were beyond redemption, the

Communists were not; that while one could not conceive of a genuine, working alliance with the Germans, such an alliance with the Russians was both possible and necessary.

To so believe, one had to have a Wilsonian idealism. Eisenhower did. Like Wilson, he believed—or more correctly, hoped—that it would be possible to overcome cultural, historic, economic, and ideological differences, and simultaneously to overcome the struggle for power inherent in the division of the world into nation states, to create a world of peace, prosperity, and progress all based on a security assured by the Great Powers acting in concert. Eisenhower was aware both of Wilson's failure and of the failure of all alliances in history to hold together after victory (even the British-French-American alliance of 1918). With Wilson's experience before him, Eisenhower was hardly naïve enough to use such phrases as "make the world safe for democracy" or "the war to end all wars." But he did say, frequently, that war had become too destructive to be an acceptable way of settling differences, and that the world therefore had to find some other system. He had seen the destruction; he felt personally involved to the greatest possible degree, as he was the man who gave the orders that sent tens of thousands of young men to their deaths; he desperately wanted a better world to emerge from the ashes. A world without an arms race, without great powers rattling sabers at one another, without hostile alliances directed against one another.

Viewed from the 1980s, it is a powerful vision. A world in which a vibrant United Nations controls the few atomic bombs in existence, a world without war, a world spared the expenses and terror of the Cold War, a world of cooperation, not confrontation. It was certainly utopian, but to Eisenhower it was worth striving for. *Something* good had to come out of the most destructive war ever fought; some effort had to be made to replace the old, discredited system.

One key would be plain and simple good will on both sides. For his part, Eisenhower was eager to show the Russians such good will. This was the real reason, above all others, that Eisenhower left Berlin and Prague to the Russians. For all his constant insistence on "military" rather than "political" factors, he avoided the two capitals for the most obvious of political reasons—to please the Russians. They wanted the honor of taking Berlin; they felt they deserved it; Eisenhower did not disagree. Nothing, he felt, would have gotten American-Russian postwar relations off to a worse start than to engage in a race for Berlin. He wanted to work with the Russians, not compete with them.

Eisenhower believed that cooperation was possible. He recognized that there would be difficulties, but thought they could be overcome by good will on both sides. In late May, he talked with Harry Hopkins and Harry Butcher about the Russians. Butcher recorded Eisenhower's comments:

> Ike said he felt that the American and British relationship with Russia was about at the same stage of arms-length dealing that marked the early contacts between Americans and the British when we first got into the war. As we dealt with each other, we learned the British ways and they learned ours. A common understanding developed and eventually we became Allies in spirit as well as on paper. Now the Russians, who have had relatively little contact . . . with the Americans and British, do not understand us, nor do we them. The more contact we have with the Russians, the more they will understand us and the greater will be the cooperation. The Russians are blunt and forthright in their dealings, and any evasiveness arouses their suspicions. It should be possible to work with Russia if we will follow the same pattern of friendly cooperation that has resulted in the great record of Allied unity demonstrated first by AFHQ and subsequently by SHAEF. Only now, in peace, the motive for cooperation is the betterment of the lot in life of the common man. If we can create singleness of purpose on this theme, as we did to win the war, then peace should be assured.[36]

It was a vivid expression of Eisenhower's experiences during the war, and of the impact they had made on him. After all, anyone who could get along with Montgomery for three years should certainly be able to get along with the Russians.

But Eisenhower's comparison between the Russian-American situation in 1945 and the Anglo-American situation in 1942 was completely inappropriate. There was no basis for the analogy and it was dangerous for Eisenhower to think there was. In 1942, the Anglo-Americans had a common enemy; in 1945, after Hitler's death, the Russians and Americans did not. In 1942, Britain and America cherished similar institutions and they had no serious territorial or spheres-of-influence disputes between them. In 1945, Russian and American institutions were as different as they could be, and Yalta had revealed that they had deep disputes over spheres of influence, in Poland and elsewhere. Eisenhower nevertheless believed that by building trust the differences between East and West could be overcome. In so believing he was following the lead of President Roosevelt. Further, Eisenhower had great faith, as did

Roosevelt and Wilson before him, in the power of personal diplomacy. Face-to-face meetings, where differences could be discussed frankly and openly, had been the way he had dealt with Churchill, Brooke, and Montgomery. Why not then with Stalin? Such an approach had a great appeal to American leaders, whether it was Wilson at Versailles in 1919, or Roosevelt at Yalta in 1945, or Eisenhower at Geneva in 1955.

Roosevelt's successor, President Harry S Truman, had less faith in summit meetings, and even less in the chances of getting along with the Russians. From the end of the war, when he cut lend-lease shipments to the Russians, to the end of his term in office, Truman followed a hard line with the Russians. By the time Eisenhower became President, the Cold War was well launched. It was too late to retrieve the situation; Eisenhower had to deal with what he found and move on from there. By that time too, his own views about the Russians had changed, to the point that he ran for the Presidency on a platform that accused Truman—of all people—of being soft on Communism. The most important reason for Eisenhower's changed attitude was, of course, Russian actions in the period 1945–1952; in this, he was no different from millions of his countrymen, who also had swung decisively away from the wartime euphoria about Russia. Even at that, Eisenhower as President retained his forlorn hope that everything could be set straight in a summit meeting.

Still, by 1952 Eisenhower was embarrassed by his 1945 pronouncements on the Russians, and by his failure to take Berlin. In various ways he tried to rewrite the historical record, asserting in his memoirs references to this or that warning he gave to this or that politician about the Russians. In *At Ease,* written in 1967, he claimed that he told FDR in January 1944 that he anticipated trouble with the Russians, but that Roosevelt would not listen. He further claimed that he warned Brooke, in 1943, that if the Allies did not get to Europe soon, the Red Army would overrun it, and that the Russians would then be impossible to deal with.[37] He way well have uttered such warnings, but he did not mention them in *Crusade in Europe,* written almost two decades before *At Ease,* nor did he ever write anything during the war to indicate that he was fearful of Russian intentions. When he claimed to have done so, it was noticeable that in both cases he said he made his point in private, and in both cases the man he made it to was dead.

Eisenhower also became highly defensive about the Berlin decision, especially after the 1948 Russian blockade of the city, and explained again and again—mainly to Republicans who feared that Stalin had made a fool of him—that he made the decision solely on military grounds, that he really was already aware of the Russian threat, and that he was warning others about the Soviets. The truth was that he may have wished by 1952 that he had taken a hard line with the Russians in 1945, but he had not. Instead, he was scrupulously fair in upholding their interests in the surrender negotiations and in the movements of his armies in the last weeks of the war.

In the spring of 1945 the Germans were eager to join the Americans in an anti-Soviet alliance. Hitler's suicide, on April 30, seemed to the remaining German leaders to eliminate the major obstacle to such an alliance. They felt that with Hitler gone, the West would be more inclined to see Germany as a bulwark against Communism in Europe. Specifically, the way Admiral Karl Doenitz, Hitler's successor, tried to speed up the East-West split and salvage something for Germany was through piecemeal surrender to the Western Allies only. Reichsfuehrer Heinrich Himmler sent an agent to Sweden to attempt to arrange for a surrender of German forces in the West. President Truman replied that the only term acceptable was unconditional surrender of all German armies to the Big Three. Churchill supported Truman; the Prime Minister told Eisenhower that "the offer looked like a last desperate attempt to create a schism between ourselves and the Russians." Eisenhower too was in complete agreement with Truman's policy. "In every move we make these days," Eisenhower assured Marshall, "we are trying to be meticulously careful in this regard."[38]

Meticulous care was essential, as by both word and act the Germans continued their effort to split the Alliance. Their soldiers on the Eastern Front, rightfully fearing above all else capture by the Red Army, fought desperately. On the Western Front, they surrendered at the first sight of an AEF unit. German civilians tried to flee to the West so that they would be inside the Anglo-American lines when the end came. And on May 1, Doenitz, in a radio address to the nation, said the Wehrmacht would "continue the struggle against Bolshevism until the fighting troops and the hundreds of thousands of families in Eastern Germany have been preserved from destruction."[39] But by May 2 or 3, Doenitz realized that Eisenhower would not accept a general surrender in the West only; he therefore tried to achieve the same end by surrendering armies and army groups to SHAEF while fighting on in the East.

The Germans facing Montgomery told him they wanted to surrender not only the troops facing 21st Army Group, but also the Wehrmacht units facing the Red Army in northeastern Germany. Eisenhower ordered Montgomery to refuse the latter offer, and he promised General

Susloparoff, who had come to Reims as the Russian liaison officer at SHAEF, that if a more general surrender did occur he would arrange "for a more formal and ceremonial surrender with Russian representatives present."[40] On the afternoon of May 4, the Germans facing 21st Army Group capitulated unconditionally on Montgomery's front. In central Germany, the units facing Hodges attempted to surrender not only their own armies but also those fighting the Russians in Czechoslovakia and Austria. The Americans refused this offer and forbade German civilians to cross the Elbe and surrender to the American troops (in fact, no real effort was made to prevent civilians from crossing into the American zone, and thousands did so).[41]

Despite the rebuffs, Doenitz kept hoping. On May 4, he sent Admiral Hans von Friedeburg to SHAEF with instructions to arrange for the surrender of the remaining German forces in the West. Eisenhower insisted that a general surrender had to take place on the Eastern and Western Fronts simultaneously, and he invited Susloparoff to attend the negotiations.[42] Smith and Strong (Strong had been military attaché in Berlin before the war and spoke perfect German) carried on the discussion with Friedeburg, for Eisenhower refused to see any German officers until the document of unconditional surrender had been signed. Smith told Friedeburg that there would be no bargaining and ordered him to sign the surrender document; Friedeburg replied that he had no power to sign. Smith insisted. He showed Friedeburg some SHAEF operational maps, which were quite convincing of the overpowering might of the AEF and the hopelessness of the German position. Friedeburg cabled Doenitz, asking for permission to sign an unconditional surrender.[43]

Late on the evening of May 5, Strong informed Eisenhower of the latest developments. Eisenhower grunted, then lay down on the cot in his office. The next morning he wrote Mamie, "Last night I really expected some definite developments and went to bed early in anticipation of being waked up at 1, 2, 3 or 4 A.M. Nothing happened and as a result I was wide awake, very early—with nothing decent to read. The Wild Wests I have just now are terrible—I could write better ones, left-handed."[44]

Doenitz did not give Friedeburg permission to sign. Instead, he made one last effort to split the Alliance, sending Generaloberst Alfred Jodl, the German Chief of Staff, to Reims to arrange for a surrender in the West only. Jodl arrived on Sunday evening, May 6. He conferred with Smith and Strong, emphasizing that the Germans were willing, indeed anxious, to surrender to the West, but not to the Red Army.

Doenitz, he said, would order all German troops remaining on the Western Front to cease firing no matter what SHAEF did about the offer to surrender. Smith replied that the surrender had to be a general one to all the Allies. Jodl then asked for forty-eight hours "in order to get the necessary instructions to all their outlying units." Smith said that was impossible. After the talks dragged on for over an hour, Smith put the problem to Eisenhower.

Eisenhower felt that Jodl was trying to gain time so that more German soldiers and civilians could get across the Elbe and escape the Russians. He told Smith to inform Jodl that "he would break off all negotiations and seal the western front preventing by force any further westward movement of German soldiers and civilians" unless Jodl signed the surrender document. But he also decided to grant the forty-eight-hour delay before announcing the surrender, as Jodl requested.

Smith took Eisenhower's reply to Jodl, who thereupon sent a cable to Doenitz, explaining the situation and asking permission to sign. Doenitz was enraged; he characterized Eisenhower's demands as "sheer extortion." He nevertheless felt impelled to accept them, and was consoled somewhat by the thought that the Germans could still save many troops from the Russians during the forty-eight-hour delay. Just past midnight, therefore, he cabled Jodl: "Full power to sign in accordance with conditions as given has been granted by Grand Admiral Doenitz."[45]

At 2 A.M. on May 7, Generals Smith, Morgan, Bull, Spaatz, Tedder, a French representative, and Susloparoff gathered in the second-floor recreation room of the École Professionelle et Technique de Garçons, Reims. Strong was there to serve as translator. The war room was L-shaped, with only one small window; otherwise, the walls were covered with maps. Pins, arrows, and other symbols showed how completely Germany had been overrun. It was a relatively small room; the Allied officers had to squeeze past one another to get to their assigned chairs, gathered around a heavy oak table. When they had all sat down, Jodl, accompanied by Friedeburg and an aide, was led into the room. Tall, perfectly erect, immaculately dressed, his monocle in place, Jodl looked the personification of Prussian militarism. He bowed stiffly. Strong found himself, to his own surprise, feeling a bit sorry for him.[46]

While the somewhat elaborate procedures for the signing went on, Eisenhower waited in his adjacent office, pacing and smoking. The signing took a half hour. In the war room, Jodl was delivering the German nation into the hands of the Allies and officially acknowledging that Nazi Germany was dead; outside, spring was bursting forth, promising new life.

Eisenhower knew that he should feel elated, triumphant, joyful, but all he really felt was dead beat. He had hardly slept in three days; it was the middle of the night; he just wanted to get it over with. At 2:41 A.M., Smith led Jodl into Eisenhower's office. Eisenhower sat down behind his desk. Jodl bowed, then stood at attention. Eisenhower asked Jodl if he understood the terms and was ready to execute them. Jodl said yes. Eisenhower then warned him that he would be held personally accountable if the terms were violated. Jodl bowed again and left.

Eisenhower went out into the war room, gathered the SHAEF officers around him (Kay and Butcher managed to sneak in too), and photographers were called in to record the event for posterity. Eisenhower then made a short newsreel and radio recording. When the newsmen left, Smith said it was time to send a message to the CCS. Everyone had a try at drafting an appropriate document. "I tried one myself," Smith later recalled, "and like all my associates, groped for resounding phrases as fitting accolades to the Great Crusade and indicative of our dedication to the great task just completed." Eisenhower quietly watched and listened. Each draft was more grandiloquent than the last. The Supreme Commander finally thanked everyone for his efforts, rejected all the proposals, and dictated the message himself. "The mission of this Allied force was fulfilled at 0241 local time, May 7, 1945."[47]

He had managed to grin while the newsreel cameras were on, to hold up the pens in a V-for-Victory sign, to walk without a limp. After signing the last message, he slumped visibly. "I suppose this calls for a bottle of champagne," he sighed. Someone brought one in; it was opened to feeble cheers; it was flat. Utter weariness now descended; everyone went to bed.

It was not at all like the image Eisenhower had held before him for three years. From the time he left Mamie in June 1942, he had sustained himself with the thought of this moment. "When the war ends"—the image of that magic moment had kept him going. When the Germans surrendered, then all would be right again. The world would be secure, he could go home, his responsibilities would be over, his duty done. He could sit beside a lazy stream with nothing but a cane pole and a bobber, and Mamie there with him, so that he could tell her about all the funny things that had happened that he had not had time to write about.

By early 1945, he had been forced to modify the fantasy somewhat, as he realized that he would have to remain in Germany for some months at least, as head of the American occupying forces. Still, he clung to the thought that Mamie could be with him immediately after the shooting stopped. Now he had the sinking feeling that even that was not going to be possible. As to escaping responsibility, decision-making, and the burden of command, he had already had to face the fact that such a release was impossible. Worst of all, he already feared that world security was threatened. There had been too many of his own officers who listened with approval to the German whisperings about an anti-Communist alliance; on the other side, the Russian suspicions about Western motives struck Eisenhower as bordering on paranoia (even before he went to bed, Eisenhower received a message that said the Russians would not accept the surrender signed in Reims and insisted on another signing, in Berlin). It made him wonder if it would be possible after all to cooperate with them in rebuilding Europe. Going to bed on that morning of May 7, Eisenhower felt as flat as the champagne.

But Eisenhower's flatness should not preclude a glance at what he had accomplished and what he had to celebrate, had he had the energy to do so. The problem is that, like Smith, one searches in vain for the fitting accolades to acknowledge the accomplishments of Dwight D. Eisenhower in the Second World War—of what he had endured, of what he had contributed to the final victory, of his place in military history. Fortunately George C. Marshall, next to Eisenhower himself the man most responsible for Eisenhower's success, spoke for the nation and its allies, as well as for the U.S. Army, when he replied to Eisenhower's last wartime message. "You have completed your mission with the greatest victory in the history of warfare," Marshall began. "You have commanded with outstanding success the most powerful military force that has ever been assembled. You have met and successfully disposed of every conceivable difficulty incident to varied national interests and international political problems of unprecedented complications." Eisenhower, Marshall said, had triumphed over inconceivable logistical problems and military obstacles. "Through all of this, since the day of your arrival in England three years ago, you have been selfless in your actions, always sound and tolerant in your judgments and altogether admirable in the courage and wisdom of your military decisions.

"You have made history, great history for the good of mankind and you have stood for all we hope for and admire in an officer of the United States Army. These are my tributes and my personal thanks."[48]

It was the highest possible praise from the best possible source. It had been earned.

CHAPTER TWENTY-ONE

Frankfurt, Berlin, London, Washington, Moscow

May 8–December 3, 1945

BY THE TIME of the surrender, Eisenhower had become the most famous and successful general of the war. By then, too, Hitler and Roosevelt were dead, so Eisenhower was one of the three best-known men in the world, just behind Stalin and Churchill. He had become the symbol of the forces that had combined to defeat the Nazis, and of the hopes for a better world. His worldwide popularity was immense. He inspired a confidence that can only be marveled at, rather than accurately measured. In the months following the surrender at Reims, whenever a big job had to be done, his name just naturally came up. Edward R. Murrow told President Truman that Eisenhower was the "only man in the world" who could make the United Nations work. Sidney Hillman, the labor politician, said that Eisenhower was the "only man" who could guide Germany into a democratic future. Alan Brooke told Eisenhower that if there were another war, "we would entrust our last man and our last shilling to your Command."[1] Democratic and Republican politicians alike felt that Eisenhower was the "only man" who could win for them in 1948. Truman himself, in July 1945, told Eisenhower, "General, there is nothing that you may want that I won't try to help you get. That definitely and specifically includes the presidency in 1948."[2]

Eisenhower's personal desire was for a quiet retirement with perhaps a bit of writing and lecturing. But fulfillment of that desire had to wait another sixteen years, because the nation continued to call him to her service, on the grounds that he was the "only man" who could do the job and it was therefore his "duty" to accept. He served in five positions—as head of the American Occupation Zone in Germany, as Chief of Staff, as president of Columbia University, as the Supreme Commander of NATO, and as President of the United States. In each instance, he accepted the responsibility reluctantly, or so at least he told himself, his friends, and the public. There can be no doubt, however, that he enjoyed the challenge, the stimulation, and the satisfaction that his work provided, and that he was, from age 54 to age 70, too active, too involved, too alive, to simply retire. Nor was he immune to the pleasures of power and its uses. But although Eisenhower's postwar career led to eight years at the pinnacle of world power, it was the case for Eisenhower, as it had been for Washington and Grant before him, that after the war the great moments of his life were behind him. Despite their success in politics, nothing that happened to Washington after Valley Forge and Yorktown, and nothing that happened to Grant after the Wilderness and Appomattox, could surpass those experiences for drama, importance, or personal satisfaction. So too for Eisenhower—nothing could ever surpass D-Day and Reims.

When news of the surrender was flashed around the world, it was, in Churchill's words, "the signal for the greatest outburst of joy in the history of mankind." For Eisenhower, the weeks that followed were full of activity—making arrangements with the Russians, occupation duties, diplomatic difficulties, redeploying the American troops in Europe to the Pacific, entertaining visiting VIPs—but most of his energy went into a hectic, exhausting, satisfying, prolonged celebration. It began on May 15, when he accepted an invitation to spend a night in London. John, Kay, Jimmy Gault, and Bradley joined him. They took along eighteen bottles of the best champagne in Reims, paid a nostalgic visit to Telegraph Cottage, ate a buffet supper at the Dorchester Hotel, then went to the theater. Kay's mother was a part of the party, and Kay sat beside the general in their box at the theater, which resulted in a famous photograph and added to the gossip about their relationship. It was the first time Eisenhower had seen a show or eaten in a restaurant in three years, indeed his first public appearance since July 1942, and he was astonished to discover how famous and popular he had become. People at the theater cheered, shouted, and called out "Speech, Speech!" when they saw him. From his box in the balcony he rose and said, "It's nice to be back in a country where I can *almost* speak the language."[3]

The grand centerpiece of the victory celebration came in June, at Guildhall, in the City of London. Churchill insisted that Eisenhower participate in the formal celebration and ignored Eisenhower's request that the ceremonies "be such as to avoid over-glorification of my own part in the victories of this Allied team."[4] Attention centered on Eisenhower. He was told that he would make the principal speech, to a large audience that would include every high-ranking military and civil official in the United Kingdom, in a historic hall filled with British pomp and circumstance at its most extreme and impressive, and that he would receive the Duke of Wellington's sword. He took the assignment with the utmost seriousness, because "this was the first formal address of any length that I had to give on my own." He worked on the speech nightly for three weeks, read it aloud innumerable times to Butcher, Kay, and anyone else who would listen. Butcher suggested that he memorize it, which would give the appearance of spontaneity and allow him to speak without wearing his spectacles. Eisenhower agreed.

The ceremony was held in the morning on June 12. An hour or so before it began, Eisenhower went for a walk in Hyde Park, alone, to collect his thoughts. He was spotted, then surrounded by a mob of well-wishers (it was the last time in his life he ever attempted to go out alone in a city). He had to be rescued by a policeman. From the Dorchester, he and Tedder rode into the City of London in a horse-drawn carriage, past the destruction and rubble around St. Paul's, to bomb-scarred Guildhall. Eisenhower received the sword from the bewigged Lord Mayor of London. Then Eisenhower began his speech by saying that his sense of appreciation for the high honor being done him was tempered by a sense of sadness, because "humility must always be the portion of any man who receives acclaim earned in blood of his followers and sacrifices of his friends." He spoke of the great Allied team and insisted that he was only a symbol, that the awards and acclaim he was receiving belonged to all the team.

"I come from the very heart of America," he said. He spoke of the differences in age and size between Abilene and London, but then pointed to the kinship between them. "To preserve his freedom of worship, his equality before law, his liberty to speak and act as he sees fit . . . a Londoner will fight. So will a citizen of Abilene. When we consider these things, then the valley of the Thames draws closer to the farms of Kansas." Then, again, he referred to "the great team" that he had led. "No man alone could have brought about [the victory]. Had I possessed the military skill of a Marlborough, the wisdom of Solomon, the understanding of Lincoln, I still would have been helpless without the loyalty, vision, and generosity of thousands upon thousands of British and Americans."

The London newspapers the following day, in what Eisenhower called "an excess of friendly misjudgment," compared the speech to the Gettysburg Address. After he finished, Churchill took him to the balcony to greet a crowd of thirty thousand in the streets below. "Whether you know it or not," Eisenhower responded to the demands for a speech, "I am now a Londoner myself. I have as much right to be down in the crowd yelling as you have." Butcher, the professional public relations man, was impressed. "[Ike's] words," he said, "came as naturally as if he had rehearsed them for a week."[5]

Eisenhower was the focus of ceremonies in Prague, Paris, and other European capitals, and most of all in the United States. Together with Marshall, he made detailed plans for the return home of his top commanders, so that Bradley, Patton, Hodges, Simpson, and the corps and division commanders would each get their share of the applause of a grateful nation. He himself came home last, because Marshall insisted that anyone who came after Eisenhower would be distinctly anticlimactic.

Eisenhower's triumphant return took place in late June. Huge crowds greeted him and he made numerous speeches. The most important was to a joint session of Congress. Marshall sent him a draft of a speech to read at the Capitol; Eisenhower thanked him for it but said he preferred to speak extemporaneously. The result was a speech full of platitudes and eternal verities, but it was spoken with such sincerity and emotion that it quite overcame the audience. The politicians gave General Eisenhower a standing ovation that was the longest in the history of Congress, and there was not a man in the hall who did not think to himself how wonderful General Eisenhower would look standing at that podium as President Eisenhower.[6]

Later that day, John joined his father for the flight to New York. As they settled into their seats, Eisenhower commented, "Well, now I've got to figure out what I am going to say when I get there." There were an estimated two million people in his audience outside City Hall. His theme was "I'm just a Kansas farmer boy who did his duty," and *The New York Times* acclaimed his speech as "masterful."[7]

He was in great demand as a speaker. Invitations came in a flood, from the rich, the famous, the heads of worthy organizations and old universities, friends, everyone wanted him to speak. All the causes were good ones; he hated to say no to any of them. But as he told a friend, "One of my greatest horrors is a garrulous general."[8] So far as possible, he held his speechmaking down to a minimum, and except for the

Guildhall address and his speech to Congress, he put in a minimum amount of preparation. He usually hit the right note. In Abilene, twenty thousand people (four times the city's population) gathered in City Park to welcome him home. "Through this world it has been my fortune, or misfortune, to wander at considerable distances," Eisenhower said. "Never has this town been outside my heart and memory." In November, when he returned to the States from Germany to testify before congressional committees on postwar organization of the armed forces, he told Marshall he would not make a formal presentation, but would "expand extemporaneously my personal beliefs and possibly embellish a bit from personal experiences." He was extremely effective in doing so; although none of his points were original and in fact reflected, even in the smaller details, Marshall's position on the issues, he made them with such force that they sounded fresh and convincing.[9]

In brief, whether as a writer, or formal speaker, or testifying before congressional committees, or making an impromptu talk to a street crowd, or just riding in an open car, waving his hands like a prizefighter and grinning broadly, and whether in Prague or Paris or London or New York, Eisenhower was a tremendous success. His first words when he stepped off the plane in Washington on June 18 made headlines the next day—"Oh, God, it's swell to be back!" Trailing along behind his triumphant parade in New York, Butcher heard numerous comments—"He waved at me." "Isn't he handsome?" "He's marvelous!"[10] In Washington, Dr. Arthur Burns, an economist at George Washington University, watched Eisenhower drive past in his convertible, caught the friendliness he projected, turned to his wife and said, "This man is absolutely a natural for the Presidency."[11]

Thus did the celebration of the victory add to the already widespread talk about Eisenhower for President. During the war, Eisenhower had responded to such suggestions with a snort or a grunt. In October 1943, George Allen, a friend, sent him some newspaper clippings about the subject, with a covering note that asked, "How does it feel to be a presidential candidate?" Eisenhower grabbed a pencil and scribbled at the bottom of Allen's note, "Baloney! Why can't a simple soldier be left alone to carry out his orders? And I furiously object to the word 'candidate'—I ain't and won't."[12] After the war, he was just as negative. When Truman said he would support Eisenhower for the Presidency in 1948, Eisenhower laughed at the idea and replied, "Mr. President, I don't know who will be your opponent for the presidency, but it will not be I." It was an interesting choice of words, as the sentence seemed to identify Eisenhower as a Republican (a subject on which there was intense speculation), and indicated that Eisenhower was shrewd enough to realize that whatever Truman was saying in 1945, Truman himself would be a candidate in 1948.[13] In August 1945, an old friend from Fort Sam Houston wrote to say he and others in San Antonio were "ready and anxious to organize an 'Eisenhower for President' Club." Eisenhower replied that he was flattered by the suggestion, "But I must tell you, with all the emphasis I can command, that nothing could be so distasteful to me as to engage in political activity of any kind. I trust that no friend of mine will ever attempt to put me in the position where I would even be called upon to deny political ambitions."[14] He made similar emphatic denials to all entreaties that he become a candidate. To Mamie, he wrote, "Many people seem astounded that I'd have no slightest interest in politics. I can't understand *them*."[15]

What he wanted to do was retire. Failing that, he wanted his wife at his side. It was sixteen years before he could achieve the first objective, six months before he realized the second.

Five days after the surrender, Eisenhower wrote his wife to say that he was at work on developing a policy that would make it possible for her to join him in Europe. He wanted her to come as soon as suitable quarters could be found, but warned that it would be difficult and might take time, because "the country is devastated. . . . It is a bleak picture. Why the Germans ever let the thing go as far as they did is completely beyond me!"[16]

On June 4, immediately after moving into a small house in Bad Homburg, near his new office in Frankfurt, Eisenhower wrote Marshall. He proposed a policy to bring to Germany wives of enlisted men and officers on occupation duty. He then made his personal case. "I will admit that the last six weeks have been my hardest of the war," he said. "My trouble is that I just plain miss my family." He said he got to see John, then assigned to the 1st Division, about once a month, which was not enough. As to Mamie, he was worried about her health (she had just entered the hospital, suffering from a persistent cold, her weight down to 102 pounds). In a heartfelt plea, he commented, "The strain of the past three years has also been very considerable so far as my wife is concerned, and because of the fact that she has had trouble with her general nervous system for many years I would feel far more comfortable about her if she could be with me." He insisted, nevertheless, that he would not want to arouse any resentment in his command, and asked for Marshall's "very frank reaction because while I am perfectly willing to carry on in this assignment . . . I really would like to make it a bit easier on myself from the personal viewpoint."[17]

Three things stand out about the letter. First, the depth of Eisenhower's love and concern for his wife. Second, his concern for what people thought of him. Third, his continued subordination of himself to Marshall. Eisenhower was, after all, Marshall's equal in rank, a five-star general. The other five-star generals—Arnold, MacArthur, *and* Marshall—had all had their wives at their sides throughout the war. Eisenhower must have known that MacArthur most certainly did not ask Marshall's permission to have Jean join him at his headquarters. Eisenhower did not have to ask Marshall's permission in order to live with his wife; all he had to do was tell her to come on over.

Marshall's response is also extraordinary and caused a subsequent furor. Marshall took the letter to the President for consultation. Truman told him "No," Mamie could not go, as it would be unfair to all the others. Decades later, long after Truman had broken with Eisenhower and at a time when Truman was approaching senility, the former President told reporter Merle Miller, for his book *Plain Speaking,* that Eisenhower had written to Marshall in June 1945 asking permission to divorce Mamie in order to marry Kay. According to Truman's story, he and Marshall agreed that they could never allow such a thing to happen. They told Eisenhower "No," threatened to ruin his career if he did go through with a divorce, and then destroyed the letter. The story was widely reported in 1973, and widely believed, but completely untrue.[18] Eisenhower did not want to divorce Mamie, he wanted to live with her.

Eisenhower's respect for Marshall and his concern about his own image were so great that, in his response to Marshall's message turning down his request, he apologized for bothering Marshall with a personal problem. Eisenhower said he understood that "from every standpoint of logic and public relations the thing is impossible."[19] He then wrote Mamie to give her the bad news and to tell her, "You cannot be any more tired than I of this long separation, particularly at my age." He said he had talked to John and persuaded him to drop his request for transfer to the Pacific, in order to be around headquarters so that they could be together. "Johnny is really anxious to go to the Pacific," Eisenhower wrote Mamie, "but he realizes I am lonely and need him."[20]

John later wrote that the postsurrender months were "probably the period in my entire life when Dad and I were closest." He was stationed within a half hour's drive. "Dad was a lonely man at that time, let down after the excitement of the war," John recognized, and he tried to help by spending as much time as possible with his father.[21] He went along on trips, including Eisenhower's whirlwind tour of the States in June.

That journey was a disappointment to Mamie, because she had to give up her man to the public. When she met her husband's plane at the Washington airport, she had only the briefest kiss and hug before Eisenhower was hustled off to the Pentagon. For the next eight days, he was constantly making public appearances. Finally, on June 25, Eisenhower, Mamie, John, and Mamie's parents went to White Sulphur Springs for a week of privacy. But as Eisenhower later wrote Charles Harger of Abilene, "In those few days the reaction from the war months and from a rapid series of celebrations was so great that I really didn't get to settle down and relax." When Eisenhower got back to Germany, Mamie wrote about her disappointment over the visit and confessed that she was "back down in the dumps." Eisenhower assured her, "If you'd just once understand how exclusively I love you and long for you then you'd realize how much the week at White Sulphur meant." He said that as a result of the trip, "My hatred of Washington is even greater than it used to be. Which is saying a lot!" and blamed her depression on the city—"I don't see how you could help it [living] in Washington."[22]

Kay was still working for Eisenhower, and still much in the news and gossip, and still much on Mamie's mind. When Eisenhower made a trip to Belfast for a celebration and ceremonies, Mamie remarked that he seemed "highly interested in Ireland." In reply, Eisenhower did not mention Kay or her Irish ancestry, but he did make sure Mamie understood that only he and two male aides had gone to Belfast, and that while there they had "carried out a schedule . . . that would kill a horse."[23]

What to do about Kay was becoming a problem. She was not a U.S. citizen and therefore could not retain her commission as a WAC or continue working for Eisenhower. In October, she decided to go to the States to take out citizenship papers. When she returned to Germany, Eisenhower asked General Lucius Clay, in Berlin, to give her a job in his office. He told Clay that "I hope you will find a really good job for her and I know that you will remember that she has not only served me with the utmost faithfulness and loyalty but has had more than her share of tragedy to bear in this war. Incidentally, she is about as close-mouthed a person about office business as I ever heard of."[24] To Smith, Eisenhower confessed that he felt badly about Kay, because he knew that "she feels very deserted and alone."[25]

Then, to Kay herself, he dictated a long, businesslike letter that explained why she could no longer work for him. He said he would "not attempt to express the depth of my appreciation for the unexcelled loyalty and faithfulness with which you have worked under my personal direction," and that he was "personally much distressed that an association which has been so valuable to me has to be terminated in this particular fashion." After promising to do anything he could to help her get started on a new career, he concluded, "Finally, I hope that you will drop me a note from time to time—I will always be interested to know how you are getting along." Then he added a handwritten postscript—"Take care of yourself—and retain your optimism."[26]

Kay left the WAC, became a U.S. citizen, and moved to New York. In late 1947 she became engaged, set a date for the wedding, and sent Eisenhower an invitation. He politely declined in a warm but formal reply.[27] Kay soon broke her engagement, however, leading Eisenhower to write in his diary on December 2, 1947, "Heard today . . . that my wartime secretary (rather personal aide and receptionist) is in dire straits." Eisenhower blamed Kay's emotional problems on the death of Colonel Arnold in North Africa in 1943, and commented, "Too bad, she was loyal and efficient and the favorite of everyone in the organization. . . . I trust she pulls herself together, but she is Irish and tragic."[28] In 1948, Kay published a book about her war experiences, *Eisenhower Was My Boss.* It was a great success and, along with the fees she earned on a lecture tour, made her financially independent. After Eisenhower moved to New York City, in 1948, Kay managed to "accidentally" run into him near his office; he was curt and, by her later account, dismissed her by saying, "Kay, it's impossible. There's nothing I can do."[29] In 1952, Kay married Reginald Morgan, a New York stockbroker. Then came the publication of *Plain Speaking* (1973), which led Kay to publish a new book of memoirs, *Past Forgetting: My Love Affair with Dwight D. Eisenhower.* In her introduction, Kay said she had been first surprised, then pleased, to discover from Truman's story that Eisenhower had wanted to divorce Mamie to marry her. As Eisenhower was by then dead, and she herself was dying of cancer, she said she had decided to tell the whole truth about their famous affair.

Whether she told the "whole truth" or not, no one can tell. If she did, then General Eisenhower was sexually impotent throughout the war. Kay's book, as a whole, was a vivid and moving account of a wartime romance that was both frustrating and exciting. Nowhere did she claim too much for her own role in his life, but she was always around, a keen and sensitive observer who was, for her part, deeply in love with her boss. Whether Eisenhower loved her in turn or not is less certain, although obviously he had strong feelings about her. In fact, she was the third most important woman in his life, behind only his mother and his wife. But he never thought of marrying Kay, and Kay knew that all along. Mamie, meanwhile, was naturally resentful about Kay, and even Eisenhower, who was so inept in such matters, realized that he could not have both Mamie and Kay. In that circumstance, he unhesitatingly chose Mamie.

No matter how successfully, coldly, even cruelly, he thereafter avoided Kay, the Eisenhower-Summersby romance was too good a story to disappear, and over the years the various rumors and gossip continued to irritate Mamie. When *Plain Speaking* and *Past Forgetting* were published, she was so upset that she authorized John to publish Eisenhower's wartime letters to her, which had previously been sealed. The book that resulted, *Letters to Mamie,* established conclusively that throughout the war years, when Eisenhower was with Kay, his love for Mamie was constant. Throughout the war, his sustaining force was the thought that when it was over he and Mamie could live together again. He loved Mamie for half a century.

But loving Mamie did not necessarily preclude loving Kay. At least, loving her under the special situation in which they lived from the summer of 1942 to the spring of 1945. He was lucky to have her around, and the Allies were lucky she was there. The best advice in attempting to pass any judgment on the Eisenhower-Summersby relationship was that given by Hughes to Tex Lee back in 1943. "Leave Kay and Ike alone. She's helping him win the war."

By the summer of 1945, two other members of Eisenhower's inner circle were writing books about their experiences. Mickey McKeogh was calling his *Sergeant Mickey and General Ike,* and asked Eisenhower for a foreword. Eisenhower said that doing so would only add to his already "acute embarrassment." When Butcher made a similar request Eisenhower replied, "If I were to do a foreword for your book, I think I would have to say that I lived with the fellow for three years and I didn't even know he could read or write."[30] Butcher had stayed in the States after the June trip, and had been given an office in the Pentagon, where he was transcribing the diary he had kept throughout the war—a diary Eisenhower had ordered him to keep and which included parts of Eisenhower's own diary, his memorandums, etc. Butcher intended to publish the manuscript in book form. When Eisenhower discovered, in late July, that Butcher had possession of the diary notes he, Eisenhower, had made while working in OPD in the first half of 1942, he directed Butcher to "destroy those personal notes of mine at once and keep no record of them whatsoever. The notes made by me personally . . . must not, repeat not, be seen by anyone."[31] Fortunately for later biographers,

Butcher did not do as ordered, although the notes were sealed for three decades. Eventually, in 1981, major portions of the wartime diary were printed. Eisenhower said that the various memorandums Butcher possessed "were not written with any thought of their ever reaching the public eye" and told Butcher not to quote from them. In this case, Butcher was even less obedient and often did use direct quotes. Meanwhile, his diary was causing a stir in the publishing world and *The Saturday Evening Post* arranged to serialize it. Eisenhower commented to his brother Milton, "Butch is apparently about to become a famous author. . . . I only hope that he does not try to go too far in an attempt to make his book an authoritative strategical treatise which he could not possibly do."[32] He was also concerned that readers might think he had collaborated on the project, because he expected Butcher's account to be flattering, and "you know my horror of self-praise."[33]

Kenneth S. Davis, meanwhile, a young Kansas State journalist, was writing a biography, with the active cooperation of the Eisenhower family. Davis had interviewed innumerable of Eisenhower's childhood friends in Abilene, then lived at Eisenhower's headquarters for several weeks in mid-1944, where he interviewed the general himself. The result was a book entitled *Soldier of Democracy,* published in late 1945 and much the best of all the early biographies, and still the most complete on Eisenhower's ancestry and childhood. Although it added to Eisenhower's popularity, he himself was not happy with the work. His complaint was that Davis put too much weight on disagreements with the British, not enough on the areas of cooperation.[34] Eisenhower wrote to Davis to object to "the poor light in which several very great men were portrayed," especially Montgomery.[35] In fact, Eisenhower had already begun what would be a lifelong effort to deny that there ever was any disagreement between himself and the field marshal. When a newspaper reported that Eisenhower "disliked" Montgomery, Eisenhower immediately wrote Montgomery to say he wanted to tell the reporter "what a skunk and a liar he is."[36]

If Eisenhower did not like what others were saying about him, he had ample opportunity to write his own version of how the war was won and his role in the victory. Publishers, agents, and magazine editors wrote asking if they could participate in the publication of his memoirs; to one of the most tempting offers, from Max Schuster of Simon and Schuster, he replied that he had given some thought to doing some memoir writing, but "I do not see how I could get enough time to do a worthwhile job—even assuming that a number of people would be interested in what I have to say."[37] Secretly, however, he had already begun some writing, as he told Milton on August 2 on a strictly confidential basis: "I am, from time to time, getting down on paper an outline of my personal story covering the war years." He was not sure he would ever allow it to be published, but "on the earnest advice of some valued friends [Smith and Bradley] I am trying to get my thoughts down on paper."[38] In September 1945, he confessed to Butcher that he was discovering "it is almost impossible to tell the story of high command without being perfectly straightforward and truthful about personalities." In short, he could not write without being critical of Montgomery and some others, and he knew that "any slightest criticism . . . is apt to be interpreted erroneously," no matter how much good he might say about the man otherwise. Therefore he thought that if he ever completed a memoir he would not allow it to be published until "after I am pushing up daisies."[39]

On May 25, 1945, Eisenhower moved his headquarters to the I. G. Farben offices in Frankfurt. The buildings were untouched by Allied bombing, according to some stories because Eisenhower had wanted to save the complex for his own later use, according to others because of financial ties between the German and American chemical corporations, according to Eisenhower simply by accident. His office, the former board room, was huge; he said it "really should belong to a sultan or to a movie star."[40] He lived twelve miles away, in Bad Homburg, on a spacious estate. He complained that he was working harder than ever. He told Butcher that "the job of fighting a war was not so wearing in its irritations and frustrations" as the job of running the occupation.[41] His powers were not as clear-cut nor as complete as they had been, he was no longer making decisions but rather carrying out someone else's policies, his administrative problems were greater and more difficult, and—worst of all—he and his command were being subjected to criticism, some of it intense and quite bitter, which was something he was not accustomed to and did not like at all. Butcher had seen this coming; in his diary a week after the surrender he had predicted that "General Ike and his entire command are in for a rough time." German-based reporters, Butcher realized, would be in keen competition for space with the Pacific war; "consequently, only critical stories of General Ike and his policies in handling . . . the occupation of Germany will find space." Butcher therefore hoped "General Ike doesn't have to stay too long [because] his standing in the near future is likely to slump."[42]

The criticism began immediately. On May 13, Marshall cabled Eisenhower to say that the War Department was "being deluged with violent protests" over the "friendly manner in which Goering and other

Nazi leaders have been received." Conservative as well as radical and liberal newspapers were carrying angry editorials, all of them referring specifically to an incident on May 9, when a U.S. Army officer had his picture taken shaking hands with Goering and later ate a meal with the Reichsmarschall. As far back as September 1944, when U.S. troops had first reached Germany, Eisenhower had forbidden any fraternization, and had placed photographs of GIs and Germans together on the censored list. In response to the Goering story, he wired his senior commanders to repeat, in strong terms, his orders against fraternization. He said the Goering incident was "shocking" and added, "After the successful conclusion of this campaign I am not going to have the whole public effect ruined in America by such ill-advised actions on the part of any officer." He added that he was "intensely displeased that my orders on nonfraternization have been so flagrantly disobeyed."[43]

In taking such a tough stance, Eisenhower was expressing accurately the spirit of his operating instructions, which were contained in a document called JCS 1067 (Joint Chiefs of Staff Paper #1067), which had been sent to him on April 26. JCS 1067 was based on the assumption that all Germans were guilty, although some were more guilty than others. It forbade any fraternization between the occupying forces and the Germans. It called for the automatic arrest of large numbers of Germans who had participated in various Nazi organizations. It insisted on denazification, primarily by removing Nazis from public office or positions of importance in public and private enterprises. It told Eisenhower that he was, as head of the occupying force in the American zone, "clothed with supreme legislative, executive, and judicial authority," and said that his most basic responsibility was "to bring home to the Germans that Germany's ruthless warfare and the fanatical Nazi resistance have destroyed the German economy and made chaos and suffering inevitable and that the Germans cannot escape the responsibility for what they have brought upon themselves."[44]

It was an impossible policy to enforce, especially the parts about fraternization and the elimination of former Nazis from all positions of responsibility. Since the formation of NATO and West Germany's emergence as one of America's staunchest allies, JCS 1067 has been almost universally denounced, and indeed many Americans in 1945, led by General Patton, were already denouncing it. But Eisenhower believed in it and tried his best to enforce it. His hatred of the Germans was wide-ranging and ran very deep. He definitely wanted them punished, humiliated, made to pay. He blamed the Germans for starting the war and for prolonging it.

The American most closely associated with the demand for a "hard peace" was Henry Morgenthau, Jr., the Secretary of the Treasury. In the so-called "Morgenthau Plan," he advocated transforming Germany from an industrial to a pastoral state, by removing all her factories, settling factory workers on small farms carved out of the feudal estates of the Junkers, and partitioning Germany. Morgenthau set forth his ideas in a book entitled *Germany Is Our Problem,* which he published in 1945. In it, he said he had gotten his ideas from Eisenhower, in a conversation he held with the general in August of 1944. In October of 1945, Morgenthau sent Eisenhower a copy of his book; Eisenhower thanked him and said he intended to read it immediately.[45] One month later, Eisenhower approved the distribution of one thousand free copies of the book to American military officials in Germany. Eisenhower insisted that free distribution did not "constitute approval or disapproval of the views expressed."[46] There can be little doubt, however, that at that time, Eisenhower definitely did approve, just as there can be little doubt that in the August 1944 conversation, Eisenhower gave Morgenthau at least some of his ideas on the treatment of Germany. Eisenhower's letters to Mamie at that time contained such statements as, "The German is a beast," and "God, I hate the Germans!"[47]

But by 1947 he had softened in his attitude toward the Germans, partly as a result of his practical experiences as head of the occupation, partly because he had hardened in his attitude toward the Russians. He no longer wanted to be associated with the Morgenthau Plan. When the State Department undertook to write a history of U.S. policy in occupied Germany, it asked Eisenhower to comment on Morgenthau's assertion that Eisenhower was the real originator of the Morgenthau Plan. Eisenhower was emphatic in his reply: "I suggested no plan and never, to anyone, expressed the opinion that Germany should or could become a pastoral state." What he did admit he had said to Morgenthau in August of 1944 was, however, stern enough: "The German people must not be allowed to escape a personal sense of guilt . . . ; Germany's war making power should be eliminated." Certain groups should be punished by Allied tribunals, including leading Nazis, Gestapo and SS members. Eisenhower recalled insisting that the German General Staff be "utterly eliminated," but said he had also told Morgenthau that "in eliminating German war making ability, care should be taken to see that Germans could make a living, else they could become a charitable charge and . . . objects of world pity."[48]

Eisenhower's shifting views on Germany partly reflected the shift in public opinion, which in 1945 was intensely hostile, but which by mid-1947 had begun to swing toward Germany. Eisenhower's concern about public opinion showed in a June 2, 1945, letter to Marshall about fraternization. He said it was almost impossible to enforce the nonfraternization rules in the case of small children, and he of course recognized that it was simply silly to forbid soldiers to talk to or give candy bars or chewing gum to German children.[49] Finally, in July, official orders on nonfraternization were amended to include the phrase "except small children." Ultimately the nonfraternization policy became a major embarrassment and was quietly dropped.

Denazification, however, was pursued with sustained vigor, and with the enthusiastic backing of General Eisenhower. His insistence on its application, in fact, was so strong that it led to a breakup of his friendship with Patton.

In Eisenhower's view, if it was a mistake to regard all Germans as guilty, it was certainly correct to regard all Nazis as guilty. In a series of general orders, he directed that no one who had ever been associated with the Nazi party be allowed to hold any position of importance in the American zone. His subordinates in the field complained that the policy was unrealistic. Patton, in command in Bavaria, was the most outspoken. On August 11, he wrote Eisenhower that "a great many inexperienced or inefficient people" were holding positions in local government as a result of the so-called de-Nazification program." Patton said that "it is no more possible for a man to be a civil servant in Germany and not have paid lip service to Nazism than it is possible for a man to be a postmaster in America and not have paid at least lip service to the Democratic Party, or the Republican Party when it is in power." He reminded Eisenhower of the Darlan Deal and AFHQ's close association with the Vichy French in North Africa, and recommended that Eisenhower follow the same collaborationist policy in Germany.

In the meantime, Patton continued to use Nazis to run Bavaria. On September 11, Eisenhower wrote Patton a letter that was designed to set him straight on the issue. "Reduced to its fundamentals," Eisenhower told Patton, "the United States entered this war as a foe of Nazism; victory is not complete until we have eliminated from positions of responsibility and, in appropriate cases properly punished, every active adherent to the Nazi party." He insisted that "we will not compromise with Nazism in any way . . . The discussional stage of this question is long past . . . I expect just as loyal service in the execution of this policy . . . as I received during the war."[50] Eisenhower followed up the letter with a personal visit to Patton to emphasize his concern. He said he wanted to extend denazification to cover the whole of German life, not just public positions. But Eisenhower could not convince Patton; as he reported to Marshall, "The fact is that his own convictions are not entirely in sympathy with the 'hard peace' concept and, being Patton, he cannot keep his mouth shut either to his own subordinates or in public."[51] Patton was trying his best to stifle himself. "I hope you know, Ike, that I'm keeping my mouth shut," he protested. "I'm a clam."[52] But he opened up on September 22, at a press conference. A reporter asked him why reactionaries were still in power in Bavaria. "Reactionaries!" Patton exploded. "Do you want a lot of communists?" After a pause, he said, "I don't know anything about parties. . . . The Nazi thing is just like a Democratic and Republican election fight."[53]

The remark caused a sensation. Eisenhower ordered Patton to report to him in Frankfurt. Patton did so. On the day he arrived, Kay recalled, "General Eisenhower came in looking as though he hadn't slept a wink. I knew at once he had decided to take action against his old friend. He had aged ten years in reaching the decision . . . When General Patton came in, followed by Beetle, the office door closed. But I heard one of the stormiest sessions ever staged in our headquarters. It was the first time I ever heard General Eisenhower really raise his voice."[54]

Eisenhower tried to convince Patton that denazification was essential to the making of a new Germany. Patton tried to convince Eisenhower that the Red Army was the real threat and that the Germans were the real friends. Red-faced, furious, shouting, dealing with the most basic issues, the two old friends reached an impasse. Eisenhower was almost horrified by some of Patton's views on the Russians, and by his loose talk about driving the Red Army back to the Volga. He later told his son that he would have to remove Patton "not for what he's done—just for what he's going to do next." Eisenhower and Patton parted in cold silence. The next day, Eisenhower relieved Patton as commander of the Third Army and put him in a paper command, head of a Theater Board studying lessons from the war.[55] According to one of his biographers, as Patton reflected on the disintegration of his friendship with Eisenhower, he "believed he saw the truth of Henry Adams' phrase that a friend in power is a friend lost."[56]

Eisenhower put Lucian Truscott in Patton's place. Before Truscott left for Bavaria, Eisenhower called him into his office and told him that the "most acute and important problems . . . were those involving denazification and the handling of those unfortunate persons who had been the victims of Nazi persecution." Eisenhower told Truscott to be "stern" toward the Nazis and to give preferential treatment to Jewish displaced persons.[57]

Eisenhower, meanwhile, on October 12, had held a press conference in Frankfurt. *The New York Times* reported that he spoke "emphatically, and at times bitterly about the Nazis" and insisted that denazification was being carried out. And it certainly was true that the arrest, trial, and punishment of former Nazis went much further in the American zone than in any of the other three zones. The Americans brought charges against some three million Germans, actually tried two million of them, and punished nearly one million.[58]

In late July, Eisenhower went to Berlin, where the President, the Secretary of State, and other officials had gathered for the Potsdam Conference. Eisenhower was an outsider at that conference. His views were unsolicited and, when put forward anyway, ignored. He urged Truman to take the Army out of the job of running the American zone and turn it over to the State Department, but was turned down. He told Truman that the United States should not encourage Russia to go to war with Japan, because it would revive old Russian claims to Far Eastern territory. And he told Truman that "rehabilitation of the Ruhr was vital to our best interests"; Truman should not therefore agree to a program of dismantling German industry.

The last point represented a shift in Eisenhower's thinking, away from a vindictive peace and toward a policy of realism with regard to European economics. The shift reflected the influence of General Lucius D. Clay on Eisenhower's thinking. Clay was Eisenhower's deputy as military governor. He had been at West Point with Eisenhower and they had served together in the Philippines. Eisenhower had a high regard for Clay's administrative abilities and had consequently delegated most of the economic, financial, and political problems of the occupation to him. Clay had been working quietly but effectively to undermine the JCS 1067 clauses that tended in the direction of the Morgenthau Plan.[59] In many long talks with Eisenhower, he convinced Eisenhower that for Europe to recover from the war, there had to be a German recovery, which in turn had to be based on a revival of the Ruhr, because only in the Ruhr could enough coal be produced to meet Europe's immediate needs. Eisenhower pointed all this out to Truman, but the President nevertheless signed the Potsdam Declaration, which called for definite limits on German production and the actual destruction of much of German industrial capacity. Clay thought the policy absolute madness.

There was one additional matter on which Eisenhower gave Truman advice and was ignored. It concerned the use of the atomic bomb.

Eisenhower first heard of the bomb during the Potsdam Conference; from that moment on, until his death, it occupied, along with the Russians, a central position in his thinking. All his military policies and decisions from then on revolved around the existence of the bomb, which in addition had a major impact on his thinking about American relations with the Soviet Union.

Secretary of War Henry L. Stimson first told Eisenhower of the bomb's existence. As the Secretary explained the weapon, Eisenhower was engulfed by a "feeling of depression." When Stimson said the United States proposed to use the bomb against Japan, Eisenhower voiced ". . . my grave misgivings, first on the basis of my belief that Japan was already defeated and that dropping the bomb was completely unnecessary, and secondly because I thought that our country should avoid shocking world opinion by the use of [atomic weapons]." Stimson was upset by Eisenhower's attitude, "almost angrily refuting the reasons I gave for my quick conclusions."[60] Three days later, on July 20, Eisenhower flew to Berlin, where he met with Truman and his principal advisers. Again Eisenhower recommended against using the bomb, and again was ignored.[61]

The bomb only added to and did not create Eisenhower's depression. All around him, in Frankfurt, in Berlin, in his trips through Germany and Europe, he saw the horrible destruction of war. Germany was pulverized almost beyond belief or repair. "The country is devastated," he told Mamie. "Whole cities are obliterated; and the German population, to say nothing of millions of former slave laborers, is largely homeless."[62] His inspection trips to German cities, to former concentration camps, to current displaced persons' camps, and his practical and immediate responsibility for handling the problems involved gave him an awareness of the consequences of war that caused him to swear to himself "never again." He told Mamie, "I hope another American shell never has to be fired in Europe," while to a friend he said, "Certainly Germany should not want to see any more high explosives for the next hundred years; I am quite sure that some of the cities will never be re-built."[63]

Worst damaged of all the nations of Europe was Russia. If Eisenhower had doubted that anything could compare to Germany, he learned better in August, when he flew from Berlin to Moscow, at only a few hundred feet of altitude. He did not see a single house standing intact from the Russian-Polish border to Moscow. Not one.[64]

The atomic bomb, then, only reinforced his conviction that war had become too terrible to ever again be a viable option. He hated to hear talk about the "next war" and would not allow his staff or subordinates to indulge in it. This was the major reason he was so furious with Patton, whose irresponsible talk about driving the Red Army beyond the Volga appalled Eisenhower.

Peace, Eisenhower knew, depended above all on Soviet-American relations. As he explained to Henry Wallace in the summer of 1945, in response to a letter from Wallace congratulating him on his success in getting along with the Russians in Germany, "So far as a soldier should have opinions about such things, I am convinced that friendship—which means an honest desire on both sides to strive for mutual understanding—between Russia and the United States is absolutely essential to world tranquility."[65] When a reporter asked him at a June press conference about a possible "Russo-American war," Eisenhower's face went red with his anger. He insisted sharply that there was no possibility of such a war. "The peace lies, when you get down to it, with all the peoples of the world," he explained, and "not just . . . with some political leader . . . If all the peoples are friendly, we are going to have peace. . . . I have found the individual Russian one of the friendliest persons in the world."[66]

It was a theme he would repeat over and over, in speeches, at congressional hearings, in his private letters, in conversation. He was not so naïve as to think that friendliness would eliminate the manifold difficulties facing the U.S.-U.S.S.R. relationship, but he was sure that there would be no success without a generally friendly and trusting spirit, while "the alternative to success seemed so terrifying to contemplate" that he insisted on approaching the Russians on the basis of friendship and trust. He hoped that in his contacts and dealings with the Russians in Berlin, where the two nations had to work together, he could establish a "spirit [that would] spread beyond Germany to our own capitals." If that could be done, "we could eventually live together as friends and ultimately work together in world partnership."[67] He also recognized that a major obstacle would be Russian suspicion and distrust of the United States. He made it a personal goal to do everything he could to alleviate that suspicion and distrust.

What the Russians were most afraid of, he knew, was the development of a German-American anti-Soviet alliance. On May 8, the day after the surrender at Reims, Eisenhower informed Marshall that arrangements had been made for another ceremony (demanded by the Russians) in Berlin, which "relieves my mind of the anxiety that I have had due to the danger of misunderstandings. This anxiety has been intensified by a very skillful German propaganda that was inspired by the German desire to surrender to us."[68]

On May 10, the Russians complained to Eisenhower that the Germans on the Eastern Front were still fighting the Red Army in order to surrender to the Americans. Eisenhower responded by ordering his commanders to hand over to the Soviets any German soldiers who tried to escape from the Russian zone. He also ordered Field Marshals Keitel and Kesselring and Generals Jodl and Warlimont placed under arrest for violating the Act of Capitulation.[69] A somewhat similar problem concerned the almost two million Soviet citizens in the American zone. Some were Red Army POWs, some slave laborers deported from the U.S.S.R., some political refugees, some Russian Jews. None wanted to go back to their homeland. The Russians wanted them all repatriated, and at Yalta the Western powers had agreed to do so. Eisenhower was scrupulous in living up to that agreement. By the late summer of 1945, almost 99 percent of the two million Soviet citizens had been forced to go home.[70]

The most vexing problem in the immediate aftermath of the war was with the zones of occupation. Eisenhower's troops had penetrated well into the zone assigned to the Soviets, and continued to occupy it. The Red Army, in turn, had taken all of Berlin, and continued to hold it, although half the city had been assigned to the Western powers. The Russians wanted the Americans to withdraw from their zone, while the Americans wanted to get their troops into Berlin. There was a similar problem along the Yugoslav-Italian border, where Tito refused to pull back from Trieste. There was talk in the West about getting tough, and it was not limited to hotheads like Patton. Churchill was indulging himself in the thought of driving Tito, and possibly even the Red Army, eastward, and Truman had told Marshall that "there is a limit to how far we can go in tolerating" Russian and Yugoslav aggression. Eisenhower recoiled from such "depressing possibilities." On May 17, he told Marshall, "I simply cannot believe, in view of tremendous efforts made by Russia during the past four years, that she would welcome any major trial of strength."[71] When the Russians asked him to pull American troops back from their forward positions and turn over to the Red Army its agreed zone of occupation, Churchill, Smith, Clay, and Patton all protested. They urged Eisenhower to hold on and to use possession of the area to force the Russians to make concessions elsewhere, especially in Austria. Eisenhower's attitude was "that to start off our first direct association with Russia on the basis of refusing to carry out an arrangement [on occupation zones] in which the good faith of our government was involved would wreck the whole co-operative attempt at its very beginning."[72]

On June 5, Eisenhower went to Berlin to meet with the Russians and to establish the Allied Control Council. He immediately struck up a warm friendship with Marshal Grigori Zhukov. Despite the language barrier, the two soldiers got on famously. They respected each other and enjoyed talking about professional matters, political philosophy, and indeed a wide range of subjects. They also found they could work together and quickly reached an agreement whereby the United States troops pulled out of the Russian zone, while the Western powers sent their forces into Berlin.

Over the weeks that followed, Eisenhower and Zhukov were often together. They studied each other's campaigns, and their admiration one for the other grew apace. Eisenhower told Montgomery that Zhukov "was in a class by himself . . . His narrative of his campaigns (and he was always at the critical point) coupled with his statement of reasons for each action that he took, including his exploitation of weapons and arms in which he had a superiority, his concern for weather, and his care in providing fully for administration before he delivered his blow, all added up to making him a standout."[73] When Zhukov came to Frankfurt for a visit, Eisenhower hosted an elaborate dinner. In a long and flattering toast to Zhukov ("To no one man do the United Nations owe a greater debt than to Marshal Zhukov"), Eisenhower said that what they both wanted was peace, and they wanted it so badly that "we are going to have peace if we have to fight for it." "This war was a holy war," he added, "more than any other in history this war has been an array of the forces of evil against those of righteousness."[74]

Stalin too wanted to meet Eisenhower. He told Harry Hopkins in late May that he hoped Eisenhower could come to Moscow on June 24 for the victory parade. Averell Harriman, the U.S. ambassador to Moscow, urged Eisenhower to accept and said there was "*no* doubt that Stalin was anxious to have him."[75] Eisenhower could not make it for the victory parade, but in August he did fly to Moscow, accompanied by Zhukov, who stayed with him throughout his trip. It was a triumphal march, although the devastation everywhere was depressing. Eisenhower saw most of the sights—the Kremlin, the subway, a collective farm, a tractor factory, etc. He attended a soccer game and delighted the crowd by throwing his arm around Zhukov's shoulder. At a sports parade in Red Square, which lasted for hours and involved tens of thousands of athletes, Eisenhower was invited by Stalin to stand on Lenin's Tomb, a unique honor for a non-Communist and non-Russian. Another unique honor came when Stalin apologized to him for the actions of the Red Army in April 1945, when it advanced toward Berlin rather than toward Dresden, as Stalin had told Eisenhower it would. As Eisenhower reported to Marshall, "Stalin explained in detail the military reasons for the last-minute change but said that I had the right to charge him with lack of frankness and this he would not want me to believe."[76]

Eisenhower made a strong impression on Stalin. The Russian dictator talked to him at great length, emphasizing how badly the Soviet Union needed American help in recovering from the war. He said that the Russians realized they needed not only American money, but American technicians and scientific assistance.[77] Eisenhower's sympathetic response was much appreciated by Stalin. When Eisenhower left, Stalin told Harriman, "General Eisenhower is a very great man, not only because of his military accomplishments but because of his human, friendly, kind and frank nature. He is *not* a 'grubi' [coarse, brusque] man like most military."[78]

Eisenhower was in his turn impressed by Stalin. He told a *New York Times* correspondent that Stalin was "benign and fatherly," and that he sensed "a genuine atmosphere of hospitality." At a press conference in Moscow, he declared, "I see nothing in the future that would prevent Russia and the United States from being the closest possible friends." But while he was in Moscow, two atomic bombs were dropped on Japan, and suddenly he did see an immediate danger to friendly relations. "Before the atom bomb was used," he told a journalist, "I would have said yes, I was sure we could keep the peace with Russia. Now, I don't know. I had hoped the bomb wouldn't figure in this war. . . . People are frightened and disturbed all over. Everyone feels insecure again."[79]

Shortly after Eisenhower returned to Frankfurt from Moscow, Marshall pressed Truman once again on the matter of his retirement. Truman had been unwilling to let Marshall go, but with the Japanese surrender in hand, the Chief of Staff became more insistent. Marshall wanted Eisenhower to replace him, and he wanted it done soon, and he had a reason that went beyond his own desire for some rest and relaxation. Marshall told Truman that Eisenhower's reputation could only suffer in the job of head of the military occupation. Marshall sent a copy of the letter to Eisenhower, and in a covering note said he hoped to be relieved early in September. Eisenhower replied that he did not want to succeed Marshall: "The most 'suitable' position for me is unquestionably a remotely situated cottage in a state of permanent retirement . . . Nothing is so near my heart's desire as to let someone else have both the headaches and the headlines." However, he added, "at the risk of appearing stuffy, I say again that I am willing to attempt anything that my superiors may direct. This, however, has nothing to do with personal desire." He would, in short, do his duty.[80]

In late October, Truman finally agreed to Marshall's retirement as Chief of Staff (although the President exacted a price—he persuaded Marshall to head a special mission to China). Eisenhower prepared to leave Germany to take up his new post in the Pentagon. Before departing, he made a trip by night train, followed by a long automobile ride, to Berlin. His sole purpose was to see Zhukov one last time. They spent a day and an evening together, talking about their various concerns. They managed to settle a number of small, but irritating, problems, such as air corridors and land routes to Berlin, and exchange of press representatives.

Then Zhukov turned to a crucial matter, reparations. The victors had agreed and announced in the Potsdam Declaration that the primary purpose of reparations was to destroy Germany's war potential, and that this would be accomplished by removing entire factories from Germany and shipping them to Russia. The Soviets, Zhukov said, had submitted a list of the factories they wanted to General Clay, but none had yet been dismantled, much less shipped to Russia. The reason was, as Eisenhower knew, that Clay wanted to keep the factories where they were, in order to get a German revival started, and thus to improve the German standard of living. Zhukov spoke to Eisenhower "rather earnestly, almost plaintively," about American concern with the living standards in France, Belgium, Holland, and "even Germany." Why, he wondered, had no American "spoken up to talk of the living standards in Russia." Eisenhower said it was because no American reporters were allowed to travel in Russia, and thus no one in the West knew what the Russian situation was. Zhukov said that "Russia would never place itself in the position of begging," but he wanted Eisenhower to know that "the standard of living in Russia today was deplorably low" and in fact worse than it was in Germany. Eisenhower was deeply moved by Zhukov's attitude, demeanor, and words. He sent a long, detailed memorandum to Clay, telling Clay to "move instantly to meet the Russians always at least half way." A few days later, Clay reported, "We were able to give Zhukov the plants he desired," which "pleased Zhukov immensely as it evidenced your good faith."[81]

• •

On November 11, 1945, Eisenhower flew to Washington. He appeared before the Senate Committee on Military Affairs, then took a train ride with Mamie to Boone, Iowa, to visit her relatives there. Scarcely had they arrived when Mamie was rushed to a hospital suffering from bronchial pneumonia. A few days later Eisenhower, after being assured that she was "on the road to recovery," returned to Washington and to more appearances before congressional committees. On November 20, Truman accepted Marshall's resignation as Chief of Staff and appointed Eisenhower in his place. Eisenhower, meanwhile, came down with a "speaker's throat," as he called it; in fact he too had bronchial pneumonia. Nevertheless, he forced himself to fly to Chicago to speak before the American Legion on the subject of postwar defense, then returned to Washington and more testifying. On November 22, the doctors put him into the hospital, at White Sulphur Springs. He stayed there for nearly two weeks. He came out on December 3, on which date he took up his duties as Chief of Staff. As he told Swede Hazlett, in a letter dictated while he was in the hospital, "The job I am taking now represents nothing but straight duty." [82]

CHAPTER TWENTY-TWO

Washington

December 1945–May 1947

IF BEING THE HEAD of an occupation force in Germany had been a thankless and unwelcome task, being Chief of Staff of the U.S. Army as it demobilized was worse. Eisenhower anticipated, correctly, interminable battles with the other members of the Joint Chiefs of Staff over the issues of universal military training and unification of the armed services, and battles with Congress over the issues of demobilization and the size and strength of the postwar Army. He entered these conflicts not as a supreme commander with a single overriding goal, but as one among equals in power within the JCS, and as a supplicant in his dealings with Congress. On every major front, he was forced to give way or give in; the contrast between the total victory he had just won in Germany and the agonizing struggles and compromises and retreats he would have to endure as Chief of Staff was complete.[1] Small wonder that shortly after taking up his duties he could write his son, John, that the Pentagon "was a sorry place to light after having commanded a theater of war."[2]

A major difficulty was the enormous amount of inescapable paper work. Millions of young men had to be brought home and discharged, while nearly every senior officer in the Regular Army had to face a reduction in rank and adjust to a new, peacetime world in which the Army had to squeeze every penny. The volume of mail addressed to the Chief of Staff on these and other subjects was overwhelming. Eisenhower wrote Smith on December 4, "I must say that in four rather busy war years, the last three days have been by far the worst."[3] A special problem for Eisenhower was his conscience—initially he tried to read every letter addressed to him. That proved to be physically impossible, so he had his staff summarize each letter. These summaries were typed on long sheets and brought to him first thing in the morning. He had the staff check each case before drafting an answer, to make certain of the facts;[4] he then read over the draft and, in about 20 percent of the cases, changed it to add a personal touch. He then signed the finished product. On the average, he signed more than a thousand letters a week.

In the first year that he was Chief of Staff, much of this correspondence concerned demobilization. The point system General Marshall had created (a man got points for length of service, for combat, for overseas duty, etc.) to govern eligibility for discharge seemed fair, but it caused Eisenhower terrific headaches, as every wife or mother or sweetheart in the country thought that her private was being cheated. Many of them wrote directly to Eisenhower; a typical plea would conclude, "*Please,* won't *you* do something about this?" Anyone who glances through the thousands of such letters cannot help being struck by the faith that nearly all the correspondents had in Eisenhower. Few if any of them trusted the Army, but they were certain that if Eisenhower himself were aware of the situation, *he* would certainly do something about it. The notable thing about their attitude was that they were right; if Eisenhower was convinced that an injustice had been done, he would correct it. In the process he got deeply involved in petty detail, something he warned others about but could not bring himself to avoid.[5]

Eventually, as his new staff came to know him and his expressions and his probable reactions better, he allowed the young officers to handle more of his correspondence. But there was a price to be paid for that system too. Every letter that came to him was opened and read by the staff; he had no genuinely private correspondence at all. When an old Army friend wrote that her husband was leaving her, Eisenhower was chagrined that a staff officer read her letter before it came to him. In making a profuse apology, Eisenhower declared that "my greatest longing seems to be for some kind of personal life." He said he knew that many officers envied him because of his job, but "they never stop to think" that in his position "the individual tends to become public property."[6] The lack of privacy extended to all phases of his existence. Every phone call that he made or received, for example, was monitored from beginning to end and recorded in a stenographer's notebook.[7]

Fortunately, he had an excellent staff to help him. His wartime family—Butch, Kay, Lee, and the others—was scattered, but a new one gathered around him. Major Craig Cannon, boyish in appearance and manner, was as efficient as Lee in running the office and supervising the secretaries; Major Robert L. Schulz, a rotund little career officer, handled all travel arrangements, Eisenhower's personal finances, and his daily schedule; Major Kevin McCann, a tall, thin officer with experience in journalism, advised him on public relations and helped write his speeches. Two men were carry-overs from the war: Sergeant Leonard Dry, who was Eisenhower's driver for twenty years, from 1942 to 1962, and Sergeant John Moaney, who was Eisenhower's personal valet and who was with Eisenhower every day for twenty-seven years.

He needed all the help he could get, because of the great demands on his time. Every organization in America, it sometimes seemed, wanted him as the principal speaker at its annual meeting, while every congressional committee that had the remotest connection with the War Department wanted the Chief of Staff to testify before it, thus giving the politicians an opportunity to have their picture taken with Eisenhower. In his first year as Chief of Staff, Eisenhower made forty-six major speeches to national organizations, or nearly one per week. He testified before Congress on thirteen occasions. In his second year, 1947, the figures were a little less—thirty and twelve. On the average, he received six invitations a day, from churches, universities, colleges, charitable and cultural associations, veterans groups, etc. For every invitation he accepted, he had to turn down almost forty. Nearly all the causes were good ones, and he confessed to his diary, "I feel a sense of guilt when I decline." His basic rule was to accept only those "where the staff insists that the welfare of the Army is involved." [8]

The feeling that as the head of the Army it was his duty to speak in its behalf dictated the theme of most of his speeches. They usually centered on the need for universal military training, or for unification of the armed forces, or for a more orderly demobilization and the continuation of selective service. On these issues, he had nothing original to say; rather, he followed the War Department line, a line that had been established by Marshall and which Eisenhower accepted unquestioningly. But no matter how derivative his point, Eisenhower made it with sufficient vigor and sincerity to impress his audience. He spoke so sincerely because he felt so deeply: "I so firmly believe we should all do our part to reawaken in our country a realization of our own blessings and what we have to do to protect them," he wrote in his diary, that he just had to speak to organizations that had "a similar purpose." [9]

He was most impressive in expressing his genuine desire for peace.

His call for a strong Army was based on his belief that American strength was necessary to keep the peace. Unlike some generals, he did not base his argument for the Army on war-scare tactics. To the contrary, he consistently condemned anything that hinted of warmongering, and he deplored talk about an inevitable conflict between Russia and the United States. In one of his first speeches as Chief of Staff, at Boston University in January 1946, he called on educators "to teach people to put the people of my profession out of a job," and he urged that students be taught that "understanding is something worthwhile, that it is greater than prejudice, that international differences are not so great that you can't resolve them."[10] His delivery was such that he could make the most commonplace utterance sound fresh and insightful. As one among innumerable examples, at the 1947 University of Pennsylvania commencement he declared, "We cannot face the future with blank despair and by stewing in pessimism." So welcome was this sage advice that *The New York Times* featured it the next day.[11]

The American public loved to hear him speak, and the content and delivery of his speeches could not have done more to add to his luster. The more often he spoke, the more the invitations poured in. He tried to hold his appearances down to a minimum; to one prominent congressman, over the telephone, he said, "Talking Generals are not a very good thing for our country," and begged to be excused.[12] In 1946, he told P. A. Hodgson, "I have always hated talking Generals—I can't understand why there is so much pressure put upon me to appear at every kind of gathering to put some more useless words on the air or over the dinner table."[13] But the requests kept coming, and he could not say no to all of them. When Gettysburg College asked him to speak in 1946, for example, he felt "impelled to accept," because the college had provided him with living quarters in 1918 when he commanded Camp Colt.[14] Financial inducements, on the other hand, he always scorned. When one state educational association offered him $1,000 as a speaking fee, he replied stiffly: "It has been my invariable practice to refuse any honorarium in fulfilling any engagement of this kind and I shall most certainly adhere to that policy as long as I occupy any type of public office."[15]

The speeches brought Eisenhower in contact with some of America's richest and most powerful men. Usually the invitations came from the chairman of the board of directors of the various universities or cultural organizations; that chairman (or whatever his title) was typically a wealthy businessman. Like most Americans, these businessmen found

Eisenhower's charm and fame irresistible; unlike the average citizen, they were in a position to get to meet and know him. A few had ulterior motives, a desire to manipulate the general for their own purposes, but most were simply hero-worshipers.

The elite of the Eastern Establishment moved in on him almost before he occupied his new office. Thomas J. Watson of IBM, for example, came to the Pentagon in early March 1946 to meet the general and insist that he speak at the Metropolitan Museum of Art in New York. The heads of other great corporations in New York all had their pet project too, and used their position in the organization or university for their initial access to Eisenhower. He had known almost none of America's business leaders before the war; he had met a few of them during the war; by 1947, he had met or at least corresponded with hundreds of them, including a high percentage of the one hundred richest and most powerful. Many became close personal friends. When Eisenhower and Mamie had last lived in Washington, twenty years earlier, their social life revolved around other obscure Army officers and their wives. From 1946 to 1948, however, their social life included almost no Army personnel; instead they spent their evenings and vacation time with Eisenhower's new, wealthy friends. When they played bridge in the thirties, it was with other majors and their wives; in the forties, it was with the president of CBS, or the chairman of the board of U.S. Steel, or the president of Standard Oil. Averell Harriman and Ely Culbertson were also participants.[16]

Eisenhower's relationships with wealthy men grew steadily from 1946 onward, to the point that his friends were almost exclusively millionaires. The effect of these relationships on Eisenhower is a matter of some dispute; his critics charge that they gave him a millionaire's view of the world and made him staunchly conservative on fiscal and other issues. According to the charge, Eisenhower was overly impressed by rich men, even a bit in awe of them. The truth was, however, more the other way around—the millionaires were awestruck by the general. For his part, Eisenhower enjoyed being with men who had proved themselves, who thought big, who had handled big problems successfully, who knew how to organize and produce, who exuded self-confidence. He also enjoyed what they could give him.

Not money—he never took money from any of his rich friends. But he would accept the use of a cottage in the north woods, or a fishing camp or hunting lodge in the Deep South, and did so often. In 1946, for example, Cason Callaway, a director of U.S. Steel and one of the largest cotton growers in the world, along with Robert Woodruff, chairman of the Coca-Cola Company, entertained Eisenhower at Callaway's Georgia plantation. The lake was well stocked; the three men caught more than two hundred largemouth bass in an afternoon. The quail hunting was also excellent.[17] The pattern lasted for the remainder of Eisenhower's life. He went hunting and fishing frequently, and it was always at the top spots in the country, in the finest conditions that money could buy. So too with his passion for golf—he could indulge it on exclusively top-quality courses. Shortly after he became Chief of Staff, Chevy Chase Club made him a member; other exclusive clubs, in New York, Georgia, and elsewhere, did too. On an income of about $15,000 per year, Eisenhower was able to enjoy, on a regular basis, recreation ordinarily reserved only for the very wealthy.

The Eisenhowers' living quarters, too, were the best they had ever had. They occupied Quarters No. One at Fort Myer, in the house Marshall had lived in and, before him, MacArthur. It was a large, sprawling, old brick house, with ample room to absorb all Mamie's furniture and a steady stream of house guests. The grounds were large too, and the Eisenhowers inherited from the Marshalls a chicken flock consisting of three roosters and two dozen Plymouth Rock hens. Eisenhower was delighted to have them—caring for the birds brought out the farmer in him—but soon tragedy struck. In June 1946, Eisenhower began a long letter to Marshall (who was in China), "This is a message of disappointment and disaster. It involves the chickens." First a rooster had died; then two of the hens; eventually half the flock was gone. Eisenhower called in a veterinarian, built a new coop, added vitamins to the feed, and tried other solutions, but to his dismay the chickens kept dying. Marshall took the news with a soldierly fortitude: "Don't worry about those hens," he replied. "Dispose of them if they are a care and a burden."[18]

For the first time in twenty years, Eisenhower had a piece of land he could dig up and plant, which he did with gusto. He went right to the top for his seeds. In 1946 they came from Henry Wallace, who was a famous plant geneticist before he became Secretary of Agriculture, and in 1947 from W. Atlee Burpee himself. He concentrated on corn, tomatoes, and peas for himself, with petunias for Mamie (Burpee named a new strain of petunia the "Mrs. Dwight D. Eisenhower"). Both years he was so anxious to get started that he planted his garden in mid-March, then had to replant after a late freeze.[19]

He and Mamie were getting along better than ever. They did a great deal of traveling together—they visited every state while he was

Chief of Staff—and he loved it, despite his complaints about his brutal schedule, because Mamie went with him. Her doctors had decided that she could be allowed to fly, if the pilot stayed below five thousand feet. They went on a number of overseas journeys, as foreign governments were just as anxious to have Eisenhower as a guest and speaker as were American universities. In 1946 alone, they visited Hawaii, Guam, the Philippines, Japan, China, Korea, Brazil, Panama, Mexico, Germany, Italy, Scotland, and England. When they returned from Brazil, Eisenhower told his son that "once we had to go up to 17,500 feet. Mamie used her oxygen mask very religiously . . . and is quite proud of herself. She is now counting the number of hours she has had in the air. I think they total about 80." The Latin Americans embarrassed Eisenhower by the number and quality of the gifts they gave him; he told his father-in-law, "I cannot imagine where we can even store some of the silver . . . Of course I am always for giving these things instantly to some museum or public institution that might have use for them. Mamie is always on the other side, since she continues to think of John's future children and so on."[20] (Nearly all such gifts ended up in the Eisenhower Museum in Abilene.)

At Quarters No. One, the Eisenhowers usually had house guests, including Mamie's parents, other relatives, and various political, business, and military leaders. Mamie was putting on weight, was up to 130 pounds. In late 1946, Eisenhower told P. A. Hodgson, "Mamie is in better health than I have ever known her to be. The only difficulty is that she has outgrown all her clothes. This is a tragedy for her."[21] A year later, she still worried about her weight and wardrobe, while her husband was still delighted by her good health. Eisenhower told P. A. that "I have been urging her to fulfill a long-held ambition, namely to buy herself a good fur coat." She agonized over the choice between a dark ranch-bred mink and a lighter wild mink, which cost twice as much. She eventually chose the cheaper coat.[22]

Eisenhower's own health was excellent too. In December 1946, he took a month at the Pratt General Hospital, in Coral Gables, Florida, where he underwent daily X-ray treatments for persistent bursitis in his left arm. The therapy included golf and fishing. Eisenhower especially enjoyed the challenge of bone fishing in the salt-water flats, the ultimate test of a fisherman. An aide reported, "After only one week, the General has shown signs which are sufficient reward to those who are devoted to him. He looks rested and is clear-eyed and tanned." His arm improved under the treatment, and Eisenhower told Beetle Smith, "I feel better than I have in many months. I am more refreshed and generally in better tone than I have been since the shooting stopped."[23] A year later, he told Smith that a checkup at Walter Reed resulted in a "very good verdict. My 'ringing' ear bothers the doctors a lot and of course my tendency to run up a bit of blood pressure when I get angry or irritated causes them to shake their heads. Aside from these things they seem to think that for an old fellow I am plugging along pretty well."[24] Photographs taken while he was Chief of Staff attest to his good spirits and trim and athletic appearance. The tension that so often showed in his eyes, his face, and his body movements during the war was replaced by a relaxed look and carriage.

John was stationed in Vienna, giving Eisenhower and Mamie a good reason for a European tour, which they took in the fall of 1946, with John along for much of the trip.[25] While they were touring together, John indicated that he was thinking about resigning his commission. When he returned to Fort Myer, Eisenhower assured his son that "you must make your own decisions in this regard," but did point out that so long as he was Chief of Staff "we would have a difficult time explaining your resignation. Personally I would want to talk it over with you at length before you took any such step."[26] When John indicated that, like almost everyone else involved, he was finding occupation duty boring and a waste of time, Eisenhower shot back some stern advice: "An officer should avoid any expression of dissatisfaction or indication of unhappiness because this invariably gives him a bad reputation . . . Everybody recoils from a whiner."[27] John stayed in the Army and stopped complaining.

John was one of the most junior officers in the Army; the most senior officer was a former resident of Quarters No. One and, for seven years, Eisenhower's boss. When Eisenhower became Chief of Staff, he technically became Douglas MacArthur's superior officer. It was, inevitably, an awkward situation for both men; they managed it by remaining, generally, at arm's length. But because MacArthur commanded the Army's second-largest overseas contingent, and was in addition the virtual U.S. satrap in Japan, some contact was necessary.

MacArthur still had his old ability to make Eisenhower go purple with rage, then leave him smoldering because there was nothing Eisenhower could do about the situation. In the fall of 1945, at a time when the Administration was attempting to ease the pressure for demobilization by emphasizing the manpower requirements of occupation duty in Germany and Japan, MacArthur undercut Washington's position by announcing that the American force in Japan could be reduced to

200,000 men within six months. This was less than half the contingent the War Department had said was necessary, so MacArthur's announcement sharply increased the pressure to speed up demobilization. Eisenhower wrote a carefully worded letter to MacArthur, outlining his manpower problems and asking for an estimate of what MacArthur's true needs would be in 1947. Amazingly, MacArthur—in a top-secret reply—said he could not possibly go below 400,000.[28] One month later, in January 1946, Truman—at Eisenhower's urging—announced that he was reducing the rate of discharge from 700,000 to 300,000 per month and abandoning the pledge to release everyone with two years' service. The immediate result was a near mutiny by American troops in Europe, the Pacific, and within the United States. MacArthur again undercut his superiors when he announced that he was speeding up the discharge rate in his theater and challenged Secretary of War Robert Patterson's statement that rapid demobilization would have an adverse effect on occupation policy.[29]

Throughout the crisis, MacArthur paid no attention whatsoever to the Chief of Staff or to Patterson, and issued his own statements without clearing them. Eisenhower wrote a four-page, single-spaced letter in which he attempted to explain the War Department position and its problems without directly accusing MacArthur of sabotage. Eisenhower spoke of the "undesirable and disagreeable results" that would come about because of a too-rapid demobilization, explained the need to make deep cuts in manpower allotments, reassured MacArthur of his own support ("Have no fear that I will battle to the death for you"), and said he was planning an early trip to Japan for a personal conference.[30]

On May 10, 1946, Eisenhower flew to Tokyo. MacArthur met him at the airport, the first time they had seen each other since their parting at the Manila docks in December 1939. Eisenhower, grinning and sticking out his hand, opened the conversation: "Well, Mac, how are you?" That evening MacArthur hosted a dinner in Eisenhower's honor. "Quick as dinner was over," Eisenhower later recalled, MacArthur said good night to the other guests "and took me and we sat in his library till about one o'clock." MacArthur told Eisenhower he *had* to run for the Presidency. Eisenhower shook his head. "You do it," he rejoined. MacArthur said No, he was too old. Eisenhower repeated that he was not interested and again urged MacArthur to become a candidate. So it went, Eisenhower said, "from about ten-thirty till about one o'clock." Neither man convinced the other. Later, Eisenhower mentioned the conversation to some friends in Washington; their instant interpretation was that MacArthur had hoped that Eisenhower would back him for the Presidency.[31] Political ambition also seemed to explain MacArthur's contradictory statements about troop strength—when he made his public announcements, he had in mind potential votes for himself, not the needs of the Army. Thus in Tokyo, MacArthur promised Eisenhower that he would make a strong public statement on the need to continue selective service (a major goal of the War Department), but once Eisenhower was gone, MacArthur remained silent. In the same way, MacArthur promised Patterson a strong statement on unification of the armed forces, but in fact never made it.[32] MacArthur stayed silent even after Eisenhower wrote him a note practically begging him to speak out, and adding that the President was "definitely disappointed" at MacArthur's failure to do so, especially since the right-wing press was spreading the rumor that MacArthur was opposed to both the draft and unification. Still MacArthur said nothing.[33]

Through the second half of 1946, Eisenhower continued patiently to woo MacArthur, without success, despite flattery and cajolery. MacArthur wanted the entire Pacific made into one theater, with himself in command; Eisenhower knew that the Navy would never agree to such a proposition, but he tried to meet MacArthur's wishes ("I do not need to assure you again of the tremendous weight I attach to your convictions").[34] Nothing worked. Ike and Mac stayed at arm's length, each man leery of the other.

Unlike MacArthur, Marshall felt neither resentment nor jealousy toward Eisenhower, and their relationship remained excellent. They had no official dealings and seldom saw each other, because Marshall was in China for much of the time, attempting to reconcile the two sides in the Chinese civil war. Eisenhower, on his trip to the Far East, stopped in to see Marshall in Nanking. He had a purpose beyond simple reunion; Truman had asked him to carry another request to Marshall. Truman was dissatisfied with Secretary of State James Byrnes and he had indicated to Eisenhower that he wanted to replace Byrnes with either Eisenhower or Marshall. Eisenhower had cut him off by saying that he would soon be seeing Marshall and would be happy to ask Marshall if he would take the job. Truman agreed; he told Eisenhower to tell Marshall "that my Secretary of State had stomach trouble and wanted to retire from office and that I wanted to know if Marshall would take the job when it became vacant."[35]

Marshall may have groaned when Eisenhower passed on the message. He had been aching to retire to his country place in Leesburg, Virginia, for some years, had expected to do so when he left the Chief of

Staff's office, and had agreed to go to China only because he thought his mission would be a short one. But Marshall's attitude was that when the President called, his duty was inescapable. He told Eisenhower that yes, he would take the post if Truman wanted him to do so, and then took the opportunity to make a sardonic comment on the frustrations of his Chinese assignment. "Eisenhower," he said, "I would do almost anything to get out of this place. I'd even enlist in the Army!"[36]

With Truman, Eisenhower's relations were correct but formal. They never established an intimacy, nor did they work closely together. Marshall had been Roosevelt's closest adviser on military and strategic matters; Eisenhower's relationship with Truman was entirely different. Truman did not turn to his Chief of Staff for advice, even on the most major decisions of his Presidency, decisions that had crucial military implications, such as the Truman Doctrine, military aid to Greece and Turkey, or the Russian blockade of Berlin. The absence of any input from Eisenhower on these and other issues was a bit surprising, because Eisenhower and Truman had so much in common. Both men came from sturdy pioneer stock of small farmers and merchants; they had grown up within 150 miles of each other; Truman and Eisenhower's older brother Arthur had been roommates in a Kansas City boarding house in 1905; both men were internationalists in outlook despite their Midwestern backgrounds. Further, they had both accepted Marshall's arguments and were advocates of his basic proposition for national defense, universal military training. Truman made UMT a part of his program and, even if he never pushed it hard, he was loyal to it until all hope of getting congressional approval was gone.[37] Eisenhower appreciated that support, as he did Truman's support for a genuine unification of the armed forces (Eisenhower himself was such a strong advocate of unification that he proposed a single uniform for the armed services, and a program of sending cadets to Annapolis and midshipmen to West Point for their third year of study). The two men shared the general Army prejudice against the Marine Corps, and, although neither could ever say so publicly, they would have liked to eliminate the Corps (indeed, according to the Marines, that was the chief objective of unification).[38]

But despite all that they had in common, Eisenhower and Truman never became friends; indeed, each man was more than a bit wary of the other. Truman could hardly avoid resenting Eisenhower's standing with the public. When the two men flew to Kansas City on the presidential plane, the *Sacred Cow,* on June 6, 1947, for example, it was Eisenhower—not the President—who attracted the reporters at the airport.

And it was Eisenhower who delivered the principal address at the homecoming reunion of the 35th Division, even though the 35th was Truman's old World War I outfit.[39] At the time of the Army "mutiny" over demobilization, Truman sent Eisenhower a handwritten letter in which he said that his own experience in the Army had taught him that the problem was poor leadership at the junior officer level, but the Commander in Chief offered his analysis with some diffidence and even a note of apology at telling Eisenhower how to run the Army. "What can I do to help?" the President concluded. Eisenhower's reply, while polite, was just on the edge of condescending: "I deeply appreciate your timely interest in this vital subject, and thank you sincerely for taking the time to write to me about it."[40] There was no mention of anything Truman might do to help.

The most difficult military problem facing the United States during Eisenhower's years as Chief of Staff was setting a policy for the atomic bomb. It was an area in which Eisenhower had, however, little influence, partly because Truman, whatever his diffidence toward Eisenhower, was determined to keep the power and responsibility in the White House, and also because Eisenhower was so busy with administrative matters, inspection trips, and speeches that he had little time to think about the implications of the new weapon. Eisenhower called the bomb "this hellish contrivance,"[41] and favored international control of the weapon, but all attempts to forge a sane nuclear policy ran afoul of the deepening American suspicions of the Soviet Union.

When Eisenhower became Chief of Staff the immediate problem with regard to the atomic bomb was that so much was unknown. How great might the explosive power of the weapon become? How long would it take other nations to make a bomb? What kind of delivery systems could be developed? What would the effect of the bomb be on diplomacy? On traditional warfare? In addition to these and many other questions, Eisenhower and the Joint Chiefs were bothered by a widespread public sentiment that held that atomic bombs made armies and navies obsolete, and that possession of an atomic monopoly by the United States constituted a sufficient defense policy by itself. Eisenhower had first of all a moral objection to such views: "I decry loose and sometimes gloating talk about the degree of security implicit in a weapon that might destroy millions overnight."[42]

The ultimate nightmare was that the bomb would be treated as just another weapon, with every nation free to build as many (and as powerful) bombs as it saw fit. But if the United States insisted on attempting to maintain its monopoly, that is exactly what would happen, and in any case monopoly as a policy had little to recommend it, because the general consensus was that within five years the Soviets would have a bomb of their own. In late 1945 Eisenhower spoke to this point in testimony before the House Military Affairs Committee, when he was asked if the United States should share the atomic secret. "Let's be realistic," Eisenhower replied. "The scientists say other nations will get the secret anyway. There is some point in making a virtue out of necessity." Pressed on the question, he went on, "I am sure of this, that if we could establish, through the United Nations Organization, a complete interchange of knowledge and a free access of every government to every other, you would at least inspire confidence, and thereby you could give such secrets to all nations."[43]

The United States made a sincere, if doomed, effort to achieve international control of atomic energy. On March 16, 1946, the State Department presented a plan (drawn up without consultation with the Joint Chiefs). Named the Acheson-Lilienthal Plan, it called for United Nations control of atomic energy, to be achieved through a series of stages. During those stages, the United States would retain its monopoly, a position that was totally unacceptable to the Soviet Union. Nevertheless, American critics of the plan protested against such a "giveaway," which led Truman, in April of 1946, to appoint Bernard Baruch the American delegate to the U.N. Atomic Energy Commission. Baruch was afraid that the Soviets might accept Acheson-Lilienthal (although Eisenhower's principal advisers told him, and he told Baruch, that Soviet acceptance was "almost unthinkable"). Baruch's worry was that if the U.N. came to control the bomb, it would be unable to use it to punish aggression because of the Russian veto in the Security Council. Eisenhower agreed with Baruch on this point; when asked his views, Eisenhower said, "If we enter too hurriedly into an international agreement . . . we may find ourselves in the position of having no restraining means in the world capable of effective action if a great power violates the agreement." Eisenhower insisted that methods of effective international control be tested and proved before the United States entered into any agreements. Therefore, "an essential primary step is to establish, and prove in operation, a system of free and complete inspection." Eisenhower's position was, in brief, that until and unless the Soviets were willing to allow American inspection teams to roam at will throughout the Soviet Union, the United States should refuse to meet Russian demands that America destroy its atomic stockpile and turn its production facilities over to the U.N. "The existence of the atomic bomb in our hands is a deterrent," he told Baruch, and in a reference to the strength of the Red Army in Central Europe, he added, "We must not further unbalance against us world power relationships."[44]

It was a prudent position, from the point of view of America's immediate security, which was of course Eisenhower's most fundamental responsibility. The trouble with the position was that by taking no chances in the immediate future, it greatly enhanced the risks America would face five or ten or twenty years down the line, when the Russians would have their own bomb, as would Britain, France, China, and others. Eisenhower was aware of this ultimate danger, but he nevertheless insisted that the Soviets make the first real move toward international control by opening their country to inspection teams. His insistence on inspection was a theme that would carry through the rest of his life and become one of the highlights of his Presidency.

In practical terms, what Eisenhower advocated did not matter, because the Truman Administration ignored him (and the other Joint Chiefs as well) on this vital military question. Neither Baruch nor the President waited to receive the JCS position on atomic matters before deciding on a policy; characteristically, Baruch was delivering his proposal before the U.N. on the same day that Eisenhower sent him his long letter of advice. Indeed, Baruch ignored the point that mattered most to Eisenhower, that of on-site inspection inside the Soviet Union. Baruch's emphasis was on majority rule in the Security Council of the U.N. to "punish" any violator or aggressor.[45]

Although there was never any chance that the Russians would accept Baruch's proposal (because it would have retained the American monopoly for five years or more), it nevertheless aroused intense criticism from those who feared America was "giving away" her greatest advantage. Newspaper columnist Dorothy Thompson, for example, wrote Eisenhower that "the United States must retain the exclusive and overwhelming power presently in our hands, and must prevent any other power from attaining it. Only the fact that we alone possess it means safety for ourselves and mankind. We must compel the rest of the world to accept our control . . . and establish a Pax Romana now."

Eisenhower recoiled from such a proposal. On a practical level, he told Thompson that biological warfare "might easily supplant the atomic bomb in destructive and disabling effect, and while we may have a temporary monopoly in the atomic field, who can say what nation is ahead in others?" Furthermore, he added in reference to the

Russians, "certain nations and peoples are peculiarly allergic to threat." Most of all, however, he rejected out of hand the idea of a Pax Americana, with the United States using its dominant position to rule the world. "Here, I submit, you are going against the very roots of American sentiment," he declared. "I cannot believe that anyone, no matter what his standing, his popularity or his persuasiveness, could develop among our people a sufficiently lively fear to lead them into the adoption of such a policy."[46]

Simultaneously with the Baruch proposal on international control, the United States was establishing its own atomic energy policy. There were two bills before the Senate. One (May-Johnson) gave the military a central position in controlling atomic developments; the other (sponsored by Senator Brien McMahon, chairman of the Special Committee on Atomic Energy) put atomic energy under civilian control, which would be exercised through an Atomic Energy Commission appointed by the President. Under the McMahon bill, the AEC would have control of the bombs and the President would make the decision on when, and if, to release them to the JCS in the event of an emergency. The McMahon bill also forbade the disclosure of atomic secrets to any foreign power. Eisenhower had originally supported May-Johnson, but Truman—without consulting the JCS—had announced that he favored the McMahon bill. In Eisenhower's view that action by the President "leaves us no recourse but to" accept it. When the House Committee on Appropriations asked him to express his personal opinion on which bill he preferred, he refused to do so. He believed the duty of the Chief of Staff was to support the President once the President had taken a stand. He therefore limited himself to saying that the McMahon bill was "acceptable."[47]

Attitudes toward atomic policy were so closely interwoven with attitudes toward the Soviet Union that the two cannot be discussed separately; thus this is the appropriate place to examine Eisenhower's evolving view of the Russians. When he returned from Germany, he remained committed to a friendly, cooperative approach to the Soviets. In November 1945, he was asked while testifying before a congressional committee to comment on the chances of Russia starting a war. He replied, "Russia has not the slightest thing to gain by a struggle with the United States. There is no one thing, I believe, that guides the policy of Russia more today than to keep friendship with the United States."[48]

Three days after taking up his duties in the Pentagon, he wrote a warm letter to Zhukov, inviting him to come to the States for a visit in the spring, and expressing the hope that many other Soviet officials could also pay a visit, because such exchanges would promote understanding and confidence. "I know that during my [visit to Russia] that my own admiration, respect and affection for the Red Army and its great leaders, and for the Russian people all the way up to the Generalissimo himself, constantly increased."[49] Zhukov replied that he hoped to come; in the meantime, he sent Eisenhower some New Year's presents, including a large white bearskin rug, which Eisenhower assured him had found a place "in my own study in my new house."[50] In March 1946, Zhukov sent Eisenhower a selection of delicacies from Russia. Eisenhower thanked him, again asked him to come for a visit, and concluded, "I still look upon the hours that I spent in friendly discussion with you as among the most pleasant and profitable that I have ever experienced."[51] By April, however, Zhukov had left Berlin for Moscow, where he stayed only briefly before going on to a command in Odessa. Beetle Smith, whom Truman had appointed ambassador to Russia, reported to Eisenhower that Zhukov had fallen from favor. It was rumored that one reason for Zhukov's virtual disappearance was his known friendship with Eisenhower.[52] There never would be a Zhukov visit to the United States.

Through 1946, Eisenhower deplored the rapidly developing breakdown of relations, the loose talk in the United States about the "inevitability" of conflict between the two systems. At a speech at the University of Richmond in March 1946, Eisenhower declared, "Although Abraham Lincoln said 'A house divided against itself cannot stand,' he did not say that two houses constructed differently, of different materials, of different appearance could not stand in peace within the same block . . . We must learn in this world to accommodate ourselves so that we may live at peace with others whose basic philosophy may be different."[53]

Late in March 1946, the FBI sent a message to the Joint Chiefs saying that "a reliable confidential source" had reported that the Russian government had directed all of its ships in U.S. ports "to be loaded immediately and clear the ports of the United States as quickly as possible." Eisenhower scoffed at the Pearl Harbor interpretation offered by the FBI. "At present," the Chief of Staff said, "there is no reason whatsoever for the U.S.S.R. to consider actual hostilities with any nation in the world."[54] In June, referring to another war scare, Eisenhower told the Reserve Officers Association, "Occasionally we hear predictions as to how and where and why the next war will be fought. Such talk is more than foolish; it is vicious."[55]

The war scares continued. On June 11, 1946, Truman called a conference at the White House. The Secretary of State and the JCS discussed the possibility of an imminent Russian offensive in Europe. Such talk made Eisenhower angry, as he felt it had no basis in fact. "I don't believe the Reds want a war," he told Truman. "What can they gain now by armed conflict? They've gained about all they can assimilate." His conclusions were based on practical considerations, not hunches or a sense of trust in the goodness of Soviet intentions. Eisenhower told Truman, forcefully, that the Russians simply were not strong enough to undertake an offensive. At this meeting, and on a number of similar occasions, he demanded evidence, hard evidence. What was there to indicate that the Russians intended suddenly to sweep across Western Europe? He knew from experience the kind of elaborate logistical support there had to be for such an offensive. Where was the evidence of the necessary buildup of supplies in East Germany? On June 11, after his meeting at the White House, Eisenhower told his staff to concentrate the intelligence effort on the area behind Russian lines in Central Europe, "to see if they are piling up any supply dumps." He added that he did not believe "for a minute that we can be wiped off the face of the earth in Germany by anything like the Russian forces now located there." The intelligence people looked, and found no Russian buildup.[56]

A month later William C. Bullitt, a former ambassador to Russia, sent Eisenhower a copy of his recent book on world affairs. Bullitt was a convinced Cold Warrior and a leader of the anti-Soviet group in the State Department. His views were simple but alarming: "The Soviet Union's assault upon the West is at about the stage of Hitler's maneuvering into Czechoslovakia," he asserted. After thus linking Stalin with Hitler, an increasingly popular analogy in Washington, Bullitt flatly declared, "The final aim of Russia is world conquest." Eisenhower thought such notions fantastic. He never for a minute believed any such thing. He told Smith that Bullitt's book was "an excoriation of Russia" and said he could not bring himself to read any more of it. Nor did he read George F. Kennan's famous "Mr. X" article, which also indicated a Russian desire for world conquest.[57]

Montgomery stood with Eisenhower. From his post as Chief of the Imperial General Staff, he wrote Eisenhower in early 1947 that "the Soviet Nation is very, very tired. Devastation in Russia is appalling and the country is in no fit state to go to war." He thought it would be fifteen or twenty years before the Russians would be able to fight another major war, and argued that in the meantime the English-speaking democracies ought to be building friendly relations with the

Soviets, rather than hurling threats and insults. Eisenhower told Montgomery that he heartily agreed.[58]

In an August 1946 letter to his father-in-law, Eisenhower said he was disturbed by "the readiness of people to discuss war as a means of advancing peace. To me this is a contradiction in terms . . . I believe that another war, even if resulting in the complete defeat of the enemy, would bring in its wake such grave disorder, dissatisfaction, and physical destruction that we would be almost certain to lose that for which we fought—namely, the system of free enterprise and individual liberty." To avoid war, and to build the basis of a permanent peace, Eisenhower was willing to go much further than halfway in meeting the Russians. "Merely because they are, from our point of view, objectionable, recalcitrant, and discourteous, should not for an instant be allowed to break down our own patience, tolerance, and spirit of conciliation in attempting to bring about better understanding." He thought that America must stand firmly for her principles, but should not be "insulting or rude in doing so." After all, he concluded, "Our own self-interest can be served only by a long period of peace."[59]

Eisenhower's belief in the vital necessity of peace combined with his faith in international cooperation to make him a strong supporter of the United Nations, far stronger than most of his peers or even his own staff. He expected that the U.N. would establish a genuine peace-keeping force, and that the United States would send a sizable contingent to it. He assigned one of his best officers, General Matthew Ridgway, to the potential peace-keeping force. As noted, he was a prudent soldier and was not ready to give up the atomic monopoly until he was assured of an adequate inspection system within the Soviet Union. But he still managed to believe that sooner or later the U.N. would have control of atomic weapons, an outcome he very much favored.[60]

Events, Soviet actions in East Europe, and the climate of opinion around him, however, were steadily eroding Eisenhower's hopes for an active cooperation with the Soviets. In Poland and elsewhere, the Soviets were acting with high-handed brutality, ignoring the promises they had made in the Yalta Agreements to hold free and unfettered elections in East Europe. In Germany, East and West were growing further apart in their policies with each passing week. In the U.N. Security Council, the U.S. and the U.S.S.R. were hurling accusations at each other. And in Greece, where a civil war raged, the Soviets appeared to be adopting new methods, "political pressure and subversive tactics" as Eisenhower called them, in an attempt to bring new territories under their control. Alarmingly, in February 1947 the British, who had been supporting the Greek monarchists, announced that they were broke and would have to pull out of Greece. Truman and the State Department reacted with speed and vigor, Truman announcing on March 12 the doctrine of containment, which went far beyond mere support for the Greek monarchists: "I believe that it must be the policy of the United States to support free peoples who are resisting attempted subjugation by armed minorities or by outside pressures." The open-ended commitment was more than Eisenhower would have advised, but Truman did not ask his opinion. On March 13, the day following the announcement of the Truman Doctrine, Eisenhower did sign a JCS paper, requested by the Secretary of War and the Secretary of the Navy, that provided a military justification for the new policy. The JCS paper assumed (as had Truman, and as did Eisenhower) that the Communist guerrillas in Greece were in fact proxies for the Kremlin, and that their victory would represent an extension of Soviet power into Greece. That would put pressure on Turkey, which would in turn threaten the entire Eastern Mediterranean. It was therefore, Eisenhower wrote, in America's interests to support the Greek king. In so saying, however, Eisenhower was also insistent on the point that "the Soviet Union currently possesses neither the desire nor the resources to conduct a major war."[61]

Two months later, under less hurried conditions, Eisenhower wrote another paper on the Truman Doctrine, this one an internal memorandum for his fellow Joint Chiefs. He indicated that he resented the crisis treatment to which the Truman Administration had subjected the military and the country, presenting the Greek situation almost as if it were another Pearl Harbor. In the future, Eisenhower said, "the U.S. must depend upon forehanded action in its foreign policy because of the high price of a continuous series of crises." He urged that American support for threatened countries be more social and economic, less military.[62]

Eisenhower also talked with Marshall, who was by then Secretary of State and who had just returned from a meeting of the foreign ministers in Moscow. Marshall, whose own hopes for a new, better world based on cooperation between the victors were as great as Eisenhower's, and who was by no means anti-Soviet, confessed that getting along with the Russians was beginning to seem impossible. The great problem, Marshall told Eisenhower, was Germany. European recovery, so obviously necessary on humanitarian grounds as well as to prevent the spread of Communism, was dependent on the recovery of German production, but Russian fears of the Germans were so great that they would not allow a German revival. Eisenhower agreed with this analysis, and with Marshall's more general point that European recovery was crucial to America's self-interest. "I personally believe," Eisenhower wrote in his diary one month before the Marshall Plan was announced, "that the best thing we could now do would be to post 5 billion to the credit of the secretary of state and tell him to use it to support democratic movements wherever our vital interests indicate. Money should be used to promote possibilities of self-sustaining economies, not merely to prevent immediate starvation."[63]

By mid-1947, then, Eisenhower was moving, reluctantly and slowly, but nevertheless surely, toward a Cold War position. He had decided that the Soviets were in fact aggressive, although certainly not in the way that Hitler had been. Unlike many Cold Warriors, he did not believe that the Soviets were preparing for war. He continued to insist that peace was possible and essential, even if active cooperation with the Russians was not likely in the immediate future. In the parlance of the day, he was "soft" on the Soviets, much softer than Truman, and much less likely to seek a military solution to the problem of coexistence.

However hopeful Eisenhower was about the possibilities of U.S.-U.S.S.R. cooperation, or about the U.N. peace-keeping force, the bedrock of American security and foreign policy remained, in his view, the Anglo-American alliance. In fact that alliance had no legal basis. There was no treaty binding the U.S. and the U.K. Nor was there any statutory authority on either side of the Atlantic for the CCS, the military brains and embodiment of the alliance. Eisenhower and the other Joint Chiefs nevertheless acted as if the CCS did have a legal basis. In so doing, however, they had to be circumspect, even conspiratorial, not only because of the obvious legal problems, but more because the Russians (and others) were bound to be suspicious of Anglo-American intentions if they knew the CCS was continuing to function, as that would indicate a secret military alliance between the U.S. and the U.K. Eisenhower and the other Chiefs—Admiral Chester Nimitz and General Carl Spaatz—therefore agreed informally among themselves to have U.S. planners meet on a most secret basis with their British counterparts, and for the planners to keep the Chiefs "informed by word of mouth only" of their progress. Thus if any of the Chiefs were asked "officially, or by civilians, they would know nothing about it and lay any blame on the Planners for unilateral action." Eisenhower went along with this system, he said, only on a temporary basis; he insisted that as soon as a genuine U.N. peace-keeping force was established, the CCS would have to be abolished. But until then, he added, "The U.S. and U.K. are so bound together in their military operations that some collaboration must continue in order to take reasonable precautions." He explained that what he had in mind was particularly code breaking and the whole Ultra setup.[64]

When the Anglo-American planners got together, as they did often, they soon discovered a fundamental difference in their views over Russian capabilities in Europe. Examining the worst case, an all-out Red Army offensive into Western Europe, the American planners advocated pulling back to and beyond the Pyrenees and the Alps. The British thought that was a gross overestimate of Russian power, and Eisenhower agreed with them. Eisenhower thought that his American planners had a bad case of the jitters; on one paper, which anticipated a pell-mell retreat out of Germany if the Red Army attacked, Eisenhower commented scathingly, "My God, it took us two months to overrun Sicily, and you expect the Russians to overrun Western Europe in two weeks?" During his visit to Berlin in October 1946, he discussed with Montgomery a "joint venture of holding a bridgehead east of the Rhine" in the event of a Russian attack (which neither of them expected in any case). Eisenhower and Montgomery agreed that a bridgehead could be held.[65]

During that same visit, Eisenhower met with the British Chiefs of Staff on a secret basis, and they agreed to develop not only common plans, but to take steps for coordination of communications (including the use of identical cipher equipment), logistics, and intelligence activities. In an *aide-mémoire,* Eisenhower made the point that "it seemed certain that in any future global war the U.S. and the British Commonwealth would be in together. It was therefore incumbent upon them to concert plans together insofar as this was possible, having regard to political susceptibilities." Eisenhower also said "we should burn this letter."[66]

A major problem in continuing the wartime cooperative spirit was the McMahon bill, because it made it illegal for the United States to divulge atomic secrets to any foreign power. The British were furious at this breach of faith (Roosevelt had promised Churchill an equal partnership in atomic matters when the British merged their research and development effort with the American Manhattan Project). Eisenhower was deeply embarrassed, as he confessed to Lord Portal, the head of the RAF, but he also emphasized that "I am personally completely removed from any kind of responsibility in the matter."[67] Four months later, in February 1947, when the British announced their withdrawal from Greece, Eisenhower's concern for the British partner and the effect of the McMahon bill increased. He feared that without adequate power (meaning possession of atomic weapons) Britain "might rapidly become a third-rate nation." Within ten years, he said, other countries (meaning Russia) would have the atomic secrets anyway, so what was the point of keeping them from the British now?[68]

Eisenhower was also embarrassed in his dealings with his many British friends by the publication of Harry Butcher's diary. The first installment appeared in *The Saturday Evening Post* on December 15, 1945. Eisenhower read it and it made him furious, because it contained a passage in which Butcher described how Eisenhower had made fun of the manner in which Churchill ate a bowl of soup. Eisenhower told Butcher it made him acutely embarrassed to think that Churchill might read it and he wanted it removed from the book (Butcher modified but did not remove it). He also wanted Butcher to eliminate any references to any other foreign official that might be construed as critical; in this connection Eisenhower specifically said he wanted no hint of a criticism of de Gaulle or Montgomery. Eisenhower explained, "You were admitted into a circle where every individual had a right to believe that the matters discussed were to remain secret . . . You know how repugnant it would be to me ever to appear in the position of having violated good faith."[69]

In January, after Eisenhower had read three installments, he was even more displeased and said he was sorry that it was ever published at all. He objected to Butcher's "human interest" angle because "by some strange quirk of fate these always center around points of momentary disagreement, so that every little point of disagreement is unfailingly dwelt upon."[70] In May 1946, Butcher's whole book came out under the title *My Three Years with Eisenhower*. It was a huge success, and added to Eisenhower's image and reputation. It was selected by the Book-of-the-Month Club, given free distribution to American servicemen overseas, provided a lecture tour for Butcher, and so on. Only the subject of the book, it seemed, was displeased.

Eisenhower wrote a series of letters of apology to his wartime companions who were discussed in the book. To Churchill, he said, "I am perfectly helpless in the matter. As long as an ex-Aide turned into a

Boswell type of reporter there is nothing I can do about it except to shudder." Churchill, in reply, was disdainful: "Great events and personalities are all made small when passed through the medium of this small mind."[71] Montgomery wrote to say it was "a great pity that Butcher should go writing these sort of things" and said he thought that "aides should be forbidden to write books about their Generals." Eisenhower replied that he agreed entirely.[72] To Tedder, Eisenhower wrote, "If ever I have to go to war again I am not going to take along with me someone that wants to write about the matter when it is all over."[73]

What bothered Eisenhower most about Butcher's diary was the revelation of disagreement in the high command. Eisenhower wanted him to emphasize the miracle of the Grand Alliance of World War II, how it held together despite the many doubters, and what it accomplished. Butcher's diary, inevitably, concentrated on the disagreements—what Montgomery did or did not promise with regard to Caen or Operation Goodwood, the dispute over a single ground commander, broad front versus single thrust, and so forth. Eisenhower wanted to cover up these disagreements, as did Montgomery. Aside from purely personal considerations of friendship, Eisenhower was concerned about the effect of the revelations on the continuing Anglo-American alliance.

The attempted cover-up was wholly ineffective. Eisenhower, on a number of occasions, as new books or articles came out, kept reassuring Montgomery that he really *did* admire him for his "outstanding characteristics," and that he recognized that Montgomery "never once failed to carry out [orders] loyally and with 100% of your effort."[74] Such statements stretched the truth considerably, but in Eisenhower's view in a good and necessary cause. When a London paper carried the headline "EISENHOWER NEARLY SACKED MONTGOMERY"—the story was based on Butcher's account of the sentiment at SHAEF in late June 1944—Eisenhower wrote the editor of the paper, saying that "any criticisms that ever came to my ears from any source concerning the qualifications of Field Marshal Montgomery for his great task were always promptly and emphatically repudiated."[75] That simply was not true. Eisenhower also assured Montgomery that his letters and cables to Eisenhower that "reveal certain differences of conviction between us have never been seen by anyone except myself," which was wishful thinking.[76]

What riled Montgomery most seriously was Butcher's revelation that he had planned before D-Day to break out on the left, at Caen, and then changed the plan after the landings. In a five-page cable to Eisenhower, Montgomery insisted that "all this idea of a change in our strategy is completely false," and said he wanted Eisenhower's comment before writing his own final report on the campaign. Montgomery claimed that "we never changed our basic strategy for one moment," a fiction Eisenhower was willing to accept. In his response, Eisenhower merely pointed out that there was "some divergence, in a tactical sense, from what we had hoped to execute."[77] A year later, Eisenhower was not inclined to be so easy on Montgomery, because de Guingand spent a few days with him as his guest at Quarters No. One and, as Eisenhower reported to Smith, "told me many things that make me believe I was too generous in my personal estimate of one of our teammates."[78]

But what really ruined the cover-up effort was Eisenhower's own commitment to the truth. From the time he became Chief of Staff, he insisted that the U.S. Army should be proud of the role it played in the war and that the full story of that role should be told. He was an early and strong supporter of the Office of the Chief of Military History and its program of selecting professional historians to write a complete, balanced, objective history of the Army's activities, out of which emerged one of the great classics in military history, the multivolume *U.S. Army in World War II.* Eisenhower personally participated in the selection of Dr. Forrest Pogue, a young combat historian, as the official historian of SHAEF. On July 26, 1946, Eisenhower sent Pogue a memorandum, which Pogue could use as necessary, in which he said, "In order to insure a complete and factual account, all records relating to your subject which are within the custody of the War Department . . . will be open for your use."[79] There was to be no censorship of any kind. The result was Pogue's magnificent work, *The Supreme Command.* Eisenhower also insisted on opening the War Department's records to historians outside the OCMH; in a memo of November 20, 1947, he declared that the Army's records were "public property, and the right of the citizens to the full story is unquestioned. Beyond this, the major achievements with which the Army is credited are in fact the accomplishments of the entire nation. The American public therefore should find no unnecessary obstacle to its access to the written record."[80] Eisenhower's stance ensured that the American people did get the first full, comprehensive accounts of the war, much earlier than did the British, with their thirty-year rule sealing the documents. The Russians are still waiting.

Eisenhower's insistence on openness was based on his fundamental conviction that no matter how much Americans criticized their British partners in accounts of the war, and vice versa, the full truth would eventually emerge and triumph, and that the full truth would strengthen, not weaken, the alliance. As he told Lord Ismay, "Extremists on both sides of the water can indulge in all the backbiting and name-calling that they please—they can never get away from the historical truth that the United States and the British Empire, working together, did a job that looked almost impossible at the time it was undertaken."[81]

CHAPTER TWENTY-THREE

Washington

June 1947–May 1948

ON JUNE 10, 1947, in the chapel at Fort Monroe, Virginia, John Eisenhower married Barbara Thompson. It had taken all the persuasive powers of the Chief of Staff, and his wife, to get the ceremony to take place there, rather than in Europe. John had met Barbara—herself an Army brat, the daughter of Colonel and Mrs. Percy Thompson—in Vienna. He had proposed in January; she had accepted; they planned to get married almost immediately. John called his parents on the telephone; they were overjoyed at first, then most unhappy at the thought of the wedding taking place in Europe, without them. Barbara then volunteered to postpone the wedding until John's tour of duty in Vienna was over; Eisenhower later told his son that Barbara's willingness to wait "made a most terrific hit with your mother."[1] In the weeks that followed, Eisenhower liked to pretend that while Mamie was all nerves and excitement, he was calm and indifferent, but in fact he was deeply involved, sending John long letters about arrangements, making suggestions on what John should do about his career before and after the wedding, manipulating the ceremony itself, purchasing a small automobile as a wedding present. John was his only child, after all, and this wedding was his only chance to play the father of the groom (given the time he put into the event, it was lucky for the U.S. Army that he did not have a daughter, because if he had been father of the bride the business of the Army would have come to a standstill for six months). As for their new daughter-in-law,

Mamie later told an interviewer, "Ike and I loved Barby on sight, and she loved us—it was as simple as that."[2] Eisenhower beamed when he learned that Barbara had a "strong foot"; he had often told John that he hoped John's tendency toward flat feet could be bred out of the family.[3] Within six weeks of the wedding, Eisenhower was beginning to hint to his son that a grandchild would be most welcome.

For the private Eisenhower, the addition of a daughter to his family was the great event of 1947, and one of his most pleasurable experiences. For the public Eisenhower, 1947 was dominated by politics, and specifically by demands that he become a candidate for President, an experience he found irksome, irritating, and almost impossible to deal with. During the war, Eisenhower had been able to brush aside various suggestions that he become a candidate. In 1946, it had not been so easy, as the number of people and groups asking him to run, and their seriousness, increased dramatically. To the hundreds of private citizens who wrote offering their support or encouraging him to run, he developed a standard reply: "Thank you for your thoughtful note. While I appreciate your interest, I want you to know I have but one ambition and that is to be a good Chief of Staff of our Army, and then take my place as a private citizen."[4] To politicians who wanted to be in on the start of an Eisenhower boom, his standard response (in this case to Senator Milton Young, Republican of North Dakota, over the telephone on January 18, 1946) was, "I'm trying to run something here [in the Pentagon] for the country rather than just for the Republicans and Democrats and it puts me in a bit of a hole to be talked of as a candidate."[5] Reporters frequently asked him about running; to them his usual answer was that he could not conceive of any circumstances under which he would enter politics. That reply seldom satisfied them. In the spring of 1946, one persistent reporter followed him into the corridor after a Pentagon press conference to ask, "Now, General, isn't there some circumstance, some very remote circumstance, that might induce you to get into politics?" Stopping dead, Eisenhower spread his feet apart, shoved his hands in his pockets, and, emphasizing each syllable, said, "Look, son. I cannot conceive of any circumstance that could drag out of me permission to consider me for any political post from dogcatcher to Grand High Supreme King of the Universe!" And he stalked off to his office.

Late in 1947, Harry Truman called Eisenhower to his office, where—according to Eisenhower—he made a most remarkable offer. If Eisenhower would accept the Democratic nomination, Truman said he would be willing to run as the vice-presidential candidate on the same ticket. At that time, Truman's chances for re-election appeared to be nil. Eisenhower assumed that Truman wanted to use him to pull the Democrats out of an impossible situation. The general wanted nothing to do with the Democratic Party; his answer was a flat "No."[6]

Most of those urging Eisenhower to run assumed that if he did so, he would win in a runaway. Eisenhower did not agree. With no party identification, no political experience or support or base, no record, and no organization, he doubted that there was any reality to an Eisenhower boom. He either was not fully aware of the depth and extent of his own popularity, or refused to believe what seemed obvious to others. When Butcher wrote him about the "many people" who had talked to him about how badly the country needed Ike for President, and predicted that Eisenhower would eventually "be forced into making a decision," Eisenhower scoffed at him. "The sentiment of which you speak is a rather thinly spread affair," he replied, "and I doubt your conclusion that I will ever have to take a stand." He thought that the boom, lacking any encouragement from the prospective candidate, would die a natural death.[7]

In November 1946, he had lunch with Douglas Southall Freeman, Robert E. Lee's biographer and editor of the Richmond *News Leader*. Eisenhower had read Freeman's great work on Lee and had deep respect for the author, so he listened carefully as Freeman "urged that I change my wholly negative attitude toward entering politics. He saw it as my simple duty to the nation." Eisenhower insisted that Freeman was wrong; he said his duty was to the Army, and he "would die a thousand deaths" before he gave "the most suspicious Congressman" the idea that he had politics in mind, because of the adverse effect that might have on Army appropriations.[8]

That he was sincere in saying that he did not want to follow the examples of Washington and Grant there can be no doubt, but he could not convince reporters or potential supporters of that fact. They assumed he was being coy. As he told Milton, "I am certain that 99% of the press representatives that I have ever met would accept instantly and without question my statement on any subject I could speak of in the world except only this one."[9] In his diary, he confessed that even his friends would not believe him.[10]

It was a mark of his self-confidence that he never said publicly, or in his private correspondence, that he did not feel qualified for the job. What he did say, emphatically and repeatedly, was that he did not want it. In Vicksburg, Mississippi, on July 4, 1947, at a time when speculation about his political future was intensifying, he replied to a question on the subject, "I say flatly, completely, and with all the force I have—I haven't a political ambition in the world. I want nothing to do with politics."[11] But even his brother Edgar did not believe him.[12] Neither could Swede Hazlett, who urged him to issue an "unequivocal statement on the subject—one that no one can shoot holes in!"[13] What Hazlett, and many others, wanted was the classic Sherman statement, "If nominated I will not run, if elected I will not serve." Anything short of that they regarded as equivocal. The fact that he would not make such a statement, combined with the well-known fact that he regarded "duty" as a sacred obligation, together with the widespread feeling that it *was* his duty to become the nation's leader, all kept the boom alive.

Eisenhower agonized over his position. He had an intense dislike for partisan politics, which did not reflect a well-thought-out position so much as it did an ingrained Army attitude. The idea of asking people for their support was alien to him, as was the thought of making political deals, fighting for a nomination and election, distributing patronage, and all the rest that goes into party politics. But the nation, from some of its biggest businessmen and most prominent politicians to tens of thousands of former GIs and other ordinary citizens, would not allow him to simply say no. The persistence of the demands that he become a candidate was forcing him to realize that there was no easy way out, and at the same time forcing him to think about what it would be like to be President. He was, after all, within a year of retirement from the Army, with no job prospect in civilian life in hand. As he told John in late August 1947, in the first hint to appear that he might be tempted to try for the White House, "Every day brings fresh evidence of world unrest and tension . . . Sometimes I wonder, though, whether I would not be even more concerned about it if I were so far removed from direct contact that all my information would have to come through the newspapers and with the uneasy feeling that I, at least, could do nothing about the matter whatsoever!"[14] But daydreaming about being President and at the center of events was much different from running for the office, and if being a candidate implied making political promises and deals, Eisenhower wanted no part of it.

A nomination and election by acclamation, on the other hand, would be a different matter. In that event, he confessed to Beetle Smith, he would be forced to regard service in the White House as his "duty." But he did not believe it would happen; indeed, he told

Smith that "someone being named by common consent, rather than by the voice and manipulations of politicians," would be an "American miracle." Nothing like it had happened since George Washington's day. If it did happen, however, he admitted that to then turn the people down and refuse to serve "would be almost the same thing as a soldier refusing to go forward with his unit."[15] But, he insisted, in an October 1947 letter to Cornelius Vanderbilt, Jr., who had urged him to run, "no man since Washington has been elected to political office unless he definitely desired it."[16] To Milton, he said that "we are not children and we know that under the political party system of this country it would certainly be nothing less than a miracle" if there ever were a genuine "draft" at a nominating convention.[17]

Having Sherman's statement thrown at him made him resentful and irritated. He insisted that there was no analogy between his situation and Sherman's. To a West Point classmate who accused him of "double-talk" and demanded a Sherman-like statement, Eisenhower responded furiously, "Did you ever look up the circumstances under which Sherman said it? For 20 years many people hounded Sherman to take a part in politics and he steadfastly refused. Finally in 1884 a political convention was actually in session. It deadlocked. The bosses communicated with him and asked him to step in as the one person around whom all might unite. Of course, under those circumstances, it was appropriate and proper for him to say exactly what he did. He was definitely offered something but certainly he did not have to feel any personal duty about engaging in an activity which was distasteful to him when he clearly understood that political leaders were merely trying to make him a convenience to pull the party out of a hole." Eisenhower took the position that it would be sheer effrontery for him to say what Sherman said, as he had not received a positive offer, as Sherman had; if that offer came his way, under similar circumstances, he insisted "emphatically" that he would do what Sherman did.[18]

With regard to the supposed analogy between Eisenhower and Sherman, certain facts are pertinent. Sherman was sixty-five and in retirement in 1884, when he made his famous statement; Eisenhower was fifty-seven and on active duty in 1948. While Sherman was certainly esteemed by his countrymen, in no way did he have the great popularity Eisenhower enjoyed. Despite Eisenhower's impression, there had been no important movement to persuade Sherman to go into politics, not even in 1884. Sherman's statement was not in response to a definite offer, as Eisenhower thought, but rather to a feeler from a hopeful delegate trying to block the nomination of James G. Blaine.[19]

But no matter how inexact the analogy, Eisenhower's failure to make a statement as unequivocal as Sherman's fed hopes that he would, if convinced that there was a popular demand and it was therefore his duty, consent to become a nominee. In December 1947, when Henry Wallace broke with Truman and became the Progressive Party candidate for President, Eisenhower thought that his own troubles were over, for as he wrote in his diary, "Wallace's third party move has completely taken me off the spot. He has increased the confidence of the Republicans that anyone can win for them."[20] Perhaps it did, but nevertheless many Republicans still wanted that "anyone" to be Eisenhower, and many Democrats much preferred him to Truman.

In January 1948, a group of New Hampshire Republicans entered a slate of delegates pledged to Eisenhower in the March 9 primary. Leonard Finder, publisher of the Manchester *Union-Leader,* endorsed Eisenhower, then in an open letter to Eisenhower said, "No man should deny the will of the people in a matter such as this." Eisenhower wrote on his copy of Finder's letter, "We'll have to answer—but I don't know what to say!"

It took him more than a week to compose an answer to Finder. He brought home various drafts every night, making many changes. On January 22, 1948, he made his reply public. He said that because the office of the President "has, since the days of Washington, historically and properly fallen only to aspirants," and as he had made it clear he had no political ambition, he had hoped that the Eisenhower boom would die. It had not. He had not issued a "bald statement" that he would not accept a nomination because "such an expression would smack of effrontery," and because he did not want to be accused of avoiding his duty. But with actual primary elections coming up, he did not want people wasting their votes, so he had decided he needed to clarify his position.

He then did so in a ringing declaration: "It is my conviction that the necessary and wise subordination of the military to civil power will be best sustained, and our people will have greater confidence that it is so sustained, when lifelong professional soldiers, in the absence of some obvious and overriding reasons, abstain from seeking high political office." (He put in the qualifying phrase—"in the absence . . ."—out of respect to MacArthur, who did want the Republican nomination; he also later wrote MacArthur to insist that he had not, as reporters were saying, intended to take MacArthur out of the campaign through his own statement.) He went on, "Politics is a profession; a serious, complicated and, in its true sense, a noble one." (That sentence went in at the suggestion of his friend James Forrestal, who said Eisenhower should be careful about politicians' feelings.) He concluded, "My decision to remove myself completely from the political scene is definite and positive."[21]

Many people, then and later, assumed that had Eisenhower answered Finder differently, had he agreed to run, he could have had the Republican nomination and the Presidency. The assumption was not tested, but Eisenhower doubted its validity, and he may well have been right. So few states held primaries in 1948 that even had he won them all, he would have gone into the convention with far less than half the delegates pledged to him. Neither Robert Taft nor Thomas Dewey, the leading Republican contenders, was likely to give up without a struggle. Considering how strong a fight Taft made in 1952, it is certainly possible that together with Dewey he could have turned back an Eisenhower nomination in 1948. That is what Eisenhower meant when he told Milton, "We are not children." He realized that his supporters were amateurs. The professional politicians who were so active in his behalf in 1952 were noticeably absent in 1948. Neither the enthusiasm of the amateurs nor Eisenhower's standing in the polls (the Gallup Poll found that he was the public's first choice, regardless of party affiliation) could produce the delegate votes necessary to capture the nomination.

Equally, however, it should be noted that Eisenhower's rejection of a candidacy in 1948 seemed to take him out of the presidential picture permanently. His assumption, and that of most political observers, was that Dewey would get the Republican nomination, then win the election. In that circumstance, Dewey could be expected to succeed himself in 1952. By the time of the 1956 election, Eisenhower would be sixty-six years old, presumably too old to be a candidate. By saying "No" in 1948, therefore, Eisenhower believed he was saying "No" for good.

The day after Eisenhower's letter to Finder was made public, the Washington *Post* ran a Herblock cartoon of a disconsolate little "Mr. American Public" seated on a curbstone, head cupped in his hands, and staring through tears at the headlines lying in the street before him. Among those *not* crying were Eisenhower himself ("I feel as if I've had an abscessed tooth pulled," he said), and of course, Taft, Dewey, and Truman. For no matter how accurate Eisenhower's judgment that nobody was going to hand him either the Republican or the Democratic nomination, the leading candidates realized that if the general had chosen to fight for it, he had an excellent chance of winning. It stretches the truth, perhaps, but only slightly, to say that Eisenhower, in 1948, turned down the Presidency of the United States.

• •

One of the remarkable aspects of the Eisenhower boom was that Eisenhower never indicated, even to his closest friends, his party preference. Democrats as well as Republicans found it easy to assume that a man as smart as Eisenhower *must* be a member of their party. (He was aware that this was a factor in his popularity, and that the moment he took a stand on a controversial issue, he would lose the support of most of those on the opposite side.) The only member of the Eisenhower family who had been involved in the Washington scene was Milton, and he had served successfully under both Democratic and Republican Administrations. General Eisenhower was careful never to say a word on domestic political issues, so no one knew where he stood on them. His commitment to internationalism was well known, of course, but at a time when a bipartisan approach to foreign policy was the norm, that stand indicated nothing about party preference.

As a career soldier, he was obliged to avoid commentary on domestic political issues, and keeping silent on such matters as deficit financing, the welfare state, government regulation of industry and agriculture, or race relations was second nature to him. The views that he did hold, he held strongly, but they were consistently in the middle of the political spectrum. Indeed he had a penchant for expressing emphatically and earnestly his belief in values that were so widely accepted and acknowledged as to be commonplace. "I believe fanatically in the American form of democracy," he said in a private letter to one of his oldest friends, Swede Hazlett, "a system that recognizes and protects the right of the individual and that ascribes to the individual a dignity accruing to him because of his creation in the image of a supreme being and which rests upon the conviction that only through a system of free enterprise can this type of democracy be preserved."[22] To cynics it sounded like pure corn, and surely, they thought, it must be a put-on. But that was the way Eisenhower talked, in private, with his friends.

For example, on September 15, 1947, Eisenhower was in Columbus, Ohio, to address the Air Force Association. After the program, back in his hotel room for a nightcap, he fell into a conversation about inflation with Tom Campbell of Montana, reputedly the largest wheat grower in the world; Everett Cook, a major cotton broker and grower from Tennessee; and Edward Curtis, a vice-president of the Eastman Company. Eisenhower reported to Milton that "the subject that came up for discussion was what to do about mounting costs of living, particularly food costs." Campbell said he was on the way to Washington to testify in favor of price controls. Cook snorted and said that in his experience anyone who advocated price controls usually had in mind a price floor and was really more concerned with a guaranteed minimum than an established maximum. This exchange "quickly launched us into the pros and cons of governmental controls and the path toward socialism as opposed to free enterprise and personal initiative. . . . We covered the waterfront. England was put on the spit and roasted well, while France and Italy came in also for their share of scorching." He confessed "that most of the conversation, in spite of its interest for me, was mostly froth." At the end of the evening, Eisenhower made a point, in great earnest, that won hearty and unanimous agreement: "It was that all of us in the United States should eat less and live more frugally." If that were done, everyone would benefit "physically, mentally and morally." He was delighted the following morning to read in the paper that Senator Taft had, in a speech in California, asked Americans to help bring down rising food prices by eating less, particularly less meat. Henry Wallace and the labor unions were severely critical of Taft for asking ordinary people to make the sacrifices necessary to reduce inflation, but Eisenhower told Milton that "I agree with Taft one hundred percent."[23]

Eisenhower consistently denounced those Americans who thought of only themselves and their needs and refused to consider the needs of the nation as a whole or to make sacrifices for the common good. Labor unions, for one, but big business too. Thus in November 1946, a week after the Republicans had just won control of Congress for the first time since 1930, after a campaign in which the power of unions was a major issue, Eisenhower wrote in his diary, with reference to labor relations, "although everyone believes in cooperation (the single key) as a principle, no one is ready to abandon immediate advantage or position in practicing cooperation. Moral regeneration, revival of patriotism, clear realization that progress in any great segment is not possible without progress for the whole, all these are necessary." He was concerned about "labor [union] dictators," but "all my sympathies are with the workers (my youth was one of such hard work, and my memories of my father's life so clear that I could do nothing else)." He wanted everyone to pull together to "produce a healthy economy, raise living standards for all, and preserve individual liberty."[24]

A year later, in December 1947, Eisenhower attended a dinner at the exclusive 1925 F Street Club in Washington. The party, given by two wealthy Pennsylvanians, brought together a number of leading East Coast industrialists and Republicans, including Senators Styles Bridges, Edward Martin, Warren Austin, Arthur Vandenberg, and Robert Taft. Eisenhower had not yet written his letter to Finder; this gathering of the Republican elite in the Senate was designed to find out what his views were. Over after-dinner drinks, the conversation turned to inflation and what to do about it. Eisenhower deplored inflation. Making one of his favorite points, he argued that if everyone would make sacrifices, inflation could be brought down. Taft asked if he had a more specific suggestion. Why, yes, Eisenhower replied, he did. Industry could set an example. Some leading industrialists, one, for example, the president of U.S. Steel (who was present), should announce that their companies, regardless of profit or loss, would not raise prices for one year.

There was a shocked silence; Eisenhower's suggestion had not gone down so well as had his remark in Columbus about people eating less. Taft and Vandenberg then pounced on the general, ridiculing his idea and insisting that it was not only impractical but dangerous. A garbled version of Eisenhower's remark was leaked to the press, to Eisenhower's great embarrassment, and he had to spend a considerable time explaining that contrary to the rumors and reports, he had *not* advocated that business give up all profits for two years in order to stem inflation.[25]

When Eisenhower talked or wrote on foreign affairs, he was on firmer ground, and his views were more sophisticated. As noted, he was a proponent of the Marshall Plan before it was announced, and a firm supporter afterward. Senator Taft was not. Taft said American money ought not be poured into a "European T.V.A." in a "vast give-away program." Along with other Republicans, Taft thought that the Europeans had gone too far in the direction of socialism already, and that they would use Marshall Plan money to nationalize basic industries, including American-owned plants. Eisenhower put his emphasis on the joint nature of the plan, which required the Europeans to get together among themselves for self-help. And he said—in a letter to Forrestal in January 1948—that "a virtual economic union" between the West European states was a precondition to success. He added that "some kind of *political* accord may have to be achieved among these European countries before they will be willing to make the required economic concessions. . . . A possible practicable approach would be to establish a Combined Chiefs of Staff for the study of common defense problems." He said that "these things are none of my business and my ideas may be completely screwy," but he knew that there were "tremendous political obstacles" to be overcome before a common market could be created, and they had to be faced. Starting with some form of defensive alliance—in practice, he was suggesting what became NATO—seemed to

Eisenhower to be in order.[26] Truman, of course, agreed. In this area, Eisenhower was much closer to the President's position than to that of Senator Taft.

So too in his developing views on the Soviet Union. By the fall of 1947, Eisenhower's feelings about the Soviets were running parallel with Truman's and those of other hard-line Cold Warriors. The Russian repression of the freedoms in Eastern Europe that Eisenhower had fought to preserve, perceived Russian aggression in Greece, Turkey, and Iran, Russian intransigence in Germany and the U.N., all a part of the intensifying Cold War, led Eisenhower to abandon his hope for friendly cooperation and instead to see an inevitable conflict between the U.S. and the U.S.S.R. "Russia is definitely out to communize the world," he wrote in his diary in September 1947. "It promotes starvation, unrest, anarchy, in the certainty that these are the breeding grounds for the growth of their damnable philosophy." He felt that "we face a battle to extinction between the two systems." To win that battle, the U.S. had to oppose Russian expansion, whether it was attempted by direct conquest or through infiltration. Eisenhower wanted to go beyond Truman's policy of containment, however, and "over the long term to win back areas that Russia has already overrun," meaning, of course, the liberation of the East European satellites. In addition, America had to help rebuild Western Europe, through the Marshall Plan, because unless their economies were restored, the peoples of Western Europe would "almost certainly fall prey to communism, and if the progress of this disease is not checked, we will find ourselves an isolated democracy in a world controlled by enemies." In the diary entry, he stated his conclusion as dramatically as he could put it: "To insure the health of American democracy," he wrote, "unity is more necessary now than it was in Overlord."[27]

Although Eisenhower had done a complete turnaround in his attitude toward the Russians, he did not in the process give way to the near hysteria that swept in waves across the country during the early Cold War, or to the view of the Russians as some kind of supermen. In October 1947, a DC-6 crashed into a mountainside, there was a large forest fire in Maine, and an airplane in Alaska had disappeared. "As a result of these incidents and others," Eisenhower reported to Smith in Moscow, "numbers of people are hinting darkly at 'sabotage.'" Eisenhower said that in the absence of proof to the contrary, he believed "they are accidents and nothing more," and he regretted that "they are added fuel to the smouldering doubts and fears that are plaguing this country."[28] In his reply, Smith said that while he had been in the States during the summer he had been "impressed with the growing uncertainty, even hysteria, which prevails at home. It is paralleled by the overpowering fear of imminent war in Western Europe." For himself, Smith thought that if America stood firm "we have little to fear." Eisenhower wholeheartedly agreed. "It is a grievous error," he said, "to forget for one second the might and power of this great republic."[29]

On October 14, 1947, Eisenhower was fifty-seven years old. He would shortly be leaving the Pentagon (Truman had promised him he would not have to serve as Chief of Staff beyond two years). He had rejected politics as a career. As a five-star general, he was technically on active duty for life, and thus drew a salary of $15,000 per year. But he had no savings, owned no property, stocks, or bonds.

What would he do? Where would he live? In his entire adult life, he had never had to answer those basic questions for himself—the Army had always provided the answer.

Offers he had, an embarrassing number. Major corporations wanted him for president or chairman of the board. They offered some "fantastic sums," Eisenhower told his father-in-law, but "I will under no circumstances take a position where I could be accused of merely 'selling a name' for publicity purposes for a corporation." And if a firm wanted him not just for his name, but for his administrative and leadership ability, that was also unsuitable, because "when I finally leave the Army I do not want to undertake any activity or employment that will keep me confined to a desk and working at high pressure." He therefore thought that the presidency of a small college somewhere would be best. After a few years of that activity, he wanted to go into full retirement. He and Mamie thought they would retire to San Antonio, and spend their summers in northern Wisconsin. "A group of men tried to give me a magnificent house up there," he told Doud, "but of course I could not accept that." However, he knew of a small cottage on a lake that would be suitable and affordable.[30] Meanwhile, Eisenhower had friends looking for a ranch near San Antonio for him. He eventually found a ranch he wanted, but finally had to turn it down because the price was too high. He confessed that, never having had a mortgage before, he was highly uncomfortable at the thought of committing himself to payments for the next twelve years.[31]

He was unsuccessful too at finding suitable employment. No small college offered him a post. The offer that attracted him most came from Amory Houghton, chairman of the board of Corning Glass and president of the Boy Scouts of America. Houghton wanted Eisenhower to become the executive director of the Boy Scouts. Eisenhower was sorely tempted, nearly accepted, but ultimately declined.[32]

• •

On April 2, 1946, Eisenhower had spoken at the Metropolitan Museum of Art, then stayed at the Waldorf-Astoria as Tom Watson's guest. Watson was a member of a Columbia University trustees' committee searching for a president to replace the aging Nicholas Murray Butler, who had finally been persuaded to retire. Watson asked Eisenhower if he would consider taking the job. Eisenhower's instant reply was that Columbia had asked the wrong Eisenhower—the university should go after Milton, who was an experienced educator. No, Watson said, Columbia wanted the general. Eisenhower said that he would not be available for nearly two years, and that he therefore could not consider the offer at that time.

Thirteen months later, Watson called on Eisenhower. "To my chagrin," Eisenhower wrote Milton, Watson again offered the Columbia position, urging "the importance of the public service I could perform in that spot" and painting "the rosiest possible picture of what I would be offered in the way of conveniences, expenses, remuneration and so on." Eisenhower repeated that Milton was the man Columbia wanted; Watson repeated that Columbia wanted the general, and pressed for an answer. Eisenhower resented the pressure and told Milton that if Watson forced him to make a quick answer, it would be "No."[33]

A month later, on June 2, 1947, Eisenhower was speaking at the West Point graduation exercises. Watson drove up from the city to meet with him and keep up the pressure. Eisenhower said he was worried about the "volume of social duties" that would devolve on Mamie. He told Watson that while Mamie was "extremely capable, she is not too strong; consequently she has to pace herself and watch her health." Because Mamie "puts out so much of herself in social contact," Eisenhower wanted to be sure that their responsibilities in such matters would be held to an absolute minimum. Watson assured him that the bulk of Columbia's entertaining was done by the trustees, all of whom were rich men. Eisenhower asked for a bit more time, and Watson gave him three weeks. Returning to Washington, Eisenhower went to the White House to discuss the proposition with Truman. The President advised him to accept and said he would be able to release Eisenhower from the Pentagon in early 1948. Eisenhower checked with Milton, who also advised him to accept.[34]

Another friend of Eisenhower's, who was also a college president—Ralph Hutchison of Lafayette College—was opposed. He said he feared Eisenhower was "being stampeded into the Columbia job" and advised the general to hang on just a little longer, because an offer from a "good men's college in a small place" was bound to "come along right soon." But when Eisenhower made this point to Watson, and added that such a situation as Hutchison described would be much preferable to him and his wife, Watson insisted that at a small college Eisenhower could not exert the influence he could at Columbia, and somehow convinced the general that "I should look upon the position [at Columbia] not merely as an opportunity for service but almost as a duty."[35]

Watson had also argued that by accepting the position, Eisenhower could remove his name from political speculation, an idea that appealed to Eisenhower mightily. It should be noted here that the popular impression that Watson and the other wealthy Republican trustees at Columbia wanted Eisenhower in order to begin grooming him for the Presidency of the United States is altogether wrong. In November 1947, Watson "exhortated" Eisenhower to "have nothing to do with this political business," and in fact Watson and most of the Columbia trustees were Dewey supporters who expected Dewey to win in 1948 and then serve until 1956.[36]

Eisenhower, who had made so many momentous decisions, found the process of making this one extremely painful. "It was almost the first decision I ever had to make in my life that was directly concerned with myself," he told Smith. In making it, he "had to struggle against every instinct I had."[37]

On June 23, 1947, Eisenhower wrote to Thomas Parkinson, chairman of the Columbia search committee, to indicate that if a formal offer were made to him, he would accept. He said that he and Mamie had gone through some "definite inner battles" and indeed experienced feelings "akin to dismay" at the prospect of living in New York City, but after hours of "anxious and prayerful thought . . . the finger of duty points in the direction of Columbia." He insisted that the trustees must understand, before they acted, the nature and extent of the verbal agreements he had made with Watson. These included no involvement in purely academic matters, no responsibility for fund raising, no excessive entertaining, and no burdensome administrative details.

What on earth would he do? He would, in his words, "devote my energies in providing internal leadership on broad and liberal lines for the University itself and promote basic concepts of education in a democracy." On those vague conditions, Columbia asked Eisenhower to become its president, at a salary of $25,000 per year. He accepted. He would take office after commencement in June 1948.[38]

Columbia got an almost immediate payoff from the appointment. Shortly after the 1947 football season ended (a season in which Columbia broke Army's thirty-two-game winning streak, 21–20), the Columbia coach, Lou Little, was offered the head coaching job at Yale. He had indicated that he would accept. Little was one of the most successful, respected, and popular coaches of his era. The Columbia alumni were dismayed. A group of alumni, headed by Wild Bill Donovan of the wartime OSS, decided that Eisenhower was the only man who could save Little for the university. They persuaded Little to come with them to the Pentagon and at least "talk to Ike" before signing a contract at Yale.

In the Chief of Staff's office, Eisenhower reminded Little that they had met once before. Little could not recall the occasion. It was back in 1924, Eisenhower said, and Little was coaching Georgetown and he was coaching Fort Meade and Little beat him by one point. As Little's mouth fell open, Eisenhower recounted the details and highlights of a game Little had long since forgotten. Then Eisenhower began asking technical questions about the new winged-T offensive Little had introduced at Columbia. Finally, Eisenhower came to the point. "Lou," he said, referring to the Yale offer, "you cannot do this to me. You're one of the reasons I am going to Columbia."

When Little got back to his hotel room in Washington, he called his wife in New York to say, "Stop packing. We're not going!" Later, Little said of Eisenhower, "He nailed me in one interview, and without a raise in salary, either. He has that rare gift from God of making you feel appreciated, valuable—yes, inspired somehow."[39]

In the middle of his twenty-seven-month tour of duty as Chief of Staff, Eisenhower had written in his diary, "It has been a most difficult period for me, with far more frustrations than progress."[40] Earlier, he had noted, "This job (C/S) is as bad as I always thought it would be."[41] In October 1946, he complained, "My life is one long succession of personnel, budgetary, and planning problems, and I am getting close to the fed up stage."[42]

As Chief of Staff, he had urged the principle of unity of command for American armed forces in the various theaters around the world; he had advocated unification of the armed forces, not through a loose federation at the top (as happened with the creation of the Department of Defense in July 1947) but through a real integration that would stretch from the high command in Washington to the smallest unit in the field; he had fought against a pell-mell, helter-skelter demobilization; he had argued for universal military training, with every American boy (and girl too, in his view) spending his or her eighteenth year either in the armed services or in some form of national service job; he had supported the idea of international control of atomic energy, if it could be achieved consistent with America's security interests; he had, until mid-1947, strongly backed the concept of cooperation with the Soviet Union both within and outside the United Nations. On every point, he had lost.

He was, therefore, glad to be handing over to Bradley. The ceremonies took place at noon on February 7, 1948. Just before leaving his office for the last time, Eisenhower dictated a final message. It was addressed "To the American Soldier." In it, he spoke of his nearly four decades of service, of his pride in the Army and its accomplishments, of the satisfaction his career had brought him. He concluded, "I cannot let this day pass without telling the fighting men—those who have left the ranks and you who still wear the uniform—that my fondest boast shall always be: 'I was their fellow-soldier.'"[43]

Then he walked across the hall to the Secretary of the Army's office, where he administered the oath of office to Bradley. President Truman pinned a third Oak Leaf Cluster to Eisenhower's DSM. By prior agreement, the Eisenhowers were to stay on at Quarters No. One until they moved to New York City in May. A few days after Bradley's swearing-in, Eisenhower bought a car, a brand-new Chrysler. The dealer brought it out to Fort Myer. After Mamie approved, Eisenhower wrote a check in full payment. Then he took Mamie by the hand, pointed to the sedan, and said, "Darling, there's the entire result of thirty-seven years' work since I caught the train out of Abilene." He was broke.[44]

His prospects, however, were, to say the least, excellent. Aside from his continuing Army salary and the salary he would soon be drawing from Columbia, he had finally managed to set aside some time—February to June 1948—to write his memoirs. Throughout 1946 and 1947, publishers had approached Eisenhower with offers for his memoirs. The one he listened to most closely was Richard Simon, of Simon and Schuster, the publishers of Butcher's diary. Simon spent an afternoon with Eisenhower and persuaded him to pick out an incident or two and write them up, as an experiment. In July 1946, Eisenhower did so, and sent the two chapters to Simon for criticism, asking Simon to be "as direct and even brutal" as necessary. Simon read the chapters, then told Eisenhower that he was delighted with them and urged Eisenhower to continue writing. Simon agreed to tell no one what he had been reading. "To be in any way associated with the telling of the story would be a great honor for any publisher," he continued. "But I wish to repeat what I told you in person; if you go ahead (which I profoundly hope you will) you are entirely free of any commitments in your final choice of a publisher."[45]

Eisenhower, however, put the writing aside. He had talked to Arthur Nevins, one of his oldest friends and a member of his staff during the war, about the possibility of Nevins helping him with the research for his memoirs, but in July 1947, Eisenhower told Nevins he had given up any thought of writing in the immediate future. Nevins should therefore not continue to hold himself available.[46] But in December, Douglas Black, president of Doubleday (and a Columbia trustee, which is how he met Eisenhower), along with William Robinson of the New York *Herald Tribune* (and a man Eisenhower liked immediately; they quickly became close friends), approached the general to argue that he owed it to "history" to write his memoirs. In *At Ease,* Eisenhower made much of this visit, writing that Black and Robinson convinced him that it was his duty to set the record straight. In fact, he had never considered *not* writing his memoirs; the problem was always one of finding the time. In addition, whenever Eisenhower talked with publishers, they made his head spin with their explanations of options and first serial rights and second serial rights and movie rights and translations and on and on. What Black and Robinson offered was much more appealing to him—a one-shot deal, in which they would pay a flat sum for all rights. Within a few days, Eisenhower had discovered that the deal they offered was even more attractive, because Joseph Davies, a former ambassador to Russia and a high-priced lawyer in Washington, who was serving informally as Eisenhower's legal representative in the talks, advised Eisenhower that he would pay a capital gains tax on the money, not a personal income tax.

That seemed too good to be true, but Eisenhower checked with the Undersecretary of the Treasury, who gave him an official ruling, which was that Davies was correct. As a nonprofessional writer, Eisenhower was entitled to pay only a capital gains tax *if* he sold the manuscript in its entirety, together with all subsidiary rights. It had often been done before, the Treasury assured Eisenhower. Eisenhower then agreed to write his memoirs. Black and Robinson paid him $635,000; he paid $158,750 in taxes; the nearly half million dollars that he got to keep made him a wealthy man. After Eisenhower had completed his manuscript and turned it over, he told the publishers he was afraid he was sticking them with a white elephant. They smiled and said that, to the contrary, they were not sure they were treating him fairly. That was indeed the truth. The book that resulted was reprinted and serialized and appeared in many different editions, and was translated into twenty-two foreign languages. It sold by the millions; indeed by some accounts only Dr. Benjamin Spock outsold Eisenhower in the twentieth century. On a regular contract, the publishers would have had to pay out far more in royalties to Eisenhower than they did in the one-lump-sum payment,

and even after paying personal income taxes on the royal
hower would have retained much more than he did get to kee
beneficiary of the deal was the publisher, not Eisenhower.[47]

In preparing himself for the task of writing the manuscript, Eisenhower began by rereading Grant's *Memoirs.* It was the best possible choice of a model, and Eisenhower used it well (he deliberately avoided rereading Pershing's memoirs, which he had thought a disaster when he first read them in manuscript). He consulted again with Richard Simon, who although he had lost out in the bid to publish the memoirs nevertheless spent an afternoon with Eisenhower helping the general get started on the book. Eisenhower was also lucky enough to find that Arthur Nevins was bored with his civilian job and happy to quit it in order to help Eisenhower with the research. Eisenhower gathered together his wartime letters, reports, diary entries, and other documents.[48] He employed three secretaries, and immediately after turning over his job to Bradley, he started writing. Or rather, dictating. His method was to begin at 7 A.M., over breakfast. At lunch, he was often joined by the two editors most directly concerned, Kenneth McCormick of Doubleday and Joseph Barnes of the *Herald Tribune.* He would continue dictating until 11 P.M. He worked at this sixteen-hour-a-day pace for most of February and all of March and April. It was a blitz, as he called it, one that few men of his age could have done. Or many younger men, either—the determination, self-discipline, and concentration he had to summon to maintain such a schedule were enormous. He never complained, indeed enjoyed reliving the war, and having all that money waiting for him when he finished—the money that would buy him and Mamie that retirement home someday—was highly motivating.

The book itself, *Crusade in Europe,* published in late 1948, "was greeted with almost unanimous critical acclaim, along with praise for its author's modesty, candor, fairness, tact, and general humanity. It was called the best American military reminiscence (with the possible exception of Grant's), and 'the work of the best soldier-historian since, perhaps, Caesar and his commentaries.'"[49] *Crusade in Europe* not only gave Eisenhower financial security; it stood the test of time (it was still selling briskly in the 1980s), and it added immeasurably to his popularity. It was a book worthy of the man and his services to the nation.

CHAPTER TWENTY-FOUR

New York

June 1948–December 1950

On May 2, 1948, immediately after finishing *Crusade,* Eisenhower left Quarters No. One. He took a month's vacation, as William Robinson's guest, at the Augusta National Golf Club. The vacation provided him and Mamie with a needed rest, and introduced him to a group of men who became and remained his closest friends. "The gang," as he called the members of the group, were all millionaires whose great passions were playing golf and bridge, and talking politics. With one exception, they were all Republicans. They were also united by their hero-worship of General Ike. For his part, Eisenhower was impressed by the gang's business success, appreciated the members' devotion to him, and enjoyed their easy banter, nonstop flow of jokes, and their eagerness to play golf and bridge with him. He sought their advice on politics, economics, and finance, both in general and with regard to his personal fortunes. He accepted from them many gifts, services, free trips, etc. To the end of his life he spent as much time with the gang as he could possibly spare; when they were separated he carried on an extensive correspondence with the members. With them, he could relax as he could with no one else.

Bill Robinson was the leader of the gang. Ten years younger than Eisenhower, Robinson had met the general in connection with *Crusade;* Robinson was the vice-president of the New York *Herald Tribune,* the newspaper that handled the syndication of Eisenhower's book. A large, beefy Irishman with a keen political sensitivity, Robinson was on intimate terms with nearly every important East Coast Republican (his newspaper was the semiofficial voice of the eastern Republican Party). He became not only Eisenhower's closest friend but also his political manager, the man who guided Eisenhower through the tortuous four-year maze that eventually ended with Eisenhower's election to the Presidency.

Next in importance was Clifford Roberts, a New York investment banker who took charge of Eisenhower's personal investments. Robert Woodruff, chairman of the board of Coca-Cola, one year older than Eisenhower, and W. Alton (Pete) Jones, six months younger and president of Cities Service Company, were other members. The only Democrat in the gang was George Allen, a rotund Mississippian who was a close friend of Truman's and a member of the Democratic National Committee. Allen, five years younger than Eisenhower, had met the general during the war. More than a bit of a clown, despite his immense success as a New York and Washington corporate lawyer, Allen had a unique ability to put Eisenhower into a state of uncontrollable laughter. Eisenhower described him to Swede Hazlett as "one of those delightful persons who has a rollicking attitude toward life and he himself is always the butt of his innumerable stories and jokes." But Eisenhower also recognized that "behind his clownish exterior he has a very shrewd clear-thinking brain."[1] Ellis (Slats) Slater, four years Eisenhower's junior and president of Frankfort Distilleries, was the last member of the gang. His wife, Priscilla, became Mamie's closest friend.

The gang made Eisenhower a member at Augusta, built him a cottage there, and put in a fish pond, well stocked with bass, for his private use. When Eisenhower moved to New York City, in June of 1948, Robinson made him a member of Blind Brook Country Club in Westchester County. Every member of the gang had his own circle of rich and powerful friends; through the gang, Eisenhower met on a social and private basis innumerable members of the American business, financial, publishing, and legal elite, nearly every one of whom, after a few minutes with the general, became an Eisenhower-for-President booster, putting their time, money, energy, experience, and contacts into the cause.

The object of their adulation, however, still insisted that he had no interest in a political career. Democrats who feared that Truman was a certain loser in 1948 continued to try to draft Eisenhower for the Democratic nomination. At Augusta, Eisenhower told Bill Robinson and the gang that he knew the Democrats "were desperately searching around for someone to save their skins," but that his friends in the Midwest "would be shocked and chagrined at the very idea of my running on a Democratic ticket for anything." When Robinson said that the right-wing Republicans might turn to MacArthur in order to block Dewey's nomination, Eisenhower blurted, "My God, anything would be better than that!" But "anything," he quickly added, did not include an Eisenhower candidacy. Nevertheless, Robinson, one of the few Republicans who doubted that Dewey could beat Truman, urged Eisenhower to step forward. Eisenhower continued to say no.[2]

In late June, the Republicans nominated Dewey. The Democrats were meeting in mid-July. Party bosses implored Eisenhower to allow them to put his name before the convention. Meanwhile, thousands of letters per day came into Eisenhower's office at Columbia, begging him to become the Democratic nominee. Truman, worried about a stampede, sent George Allen to New York to ask Eisenhower to issue a public renunciation. Eisenhower told Allen that he simply wanted to be left alone. Truman then had Secretary of the Army Kenneth Royall visit Eisenhower, again asking for a repudiation of the Eisenhower bandwagon. Again Eisenhower refused. But when Senator Claude Pepper of Florida told Eisenhower that he intended to place Eisenhower's name before the convention, with or without the general's permission, Eisenhower had to act. He wrote Pepper, "No matter under what terms, conditions, or premises a proposal might be couched, I would refuse to accept the nomination."[3] Truman was duly nominated. The furor surrounding Eisenhower subsided.

During the campaign that followed, Eisenhower refused a number of requests that he endorse Dewey, although he told his friends that he was voting for Dewey and expected him to win. He thoroughly enjoyed his freedom from political pressure, for the first time since the end of the war, and—anticipating a Dewey victory, followed by Dewey's reelection in 1952—believed that he had finally put politics completely behind him. He intended to do a good job at Columbia, retire after a few years, then perhaps do a bit of writing on national and international affairs.

That dream was shattered on election night, 1948. John Eisenhower later described November 2, 1948, as the darkest day of his life, because of the way in which Truman's upset of Dewey thrust his father's name back into the forefront of politics.[4] Eisenhower himself made no public comment on the election, which had such a momentous effect on his personal plans; he did write a letter of congratulation to Truman, praising him for his "stark courage and fighting heart," and adding, "It seems almost needless for me to reaffirm my loyalty to you as President."[5]

• •

At Columbia, in June of 1948, the Eisenhowers moved into the president's home on Morningside Drive. They were unhappy with the home, which was too palatial for their tastes; they spent most of their time on the upper two floors, which the trustees had had remodeled for them into a modern apartment. Eisenhower had a new hobby, painting in oils, which he had taken up at the urging of Churchill and after watching Thomas Stephens paint a portrait of Mamie. He did his painting in his penthouse retreat; usually his subjects were portraits. Admitting that "my hands are better suited to an ax handle than a tiny brush," he destroyed two out of every three of his attempts. Nevertheless, the activity gave him great pleasure and he tried to spend a half hour a day or more at it, usually between eleven and midnight.[6]

Time was a problem. The trustees had assured him that no heavy demands would be placed upon him, that he would be free to concentrate on general policy for the university. But after five months on the job, he confided to Bill Robinson that he feared he had made an awful mistake in coming to Columbia. He was "appalled at the terrible demands" on his time; he said he had never realized what a big operation Columbia was, with its "countless numbers" of postgraduate and professional schools.[7] Tom Watson and the other trustees had told Eisenhower that they would hold to a minimum his social obligations, but Eisenhower was dismayed to discover that he had to greet most, if not all, of the prominent visitors to New York. On one day in October 1948, for example, he shook hands with and posed for pictures with a trade mission from Tibet, an Ethiopian minister, the refugee mayor of Prague, a Boy Scout delegation, and three other groups.[8]

Neither he nor Mamie enjoyed life in the city. She felt cut off and isolated, complaining that the only time she saw her husband was on Sunday mornings. For his part, Eisenhower told a friend, "I am a country boy born and bred, and cities never fail to irritate me. I like the green grass better than paved streets and the sight of a well-fed cow more than that of a street car." As to his job, he confessed that "the work is strange, voluminous, and at times bewildering."[9]

Indeed, so fully and freely did Eisenhower exercise what he insisted was "the soldier's right to grouse"[10] about his life at Columbia that it has become a standard feature of his biographies to call these the unhappiest and least productive years of his career. And, so the story goes, Columbia suffered as much as the general did. One popular quip had it that the trustees had mistakenly asked the wrong Eisenhower; the man they really wanted was Milton, then president of Penn State. Another favorite story among the Columbia faculty was to never send the general a memorandum of more than one page, else his lips would get tired. Thus Herbert Parmet flatly declares, "Eisenhower and the super-intellectual climate of Columbia were not compatible," while Peter Lyon adds, "For him to attempt to be a university president was absurd. It was wrong all around . . . It was worse than wrong, it was cruel."[11]

There was some truth in these judgments. The general and the professors were strange to each other. Grayson Kirk, then a professor of international relations at Columbia, later Eisenhower's successor as president of the university, noted that "he had a tendency born out of his long military experience to want to have all the problems presented to him in very brief form . . . He would shoot from the hip in order to dispose of the problem . . . He felt it was better to make a decision than to postpone it." The professors, on the other hand, much preferred discussion—however protracted—to decision.[12]

Another difficulty was the lack of action. Eisenhower would make a decision, but nothing would happen. Weeks later he might ask one of his deans, "Whatever happened about that? We decided, didn't we? It was all understood by all of us. Has anything ever happened?" The dean would reply, "No, nothing's happened." John Krout, dean of the graduate faculty, noted that this situation "baffled him, that decisions could be made, and then, as so often happens in academic life . . . nothing is carried out." Faculty meetings were Eisenhower's special hell. "He thought they could be deadly dull," Krout reported. "He felt, well, here we spent an hour and a half to two hours, we haven't done a single thing. We've done a lot of talking, didn't amount to much; we haven't advanced one inch so far as doing anything for the university is concerned." After six months, he turned over the meetings to Krout.[13] At first he tried to attend committee meetings on a regular basis, but as the professors talked and talked in more and more detail about less and less consequential subjects, his eyes would glaze over with total boredom, and he soon gave that up, too.

After almost two years on the job, Eisenhower recorded in his diary, "There is probably no more complicated business in the world than that of picking a new dean within a university." As Supreme Commander during the war, Eisenhower had selected his division and corps commanders quickly and personally; as president of Columbia, he had to sit through interminable meetings while the professors argued with "an almost religious fervor" about the various candidates. "Every man's opinion is voiced in terms of urgency," Eisenhower complained. "The result is complete confusion, and I cannot see why universities have followed such a custom."[14] While he was Chief of Staff of the Army, Eisenhower had thought that there could be no bureaucracy in the world that generated so much paper work as the U.S. Army; seven months after coming to Columbia, he wrote, "One of the major surprises . . . is the paper work. . . . I thought I was leaving those mountainous white piles forever." He tried to insist that every project be presented on one typewritten page, the very idea of which reduced the prolific professors to helpless rage or laughter.[15]

For their part the professors—who had not been consulted about Eisenhower's appointment and who were, generally, unhappy at having a West Point graduate with no scholarly pretensions or advanced degree as their leader—complained that Eisenhower was inaccessible. The general had brought with him to Columbia two officers, Kevin McCann, now retired from the Army and serving as Eisenhower's assistant, and Major Robert Schulz, who became Eisenhower's administrative aide. These two guarded the entrance to Eisenhower's office; they felt that their duty was to Eisenhower personally, not to Columbia; soon they were thoroughly detested by most of the Columbia family. Mrs. Helen King, Eisenhower's secretary, who had been at Columbia for decades and loved the place, was shocked by their attitude. They were, she said, "considerably distressed by anything that had to do with the university. If I set up an appointment with a dean or faculty member, nine times out of ten Schulz would—as he said—'Kill it.' . . . He didn't want the general to be bothered." Because of his aides, Eisenhower "was completely isolated. He had a private entrance door; we didn't see him come in. But they had the place all rigged up with lights that lit and bells that rang and buzzers that buzzed according to where he was sitting and what door he was opening or closing. And then they drilled a hole in the door . . . so that they could see what he was doing without his knowing."[16]

Columbia was an outstanding university with a brilliant faculty composed of highly sophisticated specialists who were dedicated to their research. They regarded Eisenhower as hopelessly naïve. When one scholar told Eisenhower that "we have some of America's most exceptional physicists, mathematicians, chemists, and engineers," Eisenhower asked if they were also "exceptional Americans." The scholar, confused, mumbled that Eisenhower did not understand—they were research scholars. "Dammit," Eisenhower shot back, "what good are exceptional physicists . . . exceptional anything, unless they are exceptional Americans." He added that every student who came to Columbia must leave it first a better citizen and only secondarily a better scholar.[17] To the faculty, that attitude was embarrassing—Eisenhower made Columbia sound like a high-school civics class. When Eisenhower raised nearly a half million dollars for Teachers College to carry out a Citizenship Education Project, and another huge sum for a Chair of Competitive Enterprise, the embarrassment deepened.

Eisenhower wanted Columbia to be "a more effective and productive member of the American national team." If it were to remain a "mere center of independent thought," Eisenhower reasoned, it might well become "an almost monastic type of institution where professors could live and die in the most highly cultured and understanding atmosphere in the world, . . . with all sources of information in the world, and with the highest quality of people to digest all this knowledge." Such an institution was exactly what the majority of the professors wanted, but their president insisted that Columbia must find some way of "making sure that the world can profit from the whole enterprise." Columbia's work would be useless "unless it has an underlying purpose that far transcends mere discovery and imparting of knowledge."[18]

Many faculty cringed when they heard such talk. They cringed too whenever they heard the words "American Assembly." This was Eisenhower's favorite project at Columbia; he brought together at Arden House, an estate on the Hudson River given to the university by Averell Harriman, a collection of businessmen, financiers, professors, and others, to discuss major issues, such as taxes or labor legislation. His thought was that mixing the professors with practical men could lead to ideas that would save America. From what? As Eisenhower explained to one potential donor, "We have always known that democracy could be destroyed by creeping paralysis from within. Bureaucratic controls, deficit spending, subsidies, and just plain hand-outs may, in certain emergencies, be required; but their cumulative effect *could* produce dictatorship."[19] Small wonder the professors saw the Assembly as simply another rich man's anti-New Deal organization.

Other complaints included Eisenhower's frequent absence from the campus. Eisenhower insisted that the trustees give him more assistants, then delegated to them—especially the provost, Albert Jacobs—virtually all the tasks a university president normally performs.[20] On Wednesday afternoons, Eisenhower always played golf at Blind Brook with his gang. The rest of the week, it sometimes seemed, he was on the road, delivering speeches all across the country, speeches that seldom had Columbia and its needs as the theme. Eisenhower's ignorance of things academic rankled. He did not know what to call deans and directors, and pleaded total ignorance when asked to make a judgment on fraternities on campus.[21] On another perennial academic issue, Eisenhower came down on the wrong side, at least in the view of most of his faculty, when he declared that "our universities must be alert against all the insidious ways in which freedom can be lost" and he defended the university for firing a Communist professor.[22]

Clearly the general and the professors were incompatible. Clearly, from the professors' point of view, the trustees had done Columbia a major disservice by hiring Eisenhower, although many of them would have accepted Peter Lyon's softer conclusion, that Eisenhower "was not a bad president because he was no president at all."[23]

That was a legitimate point of view, but there is another perspective. To begin with one of the most persistent complaints, that Eisenhower was inaccessible, it is necessary to note that only a tiny minority of professors at any large university ever have a private meeting with their president. There is a good reason: they have no real business to discuss with him. In Eisenhower's case, however, they definitely did want some private time with General Ike. Few of them had ever been alone with Eisenhower's predecessor, Nicholas Murray Butler; fewer of them cared. But many of them wanted to use their academic credentials to gain access to Eisenhower, just as the millionaires used their money to get close to Ike. Although they never would have admitted it, like the millionaires, the professors were hero-worshipers.

Eisenhower, eager to learn, visited various classes and departments on the campus, an almost unique event at any major university. He was especially interested in the history and physics departments. He gathered together the younger historians and gave them a talk on their duties and obligations (it backfired; these recent Ph.Ds were embarrassed by his stress on teaching military history and patriotism).[24] The physics department was his favorite; he was fascinated by atomic energy and went to the department for instruction. He developed a close relationship with Nobel Prize winner Isidor Rabi (who would later, in 1957, become a member of the President's Science Advisory Committee). When Rabi was offered a post at the Institute for Advanced Study in Princeton, where he would have daily association with his close friend Albert Einstein and enjoy a much higher salary, Eisenhower turned on the full Ike treatment to keep Rabi at Columbia. Eisenhower told Rabi that Columbia needed him, that he personally needed him, that the university's reputation would suffer a tremendous blow if Rabi left, etc. Rabi succumbed and agreed to stay.[25]

That was a clear gain for Columbia. There were many others. In his two and a half years at the university, where he was actually on the job less than half the time, Eisenhower started a series of programs that brought prestige, money, and a more vibrant intellectual climate to the school. For all the faculty disdain about the American Assembly, it generated funds and publicity unattainable elsewhere. Eisenhower raised the money for and started a program for the Conservation of Human Resources, under the directorship of world-famous economist Eli Ginzberg. Eisenhower said that he found it "almost incomprehensible that no American university has undertaken the continuous study of the causes, conduct and consequences of war."[26] To remedy the situation, he raised funds for an Institute of War and Peace Studies. He tried to persuade George Kennan to take the chair; when Kennan declined, he persuaded William Fox to leave Yale to take the post. Fox made the institute into an ongoing and successful operation.[27] Eisenhower created a program to study the "erosion and wastage" of the soil, America's "greatest resource," and used his connections to bring in national leaders in the field.[28] He also established a new Engineering Center. As the endowment went up, so did faculty salaries. The graduate schools prospered. Taken all together, Eisenhower accomplished more in the way of starting new programs at Columbia in his brief tenure than most university presidents do in a decade.

As to Eisenhower's supposed anti-intellectualism, there was another side to that too. When his rich friends complained about all the Reds in the universities, Eisenhower responded that they did not know what they were talking about; when they complained about the teaching of Communist theory in the classroom, Eisenhower replied that there would be no "intellectual iron curtain" at Columbia and defended the teaching of "the facts of Communism." In the face of numerous loud protests, he accepted $30,000 from the Communist Polish government for a chair in Polish studies. He refused to interfere with the right of students to form radical clubs and promote left-wing politics. There were definite limits to his tolerance, however; he insisted that he would dismiss at once any teacher "infiltrating our university with inimical philosophies."[29]

With regard to fund raising, Eisenhower was a genius at it. He never directly solicited funds, but he wrote innumerable letters to his rich friends and acquaintances explaining this or that aspect of Columbia's program. He made it clear to them that he would regard it as a personal favor if they would "help Columbia help America" by contributing. On a special trip to Texas to meet with some oil millionaires (led by the fabulously wealthy Sid Richardson, whom Eisenhower had first met in December 1941, riding the train to Washington), Eisenhower managed to raise nearly $500,000 for Columbia from men who had to be told where Columbia was located. Eisenhower was able to attract large sums of money partly because of his presentation and enthusiasm, but mainly because the contributors knew it was the way to create or maintain good relations with the general.

Eisenhower brought other benefits to Columbia. Big as the university was, it was tiny in comparison to the U.S. Army, and the former Chief of Staff quickly established control over the budget, which had been a mess. Within two years Eisenhower had eliminated a large deficit and had Columbia running on a businesslike basis.[30] On numerous occasions he used his connections in Washington to solve bureaucratic problems for the veterans on campus. When graduate students in Asian studies complained to him that General MacArthur was not allowing any American scholars to study in Japan, Eisenhower went directly to the Secretary of the Army to gain entry for them.[31]

The image that Eisenhower was unhappy at Columbia also requires re-examination. When Swede wrote that he was disturbed by all the reports about Eisenhower's dissatisfaction with his job, Eisenhower replied, "If a man were able to give his full or nearly full attention to such a job as this, he would find it completely absorbing." He said that the opportunity to be in the presence of such outstanding scholars was a rare and happy one. "I love to partake in or, at least, to listen to discussions on such subjects as economics, history . . . physical science, etc. Living with a distinguished faculty gives to me many wonderful hours that I could never have in any other environment."[32]

Eisenhower's problem at Columbia was not that he could not adjust to the academic environment after a lifetime in the Army. As Dean Krout put it, "He learned with amazing speed. I was always astounded at the rapidity with which he did master things."[33] The real problems were the demands on his time, from the defense establishment and from politics, and the relative importance of the job. True, the faculty liked to think of Columbia as the center of the world, but to the former Supreme Commander, a university presidency offered little challenge.

After seven years at the center of world events, accustomed to seeing the latest top-secret intelligence every morning, to making decisions involving millions of men, to dealing on a daily basis with men like Churchill and de Gaulle, Eisenhower felt left out at Columbia. He could only comment upon, not shape, events; his decisions affected only a few thousand people; his contacts were social ones with his millionaire friends, not business meetings with heads of government. The worst part was that he seemed to be working as hard as ever, but had little to show for it.

The Truman Administration was anxious to get Eisenhower involved, in part because it was obviously prudent for the Administration to draw upon the general's reputation and experience, but more to make him a supporter of Administration policy. As a five-star general he was, by law, on active duty for life, and thus available. In 1947 Congress passed the National Defense Act, creating the office of Secretary of Defense and bringing the three services together in a loose federation. In December 1948, Truman asked Eisenhower to come to Washington for "two or three months" to act as a military consultant to the first Secretary of Defense, James Forrestal. Forrestal was involved in the thankless task of trying to bring about some genuine unification among the services.

When Eisenhower arrived in Washington in January 1949, he was appalled. The "Revolt of the Admirals" had broken out; the Navy wanted a much larger share of the Department of Defense's money than it had been appropriated, and went after it by ridiculing the Air Force and the Army, meanwhile demanding a larger role for the Navy. Eisenhower told Swede that "our present Navy can scarcely be justified on the basis of the naval strength of any potential enemy." He thought the Navy's proposed super-carrier would just be a super-target. He objected to the Navy's insistence on a strong Marine Corps. Why, he asked Swede, should the Navy have its own land army of hundreds of thousands of men?[34]

What bothered Eisenhower most was the way in which the Joint Chiefs were going before Congress as individuals to plead their special cases. Eisenhower feared that "some of our seniors are forgetting that they have a commander in chief."[35] Forrestal was having a terrible time trying to get the Chiefs to concentrate their attention on the Russians, instead of one another. He thought Eisenhower was just the man to straighten things out. Eisenhower had his doubts. Forrestal, he wrote in his diary, "is apparently highly discouraged. He exaggerates greatly the possibility that I will materially help in his task of 'unifying' the services." After two weeks in Washington, Eisenhower wrote in the diary, "Except for my liking, admiration, and respect for his great qualities I'd not go near Washington, even if I had to resign my commission completely."[36]

Eisenhower's advice to Forrestal was to establish a "majority rule" principle for the JCS. The Chiefs should be free to argue for their services when the budget was being drawn up, but all their votes should be secret, and once decisions had been reached, they should "carry [them] out faithfully, loyally, enthusiastically." Over the next two years, Eisenhower continued to take the train to Washington once a week; he sent long letters of advice and suggestions on reorganization to Forrestal; he continued to advocate his own program of universal military training; but he was more politely tolerated than listened to, because he always remained an outsider.[37] Truman wanted his prestige, not his advice; Forrestal was, in Eisenhower's words, "nervous, upset, preoccupied, and unhappy."[38] (In May 1949, Forrestal committed suicide.) Meanwhile, the Chiefs continued to bicker, loudly and in public. "The situation grows intolerable," Eisenhower noted. "I am so weary of this interservice struggle for position, prestige and power that this morning I practically 'blew my top.' I would hate to have my doctor take my blood pressure at the moment."[39]

In the spring of 1949, Truman asked Eisenhower to serve as the informal chairman of the JCS. The position had no legal basis and, as Eisenhower was in Washington for only a day or two per week, no real clout. He could not possibly keep up with the details of the arguments between the Chiefs, and in that atmosphere, mastery of detail was crucial. He urged Truman to spend more money on defense, but the President insisted on attempting to balance the budget and would not go above $15 billion. Eisenhower had a feeling of déjà vu; "Of course the results [of an inadequate defense policy] will not show up until we get into serious trouble," he predicted in June 1949. "We are repeating our own history of decades, we just don't believe we ever will get into a real jam."[40] Being a part-time, informal chairman of the JCS gave Eisenhower maximum exposure and minimum influence, which suited the Truman Administration nicely, but left the general depressed. Despite Eisenhower's logic, his reputation, and his charm, the Chiefs continued to bicker among themselves. "The bitter fight still goes on," Eisenhower wrote in his diary. "The whole performance is humiliating—I've seriously considered resigning my commission, so that I could say what I pleased, publicly."[41]

For much of his life, Eisenhower had suffered from occasional stomach cramps. The attacks were isolated and capricious and without apparent cause. On March 21, 1949, while he was in Washington, Eisenhower had an acute attack. His friend and personal physician, General Howard Snyder, suspected some form of enteritis (the ailment was in fact chronic ileitis) and kept Eisenhower in bed for a week on a liquid diet. Truman offered Eisenhower the use of the Little White House that he maintained in Key West. Eisenhower accepted the offer and spent three weeks recuperating in the sun. In April, he moved north to Augusta, where he spent the next month with the gang, playing golf and bridge, fishing, and loafing.

While he was at Key West, Eisenhower had been told by Snyder that he would have to cut down from four packs of cigarettes per day to one. After a few days of limiting his smoking, Eisenhower decided that counting his cigarettes was worse than not smoking at all, and he quit. He never had another cigarette in his life, a fact that amazed the gang, his other friends, the reporters who covered his activities, and the public. Eisenhower was frequently asked how he did it; he replied that it was simple, all he did was put smoking out of his mind. It helped, he would add with a grin, to develop a scornful attitude toward those weaklings who did not have the will power to break their enslavement to nicotine. He told Cliff Roberts, "I nursed to the utmost . . . my ability to sneer."[42]

Shortly after Eisenhower returned to Columbia, John—currently an instructor in English at West Point—and Barbara had their second child, Barbara Anne. The Eisenhowers' first grandchild, Dwight David Eisenhower II, had been born fourteen months earlier. A third, Susan Elaine, was born in 1951. The Eisenhowers were doting grandparents. The general wanted his grandchildren with him for as long and as often as possible; he loved playing with them, teaching them things, buying them presents, giving them lectures. His relationship with his namesake—who was called David, not Dwight—was especially close, and grew even closer as David grew older.

With the coming of grandchildren, Mamie wanted a place of her own more than ever. In thirty-four years of marriage, she had never had one. In the fall of 1950, Eisenhower found one for them, near a farm George Allen had purchased outside Gettysburg, Pennsylvania (Allen later bought up all the land around the Eisenhower farm so that it would be completely protected from encroachment). The farm appealed to the Eisenhowers because of its location, Gettysburg's historic significance, and the worn-out nature of the soil. Eisenhower looked forward to building the soil back up again, restoring it to the condition it was in when the Eisenhowers first came to Pennsylvania from Germany. Mamie looked forward to restoring the old farmhouse; eventually, however, it had to be torn down and a new home built. Mamie designed it for a retirement home, with large, airy rooms and lovely views.[43] Eisenhower began raising cattle in partnership with Allen.

• •

In the late summer of 1949, Eisenhower severed all his ties with the Administration. The issue was the budget.[44] Truman was determined to cut spending on defense to below $15 billion a year; Eisenhower wanted it raised to $16 billion. Secretary Johnson asked Eisenhower to help him distribute the allocation (about $13.5 billion) among the three services. Eisenhower did so, but he fought with Johnson at nearly every step of the way, and when the process ended he asked to be relieved of his assignment. He returned to Columbia, "convinced that Washington would never see me again except as an occasional visitor."[45]

For a man who expected never to return to Washington to live, and for a man who continued to insist that he had no interest in any political career, Eisenhower was acting suspiciously like a man who in fact planned to be the Republican candidate for the Presidency in 1952. He could not avoid thinking about his intentions, because his friends, and a virtual army of citizens, were urging him to enter the race.

Daily, in one form or another, he was asked, "Don't you want to be President?" He emphatically denied it, in his private conversations with his family, the gang, his other intimate friends; he denied it in his private diary; he denied it in his correspondence; he denied it in every public utterance he made on the subject. There is not a single item in the massive collection at the Eisenhower Library prior to late 1951 that even hints that he would seek the job or that he was secretly doing so.

And yet, his actions could not have been better calculated to put him into the White House. His numerous public appearances, his association with the rich and powerful, and the content of his speeches all increased the demand that he become a candidate. No professional politician could have plotted a campaign for the general as successful as the one he directed himself.

To be a successful candidate, he had to appear to be a reluctant candidate. Until after a nomination, he had to avoid partisanship. His speeches had to be forceful without being controversial, seeking the great middle ground of American politics while avoiding any position on current specific disputes. He needed to make himself visible around the country, not as a candidate pleading for votes but as a public servant speaking out on some great issue on which the majority already agreed. He had to put some distance between himself and the Democrats without appearing ungrateful to FDR and Truman for the opportunities they had given him. He had to have access to men of great wealth, and to assure them that his views, especially on taxes and the economy, were safely conservative. He had to keep his image as the Supreme Commander—tough, decisive, highly intelligent, dignified, a man at ease with Churchill and de Gaulle and the other great men of the age—as well as his image as "Ike"—friendly, outgoing, personable, just plain folks, the Kansas farm boy who retained his modesty and was a bit bemused by all the attention that surrounded him, just a simple soldier trying to do his duty.

All this he did, and it led unswervingly to the White House. Yet at every step of the way he protested that he had no ambition to serve as President. He frequently complained that no one, not even the gang, believed his denials, but then how could they, given his actions? None of this recital of his ambivalent behavior is meant to suggest that he sat down, sometime after the night of Truman's re-election, and charted a course for himself that had as its goal the White House. Most of what he did in the period from November 1948 to the end of 1950 he would have done even had Dewey won in 1948 and thus ended all talk about Eisenhower for President. But, as he knew better than anyone else, his activities kept his political options open. He did not decide that he wanted to be President and gear his actions to that end, but he carefully made certain that the possibility remained open, indeed that it increased. He did not seek the Presidency, but he so successfully managed his public and private life that, more so than any other candidate in American history, save only George Washington, the Presidency sought him.

He said that he would never willingly seek a vote, and he would never consent to becoming a candidate unless there was an overwhelming popular demand and unless he could be convinced that it was his duty to serve. Then, with the aid of his friends, he created the conditions that both led to an overwhelming demand and convinced him that it was his duty to run.

Eisenhower's progress toward the White House began the day after Truman's re-election. Ed Bermingham of Alabama, a highly successful investment broker, asked Eisenhower to be the guest of honor at a dinner in Chicago that would have as its audience the leading businessmen, publishers, and bankers in the Midwest. Eisenhower instantly accepted; his remarks at the dinner about the dangers of big government and big labor, high taxes, and creeping socialism were greeted with sustained applause. Shortly after he returned to New York, he was the honored guest of Winthrop Aldrich of the Chase Manhattan Bank at a dinner party at the Racquet & Tennis Club in Manhattan. When Frank Adams, chairman of Standard Oil of New Jersey, asked him to give a little off-the-record talk to his company's top officials on the "broad economic, political and social problems" of the day, Eisenhower accepted the next day.[46] He thus established a pattern that continued, without letup, for the next two years. By the end of that time, there was scarcely a successful businessman, publisher, or financier in the country who had not experienced Eisenhower's firm handshake, seen that big grin, reacted to that bouncy enthusiasm, been impressed by "Ike's" grim determination.

Meanwhile, he tried to avoid the politicians, but they came to him, usually secretly, or through an emissary. The man he least wanted to be seen with in public was Governor Dewey. Thus when Dewey asked for a private meeting in July 1949, Eisenhower agreed, but only if Dewey would come in via the back door and without any publicity. Eisenhower had first met Dewey at a banquet in 1945; at that time, Eisenhower later related, Dewey "spent the entire evening trying to convince me that I should not allow myself to be plunged into politics."[47]

By July 1949, Dewey had "changed his tune." The governor told Eisenhower that he was "a public possession," that his standing with the citizenry was "likewise public property," and that he had to "carefully guard" his image so that it could be used "in the service of all the people." The governor explained that Eisenhower was the "only" man who could "save this country from going to hades in the handbasket of paternalism, socialism, dictatorship." Eisenhower replied that he would never "want to enter politics," that he would never seek a vote, that he would of course do his duty, but that "I do not believe that anything can ever convince me that I have a duty to seek political office."[48] That only made plainer to Dewey what he already knew—that his task was to "convince" Eisenhower where his "duty" lay.

Eisenhower also declined another offer from another prominent politician, Harry Truman, who had his own reasons for wanting Eisenhower out of the way. In August 1949, while Eisenhower was vacationing with his gang in Colorado, Truman had George Allen offer the general the Democratic nomination for senator in New York State. Eisenhower sent Allen back to Truman with a message of his own: he would not consider it for an instant.[49]

While he was in Denver, Eisenhower heard some political advice from Bill Robinson, advice Robinson had gotten from Clarence B. Kelland, a former executive director of the Republican National Committee. Kelland had told Robinson to encourage Eisenhower to speak "at decent intervals" on the subject of the "restoration and preservation of human liberty." He thought the general should stick to the middle of the road, avoiding the "radicals to the right as well as the radicals to the left." He also advised Robinson to have Eisenhower "win the personal friendship of party leaders in a private way." Then, in a year or two, "it would be easy to bring about spontaneous movements . . . to demand a draft. These things do not happen of themselves but require organization and skillful handling . . . Let there seem to be . . . a voluntary public demand dissociated from obvious party leaders." Kelland warned again, "These things do not happen. They must be contrived. And they cannot be contrived by amateurs."[50] It was an almost perfect description of the way in which Eisenhower eventually captured the Republican nomination.

A week after his Denver vacation, Eisenhower delivered a speech to the American Bar Association in St. Louis. He followed Kelland's advice, calling for Americans to seek the "middle way." Using military metaphors, he said that "the frightened, the defeated, the coward, and the knave run to the flanks," while "the clear-sighted and the courageous . . . keep fighting in the middle . . . They are determined that we shall not lose our freedoms, either to the unbearable selfishness of vested interest, or through the blindness of those who . . . falsely declare that only government can bring us happiness, security, and opportunity." He deplored the labor strife rampant in the country and called for a unity between labor and management, so that they could be bound "into a far tighter voluntary cooperative unit than we now have."[51]

It was all pretty much pap—Eisenhower confessed to Swede that it was "rather difficult for an old soldier" to make a speech that was anything more than "a disjointed collection of empty platitudes and aphorisms"[52]—but it got an enthusiastic reception from the lawyers. When Eisenhower got more specific, however, he got into trouble. In Texas in December, Eisenhower told one audience that "if all Americans want is security they can go to prison," and that those who died for freedom "believed in something more than trying to be sure they would not be hungry when they were sixty-seven."[53] Kelland sent a hasty note to Robinson: "For God's sake get your boy to close his trap and crawl into a hole for a while. A few more speeches and he'll be up the creek without a bucket."[54]

Robinson fully agreed; he also agreed with Bruce Barton, former Republican congressman from New York and the nation's most famous public relations and advertising executive, who told Robinson that "when we nominated Willkie in 1940 . . . the Democrats were the most completely demoralized and unhappy individuals you can imagine. They were ready to concede the election." A few weeks later a Democrat told Barton, "Bruce, we aren't worried any more, not since Willkie began to talk. He will talk himself out of it." And, Barton added, "He did."[55] Eisenhower, when told by Robinson of the negative effects of his unfortunate remark, complained that "I am one person in the United States who does not enjoy the privilege of 'freedom of speech.' If I open my mouth on any subject from poverty to flat feet, I am accused of political aspirations." But he also stopped comparing the welfare state to prison.[56]

Throughout 1949 and on into 1950, Eisenhower repeatedly stated in his diary, "I am not, now or in the future, going willingly into politics," but always there was the "unless." "If ever I do so it will be as the result of a series of circumstances that crush all my arguments, that there appears to me to be such compelling reasons to enter the political field that refusal to do so would always thereafter mean to me that I'd failed to do my duty."[57] He said he could not believe he could be so convinced, and added that "if I should ever, in the future, decide affirmatively . . . it will be because I've become oversold by friends."[58] Then he gave his friends every reason to try to so convince him, as he went around the country decrying the state of the nation's defenses, America's position in the world, and the drift to socialism and dictatorship.

Through the first half of 1950, Eisenhower continued to tour the country, presumably on behalf of the American Assembly, and to meet with such men as H. L. Hunt in Texas, Robert Cutler of the Old Colony Trust Company in Boston, Harry Bullis, the chairman of General Mills, and so on. To them, he deplored "those paternalistic and collectivistic ideas which, if adopted, will accomplish . . . the collapse of self-government."[59] Then he would ask—although never directly—for a contribution to the Assembly to help combat such insidious doctrines. When the millionaires would respond that Eisenhower could do a great deal more to combat the forces of evil as President of the United States than as president of Columbia, he would grin and say, "No, not me. Never."

In July of 1950 he went to the very heart of right-wing Republicanism, the Bohemian Grove, a retreat in California where millionaires gathered each year to talk, listen to speeches, play, drink, relax, and establish contacts. Herbert Hoover was the reigning figure at the Grove; members called him "The Chief." Eisenhower made the trip on a special train provided for him by the president of the Santa Fe Railroad; in California, he delighted the men at the Grove (including Congressman Richard Nixon, who chatted briefly with Eisenhower at this, their first meeting) by his informality, friendliness, and attacks on the New Deal.[60]

On June 25, 1950, the North Koreans invaded South Korea. Truman reacted immediately; the United Nations adopted an American resolution denouncing the aggression and committing the U.N. to the defense of South Korea, while Truman sent in the U.S. Navy and Air Force, with ground troops to follow.

No one in the Administration thought to invite General Eisenhower to Washington for consultation, but he went anyway, three days after the war began. At the Pentagon he talked with the high command, and was disappointed. "I went in expecting to find them all in a dither of effort, engaged in the positive business of getting the troops, supplies, etc., that will be needed to settle the Korean mess," he wrote in his diary. But "they seemed indecisive." Eisenhower assured them that he supported Truman's decision, then emphasized that an "appeal to force cannot, by its nature, be a partial one. . . . for God's sake, get ready!" He told his friends, "Remember, in a fight we . . . can never be too strong," and urged "action in a dozen directions . . . We must study every angle to be prepared for whatever may happen, even if it finally came to the use of an A-bomb (which God forbid)."[61] He returned to Washington a week later, to meet with Pentagon officials, testify before a Senate committee, and have lunch with Truman and George Marshall. Eisenhower and Marshall told Truman that they "earnestly supported" his actions, then advised him to put as much strength, as quickly as possible, into Korea. But although Truman and the Pentagon officials assured Eisenhower that in Korea General MacArthur was getting "all he asked for," Eisenhower felt "there seems no disposition to begin serious mobilizing. . . . [Truman's] military advisers are too complacent."[62]

The mood in Washington in late June and July of 1950 was not at all similar to the mood of urgency and dedication that characterized December 1941. For Eisenhower personally, being an outsider commenting on events without benefit of the latest information, rather than being at the center of the action, as he had been in 1941, was frustrating. But whatever the drawbacks to being an outsider, there were advantages. Eisenhower was in the happy position of being able to give advice without having to make decisions. Thus he could tell Truman to undertake a rapid rearmament program, without having to consider all the President's legal, economic, and political problems. Thus he could argue—as he did, later, when it became an issue—that he had advised the government to do more in Korea, but had been ignored.

The government, meanwhile, was trying to put the blame on him, his attacks on the New Deal in his speeches having made it clear to most Administration officials that if Eisenhower ever did run, it would not be as a Democrat. In late August, Earl Schaefer of the Boeing Airplane Company wrote Eisenhower to inform him that at a recent meeting with top Department of Defense people, Democratic officials had charged that the U.S. armed services were in poor shape to meet the Korean crisis because of the recommendations on the budget Eisenhower had made in 1949. It was Eisenhower's budget, the Democrats charged, and he was thus responsible for the lack of preparedness. Schaefer added that one Democrat had told him that if Eisenhower did become the Republican candidate, "we will pull the file on the General . . . and will show that our Korean embarrassment is at his door step."[63] Eisenhower defended himself, telling Schaefer that his only role in preparing the budget was to supervise the distribution of a finite sum among the three services. He pointed out that in public speeches, in testimony before a Senate committee, and in internal memorandums to the President, he had protested that not enough was being spent. Eisenhower professed unconcern about any threats, but said that if the Democrats wished to make an issue of it, "the record would be anything but a comfort to them." He concluded, "What . . . these so-and-so's cannot possibly realize is that there just might be one American who believes he has enough work to do without trying to be President of the United States." He then sent Schaefer's letter and his response to Robinson, so that Robinson would know the facts "in case you hear the same kind of propaganda." Eisenhower told Robinson that "this information is personal," but added in a postscript, "I don't object to your showing it to members of our own crowd."[64]

By the fall of 1950, Eisenhower clearly needed to get out of Columbia. The nation was at war, the world in crisis, and the old soldier wanted to be in on the action.

His luck held, his opportunity came. In 1949, the United States had joined with the nations of Western Europe in the North Atlantic Treaty Organization (NATO). European rearmament, almost nonexistent before the Korean War began, was now under way. Truman had committed the United States to a massive program of rearmament and indicated that he would send a goodly portion of the forces raised to Europe, to join in a NATO military organization. Leaders on both sides of the Atlantic unanimously agreed that Eisenhower was the "only man" who could take command of the NATO forces. In October 1950, Truman called Eisenhower to a meeting at the White House, where he "requested" the general to accept the appointment. Eisenhower took the position that "I am a soldier and am ready to respond to whatever orders my superiors . . . may care to issue to me." He insisted that Truman "order" him to the post, not "request" that he accept it.[65]

Eisenhower's semantic objections aside, it was an ideal appointment for him. As NATO commander, with headquarters in Paris, he could avoid making any comments about domestic and partisan issues. His return to Europe would insure front-page coverage around the world. He could speak out, forcefully, on the issue closest to his heart, the Atlantic Alliance. He would be in daily working contact with the heads of government of Western Europe, which would only add to his image as one of the world's leading statesmen. His reputation as the Western world's greatest soldier would be enhanced. The post put Eisenhower at the center of great events. It represented a challenge worthy of his talents. As he explained to his son, John, "I consider this to be the most important military job in the world."[66] He could renew and strengthen his relations with his many British and French friends, and establish new ones with the West German leaders. His only worry, he said, was his wife; Mamie's "heart condition deteriorates a bit year by year and I hate to contemplate" forcing her to move once again. But as for himself, he knew he would be happy when he could feel that "I am doing the best I can in what I definitely believe to be a world crisis."[67] Best of all, he would be in a position to preserve the victory he had directed in 1945; the specter of the Europe that he had liberated being overrun and enslaved by the Red Army—a prospect that in late 1950 seemed entirely possible—was too painful to contemplate. He told Swede, "I rather look upon this effort as about the last remaining chance for the survival of Western civilization."[68]

But if Truman had provided Eisenhower with a perfect platform, it was still Eisenhower who would have to perform. The job was hardly ceremonial; the challenges were real; there was a definite possibility of failure. The only firm decision that the NATO Council of Ministers had made was that they wanted Eisenhower for the Supreme Command. But of what? A multinational force? Independent national armies joined together in a loose alliance? How many troops? Where would they come from? Truman had said he intended to send more American divisions to Germany—there were two there already—but Taft and other Old Guard Republicans had challenged the President's right to ship American troops to Europe in peacetime. And although few dared to say so publicly, all the NATO partners knew that NATO without German troops would never be able to match the Red Army. Eisenhower himself felt that "the safety of Western Europe demands German participation on a vigorous scale,"[69] but West Germany was not yet sovereign, was not a member of NATO, and in any case the French, Dutch, Belgians, and others were horrified at the prospect of rearming the Germans only five years after they had been liberated from the Nazis. German rearmament was going to be a hard sell. So too would be general European rearmament. To the Europeans, NATO meant a guarantee that the United States would not desert them, that they could count on the atomic bomb to deter the Red Army. They could see no reason to add a significant military component to NATO, especially when the price would include German rearmament as well as higher taxes and more sacrifices for their economies, at a time when they were just beginning to emerge from the ashes of World War II. Rearmament would merely provoke the Russians, critics said, without creating sufficient strength to repel them—at least without using atomic bombs, which was already assured by American participation in NATO. To succeed as Supreme Commander, Eisenhower would have to persuade the Europeans that the Germans were their allies, not their enemies; that they could build ground and air forces strong enough to hurl back the Red Army; that a genuine military alliance of the NATO partners was, even if unique in history, nevertheless workable.

Everything about the job was "vague," Eisenhower complained in his diary, but he realized that the vagueness was inevitable. In a trip to Washington in early November he was further disturbed by the sense of "hysteria" gripping the capital after the Chinese had entered the Korean War. Pentagon officials, and some top politicians, were arguing that once the Communists had drawn enough American strength off to Korea, the Red Army was going to march across the Elbe River. Eisenhower also objected to the attitude, so frequently voiced, that "'In Europe Eisenhower can solve all the problems.'" He thought that was "sweet, but valuable only as an opiate."

Most of all, he was disturbed by American leadership. Taft and his fellow isolationists in the Republican Party were simply hopeless. Truman was not much better. There was no sense of direction, Eisenhower complained, "and poor HST [is] a fine man who, in the middle of a stormy lake, knows nothing of swimming. . . . If his wisdom could only equal his good intent."[70] On December 5, 1950, as the Chinese armies rolled southward in Korea, as the Europeans continued to resist either German or their own rearmament, and as the Americans continued to bicker among themselves about the size of their commitment to NATO, Eisenhower wrote in his diary, "Something is terribly wrong."[71]

His friends kept telling him that he was the "only man" who could lead America and the Atlantic Alliance out of its morass. He was finding it increasingly difficult to disagree with them. He still insisted that there were many fine men around and that he wanted no part of politics, but hardly anyone believed him. By December, Eisenhower had been convinced that one more Democratic victory would end the two-party system in the United States, but he was not convinced that Taft could not win the 1952 election. His concern was with Taft's policies, not on domestic matters, where the two men thought alike, but in foreign affairs, and most of all with Taft's commitment to NATO (Taft had voted against the treaty). Eisenhower was disturbed by Taft's endorsement of Herbert Hoover's call for an "American Gibraltar," defended by atomic bombs and living in isolation from the rest of the world. Eisenhower's own response to Hoover's statement was to write in his diary that while he had admired Hoover "extravagantly, I'm forced to believe he's getting senile."[72] So, before leaving for Europe, Eisenhower arranged a meeting with Taft. He wanted Taft's support for NATO; if he got it, he was ready to "kill off any further speculation about me as a candidate for the Presidency." Before Taft arrived, Eisenhower wrote out a statement he intended to issue that evening, if Taft would agree to the principles of collective security and an all-out American commitment to NATO. Eisenhower's statement read, "Having been called back to military duty, I want to announce that my name may not be used by anyone as a candidate for President—and if they do I will repudiate such efforts."

But the talk with Taft was disheartening. The senator objected to Truman's program of sending additional American divisions to Europe, said that the President did not have the right to do so. Eisenhower insisted that the President certainly did have such a right. Then Eisenhower asked Taft if he and his followers would "agree that collective security is necessary for us in Western Europe" and would support NATO as a bipartisan policy. Taft equivocated. He seemed to Eisenhower to be "playing politics," and appeared to be primarily interested "in cutting the President, or the Presidency, down to size." He moved the discussion from principle to detail, mumbling several times, "I do not know whether I shall vote for four divisions or six divisions or two divisions." Eisenhower said he had no interest in such details (although he had told Marshall, who had recently become Secretary of Defense, that he wanted "ten to twenty American divisions during the critical and risky stages of this venture"). Eisenhower said that he wanted support for the concept of NATO, but Taft would not respond. After the senator left, Eisenhower called in two aides and in their presence tore up his drafted statement, which was Sherman-like enough to take him out of the presidential race forever. He decided to retain "an aura of mystery" about his plans.[73]

When Eisenhower took the NATO assignment, he tried to resign at Columbia, but the trustees insisted that he take a leave of absence instead. He had a series of conferences with Marshall and officials at the Pentagon, talked with Truman, met with congressmen, briefed the press. On January 1, 1951, he returned to Europe.

CHAPTER TWENTY-FIVE

Paris

January 1951–May 1952

EISENHOWER'S LAST ACT in New York was to call General Ed Clark, an old Army friend who was attempting to organize an Eisenhower-for-President movement, to remind Clark that he had not changed his mind about politics. Using his standard line on the subject, Eisenhower said, "I hope always to do my duty to my country; but I cannot even conceive of circumstances as of this moment that could convince me I had a duty to enter politics."[1]

As always, the words were carefully chosen. Eisenhower never expressed any personal ambition to be President, but he indicated that he was willing to serve if he could be convinced that he was responding to the voice of the people and that he was the only alternative to either a Taft or a Truman victory. He would never allow himself to be portrayed as a supplicant. He had always followed orders, even ones as distasteful as those that had kept him in the Philippines for all those years under MacArthur. His superiors had always come forward to tell him where his duty lay and where he could make his greatest contribution. If the American people "ordered" him to be their leader, he would accept their mandate. So he let his friends go on trying to convince him that only he could save the country from isolationism or socialism. They could still believe that he would reluctantly respond, even though he would never seek the job.

Presidential preference polls indicated that he was the first choice among American voters of all persuasions. The Republican Party was growing more isolationist and negative. Taft continued to resist sending American troops to Germany and American money to NATO.[2] Meanwhile, the McCarthyites were becoming more extreme in their assaults on the Democrats. Eisenhower bemoaned the "sorry picture" they created and called Taft, McCarthy, and other Republicans "disciples of hate."[3] The Democrats were little if any better; in Washington, Eisenhower said, "unworthy men . . . guide our destinies."[4] He was concerned about the deficit spending of the Truman Administration, its lack of popular support, and its inability to chart a course. "How we need some brains (on both sides) and some selflessness," he commented.[5] He was glad to get out of the States, especially since he had a job to do, one that he could consider bipartisan and that he regarded as crucial to the future of Western civilization.[6]

Eisenhower began his tour as Supreme Allied Commander, Europe (SACEUR) with a January trip that took him to the eleven European capitals of the NATO countries. He started in Paris, where he made a Europe-wide radio broadcast. He took the opportunity to assert his great love for Europe: "I return with an unshakable faith in Europe—this land of our ancestors—in the underlying courage of its people, in their willingness to live and sacrifice for a secure peace and the continuance and the progress of civilization."[7] He said that he had no "miraculous plans," and that he brought with him no troops or military equipment, but he did bring hope.

And his name, the power of which he knew. At the initial NATO planning session, General Lauris Norstad of the U.S. Air Force recalled, "I've never heard more crying in my life." All the staff officers from the various countries said they did not have this, they did not have that, how weak they were. "And I could see General Eisenhower becoming less and less impressed with this very negative approach, and finally he just banged that podium . . . got red faced . . . and said in a voice that could have been heard two or three floors below that he knew what the weaknesses were . . . 'I know there are shortages, but I myself make up for part of that shortage—what I can do and what I can put into this—and the rest of it has to be made up by you people. Now get at it!' And he banged the podium again and he walked out. Just turned around, didn't say another word, just walked out. And believe me there was a great change in the attitude. Right away there was an air of determination—we *will* do it."[8]

One of Eisenhower's goals on the January trip was to get from the Europeans positive commitments to NATO that he could use back in the States to counter Taft, Hoover, and the others who were charging that since the Europeans were unwilling to rearm, the United States should not bear the burden and the cost. In Lisbon, Eisenhower told Prime Minister Salazar that the Europeans would have to develop "the same sense of urgency and desire for unity and common action to preserve peace as existed in the United States," and asked Salazar to give him "concrete evidence to take back to the American people that the European countries were giving their defense effort chief priority."[9] He repeated these demands at every stop, and he could be blunt and direct in doing so. He told the Danes, for example, that the 4 percent of their national product that they were spending on defense was entirely inadequate.[10] He told the Dutch that The Hague was not "showing a sense of urgency, readiness to sacrifice, and determination to pull its full share of the load," and that he could "not understand why a country of ten million people should not plan to build a five division army." In every capital, he urged the leaders to be an example to the others.[11] The United States, he emphasized, had to be convinced "that a nation is going full out in developing its own human and material resources for defense, as a condition of receiving American aid . . . There is no time to lose!!"[12]

Eisenhower also used the trip to give pep talks to the Europeans. He was at his most dramatic in Paris, where he told Premier Pleven "that the French do not have enough confidence in their own potentialities; that, after all, they have only been defeated once and that the public officials in a country of such glorious traditions should be constantly exhorting the people to again rise to the height of which the French people are capable." He urged Pleven to "beat the drums to reaffirm the glory of France." The official recorder noted that "the impression Eisenhower made on M. Pleven was very noticeable. M. Pleven said, 'I thank you; you have aroused new confidence in me already.'" When Eisenhower's chief of staff, Alfred Gruenther, told him he had been "superbly eloquent," Eisenhower grunted, "Why is it that when I deliver such a good talk it has to be to an audience of one!"[13]

Part of the pep talk included urging the Europeans to get along with one another. He asked Prime Minister de Gasperi of Italy, for example, if it was not possible "for the Italians to think in friendly terms about Yugoslavia," as he had high hopes of eventually including Yugoslavia in NATO in order to strengthen his southern flank. (His overtures to Marshal Tito, a sort of Darlan Deal in reverse, aroused the fury of Republicans, who were upset enough at the thought of helping Europe's socialist governments. The idea of giving military aid to Communist Yugoslavia made them livid. But Eisenhower in 1951, as in November 1942, would take allies wherever he could find them.) De Gasperi, citing the struggle between Italy and Yugoslavia for control of Trieste, noted that "it was a sad fact that in Europe nations were usually friendly with other nations which were not their neighbors."[14]

Two neighbors who shared a long frontier and deep hatreds were France and West Germany. When talking with the French, Eisenhower avoided the delicate subject of German rearmament, but he did begin to lay a basis for the creation of a German army by making a trip to the U.S. Rhein-Main air base in West Germany, where he held a press conference. He opened by saying that when he had last come to Germany "I bore in my heart a very definite antagonism toward Germany and certainly a hatred for all that the Nazis stood for, and I fought as hard as I knew how to destroy it." But, he added, "for my part, by-gones are by-gones," and he hoped that "some day the great German people are lined up with the rest of the free world, because I believe in the essential freedom-loving quality of the German people." When a German reporter pointed out that many Frenchmen wanted a permanently neutralized Germany, Eisenhower replied that "in this day and time to conceive of actual neutrality . . . is an impossibility." When asked whether he thought a German contribution was essential to the defense of Europe, he hedged a bit, but finally admitted "the more people on my side the happier I will be."[15]

In late January, Eisenhower flew back to the States, where he spent four days at the Hotel Thayer at West Point, writing a speech for delivery to Congress. He found it one of the most difficult of his entire career to prepare, because of the number of seemingly contradictory themes that he had to expound. He had to simultaneously convince the American politicians that the danger was great and imminent, but that it would not cost America an excessive amount of money to meet it; that the West Europeans were too weak to defend themselves, but that they had the spirit and dedication to do so if given American help; that he needed American troops in Europe, immediately, but that he would not need too many of them nor for too long a duration. As he told Robert Lovett, "NATO needs an eloquent and inspired Moses as much as it needs planes, tanks, guns and ships," and he intended to be that Moses.[16]

In his speech, delivered on February 1 before an informal joint session of Congress, he assured the audience that the United States, by itself, would not be responsible for defending Europe from the Russians; that with forty divisions, NATO could mount an effective defense; that only six of those divisions need be American; that the most urgent need was not U.S. troops, but an immense flow of American-produced military equipment for the Europeans; that he was fully aware of the worldwide nature of the Communist threat, which meant he recognized that "we cannot concentrate all our forces in any one sector, even one as important as Western Europe." He emphasized the moral factor, assuring the congressmen that if they showed the Europeans that the United States was behind them, they would respond with a vigorous rearmament program of their own.

Eisenhower carefully avoided the German question, although in executive session testimony before the Armed Services and Foreign Affairs Committees, he stressed that all the talk and bickering about German rearmament had given the Germans the idea that "they can sit there and blackmail us." He explained that the Germans—many of whom were opposed to the creation of a new German army—were saying that the price of their joining NATO was a restoration of their sovereignty, and that if they did not get it they just might have to turn to the Russians for help. To this threat, Eisenhower said, he had told the Germans, "I am not going to come on my hands and knees for anything. If you people don't see your welfare lies with the free West, I am not going to beg you, a conquered nation." He pointed out that Europeans who had "seen their own sons tortured to death in German camps are not going to think very nicely about seeing Germany rejuvenated in any way," but he also admitted that the Germans were in a strong position to force concessions from the occupying powers in return for their rearmament, because "the Western European situation is really not going to be stable until that day arrives that we have Germany a decent respectable member, contributing its regular part."[17]

It was, all together, a convincing performance. Reporters concluded that Eisenhower was far more effective in presenting NATO's case than the Truman Administration had been. Two months later, Congress approved the dispatch of four divisions, plus supporting naval forces and air wings, to Europe. It also voted increased appropriations for the Mutual Defense Assistance Program (MDAP). With these American contributions, NATO by mid-1951 was beginning to create a genuine military force.

But it was only a start, as Eisenhower well knew, and in the months following his return to Europe and the establishment of his headquarters outside Paris, he devoted most of his time to building more support for NATO both in Europe and back in the States. He called this goal his most important objective[18] and carried out a brutal schedule to meet it—press conferences, numerous trips to the various capitals, where he was careful to talk not only to government figures but also to opposition party leaders, trade union officials, intellectuals, and molders of public opinion. "Our problem," he told Army Chief of Staff Joseph Collins, "is one of selling and inspiring."[19]

In his extensive private correspondence, with the gang, with other millionaires, with politicians and publishers, Eisenhower concentrated on selling NATO. Most of the incoming letters were pleas that he run for the Presidency; his standard reply was that he had no interest in politics and that in any event the job he held was so important that he had to concentrate his full energy and time on it. Then he would launch into a sales pitch for NATO, usually ending by urging the recipient to spread the word.

The word was that "the future of civilization, as we know it, is at stake." The word was that the true defense of the United States was on the Elbe River. The word was that the American way of life was dependent upon raw materials that could come only from Europe and its colonies, and upon trade and scientific exchanges with Europe and the rest of the free world. The word was that by supporting European rearmament, the United States could buy as much security for itself by spending $1 as it could by spending $4 to build up American forces. The word was that only through collective security could the United States and Europe meet the Soviet threat.[20]

In his correspondence, Eisenhower dealt directly with the two major objections to American support for NATO. The first was that the Europeans, led by the Labour Party in Britain, were going socialist, which led many of Eisenhower's friends to demand, "Why in hell should we support a bunch of pinkos?" Eisenhower reassured them that Europe was fully committed to a free, democratic way of life, that it was not about to go Communist (unless the United States abandoned it), and that "it would be a terrific mistake to demand conformity in all political and economic details. We would soon fall apart!"[21]

The second objection, far more serious, was that the United States was committing itself to an indefinite defense of Europe, at a tremendous cost that would continually go higher. Eisenhower admitted the force of the objection. "We cannot be a modern Rome guarding the far frontiers with our legions," he said. He recognized that the economic strength of the United States was the greatest asset the free world had, and he agreed that the expenditure of billions of dollars for defense would, in the long run, bankrupt the United States, thus presenting the Soviets with "their greatest victory." But he insisted that a program of support for NATO was a short-run proposition. American aid for NATO was essential now, in 1951, but it could be phased out rather quickly. To Ed Bermingham, he flatly declared, "If in ten years, all American troops stationed in Europe for national defense purposes have not been returned to the United States, then this whole project will have failed."[22]

In addition to his correspondence, Eisenhower used his persuasive powers on the "veritable stream of American visitors passing through my office." Every American who came to Europe in 1951, it seemed, wanted to meet with the general and hear about NATO; many, especially politicians, came to Paris expressly for that purpose. Eisenhower gave all of them at least a few minutes; to congressional delegations he devoted days of his time. His theme was always the same. "Our wisest course," he told one group, "would appear to strive for a very intensive but relatively short program of American assistance which should begin to pass its peak, especially in ground force content, within two and one-half or three years."[23] He was dissembling. To Truman, Eisenhower estimated more candidly that "it should be possible, within some 4–8 years, to reduce the American ground forces stationed here," which was far short of his implied promise to congressional visitors that he could bring all the boys home in three years or less.[24]

Within Europe, Eisenhower considered morale to be his biggest problem. Less than six years after the most destructive war in history, Europeans just did not want to think about fighting—or building the forces to fight—another war. Further, the figures on ground strength were so stark and discouraging—NATO had only 12 divisions, the Russians 175—that it seemed impossible to stop the Red Army without using atomic bombs, and if the Americans were going to use atomic bombs anyway, why bother to build European ground strength, especially when it would be so expensive, would slow or halt economic recovery, and would only provoke the Russians?

Eisenhower thought that sufficient conventional strength could be built and that it was both mad and immoral to rely upon the atomic bomb. In his talks with the European leaders, Eisenhower attempted to build their confidence. Inevitably, he had to ask them to dig deeper, spend more, but he did so within the context of recognizing political realities. As his principal aide, Andrew Goodpaster, later explained, "He had a great sense of how the governments of the various countries worked and what the practical constraints were on the political leaders, that you couldn't crowd them too far, you couldn't ask too much of them . . . But at the same time he was constantly able to point to the basic scope of resources on which we in the West could draw if we could simply mobilize them and organize them properly."[25] Eisenhower therefore emphasized morale, which cost little or nothing to build. "Civilian leaders talk about the state of morale in a given country as if it were a sort of uncontrollable event or phenomenon, like a thunderstorm or a cold winter," he complained in his diary, while "the soldier leader looks on morale as . . . the greatest of all his problems, but also as one about which he can and must do something."[26]

He told Averell Harriman, "The last thing that a leader may be is pessimistic if he is to achieve success."[27] To Omar Bradley, serving as chairman of the JCS, Eisenhower said that "men in uniform . . . are the only ones who can educate and inspire our civil leaders."[28] Thus he continued to urge, cajole, encourage. He asked the governments to remind each and every citizen daily "of his own conceptions of the dignity of man and of the value he places upon freedom; this must be accompanied by the reminder that freedom is something that must be earned every day that one lives!"[29] On the seventh anniversary of Overlord, Eisenhower went to Normandy to deliver a Europe-wide radio broadcast that reminded the Europeans of what was at stake. "Never again," he said, "must there be a campaign of liberation fought on these shores."[30]

Germany remained Eisenhower's most delicate problem. No matter how successful he was in persuading the other nations of Western Europe to increase their defense spending, his goal of forty divisions was simply unattainable without a German army.[31] Eisenhower had extracted from the French a promise of twenty-four divisions for NATO, but in fact the French had only three divisions in West Germany and six in France, with no immediate prospect of making any further contribution, because ten French divisions were tied down in Indochina in an apparently endless war. Whenever Eisenhower asked the French for more support for NATO, they countered with a request for more American support for their effort in Indochina. "I'd favor heavy reinforcement to get the thing over at once," Eisenhower wrote in his diary, "but I'm convinced that no military victory is possible in that kind of theater."[32] In his view, the French had to give Vietnam, Laos, and Cambodia their independence, then let them fight their own war, while the French army came home to defend France. But he could not convince any French leader of the wisdom of that course, which meant that the only alternative for NATO was to create a German army, but the French would not allow that either.

"We are either going to solve this German problem," Eisenhower believed, "or the Soviets will solve it in their favor."[33] Or as Chancellor Konrad Adenauer put it, "The Western Allies, especially France, have to . . . answer the question of which danger is the greater: the Russian threat or a German contribution to a European defense community."[34] After going through various contortions, including a proposal that the Germans provide the enlisted men while the French supplied the officers, the French finally offered the "Pleven Plan." The Germans would build an army that would have no unit larger than a division, as part of an integrated NATO force commanded by Eisenhower; the German contribution would be limited to 20 percent of the integrated force.

Originally Eisenhower did not think much of the Pleven Plan; he feared that it would be "more divisive than unifying in its effect," as it included "every kind of obstacle, difficulty, and fantastic notion that misguided humans could put together in one package."[35] But after a half a year as SACEUR, Eisenhower changed his mind. "I am shifting my position" with regard to a European army, he reported to Marshall, because NATO needed "some spectacular accomplishment" to keep American public opinion behind the organization and to spur the Europeans to do more toward their own defense. Further, "the plan offers the only immediate hope that I can see of developing, on a basis acceptable to other European countries, the German strength that is vital to us." In addition, he had a larger goal. "I am certain that there is going to be no real progress towards a greater unification of Europe except through the medium of specific programs of this kind."[36] In other words, rather than waiting for the creation of a United States of Europe to achieve an all-European army, he felt that by forming the army first, the political unification would naturally follow.

He thought the new super-nation should include all the European NATO members, plus Greece, Sweden, Spain, and Yugoslavia. A United States of Europe, he argued, would "instantly . . . solve the real and bitter problems of today . . . So many advantages would flow from such a union that it is a tragedy for the whole human race that it is not done at once." He brushed aside objections. "I get exceedingly weary of this talk about a step-by-step, gradual cautious approach," he told Harriman. He saw no reason why a "socialist Sweden could [not] live alongside a capitalist Germany" so long as there was a simple bill of rights in the constitution, and the elimination of trade barriers and all economic and political restraint on free movement. He thought the United States could and should go to "any limit" to support such a venture.[37]

In December 1951, he urged Premier Pleven to issue a call to the European members of NATO "to meet in an official constitutional convention to consider ways and means for promoting a closer union." Such a "dramatic and inspiring call to action," he said, would be a great help in getting a European army under way. But although Pleven was the sponsor of the European army idea, and although Eisenhower carefully flattered Pleven (telling him that "you are the one person in Europe who, by reason of nationality and political, intellectual, and moral leadership, is outstandingly qualified to take such an action"), Pleven did not respond.[38] The French, in short, could not yet answer Adenauer's question: Which do you fear most, the Red Army or a new German army?

The British too had to be wooed. They were not so opposed to a German army as were the French, but a united Europe was "anathema to them." Eisenhower went after the British in his typical fashion—public speeches, private meetings with politicians, and an extensive correspondence with his many friends in the British government. On July 3, 1951, he delivered a major address to the English-Speaking Union at Grosvenor House on Park Lane, to an audience of 1,200 British leaders. Foreign Secretary Herbert Morrison introduced him as "the First Citizen of the Atlantic"; Prime Minister Attlee referred to him as "the man who won the war"; the then opposition leader, Winston Churchill, led the standing ovation. The attitude of the audience toward Eisenhower, according to Bill Robinson, who was there, "amounted to worship." In his speech, Eisenhower issued a ringing call for a United States of Europe. He recognized the difficulties—"this project faces the deadly danger of procrastination, timid measures, slow steps and cautious stages"—then held out the vision of what could be gained: "With unity achieved, Europe could build adequate security and, at the same time, continue the march of human betterment that has characterized Western civilization. Once united, the farms and factories of France and Belgium, the foundries of Germany, the rich farmlands of Holland and Denmark, the skilled labor of Italy, will produce miracles for the common good." The next day Churchill told Eisenhower that he was too deaf to have heard the speech, but having now read it, he wanted to say "I am sure this is one of the greatest speeches delivered by any American in my lifetime."[39]

Throughout the winter, Eisenhower pushed the project. To Harriman, he declared, "Every day brings new evidence that Western Europe must coalesce both politically and economically, or things will get worse instead of better. It seems remarkable that all European political leaders recognize the truth of this statement but just sit down and do absolutely nothing about it."[40] By March of 1952, enough progress had been made toward the European army to initiate detailed discussions about tables of organization and equipment. Progress was satisfactory.[41]

At his home outside Paris, Eisenhower had Mamie with him, as well as Schulz (now a lieutenant colonel), Moaney as his valet, Sergeant Dry as his driver, and Colonel Craig Cannon as his personal aide. There was a golf course on the property, as well as a fish pond well stocked with trout, and room for a vegetable garden. Initially the house was too French for Mamie's taste; too grand in its appearance, both inside and out, while the plumbing and electricity were unreliable. But after it was fixed up it became one of her favorite homes. There was plenty of room for guests, and every member of the gang managed to make at least one trip to Paris to stay with the Eisenhowers and play some golf and bridge, as well as engaging in political talk. Eisenhower was terribly concerned about his friends' health; to both Bill Robinson and George Allen he sent numerous letters, and gave many lectures, on holding down their drinking and eating. The aches and pains of advancing age were getting to him; on his sixty-first birthday he told one friend that "the years are getting so they flash past me like pickets in a fence." He had a sore wrist that required daily heat treatments and for some months prevented him from playing golf.[42]

He took great pleasure in his garden and his painting. "We have had sweet corn, two kinds of beans, peas, radishes, tomatoes, turnips, and beets . . . in great quantity," he told his son in September, and bragged that "our corn did better than almost any other we have ever planted."[43] His painting abilities had not improved, he told Swede; there was still "no faintest semblance of talent." But he added that because he could no longer indulge himself in "serious and steady reading," he needed "some kind of release" and he found it in painting. "For me the real benefit is the fact that it gives me an excuse to be absolutely alone and interferes not at all with what I am pleased to call my 'contemplative powers.'"[44]

He needed all his contemplative powers to deal with the complex pressures of a possible political career. At a lunch with his gang, his friends said they were anxious to devote their full energies to his candidacy. He hinted that if it appeared that he was the only man who could stop Taft, and if there was a genuine draft, he would consent to run.

When Bill Robinson offered to move to France to help Eisenhower, Eisenhower told him, "I do not see how you could occupy a more advantageous position than you already do for potential assistance to me."[45]

There was much to be done. In March, Robinson informed Eisenhower that the Chicago *Tribune,* the Hearst papers, and other right-wing publications were charging that by accepting the NATO post, Eisenhower had "embraced almost all the foreign, domestic and political policies of the Administration." Robinson added that Truman and his colleagues would make no denial of these stories; instead, the Democrats "will gleefully welcome the planting of this idea." Robinson assured Eisenhower that through the *Herald Tribune,* and through his many contacts with the moderate Republican press, he would do what he could to refute the charges, but warned that Eisenhower himself would have to carry the main burden.[46]

Eisenhower responded handsomely. He wrote a series of letters to his big-business friends, assuring them that he had not "joined the Administration" and that he violently disagreed with the Democrats on domestic policies. His every public and private utterance, he insisted, "has been *against* planned economy, the 'hand out' state, and the trend toward centralization of economic and political power in the hands of Washington bureaucrats."[47] When the Democrats began alleging that Eisenhower was the man responsible for American demobilization after 1945, Eisenhower heatedly denied it. He told Robinson—and asked him to tell others—that they were "unwarranted and baseless" statements, that in fact he had urged universal military training at that time, only to be sabotaged by MacArthur.[48]

One of the most dramatic events of early 1951 was Truman's firing of MacArthur. Reporters inevitably wanted Eisenhower's reaction. Lucius Clay, who had retired from the Army and was serving as chairman of Continental Can in New York (but spending most of his time working with Robinson and the others on the Eisenhower-for-President movement), immediately wrote Eisenhower an "earnest request: that you let no one maneuver you into any . . . comment on the MacArthur incident." Clay said that he had inside information that the Taft people were going to attempt to do so, "thus aligning you with the President and indirectly with his party and its inept conduct of government." As a general rule, Clay advised that "you must keep yourself aloof from present controversies."[49] Eisenhower replied, "I assure you that I am going to maintain silence in every language known to man."[50] He then wrote MacArthur—he had earlier sent his old boss hearty congratulations on the brilliant landing at Inchon—to denounce the "sensation-seeking columnists" who were trying to "promote the falsehood that you and I are mortal enemies." He wished he could put an end to this "curious lie." MacArthur assured Eisenhower that "I pay absolutely no attention to scuttlebutt."[51]

Besides denying any secret New Deal tendencies and keeping silent on MacArthur and other volatile issues, Eisenhower's friends told him he needed to affirm what he was for, not so much for their sake but so that they could show his statements to their associates. There was, for example, the fear that he was too much an internationalist, a fear that was strengthened by all his pro-NATO and United States of Europe pronouncements. Again and again, Eisenhower assured his friends that he put America first, but within the context of America's need for the rest of the world. "From my viewpoint," he told Earl Schaefer of Boeing Aircraft, "foreign policy is, or should be, based primarily upon one consideration. That consideration is the need for the United States to obtain certain raw materials to sustain its economy and . . . to preserve profitable foreign markets for our surpluses." To achieve these goals, America had to have friends.[52]

More specifically, Eisenhower's friends worried about his attitude toward Russia. He was vulnerable on that point because of his well-known friendship with Zhukov, his failure to take Berlin in 1945, and his attempts to get along with the Russians when he was in command of the occupation forces in Germany. His position as SACEUR gave him an opportunity—which he seized—to speak out frequently about the Communist threat and to denounce the Soviet Union for its actions and intentions. The hopes that he had felt in 1945 for a better world had almost disappeared. By 1951 he was a complete Cold Warrior, unwilling to trust the Russians on any issue, suspicious of their every proposal, determined to turn back the Red tide. The only way to deal with the Russians, he said in his speeches, in his letters, and in his private conversations, was with firmness backed up by military strength.[53]

How much military strength posed a dilemma. Back in 1940, he had asked how long America would be willing to make "such great expenditures in money, time, resources and effort" just to meet a threat; how long would it be "before public opinion decides that it will eventually be cheaper to *remove* the threat?"[54] In 1951, that question inevitably raised the possibility of a preemptive atomic strike against the Soviets, a possibility that had often been discussed by the

JCS.[55] Eisenhower would not consider it, for political, moral, and practical reasons. He thought "it is obviously impossible for a democracy to mobilize secretly . . . to make a surprise attack." He continued to refer to the bomb as "that awful thing" and to wish that it had never been invented or used against the Japanese. And he pointed out that Russia had its own bomb, which it could use against the great cities of Europe and possibly even against American cities. He also noted that the Red Army could overrun Europe even as American bombs were falling on Moscow.[56]

Since nothing realistic could be done to remove the threat, and since it had to be met, the dilemma deepened. The cost of meeting the threat was horrendous. Truman's 1952 budget called for spending $85 billion, with a contemplated deficit of $14 billion; nearly $65 billion of that money would go for defense. Eisenhower was appalled by such figures, even though he knew that his own activities in demanding more for NATO were a part of the problem. But he feared that "we are risking damage from the other horn of our dilemma—that is, the danger of internal deterioration through the annual expenditure of unconscionable sums on a program of indefinite duration, extending far into the future."[57] To Charles Wilson, president of General Motors, Eisenhower said that "any person who doesn't clearly understand that national security and national solvency are mutually dependent, and that permanent maintenance of a crushing weight of military power would eventually produce dictatorship, should not be entrusted with any kind of responsibility in our country."[58]

As SACEUR, Eisenhower had to insist that both Europeans and Americans do more to bolster their defenses, but as a strict conservative on financial issues, he was committed to both a balanced budget and lower taxes. That program could only be accomplished through drastic cuts in defense spending, and the most obvious place to cut was MDAP and American forces in Europe. The Korean War was still being fought; the French in Indochina needed more assistance; massive expenditures were crucial to keeping ahead of the Russians in atomic warfare.

Eisenhower's solution was to cut American costs by persuading the Europeans to do more in their own defense and by reducing overall NATO expenditures. Thus he rejected the U.S. Navy's arguments for super-carriers, which were too expensive; thus he argued for trimmer divisions with more fighting men and fewer support systems; thus he rejected the Army's argument for more, and heavier, tanks. He had been one of the Army's first proponents of the tank; now he was the first detractor. He believed that developments in recoilless weapons that could hurl projectiles three thousand yards with remarkable accuracy and with great destructiveness had made "the expensive tank . . . about as valuable as a piece of warm butter." The tank would soon go the way of the dreadnaughts; thus what he wanted was not heavier tanks, but lighter, cross-country vehicles of "great speed, reliability, and low silhouette."[59]

Beyond the question of tactical weapons, Eisenhower kept his emphasis on the Europeans assuming their fair share of the defense burden, so that American troops would not have to stay in Europe for too many years and so that MDAP shipments could be reduced, perhaps even eliminated, by the mid-1950s.[60] Continued deficit spending would bankrupt the United States; it would cause unbearable inflation, which Eisenhower feared as much as he feared the Russians; it would continue and increase the evils of big government and creeping socialism. Worst of all, deficit spending was habit-forming; to George Sloan of Chrysler, Eisenhower compared deficit spending to the taking of drugs—"each dose increases the need for the next one."[61]

To W. M. Clement of the Pennsylvania Railroad, Eisenhower expressed his feelings about the dangers facing America. "Among other things," he said, "they include expenditures so high as to be frightening; taxes so high as to approach the point of destroying initiative; enormous portions of our labor and materials flowing into the negative and sterile organizations known as armies, navies, and air forces; a corresponding lack of many things that people want and need; a constant spiral of rising commodity prices and the costs of everything that go into the production of commodities; . . . and the increasing tendency to depend upon government instead of self."[62]

Such sentiments were exactly what Eisenhower's friends wanted to hear. They responded, in the summer of 1951, by forming—with his knowledge and more or less with his approval—a volunteer organization, Citizens for Eisenhower. Cliff Roberts financed the effort, with help from Ellis Slater, Pete Jones, and the rest of the gang, along with such Republican financiers as John Hay Whitney, L. B. Maytag, and George Whitney, the president of J. P. Morgan & Company. Citizens for Eisenhower then oversaw and encouraged the innumerable Ike Clubs that began springing up around the country. Because the group included no professional politicians, the movement gave the appearance of a spontaneous grass-roots demand.

Eisenhower, meanwhile, began to prepare himself for broader duties. He asked for, and got, "lectures on economics" from such men as Whitney and Paul Hoffman, currently the director at the Ford

Foundation, earlier the administrator of the Marshall Plan.[63] He discussed with Whitney the possibility of going back to the gold standard.[64] He asked Hoffman to have the experts in the Ford Foundation provide him with an education on "the farm problem" and on the "practicability of substituting State Government for Federal in those instances where certain types of controlled group action appear desirable or necessary."[65] With Bernard Baruch, Herbert Bayard Swope, and others, he discussed, endlessly, the dangers of inflation.[66]

As the Ike Clubs boomed, inevitably the professional politicians began to get involved, through letters, telegrams, speeches, and visits to Paris. Eisenhower was polite to all of them. Senator McCarthy sent him a copy of one of his speeches; Eisenhower made a noncommittal, but friendly, reply.[67] Senator Richard Nixon made a special trip to Paris in late May to meet the general and express his support for NATO.[68]

Insofar as the Ike Clubs claimed to be nonpartisan, and insofar as Eisenhower was so much closer to the Democrats than the Taft-dominated Republicans on foreign policy, and insofar as Eisenhower would be an absolutely sure thing as a Democratic candidate, some Democrats still had hopes of capturing the general. In August 1951, Oregon Democrats filed petitions putting him on the Democratic primary ballot. Eisenhower protested that as SACEUR he could not take a partisan position and asked that his name be removed.[69] Truman, meanwhile, was remaining as mysterious about his plans as Eisenhower was; it was generally acknowledged that he could have the Democratic nomination if he wanted it, but most observers felt he would not have much chance in the general election (his approval rating in the polls was below 30 percent). In November, when Eisenhower was in Washington for consultation on NATO matters, Truman met him privately in Blair House and there repeated an offer he had made earlier through George Allen—the President would "guarantee" Eisenhower the Democratic nomination and give him his full support. "You can't join a party just to run for office," Eisenhower replied. "What reason have you to think I have ever been a Democrat? You know I have been a Republican all my life and that my family have always been Republicans." Truman pressed the offer; Eisenhower rejoined that his differences with the Democrats over domestic issues, especially labor legislation, were too vast for him to even consider accepting.[70]

Had Eisenhower accepted, given that he had more support from Democratic than Republican voters, he would have won a certain victory, probably bringing a Democratic majority to Congress with him. But he would not consider it. For one thing, the Republican Party had to be saved from itself; for another, there were the general's personal feelings. As he noted in his diary, "I could never imagine feeling any compelling duty in connection with a Democratic movement of any kind."[71]

Tom Dewey, titular leader of the Republican Party, also wanted Ike. In October 1950, he had announced that he would prefer Eisenhower as the Republican nominee in 1952. Eisenhower's public response was, "I don't know why people are always nagging me to run for President. I think I've gotten too old."[72] Privately, however, Eisenhower was more receptive. In May 1951, Winthrop Aldrich came to Paris as an emissary from Dewey to discuss tactics. Aldrich said that both he and Dewey felt strongly that, for the present, Eisenhower should "keep still." Eisenhower insisted that his present duty was to NATO: "If I should ever have to do any other, I shall have to be *very clear* that I know it to be *duty*." He admitted, however, that he was impressed by the argument that if he did not run, the Republican Party would disappear, which he regarded as "a disastrous possibility." Nevertheless, because of his NATO position he would not announce his party preference, although he knew it made him appear "evasive and coy."[73]

Taft, meanwhile, was piling up delegates. Equally alarming to Eisenhower's political supporters, the Citizens for Eisenhower group was plagued by problems—internal bickering, fighting for position, poor organization. On September 4, 1951, Senator Henry Cabot Lodge of Massachusetts visited Eisenhower in Paris. He came as a spokesman for numerous East Coast Republicans, and he insisted that it was time to put some professional expertise into the Eisenhower campaign. Getting the nomination would be the hard part, Lodge said. The election was a cinch. Lodge therefore insisted that Eisenhower had to permit the use of his name in the Republican primaries, and to allow professionals to take control of the Citizens for Eisenhower organization. Speed was essential; otherwise Taft soon would have the nomination sewed up. Eisenhower promised to think it over.[74]

In the States, meanwhile, the professionals were trying to infiltrate the Citizens organization. Lucius Clay sent Eisenhower a series of reports on their activities, all done in a simple code. ("Our Friend up the river" was Dewey; "F" was Harold Stassen; "G" was Taft; "A" was Senator James Duff of Pennsylvania; etc.) Clay was disturbed by their infighting—F would not join up if A was a part of the movement; Our

Friend did not like A; and so it went. On a more positive note, Clay reported that "I am convinced that the President will not run if you run. He has made this statement to two separate and reliable persons. He will run if G does, and in my opinion would beat G to a frazzle."[75] Eisenhower responded that he would do whatever duty dictated. He then added that he had been assured by Stassen, who had made a strong bid for the Republican nomination in 1948 and was attempting to do so again in 1952, that at the proper moment he, Stassen, would deliver his delegate votes to Eisenhower. Eisenhower also assured Clay that "you need not worry that I shall ever disregard Our Friend," then ended with a heartfelt handwritten postscript: "Wouldn't it be nice if we could just forget all this kind of thing?"[76]

That was obviously impossible. On November 10, Clay met in New York with Dewey, Duff, Lodge, and a number of Dewey's high command from 1948, including his campaign manager, New York lawyer Herbert Brownell, and his economic adviser, Gabriel Hauge. The group agreed to name Lodge as Eisenhower's campaign manager. Lodge was free of the onus of being a Dewey man (he had supported Arthur Vandenberg in 1948) and had enthusiasm, drive, and professional know-how. As the meeting broke up, Dewey said, "And don't forget, let's get a hell of a lot of money." Harold Talbott of Chrysler, who had made a personal fortune selling airplanes in World War I and who had raised the money for the 1948 Dewey campaign, promised to do just that. So did John Hay Whitney. Sig Larmon of the Young and Rubican ad agency, and an Eisenhower golf crony, would handle publicity. Hauge would do research and establish an economic intelligence unit.[77]

On October 25, Robinson wrote a front-page editorial for the *Herald Tribune* endorsing Eisenhower. "At rare intervals in the life of a free people the man and the occasion meet," Robinson declared. "We believe that for the Republican Party the occasion has now come." Eisenhower had "the vision of the statesman, the skill of the diplomat, the supreme organizing talents of the administrator, and the human sympathies of the representative of the people." Robinson also confidently declared that Eisenhower "is a Republican by temper and disposition . . . by every avowal of faith and solemn declaration." In a private letter to Eisenhower, Robinson said he hoped the editorial "did not cause you too much displeasure or irritation," that it was necessary to slow Taft's momentum, and that the response had been "terrific."[78]

Eisenhower replied that he had been "highly complimented, and I mean highly," by the editorial. What pleased him most was the way in which Robinson had given "encouragement to a great underlying sentiment that might be called a truly grass roots, but definitely inarticulate one." Then he repeated, yet again, that he would never "get tangled up in any kind of political activity unless forced to do so as the result of a genuine and deep conviction expressed by a very large segment of our people."[79]

When Eisenhower flew to New York in November, he spent three hours sitting in the airplane at LaGuardia Airport while Mamie went to Morningside Heights to collect a few things. On the plane, Eisenhower held a meeting with the gang. Milton Eisenhower and Clay also were there. Throughout his brief stay in the States, Eisenhower had been harassed by reporters wanting to know his political preference; he had just come from Washington, where he had turned down Truman's offer; he was exhausted, irritable, and unhappy. But he was also moved by Milton's position, which was that if the choice before the voters in 1952 was to be Truman or Taft, then "any personal sacrifice on the part of any honest American citizen is wholly justified." Robinson pointed out that "in no circumstance could you ever avoid the burden of worry over the country's future course, and there would seem to be fewer frustrations for the leader than there would be for the commentator." Eisenhower replied that he would respond to a genuine draft, that he would do nothing to bring it about, that he would not repudiate the efforts of the Citizens for Eisenhower, and that he wished the whole thing were over, because he certainly did not want to be President.[80]

What it came down to was that Eisenhower wanted to be nominated by acclamation, but his friends knew that was impossible. He was expecting too much; he would have to enter the fight for delegates before Taft had them all. Eisenhower refused. He cited his NATO job, the need for him to remain above politics, and—most of all—Army regulations, which forbade a serving officer from seeking political office. At least, his friends said, allow us to announce that you are a Republican, because Taft's great advantage in the struggle for delegates was his argument that no one knew what political party the general belonged to. Still Eisenhower refused, but he did agree that Milton could make a statement to the effect that the Eisenhower family had always been Republican. Even that statement was unsatisfactory, however; the press and politicians wanted the word from the man himself. *McCall's* magazine even offered Eisenhower a $40,000 check for a yes or no answer to the question "Are you a Republican?" Eisenhower would not say.[81]

• •

Growing pressure caused growing resentment. The more he saw of professional politicians, the less he liked them. "Politics . . . excites all that is selfish and ambitious in man," Eisenhower told Sid Richardson.[82] Shortly after returning to Paris in November, he wrote Robinson, "Every passing day confirms and hardens my dislike of all political activity as a personal participant."[83] Because of that reaction he was increasingly ambiguous, increasingly doubtful that he wanted to pay the price of a political career. In November, Democratic Senator William Benton of Connecticut came to his office to argue that Eisenhower had "no true spiritual and intellectual affinity with the Republicans" and should run as a Democrat. Benton insisted that "there are more ignorant, venal, repulsive individuals in positions of influence in the Republican Party than in the Democratic," which was the kind of political talk that made Eisenhower impatient and irritated. If that was politics, he wanted no part of it.[84] On the other hand, he made moves that indicated a determination to remain politically available. Sid Richardson had been investing some of Eisenhower's *Crusade* money in Texas oil wells; now Eisenhower had to worry about the possibility of making some fantastic profit, which could be used against him in a campaign. Therefore he felt it necessary to tell Richardson to sell his shares for what he had paid for them; "In no case am I to have any profit."[85] That was not the decision of a man planning retirement.

He was distressed by reports from Clay of trouble in the organization. Senator Duff was "full of ego and determined to be the 'anointed.'" Duff did not like Lodge; Lodge could not stand Duff; Dewey was doubtful about both Duff and Lodge; no one trusted Stassen; there were difficulties with the finance managers, as Talbott was suspicious of Winthrop Aldrich, while Aldrich was jealous of Whitney. Strategy sessions were fights rather than discussions, the major issue being when the general should announce his willingness to accept a Republican nomination. It all made Eisenhower's head spin.[86]

The pressure mounted. Paul Hoffman, whom Eisenhower admired enormously (he had urged Hoffman to be a candidate for the Presidency himself and pledged his support if Hoffman would do so), wrote Eisenhower on December 5: "Whether you like it or not, you have to face the fact that you are the one man today who can (1) redeem the Republican party, (2) change the atmosphere of the United States from one impregnated with fear and hate to one in which there will be good will and confidence, and (3) start the world down the road to peace."[87] Clay, Robinson, and dozens of other men Eisenhower respected bombarded him with similar statements. Aldrich sent him a poll taken in Texas that indicated Eisenhower would carry the state by a wide margin.[88] It was that prospect—that all he had to do was say yes and he could be President, and that as President he could save the country—that kept him from repudiating the efforts in his behalf. That, and his feeling that "the presidency is something that should never be sought, [but] could never be refused." He finally admitted in his diary that if the nomination came to him "without any direct or indirect assistance or connivance on my part," it would "place upon me a transcendent duty."[89]

Then, on December 8, what Eisenhower called a crisis arose. Lodge told him that he simply had to return to the States and make a positive announcement or "the whole effort is hopeless." Eisenhower's response was immediate and negative. To involve himself in preconvention activity, he said, "would be a dereliction in duty—almost a violation of my oath of office . . . I shall do no such thing."[90] He told Lodge that "the program in which you and your close political associates are now engaged should, logically, be abandoned." He wanted Lodge to announce that since Eisenhower's backers had concluded that his nomination without his active participation was impossible, and since "it is impossible for me in my position as a military commander" to campaign, the Citizens for Eisenhower group was being disbanded. In his diary, he outlined these developments, then wrote "Hurrah." As far as he was concerned, it was over—or so it seemed.[91]

Getting out was hardly going to be that easy. Stassen flew over to see him and argue for the cause. Clay wrote a long letter, in effect accusing Eisenhower of going back on his word, given at the LaGuardia Airport meeting, that "if a group could prove it was your duty, on their advice you would return home."[92] Eisenhower was disturbed at the charge. He told Clay that he could not bear the thought of returning to the States, that when he was in Washington in November "my life was almost unendurable," and reminded him again of Army Regulations 600-10: "Members of the Regular Army, while on active duty, may accept nomination for public office, provided such nomination is tendered without direct or indirect activity or solicitation on their part."[93] To reporter Cy Sulzberger, who was a house guest in Paris, Eisenhower insisted that he had "no intention of making any move to help those political leaders . . . either covert or overt." He would respond to a draft but he hoped "this will not occur."[94]

Cliff Roberts and Bill Robinson flew over to Paris. He told them that his "feeling midway between aversion and reluctance is 100% real," and that he was "more devoted to the success of his [NATO] mission than intrigued by the idea of being President." Then he came down from Olympus, explaining his own political judgment and in the process revealing political calculations of his own. There were, he said, advantages to his staying at his post and making no political statements. First of all, his success in Europe was the *sine qua non* of a successful bid for the Presidency. He could not claim success until the late February meeting of the NATO Council of Ministers in Lisbon, or until he had issued his Annual Report, in April. Next, he pointed out that "the seeker is never so popular as the sought. People want what they think that they can't get." His nonparticipation in the delegate struggle insured that he had made no deals nor incurred any obligations. If he returned to the States and began to campaign, he would have to take a stand on various emotional issues, which would "alienate more strength than it would develop." Further, he would be subjected to more direct and severe attacks than his opponents would dare risk while he was SACEUR. By avoiding a debate with Taft, he might be able to prevent a split in the party and a bitter personal rivalry.

These were powerful arguments, and they convinced his friends. Robinson's conclusion was that "it would seem that there is more to be gained than lost by staying on the job in Europe."[95]

Like Eisenhower, Truman was keeping his options open. In late December, the President sent Eisenhower a handwritten note, saying that while he would like to retire, his immediate duty was to keep the isolationists out of the White House. He wanted to know Eisenhower's intentions. Eisenhower took two weeks to reply; when he did, his answer left Truman as uncertain as ever. Eisenhower said that he too wanted to retire, but "I've found that fervent desire may sometimes have to give way to a conviction of duty." He would not seek a nomination, and therefore "the possibility that I will ever be drawn into political activity is so remote as to be negligible."[96] Then at a press conference a reporter asked Truman a loaded question designed to produce an anti-Eisenhower statement. The President refused to comment and sent a recording of the conference to Eisenhower. In thanking him, Eisenhower said he too would do all he could to avoid creating any "irritation or mutual resentment between us." Truman replied, "You can rest assured that no matter what the professional liars and the pathological columnists may have to say, you and I understand each other."[97]

Robinson, meanwhile, had carried back to Lodge the arguments Eisenhower had made against his returning home and announcing that he was a Republican. Lodge was unconvinced. The general's position, Lodge agreed, would be a positive factor in winning a general election, but it would not help him win the nomination. Lodge's job was to win delegates, and he could not do so for a man who would not even identify himself as a Republican. Lodge decided to force the issue. On January 6, 1952, he announced that he was entering Eisenhower's name on the Republican ballot in the New Hampshire primary. In response to questions, Lodge told reporters that Eisenhower was indeed a Republican, that he would accept the Republican nomination if it were offered to him, and that the general himself would confirm these statements.[98]

Eisenhower was furious. Lodge's presumption, he told Roberts, "has caused me a bit of bitter resentment."[99] He sent a sharp letter of rebuke to Clay,[100] then issued a coy statement of his own. He did not directly confirm Lodge's claim that he was a Republican, but admitted that he did vote for that party. He did not say he would accept a Republican nomination, but did admit that Lodge and his associates had the right "to place before me next July a duty that would transcend my present responsibility." He did not give his approval to the actions of the Citizens, although he added that all Americans were free "to organize in pursuit of their common convictions." He ended with a promise: "Under no circumstances will I ask for relief from this assignment in order to seek nomination for political office, and I shall not participate in . . . preconvention activities."[101]

The pressure continued. Clay told Eisenhower that if he did not allow the use of his name in the primaries, Taft would capture them all, and the nomination with them.[102] Ellis Slater reported to Robinson that on a delegate-hunting trip to Syracuse, he found far more Taft support than he anticipated. Syracuse was an industrial city, and Slater learned that every manufacturer, banker, and lawyer in town was for Taft, because Taft had done "such a grand job in fighting the unions."[103] Hoffman joined the Citizens on a full-time basis, and he too told Eisenhower to come home.

The pleas that he return were making the general testy. He told Clay, "I fail to see why something of a virtue cannot be made of my refusal to have my attention diverted from my assigned duty."[104] And he told Hoffman, "Some insist that I come home (possibly, I suppose, as a deserter)."[105] He asked Robinson to tell the politicians to lay off, that the more they pleaded with him the more he would dig in his heels. "While I might possibly be induced to make some slight modification of my predetermined course of action," he added, "it would be only on the advice of some such group as one composed of you, Cliff, Pete Jones,

Clay, Milton, and Slats. Others may as well save their time and effort!"[106]

But events continued to drive him toward a different course. On January 21, Truman submitted his budget, with its $14 billion deficit, to Congress, which led Eisenhower to dictate an eight-page furious protest in his diary. On February 8, Herbert Hoover joined Taft and sixteen other prominent Republicans in a statement that urged that "American troops should be brought home" from Europe.[107] Which was worse, the danger of bankruptcy or isolation, Eisenhower hardly knew, but he felt he had to stop both trends.

There was also the pressure of being wanted as well as needed. It was the pressure he was apparently waiting to see. His friends and the politicians kept telling him how much the American people yearned for his leadership, and on February 11, he got a dramatic demonstration of how right they were. Jacqueline Cochran, the famous aviator and wife of Floyd Odlum, the financier, flew to Paris with a two-hour film of an Eisenhower rally in Madison Square Garden, held at midnight following a boxing match. It had been carefully stage-managed by Eisenhower's friends and the Citizens. Some fifteen thousand people attended, despite—according to Cochran—a total lack of cooperation from the city officials (all, of course, Democrats). The film showed the crowd chanting in unison, "We want Ike! We want Ike!" while waving "I Like Ike" banners and placards. Eisenhower and Mamie watched in their living room and were profoundly moved.

When the film was over, Eisenhower got Cochran a drink. As they raised their glasses, she blurted out a toast: "To the President." She later recalled, "I was the first person to ever say this to him and he burst into tears . . . Tears were just running out of his eyes, he was so overwhelmed . . . So then he started to talk about his mother, his father and his family, but mostly his mother, and he talked for an hour." Then Cochran told him that he would have to declare himself and go back to the States, that "I'm as sure as I'm sitting here and looking at you that Taft will get the nomination if you don't declare yourself." Eisenhower told her to return to New York and tell Clay to come to Europe for a talk, then added, "You can go tell Bill Robinson that I'm going to run."[108]

The next morning Eisenhower dictated a series of letters to his closest friends (some thirty pages of single-spaced typing in all). Each expressed his astonishment and emotion. To Swede, for example, he said the film "brought home to me for the first time something of the depth of the longing in Americans today for a change . . . I can't tell you what an emotional upset it is for one to realize suddenly that he himself may become the symbol of that longing and hope."[109] In another letter, he spoke of a "mandate" from the people, how touched he was by the evidence that the people wanted him, and that "if any American could fail to feel . . . a deep sense of overpowering pride in such confidence, then I should say he would be scarcely human."[110]

Five days later, Eisenhower met with Clay, Richardson, and George Allen in London, where he had gone to attend the funeral of King George VI. Clay told him that Taft already had 450 pledged delegates (it took 604 to nominate), with another 70 or so leaning his way. Clay thought that Eisenhower also had about 450 delegates, and that most of the uncommitted would stay that way until just before the convention. Therefore, Eisenhower need not come home before June 1, "when the heat is on," to fight it out for those 300 votes. Then, Clay said, "you will be a fresh figure, untouched by all the campaigning that is now going on, and a certain Republican winner." Eisenhower could kick off his campaign with a speech in Abilene.[111]

That program suited Eisenhower perfectly. The NATO meeting in Lisbon would be over by then, he would have issued his Annual Report, and he could safely resign as SACEUR, satisfied that he had gotten NATO off to a good start and unhampered by feelings of being a deserter. He and Clay shook hands on it. The commitment had been made.

On March 11, 1952, in the New Hampshire primary, Eisenhower beat Taft and Stassen with 50 percent of the vote to their 38 percent and 7 percent. A week later, in Minnesota, Eisenhower received 108,692 write-in votes while Stassen, his name on the ballot in his home state, got 129,076 (Taft did not run). As Stassen had privately assured Eisenhower of his support at the convention, those delegates could be added to the Eisenhower total. He was on his way.

He was not entirely happy about it. Robert Anderson, a forty-two-year-old Texas lawyer, politician, and financier, who flew to Paris to consult with the candidate about the Federal Reserve Board, found Eisenhower "working himself into physical exhaustion" as he tried to finish his NATO duties and prepare himself for the campaign.[112] Cy Sulzberger came to play golf; he noted that the general was crotchety, tired, and pale. In the locker room after one round, Eisenhower growled, "Anybody is a damn fool if he actually seeks to be President. You give up four of the very best years of your life."[113]

To Clay, Eisenhower wrote, "When I was a boy, I had one pastime that was rather fascinating to me. I would go out to the corral in the morning and watch one of the men trying to get a loop over the neck of a horse. I was always pulling for the horse but . . . he was always caught—no matter how vigorously he ducked and dodged and snorted and stomped. Little did I think, then, that I would ever be in the position of the horse!"[114]

Caught unwillingly or not, Eisenhower was not going to go into a battle expecting to lose. He had earlier told Robinson, "If ever I get into this business, I am going to start swinging from the hips and I am going to keep swinging until completely counted out."[115] He was ready to start swinging, although not ready to begin making statements on the issues. As he explained to George Sloan of Chrysler, "A premature consumption of all the ammunition in a battle is certain to bring defeat—everything must be so calculated that the effort constantly increases in its intensity towards its ultimate maximum, which is the moment of victory."[116] Privately, he sent long letters to his business friends, bemoaning high taxes and government bureaucracy; he counted on them to pass the letters around. He met regularly, if secretly, with prominent Republican politicians. He assured Texans that he was on the side of states' rights in the tidelands oil dispute with the federal government. He assured doctors that he was completely opposed to socialized medicine. He wrote a long, friendly letter to Drew Pearson on the subject of Christianity versus Communism. He opened a correspondence with various Republican governors.[117]

He continued to arm himself for battle. He asked experts for background papers on mortgage financing, farm subsidies, public housing, and a myriad of other subjects.[118] He asked John Foster Dulles to give him a statement on the problems of dealing with the Russians.[119] Herb Brownell came over to Paris to assure Eisenhower that Dewey had the New York delegation solidly behind the general, and could deliver other East Coast delegations. The two men discussed the mechanics of a presidential campaign, scheduling, speeches, platforms, organization needs, and such issues as Social Security, race relations, and the budget.[120]

On the personal side, Eisenhower told Cliff Roberts that after he retired from the Army, he would need financial help to retain the services of Moaney and Dry, for without them "I could not possibly carry the load that each day brings to me." Roberts had already assured him that the gang would take care of such expenses, but Eisenhower wanted to make certain it was done legally and on the "up-and-up." Roberts said that could be done.

The intense activity—Eisenhower said he could never recall being busier—made him fear he was "heading directly for the psychoneurotic ward. I'm getting so I'm almost afraid to pass a doctor in the hall."[121]

In early April 1952, Eisenhower issued his NATO report. It was decidedly upbeat. ("The tide has begun to flow our way and the situation of the free world is brighter than it was a year ago . . . Our active forces have increased to a point where they could give a vigorous account of themselves, should an attack be launched against us.")[122] Then he sent his request for relief from his assignment, effective June 1, to Truman (who, having heard from George Allen of Eisenhower's plans, had recently announced that he would not be a candidate for re-election). NATO, Eisenhower assured the President, was in good shape. "Patterns of development have been devised, security plans prepared, organizations set up, logistic and support measures initiated, first candid reexaminations made and, from now on, progress will . . . follow the lines . . . already marked out."[123] Truman responded with a handsome handwritten letter. He said Eisenhower's resignation "makes me rather sad . . . I hope you will be happy in your new role."[124]

Eisenhower's upbeat conclusions about NATO represented the kind of self-serving assessment any presidential candidate would make of his own performance in his most recent job. He ignored the many unsolved problems he was leaving behind, but which he would have to face again if and when he won the election. NATO was still woefully short of matching the Red Army and its allies on the ground; despite Eisenhower's hopes, the United States was no closer to being able to withdraw American ground strength from Europe; the European army did not exist; the United States of Europe was still a long way off; the command structure of NATO was a hopeless muddle.

Nevertheless, there had been accomplishments in which Eisenhower could take justifiable pride. NATO was far stronger in April 1952 than it had been in December 1950. European belief in the NATO concept was growing. The capstone came on May 27, when the foreign ministers of France, West Germany, Italy, and the Benelux countries signed the treaty creating the European Defense Community (EDC). Although the treaty still had to be ratified by the various legislatures, the basis for a European army had been laid. As President, Eisenhower could expect to continue such progress. He was satisfied with what he had done, and with the direction NATO was taking.

Now he was a full-time candidate, pure and simple. His supporters began to bombard him with advice, telling him what he should say on this or that issue. The advice was often cynical. "It seems necessary to walk around some of the questions presented," he wrote Milton. "I seem to sense a difference between a man's convictions and what he believes to be politically feasible."[125] The politicians wanted Eisenhower to "take a stand." He resisted. "Frankly," he told Clay, "I do not consider either race relations or labor relations to be issues. And I don't believe the problems arising within either of them can be ended by punitive law or a statement made in a press conference."[126] When he did express his views, he got into trouble. After his pro-Texas views on the tidelands matter became known, Lodge wrote in alarm—Eisenhower's stand would hurt him in the Northeast, and he should retreat from a flat endorsement of the Texas claims. Eisenhower replied, "I am compelled to remark that I believe what I believe." He said the original treaty between Texas and the United States specifically guaranteed the tidelands to the state, which as far as he was concerned settled the matter. He added that he would not "tailor my opinions and convictions to the one single measure of net vote appeal."[127]

With all the conflicting advice, with all that Brownell had told him about the rigors of a presidential campaign, with the attacks on him that the Taft people were already launching, with the wrench that came with packing up and moving again, Eisenhower's mood was glum. "Soon I shall be coming home," he wrote Cliff Roberts on May 19, "and I really dread—for the first time in my life—the prospect of coming back to my own country."[128]

Why then was he going? Of all the arguments used to induce him to enter the campaign, three were decisive. First was the matter of duty, and the man who had presented that case in a decisive fashion was his brother Milton. Milton had been opposed to his brother's entering politics and thereby endangering his reputation and his place in history, not to mention the personal sacrifices involved. But when Milton told Dwight that if he did not run, the nation would have to choose between Taft or Truman, and that in such circumstances any sacrifice by any individual who could prevent such a disaster was justified, Dwight had to agree. Second was the matter of a mandate, and the woman who made it clear to him that he had one was Jacqueline Cochran. "Even though we agree with the old proverb, 'The voice of the people is the voice of God,'" Eisenhower had written Clay, "it is not always easy to determine just what that voice is saying."[129] Cochran's dramatic presentation of the Madison Square Garden rally convinced him that the people wanted him.

But the most decisive argument was the one put forward by Bill Robinson, sitting in the airplane at LaGuardia Airport. "In no circumstance could you ever avoid the burden of worry over the country's future course," Robinson had said, "and there would seem to be fewer frustrations for the leader than there would be for the commentator." The truth was that Eisenhower was not ready to retire or abandon his country to others. At sixty-one years of age, he was in excellent health. Indeed, despite his irritability at being pushed and pulled in every direction, most observers thought that he had never looked better. As he had done for the past decade, he was working a twelve-to-fourteen-hour day, seven days a week. He was intensely involved, totally active. And, despite his oft-expressed modesty, he was supremely self-confident, certain that of all the candidates for national leadership, he was the best prepared for the job. Although he never said so, even to himself, he knew that he was smarter, more experienced, and had better principles than his competitors, and thus was the right man to lead America through the world crisis. He wanted what was best for his country, and in the end he decided that he was the best and would have to serve.

As he prepared to leave Paris, he received a farewell letter from an old British associate with whom he had had many a battle during the war. If he needed any confirmation of the wisdom of his agreeing to be a candidate, Field Marshal Alan Brooke supplied it. "Personally I thank God that you have decided to do so," Brooke wrote, "for I feel that the future security of the world depends on your now assuming this great office and of being in a position to guard the steps of your great country during the critical years to come."[130]

CHAPTER TWENTY-SIX

Abilene, New York, Denver, Chicago

June–August 1952

ON JUNE 1, Eisenhower returned to the States. The following day he paid Truman a courtesy call. They got to talking politics. Already the Taft people were circulating stories about Mamie's alleged drinking habits, about Eisenhower's supposedly being Jewish, about Eisenhower's presumed secret and continuing love affair with Kay Summersby, and other slanderous material. Truman expressed his sympathy, then said, "If that's all it is, Ike, then you can just figure you're lucky."[1] Eisenhower then flew off to Kansas City. There he was met by Governor Dan Thornton of Colorado, a big, outgoing man wearing cowboy boots, a ten-gallon hat, and a huge smile. "Howya, pardner!" Thornton boomed as he gave Eisenhower a powerful slap on the back. A reporter noted, "There was a tense moment as the General's eyes blazed and his back stiffened. Then, with great control, he gradually unfroze into a smile and reached out his hand to say, 'Howya, Dan.'"[2]

Politics, American style. In England, Eisenhower ruefully noted, men "stood" for office, but in America they had to "run." He had feared that he was going to hate the whole process; now he was sure he had been right. Still, he had promised Bill Robinson that "if ever I get into this business, I am going to start swinging from the hips," and he told "Gee" Gerow that "having put my hand to the plow I intend to see the job through to the end of the furrow."[3] He was determined to win, even if it meant ignoring base slurs on his personal life, mindless attacks on his public record, and affronts to his dignity. He was also willing to pander to those whose support he needed, even if it meant tailoring his views to meet their desires.

The Republican Party of 1952, after twenty years without power or responsibility, was frustrated, angry, negative. What it did best was to criticize, charge, accuse. When it went after the New Deal in general, Eisenhower was in perfect agreement, although on such specific issues as Social Security he was more inclined to take a moderate position. But on foreign policy, he had a major problem. Senator McCarthy's assault against George Marshall ("part of a conspiracy so immense, an infamy so black, as to dwarf any in the history of man") was perhaps a bit more extreme than most Republicans would indulge in, but only a bit. But it was from the midwestern and western Republicans, men who had voted against the Marshall Plan and NATO, that Eisenhower would have to find the delegate votes to beat Taft. Therefore his initial national appearances would not be national at all, but rather appeals to the right wing of the GOP. And for the Old Guard, of all the infamies committed by the Democrats in their "twenty years of treason," the greatest were Yalta and the loss of China. To them, Yalta was the focal point of their hatred of FDR, China of their hatred of Truman.

Now, the truth was that Eisenhower had been one of FDR's principal agents in carrying out his foreign policy in Europe during the war, and Truman's Chairman of the JCS when China was "lost." Eisenhower was hardly an unwilling agent. No matter how much he dodged, equivocated, denied, or explained his actions, it was inescapable that he had loyally, indeed enthusiastically, helped implement FDR's policy. His refusal to race the Russians to Berlin or Prague and his attempts to get along with Zhukov in the second half of 1945 gave the strongest possible support to the Yalta agreements. His close involvement with the Truman Administration in 1948 and 1949 had given at least implied consent to the China policy. These facts were the major obstacle to his winning the nomination. He knew it, and knew he had to leap over it.

At Abilene, on June 4, he gave his first nationally televised political speech. It was, taken all together, a dismal affair. It was raining; the grandstand was half empty; he looked odd in his civilian raincoat; he read, without emotion and indistinctly, from a prepared text; his phrases were repetitious and familiar. But what he accomplished was more important than the appearance, because he reassured the Old Guard. He was an enemy of inflation, he said, and of excessive taxation, of centralization of government, of dishonesty and corruption, etc. Most of all, he deplored the secrecy of Yalta and the loss of China. Although he did condemn "the utter futility of any policy of isolation," his emphasis on Yalta and China was exactly what the uncommitted delegates wanted to hear; it also set the tone for the campaign that followed.[4]

The next day Eisenhower held a press conference. Reporters agreed that in contrast to his prepared speech, the general's spontaneous response to specific questions was superb. James Reston thought that Eisenhower was the greatest master of the press conference since FDR: indeed, he was better than Roosevelt because he avoided petulance and sarcasm. "He is direct," Reston wrote, "and what is equally important, he seems to be more direct in answer to some questions than he actually is. He speaks in sentences and avoids intellectual detours."[5] On the specific issues, Eisenhower said he had no secret formula for ending the Korean War, pointed to the risks of bombing across the Yalu River, and said he would work for a "decent armistice." He favored civil rights, but thought the responsibility should be left to the individual states and thus he opposed the Fair Employment Practices Commission (FEPC). He would rid the economy of "artificial direct legislative controls" and rely on a free marketplace. He attacked socialized medicine while arguing that "every American has the right to decent medical care." And so on. The loaded question came: "Would he support the re-election of Senator McCarthy?" The candidate replied that he would not indulge in personalities—the first of countless times he would duck the McCarthy question with that response—but he added that no one was more determined than he was that "any kind of Communistic, subversive or pinkish influence be uprooted from responsible places in our government." Would he say who was responsible for the loss of China? Again, he refused to indulge in personalities.[6]

It was nicely pitched to win delegates; it followed the advice he received from Lodge, Brownell, Dewey, and the others; it made him squirm. Politics is a strange business, he wrote Al Gruenther in Paris: "Everything is calculated; the natural and the spontaneous are frowned upon severely."[7] But he had to fight according to the rules of the game, insofar as there were any, and he was prepared to do so. A major worry of the uncommitted Republican delegates about Eisenhower, aside from his position on Yalta and China, was what kind of a candidate he would make. Concerned about their own election, they wanted to know what Eisenhower could contribute to it. Did he have the energy for a campaign? Would he repeat an acceptable GOP litany? Would he, unlike Willkie, work within the organization? Did he have the kind of voter appeal that would bring out their constituents on election day? As Supreme Commander and as SACEUR, Eisenhower had been treated by reporters with deference, but now that the Presidency was at stake, he could expect a barrage of hostile questions. Could he stand up to them? Eisenhower could answer these questions most effectively through face-to-face, private meetings with the various state delegations, and he began to do so on June 6, in Abilene, with a series of conferences.

The meetings were triumphs. There was nothing like the feel of the man, the firm handshake, that marvelous grin, the enthusiasm, the just-plain-folks touch, the confidence, determination, knowledge, intelligence, the total presence. Quintessentially the best way to sell General Eisenhower was to let people meet him. Eisenhower met many delegates; most came away convinced. Partly this response was due to his ability to hold his temper in the face of boorish questions. It must have taken a tremendous effort of will, for example, for Eisenhower to remain calm when a delegate from Nebraska told him, "General, we're not worried about what you stand for. We think we understand that pretty well. But we're worried about your wife." Quietly, without rancor, Eisenhower said, "Yes?" "We hear she's a drunk." Eisenhower leaned back, took a short breath, and said, "Well, I know that story has gone around, but the truth of the matter is that I don't think Mamie's had a drink for something like eighteen months." Eisenhower was, Merriman Smith recalled, "very bland. Never ruffled him at all."[8] After that, none of the Nebraska delegates, at least, ever doubted his ability to take whatever hostile reporters might throw at him.

From Abilene, Eisenhower returned to New York, where he and Mamie took up residence in Morningside Heights (he was still technically the president of Columbia), and held a week of meetings with East Coast delegations. The most important of these was Pennsylvania. There, Governor John Fine headed a delegation that was split, 20 for Eisenhower, 18 for Taft, and 32 uncommitted. Eisenhower had a private three-hour meeting with Fine, which was indecisive, as Fine wanted to keep his delegates uncommitted for as long as possible in order to extract the maximum price for their votes. Fine did agree to bring 120 delegates and alternates to Eisenhower's Gettysburg farm on June 13 for a picnic. It was a success; Eisenhower joked and bantered with the politicians, answered their questions in his simple, forthright manner, and gave them a flash of Eisenhower anger. When he was asked whether he was prepared to wage an enthusiastic campaign, he snapped that it was a "funny kind of question to put to a man who has spent forty years of his life fighting."[9]

When the New Hampshire delegation came to Morningside Heights, Eisenhower met Governor Sherman Adams for the first time. Few people actually liked Adams—thin, nervous, crisp to the point of rudeness, Adams had a face that looked as if it had been carved from New Hampshire granite, a demeanor as cold as a New Hampshire winter—but Eisenhower saw in him many of the qualities that Bedell Smith possessed, and sensed that he would have the same kind of loyalty and efficiency. Eisenhower therefore agreed to Lodge's suggestion that Adams be designated the floor manager for the Eisenhower forces at the convention.[10]

After a week in New York, the Eisenhowers took the train to Denver, stopping en route to address forty thousand people in Cadillac Square in Detroit. He had a prepared speech, but announced that he was abandoning it to talk from the heart. Then he asserted that he had had no personal responsibility for the diplomatic blunders at Yalta and Potsdam, that he had had no part in the formation of the Morgenthau Plan, and that the decision not to go into Berlin was a political one beyond his control. Then he defended that decision, and in effect contradicted himself, when he reminded the audience that "none of these brave men of 1952 have yet offered to go out and pick the ten thousand American mothers whose sons would have made the sacrifice to capture a worthless objective." He concluded by leading the crowd in reciting the Pledge of Allegiance.[11]

In Denver, he set up headquarters in the Brown Palace Hotel, where he received delegations from the Midwest and West. In these meetings, he followed the advice given him by Bill Robinson, who said that since his return to the States, "you have dispelled completely the Taft forces' charges that you were a New Dealer; you were beholden to Roosevelt and Truman; you were another Willkie; you are not a valid Republican." Therefore, Robinson said, within the Republican Party "there is virtually no concern about your political philosophy on domestic problems," which meant that Eisenhower could from then on concentrate on foreign affairs, where his experience and record were in sharp contrast with Taft's ignorance and inexperience.[12] Taft, while continuing to oppose an American commitment to NATO, had joined with MacArthur in calling for "unleashing" the Nationalist Chinese against the mainland and for an all-out offensive designed to bring about a victory in Korea. Eisenhower told the delegates from Oregon and Arizona that such a program would risk a general war over a country whose strategic position did not justify it. Japan, he asserted, was "the real outpost of our civilization" in the Far East, and Japan "must not be jeopardized by ill-advised ventures in Korea and Formosa."[13]

The delegate meetings, Eisenhower told Cliff Roberts, "are always on an informal and friendly basis and I know have been productive of mutual respect, and in many cases even liking." Unfortunately, when the delegates were met by the press afterward, "they do not always accurately reflect what I have said." That morning, for example, blazing headlines proclaimed that Eisenhower had a plan to win the Korean War. What he actually said, Eisenhower told Roberts, "was that there was no easy way out of the Korean war and that the only program I could offer was . . . to organize and arm the necessary number of South Koreans to defend their own front lines and withdraw our own troops into reserve positions." He recognized that "this is far from a satisfactory solution but it is the only one that looks to me to have any sense at this moment."[14]

Eisenhower's moderate position on Korea was crucial to his campaign. "Give the people what they most need," Robinson had told him, "the hope and the confidence that peace and security can be achieved."[15] When Taft claimed that there was little difference between them on foreign policy, Eisenhower hooted, then contrasted Taft's adventurousness in the Far East with his own prudent approach, and Taft's willingness to abandon Europe with his own determination to defend it. On domestic issues, meanwhile, Eisenhower continued to take positions that were, if anything, to the right of Taft. He also continued to pour out the key words Republicans wanted to hear. On June 26 he gave a national radio-TV address before a Denver Coliseum crowd of eleven thousand that had been warmed up by such movie stars as Humphrey Bogart and Susan Hayward.* Eisenhower denounced Yalta, blamed the Democrats for the loss of China, and accused Truman of being too soft on corruption at home and on Communism abroad. "If we had been less trusting," Eisenhower said, "if we had been less soft and weak, there would probably have been no war in Korea!" He repeated his commitment to sound fiscal practices: "A bankrupt America is a defenseless America."[17]

The next morning he embarked on a ten-day trip back and forth across the Great Plains, Taft country. He met privately with politicians, and gave a series of public addresses, with the emphasis on the positive things he could accomplish. One new theme was the need to get young people into the GOP; he insisted that the time had come to give eighteen-year-olds the vote. Another was that within the United States "we have a vast reservoir of good will just waiting to be tapped." He deplored the way the politicians "stirred people up," and the "scary talk about Russia." He said he did not believe "every Russian is fourteen feet high." If the American people would pull together, then there was no

* Taft had movie stars among his supporters too, including John Wayne, who angrily asked an ex-GI carrying an Ike banner, "Why don't you get a red flag?"[16]

more reason to fear the Russians "than there is to fear polywogs swimming down a muddy creek." He said that the third world war should be directed "against intolerance, ignorance, indifference, hunger, disease and hopelessness."[18]

Taken all together, it was an adroit campaign. It was by no means, however, a complete success. Old Guard delegates enjoyed meeting the general; they were impressed by him and by the response his foreign policy positions brought forth from their constituents; they were satisfied that the general's domestic views were safe. But their hearts belonged to Taft, and if not their hearts, then their pocketbooks did, because Taft controlled the party machinery and had been nurturing for years the party faithful who made up the delegates. On the eve of the convention, the Associated Press calculated that Taft had 530 delegates, Eisenhower 427.

Many of the delegates still chafed under their party's defeat in 1948, and "Mr. Republican" was determined to use his lead to stop Eisenhower by portraying Eisenhower as a front man for the hated Dewey. Taft now brought to the fight his finely honed skills as a practical politician. He was, after all, the son of William Howard Taft, the man who had kept the 1912 GOP nomination from that most popular of all early-twentieth-century Republicans, Theodore Roosevelt.

In 1912, President Taft had lost in the primaries to Roosevelt, badly, but Taft used his control of the party machinery to capture the delegations from those states (a majority) that selected the delegates at a party convention. The South was the key; there were no primaries in the area, for the good reason that there were practically no Republicans. Those that did exist usually worked for the federal government, which meant that they worked for President Taft in 1912. Attempts by pro-Roosevelt voters to take control of these rotten boroughs were ruthlessly turned back by the Taft forces, who then used their domination of the Republican National Committee (RNC) to reject contesting Roosevelt delegations. Roosevelt and his followers then walked out of the GOP convention, formed the Progressive Party, and ran TR for President. The Republican split led to Woodrow Wilson's election and gave the Democrats eight years in the White House. Each Republican faction blamed the other for this disaster.

In 1952, Taft's son was trying to use his father's tactics to capture the nomination. True, he did not control federal patronage, but he had the support of many state party leaders, conservative businessmen who controlled many of the delegates and the machines of the party at local levels in the South. Republican party structures in the South were little more than clubs resuscitated just before national conventions. Despite their meager constituencies, these rotten boroughs controlled almost a third of the convention delegates. None were elected by primaries. All were handpicked by party bosses. As in 1912, there were a number of contested delegations from the South, the most important from Texas. There, on May 3, 1952, some 185 precinct conventions were held. Normally these were small, friendly affairs with foregone conclusions. But in 1952 thousands of Texans showed up, signed a pledge that committed them to participate in Republican Party activities, and then voted overwhelmingly for pro-Eisenhower delegates to the state convention. The Texas national committeeman, Henry Zweifel, charged that these "one-day Republicans" were actually Democrats set on stealing the Republican Party from its rightful owners. He also launched a smear campaign against Eisenhower, creating such headlines as "REDS, NEW DEALERS USE IKE IN PLOT TO HOLD POWER" and "IKE CODDLED COMMUNISTS WHILE PRESIDENT OF COLUMBIA UNIVERSITY." Then, on May 27, when the Eisenhower delegates showed up at the state convention at Mineral Wells, Zweifel rejected them and selected a delegation that was thirty for Taft, four for MacArthur, and four for Eisenhower. The Eisenhower forces, meanwhile, held a rival convention and picked a delegation that was thirty-three for Eisenhower, five for Taft.[19]

Eisenhower was outraged, shocked, incredulous—at least in public. "The rustlers stole the Texas birthright instead of Texas steers," he charged in a Dallas speech on June 21.[20] Actually, his managers had known in advance what would happen, warned Eisenhower about it, and decided that taking the high ground of moral outrage was their only hope of stealing the delegation back from Taft. Lodge and Brownell knew that the Taft people had a solid argument—the credentials of the Eisenhower "Republicans" in Texas were certainly suspect—and, far more important, control of the RNC. Under existing party rules, the RNC would decide between contesting delegations. It could be expected to give Texas, and other disputed southern delegations, to Taft; with those votes, he would have more than the 604 required for nomination. The only hope for the Eisenhower people was to change the rules.

While Eisenhower toured the Great Plains, denouncing rotten boroughs and corrupt political practices, Lodge did the work. He first had to turn back a spurious offer of compromise from Herbert Hoover, who said he would be willing to sit with two other "eminent persons" to work out an agreement. As Hoover was a Taft supporter, Lodge knew that that way lay disaster, and he boldly maintained that there was nothing to mediate. He loftily declared, "It is never right to compromise with dishonesty."[21] Lodge then offered the "Fair Play Amendment," which would change the party rules by denying the national committee the right to seat contested delegates on a temporary basis. That possibility was the great danger, because if the Taft people from Texas were seated, even temporarily, they could then join the other Taft delegates in voting themselves into permanent seats. If the full convention voted for Fair Play, before the disputed delegates were seated, then the delegates as a whole would choose between the disputed southern delegations. In that case the Eisenhower people, joined by delegates pledged to various favorite sons (who also had to stop Taft), would prevail.

Eisenhower, taking his instructions from Lodge, declared, "I'm going to roar out across the country for a clean, decent convention. The American people deserve it."[22] But however loudly the general roared, the real action was in the smoke-filled rooms in Chicago, site of the convention, and there everything depended on Lodge. Eisenhower was more a bystander than a participant in this process.

Lodge, like Taft, had a famous forebear. In 1912, ironically, Senator Henry Cabot Lodge had stayed with the Regular Republicans and supported President Taft. In 1920, his eighteen-year-old grandson and namesake had watched him secure the nomination for Warren Harding. An urbane Harvard graduate, former editorial writer for the *Herald Tribune,* a bit pudgy but possessing an aristocratic look highlighted by his penchant for pin-striped three-piece suits, the younger Lodge proved himself to be a master of political intrigue and the perfect choice as Eisenhower's manager. He could count on votes for Fair Play from Stassen; Dewey had the New York delegation firmly in hand; the key state was California. There Governor Earl Warren, Dewey's running mate in 1948, was the favorite son. Warren was hoping for a deadlocked convention between Eisenhower and Taft, from which he might emerge as the compromise choice. He therefore wished to avoid alienating either side, and thus wanted to split the California vote on Fair Play down the middle. If that happened the amendment would probably lose.

Lodge had to go around Warren (and California Senator William Knowland, who was backing Warren but was eager to jump over to Taft at the right moment). To do so, he turned to California's junior senator, Richard Nixon. "I couldn't think of anybody else who could keep the California delegation in line," Lodge later explained.[23] On the Senate floor one month before the convention, Lodge whispered discreetly to Nixon that he was being considered for the second place on an Eisenhower ticket.[24] When Nixon made a speech in New York,

Dewey also hinted to him about a possible vice-presidential nomination. Nixon then went to work. Following the June 3 California primary, which Warren won easily (Eisenhower was not on the ballot), Nixon conducted a private poll of twenty-three thousand constituents, asking their opinion of "the strongest candidate that Republicans could nominate for President." This action represented a virtual break with Warren (Eisenhower won Nixon's poll handily) and led to an open struggle for control of the California delegation. In public, Nixon denounced the "Texas grab" and declared that if the GOP gave the contested seats to Taft, the Republicans would lose the "corruption issue." He also warned that the party "can't hope to win this November if it limits its membership to the minority."[25] In private, on the train ride from California to Chicago, Nixon worked on individual delegates with a combination of promises and threats. Then, in a heated caucus, Nixon took control of the delegation from Warren and committed it to Fair Play.[26]

In Chicago, meanwhile, on July 1, the RNC convened to study the credentials of the contested delegations. The Taft people offered a compromise to Lodge, one that would have given Taft half the disputed votes (and thus, probably, the nomination). Lodge refused. Simultaneously, at a national governors' conference in Houston, Sherman Adams maneuvered the Republican governors, including Taft's supporters, into signing a telegram to Guy Gabrielson, the chairman of the RNC, urging him to "support a ruling that no contested delegate may vote to determine the outcome of any contest." That key phrase was buried on page two of the telegram and the pro-Taft governors did not know what they had signed.[27]

On July 5, Eisenhower arrived in Chicago. He set up headquarters in the Blackstone Hotel, where he met delegates on a nonstop basis, one group waiting in one of his living-room suites while he talked to a different delegation in the other one. He also met privately with Governor Fine and Arthur Summerfield, who controlled the Michigan delegation. Each man said he favored the general but was not yet ready to make a public announcement to that effect. They were also coy about how their delegations would vote on Fair Play.

Eisenhower had his longest talk with Warren. After the California governor left, Eisenhower told reporters that he liked the man because they shared middle-of-the-road views. "Neither Warren nor I is going to get involved with a lot of pinkos," Eisenhower said, "but we're not going to get dragged back by a lot of old reactionaries either." To many visitors, he seemed curiously detached. He kept repeating Fox Conner's advice to "always take your job seriously, never yourself." He said that what happened to him was unimportant; what was of "paramount importance" was the principle of Fair Play.[28]

Taft, meanwhile, had good reason for optimism. His people controlled the convention machinery. General MacArthur would be the keynote speaker, Hoover and Senator McCarthy were scheduled to give major addresses, and other Taft supporters had prominent roles. On July 4, Taft made his major play. He wrote a public letter to Gabrielson, offering yet another compromise. He would split the Texas delegation with Eisenhower, giving the general sixteen seats and leaving himself twenty-two, which was eight less than he had. "If General Eisenhower and his managers hold with me that the good of the party comes first," Taft wrote, "they will not hesitate to accept my proposal. While I will suffer a delegate loss in making this proposal, I am doing so because I think it is so generous that its equity cannot be questioned, and I am willing to take that loss as a contribution to the strengthening of the Republican Party."[29]

Eisenhower had spent his life working out compromises between strong-willed people. Taft's proposal seemed to him to be exactly what Taft said it was, fair and generous. "Gee, that sounds good," Eisenhower told reporters when they informed him of Taft's offer. "That's swell."[30]

With those words, he nearly lost everything, because he had fallen into a trap. A compromise settlement would concede that there were two possible versions to the Texas story, and it would thus deprive Lodge of his most persuasive issue, the moral one. More important, it would give Taft the votes to prevail.

Lodge recognized this immediately. It was his finest hour. He rushed forward to denounce the Taft maneuver and coldly reject any compromise. He carefully explained to Eisenhower how naïve and foolish the general had been and told Eisenhower to thereafter stay in his suite and keep his reactions to himself. Then he went out to begin a complex process of managing a series of procedural votes leading up to the adoption of Fair Play.[31]

All that followed was anticlimax, although it made for spectacular TV viewing (this was the first national convention to be covered by live TV). Along with most of the rest of the nation, Eisenhower watched the proceedings, nearly as bemused by what was happening as was the public. The parliamentary maneuvering was as foreign to him as the duties of the president of Columbia had been. He eventually learned to leave everything to his managers, especially Lodge, Adams, and

Brownell. The general's "above the battle" posture infuriated the Taft people, who blamed Dewey for their woes. Westbrook Pegler wrote that "this Dewey, who was such a mincing, falsetto campaigner . . . is manipulating Taft right out of his nomination . . . with Ike just standing around and doing as he is told and wondering what it is all about."[32]

There was truth in the charge. Increasingly, Eisenhower was spending his time with his brothers, who had gathered with him at the Blackstone, talking about the old days in Abilene. He was also greatly worried about Mamie, who had an infected tooth and proved allergic to the antibiotics prescribed. She was in bed, suffering excruciating pain. Regularly the general would break away from the TV set or reminiscences with his brothers to check on her condition.[33]

The convention rolled forward. MacArthur delivered a bombastic, right-wing assault on the Democrats. McCarthy got thunderous applause for his ringing declaration that "one Communist in a defense plant is one Communist too many. . . . One Communist among the American advisers at Yalta was one Communist too many. And even if there were only one Communist in the State Department, that would still be one Communist too many."[34] When the convention began to discuss the contested seats from Georgia, Senator Everett Dirksen of Illinois asked the delegates to "search their hearts" before voting for the Eisenhower supporters. Staring down at Dewey, who sat well below and to the right of the podium, Dirksen shook his finger at the governor. "We followed you before and you took us down the path of defeat. Don't do it to us again."[35] Boos reverberated through the hall, some directed at Dirksen, some at Dewey. Fistfights broke out. Turmoil swept the galleries. When order was finally restored, Dirksen pleaded, "This is no place for Republicans to be booing any other Republicans."

It was all hoopla, shadow without substance. Lodge already had the votes lined up to carry Fair Play—Nixon was holding California in line, Fine and Summerfield were delivering Pennsylvania and Michigan, Stassen's Minnesota votes were with Eisenhower. Fair Play was adopted, 658 votes to 548. Then the convention rejected the decision of the RNC to seat the Taft delegation from Georgia by a vote of 607 to 531; next it gave unanimous approval to seating the Texans for Eisenhower.

The following day, Eisenhower watched Dirksen nominate Taft, while Governor Theodore McKeldin of Maryland placed his name before the convention. He was filled with a "feeling of indifference, or perhaps numbness, toward the outcome." The "fatigue and strain" of the convention had left him exhausted and confused. He said he really did not care, at that moment, who won.[36] At the end of the first ballot, he had 595 votes, 9 short of victory. Senator Edward Thye of Minnesota, head of the delegation, which had cast 19 votes for Stassen, demanded the floor. The chairman recognized Warren Burger of the Minnesota delegation, who turned the mike over to Thye, who announced that "Minnesota wishes to change its vote to Eisenhower." Other switches then brought Eisenhower's total to 841, but when Knowland moved to make the choice unanimous he was turned back by furious die-hard Taft supporters, who screamed "No!"[37]

Nevertheless, it was over. Eisenhower was the Republican nominee for the Presidency in 1952.

After winning the prize, Eisenhower's first impulse was to be conciliatory. After checking on Mamie, he called Taft on the telephone to ask if he could come across the street to call upon the senator. Taft, surprised, agreed. Eisenhower's advisers, the men who had fought it out in the trenches with the Taft forces and were still bitter (some of them had been spat upon), were all against it. They wanted to relish their triumph and told Eisenhower that a trip to Taft would violate precedent. But Eisenhower was now the nominee, the man in command. His staff could not push him around anymore, and he insisted.

He did so because, although he might be bewildered by the actions of the politicians gathered in convention, an area in which even a lifelong expert like Taft could get lost, Eisenhower knew better than any politician how to exert leadership on a national stage. He was determined to lead a team, and to have a team he had to bring the Taft people back into the mainstream of the Republican Party. Not so much for the vote in November, which he had been told, and believed, was a sure thing. He wanted—he had to have—a team in order to govern, beginning in January 1953. He had to have a united Republican Party to achieve his program. He had not sought the Presidency for personal reasons, and he felt no great sense of personal triumph over Taft. Rather his first thought was to get Taft on the team, for without him there would be no team and nothing could be accomplished.

The meeting itself was matter-of-fact. It took Eisenhower a half hour to work his way through the crowd of cheering supporters. When he finally got to Taft's hotel room (passing in the hall Taft workers who were weeping), he told the senator, "This is no time for conversation on matters of any substance; you're tired and so am I. I just want to say that I want to be your friend and hope you will be mine. I hope we can work together." Taft thanked him; they went into the hall for photographs; Eisenhower returned to the Blackstone.[38]

That was all. But crossing that Chicago street set Eisenhower on a path that he would follow for the next eight years, a path whose destination was an accommodation with the Old Guard, one based on the Old Guard's acceptance of NATO and all that it implied. Through his Presidency, Eisenhower stuck to the path, often complaining along the way about the hopelessness, ignorance, or perfidy of various Republican right-wing senators. He never really made it to his destination, and the right wing never came out of its room to meet him halfway. But he never stopped trying to educate and appease the Old Guard.

Eisenhower's second step on the path was his selection of a running mate. On this decision, his advisers were completely with him, because they too recognized the obvious factors in the situation that dictated who the running mate would be. The criteria, in order of importance, were a card-carrying member of the Old Guard who nonetheless was acceptable to the moderates, especially the Dewey people; a prominent leader of the anti-Communist cause; an energetic and vigorous campaigner; a relatively young man, to offset Eisenhower's age; a man from the West, to offset Eisenhower's association with Dewey and New York; a man who had made a contribution to Eisenhower's winning the nomination.

Taft, knowing that the choice was being made, telephoned Eisenhower's suite in the Blackstone and recommended Dirksen. In view of what Dirksen had said on the floor of the convention, that was obviously impossible. ("After what he said," one of the advisers declared, "I wouldn't wipe my feet on that fellow.") Eisenhower submitted a short list of people acceptable to him. Nixon's name was first, followed by Knowland, Charles Halleck, Walter Judd, and Dan Thornton. The only name on the list to satisfy all the criteria was, as Eisenhower well knew, Nixon's. So it was done. Brownell called Nixon and asked him to come over to the Blackstone to meet Eisenhower.[39]

Eisenhower was coldly formal. He told Nixon he wanted his campaign to be a crusade for all that he believed in and the things he thought America stood for. "Will you join me in such a campaign?" Nixon, somewhat bemused by the pretentious lines, answered, "I would be proud and happy to."

"I'm glad you are going to be on the team, Dick," Eisenhower said. "I think that we can win, and I know that we can do the right things for this country." Then he smacked his forehead with the palm of his hand. "I just remembered," he said. "I haven't resigned from the Army yet!" He dictated a telegram to the Secretary of the Army, resigning his commission. The scene brought tears to Milton and Arthur Eisenhower's eyes.[40]

• •

Eisenhower's third step along the path of accommodation to the Old Guard was his acceptance of the party platform. This was an extreme right-wing document; by asserting that he could and would campaign on it, Eisenhower reached out for party unity. The platform charged that the Democrats "have shielded traitors to the Nation in high places," and sanctimoniously declared, "There are no Communists in the Republican Party." The GOP, it promised, "will appoint only persons of unquestioned loyalty." The foreign policy section, drafted by John Foster Dulles, who hoped to be Secretary of State, pledged the GOP to "repudiate all commitments contained in secret understandings such as those of Yalta which aid Communist enslavement." It damned Truman's containment policy (of which NATO was the most important part) as "negative, futile and immoral," because containment "abandons countless human beings to a despotism and godless terrorism." Then, in an open appeal not only to the Old Guard, which had been thundering about Yalta since 1945, but also to the normally Democratic ethnic vote, Dulles' platform said that a Republican Administration would look "happily forward to the genuine independence of those captive peoples" of Eastern Europe, whom the Democrats had "abandoned . . . to fend for themselves against Communist aggression." (The Old Guardsmen were, indeed, a strange set of isolationists. They doubted the wisdom of giving any help to Western Europe, but claimed to be ready to liberate Eastern Europe and Asia.) The platform did contain, at Eisenhower's insistence, an endorsement of NATO, but to balance that pledge it renounced any intention of sacrificing the Far East to preserve Western Europe.[41]

In his acceptance speech, Eisenhower avoided foreign policy. Instead, he spoke positively. "I know something of the solemn responsibility of leading a crusade," he told the convention. "I accept your summons. I will lead this crusade." He would bring an end to the "wastefulness, the arrogance and corruption in high places, the heavy burdens and the anxieties which are the bitter fruit of a party too long in power." He vowed a "program of progressive policies, drawn from our finest Republican traditions." He asked all the delegates to join his team, then concluded that "since this morning I have had helpful and heartwarming talks with Senator Taft, Governor Warren and Governor Stassen. I want them to know, as I want you now to know, that in the hard fight ahead we will work intimately together." Nixon followed with his acceptance speech, in which he praised Taft to an almost embarrassing degree.[42]

• •

The following day Eisenhower devoted to his family. Mamie was feeling better, and naturally was delighted, proud of her husband, and apprehensive about the rigors of the forthcoming campaign. John spent the day with them; he was en route to Korea, where he was due to join a front-line battalion. His father talked to him, alone, about the possibility of capture, and the danger that the Chinese might use him for blackmail if his father became President. "If you're captured," Eisenhower said, "I suppose I would just have to drop out of the presidential race." But John's years at West Point had taught him the proper response. "You may be confident," John solemnly assured his father, "that I will never be captured."[43]

On July 14, the Eisenhowers flew to Denver, where he again set up a headquarters in the Brown Palace Hotel. One of his first acts was to reply to a handwritten letter from George Marshall. It began, as always, "Dear Eisenhower." After congratulating Eisenhower on his "fine victory," Marshall said that he had "carefully refrained from any communication with you because of a continued effort to keep entirely clear of political affairs. But more than that, I felt because of the vigorous attacks on me by various Republicans any communication with you might be picked up as the basis of some strictures detrimental to your cause." Eisenhower's reply—which began, as always, "Dear General"—expressed his astonishment at the turn of events that had placed him in his present position. "In any event here I am," he continued, "and I shall, of course, fight as hard as I can with the single limit on my efforts defined by honor, fairness and decency." He did not thank Marshall directly for helping him by refusing to comment on the charges of treason brought against him by various Republicans, and he ignored Marshall's gentle reference to Eisenhower's new associates.[44]

Instead, he continued to seek accommodation with the Old Guard. When he read an interview Paul Hoffman had given a California paper, in which Hoffman lambasted the Taft wing of the party, Eisenhower immediately dictated a letter to Hoffman. "I want to point out," he began, "that in our struggle to keep the crusade moving along and to insure its success in November, we should avoid pouring salt in the wounds of the defeated. In every conversation and in public statements, I am careful to see that the principles on which we fought out this campaign are all restated." He explained that, once these principles had been accepted, "I then do my best to enlist the support of those who have been on the other side of the fence—or sitting on the fence. Speaking generally, I believe this is the clearly indicated course of action." His conclusion was direct and to the point: "I trust you agree." Hoffman gave no more interviews.[45]

After writing Hoffman, Eisenhower was off for a ten-day vacation at Aksel Nielsen's ranch at Fraser, Colorado. At 8,700 feet, on the western slope of the Divide, it was a perfect place to be in late July. Eisenhower fished, cooked steaks and trout, and painted. George Allen and other members of the gang were there; Allen insisted on listening to the Democratic convention on the radio. Eisenhower joined him to listen to the acceptance speech of the nominee, Governor Adlai Stevenson of Illinois. Eisenhower was impressed by Stevenson's speaking ability. Allen snorted, "He's too accomplished an orator; he will be easy to beat."[46]

Eisenhower was not so sure. With the nomination behind him, and a specific rival to worry about, the candidate and his advisers could suddenly think of all sorts of things that might go wrong. Dewey's supreme confidence, right up to election night in 1948, was always there to haunt them. The Democratic Party was by far the majority party in the country, it controlled federal patronage, it was accustomed to winning against the heaviest of odds. Taft had withdrawn into a shell; his supporters continued to snarl at Eisenhower; the Republican Party was beset by the twin obstacles of overconfidence and internal division. At Fraser, Eisenhower began preparing for his campaign, working almost as hard as he had in preparing Overlord.

The first problem, as with Overlord, was to pick a staff. Lodge, the obvious man to serve as campaign manager and chief of staff, had his own senatorial campaign to run in Massachusetts. Eisenhower had been much impressed by Sherman Adams' performance at the convention and asked Adams to travel with him through the campaign and serve as his chief of staff. Summerfield, the new chairman of the RNC, was given the title of campaign manager, but the real power lay with Adams. Arthur Vandenberg, Jr., son of the late senator from Michigan and an early Eisenhower-for-President worker, was named as executive assistant. Ex-Dewey aide Thomas Stephens was put in charge of appointments, and James C. Hagerty, Dewey's press secretary, took on that job for Eisenhower.

With these men, and others (including Nixon, who came to Fraser for a few hours' visit), Eisenhower then planned his campaign. The professionals were anxious to get started, eager to hit out at the Democrats. Eisenhower was not. "I alone had to be the judge of my reserve of physical energy," he wrote in his memoirs, "realizing that to start too soon could well result in exhaustion for the candidates and fatigue in the electorate, while to start too late would limit the scope of the effort and might raise again the charge of complacency." Indeed, such charges were already being made against him. But he judged that he could go at full speed for some eight or nine weeks, so he fixed September 1 as the starting date of his active campaigning.[47] It was a wise decision. Not only did he not want to peak prematurely, he was also aware of the risk to his popular image if he appeared too eager for the job.

Eisenhower was also smarter than the professionals on the question of where he should campaign. He insisted on going into the South. The politicians were "flatly opposed." The only electoral votes the Republicans had won in Dixie since Reconstruction had come in 1928, and then only because of Al Smith's religion. But Eisenhower insisted. He had lived for years in the South; he liked southerners; he wanted to be President of all the people;[48] most of all, he thought he had a chance to carry some of the southern states, especially Texas, where he had so many friends and where his position on the tidelands issue was popular. He and Mamie were going to undertake a whistle-stop campaign across the country, and the country included Dixie. That was that.

He was in full command now, although some of the professionals did not yet realize it. At one strategy session, he listened without comment to their chatter. When it was over, he told Adams, "All they talked about was how they would win on my popularity. Nobody said I had a brain in my head."[49] But whatever his staff thought, he was going to be himself, which meant that he was going to be in charge. "I simply hold fast to a few simple rules," he wrote Slats Slater: "(a) to form my own convictions about important . . . matters; (b) never to violate these basic convictions . . . ; (c) to deal honestly with everybody; (d) to work as hard as I can . . . My greatest hope . . . is that every individual who is my good friend at its beginning will likewise be such at its end."[50]

Obviously such high-minded hopes would have to give place, at least occasionally, to practical needs, of which satisfying the Old Guard remained paramount. Much of that work could be done by Nixon, who was already out campaigning, making charges against the Democrats that were nearly as extreme as McCarthy's and in the process delighting the right wing. But the presidential candidate himself would also have to participate in the appeasement of the right.

Thus one of Eisenhower's most important and fateful declarations during the August precampaign period was his support for "liberation of the satellite countries." He had already met with a number of Old Guard senators to bring them onto the team; now, on August 13, he met with Congressman Charles Kersten, the chief congressional spokesman for liberation. As Kersten was one of the leading knights in the anti-Communist crusade, Eisenhower turned to him for help in lifting the tone of that crusade. "What can we do about McCarthy making unproved charges?" he asked Kersten.[51] Unfortunately Kersten, like Eisenhower, did not know what to do about McCarthy.

After Eisenhower talked with Kersten, they held a joint press conference. Eisenhower, who had already warned Dulles about going too far with the liberation talk, was beginning to realize how far he himself had already gone. So, he pledged to initiate a policy that offered hope "of obtaining by peaceful means freedom for the people now behind the Iron Curtain," but he put the emphasis on the word "peaceful." Kersten, speaking next, denounced Yalta as "immoral, unethical and un-American," and said that foreign policy should aim at the "ultimate" freedom for the "captive nations." A beginning, Kersten added, would be to create army units composed of refugees from the satellite countries, then unleash them to break "Stalin's hold" on the "enslaved nations." When Kersten finished, Hagerty rushed to the mike to explain to the press that Eisenhower's earlier statement was "in no way an endorsement" of Kersten's bellicose views.[52]

It was, nevertheless, a theme Eisenhower could not leave alone. Despite the obvious dangers and risks of a call for liberation, the rewards were too great to ignore. Liberation was what the Old Guard wanted to hear; it helped disassociate Eisenhower from Yalta and FDR; it would bring thousands of voters of Eastern European backgrounds into the GOP camp for the first time. So, when Eisenhower went to New York on August 24 to speak to the American Legion convention, and to set up a new headquarters in the city, he brought the theme with him. He told the Legion that the United States should use its "influence and power to help" the satellite nations throw off the "yoke of Russian tyranny." He said that he would inform the Soviet Union that the United States would "never" recognize the "permanence" of the Soviet occupation of Eastern Europe, and that American "aid" to the "enslaved" peoples would not stop until their countries were free.[53]

But Eisenhower was never comfortable with loose talk about war, much less thinly veiled threats to use the atomic bomb. Earlier, in April, when Dulles had said that the United States should develop the will and the means to "retaliate instantly against open aggression by Red armies, so that if it occurred anywhere, we could and would strike back where it hurts, by means of our own choosing," Eisenhower had protested. What if the Communists moved politically, Eisenhower asked, as in Czechoslovakia, to "chip away exposed portions of the free world?

. . . Such an eventuality would be just as bad for us if the area had been captured by force. To my mind, this is the case where the theory of 'retaliation' falls down."[54] Dulles, always anxious to please, replied that Eisenhower had put his finger on a weakness in his theory.

Then just before the convention, Eisenhower had again written Dulles: "Peace is our objective. We reject all talk and proposals of preventive war," and he demanded the deletion of any reference to "retaliation" in the platform.[55] Dulles agreed to do so. But in late August, Dulles told reporters, "What we should do is try to split the satellite states away from the control of a few men in Moscow." Averell Harriman, much alarmed, warned that the loose talk about liberation was spreading the fear of war in Europe and could only lead to premature uprisings like the tragic Warsaw revolt of 1944.[56]

Eisenhower agreed with Dulles' position that it would be immoral to abandon the peoples of Eastern Europe, but he insisted that moral means had to be used for moral purposes, and he was upset at Dulles' continuing belligerent tone. He got Dulles on the telephone and told him that from then on he absolutely had to use the words "all peaceful means" whenever he discussed liberation. Dulles mumbled that the omission was just an oversight; Eisenhower accepted his explanation.[57]

Having given the Old Guard what it wanted on liberation, Eisenhower tried to put some distance between himself and McCarthy. At an impromptu press conference in late August, reporters confronted him with a recent Nixon statement that Eisenhower would support McCarthy and other Old Guard senators as members of the Republican team. Eisenhower said he would support McCarthy "as a . . . Republican," but added forcefully, "I am not going to campaign for or give blanket endorsement to any man who does anything that I believe to be un-American in its methods and procedures." Pressed about McCarthy's charges against Marshall, Eisenhower became angry, got up from his desk, began to pace around the room. "There is nothing of disloyalty in General Marshall's soul," he said, stating what most would have thought to be the obvious with great emphasis. He described Marshall as "a man of real selflessness." In an oblique reference to McCarthy (whom he never mentioned by name), Eisenhower said, "I have no patience with anyone who can find in his [Marshall's] record of service for this country anything to criticize."[58]

Simultaneously, Eisenhower kept his distance from Truman. In mid-August, Truman invited Eisenhower to a White House luncheon with the Cabinet. Bedell Smith, then the CIA director, would give Eisenhower a briefing on the international situation. Eisenhower coldly turned down the President. He said no "grave emergency" required such a meeting, and maintained that it was his "duty to remain free to analyze publicly the policies and acts of the present administration whenever it appears to me to be proper and in the country's interests." He might have added, but did not, that it was unthinkable that Smith might know something of transcendent importance and not pass it along. In a handwritten reply, Truman said that what he had in mind was "a continuing foreign policy. You know that is a fact, because you had a part in outlining it." That was exactly the point Eisenhower wished to avoid—his own involvement in postwar foreign policy. Truman then pontificated that "politics should stop at the boundaries the [*sic*] the United States. I am extremely sorry that you have allowed a bunch of screwballs to come between us."[59] The relationship, never warm, had now gone past the breaking point.

Before leaving Denver for New York, Eisenhower had written Joe Collins. He ruefully noted the possibility that "some day I shall conclude that I made a mistake in allowing myself to be drawn into the political whirlpool. However, that is past history—and Mamie and I both are determined to give our best to the task that lies before us." He admitted that "it is not easy; we simply never allow ourselves to think of the serene, peaceful life that could be ours if I had not allowed friends and others to persuade me as to my public duty back in 1949, '50, or '51. Or indeed, if the fates had decided differently in Chicago."[60]

But that was, as Eisenhower had said, history. Now he had a campaign to run, and campaigns had always brought out the best in him. He looked forward to this one.

CHAPTER TWENTY-SEVEN

U.S.A.

September–November 1952

ON SEPTEMBER 2, Eisenhower began his campaign with a swing through the South, where he visited every state except Mississippi. He traveled on a special train, nicknamed the "Look Ahead, Neighbor," accompanied by Mamie, Adams, more than three dozen political advisers and staff members, and the working press.

Eisenhower was in command on the train. He created the organization and picked the team. Adams was his administrative assistant who carried out his wishes and followed his orders. For example, Eisenhower told Adams he wanted at least one Jew and one Catholic among his advisers; Adams found them. Eisenhower wanted to give Summerfield (and through him, the RNC) the feeling "that he was represented in some definite way on our train," and Adams found a man close to Summerfield to come along. Eisenhower wanted a doctor present—Howard Snyder came. He wanted a schedule worked out well in advance, as "advance preparation saves wear and tear on the nerves." To keep Adams from feeling that he was merely an errand boy, Eisenhower added to one long memorandum of orders, "I scarcely need to remind you that all the above is intended as suggestion only—you, of course, must make the decisions." Adams, of course, did exactly what Eisenhower told him to do.[1]

Speeches were written in the New York headquarters by a team that included C. D. Jackson and Emmet John Hughes, both on loan from Time Inc., Stassen and Brownell, and on the train by Milton

Eisenhower and Gabriel Hauge. As was his lifelong habit, Eisenhower went over every formal speech with his blue pencil, changing single words here, crossing out entire paragraphs there, substituting his own phrases. Hughes was amazed by his powers of concentration, the way he could listen to a reading of a first draft, then pounce on it. "Right," Eisenhower would say when Hughes finished. "Now at one point, along about the second page, you say . . . This doesn't seem right to me because . . ." The criticism would range from details of substance to points of style, sentence structure, questions of grammar. His greatest aversion, Hughes discovered, "was the calculatedly rhetorical device. . . . All oratorical flourishes made the man uneasy."[2] Eisenhower deliberately avoided anything that smacked of intellectualism; once he apologized during a speech after using the words "status quo," saying that Stevenson, not he, was the intellectual candidate.

Eisenhower's was the last, and one of the best, whistle-stop barnstormers. It was patterned after Truman's successful whistle-stop campaign of 1948, and it rejected Dewey's slow-motion campaign of that year. All the hoopla of American politics was there. The train would stop; the local Republicans would have the crowd waiting; Eisenhower would appear on the rear platform, accompanied by Mamie; he would deliver a set speech that concentrated on cleaning up the mess in Washington and asking the audience to join him in his "crusade"; the whistle sounded; they were off again. Between stops, Eisenhower conferred with local Republican candidates, all of whom wanted their pictures taken with the general.

He carried out a brutal schedule. So brutal, indeed, that the Democrats never dared make an issue of his age. At sixty-one, he was a much more vigorous, active, energetic campaigner than Stevenson, who was nine years his junior. He traveled more than his opponent, spoke more, held more press conferences, and never displayed the kind of utter exhaustion that Stevenson sometimes did. In private, he exercised the soldier's right to grouse. "Those fools on the National Committee!" he once growled when told of yet another motorcade. "Are they trying to perform the feat of electing a dead man?" But he always bounced back, ready to go full speed again the next morning, after enjoying what Hughes described as "the physical miracle that is a soldier's night's sleep."[3] In the eight-week campaign, Eisenhower traveled 51,376 miles, through 45 states, and gave a speech in 232 towns and cities.[4]

As always, the crowds responded to his presence, the power of his personality, his appearance, his confidence and sincerity. No matter how corny his speech—in truth, the more corny it was—he managed to make the most commonplace utterances sound like inspired insights, the most unsophisticated and timeworn expressions of his patriotism and religious beliefs sound like fresh and profound conviction. One of Hauge's assistants recalled years later that Eisenhower knew how to make "sophisticated use of the unsophisticated side of himself."[5] Unlike Stevenson, he did not have to establish an identification; everyone knew who he was, everyone had seen photographs of that famous grin, the arms stretched upward in the classic pose. But seeing him in person was far more satisfying than seeing his picture in the newspapers, and he left an indelible impression on the millions who gathered around the back of the train.

Mamie proved to be a great asset. She was uneasy with crowds, did not much like politicians, gave no speeches, granted no interviews, and found the whole experience exhausting. But she was a trouper and she seized this opportunity to make a positive, public contribution to her husband's career. No matter how weary, she roused herself at every stop, stood by her husband's side, smiled and waved at the appropriate moments. She looked smashing; her bangs became an overnight fad. The most famous picture of the campaign came in Salisbury, North Carolina, when a crowd gathered around the train at 5:30 A.M. and began chanting for Eisenhower. The general and his wife woke, groaned, put on their bathrobes, and groped their way to the rear platform, where they waved back at the crowd.[6] Ike had his arm around Mamie's shoulder; they both had big grins spreading across their faces. The photograph, as Jim Hagerty said, was "dynamite."

On September 9, the train swung up into Indiana, where Eisenhower appeared before an overflow crowd of twenty thousand in the Butler University Field House. Senator William Jenner was on the platform with him. Jenner was one of the worst of the Old Guardsmen, an opponent of the U.N., NATO, the Marshall Plan, foreign aid, and virtually every piece of New Deal legislation. He was McCarthy's strongest supporter in the Senate; he had denounced Marshall as a "front man for traitors" and "a living lie." Indianapolis was Taft country, and Eisenhower gave the audience what it wanted to hear. He said he had decided to run because he could not sit by while his country was "the prey of fear-mongers, quack doctors and bare-faced looters," and he asked for support for the entire Republican ticket "from top to bottom." He did not mention Jenner by name, but each time he was applauded, Jenner reached out, grabbed his arm, and thrust it aloft in a display of joyous approval. When Eisenhower finished, Jenner jumped to his feet and embraced him as flash bulbs popped all around. Furious,

Eisenhower turned to Congressman Charles Halleck and muttered, "Charlie, get me out of here!" Later, Eisenhower told Hughes that he "felt dirty from the touch of the man."[7] But that was a private reaction; to the press and to the public, Eisenhower had endorsed Jenner. Steve Young, one of the vice-chairmen of the National Young Republican Clubs, resigned his post, telling the press, "It is too much for an honest man to swallow."[8]

There was more to come. On September 12 the train returned to New York, where Eisenhower held a breakfast meeting in Morningside Heights with Taft. The senator had brought along a statement that he intended to distribute to the press after the meeting. Eisenhower glanced at it and approved. He was keenly aware that the Old Guard, despite his appearance with Jenner, was holding back; an Indiana national committeeman had been quoted as saying, "Until Bob Taft blows the bugle, a lot of us aren't going to fight in the army."[9] Taft's statement that Eisenhower approved amounted to Taft's own platform, had he been the candidate. It said the real issue was one of "liberty against creeping socialization" and called for drastic reductions in federal spending and taxes. It dismissed the differences between Eisenhower's and his own foreign policy views as matters of "degree" only, because "we are both determined to battle communism throughout the world and in the United States."[10] Taft then urged his own supporters to back Eisenhower.

The Democrats eagerly jumped on "the Surrender at Morningside Heights." Stevenson charged that "Taft lost the nomination but won the nominee." But the charge of hypocrisy hardly convinced, coming as it did from a candidate who was running on a platform pledged to civil rights, but with a southern senator (John Sparkman of Alabama) as his running mate. Eisenhower was the real winner. Taft had blown his bugle and his troops were forming up for the battle. The incident helped Eisenhower far more with the Old Guard than it hurt him with independents. As one of Stevenson's observers perceptively put it, "the lower Eisenhower sinks, the harder he gets to beat."[11]

Nixon, meanwhile, was campaigning vigorously, concentrating on K_1C_2 (Korea, Communism, and corruption). He called Stevenson a graduate of Dean Acheson's "Cowardly College of Communist Containment," criticized him for having given a deposition that vouched for Alger Hiss's reputation, and poked fun at Stevenson's urbane manner and intellectualism. He also took a holier-than-thou attitude toward the corruption that had plagued the Truman Administration in its last years, where gift giving of such items as home freezers and fur coats to public officials had assumed—according to Nixon—alarming and scandalous proportions. Repeatedly, Nixon assured audiences that the Eisenhower "crusade" would clean the crooks and Communists out of Washington.

On September 18, Nixon was hoist with his own petard. "SECRET NIXON FUND!" screamed the headline in the New York *Post*. "SECRET RICH MEN'S TRUST FUND KEEPS NIXON IN STYLE FAR BEYOND HIS SALARY." Despite the sensationalism, there was no more substance to the charges than there was to Nixon's accusations about the Democrats surrendering to Communism and corruption. The *Post* story said that Nixon had accepted contributions in the amount of some $18,000 from California millionaires, but that was such a relatively small amount, and the practice of accepting such contributions was so widespread in Washington, that most editors dismissed the story as a political stunt. But it was too good to pass up, primarily because of the brazen hypocrisy of Nixon in attacking the Democrats for accepting gifts in return for influence peddling. Nixon helped blow the story up by his own overreaction; he immediately, and instinctively, labeled the story a smear by the Communist elements that were out to get him. Then the Democratic National Chairman, Stephen Mitchell, went on the offensive, demanding that Nixon either be thrown off the ticket or else keep his mouth shut about corruption.

At this point, something akin to panic began to spread among the Republicans. It even affected Eisenhower's gang. His friends were unanimous in advising Eisenhower to dump Nixon, quick. They could not bear the thought of their hero's reputation being besmirched, and they felt a personal responsibility for having put him into such an awkward and embarrassing position. Robinson wrote an editorial for the *Herald Tribune* that concluded, "The proper course of Senator Nixon in the circumstances is to make a formal offer of withdrawal from the ticket. How this offer is acted on will be determined by an appraisal of all the facts in the light of General Eisenhower's unsurpassed fairness of mind."[12] Most of Eisenhower's professional advisers (although not Dewey) also urged him to get rid of Nixon. The reporters on the Eisenhower train were forty to two in favor of dropping Nixon, and they told Eisenhower that unless he did so, his crusade was doomed.

Eisenhower, the supposed political novice, realized immediately how much was at stake. His first comment to Adams was "Well, if Nixon has to resign, we can't possibly win."[13] He was one of the few—Dewey was another—to recognize this central fact (George McGovern would have done well to study Eisenhower's response to the Nixon crisis before he acted in 1972 on the Eagleton affair). Further, Eisenhower had been through more than enough crises in his life to be thrown by this one. Indeed, his first thought, upon being informed, was of George Patton, another subordinate who had shot off his mouth too much and had to be rescued by his boss, who needed him.[14] In a way it was like the Battle of the Bulge—the opposition had launched a daring, surprise assault that threw most of those around Eisenhower into near panic; but Eisenhower felt instinctively that the Democrats, like the Germans in 1944, did not in fact have the resources to sustain the attack. Eisenhower's response was therefore patient, calculated, clear-headed, and in the end he turned apparent disaster into stunning triumph. In the process, however, both men lost whatever chance there was of establishing a warm, close, trusting relationship.

Eisenhower scarcely knew Nixon. The two men had met fewer than half a dozen times, only once alone, and all their discussions had been formal affairs, primarily about scheduling speeches and other campaign appearances. They had held no philosophical or political discussions of any substance; they had never played cards together, or shared a meal, or a drink. At thirty-nine years of age, Nixon was young enough to be Eisenhower's son. Eisenhower's reputation rested on a lifetime of accomplishments as manager, organizer, commander; Nixon's reputation, aside from his slashing campaign style, rested on a single investigation, that of Alger Hiss. Except for the delivery of the California vote on Fair Play at the convention, Eisenhower owed Nixon nothing. And Eisenhower's advisers, led by Stassen and Robinson, told him that there was a substitute candidate available, Senator Knowland, who would bring to the ticket everything that Nixon could, except for youth, a factor that was counterbalanced by Knowland's presumed innocence of any hint of scandal.

The Old Guard, meanwhile, led by Taft and Summerfield, demanded that Eisenhower stand by Nixon and condemn the trumped-up charges. Eisenhower even received conflicting advice from his own brothers: Milton wanted to dump Nixon, while Edgar told Dwight he had to give Nixon an instant and full endorsement.[15]

Eisenhower's virtues included patience and fair-mindedness. "Make no mistakes in a hurry" was one of his favorite maxims, and it would have been patently unfair to simply dump Nixon without hearing his side, just as it would have been foolish to endorse him without knowing the facts. Eisenhower also wanted to let the uproar die down a bit before taking any action, if only to gauge the public response.

Eisenhower's first step was to draft a letter to Nixon. He said that the "critical question is the speed and completeness of your presentation of fact to the public," and suggested that Nixon immediately make public all the details about the fund—where it came from, how the money was spent. "Any delay will be interpreted I think as reluctance to let the light of day into the case and will arouse additional doubt of suspicion." (Nixon would have done well to follow that advice when the Watergate story broke.) Eisenhower suggested that Nixon invite Senator Paul Douglas, the Democratic chairman of the Committee on Ethics in Government, "to examine your complete records and to make his findings public."[16] Then Eisenhower had second thoughts, and he did not send the letter. A good thing, too, as even a hint that Nixon should put his fate in the hands of a Democratic senator would have sent Nixon into a towering rage.

Instead of writing Nixon, Eisenhower issued a defensive public statement. "I have long admired and applauded Senator Nixon's American faith and the determination to drive Communist sympathizers from offices of public trust," it began. "There has recently been leveled against him a charge of unethical practices. I believe Dick Nixon to be an honest man. I am confident that he will place all the facts before the American people fairly and squarely." Eisenhower concluded, "I intend to talk with him at the earliest time."[17] He did not mean it; in fact he was carefully avoiding any conversation with his running mate. Instead, he had Adams place a call to Nixon, with instructions to tell Nixon to make a full public disclosure. Nixon refused to accept the call; he had an aide tell Adams that he would not talk with anyone except Eisenhower himself.[18]

Eisenhower was not ready to talk to Nixon. He did write to Bill Robinson, who was leading the dump-Nixon movement in New York. Eisenhower said he would not prejudge the case, and gently reminded Robinson that he, Eisenhower, had selected Nixon, and thus his own reputation was involved: "I could not jump to the conclusion that a man, whom I trusted to be my running mate, is bad." Eisenhower continued, "I have a feeling that in matters of this kind no one can afford to act on a hair-trigger. But if there is real wrong at stake, there will be prompt and conclusive action by me. That has always been my way of acting."[19] Robinson was not convinced; he sent a telegram to Eisenhower that concluded, "My own personal view is that Nixon's continuation on the ticket seriously blunts and dilutes the sharp edge of corruption issue and burdens you with heavy and unfair handicap Stop. This view shared by Cliff [Roberts]."[20]

Eisenhower, meanwhile, held an informal press conference on his train. "I don't care if you fellows are forty to two [against Nixon]," he declared. "I am taking my time on this. Nothing's decided, contrary to your idea that this is a setup for a whitewash of Nixon." Then he added, "Of what avail is it for us to carry on this crusade against this business of what has been going on in Washington if we, ourselves, aren't clean as a hound's tooth?" The following day, the colorful "hound's tooth" phrase made headlines across the country.[21] Nixon was coming to understand how George Patton had felt when he got into trouble and Eisenhower made him sweat it out before taking him back on the team.

At this point Dewey, always the broker, called Nixon to suggest that Nixon go on national TV to explain the fund. Dewey said that the people around Eisenhower, both on the train and in the New York headquarters, constituted a "hanging jury" and that the proposed appearance was the only way to take the decision out of their hands. "At the conclusion of the program," Dewey advised Nixon, "ask people to wire their verdict in to you." If the replies ran no better than 60–40 in Nixon's favor, he should offer his resignation; if they were 90–10, he could stay on. "If you stay on," Dewey concluded, "it isn't blamed on Ike, and if you get off, it isn't blamed on Ike."[22] Dewey, it is important to note, had *not* cleared this suggestion with Eisenhower, who had no intention of leaving the decision in Nixon's hands.

Robert Humphreys, Summerfield's principal assistant at the RNC, then began to round up support for the idea of a national broadcast. The Old Guard was all for it; Eisenhower's advisers were opposed. "I wouldn't put him on TV, Bob," Robinson said. "I'd throw him off the ticket." Humphreys flew to St. Louis, got on the Eisenhower train, and confronted Adams, only to discover that Adams wanted to get rid of Nixon. "He may be a sonofabitch," Humphreys yelled at Adams, "but he's *our* sonofabitch!" Adams shouted back, "General Eisenhower doesn't have sonsofbitches running with him." Humphreys insisted that Eisenhower had to call Nixon and talk to him. Adams demurred. Humphreys exploded, "Do you expect the American people to *believe* that in three days Eisenhower can't find a way to talk to Nixon? Hell, all he has to do is pick up the phone."[23]

That evening, Eisenhower did place the call. He told Nixon he had not decided what to do, then paused waiting for a reply. Nixon let the line hang silent. Finally Eisenhower said, "I don't want to be in the position of condemning an innocent man. I think you ought to go on a nationwide television program and tell them everything there is to tell, everything you can remember since the day you entered public life."

Nixon asked if, after the program, an announcement could be made, "one way or the other." Eisenhower quibbled. Nixon, furious, said that there came a time to stop dawdling, that once he had made his speech, the general ought to decide.

"There comes a time in matters like this when you've either got to shit or get off the pot," Nixon said. Catching himself, he added apologetically, "The great trouble here is the indecision."

There was another long silence, as Eisenhower caught his breath and regained his composure. Then he said, "We will have to wait three or four days after the television show to see what the effect of the program is."[24] Eisenhower was, in short, going to let Nixon hang, twisting slowly in the wind, until he—Eisenhower—had had an opportunity to judge the speech itself, and its impact.

The conversation was a crucial moment in their relationship. Nixon's people were already outraged at Eisenhower's people for their obvious anti-Nixon attitude, and for their determination to protect the general's reputation, no matter at what expense to Nixon's career. From the time of the fund incident onward, the relationship between the two camps was always characterized by tension, hostility, mistrust. As for the two principals, Nixon could never forget or forgive Eisenhower for not backing him unhesitatingly during this crisis, while Eisenhower would never forget Nixon's unfortunate phrase—no one, not Churchill, not de Gaulle, not FDR, not Marshall, had ever presumed to talk to Eisenhower like that.

So far as the Eisenhower-Nixon relationship was concerned, there was worse to come. The RNC gathered the money; Nixon went on television. Eisenhower, together with Mamie and a couple of dozen members of his team, watched in Cleveland, where he was about to make an appearance. Nixon's speech itself is one of the great classics of American political folklore, so well known that it need not be even summarized here. There was, however, one part to the speech that affected Eisenhower directly and personally which has not received the attention that has been given to the dog Checkers or Pat Nixon's cloth coat. It had just been revealed that Stevenson too had a fund, which he had not accounted for and which he used to supplement the salaries of some of his personal appointees in Springfield. Further, Nixon knew that Sparkman had his wife on his Senate payroll. After Nixon had laid bare his own (modest) financial position, and demonstrated that he had used the fund for legitimate political expenses, he called on Stevenson and Sparkman to make full revelations of their financial history, because, Nixon said, "a man who's to be President and a man who's to be Vice-President must have the confidence of all the people."

Eisenhower had a pad of legal paper in one hand, a pencil in the other. When Nixon called for full financial disclosure from Stevenson and Sparkman, Eisenhower jabbed the pencil into the pad so hard that he broke the pencil point and made a hole in the paper. The blood rushed to his face. Only Humphreys noticed this; all the others in the room were staring fixedly at the TV screen. Humphreys realized immediately what Nixon had done: he had turned the spotlight on Eisenhower, because if three out of the four candidates made their finances public property, Eisenhower would have to do so too. Humphreys said that "Eisenhower got the point. He was the only man smart enough in that room to get it."

Eisenhower had spent a lifetime learning how to control his temper. He realized that Nixon had saved himself with his brilliant presentation, that he was now stuck with Nixon. (Not everyone did at first. Lucius Clay thought the speech "the corniest thing I ever heard"; he later said he realized he was wrong "when I saw the apartment elevator operator crying." Robinson, on the other hand, was now enthusiastically pro-Nixon.) When Nixon concluded, Eisenhower gathered himself together and remarked to Summerfield, "Well, Arthur, you sure got your money's worth!"[25] He then dictated a message to Nixon, praising him for his "magnificent" performance, but still leaving Nixon hanging: "My personal decision is going to be based on personal conclusions." (At the end of his speech, Nixon had asked viewers to write or wire the RNC as to whether or not he should remain on the ticket, a bold attempt to take the decision out of Eisenhower's hands.) Just in case Nixon still did not get the point as to who was in charge, Eisenhower added, "I would most appreciate it if you can fly to see me at once. Tomorrow I will be at Wheeling, W.Va." He concluded, "Whatever personal affection and admiration I had for you—and they are very great—are undiminished." Not enhanced, just undiminished. Nixon was distraught. "What more can he possibly want from me?" he angrily asked one of his aides. He said he would not go to Wheeling, that he would not humiliate himself any further.[26] Calmer heads in his camp prevailed, and he agreed to go.

Eisenhower, meanwhile, went out to face the Cleveland audience. It had listened to Nixon over the radio, and it roared with enthusiasm: "We want Dick! We want Dick!" Eisenhower had anticipated that reaction, and when the crowd finally quieted down, he declared, "I like courage. Tonight I saw an example of courage. . . . When I get in a fight, I would rather have a courageous and honest man by my side than a whole boxcar full of pussyfooters."[27]

Inwardly, he continued to seethe. Stevenson and Sparkman both said the following week that they would release their tax returns extending over the past decade. Reporters asked Hagerty whether Eisenhower would also make his financial situation public property. Hagerty said he did not know, but turned to Milton, who was with him. Milton said that of course Eisenhower would follow the example of the others. Twenty years later, Hagerty—who was at Eisenhower's side daily through eight years—recalled that he never, ever, saw Eisenhower madder than when he was informed of Milton's remark. Eisenhower "blew his stack." He told Hagerty that he would not do it, ever. Eventually, of course, he had to yield. In early October, Hagerty released Eisenhower's tax returns, which showed earnings over the past ten years of $888,303, including $635,000 for the one-time sale of the rights to *Crusade,* and taxes of $217,082, including $158,750 in capital gains taxes on the book.[28] No one protested or raised any questions, but Eisenhower nevertheless was furious. He hated having to make his private finances public knowledge. It went against every fiber of his being. And he never forgave Nixon for making him do it.

Actually, he was lucky, both in the personal and in the political sense. Like Nixon and Stevenson, he could have been put into a terribly embarrassing position if any reporters had started asking him about gifts, trips, and other favors he had accepted from his rich friends, many of whom did extensive business with the federal government. None did; as always, the reporters on the Eisenhower train liked and respected the general enormously. His political luck was even greater. He was lucky that the Democrats had attacked with insufficient ammunition. Nixon was in fact as clean as a hound's tooth. Whatever his sins, Nixon was no crook. Eisenhower was also lucky that the Stevenson fund existed and became public knowledge. But his own political acumen had also been crucial. Eisenhower was exactly right—to have condemned, or endorsed, Nixon too early would have been fatal. Eisenhower's patience was the key to the Republican triumph.

But triumph aside, the incident always rankled, with both men. It also elevated Nixon to a position he could not possibly have attained had it not happened. It gave Nixon a solid power base of his own. Much more than the Hiss investigation, or than his nomination for the Vice-Presidency, the Checkers speech made Nixon a national, and extremely visible, love-hate figure. Henceforth, Eisenhower would have to deal with Nixon as he had had to deal with de Gaulle, as a man who brought considerable strength of his own to their alliance and had to be treated accordingly.

Still, Eisenhower emerged from the crisis as the man unquestionably in command. He had not panicked when others had; he had resisted the pressure from both wings of the Republican Party to either endorse or dump Nixon; he had kept the final decision in his own hands. If anyone, including Nixon, had any doubts on the point of who was the commander in chief, Eisenhower set them straight in his first words to Nixon when they met at the Wheeling airport. By that time, the evening after the speech, it was obvious that Nixon had received an overwhelmingly positive response from the public. As Nixon was helping his wife put on her now famous coat, Eisenhower rushed up the steps to the plane, hand outstretched. Astonished, Nixon mumbled, "General, you didn't need to come out to the airport." "Why not?" Eisenhower grinned. "You're my boy!"[29] As far as Eisenhower was concerned, that "my boy" phrase put their relationship in the proper perspective.

In the weeks that followed, Eisenhower prudently toned down his remarks about Democratic corruption, while he and other Republicans increased their attacks on Communist sympathizers in government. The note of strident anti-Communism bothered some of Eisenhower's East Coast supporters, especially Edward Mead Earle, the distinguished scholar of international relations at Princeton's Institute for Advanced Study. Earle wrote Eisenhower of the "mental pain" he experienced as he listened to or read the diatribes. Eisenhower had great respect for Earle (he had tried to lure him to Columbia a few years earlier), and Earle obviously touched a sore nerve, perhaps even some guilt. Eisenhower sent a long, handwritten, thoughtful reply. "I sincerely believe," Eisenhower wrote, "that some years ago, subversion and communism had succeeded in penetrating dangerously into important regions of our government and our economic life." He reminded Earle that before Hiss had been found guilty of perjury, Truman and others had "shouted 'red herring.'" He continued, "No matter how bitterly we condemn un-American practices applied against the individual, we must not forget that governmental neglect, indifference and arrogance, gave to extremists an excuse to indulge in these practices." In Eisenhower's view, in short, the Democrats had made McCarthyism possible. Still, he "condemned unjust accusation" and said that "I do not condone unfairness."

Turning to McCarthy himself, whom Earle had asked Eisenhower to denounce, Eisenhower said that Earle should realize that McCarthy had just won a primary victory by some 100,000 votes. To Eisenhower's mind, this meant that if "I should oppose him on the ground that he is morally unfit for office, I would be indirectly accusing the Republican electorate of stupidity, at the least, and of immorality, at the most." He agonized over the problem of McCarthy (when it was typed up, his letter to Earle covered four single-spaced pages). He said he had resisted attempts to induce him to bring his campaign train into Wisconsin. But, "having consented to lead a crusade, based firmly on moral values—I want to carry my message to the people of Wisconsin." Further, he was the leader of the Republican Party, he believed in the two-party system, and he had therefore concluded that "I *could not* ask for the defeat of any duly nominated Republican, and this, stated backward, means that, politically, I want to see them elected." Denying the obvious, he claimed that "I am neither defending nor rationalizing." He insisted that he was not compromising his principles, then concluded by introducing a fantasy that he would continue to nurture over the next eight years, without ever bringing it to fruition: "Of course—if a 3rd party had been started, and I had joined, then we could have excluded all with whom we did not agree on some major issue."[30]

A third party, located midway between the Democrats and the Old Guard Republicans, was the will-of-the-wisp Teddy Roosevelt had pursued with the Progressive Party in 1912, with results that Eisenhower well knew. Besides, it was McCarthy's methods, not his objectives, that Eisenhower objected to. He could not but condemn the wild accusations that were so closely identified with McCarthy, and his logical, orderly mind, coupled with his lifelong devotion to the proper chain of command, made him abhor McCarthy's freewheeling, irresponsible "investigations." Eisenhower's position was that the executive branch of the government should assume the responsibility for rooting out the Reds. He promised to do just that. In Billings, Montana, he pledged his Administration to "find the men and women who may fail to live up to these standards; we will find the pinks; we will find the Communists; we will find the disloyal."[31]

But Eisenhower's distinction between his methods and McCarthy's was much too fine to have a public impact. What people wanted to know was, Would he repudiate McCarthy or not? What made it a major question was not just McCarthy's popularity with the right wing of the party, and indeed with Republicans throughout Wisconsin, the Midwest, and the West, but more to the point, McCarthy's assaults on Marshall. The question became, in other words, Would Eisenhower stand up for Marshall?

Now in fact, Eisenhower had already done so, in his August 22 press conference in Denver, and would do so three more times during the campaign, in Salt Lake City, in New York, and in Newark. But neither Utah nor the East Coast was Wisconsin, and defending Marshall in those places was not standing up for his mentor in McCarthy's home state. Especially after the Jenner episode, many of the general's backers, including the gang, urged him to tell McCarthy off in his own back yard. Marshall, incidentally, stayed circumspectly out of the picture, refusing to make any public comment on the campaign and, save for his note of congratulations to Eisenhower on winning the nomination, sending no letters or communications of any kind to Eisenhower.

In late September, Eisenhower flew to New York for strategy sessions before embarking on a train trip through the Midwest. After Illinois, he was going to Wisconsin, which meant that the question of what to do about McCarthy had to be faced. Smarting from the criticisms his appearance with Jenner had brought forth, Eisenhower said to Emmet Hughes, "Listen, couldn't we make this an occasion for me to pay a personal tribute to Marshall—right in McCarthy's back yard?" Hughes, the self-styled liberal in Eisenhower's headquarters, was enthusiastic. He drafted a paragraph that praised Marshall "as a man and as a soldier, . . . dedicated with singular selflessness and the profoundest patriotism to the service of America." Charges of disloyalty against Marshall, the paragraph concluded, constituted "a sobering lesson in the way freedom must *not* defend itself."[32]

Someone at headquarters—it was never discovered who—told the Wisconsin Republicans of Eisenhower's intentions. On October 2, while Eisenhower's train was in Peoria, Illinois, for an overnight stop before heading north to Wisconsin, the Wisconsin governor, Walter Kohler, the national committeeman, Henry Ringling, and the junior senator, Joe McCarthy, flew by private plane to Peoria to confront the general. Eisenhower, staying at the Pere Marquette Hotel, was told that they were in town and wanted to see him. He said he would meet with McCarthy, alone. ("When I saw [McCarthy] go up in that elevator," Hauge recalled, "I felt sick.") The private meeting lasted a half hour. According to Kevin McCann, recalling the event years later, "[Eisenhower] just took McCarthy apart. I never heard the General so cold-bloodedly skin a man. The air turned blue—so blue in fact that I couldn't sit there listening. McCarthy said damned little. He just grunted and groaned. . . . He was no heavyweight anyway. And under the attack he just went into shock."[33] Perhaps it did happen that way, or perhaps that is the way McCann wished it would have happened. But *The New York Times* reported the next day that McCarthy asked Eisenhower to make his defense of Marshall in another state; Eisenhower evidently refused. When McCarthy emerged from the meeting, nevertheless, he told reporters that he had had a "very, very pleasant" conversation with the general and that he, Kohler, and Ringling would be on the general's train as it rolled through Wisconsin.[34]

The following day, as the train headed toward Green Bay, Adams showed Kohler the draft of Eisenhower's Milwaukee speech, his major address in Wisconsin. It was pretty much standard Republican anti-Communist rhetoric, well laid on—for all his liberalism, Hughes was as anxious to get the Reds as anyone at Eisenhower's headquarters—but it did contain, almost as a gratuitous afterthought, and certainly out of place, Hughes's paragraph defending Marshall. Kohler told Adams he liked the speech but wanted the Marshall paragraph removed, as it was unnecessarily insulting to McCarthy in his home state. He suggested that Eisenhower could defend Marshall somewhere else. At this point, it becomes impossible to determine who said what to whom. By some accounts, Adams agreed with Kohler; by others, he was strongly opposed to removing the paragraph. Supposedly Hauge and Boston banker Robert Cutler, a member of Eisenhower's staff and a wartime aide to Marshall, were adamant about retaining the remarks. The general himself, according to some of those present, insisted on keeping it; others could not recall his participating in the conversation. In his memoirs, Eisenhower was extremely vague about the whole thing, saying only that he told McCarthy, sometime during the train ride, that he intended to speak out against McCarthy's methods in Green Bay. McCarthy replied, "If you say that, they will boo you." Eisenhower responded "with some heat" that he had been criticized before for his actions, that it did not bother him, and that he would "gladly be booed for standing for my own conceptions of justice."[35]

If Eisenhower did indulge in such tough talk, his speech in Green Bay must have been a major disappointment to Hauge and Cutler, and it certainly gave McCarthy nothing to worry about. Eisenhower asked the audience "to elect the entire slate of those we have nominated on our party tickets" and added that the purposes McCarthy and he had "of ridding this government of the incompetents, the dishonest and above all the subversive and disloyal are one and the same and we differ only over methods." He then stated that the Reds could be rooted out "with absolute assurance that American principles of trial by jury, of innocence until proven guilty, are all observed, and I expect to do it."[36]

From Green Bay, the train headed south, stopping first in Appleton, McCarthy's home town. Again, the sources differ. According to some, Eisenhower objected to being introduced by McCarthy, but ultimately yielded; others have no such memory. In any event, McCarthy did make the introduction and stood by the general's side as he delivered a twelve-minute address that contained no reference to McCarthy or his methods.[37] As the train moved toward Milwaukee, the argument over the Marshall paragraph continued. Kohler told Adams that he felt it stood out as an "unnecessarily abrupt rebuff to McCarthy" and said that it would cause serious problems for the Republicans in Wisconsin in the election (Wisconsin had gone Democratic in 1948). Eisenhower had already defended Marshall in Denver, Kohler argued, and he also insisted that it was Jenner, not McCarthy, who had called Marshall a traitor.

Adams then went to the rear of the train to argue Kohler's case with Eisenhower. "Are you suggesting that the reference to George Marshall be dropped from the speech tonight?" Eisenhower asked. Adams responded, "Yes, not because you're not right, but because you're out of context." The general then said, "Well, drop it. I handled the subject pretty thoroughly in Denver and there's no reason to repeat it tonight." Hauge and Cutler protested, to no avail.[38]

In their various reminiscences, Eisenhower's staff tried to make it all sound just that simple—the general dropped the paragraph because it was out of place—and they expressed surprise at the uproar that followed, which came about, they claimed, because someone had leaked an advance copy of the speech and thus the excision of the paragraph became known.[39] But Hauge, Cutler, and others had been telling reporters all day, "Just wait till we get to Milwaukee, and you will find out what the general thinks of Marshall." Everybody on the train was talking about the stinging rebuke McCarthy was going to get. Further, Eisenhower did not merely remove the paragraph; in deference to the senator he also weakened some paragraphs denouncing McCarthy's methods.[40]

In Milwaukee, Eisenhower made no reference to Marshall. Instead, he said that the Truman Administration had been infiltrated by Communists. The loss of China and the "surrender of whole nations" in Eastern Europe to the Communists was due, he said, to the Reds in Washington. Their penetration of the government, he added, in his most McCarthy-like statement of the campaign, "meant—in its most ugly triumph—treason itself." Lamely, he added that "freedom must defend itself with courage, with care, with force and with fairness," and he called for "respect for the integrity of fellow citizens who enjoy their right to disagree. The right to question a man's judgment carries with it no automatic right to question his honor."[41] As much as the general may have been convinced that he had thereby established a clear distinction between himself and McCarthy, as Guenter Bischof has observed, "With McCarthy behind him on the stage they sounded like pretty naïve quibbles." When Eisenhower finished, McCarthy reached awkwardly over a few rows of chairs to vigorously shake Eisenhower's hand.

The reaction was immediate and intense. *The New York Times* editorialized, "Yesterday could not have been a happy day for General Eisenhower . . . nor was it a happy day for many supporters." *Times* publisher Arthur Hays Sulzberger privately cabled Adams, "Do I need to tell you that I am sick at heart?" Hauge thought of resigning. Senator Wayne Morse of Oregon did resign from the GOP because of "reactionaries running a captive general for President." Joseph Alsop later reported that Eisenhower's personal staff on the train were soon referring to the Milwaukee visit as "that terrible day." Herblock published a cartoon in the Washington *Post* (which was supporting Eisenhower) showing the leering ape-man McCarthy standing in a pool of filth and holding a sign reading, "ANYTHING TO WIN." About the only public figure who had no public reaction, either then or later, was Marshall himself.[42]

Even Harold Stassen complained, which led Eisenhower, on October 5, to make his only defense of his decision. He told Stassen that "in principle I agree with the criticism you make on the revisions made in the Milwaukee talk," then explained his reasoning. First, the staff was "practically a unit" in recommending the deletion (which was not true). Second, the speech was well balanced "between the hunt for Communism and the methods used in the hunt." Third, "A considerable amount of argument was presented to show that Senator McCarthy had never made the flat allegation that General Marshall was traitorous in design." Fourth, Kohler was so insistent upon "revision that I felt it difficult to campaign through his state if I completely disregarded his advice." Then Eisenhower promised that "from here on out I shall try—in every talk—to emphasize the liberal side of our program. Certainly I shall try to make it clear that I am no man's creature."[43]

Perhaps the best thing that can be said about the incident is that Eisenhower, having decided to run for the Presidency, was so determined to win that he was willing to do whatever seemed necessary to do so. That he was ashamed of himself there can be little doubt. After writing Stassen, he tried never again to refer to the Milwaukee speech. When he came to write his memoirs, ten years later, he wanted to ignore it altogether; when his aides insisted that he could not simply pass it over, he wrote, discarded, wrote again, discarded again, and finally printed a version in which he said that if he had realized what the reaction to the deletion was going to be, "I would never have acceded to the staff's arguments, logical as they sounded at the time." He claimed that the reaction constituted a "distortion of the facts, a disortion that even led some to question my loyalty to General Marshall."[44] That was as close as he ever came to making a public apology to Marshall; whether he made a private apology or not is unknown.

Five days after Eisenhower's Milwaukee speech, Stevenson campaigned in Wisconsin. Eisenhower had been attacking him for cracking jokes during a serious campaign. "My opponent has been worrying about my funnybone," Stevenson gibed. "I'm worrying about his backbone." Then Stevenson gave what must be the last word on the Marshall deletion. He called the whole thing a "melancholy spectacle."[45]

The Nixon fund and the never-delivered Marshall paragraph were the two most famous incidents of the campaign, the ones remembered for decades afterward. Other incidents, recalled with fondness, chagrin, or disgust, depending on the point of view, included McCarthy's "slip of the tongue" when he confused the names "Alger" and "Adlai"; Nixon's rampaging assaults on the Democrats, highlighted by his constant association of Stevenson and Hiss; and Truman's late but enthusiastic entry into the debate, as the President gave back a bit of what the Republicans were dishing out, including some personal attacks on Eisenhower. The campaign was also notable for Eisenhower's cracking the Solid South. His trips there, plus his advocacy of states' rights on the tidelands oil issue, and most of all his refusal to endorse FEPC, won him the endorsement of Governor Robert Kennon of Louisiana, Governor Allan Shivers of Texas, Governor Jimmy Byrnes of South Carolina, and the neutrality of Senator Harry Byrd of Virginia, who refused to support Stevenson (who had advocated FEPC). Taken all together, 1952 is recalled as one of the bitterest campaigns of the twentieth century, and the one that featured the most mudslinging. Few, if any, of the participants could look back on it with pride.

But there was a serious, positive side to the Republican campaign, although little noticed by the press at the time or historians later. Eisenhower was not by nature a negative man, and for all his cynical compromises with the Old Guard, he felt little if any of the personal animosity toward his opponents that animated Nixon, McCarthy, and others. He did believe, truly and deeply, in the Republican slogan, "It's time for a change," and he tried to concentrate his campaign on telling the American people exactly what changes he would make, and why. His proposed changes went far beyond simply cleaning the crooks and the Commies out of Washington, but they did not include a wholesale repudiation of twenty years of Democratic legislation. He promised to lower taxes, halt the spread of big government, and balance the budget, but all within the context of a determination "to improve and extend the Federal program of Social Security." He said he would get "the best kind of business management this nation can produce to help us run this government." The resulting efficiencies would be a start toward bringing spending under control.

He was specific about where other budget cuts would come from: "But the big spending is, of course, the 60 billion dollars we pay for national security. Here is where the largest savings can be made." The Republicans, he said, would call a halt "to stop-and-start planning." They would not "demobilize and then hurriedly remobilize, or swing from optimism to panic." They would, instead, "plan for the future on something more solid than yesterday's headlines."

With regard to Taft-Hartley, Eisenhower favored amending the law, but said he would not support any changes that "weaken the rights of working men and women," and he promised to consult labor leaders as well as management before suggesting specific amendments. He was opposed to any bill that would give to the President the power to compel arbitration in an industrial dispute; he wanted to encourage collective bargaining and the right to strike. He said he realized that many people felt Taft-Hartley could be used to break unions. "That must be changed. America wants no law licensing union-busting. And neither do I." On one of the most controversial elements of Taft-Hartley, he said that "since patriotic American union leaders must swear that they are not Communists, then the employers with whom they deal should be subject to the same requirement."

On foreign policy, Eisenhower's most important commitment was to collective security. "We need allies," he flatly declared. He also pledged "unwavering support of the United Nations." In addition, "Never will we be backward in proposing or accepting any program for disarmament that carries dependable assurances of good faith." He consistently avoided the specific subject of NATO in his speeches, but in reply to a question at a press conference he insisted on its importance to the United States. Another unpopular program he seldom mentioned was foreign aid, but when he did he was firm in his support. He wanted to lower tariff barriers and promote more free trade. He insisted that "the problem of re-establishing the economies of Japan and West Germany must be recognized as a problem of the entire free world," and pledged the Republicans to help those countries find markets for their products and replace their lost markets in China and East Europe. He did not use the word "liberation" himself, but he did say he would "aid by every peaceful means, but only by peaceful means, the right to live in freedom."

Korea, not crooks or Communists, was the major concern of the voters. Eisenhower explicitly and vigorously rejected the extreme solutions; he would not withdraw, as Taft advocated, nor would he go all out for victory, as MacArthur demanded. He ridiculed those who wanted to invade or bomb China as people who did not know what they were talking about; he was equally scornful about those who were willing to leave the South Koreans in the lurch. He promised prudence in Korea, backed by firmness, and directed toward securing a just and lasting peace.[46]

The high point of Eisenhower's campaign came in Detroit, on October 24, when he announced that, immediately after his election, he would "forego the diversions of politics and concentrate on the job of ending the Korean war . . . That job requires a personal trip to Korea. I shall make that trip. Only in that way could I learn how best to serve the American people in the cause of peace. I shall go to Korea."

It was an electrifying announcement, coming less than two weeks before the election, and it practically guaranteed the result (one Associated Press reporter heard the speech, packed up his typewriter, and left the campaign trail, declaring that it was all over). Eisenhower had always maintained a comfortable lead in the polls; Stevenson had been moving up a bit in October; with Eisenhower's Korean announcement, he re-established and then added to his lead.

Stevenson wisely kept quiet about Eisenhower's pledge, but Truman denounced it as a gimmick of the worst sort, and said that if Eisenhower really wanted to seek peace he should go to Moscow, not Korea. But it was no gimmick; it was so obviously something that the President-elect should do that Stevenson himself, some weeks earlier, had decided that if he won he would make such a trip. But he and his advisers realized that for the governor of Illinois to make such a pledge would most certainly look like a grandstand play, and they could only hope that the idea of such an announcement would not occur to General Eisenhower.[47] But it had always been in Eisenhower's mind to make such a trip, which he equated with his frequent visits to the front lines during the war. In 1952, as in 1942–1945, he wanted to see for himself. The thought of making his intention public first occurred to Emmet Hughes; C. D. Jackson brought a draft of the speech to Eisenhower, read it to him, and got the general's immediate endorsement.[48]

The response was enthusiastic. The nation's number-one hero, her greatest soldier and most experienced statesman, was promising to give his personal attention to the nation's number-one problem. It was reassuring, it was exciting, it was exactly what people wanted to hear. He had not, it is important to note, made any promises about what he would do once in Korea. Those who thought a military victory was still possible could imagine that General Ike would find a way to achieve it; those who wanted an early end to the war could believe that Eisenhower was the one man who could deliver it. This ambiguity was not only helpful in the quest for votes; more important to Eisenhower, who was going to win anyway, it kept his options open. The truth was that he did *not* know what he was going to do about Korea; he wanted to reserve judgment until he had seen for himself; in the meantime, his pledge was a dramatic and effective way to use his prestige and reputation to win votes while retaining flexibility.

In the last week of the campaign, Eisenhower directed his appeal to the independents. In Chicago, he indirectly attacked McCarthy when he told his audience that there was rightful concern about the methods being used to combat Communism in government. He stressed his moderation on labor legislation, Social Security, civil rights, and other issues. In Boston, on the campaign's last day, he closely identified himself with Wendell Willkie and progressive Republicans.

Overall, with the notable exception of the Marshall incident in Milwaukee, the campaign went almost exactly the way Eisenhower wanted it to go. He successfully appeased the Old Guard, which infuriated the Democrats but scarcely hurt him with the critical independent vote. He strengthened his image as a fair-minded, decent man, highly intelligent but with a common touch, accustomed to keeping his head in a crisis, experienced, a born leader. He also preserved his image as a man who was accepting the responsibility of the Presidency because it was his duty to do so, rather than a man who was seeking a job for ambitious personal reasons. He promised the American people that, if elected, he would give them peace with prosperity, a balanced budget, a reduction in the size and scope of the federal government, dignity in the White House, and an end to Communism and crookedness in Washington. He was willing to bet that was what most Americans wanted.

• •

After his Boston appearance, Eisenhower and Mamie took the train to New York, where they arrived early on Election Day, November 4. They voted, then went to Morningside Heights and went to bed. Although the professional pollsters, so badly burned in 1948, were hedging, Eisenhower was confident of success. He was right, of course. The early returns that evening showed a massive switch to the Republicans. Across the country, Eisenhower was getting 55 percent of the vote. His decision to campaign in the South was justified, as he carried Texas, Tennessee, Virginia, Florida, and Oklahoma, and barely missed in Louisiana and South Carolina, thereby beginning the historic process of breaking up the Solid South.

Eisenhower got 33,936,234 votes to Stevenson's 27,314,992, or 55.1 percent to 44.4 percent. Eisenhower received 442 electoral votes to Stevenson's 89 (from West Virginia plus eight Deep South states). Eisenhower ran ahead of the Republican ticket everywhere, and was especially pleased that he got 100,000 more votes in Wisconsin than McCarthy received. He did manage to bring a Republican Congress with him, although by the slimmest of majorities (eight in the House; a tie in the Senate, which with Vice-President Nixon's vote meant Republican control).

It was a smashing victory. Millions of middle-aged Republicans who voted for Eisenhower had never before cast their ballot for a presidential winner. After five successive victories the Democrats, if not repudiated, were certainly rebuffed. By far the most important reason was Eisenhower's personal popularity; it was, every analyst agreed, much more his triumph than the Republicans'.

As the returns came in, the Eisenhowers watched on TV in their suite at the Commodore Hotel. The gang, plus Milton and a few other close friends and political associates, joined them. Mamie sat on the floor, tears running down her cheeks.[49] When Stevenson conceded, at 1:30 A.M., the Eisenhowers joined the celebration in the ballroom long enough for the President-elect to make a brief speech, then returned to their suite. Eisenhower threw himself down on a bed, exhausted. Clare Boothe Luce approached him. "Mr. President," she said, "I know how tired you are. But there is one more thing you *have* to do." She told him what it was. Groaning, he went to the phone and put through a call to the last Republican President, Herbert Hoover.[50] Then he and Mamie decided to return to Morningside Heights. When they got into their car, on Park Avenue, they were momentarily astonished to see that

Sergeant Dry had been replaced by two complete strangers. They were Secret Service men.[51]

Now he was President-elect. He was in that position because of his proved competence as a general, as a statesman, and as a leader. People had turned to Eisenhower not so much because of what he stood for, although that counted, as because of who he was and what he had accomplished. He was the hero who could be trusted to lead the nation to peace and prosperity. In ten weeks, he would become the most powerful man in the world. (Just how powerful was exemplified by an event that occurred on the last weekend of the campaign. On November 1, at Eniwetok, the United States exploded its first hydrogen device, 150 times more powerful than the atomic bomb dropped on Japan.) He would be directly responsible for dealing with the world's most pressing problems. Despite his penchant for portraying himself as a political novice, few of these problems would be new ones to him. Indeed, it can be argued that no man elected to the Presidency was ever better prepared for the demands of the job than Eisenhower. The man who had organized and commanded Overlord was confident that he could organize and run the United States as it faced the challenges of the Cold War. For all his reluctance as a candidate, he was eager to assume the duties and responsibilities of his new office.

NOTES

Chapter One

1. The most complete treatment of the Eisenhower ancestry is Davis, *Soldier of Democracy* (full citations are in the Bibliography), the first serious biography and still much the best on his early life. See also Kornitzer, *The Great American Heritage,* which is based on interviews with the five surviving brothers. Miller, *Eisenhower,* and Neal, *The Eisenhowers,* also have material on the family.
2. Davis, *Soldier of Democracy,* 18.
3. *Ibid.,* 19.
4. *Ibid.,* 28.
5. Interviews with DDE and Milton Stover Eisenhower (MSE).
6. Neal, *The Eisenhowers,* 8; Davis, *Soldier of Democracy,* 28–29.
7. Interview MSE.
8. Kornitzer, *Great American Heritage,* 9.
9. *Ibid.,* 10.
10. Davis, *Soldier of Democracy,* 33.
11. Interview MSE.
12. Davis, *Soldier of Democracy,* 35; Kornitzer, *Great American Heritage,* 11–12.
13. Davis, *Soldier of Democracy,* 37.
14. DDE, *At Ease,* 32.
15. Davis, *Soldier of Democracy,* 44.
16. *Ibid.,* 45.
17. Kornitzer, *Great American Heritage,* 26.
18. Interview MSE.
19. *Ibid.*
20. See Kornitzer, *Great American Heritage,* 22–27; interviews MSE and DDE; DDE, *At Ease,* 31.

21. Kornitzer, *Great American Heritage,* 32.
22. *Ibid.,* 52.
23. DDE, *At Ease,* 36.
24. Interview DDE.
25. Interview MSE.
26. Kornitzer, *Great American Heritage,* 23.
27. *Ibid.,* 24.
28. Davis, *Soldier of Democracy,* 67–68.
29. DDE, *At Ease,* 35.
30. Kornitzer, *Great American Heritage,* 19.
31. *Ibid.,* 53.
32. DDE, *At Ease,* 36–37.
33. Kornitzer, *Great American Heritage,* 1.
34. *Ibid.,* 27.
35. *Ibid.,* 19.
36. *Ibid.,* 33.
37. Interview MSE.
38. *Ibid.*
39. DDE to Pelagius Williams, Oct. 30, 1947, Eisenhower Library, Abilene.

Chapter Two

1. Davis, *Soldier of Democracy,* 67.
2. Kornitzer, *Great American Heritage,* 46, 88; DDE, *At Ease,* 33.
3. DDE, *At Ease,* 33.
4. *Ibid.,* 94; Davis, *Soldier of Democracy,* 76–77; Kornitzer, *Great American Heritage,* 45–46.
5. DDE, *At Ease,* 51–52.
6. Davis, *Soldier of Democracy,* 68.
7. Kornitzer, *Great American Heritage,* 50–51; Davis, *Soldier of Democracy,* 70–71.
8. DDE, *At Ease,* 88–90.
9. *Ibid.,* 94–96.
10. *Ibid.,* 39.
11. *Ibid.*
12. Davis, *Soldier of Democracy,* 83.
13. DDE, *At Ease,* 42–43.
14. *Ibid.,* 40.
15. *The Helianthus,* 1909.
16. DDE, *At Ease,* 99.
17. Davis, *Soldier of Democracy,* 85.
18. *Ibid.,* 82–83.
19. Miller, *Eisenhower,* 80.
20. The card is in the Eisenhower Museum, Abilene.
21. Miller, *Eisenhower,* 80.
22. DDE to Lucy Eldredge, 1/17/1946, Eisenhower Library, Abilene.
23. DDE, *At Ease,* 98–99; Davis, *Soldier of Democracy,* 97–98; *The Helianthus,* 1909.
24. The card is in the Eisenhower Museum, Abilene.
25. DDE, *At Ease,* 90–91, 108.
26. *Ibid.,* 96–97; Kornitzer, *Great American Heritage,* 43–44; Davis, *Soldier of Democracy,* 79–80.

27. Kornitzer, *Great American Heritage,* 44.
28. DDE, *At Ease,* 97.
29. Kornitzer, *Great American Heritage,* 147.
30. DDE, *At Ease,* 104.
31. Miller, *Eisenhower,* 79, 81.
32. *Ibid.,* 79.
33. Interview DDE.
34. DDE, *At Ease,* 104.
35. Neal, *The Eisenhowers,* 19.
36. *Ibid.*; DDE, *At Ease,* 105; Davis, *Soldier of Democracy,* 110–13.
37. The original is in the Bristow Papers at the Kansas Historical Society, Topeka.
38. *Ibid.*
39. Davis, *Soldier of Democracy,* 112.
40. These records are in the Bristow Papers in the Kansas Historical Society, Topeka.
41. Davis, *Soldier of Democracy,* 113; Neal, *The Eisenhowers,* 21.
42. DDE, *At Ease,* 106.
43. *New York Times,* July 8, 1954; Kornitzer, *Great American Heritage,* 87, 152.
44. Miller, *Eisenhower,* 82.
45. DDE, *At Ease,* 108.
46. Davis, *Soldier of Democracy,* 84–85.
47. *Ibid.*; Miller, *Eisenhower,* 79–80.

Chapter Three

1. DDE, *At Ease,* 4.
2. Ambrose, *Duty, Honor, Country,* 223–26.
3. DDE, *At Ease,* 6.
4. Ambrose, *Duty, Honor, Country,* 225.
5. DDE, *At Ease,* 4–5.
6. Davis, *Soldier of Democracy,* 131.
7. DDE, *At Ease,* 18.
8. Ambrose, *Duty, Honor, Country,* 250, 251.
9. DDE, *At Ease,* 19–20.
10. Ambrose, *Duty, Honor, Country,* 240; Davis, *Soldier of Democracy,* 134.
11. Ambrose, *Duty, Honor, Country,* 252.
12. *The Howitzer,* 1915.
13. Ambrose, *Duty, Honor, Country,* 156–57, 163.
14. DDE, *At Ease,* 17.
15. *Ibid.,* 12.
16. Neal, *The Eisenhowers,* 30.
17. DDE, *At Ease,* 8.
18. *Ibid.,* 12.
19. *Ibid.,* 13–14.
20. Neal, *The Eisenhowers,* 25; Davis, *Soldier of Democracy,* 135.
21. *The Howitzer,* 1913.
22. Interview MSE.
23. DDE, *At Ease,* 14–15.
24. These undated letters are in the Ruby Norman file, Eisenhower Library, Abilene.
25. Lyon, *Eisenhower,* 45; DDE, *At Ease,* 16.

26. Davis, *Soldier of Democracy,* 140; *The Howitzer,* 1915.
27. Davis, *Soldier of Democracy,* 140–41.
28. Norman file, Eisenhower Library; Neal, *The Eisenhowers,* 29–30.
29. DDE, *At Ease,* 16.
30. Davis, *Soldier of Democracy,* 147.
31. *Ibid.,* 146.
32. DDE, *At Ease,* 26.
33. See Ambrose, *Duty, Honor, Country,* 330–33.
34. See Huntington, *The Soldier and the State,* Chapter 9, "The Creation of the American Military Profession," and especially the subsection, "The Making of the American Military Mind."
35. Quoted in *ibid.,* 259.

Chapter Four

1. DDE, *At Ease,* 24–25, 111.
2. *Ibid.,* 121–25.
3. *Ibid.,* 119–20.
4. *Ibid.,* 129.
5. Davis, *Soldier of Democracy,* 157; Lyon, *Eisenhower,* 48.
6. DDE, *At Ease,* 113.
7. Neal, *The Eisenhowers,* 35; Hatch, *Red Carpet for Mamie,* 69–70.
8. Hatch, *Red Carpet for Mamie,* 73.
9. DDE, *At Ease,* 113–14, 118.
10. DDE, *At Ease,* 117; Hatch, *Red Carpet for Mamie,* 83.
11. DDE, *At Ease,* 123.
12. *Ibid.,* 123; Brandon, *Mamie Doud Eisenhower,* 72; Hatch, *Red Carpet for Mamie,* 97–98.
13. Neal, *The Eisenhowers,* 38.
14. Hatch, *Red Carpet for Mamie,* 114; Brandon, *Mamie Doud Eisenhower,* 42–43; Neal, *The Eisenhowers,* 43.
15. Neal, *The Eisenhowers,* 43; DDE, *At Ease,* 132–33; Lyon, *Eisenhower,* 50–51; Davis, *Soldier of Democracy,* 174–75; Lt. Ed. Thayer to his mother, Jan. 1918, Eisenhower Library, Abilene.
16. DDE, *At Ease,* 137.
17. *Ibid.,* 137.
18. *Ibid.,* 140.
19. Davis, *Soldier of Democracy,* 177–78.
20. Miller, *Eisenhower,* 172.
21. DDE, *At Ease,* 144–45.
22. Neal, *The Eisenhowers,* 45.
23. Hatch, *Red Carpet for Mamie,* 112.
24. DDE, *At Ease,* 147.
25. *Ibid.,* 152–53; Randolph to Eisenhower, 6/20/1945, Eisenhower Library, Abilene.
26. Miller, *Eisenhower,* 173.
27. Davis, *Soldier of Democracy,* 180.

Chapter Five

1. Weigley, *History U.S. Army,* 396, 403.
2. DDE, *At Ease,* 155.

3. *Ibid.,* 157–67.
4. Davis, *Soldier of Democracy,* 206–17.
5. Weigley, *History U.S. Army,* 409.
6. DDE, *At Ease,* 169; Davis, *Soldier of Democracy,* 187; Lyon, *Eisenhower,* 55; Blumenson, *Patton Papers,* Vol. I.
7. DDE, *At Ease,* 170.
8. DDE, "A Tank Discussion."
9. Weigley, *Eisenhower's Lieutenants,* 6.
10. DDE, *At Ease,* 173.
11. *Ibid.,* 174.
12. Interview DDE.
13. Lyon, *Eisenhower,* 56; DDE, *At Ease,* 178; Davis, *Soldier of Democracy,* 188.
14. DDE, *At Ease,* 178–79.
15. *Ibid.,* 181.
16. Neal, *The Eisenhowers,* 64–65.
17. *Ibid.,* 65; DDE, *At Ease,* 182.
18. Brandon, *Mamie Doud Eisenhower,* 126–27, 131–32.
19. Neal, *The Eisenhowers,* 67.
20. DDE, *At Ease,* 195; Davis, *Soldier of Democracy,* 197; McCann, *Man from Abilene,* 78.
21. DDE, *At Ease,* 187.
22. Brandon, *Mamie Doud Eisenhower,* 134.
23. Conner's efficiency reports are in Eisenhower Library, Abilene.
24. Davis, *Soldier of Democracy,* 198–99; McCann, *Man from Abilene,* 80.
25. John Eisenhower, *Strictly Personal,* 9–10; Brandon, *Mamie Doud Eisenhower,* 141.
26. Davis, *Soldier of Democracy,* 202–3; Eisenhower, *At Ease,* 200.
27. DDE, *At Ease,* 201.
28. Weigley, *Eisenhower's Lieutenants,* 7.
29. DDE, *At Ease,* 202–3.
30. John Eisenhower, *Strictly Personal,* 2.
31. Mrs. Doud to DDE, June 16, 1926, Eisenhower Library, Abilene.
32. Davis, *Soldier of Democracy,* 205.
33. Patton to DDE, 7/9/26, Eisenhower Library.
34. DDE, *At Ease,* 204.
35. Interviews DDE and MSE.
36. Interview MSE.
37. *Ibid.;* Lyon, *Eisenhower,* 64.
38. Pershing to DDE, 8/15/27, Eisenhower Library, Abilene.
39. Interviews DDE and Forrest Pogue; DDE, *At Ease,* 207–9.
40. Lyon, *Eisenhower,* 63.

Chapter Six

1. Davis, *Soldier of Democracy,* 225.
2. Brandon, *Mamie Doud Eisenhower,* 167.
3. DDE Diary, 11/30/32 and 2/28/32, Eisenhower Library, Abilene.
4. John Eisenhower, *Strictly Personal,* 8–10.
5. Neal, *The Eisenhowers,* 75; Davis, *Soldier of Democracy,* 222, 224–25; Lyon, *Eisenhower,* 64; Hatch, *Red Carpet for Mamie,* 152–53.
6. Quoted in James, *The Years of MacArthur,* I, 383.
7. Lyon, *Eisenhower,* 75.
8. DDE, *At Ease,* 213.

9. DDE to Clark, 9/17/40, Eisenhower Library, Abilene (hereinafter cited as EL); James, *Years of MacArthur,* I, 674; Moseley's efficiency report is in EL.
10. James, *Years of MacArthur,* I, 343; DDE, *At Ease,* 212.
11. DDE speech, "Brief History of Planning . . . ," 10/2/31, EL.
12. Weigley, *History U.S. Army,* 408; James, *Years of MacArthur,* I, 461.
13. James, *Years of MacArthur,* I, 462.
14. The best source on the commission is DDE, "War Policies," 25–29.
15. *Ibid.,* 29; James, *Years of MacArthur,* I, 462–63.
16. DDE, "War Policies," 27.
17. *Ibid.,* 26.
18. James, *Years of MacArthur,* I, 466–67.
19. MacArthur to DDE, 10/12/32, EL.
20. MacArthur to DDE, 11/4/31, EL; MacArthur's efficiency reports are in EL.
21. *Ibid.*
22. James, *Years of MacArthur,* I, 564.
23. DDE, *At Ease,* 214; Lyon, *Eisenhower,* 69.
24. DDE Diary, 9/26/36 and 11/15/36, EL. Large portions of this diary, which was kept in several different forms, have been published as *The Eisenhower Diaries,* edited by Robert H. Ferrell.
25. DDE, *At Ease,* 213.
26. Merriman Smith interview.
27. DDE, *At Ease,* 215–16.
28. MacArthur, *Reminiscences,* 93.
29. DDE, *At Ease,* 216; ACW Diary, 12/4/54, EL.
30. James, *Years of MacArthur,* I, 394–97; Lyon, *Eisenhower,* 70.
31. Interview DDE; DDE, *At Ease,* 216; James, *Years of MacArthur,* I, 398–99.
32. James, *Years of MacArthur,* I, 400–401.
33. DDE, *At Ease,* 217.
34. *Ibid.,* 217–18.
35. James, *Years of MacArthur,* I, 403–4.
36. DDE, *At Ease,* 217.
37. James, *Years of MacArthur,* I, 409.
38. Interview DDE; James, *Years of MacArthur,* I, 413.
39. Weigley, *History U.S. Army,* 414.
40. James, *Years of MacArthur,* I, 443.
41. Davis, *Soldier of Democracy,* 242.
42. Neal, *The Eisenhowers,* 93–94.
43. Interview MSE; Neal, *The Eisenhowers,* 94; Davis, *Soldier of Democracy,* 239–40.
44. James, *Years of MacArthur,* I, 485, 530; DDE, *At Ease,* 220–21.
45. MacArthur to DDE, 9/30/35, EL.

Chapter Seven

1. DDE to MSE, 1/3/39, EL.
2. James, *Years of MacArthur,* I, 481.
3. DDE Diary, 12/27/35; DDE, *At Ease,* 221; James, *Years of MacArthur,* I, 501.
4. DDE Diary, 12/27/35.
5. James, *Years of MacArthur,* I, 504.
6. DDE Diary, 5/29/36.
7. DDE Diary, 2/15/36.
8. Lyon, *Eisenhower,* 78.

9. DDE Diary, 7/1/36.
10. James, *Years of MacArthur,* I, 505–6.
11. Brandon, *Mamie Doud Eisenhower,* 178–80, 184–85; Hatch, *Red Carpet for Mamie,* 156–57.
12. John Eisenhower, *Strictly Personal,* 18–20.
13. Brandon, *Mamie Doud Eisenhower,* 190–91.
14. Hatch, *Red Carpet for Mamie,* 158.
15. Brandon, *Mamie Doud Eisenhower,* 192.
16. *Ibid.,* 198–99; DDE Diary, June–Dec., 1937.
17. Interview DDE.
18. *Ibid.*
19. DDE Diary, 1/20/36.
20. See DDE to MacArthur, 8/23/38 and 9/16/38, EL.
21. James, *Years of MacArthur,* I, 514.
22. *Ibid.,* 517–18.
23. DDE Diary, 7/9/37.
24. James, *Years of MacArthur,* I, 509.
25. DDE, *At Ease,* 225–26.
26. Lyon, *Eisenhower,* 79.
27. *Ibid.,* 78.
28. MacArthur to DDE, undated, EL.
29. Quezon to DDE, 3/10/37, EL.
30. DDE to Mrs. E. T. Spencer (Ord's sister), 3/26/38, EL.
31. DDE, *At Ease,* 228.
32. *Ibid.,* 229–30.
33. Interview DDE.
34. DDE to MSE, 1/3/39, EL.
35. DDE to MSE, 9/3/39, EL; McCann, *Man from Abilene,* 52–53.
36. Patton to DDE, 10/1/40, EL.
37. DDE to Gerow, 10/11/39, EL.
38. DDE, *At Ease,* 231.
39. DDE to Gerow, 10/11/39.
40. See Vargas to DDE, 12/9/39, EL, and DDE, *At Ease,* 246–47.
41. MacArthur to DDE, 12/9/39, EL.
42. Davis, *Soldier of Democracy,* 252.
43. DDE, *At Ease,* 240–41.

Chapter Eight

1. DDE to Bradley, 7/1/40, EL.
2. DDE to Gerow, 8/23/40, EL.
3. DDE, *At Ease,* 237.
4. DDE to MSE, 11/6/40, EL.
5. DDE to MSE, 11/7/40, EL.
6. See the John S. D. Eisenhower and the MSE files in EL for the considerable correspondence on the subject of John's appointment.
7. DDE to Hughes, 11/26/40, EL.
8. Davis, *Soldier of Democracy,* 256.
9. Weigley, *Eisenhower's Lieutenants,* 2, 12.
10. DDE, *At Ease,* 383–84.
11. John Eisenhower, *Strictly Personal,* 29.
12. Davis, *Soldier of Democracy,* 257.
13. DDE to Gerow, 8/23/40, EL.

14. DDE to Hughes, 11/26/40, EL.
15. DDE to Patton, 9/17/40, EL.
16. Patton to DDE, 10/1/40, EL.
17. DDE to Clark, 10/31/40, EL; see also almost any letter written by DDE in Oct.–Nov. 1940, EL.
18. Patton to DDE, 11/1/40, EL.
19. DDE to T. J. Davis, 11/14/40, EL.
20. DDE to Gerow, 11/18/40, EL.
21. DDE to Gerow, 11/23/40, EL.
22. Davis, *Soldier of Democracy,* 263.
23. Lyon, *Eisenhower,* 82–83.
24. Hatch, *Red Carpet for Mamie,* 174; Brandon, *Mamie Doud Eisenhower,* 206.
25. Davis, *Soldier of Democracy,* 266–68.
26. DDE to Gerow, 8/5/40, EL.
27. DDE, *At Ease,* 243; Davis, *Soldier of Democracy,* 269–72.
28. Lyon, *Eisenhower,* 83; DDE to Gerow, 9/25/40, EL.
29. *New York Times,* 9/17/40.
30. Quoted in Davis, *Soldier of Democracy,* 272.
31. DDE to Gerow, 10/4/41, EL.
32. Nielsen to DDE, 10/28/40, and DDE to Nielsen, 10/31/40, EL.
33. DDE to Clark, 10/7/41, EL.
34. DDE to Gerow, 10/25/41, EL.
35. Davis, *Soldier of Democracy,* 276.
36. Ambrose, *Supreme Commander,* 3.

Chapter Nine

1. Interview DDE; Pogue, *Ordeal and Hope,* 237–39; DDE, *Crusade,* 14–22. "Steps to Be Taken" is reprinted in the Eisenhower Papers (hereinafter cited as EP). Documents in EP are printed in chronological order and will here be cited only by date.
2. Interview DDE; Pogue, *Ordeal and Hope,* 95–98.
3. DDE Diary, 10/5/42; DDE, *At Ease,* 248.
4. DDE, *Crusade,* 34–35.
5. Interview DDE.
6. *Ibid.*
7. Ambrose, *Supreme Commander,* 9–11.
8. DDE Diary, 1/13/42.
9. *Ibid.,* 1/1, 12, 17/42.
10. Ambrose, *Supreme Commander,* 11–13.
11. DDE to Marshall, 9/25/44, EP.
12. DDE Diary, 1/19/42.
13. *Ibid.,* 1/23/42.
14. *Ibid.,* 1/29/42.
15. *Ibid.,* 2/3, 8/42.
16. Ambrose, *Supreme Commander,* 18.
17. DDE Diary, 2/9/42.
18. FDR to MacArthur, 2/9/42.
19. DDE Diary, 2/23/42.
20. *Ibid.,* 3/19/42.
21. *Ibid.,* 3/31/42.

22. *Ibid.*, 5/6/42.
23. *Ibid.*, 2/10/42.
24. *Ibid.*, 2/17/42.
25. *Ibid.*, 2/28/42.
26. *Ibid.*, 3/14/42.
27. *Ibid.*, 3/10/42.
28. DDE, *At Ease*, 252.
29. Interview MSE.
30. McKeogh and Lockridge, *Sergeant Mickey and General Ike*, 21.
31. DDE Diary, 2/22/42.
32. *Ibid.*, 1/27/42.
33. *Ibid.*, 1/24/42.
34. *Ibid.*, 3/10, 11, 12/42.
35. Interview DDE; DDE, *At Ease*, 248–49.
36. DDE Diary, 3/21/42.
37. *Ibid.*, 3/30/42.
38. DDE, *At Ease*, 250.
39. Truscott, *Command Missions*, 21–22.
40. DDE, *Crusade*, 38.
41. *Ibid.*, 32–33.
42. DDE Diary, 2/23/42.
43. *Ibid.*, 1/6/53.
44. *Ibid.*, 1/5/42.
45. *Ibid.*, 1/10/42.
46. *Ibid.*, 2/5/42.
47. *Ibid.*, 1/30/42.
48. *Ibid.*, 1/17, 22, 27/42.
49. *Ibid.*, 2/22/42.
50. *Ibid.*, 2/19/42.
51. DDE's undated plan is EP No. 160.
52. DDE's plan of 3/27/42 is in EP; see also Harrison, *Cross-Channel Attack*, 12–19.
53. DDE Diary, 4/20/42.
54. Marshall to FDR, 5/4/42, EP.
55. Ambrose, *Supreme Commander*, 41–42.
56. DDE Diary, 5/5/42.
57. *Ibid.*, 5/6/42.
58. *Ibid.*, 5/21/42; Pogue, *Ordeal and Hope*, 338–39.
59. DDE Diary, 5/23, 24, 25/42; Summersby, *Eisenhower Was My Boss*, 5–9.
60. DDE, *Crusade*, 50.
61. DDE Diary, 5/27/42.
62. Bryant, *Turn of the Tide*, 285.
63. Ambrose, *Supreme Commander*, 45.
64. DDE Diary, 6/4/42.
65. DDE, *Crusade*, 50.
66. Pogue, *Ordeal and Hope*, 338–40; Lyon, *Eisenhower*, 123–24.
67. DDE, *Crusade*, 50; Ambrose, *Supreme Commander*, 47.
68. DDE Diary, 6/8/42.
69. Pogue, *Ordeal and Hope*, 338.
70. DDE, *Crusade*, 51.
71. DDE Diary, 6/20/42; see Ferrell, *Eisenhower Diaries*, 404–5, note 1.
72. Brandon, *Mamie Doud Eisenhower*, 216–17; Hatch, *Red Carpet for Mamie*, 182.
73. DDE to Akin, 6/19/42, EP.

Chapter Ten

1. Davis, *Soldier of Democracy,* 317, 322.
2. McKeogh and Lockridge, *Sergeant Mickey and General Ike,* 30; Davis, *Soldier of Democracy,* 314.
3. Davis, *Soldier of Democracy,* 315–16.
4. Hatch, *Red Carpet for Mamie,* 184–87.
5. Butcher Diary, 6/26/42. Butcher printed parts of his diary as *My Three Years with Eisenhower.* I have used the original throughout; there is a copy in EL.
6. Interview Thor Smith.
7. Quoted in Lyon, *Eisenhower,* 156.
8. DDE to Hartle and others, 7/19/42, EP.
9. *Ibid.*
10. DDE to Prichard, 8/27/42, EP.
11. DDE, *At Ease,* 281–82.
12. DDE Diary, 7/5/42.
13. *Ibid.,* 7/1, 2/42.
14. Interview DDE; DDE, *Crusade,* 89.
15. Ambrose, *Supreme Commander,* 97.
16. Bryant, *Turn of the Tide,* 341.
17. DDE memorandums, 7/19/42, EP.
18. DDE Diary, 7/20/42.
19. DDE to Somervell, 7/27/42, EP.
20. Butcher Diary, 7/23/42.
21. DDE Diary, 7/26/42.
22. See Wilt, *The Atlantic Wall.*
23. Churchill, *The Hinge of Fate,* 439.
24. Butcher Diary, 7/16/42.
25. DDE, *At Ease,* 252.
26. Interview DDE; Pogue, *Ordeal and Hope,* 348; DDE, *Crusade,* 71.
27. Pogue, *Ordeal and Hope,* 403.
28. DDE to Marshall, 8/17/42, EP.
29. DDE Diary, 9/2/42.
30. Butcher Diary, 8/26/42.
31. *Ibid.,* 8/15/42.
32. EP No. 444, note 1.
33. Butcher Diary, 8/10/42.
34. Salmon, *History of AFHQ,* 17.
35. Interview DDE.
36. Ismay, *Memoirs,* 258, 263.
37. Interview DDE; DDE, *Crusade,* 83.
38. Interview DDE.
39. *Ibid.*; interviews Frederick Morgan and Ian Jacob; DDE, *Crusade,* 55.
40. Interview Forrest Pogue.
41. Interview DDE.
42. DDE to Gailey, 9/19/42, EP.
43. DDE, *Letters to Mamie,* 28.
44. *Ibid.,* 35.
45. *Ibid.,* 26, 41, 48, 50, 51.
46. *Ibid.,* 44, 35–36.
47. *Ibid.,* 23, 50.

48. *Ibid.,* 38.
49. *Ibid.,* 33.
50. DDE to Marshall, 8/26/42, EP.
51. Interview DDE; DDE, *Crusade,* 62.
52. DDE to Patton, 8/31/42, EP.
53. DDE to Handy, 9/5/42, EP; Churchill, *Hinge of Fate,* 542–43.
54. DDE Diary, 9/2/42.
55. *Ibid.,* 9/15/42.
56. Pogue, *Ordeal and Hope,* 402.
57. DDE Diary, 9/13/42.
58. *Ibid.,* 9/15/42.

Chapter Eleven

1. Butcher Diary, 9/17/42; DDE to Marshall, 9/19/42, EP.
2. DDE to Marshall, 10/12/42, EP.
3. Churchill to FDR, 9/22/42, in Loewenheim, *Roosevelt and Churchill,* 255.
4. DDE to Marshall, 9/21/42, EP.
5. Ambrose, *Supreme Commander,* 105.
6. DDE to Marshall, 10/17/42, EP.
7. Butcher Diary, 10/17/42; interview DDE; Clark, *Calculated Risk,* 67–72.
8. Clark, *Calculated Risk,* 71.
9. Butcher Diary, 10/24/42.
10. Ambrose, *Ike's Spies,* 34–36.
11. Clark, *Calculated Risk,* 90.
12. DDE, *Crusade,* 88.
13. DDE to Marshall, 10/20/42, EP.
14. DDE to Marshall, 10/29/42, EP.
15. DDE, *Letters to Mamie,* 50–51.
16. DDE, *Crusade,* 95.
17. DDE Diary, 11/9/42.
18. Butcher Diary, 11/6/42.
19. DDE to Marshall, 11/7/42, EP.
20. DDE, *Crusade,* 101; Butcher Diary, 11/8/42.
21. Butcher Diary, 11/9/42.
22. *Ibid.*
23. DDE to Smith, 11/9/42, EP.
24. DDE to Marshall, 11/9/42, EP.
25. DDE to Smith, 11/11/42, EP.
26. Viorst, *Hostile Allies,* 119–21.
27. DDE to Smith, 11/13/42, EP.
28. DDE to Edgar Eisenhower, 2/18/43; DDE, *Crusade,* 107.
29. DDE to John Eisenhower, 4/8/43, EP.
30. Macmillan, *Blast of War,* 174.
31. DDE to Col. Wm. Lee, 10/29/42, EP.
32. DDE, *Letters to Mamie,* 66.
33. Butcher Diary, 12/7/42.
34. Ambrose, *Supreme Commander,* 130.
35. DDE to CCS, 11/14/42, EP; DDE to Churchill, 11/14/42, EP.
36. Viorst, *Hostile Allies,* 122–23.
37. Ambrose, *Supreme Commander,* 131.
38. Darlan to Clark, 11/21/42, EP.

39. Murphy, *Diplomat Among Warriors,* 150–51.
40. Viorst, *Hostile Allies,* 126.
41. DDE to Smith, 11/12/42, EP.
42. Butcher Diary, 11/29/42.
43. DDE Diary, 12/15/42.
44. DDE, *Crusade,* 121; DDE to Marshall, 11/30/42, EP.
45. DDE to Handy, 12/7/42, EP.
46. Patton to DDE, 7/9/26, EL.
47. Butcher Diary, 12/9/42.
48. DDE, *Crusade,* 126.
49. DDE Diary, 12/10/42.
50. Butcher Diary, 12/9/42.
51. DDE Diary, 12/10/42.
52. DDE, *Letters to Mamie,* 63–68.
53. Butcher Diary, 12/23/42.
54. Sir Ian Jacob diary (loaned to the author), 12/30/42.
55. Bryant, *Turn of the Tide,* 430.
56. DDE, *Letters to Mamie,* 74.
57. Quoted in Lyon, *Eisenhower,* 174.
58. DDE to CCS, 12/24/42, EP; DDE, *Crusade,* 124.
59. Murphy, *Diplomat Among Warriors,* 143.
60. Ambrose, *Ike's Spies,* 39–56.
61. Clark, *Calculated Risk,* 128–31.
62. DDE, *Letters to Mamie,* 75.
63. Ambrose, *Supreme Commander,* 148.

Chapter Twelve

1. Jackson, *North African Campaign,* 346–47.
2. Brereton, *Diaries,* 172, 175.
3. DDE Diary, 1/19/43.
4. DDE, *Letters to Mamie,* 98; Butcher Diary, 1/23/43.
5. DDE, *Letters to Mamie,* 88.
6. Jacob Diary, 1/1/43.
7. *Ibid.,* 1/13/43.
8. Wedemeyer, *Wedemeyer Reports!,* 192.
9. DDE to Handy, 1/28/43, EP.
10. Bryant, *Turn of the Tide,* 452–55.
11. See EP, #811, note 2.
12. DDE to Marshall, 2/8/43, EP.
13. DDE, *Letters to Mamie,* 94–95.
14. *Ibid.,* 111.
15. *Ibid.*
16. *Foreign Relations, 1943, Europe,* 24.
17. Butcher Diary, 1/3/43.
18. Ambrose, *Supreme Commander,* 157.
19. DDE, *Crusade,* 136.
20. *Ibid.,* 146.
21. DDE, *At Ease,* 260; Lyon, *Eisenhower,* 197.
22. DDE, *Letters to Mamie,* 83, 97–105.
23. DDE to Hartle and others, 1/15/43, EP.
24. DDE Diary, 2/25/43.
25. DDE to Fredendall, 2/4/43, EP; Blumenson, *Kasserine Pass,* 86–87; DDE, *Crusade,* 141.

26. DDE to Fredendall, 2/4/43, EP, and notes.
27. Blumenson, *Kasserine Pass,* 94–95; DDE, *Crusade,* 142.
28. Blumenson, *Kasserine Pass,* 163.
29. DDE Diary, 2/25/43.
30. Blumenson, *Kasserine Pass,* 278–79.
31. Fredendall to DDE, 2/19/43, EP.
32. Butcher Diary, 2/20/43.
33. DDE to Truscott, 2/16/43, EP.
34. DDE to Marshall, 2/15/43, EP.
35. Blumenson, *Kasserine Pass,* 282–83; DDE, *Crusade,* 145–46.
36. Blumenson, *Kasserine Pass,* 297, 306.
37. DDE to Patton, 3/6/43, EP.
38. DDE to Gerow, 2/24/43, EP.
39. Jackson, *North African Campaign,* 354–55.
40. Tedder, *With Prejudice,* 410–11.
41. *Ibid.,* 411.
42. *Ibid.*
43. Jackson, *North African Campaign,* 358.
44. DDE to Marshall, 3/29/43, EP.
45. Lyon, *Eisenhower,* 196.
46. Marshall to Eisenhower, 4/14/43, EP.
47. DDE to Marshall, 4/15/43, EP.
48. DDE to Bradley, 4/16/43, EP.
49. Butcher Diary, 4/25/43.
50. DDE to Alexander, 4/30/43, EP.
51. DDE, *Letters to Mamie,* 99.
52. DDE to Arthur Eisenhower, 5/18/43, EP; DDE to John Eisenhower, 5/22/43, EP.
53. DDE to Marshall, 5/13/43, EP.
54. DDE Diary, 6/11/43.
55. Macmillan, *Blast of War,* 263; Lyon, *Eisenhower,* 204–5.

Chapter Thirteen

1. DDE to CCS, 6/10/43, EP.
2. *Foreign Relations,* 1943, Vol. II, 152–55.
3. FDR to Churchill, 6/17/43, EP.
4. Churchill to FDR, 6/18/43, EP.
5. DDE to FDR, 6/18/43, EP.
6. DDE to Marshall, 6/19/43, EP.
7. DDE to Marshall, 6/22/43, EP.
8. Churchill, *Closing the Ring,* 179; FDR to DDE, 7/8/43, EP.
9. DDE to Marshall, 7/22/43, EP.
10. Funk, *De Gaulle,* 158–60; Churchill, *Closing the Ring,* 182–83.
11. DDE to Marshall, 4/19/43, EP.
12. Butcher Diary, 5/30/43; Bryant, *Turn of the Tide,* 522.
13. DDE, *Crusade,* 168.
14. These debates are treated in detail in Ambrose, *Supreme Commander,* 204–14.
15. Brandon, *Mamie Doud Eisenhower,* 218.
16. DDE, *Letters to Mamie,* 128.
17. *Ibid.,* 137.
18. *Ibid.,* 136.

19. Quoted in Irving, *War Between the Generals,* 46–47.
20. *Ibid.,* 65.
21. DDE, *Letters to Mamie,* 132.
22. Cunningham, *A Sailor's Odyssey,* 540; DDE, *At Ease,* 264–65.
23. DDE to Marshall, 6/11/43, EP.
24. Interview DDE.
25. DDE to Marshall, 7/1/43, EP.
26. Garland and Smyth, *Sicily,* 11, 88; Wedemeyer, *Wedemeyer Reports!,* 192.
27. Butcher Diary, 7/8/43.
28. DDE to Marshall, 7/9/43, EP; Garland and Smyth, *Sicily,* 108–9.
29. DDE, *Letters to Mamie,* 134–35.
30. Butcher Diary, 7/10/43.
31. Baldwin, *Battles Lost and Won,* 460–61, note 116.
32. Butcher Diary, 8/4/43.
33. DDE to CCS, 8/5/43, EP.
34. Ambrose, *Supreme Commander,* 228–29.
35. DDE to Patton, 8/17/43, EP.
36. Ambrose, *Supreme Commander,* 230–31.
37. Patton to DDE, 8/29/43, EP.
38. DDE to Marshall, 8/27, 28/43, EP.
39. Butcher Diary, 8/14/43.
40. Garland and Smyth, *Sicily,* 281.
41. Churchill, *Closing the Ring,* 55–65.
42. Macmillan, *Blast of War,* 305.
43. DDE to Churchill, 7/18/43, EP.
44. DDE to CCS, 7/26/43, EP.
45. DDE to CCS, 7/27/43; DDE to Churchill, 7/27/43; DDE to Marshall, 7/29/43, EP; Macmillan, *Blast of War,* 308–9.
46. DDE, *Letters to Mamie,* 125.
47. Garland and Smyth, *Sicily,* 283–88.
48. DDE to CCS, 8/4/43, EP.
49. For a detailed account, see Ambrose, *Supreme Commander,* 246–50.
50. DDE to CCS, 8/17/43, EP.
51. EP, No. 1120, note 1.
52. CCS to DDE, 8/18/43, EP.
53. Macmillan, *Blast of War,* 307–8; the long terms are reprinted in Garland and Smyth, *Sicily,* 559–64.
54. Garland and Smyth, *Sicily,* 474–79. This great work is the indispensable guide through the maze of the Italian surrender negotiations.
55. DDE to CCS, 9/1/43, EP.
56. Garland and Smyth, *Sicily,* 484.
57. *Ibid.,* 501–5.
58. DDE to CCS, 9/8/43, EP.
59. DDE to Badoglio, 9/8/43, EP; Garland and Smyth, *Sicily,* 506–7.
60. Garland and Smyth, *Sicily,* 509.
61. Butcher Diary, 9/9/43.
62. DDE, *Letters to Mamie,* 146–47.
63. DDE to Marshall, 9/6/43, EP.

Chapter Fourteen

1. Garland and Smyth, *Sicily,* 515–20.
2. DDE to Badoglio, 9/10/43, EP.
3. DDE to CCS, 9/9/43, EP.

4. DDE to CCS, 9/13/43, EP; DDE to Wedemeyer, 9/13/43, EP.
5. Butcher Diary, 9/13/43; DDE to Marshall, 9/13/43, EP; DDE Diary, 9/14/43.
6. DDE, *Crusade,* 188; Clark, *Calculated Risk,* 199; DDE Diary, 9/14/43.
7. Marshall to DDE, 9/23/43, EP.
8. Butcher Diary, 9/25/43; DDE to Marshall, 9/25/43, EP.
9. DDE to Dill, 9/30/43, EP.
10. Butcher Diary, 12/19/43.
11. Summersby, *Eisenhower Was My Boss,* 114; DDE to Spaatz, 12/24/43, EP.
12. DDE, *Letters to Mamie,* 150.
13. *Ibid.,* 154, 156–58.
14. Butcher Diary, 9/16/43.
15. DDE to Arthur Eisenhower, 10/20/43, EP.
16. DDE to Moseley, 10/7/43, EP.
17. DDE, *Crusade,* 197; DDE Diary, 12/6/43; Butcher Diary, 11/21/43.
18. DDE, *Crusade,* 200; DDE, *At Ease,* 266.
19. Pogue, *Supreme Command,* 30–32.
20. Butcher Diary, 12/4/43.
21. Cunningham to DDE, 10/21/43, EP.
22. Bryant, *Triumph in the West,* 74.
23. DDE to Nielsen, 12/6/43, EP.
24. Montgomery, *Memoirs,* 484.
25. DDE, *Crusade,* 206–7.
26. Butcher Diary, 12/8/43.
27. *Ibid.,* 1/14/44.
28. DDE to Marshall, 12/17/43, EP.
29. DDE to Patton, 11/24/43, EP.
30. DDE, *Letters to Mamie,* 159.
31. Interview DDE.
32. Marshall to DDE, 12/29/43, EP.
33. Ambrose, *Supreme Commander,* 318.

CHAPTER FIFTEEN

1. DDE, *Letters to Mamie,* 162; Brandon, *Mamie Doud Eisenhower,* 221.
2. Interview DDE.
3. Smith to DDE, and DDE to Smith, 1/5/43, EP.
4. Morgan, *Past Forgetting,* 199.
5. Davis, *Soldier of Democracy,* 456–57.
6. EP, No. 1539, note 2.
7. Arnold to DDE, no date, EP, No. 1539, note 2.
8. Butcher Diary, 12/31/43; de Gaulle, *Unity,* 216–17.
9. Pogue, *Supreme Command,* 140; DDE, *Crusade,* 218.
10. This issue is discussed at length in Ambrose, *Supreme Commander,* 387–91.
11. Hatch, *Red Carpet for Mamie,* 192.
12. DDE, *Letters to Mamie,* 164–65.
13. DDE to Haislip, 1/24/44, EP.
14. DDE, *Crusade,* 220.
15. DDE to Marshall, 1/22/44, EP.
16. DDE to Somervell, 4/4/44, EP.
17. DDE, *Letters to Mamie,* 170.
18. DDE to Cunningham, 2/23/44, EP.
19. Harrison, *Cross-Channel Attack,* is the classic study of the operation.
20. DDE to CCS, 1/23/44, EP.

21. The debate is covered in detail in Ambrose, *Supreme Commander,* 349–62.
22. Harrison, *Cross-Channel Attack,* 68.
23. Butcher Diary, 1/25/44.
24. DDE Diary, 2/7/44.
25. Marshall to DDE, 2/7/44, EP.
26. DDE to Marshall, 2/8/44, EP.
27. Morgan, *Past Forgetting,* 194.
28. DDE, *Letters to Mamie,* 179.
29. Tedder, *With Prejudice,* 508; Harrison, *Cross-Channel Attack,* 219.
30. Quoted in Irving, *War Between the Generals,* 79.
31. Quoted in *ibid.,* 81.
32. Tedder, *With Prejudice,* 510–12; Pogue, *Supreme Command,* 124; Harrison, *Cross-Channel Attack,* 219–20.
33. DDE Diary, 3/22/44.
34. Tedder, *With Prejudice,* 524.
35. DDE to Churchill, 4/5/44, EP.
36. Tedder, *With Prejudice,* 528–30.
37. *Ibid.,* 531–33.
38. Churchill, *Closing the Ring,* 529–30.
39. Weigley, *Eisenhower's Lieutenants,* 58–64, takes a dim view of the Transportation Plan, as do the official U.S. Army Air Force historians.
40. Pogue, *Supreme Command,* 132.
41. Harrison, *Cross-Channel Attack,* 224, 230.
42. Interview DDE.
43. For a detailed discussion, see Ambrose, *Ike's Spies,* 75–95.
44. Pogue, *Supreme Command,* 162–63; DDE to British Chiefs, 3/6/44, EP.
45. Pogue, *Supreme Command,* 163–64.
46. DDE to Marshall, 5/21/44, EP.
47. Butcher Diary, 5/12/44.
48. DDE, *Letters to Mamie,* 172, 175–76.
49. DDE, *Crusade in Europe,* 238.
50. Interview Thor Smith.
51. DDE to Marshall, 1/29/44, EP.
52. DDE to Marshall, 4/30/44, EP; Butcher Diary, 5/3/44.
53. DDE to Marshall, 2/9/44, EP.
54. Quoted in Weigley, *Eisenhower's Lieutenants,* 121–22.
55. DDE to Marshall, 4/29/44, EP.
56. *Ibid.,* notes.
57. DDE to Patton, 4/29/44, EP.
58. DDE to Marshall, 4/30/44, EP.
59. *Ibid.,* note 1.
60. DDE, *At Ease,* 270; DDE to Marshall, 5/3/44, EP; Farago, *Patton,* 421–23.
61. Butcher Diary, 5/1/44.
62. DDE, *Crusade,* 225.
63. DDE Diary, 2/7/44.
64. Bradley, *Soldier's Story,* 239.
65. *Ibid.,* 241–42; Bryant, *Triumph in the West,* 189–91; de Guingand, *Operation Victory,* 317.
66. Butcher Diary, 5/15/44.
67. Bryant, *Triumph in the West,* 139.
68. Sir Ian Jacob Diary, 5/15/44.
69. DDE, *At Ease,* 273, 275; Butcher Diary, 5/13/44.
70. DDE Diary, 1/22/42; DDE, *At Ease,* 275.

Chapter Sixteen

1. DDE, *Letters to Mamie,* 183.
2. *Ibid.,* 182; Morgan, *Past Forgetting,* 209; Butcher Diary, 5/28/44.
3. Leigh-Mallory to DDE, 5/29/44, EP.
4. DDE to Leigh-Mallory, 5/30/44, EP; DDE, *Crusade,* 246–47.
5. Butcher Diary, 6/4/44.
6. de Gaulle, *Unity,* 255–56; Funk, *de Gaulle,* 257–59.
7. EP, No. 1732.
8. Interview DDE; de Gaulle, *Unity,* 256.
9. DDE Diary, 6/3/44.
10. DDE, *Letters to Mamie,* 185.
11. DDE, *Crusade,* 249.
12. Pogue, *Supreme Command,* 169; Harrison, *Cross-Channel Attack,* 272.
13. Tedder, *With Prejudice,* 545; DDE, *Crusade,* 249.
14. de Guingand, *Operation Victory,* 302.
15. Tedder, *With Prejudice,* 545.
16. Interviews with DDE, Sir Kenneth Strong, Sir Arthur Tedder; Butcher Diary, 6/5, 6, 7/44; Pogue, *Supreme Command,* 170; Harrison, *Cross-Channel Attack,* 274; DDE, *Crusade,* 250.
17. Butcher Diary, 6/6/44.
18. *Ibid.*
19. Interview DDE; Butcher Diary, 6/6/44; DDE, *Crusade,* 252.
20. Morgan, *Past Forgetting,* 216; Butcher Diary, 6/7/44.
21. DDE to Marshall, 6/6/44, EP.
22. Butcher Diary, 6/7/44.
23. Harrison, *Cross-Channel Attack,* 302–36.
24. Butcher Diary, 6/7/44.
25. Pogue, *Supreme Command,* 173.
26. DDE to CCS, 6/9/44, and DDE to Smith, 6/11/44, EP.
27. DDE to Smith, 6/16/44, EP.
28. Quoted in Ambrose, *Supreme Commander,* 424.
29. EP, No. 1772.
30. DDE, *Letters to Mamie,* 189–90.
31. Morgan, *Past Forgetting,* 220–21.
32. Quoted in Neal, *The Eisenhowers,* 184.
33. DDE, *Letters to Mamie,* 190.
34. *Ibid.,* 190–92.
35. Morgan, *Past Forgetting,* 221–22.
36. John Eisenhower, *Strictly Personal,* 63.
37. Interview John Eisenhower.
38. Butcher Diary, 6/19/44; Irving, *War Between the Generals,* 170–71; Morgan, *Past Forgetting,* 223–24; John Eisenhower, *Strictly Personal,* 64.
39. John Eisenhower, *Strictly Personal,* 58–62.
40. *Ibid.,* 72.
41. DDE, *At Ease,* 288.
42. Montgomery, *Memoirs,* 43; Weigley, *Eisenhower's Lieutenants,* 210.
43. Interview Brigadier Kenneth G. McLean.
44. Montgomery to DDE, 6/25/44, EP.
45. Butcher Diary, 6/26/44.
46. Bryant, *Triumph in the West,* 178.
47. Tedder, *With Prejudice,* 582.

48. DDE to Bradley, 7/1/44, EP.
49. DDE, *At Ease,* 288–89.
50. Eisenhower Office Diary, July 5, 1944, EL.
51. *New York Times,* July 6, 1944.
52. DDE, *Letters to Mamie,* 195–96.
53. Tedder, *With Prejudice,* 557.
54. Irving, *War Between the Generals,* 232.
55. Montgomery to DDE, 7/7/44, EP, note 1.
56. Pogue, *Supreme Command,* 188.
57. DDE to Montgomery, 7/14/44, EP.
58. Bryant, *Triumph in the West,* 170; Tedder, *With Prejudice,* 558–61; interview Eisenhower.
59. Blumenson, *Breakout and Pursuit,* 193–94.
60. Butcher Diary, 7/21/44.
61. *Ibid.*
62. Interview Eisenhower.
63. Tedder, *With Prejudice,* 565–67.
64. DDE to Montgomery, 7/21/44, EP.
65. Tedder, *With Prejudice,* 567.

Chapter Seventeen

1. Pogue, *Supreme Command,* 192–96; Blumenson, *Breakout and Pursuit,* 175–84.
2. Bradley, *Soldier's Story,* 343.
3. DDE to Bradley, 7/24/44, EP.
4. Wilmot, *Struggle for Europe,* 362.
5. Bryant, *Triumph in the West,* 181–82; Wilmot, *Struggle for Europe,* 362.
6. Butcher Diary, 7/25/44.
7. Bradley, *Soldier's Story,* 349; DDE, *Crusade,* 272.
8. DDE to Bradley, 7/26/44, EP.
9. DDE to Montgomery, 7/28/44, EP.
10. Pogue, *Supreme Command,* 200–201.
11. Butcher Diary, 8/2/44.
12. DDE to Marshall, 8/2/44, EP.
13. DDE to Montgomery, 8/2/44, EP.
14. Pogue, *Supreme Command,* 207.
15. Tedder, *With Prejudice,* 575; DDE to Marshall, 8/9/44, EP.
16. Butcher Diary, 8/8/44.
17. DDE, *Crusade,* 281.
18. Pogue, *Supreme Command,* 218–33.
19. DDE to Marshall, 8/5/44, EP.
20. DDE to Marshall, 8/5/44, EP.
21. DDE to Marshall, 8/11/44, EP; DDE to Churchill, 8/11/44, EP; Pogue, *Supreme Command,* 225; DDE, *Crusade,* 281–83.
22. DDE to Marshall, 8/24/44, EP.
23. Interview DDE; Ambrose, *Supreme Commander,* 458.
24. Butcher Diary, 8/8/44.
25. Bradley, *Soldier's Story,* 377; Wilmot, *Struggle for Europe,* 424–25.
26. Butcher Diary, 8/14/44.
27. Pogue, *Supreme Command,* 546–47.
28. DDE, *Letters to Mamie,* 204, 210.
29. DDE to Smith, 5/20/44, and to Marshall, 5/27/44, EP.

30. Butcher, *My Three Years,* 644–46.
31. DDE to Marshall, 8/17/44, EP.
32. SHAEF Office Diary, 8/29/44, EL.
33. DDE, *Crusade,* 279.
34. DDE, *Letters to Mamie,* 203.
35. EP, No. 1908.
36. Blumenson, *Breakout and Pursuit,* 604–5.
37. Bradley, *Soldier's Story,* 394–95; DDE, *Letters to Mamie,* 209, 211.
38. DDE, *Crusade,* 297–99; Blumenson, *Breakout and Pursuit,* 622; Pogue, *Supreme Command,* 242; Bradley, *Soldier's Story,* 394–95.
39. *Foreign Relations,* 1944, III, 742–43.
40. White, *Seeds of Discord,* 357.
41. Pogue, *Supreme Command,* 244–45.
42. Ambrose, *Supreme Commander,* 510.
43. Pogue, *Supreme Command,* 245.
44. DDE to Marshall, 8/24/44, EP.
45. DDE to Marshall, 8/31/44, EP.
46. Butcher Diary, 8/7/44.
47. Pogue, *Supreme Command,* 263–64.
48. DDE to Marshall, 8/19/44, EP.
49. Montgomery, *Memoirs,* 240.
50. John Eisenhower, *Strictly Personal,* 62–63.
51. Montgomery, *Memoirs,* 241; DDE to Montgomery, 8/24/44, EP.
52. Montgomery, *Memoirs,* 243.
53. Quoted in Irving, *War Between the Generals,* 250–51.
54. DDE to commanders, 8/29/44, EP.
55. Pogue, *Supreme Command,* 259.
56. de Guingand, *Operation Victory,* 329–30.
57. Bryant, *Triumph in the West,* 213.

Chapter Eighteen

1. Davis, *Soldier of Democracy,* 507; Irving, *War Between the Generals,* 256.
2. Patton, *War As I Knew It,* 120; Wilmot, *Struggle for Europe,* 469.
3. Quoted in Weigley, *Eisenhower's Lieutenants,* 266.
4. DDE to Montgomery, 9/5/44, EP.
5. Montgomery, *Memoirs,* 242–46.
6. Morgan, *Past Forgetting,* 239–40; DDE, *Letters to Mamie,* 210–11.
7. Interview DDE; Wilmot, *Struggle for Europe,* 488–89.
8. Tedder, *With Prejudice,* 590–91; SHAEF office diary, 9/11/44, EL.
9. Tedder, *With Prejudice,* 590–91.
10. SHAEF office diary, 9/11/44, EL.
11. Ambrose, *Supreme Commander,* 518.
12. DDE to Marshall, 9/18/44, EP.
13. Montgomery, *Memoirs,* 250–51.
14. DDE to Marshall, 9/21/44, EP.
15. Morgan, *Past Forgetting,* 240.
16. DDE, *Letters to Mamie,* 210–12.
17. DDE to Montgomery, 9/22/44, EP.
18. Bradley, *Soldier's Story,* 422–23; Pogue, *Supreme Command,* 293–94; Patton, *War As I Knew It,* 120; Irving, *War Between the Generals,* 285.
19. Patton, *War As I Knew It,* 120, 125, 133.
20. DDE to Montgomery, 10/9/44, EP.

21. EP, No. 2032, note 1.
22. DDE to Montgomery, 10/10/44, EP.
23. Interview Sir Frederick Morgan.
24. Lyon, *Eisenhower,* 296.
25. DDE to Montgomery, 10/13/44, EP.
26. EP, No. 2038, note 1; Pogue, *Supreme Command,* 298.
27. MacDonald, *Siegfried Line Campaign,* 220.
28. Pogue, *Supreme Command,* 299–301.
29. Bryant, *Triumph in the West,* 219.
30. DDE to Marshall, 11/11/44, EP.
31. DDE, *Crusade,* 323.
32. DDE to Early, 11/26/44, EP.
33. DDE to Marshall, 11/11/44, EP.
34. DDE, *Letters to Mamie,* 222.
35. DDE to American commanders, 11/6/44, EP.
36. DDE to CCS, 12/3/44, EP.
37. DDE, *Letters to Mamie,* 219–21, 224, 228.
38. *Ibid.,* 218–19.
39. Bryant, *Triumph in the West,* 259.
40. *Ibid.,* 255–60.
41. DDE to Montgomery, 12/1/44, EP.
42. Tedder, *With Prejudice,* 620–23; Montgomery, *Memoirs,* 270–74; Pogue, *Supreme Command,* 316–17; Bryant, *Triumph in the West,* 264–65.
43. Bryant, *Triumph in the West,* 266.
44. DDE, *Letters to Mamie,* 213–14.
45. *Ibid.,* 219–20.
46. *Ibid.,* 216.
47. Wilmot, *Struggle for Europe,* 573–74.
48. DDE to Montgomery, 12/16/44, EP.

Chapter Nineteen

1. Morgan, *Past Forgetting,* 242; Irving, *War Between the Generals,* 338.
2. DDE Diary, 12/23/44; Weigley, *Eisenhower's Lieutenants,* 457–58; Bradley, *Soldier's Story,* 464–65; Pogue, *Supreme Command,* 372–74.
3. Weigley, *Eisenhower's Lieutenants,* 574.
4. DDE to Somervell, 12/17/44, EP.
5. DDE to Bradley, 12/18/44, EP.
6. Bradley, *Soldier's Story,* 470; DDE, *Crusade,* 350.
7. DDE to CCS, 12/19/44, EP; Pogue, *Supreme Command,* 376–77.
8. Bradley, *Soldier's Story,* 476; interview Sir Kenneth Strong; Weigley, *Eisenhower's Lieutenants,* 503.
9. Interview Sir Kenneth Strong; SHAEF office diary, 12/20/44, EL.
10. Bryant, *Triumph in the West,* 272.
11. *Ibid.,* 273.
12. DDE to Marshall, 12/21/44, EP.
13. DDE to Simpson and Hodges, 12/22/44, EP.
14. DDE to CCS, 12/20/44, EP.
15. DDE, *At Ease,* 292.
16. Ambrose, *Supreme Commander,* 561.
17. DDE to Lee and Bradley, 12/19/44, EP.
18. Bradley, *Soldier's Story,* 475–76.
19. Butcher, *My Three Years,* 727–28.

20. *Ibid.*, 728.
21. *Ibid.*
22. EP, No. 2194.
23. Tedder, *With Prejudice*, 629.
24. Bryant, *Triumph in the West*, 278.
25. SHAEF office diary, 12/26/44, EL.
26. *Ibid.*
27. *Ibid.*, 12/27/44.
28. DDE to Montgomery, 12/29/44, EP; DDE, *Crusade*, 360–61; Montgomery, *Memoirs*, 284.
29. Tedder, *With Prejudice*, 631.
30. Interviews with DDE and Sir Arthur Tedder.
31. Tedder, *With Prejudice*, 632–33.
32. Montgomery, *Memoirs*, 284–85.
33. DDE to Bradley and Montgomery, 12/31/44, EP.
34. DDE to Montgomery, 12/31/44, EP.
35. Interview with Freddie de Guingand.
36. de Guingand, *Operation Victory*, 348; Montgomery, *Memoirs*, 286.
37. Montgomery, *Memoirs*, 289.
38. DDE, *Letters to Mamie*, 228.
39. DDE to de Gaulle, 1/3/45, EP.
40. DDE to Marshall, 1/6/45, and to de Gaulle, 1/5/44, EP; DDE, *Crusade*, 362–63.
41. DDE to Marshall, 2/20/44, EP.
42. DDE, *Letters to Mamie*, 228–29.
43. *Ibid.*, 229–30, 242.
44. Pogue, *Supreme Command*, 387–88; Bradley, *Soldier's Story*, 484.
45. Quoted in Irving, *War Between the Generals*, 362.
46. Weigley, *Eisenhower's Lieutenants*, 580–81; Irving, *War Between the Generals*, 384–85.
47. DDE, *Letters to Mamie*, 231–32.
48. DDE to Marshall, 1/15/45, EP.
49. Weigley, *Eisenhower's Lieutenants*, 572, 605.
50. DDE, *Letters to Mamie*, 234–35.
51. DDE to Marshall, 1/15/45, and to Montgomery, 1/17/45, EP; Smith, *Eisenhower's Six Great Decisions*, 125; interview DDE.
52. Ryan, *The Last Battle*, 241.
53. Quoted in Ambrose, *Supreme Commander*, 612.
54. John Eisenhower, *Strictly Personal*, 80; Eisenhower Press Conference, 12/2/1954.
55. DDE, *Letters to Mamie*, 233, 234, 240–41.
56. *Ibid.*, 233; Morgan, *Past Forgetting*, 244–45; John Eisenhower, *Strictly Personal*, 80.
57. DDE to Marshall, 2/20/45, EP.
58. Butcher Diary, 3/27/45.
59. Pogue, *Supreme Command*, 423–29.
60. DDE to Marshall, 3/26/45, EP.

Chapter Twenty

1. Bradley, *Soldier's Story*, 510–12; DDE, *Crusade*, 378–80; Butcher Diary, 3/8/45.
2. DDE to CCS, 3/8/45, EP.
3. Irving, *War Between the Generals*, 392–93; DDE, *Letters to Mamie*, 243–44.

4. Quoted in Irving, *War Between the Generals,* 403.
5. Morgan, *Past Forgetting,* 244–45.
6. DDE, *Letters to Mamie,* 246–47.
7. *Ibid.,* 243–49.
8. DDE to CCS, 3/21/45, EP.
9. Churchill, *Triumph and Tragedy,* 442–43.
10. Wilmot, *Struggle for Europe,* 690.
11. Quoted in Ambrose, *Supreme Commander,* 629–30.
12. Butcher Diary, 3/27/45.
13. Bradley, *Soldier's Story,* 535.
14. Ryan, *The Last Battle,* 241.
15. DDE to Stalin, 3/28/45, EP.
16. The authoritative account is Ziemke, *Stalingrad to Berlin,* 467–99.
17. Bryant, *Triumph in the West,* 336–41.
18. Pogue, *Supreme Command,* 442.
19. DDE to Marshall, 3/30/45, EP.
20. Pogue, *Supreme Command,* 442; Churchill, *Triumph and Tragedy,* 463–65; DDE to Churchill, 3/30/45, EP.
21. DDE to Churchill, 4/1/45, EP.
22. Bryant, *Triumph in the West,* 339.
23. Ambrose, *Supreme Commander,* 639.
24. DDE to Montgomery, 4/8/45, EP, note 1.
25. Quoted in Ambrose, *Eisenhower and Berlin,* 64–65.
26. DDE to Marshall, 4/7/45, EP.
27. Pogue, *Supreme Command,* 448–49.
28. Quoted in Weigley, *Eisenhower's Lieutenants,* 698.
29. DDE to Marshall, 4/15/45, EP.
30. Churchill, *Triumph and Tragedy,* 515–16.
31. Pogue, *Supreme Command,* 468.
32. DDE to Marshall, 4/29/45, EP.
33. DDE to Deane, 4/30 and 5/6/45, EP; Pogue, *Supreme Command,* 469.
34. DDE, *Letters to Mamie,* 248.
35. DDE to Marshall, 4/15/45, EP.
36. Butcher Diary, 5/25/45.
37. DDE, *At Ease,* 264, 268.
38. Pogue, *Supreme Command,* 476–77; DDE to Marshall, 4/27/45, EP.
39. Quoted in Ambrose, *Supreme Commander,* 661.
40. DDE to CCS, 5/2/45, EP.
41. Pogue, *Supreme Command,* 480–83.
42. DDE to CCS, 5/4/45, EP.
43. DDE to CCS, 5/5/45, EP.
44. DDE, *Letters to Mamie,* 250.
45. Pogue, *Supreme Command,* 486–87.
46. Interview Sir Kenneth Strong.
47. Interviews with DDE and Sir Kenneth Strong; Butcher Diary, 5/7/45; DDE to CCS, 5/7/45, EP; Smith, *Eisenhower's Six Great Decisions,* 229; Pogue, *Supreme Command,* 488–89.
48. Marshall to DDE, 5/8/45, EP.

Chapter Twenty-one

1. See DDE to Butcher, 9/27/45, and to Marshall, 10/13/45, EP.
2. DDE, *Crusade,* 444.
3. Morgan, *Past Forgetting,* 250–53; DDE, *Letters to Mamie,* 254.

4. DDE to Churchill, 5/19/45, EP.
5. Butcher Diary, 6/2/45 and 6/13/45; DDE, *At Ease,* 298–300; Morgan, *Past Forgetting,* 257.
6. Butcher Diary, 6/21/45; DDE to Marshall, 6/11 and 6/14/45, EP.
7. Butcher Diary, 6/21/45; *New York Times,* 6/20/45.
8. DDE to Lewis Douglas, 9/11/45, EP.
9. DDE to Marshall, 11/10/45, EP; Neal, *The Eisenhowers,* 224.
10. Butcher Diary, 6/21/45.
11. Lyon, *Eisenhower,* 27.
12. DDE to Allen, 10/28/43, EP.
13. DDE, *Crusade,* 444.
14. DDE to Neill Bailey, 8/1/45, EP.
15. DDE, *Letters to Mamie,* 256.
16. *Ibid.,* 253–54.
17. DDE to Marshall, 6/4/45, EP; Brandon, *Mamie Doud Eisenhower,* 229.
18. Merle Miller, *Plain Speaking,* 339–40.
19. DDE to Marshall, 6/9/45, EP.
20. DDE, *Letters to Mamie,* 259.
21. John Eisenhower, *Strictly Personal,* 113–14.
22. DDE to Harger, 10/31/45, EP; DDE, *Letters to Mamie,* 264–66.
23. DDE, *Letters to Mamie,* 270.
24. DDE to Clay, 11/22/45, EP.
25. DDE to Smith, 12/4/45, EP.
26. DDE to Kay Summersby, 11/22/45, EP.
27. DDE to Kay Summersby, 11/12/47, EP.
28. DDE Diary, 12/2/47.
29. Morgan, *Past Forgetting,* 277.
30. DDE to McKeogh, 11/6/45, EP; Butcher Diary, 7/10/45.
31. DDE to Butcher, 7/31/45, EP.
32. DDE to MSE, 9/11/45, EP.
33. DDE to Butcher, 12/10/45, EP.
34. DDE to MSE, 9/27/45, EP.
35. DDE to Davis, 2/4/46, EP.
36. DDE to Montgomery, 10/9/45, EP.
37. DDE to Schuster, 7/18/45, EP.
38. DDE to MSE, 8/2/45, EP.
39. DDE to Butcher, 9/11/45, EP.
40. DDE to Douglas, 5/27/45, EP.
41. DDE to Butcher, 10/12/45, EP.
42. Butcher Diary, 5/14/45.
43. DDE to Marshall, 5/14/45, and to Bradley and others, 5/14/45, EP.
44. Ruhm von Oppen, *Documents on Germany,* 13–27.
45. DDE to Morgenthau, 10/9/45, EP.
46. See DDE to Patterson, 11/8/45, EP.
47. DDE, *Letters to Mamie,* 209–10.
48. DDE to Cannon, 8/19/47, EP; see also DDE, *Crusade,* 287.
49. DDE to Marshall, 6/2/45, EP.
50. DDE to Patton, 9/11/45, EP.
51. DDE to Marshall, 9/29/45, EP.
52. DDE, *At Ease,* 307.
53. Lyon, *Eisenhower,* 361, has the best account of this press conference.
54. Summersby, *Eisenhower Was My Boss,* 278.
55. DDE to Patton, 9/29/45, EP; John Eisenhower, *Strictly Personal,* 114.
56. Farago, *Patton,* 818; see also Blumenson, *Patton Papers,* II, 782–94.

57. Truscott, *Command Mission,* 508.
58. Zink, *U.S. in Germany,* 150–68.
59. Clay, *Decision in Germany,* 18.
60. DDE, *Mandate,* 312–13; John Eisenhower, *Strictly Personal,* 97.
61. DDE to Harry Vaughan, 7/19/45, especially note 2, EP.
62. DDE, *Letters to Mamie,* 253.
63. DDE to Carlson, 5/12/45, EP.
64. DDE, *Crusade,* 469.
65. DDE to Wallace, 8/28/45, EP.
66. Butcher Diary, 6/15/45; Lyon, *Eisenhower,* 25–26.
67. DDE, *Crusade,* 458–59.
68. DDE to Marshall, 5/8/45, EP.
69. DDE to Deane and Archer, 5/10/45, EP.
70. See DDE to Truman, 9/18/45, EP, especially note 4.
71. DDE to Marshall, 5/17/45, EP.
72. DDE, *Crusade,* 474.
73. DDE to Montgomery, 2/20/47, EP.
74. Butcher Diary, 6/10/45, EP.
75. See DDE to Marshall, 6/15/45, note 1, EP.
76. DDE to Marshall, 8/16/45, EP.
77. DDE, *Crusade,* 461–62.
78. DDE to Harriman, 8/22/45, note 1, EP; DDE to Marshall, 8/29/45, note 1, EP.
79. Quoted in Lyon, *Eisenhower,* 356.
80. DDE to Marshall, 8/27/45, EP.
81. DDE to Clay, 11/8/45, note 9, EP.
82. DDE to Hazlett, 11/27/45, EP.

Chapter Twenty-two

1. See the Louis Galambos introduction to Vol. VI of EP.
2. DDE to John Eisenhower, 12/15/45, EP.
3. DDE to Smith, 12/4/45, EP.
4. McCann, *Man from Abilene,* 131.
5. See for example DDE to Mrs. Murphy, 12/17/45, EP.
6. DDE to Marion Huff, 1/3/46, EP.
7. DDE, *At Ease,* 321.
8. DDE to Wainwright, 6/28/46, EP; DDE Diary, 3/8/47.
9. DDE Diary, 3/8/47.
10. *New York Times,* Feb. 1, 1946.
11. *Ibid.,* 6/19/47.
12. See note 5, DDE to Marsh, 1/14/47, EP.
13. DDE to P. A. Hodgson, 10/30/46, EP.
14. See DDE to Clothier, 1/3/46, EP.
15. DDE to Hold, 8/18/47, EP.
16. See DDE to Hodgson, 11/28/47, EP.
17. DDE to Callaway, 6/14/47, EP.
18. DDE to Marshall, 6/15/46, EP.
19. See DDE to Wallace, 3/26/46, and to Burpee, 3/12/47, EP.
20. DDE to Doud, 8/23/46, and to John Eisenhower, 8/23/46, EP.
21. DDE to Hodgson, 10/30/46, EP.
22. DDE to Hodgson, 10/23/47, EP.
23. DDE to Smith, 12/7/46, EP.

24. DDE to Smith, 12/10/47, EP.
25. DDE to John Eisenhower, 4/23/46, EP.
26. DDE to John Eisenhower, 7/1/46, EP.
27. DDE to John Eisenhower, 1/22/47, EP.
28. See DDE to MacArthur, 12/8/45, EP.
29. See DDE to Patterson, 1/15/46, EP.
30. DDE to MacArthur, 1/28/46, EP.
31. Lyon, *Eisenhower,* 372.
32. See DDE to MacArthur, 5/15/46, EP.
33. DDE to MacArthur, 5/28/46, EP.
34. DDE to MacArthur, 8/28, 9/2 and 10/25/46, EP.
35. Truman, *Memoirs,* Vol. I, *Year of Decisions,* 546–53.
36. DDE, *Mandate,* 81.
37. See DDE to Baruch, 1/5/46, EP.
38. See DDE to Surles, 5/9/46, especially note 3, and DDE to Aurand, 12/26/45, and DDE to Taylor, 7/21/47, EP.
39. See DDE to Rutherford, 6/4/47, note 1, EP.
40. DDE to Truman, 1/30/46, EP.
41. DDE to Hazlett, 7/1/46, EP.
42. Quoted in Neal, *The Eisenhowers,* 241.
43. Quoted in Lyon, *Eisenhower,* 366.
44. DDE to Baruch, 6/14/46, EP.
45. See notes 2 and 3 in *ibid.*
46. DDE to Thompson, 6/25/46, EP.
47. See DDE to Patterson, 6/4/46, note 2, EP.
48. Quoted in Lyon, *Eisenhower,* 365.
49. DDE to Zhukov, 12/6/45, EP.
50. DDE to Zhukov, 1/3/46, EP.
51. DDE to Zhukov, 3/13/46, EP.
52. DDE, *Crusade,* 473; DDE to Smith, 4/11/46, EP.
53. DDE to Boatwright, 2/13/46, note 4, EP.
54. DDE to Patterson, 3/29/46, EP.
55. DDE to Lippmann, 6/5/46, EP.
56. See DDE memo to JCS, 6/7/46, note 3, EP.
57. DDE to Smith, 7/29/46, EP; Bullitt, *The Great Globe Itself,* 69; Ambrose, *Rise to Globalism,* 123.
58. See DDE to Montgomery, 2/20/47, and note 1, EP.
59. DDE to Doud, 8/23/46, EP.
60. See DDE memo to JCS, 4/19/46, and to Norstad, 9/19/46, and to Ridgway, 7/13/46, EP.
61. DDE to Patterson and Forrestal, 3/13/47, EP.
62. DDE to JCS, 5/10/47, EP.
63. DDE Diary, 5/15/47.
64. See DDE memo for Nimitz, 6/29/46, EP.
65. See note 5 in *ibid.*
66. DDE to Ismay, 10/28/46, EP.
67. DDE to Portal, 10/30/46, EP.
68. DDE to Patterson, 2/14/47, EP.
69. DDE to Butcher, 12/26/45, EP.
70. DDE to Ismay, 1/29/46, EP.
71. DDE to Gault, 12/17/45, and to Churchill, 12/18/45, EP.
72. DDE to Montgomery, 2/12/46, EP.
73. DDE to Tedder, 3/4/46, EP.
74. DDE to Montgomery, 2/4/46, EP.

75. DDE to Eade, 2/4/46, EP.
76. DDE to Montgomery, 2/12/46, EP.
77. DDE to Montgomery, 5/23/46, EP.
78. DDE to Smith, 3/18/47, EP.
79. DDE to Pogue, 7/26/46, EP.
80. DDE to Chiefs of Divisions, 11/20/47, EP.
81. DDE to Ismay, 7/13/46, EP.

Chapter Twenty-three

1. DDE to John Eisenhower, 1/22/47, EP.
2. Brandon, *Mamie Doud Eisenhower,* 253.
3. DDE to John Eisenhower, 7/23/47, EP; John Eisenhower, *Strictly Personal,* 128.
4. DDE to Lieberman, 1/17/46, EP.
5. See note 1 in *ibid.*
6. McCann, *Man from Abilene,* 140–41; pre–Press Conference notes, ACW Diary, 9/11/56.
7. DDE to Butcher, 7/10/46, EP.
8. DDE, *At Ease,* 334; DDE to Freeman, 10/28/46, EP.
9. DDE to MSE, 10/16/47, EP.
10. DDE Diary, 11/12/46.
11. See DDE to Carley, 7/10/47, note 3, EP.
12. See DDE to Edgar Eisenhower, 5/17/47, EP.
13. See DDE to Hazlett, note 3, 10/29/47, EP.
14. DDE to John Eisenhower, 8/28/47, EP.
15. DDE to Smith, 9/18/47, EP.
16. DDE to Vanderbilt, 10/29/47, EP.
17. DDE to MSE, 10/16/47, EP.
18. DDE to Price, 10/31/47, EP.
19. See Morgan, *From Hayes to McKinley,* 176.
20. DDE Diary, 12/31/47, EP.
21. DDE to Finder, 1/22/48, and notes; DDE to MacArthur, 2/7/48, EP.
22. DDE to Hazlett, 7/19/47, EP.
23. DDE to MSE, 9/16/47, EP.
24. DDE Diary, 11/12/46.
25. Krock, *Memoirs,* 282–83; DDE to Browning, 1/27/48, EP.
26. DDE to Forrestal, 1/31/48, EP.
27. DDE Diary, 9/16/47.
28. DDE to Smith, 10/29/47, EP.
29. DDE to Smith, 11/28/47, EP.
30. DDE to Doud, 1/31/47, EP.
31. See DDE to Moore, 4/29/47 and 5/16/47, EP.
32. DDE to Houghton, 6/19/47, EP.
33. DDE to MSE, 5/29/47, EP.
34. See DDE to Watson, 6/14/47 and to MSE, same date, EP.
35. DDE to Hutchison, 6/25/47, EP.
36. See DDE to Watson, 11/17/47, EP.
37. DDE to Smith, 7/3/47, EP.
38. DDE to Parkinson, 6/23/47, EP.
39. DDE, *At Ease,* 346–47; Neal, *The Eisenhowers,* 246.
40. DDE Diary, 11/12/46.

41. DDE Diary, 12/15/45.
42. DDE to Hodgson, 10/30/46, EP.
43. DDE to American soldiers, 2/7/48, EP.
44. McCann, *Man from Abilene,* 154–55.
45. DDE to Simon, 7/31/46, EP, note 1.
46. DDE to Nevins, 7/10/47, EP.
47. DDE to Robinson, 12/17/47; to Davies, 12/23/47 and 12/31/47, EP; DDE, *At Ease,* 324–29.
48. DDE to Simon, 1/27/48; DDE to Nevins, 1/3/48, EP.
49. See the introduction to the 1977 Da Capo Press edition of *Crusade in Europe,* written by Manfred Jonas.

Chapter Twenty-Four

1. DDE to Hazlett, 10/6/48, EL.
2. Robinson memo of 4/1/48, and Robinson to Leo Perpen, 6/12/48, Robinson Papers.
3. DDE memo to Harron, 7/5/48, EL; Lyon, *Eisenhower,* 386–87; DDE to E. Lindley, 6/19/48, EL.
4. Interview John Eisenhower.
5. DDE to Truman, 11/18/48, EL.
6. DDE, *At Ease,* 339–41; DDE to Hazlett, 8/12/49, EL.
7. Robinson notes, 10/17/48, Robinson Papers.
8. Ira H. Freeman, "Eisenhower of Columbia," *New York Times Magazine,* 11/7/48.
9. DDE to Drew Middleton, 6/21/48, EL.
10. DDE to Hazlett, 2/24/50, EL.
11. Parmet, *Eisenhower,* 15; Lyon, *Eisenhower,* 383.
12. Kirk interview, EL.
13. John Krout interview, EL.
14. DDE Diary, 4/5/50.
15. Neal, *The Eisenhowers,* 251.
16. Helen King interview, EL.
17. Neal, *The Eisenhowers,* 249–50.
18. DDE to Harry Bullis, 7/10/50, and DDE to Wm. Benton, 12/8/48, EL.
19. DDE to A. Andrews, 9/29/50.
20. See DDE to Douglas Black, 2/19/49, and to Grayson Kirk, 6/13/50, EL.
21. DDE to P. Fleming, 10/15/48, EL.
22. DDE to Bullis, 7/10/50, EL; Freeman, "Eisenhower of Columbia."
23. Lyon, *Eisenhower,* 383.
24. Interview David Donald.
25. Interview John Krout, EL; DDE, *At Ease,* 347–48.
26. DDE to Ed Clark, 4/5/50, EL.
27. John Krout interview, EL; DDE to Churchill, 5/1/50, EL.
28. See DDE to C. M. Malone, 7/10/48, EL.
29. Freeman, "Eisenhower of Columbia."
30. See DDE to Douglas Black, 11/17/48, EL.
31. DDE to Royall, 1/13/49, EL.
32. DDE to Hazlett, 2/24/50, EL.
33. John Krout interview, EL.
34. DDE to Hazlett, 1/27/49, EL; DDE Diary, 1/8/49.
35. DDE Diary, 1/8/49.

36. *Ibid.,* 2/2, 1/8/49.
37. *Ibid.,* 1/7/49; see also DDE to Eberstadt, 9/20/48, and to Forrestal, 11/24/48 and 2/4/48, EL.
38. DDE Diary, 3/19/49.
39. *Ibid.;* DDE to Hap Arnold, 3/14/49, EL.
40. DDE Diary, 6/4/49.
41. *Ibid.,* 10/14/49.
42. Interview DDE; DDE, *At Ease,* 554–55; DDE to Roberts, 5/3/51, EL.
43. DDE, *At Ease,* 358–60.
44. On the issue of sharing the atomic "secret" with the British, see Lilienthal, *The Atomic Energy Years,* 544–48.
45. DDE, *At Ease,* 355.
46. Adams to DDE, 6/21/49, and DDE to Adams, 6/23/49, EL.
47. Whitman Diary, 6/15/54, ACWD.
48. DDE Diary, 7/7/49.
49. Robinson memo, 8/29/49, Robinson Papers.
50. Kelland to Robinson, 9/6/49, and Robinson to Kelland, 9/9/49, Robinson Papers.
51. *New York Times,* 9/6/45; DDE, *Mandate,* 11–12.
52. DDE to Hazlett, 9/12/50, EL.
53. Quoted in Parmet, *Eisenhower,* 36.
54. Kelland to Robinson, 12/11/49, Robinson Papers.
55. Barton to Robinson, 12/9/49, *ibid.*
56. DDE to Paul Carroll, 12/21/49, EL.
57. DDE Diary, 11/3/49.
58. *Ibid.,* 9/27/49.
59. Lyon, *Eisenhower,* 410.
60. See DDE to Wedemeyer, 5/20/50, and to James Black, 5/31/50, EL.
61. DDE Diary, 6/30/50.
62. *Ibid.,* 7/6/50.
63. Schaefer to DDE, 8/26/50, EL.
64. DDE to Schaefer, 8/31/50, and to Robinson, 8/30/50, EL.
65. DDE Diary, 10/28/50.
66. Memo, 7/6/60, DDE Diary series, AWF.
67. DDE Diary, 10/28/50.
68. DDE to Hazlett, 11/1/50, EL.
69. DDE Diary, 10/28/50.
70. *Ibid.,* 11/6/50.
71. *Ibid.,* 12/5/50.
72. *Ibid.,* 3/5/51.
73. DDE, *At Ease,* 371–72; DDE, *Mandate,* 14; DDE to George Marshall, 12/12/50, EL.

Chapter Twenty-five

1. DDE Diary, 1/1/51.
2. *History JCS,* Vol. IV, 221–22.
3. DDE Diary, 6/14/51.
4. *Ibid.,* 4/27/51.
5. *Ibid.,* 6/14/51.
6. *Ibid.,* 3/13/51.
7. DDE, *At Ease,* 366.

8. Lauris Norstad interview, EL.
9. Memo of conversation with Salazar, 1/17/51, EL.
10. Memo of conversation in Copenhagen, 1/12/51, EL.
11. DDE to Selden Chapin, 1/13/51, EL.
12. DDE to Harriman, 1/14/51, EL.
13. Memo of conversation with Pleven, 1/24/51, EL.
14. Memo of conversation with De Gasperi, 1/11/51, EL.
15. Press conference notes, 1/20/51, EL.
16. DDE to Lovett, 9/25/51, EL.
17. Notes, Executive Session, 2/2/51, EL; *New York Times,* 2/2/51; Osgood, *NATO,* 78–79; *History JCS,* Vol. IV, 222–23.
18. DDE, *At Ease,* 373.
19. DDE to Collins, 6/19/51, EL.
20. See DDE to Lodge, 4/4/52, and to Woodruff, 8/27/51, and to McConnell, 6/29/51, and memo of briefing for Senate Foreign Relations Committee, 7/9/51, all in EL.
21. DDE to Lovett, 9/25/51, EL.
22. DDE to Bermingham, 2/28/51, EL.
23. See DDE to Wigglesworth, 7/6/51, and to Marshall, 7/21/51, EL.
24. DDE to Truman, 2/24/51, EL.
25. Andrew Goodpaster interview, EL.
26. DDE Diary, 10/10/51.
27. DDE to Harriman, 6/1/51, EL.
28. DDE to Bradley, 3/30/51, EL.
29. DDE to Lovett, 9/25/51, EL.
30. Eisenhower address text, 6/6/51, EL.
31. Memo of conversation with Chaban-Delmas, 3/20/51, EL.
32. DDE Diary, 3/17/51.
33. DDE to Paley, 3/29/52, EL.
34. Quoted in *History JCS,* Vol. IV, 195.
35. DDE to Marshall, 8/3/51, EL.
36. *Ibid.*
37. DDE Diary, 6/11/51; DDE to Harriman, 6/30/51, EL.
38. DDE to Pleven, 12/24/51, EL.
39. Robinson notes on Eisenhower speech, Robinson Papers; *New York Times,* 7/4/41; Churchill to DDE, 7/5/51, EL.
40. DDE to Harriman, 3/11/52, EL.
41. Memo of conversation with Juin, 3/29/52, EL.
42. DDE to Robinson, 7/12/51; to Tom Watson, 8/25/51; to Hoyt Vandenberg, 10/5/51, and to Cliff Roberts, 9/27/51, all in EL.
43. DDE to John Eisenhower, 9/27/51, EL.
44. DDE to Hazlett, 9/4/51, EL.
45. DDE to Robinson, 2/16/51, Robinson Papers.
46. Robinson to DDE, 3/13/51, Robinson Papers.
47. See DDE to Bermingham, 2/28/51, and to Robinson, 3/6/51, and to Fred Gurley, 9/22/51, all in EL.
48. DDE to Robinson, 10/19/51, Robinson Papers.
49. Clay to DDE, 4/13/51, EL.
50. DDE to Clay, 4/16/51, EL.
51. DDE to MacArthur, 5/15/51, and MacArthur to DDE, 5/18/51, EL.
52. DDE to Schaefer, 12/27/51, EL.
53. See for example DDE to L. C. Stevens, 2/22/51, and to Tom Campbell, 9/1/51, EL.

54. DDE to Hughes, 11/26/40, EL.
55. See Herken, *The Winning Weapon.*
56. DDE to Paul Hoffman, 8/28/51, EL.
57. DDE Diary, 1/22/52.
58. DDE to Wilson, 10/20/51, EL.
59. Memos to Gruenther, 3/23/51 and 9/26/51; DDE to Clark, 10/8/51, EL.
60. DDE to Bermingham, 2/28/51, EL.
61. DDE to Sloan, 1/29/52, EL.
62. DDE to Clement, 12/4/51, EL.
63. See DDE to Whitney, 3/2/51, and to Hoffman, 10/4/51, EL.
64. DDE to Whitney, 11/24/51, EL.
65. DDE to Hoffman, 1/24/52, EL.
66. DDE to Swope, 4/20/51, EL.
67. DDE to McCarthy, 3/15/51, EL.
68. See Nixon to DDE, 1/17/52, EL.
69. DDE to Bert Andrews, 8/31/51, EL.
70. Krock, *In the Nation,* 194–95; Krock, *Memoirs,* 267–69. When Arthur Krock broke the story in *The New York Times,* both Eisenhower and Truman denied it. Eisenhower wrote Arthur Sulzberger a private denial, but did not send the letter. See DDE to Sulzberger, 1/10/51, EL. In his *Memoirs,* Krock revealed that Justice William O. Douglas was his source and that Eisenhower later "obliquely" confirmed the story.
71. DDE Diary, 9/25/51.
72. Gunther, *Eisenhower,* 137–38.
73. DDE to Clay, 5/30/51, EL.
74. DDE, *Mandate,* 18.
75. Clay to DDE, 9/29/51, EL.
76. DDE to Clay, 10/3/51, EL.
77. Smith, *Dewey,* 579.
78. New York *Herald Tribune,* 10/25/51; Robinson to DDE, 10/26/51, Robinson Papers.
79. DDE to Robinson, 10/31/51, Robinson Papers.
80. See DDE to Duff, 11/13/51, to Leithead, 11/8/51, to Robinson, 11/8/51, to Milton Eisenhower, 11/20/51, and Robinson to DDE, 11/15/51, all in EL.
81. Lyon, *Eisenhower,* 430.
82. DDE to Richardson, 6/20/51, EL.
83. DDE to Robinson, 11/24/51, Robinson Papers.
84. DDE Diary, 11/9/51.
85. DDE to Richardson, 11/8/51 and 12/26/51, EL.
86. Clay to DDE, 12/7/51, EL.
87. Hoffman to DDE, 12/5/51, EL.
88. Aldrich to DDE, 11/26/51, EL.
89. DDE Diary, 10/29/51.
90. DDE to Cliff Roberts, 12/8/51, and to Bill Burnham, 12/11/51, EL.
91. DDE to Lodge, 12/12/51, EL; DDE Diary, 12/11/51.
92. Clay to DDE, 12/21/51, EL.
93. DDE to Clay, 12/27/51, EL.
94. Lyon, *Eisenhower,* 430.
95. Robinson Memo, 12/29/51, Robinson Papers.
96. DDE to Truman, 1/1/52, EL; see also DDE, *Mandate,* 18–19.
97. DDE to Truman, 1/23/52, and Truman to DDE, 1/31/52, EL.
98. *New York Times,* 1/7/52.

99. DDE to Roberts, 1/11/52, EL.
100. DDE to Clay, 1/8/52, EL.
101. *New York Times,* 1/8/52.
102. Clay to DDE, 1/16/52, EL.
103. Slater to Robinson, 1/23/52, Robinson Papers.
104. DDE to Clay, 1/28/52, EL.
105. DDE to Hoffman, 2/9/52, EL.
106. DDE to Robinson, 1/19/52, EL.
107. DDE to Clay, 2/9/52, EL.
108. Jacqueline Cochran interview, EL.
109. DDE to Hazlett, 2/12/52, EL.
110. DDE to Reed, 2/12/52, EL.
111. Don Cook notes on Clay/Eisenhower meeting, 2/17/52, Robinson Papers.
112. Parmet, *Eisenhower,* 54–55.
113. Sulzberger, *Candles,* 752.
114. DDE to Clay, 3/28/52, EL.
115. DDE to Robinson, 11/24/51, EL.
116. DDE to Sloan, 2/21/52, EL.
117. See DDE to McKeldin, 3/26/52, to Brownell, 3/18/52, to Pearson, 3/27/52, to Porter, 3/28/52, to Odlum, 2/29/52, all in EL.
118. See DDE to Aksel Nielsen, 4/3/52, EL.
119. DDE to Dulles, 4/15/52, EL.
120. Smith, *Dewey,* 583.
121. DDE to Roberts, 4/4/52, EL.
122. SACEUR's First Annual Report, April, 1952, EL.
123. DDE to Truman, 4/2/52, EL.
124. Truman to DDE, 4/6/52, EL.
125. DDE to Milton Eisenhower, 4/4/52, EL.
126. DDE to Clay, 5/20/52, EL.
127. DDE to Lodge, 5/20/52, EL.
128. DDE to Roberts, 5/19/52, EL.
129. DDE to Clay, 2/20/52, EL.
130. Brooke to DDE, 5/17/52, EL.

Chapter Twenty-six

1. Lyon, *Eisenhower,* 439.
2. Parmet, *Eisenhower,* 57.
3. DDE to Gerow, 6/28/52, WHCF P.I.
4. *New York Times,* 6/5/52; DDE, *Mandate,* 33.
5. *New York Times,* 6/6/52.
6. *Ibid.*
7. DDE to Gruenther, 6/19/52, EL.
8. Merriman Smith interview, EL.
9. *New York Times,* 6/14/52; Parmet, *Eisenhower,* 64–65.
10. Sherman Adams interivew, EL.
11. *New York Times,* 6/15/52.
12. Robinson to DDE, 6/19/52, Robinson Papers.
13. *New York Times,* 6/19/52.
14. DDE to Roberts, 6/19/52, EL.
15. Robinson to DDE, 6/19/52, Robinson Papers.
16. Parmet, *Eisenhower,* 96.

17. *New York Times,* 6/27/52.
18. See DDE to Waldmire, 6/24/52, WHCF P.I.; *New York Times,* 6/17/52.
19. Parmet, *Eisenhower,* 76–77.
20. DDE, *Mandate,* 39.
21. Smith, *Dewey,* 587.
22. *New York Times,* 7/3/52.
23. Smith, *Dewey,* 595.
24. Parmet, *Eisenhower,* 92.
25. *New York Times,* 7/3/52.
26. Smith, *Dewey,* 596.
27. *New York Times,* 7/3/52; Parmet, *Eisenhower,* 73–82.
28. Parmet, *Eisenhower,* 88.
29. *New York Times,* 7/5/52.
30. *Ibid.*
31. Smith, *Dewey,* 589.
32. *Ibid.,* 592–93.
33. DDE, *Mandate,* 43–44.
34. Reeves, *McCarthy,* 426.
35. Smith, *Dewey,* 593.
36. DDE, *Mandate,* 44.
37. Parmet, *Eisenhower,* 99–100; Smith, *Dewey,* 594.
38. DDE, *Mandate,* 45.
39. *Ibid.,* 46; Smith, *Dewey,* 596–97; Parmet, *Eisenhower,* 100.
40. Nixon, *Memoirs,* 87; Milton Eisenhower, *The President Is Calling,* 249–50.
41. Parmet, *Eisenhower,* 97–98; Theoharis, *Yalta Myths,* 143–45.
42. Parmet, *Eisenhower,* 101; Nixon, *Memoirs,* 90.
43. DDE, *Mandate,* 48–49; John Eisenhower, *Strictly Personal,* 134.
44. Marshall to DDE, 7/12/52, and DDE to Marshall, 7/17/52, AWNS.
45. DDE to Hoffman, 7/17/52, WHCF, P.I.
46. DDE, *Mandate,* 49–50.
47. *Ibid.,* 54–55.
48. *Ibid.*
49. Adams, *Firsthand Report,* 20.
50. Slater, *The Ike I Knew,* 23–24.
51. Reeves, *McCarthy,* 436.
52. Theoharis, *Yalta Myths,* 145.
53. *New York Times,* 8/25/52.
54. DDE to Dulles, 4/15/52, EL.
55. DDE to Dulles, 6/25/52, EL.
56. *New York Times,* 8/26/52 and 8/27/52.
57. Interview DDE.
58. Reeves, *McCarthy,* 436–37.
59. DDE to Truman, 8/14/52, and Truman to DDE, 8/16/52, AWNS.
60. DDE to Collins, 8/5/52, WHCF P.I.

Chapter Twenty-seven

1. Memo, DDE to Adams, 8/27/52, AWNS.
2. Hughes, *Ordeal,* 24–25.
3. *Ibid.,* 22.
4. DDE, *Mandate,* 58–59.
5. Parmet, *Eisenhower,* 117.

6. DDE, *Mandate,* 63.
7. Parmet, *Eisenhower,* 127–28; *New York Times,* 9/10/52; Hughes, *Ordeal,* 41.
8. *New York Times,* 9/11/52.
9. Lyon, *Eisenhower,* 449.
10. *New York Times,* 9/13/52.
11. Martin, *Stevenson,* 683.
12. New York *Herald Tribune,* 9/20/52.
13. Adams interview, COHP.
14. Ewald, *Eisenhower,* 49.
15. *Ibid.,* 51; DDE, *Mandate,* 66.
16. DDE to Nixon, draft, 9/19/52, AWNS.
17. DDE, *Mandate,* 66.
18. Nixon, *Memoirs,* 96.
19. DDE to Robinson, 9/20/52, AWNS.
20. Robinson to DDE, 9/22/52, Robinson Papers.
21. Nixon, *Memoirs,* 96.
22. *Ibid.,* 97.
23. Ewald, *Eisenhower,* 51–52.
24. Nixon, *Memoirs,* 97–98.
25. Ewald, *Eisenhower,* 55.
26. Nixon, *Memoirs,* 105–6.
27. DDE, *Mandate,* 69.
28. Ewald, *Eisenhower,* 56–57.
29. Nixon, *Memoirs,* 106.
30. DDE to Earle, 9/2/52, EL.
31. *New York Times,* 10/6/52.
32. Hughes, *Ordeal,* 41–42.
33. Ewald, *Eisenhower,* 60.
34. *New York Times,* 10/3/52; Bischof, "Before the Break," 72.
35. DDE, *Mandate,* 318–19; Ewald, *Eisenhower,* 61; Bischof, "Before the Break," 73; Reeves, *McCarthy,* 438; Adams interview, COHP.
36. *New York Times,* 10/4/52.
37. *Ibid.* Bernhard Shanley Diary, EL; Kohler interview, COHP; Bischof, "Before the Break," 74.
38. Adams interview, COHP.
39. See for example Ewald's treatment in *Eisenhower,* 62–63, and the Adams interview, COHP.
40. Griffith, "The General and the Senator," 27.
41. *New York Times,* 10/4/52.
42. *New York Times,* 10/4/52; Parmet, *Eisenhower,* 133; Bischof, "Before the Break," 75–76; Reeves, *McCarthy,* 440.
43. DDE to Stassen, 10/5/52, AWNS.
44. DDE, *Mandate,* 318.
45. Martin, *Stevenson,* 713.
46. All quotations are taken from the file Political Campaign Series, Political Speeches, 1952, in AWF.
47. Martin, *Stevenson,* 741.
48. DDE, *Mandate,* 73.
49. Slater, *The Ike I Knew,* 27.
50. DDE interview; Hughes, *Ordeal,* 46.
51. DDE, *Mandate,* 75.

ACKNOWLEDGMENTS

My debts are deep. My agent, John Ware, has provided support and encouragement throughout the process of writing this book, and indeed for a decade before I began the writing. Alice Mayhew of Simon and Schuster gave me badly needed assistance at a critical moment in the writing. The library staff and the Department of Modern History at University College, Dublin, where I spent the academic year of 1981–1982, provided essential help. My chairman at the University of New Orleans, Joseph Logsdon, read the entire manuscript with his unexcelled critical eye, forcing me to rethink many conclusions and to rewrite entire sections. Although he is one of my dearest friends, Joe is my sternest critic, and his contribution to this volume is invaluable. Dr. Julian Pleasants of the University of Florida read the early chapters and provided me with innumerable suggestions. The staff of the library at the University of New Orleans was unflagging in its support of my research. I am grateful to all of Eisenhower's associates who granted me interviews; special thanks are due to Milton and John Eisenhower for giving me fully and freely of their time and knowledge.

The director of the Eisenhower Library in Abilene, Kansas, Dr. John Wickman, and his staff—especially Rod Soubers, Martin Teasley, Hazel Hartman, Jim Leyerzapf, and David Haight—were the *sine qua non* of this effort. The library is a model of presidential libraries. The research room is an ideal place to work; the millions of documents are superbly organized; the staff is thoroughly familiar with the thousands of files, eager to help the researcher, anxious to obtain clearance of classified material, outstanding in its preparation of finding aids, and invaluable in guiding the researcher to the right documents. As a bonus, the staff is both a friendly one and has a real sense of being part of a team (Dwight Eisenhower, who emphasized the importance of teamwork from his pre-teen-age years to his death, would have liked that). Not only in the research room, but at coffee breaks, lunches, and social occasions after closing hours, the people at the Eisenhower Library made my many trips to Abilene memorably pleasant occasions.

Elizabeth Smith joined me in Abilene to go through the documents and to select from them the ones that had to be Xeroxed and brought back to my writing desk in New Orleans (some fifteen thousand copies for the period 1948 to 1953 alone). Betty, who began her work on Eisenhower as a secretary at the Eisenhower Project at Johns Hopkins University in the early 1960s under the then editor Alfred D. Chandler, Jr., and who became an associate editor of the Eisenhower Papers in the 1970s under editor Louis Galambos, is one of Eisenhower's greatest fans and highly knowledgeable about the man. She is also an old and close friend. As a labor of love (she refused compensation) she typed the entire manuscript for me. My thanks to her are heartfelt, sincere, and entirely inadequate.

My wife, Moira Buckley Ambrose, has lived with me—and Eisenhower—for almost two decades. She does more than put up with us. She listens as I read aloud to her each chapter when the first draft is finished. She provides suggestions that are almost invariably adopted. She loves Ike as I do, and her enthusiasm for the man helps keep my own enthusiasm high. She is a gifted teacher of learning-disabled children in the New Orleans high-school system, a most taxing and nerve-racking job, and is also the mother of five children. She deserves her vacations. But she gives them up to come to Abilene with me to spend eight hours a day, six days a deek, week after week, sitting at a desk in the research room, poring over the documents, interviews, and photographs, making selections. No man could ask for more, but in addition to all this she spoils me shamelessly, both in running the house to satisfy my needs and whims, and in bolstering my ego and self-confidence when necessary (almost daily). Without Moira's support, encouragement, strength, and love, I could not possibly have written this book.

STEPHEN E. AMBROSE

Innsbruck, Austria (June–September 1981)
Dublin, Ireland (October 1981–May 1982)
Abilene, Kansas (June–August 1982)
New Orleans, Louisiana (September–December 1982)

BIBLIOGRAPHY

The vast majority of citations are to Eisenhower's own writings, and come from two basic sources. The first is *The Papers of Dwight David Eisenhower*, published in nine volumes to date, covering the period December 1941 to February 1948. Quotations taken from these volumes are cited by date, as they appear chronologically in the Papers, which are identified as EP. The second source is the Eisenhower Papers at the Eisenhower Library in Abilene, Kansas. There is a bewildering array of boxes, files, and collections within the Eisenhower Papers, but the overwhelming majority used for this work come from one file, identified by the staff of the library as the "1652" file (because it covers the period 1916–1952). Citations to quotations from that file are listed as EL (for Eisenhower Library).

Additional Manuscript Collections

Bristow Papers, Kansas Historical Society, Topeka
Harry Butcher Diary, EL
Eisenhower Diary Series, EL
Sir Ian Jacob Diary, author's possession
William Robinson Papers, EL
SHAEF Office Diary, EL
Bernhard Shanley Diary, EL
Ann Whitman Diary, EL
Ann Whitman File, EL (AWF)
Ann Whitman Name Series, EL (AWNS)
Ann C. Whitman Diary file (ACWD)
White House Central File, Pre-Inaugural, EL (WHCF, P.I.)

Interviews by the Author

Omar Bradley; Sir Francis de Guingand; David Donald; Dwight D. Eisenhower; John S. D. Eisenhower; Milton S. Eisenhower; Andrew Goodpaster;

Sir Ian Jacob; Sir Frederick Morgan; Forrest Pogue; Thor Smith; Sir Kenneth Strong; Sir Arthur Tedder.

INTERVIEWS BY THE STAFF OF THE EISENHOWER LIBRARY

Sherman Adams; Helen King; Grayson Kirk; John Krout; Merriman Smith.

INTERVIEWS BY THE COLUMBIA ORAL HISTORY PROJECT (COHP)

Sherman Adams, Walter Kohler.

LIST OF PUBLISHED WORKS CITED

Adams, Sherman. *Firsthand Report: The Story of the Eisenhower Administration*. New York: Harper & Bros., 1961.
Ambrose, Stephen E. *Duty, Honor, Country: A History of West Point*. Baltimore: Johns Hopkins Press, 1966.
———. *Eisenhower and Berlin, 1945: The Decision to Halt at the Elbe*. New York: W. W. Norton & Co., 1967.
———. *Ike's Spies: Eisenhower and the Espionage Establishment*. Garden City, N.Y.: Doubleday & Co., 1981.
———. *Rise to Globalism: American Foreign Policy Since 1938*. New York: Penguin, 1972.
———. *The Supreme Commander: The War Years of General Dwight D. Eisenhower*. Garden City, N.Y.: Doubleday & Co., 1970.
Baldwin, Hanson. *Battles Lost and Won: Great Campaigns of World War II*. New York: Harper & Row, 1966.
Bischof, Guenter. "Before the Break: The Relationship Between Eisenhower and McCarthy, 1952–1953." Unpublished thesis, University of New Orleans.
Blumenson, Martin. *Breakout and Pursuit*. Washington: U.S. Department of the Army, 1961.
———. *Kasserine Pass*. Boston: Houghton Mifflin Co., 1967.
———. *The Patton Papers*. 2 vols. Boston: Houghton Mifflin Co., 1972, 1974.
Bradley, Omar. *A Soldier's Story*. New York: Henry Holt and Co., 1951.
Brandon, Dorothy. *Mamie Doud Eisenhower*. New York: Charles Scribner's Sons, 1954.
Brereton, Lewis H. *The Brereton Diaries*. New York: William Morrow and Co., 1946.
Bryant, Sir Arthur. *Triumph in the West*. London: Collins, 1959.
———. *The Turn of the Tide*. New York: Doubleday & Co., 1957.
Bullitt, William C. *The Great Globe Itself: A Preface to World Affairs*. New York: Charles Scribner's Sons, 1946.
Butcher, Harry. *My Three Years with Eisenhower*. New York: Simon and Schuster, 1946.
Churchill, Winston S. *The Second World War* (especially *The Hinge of Fate*, *Closing the Ring*, and *Triumph and Tragedy*). Boston: Houghton Mifflin Co., 1948–1953.
Clark, Mark Wayne. *Calculated Risk*. New York: Harper & Bros., 1950.
Clay, Lucius D. *Decision in Germany*. New York: Doubleday & Co., 1950.
Cunningham of Hyndhope, Viscount. *A Sailor's Odyssey*. London: Hutchinson & Co., 1951.
Davis, Kenneth S. *Soldier of Democracy: A Biography of Dwight Eisenhower*. Garden City, N.Y.: Doubleday, Doran & Co., 1945.

de Gaulle, Charles. *The War Memoirs of Charles de Gaulle,* Vol. II, *Unity.* New York: Simon and Schuster, 1959.

de Guingand, Sir Francis. *Operation Victory.* New York: Charles Scribner's Sons, 1947.

Eisenhower, Dwight D. *At Ease: Stories I Tell to Friends.* Garden City, N.Y.: Doubleday & Co., 1967.

———. *Crusade in Europe.* Garden City, N.Y.: Doubleday & Co., 1948.

———. *Letters to Mamie,* ed. John S. D. Eisenhower. Garden City, N.Y.: Doubleday & Co., 1978.

———. *Mandate for Change.* Garden City, N.Y.: Doubleday & Co., 1963.

———. *The Papers of Dwight David Eisenhower* (Vols. I through V edited by Alfred D. Chandler, Jr., *et al.;* Vols. VI through IX edited by Louis Galambos, *et al.*). Baltimore: Johns Hopkins University Press, 1970, 1978.

———. "A Tank Discussion." *Infantry Journal,* Nov. 1920.

———. "War Policies." *Cavalry Journal,* Nov.–Dec. 1931.

Eisenhower, John S. D. *Strictly Personal.* Garden City, N.Y.: Doubleday & Co., 1974.

Eisenhower, Milton S. *The President Is Calling.* Garden City, N.Y.: Doubleday & Co., 1974.

Ewald, William Bragg, Jr. *Eisenhower the President.* Englewood Cliffs, N.J.: Prentice-Hall, 1981.

Farago, Ladislas. *Patton: Ordeal and Triumph.* New York: Astor-Honor, Inc., 1964.

Feis, Herbert. *Churchill, Roosevelt, Stalin: The War They Waged and the Peace They Sought.* Princeton: Princeton University Press, 1957.

Ferrell, Robert H., ed. *The Eisenhower Diaries.* New York: W. W. Norton & Co., 1981.

Freeman, Ira H. "Eisenhower of Columbia." *New York Times Magazine,* Nov. 7, 1948.

Funk, Arthur. *Charles de Gaulle: The Crucial Years, 1943–1944.* Norman, Okla.: University of Oklahoma Press, 1959.

———. *The Politics of Torch.* Lawrence, Kans.: The University Press of Kansas, 1974.

Garland, Albert N., and Howard McGaw Smyth. *Sicily and the Surrender of Italy.* Washington: U.S. Department of the Army, 1965.

Griffith, Robert. "The General and the Senator." *Wisconsin Magazine of History,* Autumn 1970.

Gunther, John. *Eisenhower: The Man and the Symbol.* New York: Harper & Bros., 1952.

Harrison, Gordon A. *Cross-Channel Attack.* Washington: U.S. Department of the Army, 1951.

Hatch, Alden. *Red Carpet for Mamie.* New York: Henry Holt and Co., 1954.

Herken, Gregg F. *The Winning Weapon.* New York: Knopf, 1981.

History of the Joint Chiefs of Staff, 4 vols. Washington: Government Printing Office, 1982.

Hughes, Emmet John. *The Ordeal of Power.* New York: Atheneum, 1963.

Huntington, Samuel. *The Soldier and the State.* Cambridge, Mass.: Harvard University Press, 1957.

Irving, David. *The War Between the Generals.* New York: Congdon & Lattès, 1981.

Ismay, Hastings L. *The Memoirs of General Lord Ismay.* New York: Viking Press, 1960.

Jackson, W. G. F. *The North African Campaign, 1940–1943.* London: Batsford, 1975.

James, D. Clayton. *The Years of MacArthur,* Vol. I, 1880–1941. Boston: Houghton Mifflin, 1970.

Kornitzer, Bela. *The Great American Heritage: The Story of the Five Eisenhower Brothers.* New York: Farrar, Straus and Cudahy, 1955.

Krock, Arthur. *In the Nation: 1932–1966.* New York: McGraw-Hill, 1966.

———. *Memoirs: Sixty Years on the Firing Line.* New York: Funk & Wagnalls, 1968.

Lilienthal, David E. *The Journals of David E. Lilienthal,* Vol. II, *The Atomic Energy Years, 1945–1950.* New York: Harper & Row, 1964.

Loewenheim, Francis, Harold Langley, and Manfred Jonas, eds. *Roosevelt and Churchill: Their Secret Wartime Correspondence.* London: Barrie & Jenkins, 1975.

Lyon, Peter. *Eisenhower: Portrait of the Hero.* Boston: Little, Brown and Co., 1974.

MacArthur, Douglas. *Reminiscences.* New York: McGraw-Hill, 1964.

MacDonald, Charles. *Siegfried Line Campaign.* Washington: U.S. Department of the Army, 1963.

Macmillan, Harold. *The Blast of War: 1939–1945.* New York: Harper & Row, 1968.

Martin, John Bartlow. *Adlai Stevenson of Illinois.* Garden City, N.Y.: Doubleday & Co., 1976.

McCann, Kevin. *Man from Abilene.* Garden City, N.Y.: Doubleday & Co., 1952.

McKeogh, Michael, and Richard Lockridge. *Sergeant Mickey and General Ike.* New York: G. P. Putnam's Sons, 1946.

Miller, Francis Trevelyan. *Eisenhower: Man and Soldier.* Philadelphia: John C. Winston Co., 1944.

Miller, Merle. *Plain Speaking: An Oral Biography of Harry S. Truman.* New York: Berkley Publishing Corp., 1973.

Montgomery, Bernard Law. *Memoirs.* Cleveland: World Publishing Co., 1958.

Morgan, H. Wayne. *From Hayes to McKinley.* Syracuse: Syracuse University Press, 1969.

Morgan, Kay Summersby. *Past Forgetting: My Love Affair with Dwight D. Eisenhower.* New York: Simon & Schuster, 1976.

Murphy, Robert. *Diplomat Among Warriors.* Garden City, N.Y.: Doubleday & Co., 1964.

Neal, Steve. *The Eisenhowers: Reluctant Dynasty.* Garden City, N.Y.: Doubleday and Co., 1978.

Nixon, Richard. *Memoirs.* New York: Grosset & Dunlap, 1978.

Osgood, Robert E. *NATO: The Entangling Alliance.* Chicago: University of Chicago Press, 1962.

Parmet, Herbert S. *Eisenhower and the American Crusades.* New York: Macmillan Co., 1972.

Patton, George S., Jr. *War As I Knew It.* Boston: Houghton Mifflin Co., 1947.

Pogue, Forrest C. *George C. Marshall: Ordeal and Hope, 1939–1942.* New York: Viking Press, 1966.

———. *George C. Marshall: Organizer of Victory, 1943–1945.* New York: Viking Press, 1973.

———. *The Supreme Command.* Washington: U.S. Department of the Army, 1954.

Reeves, Thomas C. *The Life and Times of Joe McCarthy.* New York: Stein and Day, 1982.

Ruhm von Oppen, Beate, ed. *Documents on Germany Under Occupation.* London: Oxford University Press, 1955.

Ryan, Cornelius. *The Last Battle.* New York: Simon and Schuster, 1966.

Salmon, E. Dwight. *History of Allied Force Headquarters* (internal Army study). Lithograph copy in author's possession.

Slater, Ellis D. *The Ike I Knew*. N.P., 1980.

Smith, Richard Norton. *Thomas E. Dewey and His Times*. New York: Simon and Schuster, 1982.

Smith, Walter B. *Eisenhower's Six Great Decisions*. New York: Longmans, Green and Co., 1956.

Sulzberger, C. L. *A Long Row of Candles*. New York: Macmillan, 1969.

Summersby, Kay. *Eisenhower Was My Boss*. New York: Prentice-Hall, 1948.

Tedder, Sir Arthur. *With Prejudice*. London: Cassell, 1966.

Theoharis, Athan G. *The Yalta Myths: An Issue in U.S. Politics, 1945–1955*. Columbia, Mo.: University of Missouri Press, 1970.

Truman, Harry S. *Memoirs*, Vol. I, *Year of Decisions*. Garden City, N.Y.: Doubleday & Co., 1955.

Truscott, Lucian K., Jr. *Command Missions*. New York: E. P. Dutton and Co., 1954.

Viorst, Milton. *Hostile Allies: FDR and Charles de Gaulle*. New York: Macmillan Co., 1965.

Wedemeyer, Albert C. *Wedemeyer Reports!* New York: Henry Holt & Co., 1958.

Weigley, Russell. *Eisenhower's Lieutenants: The Campaign of France and Germany*. Bloomington, Ind.: Indiana University Press, 1981.

———. *History of the United States Army*. New York: Macmillan Co., 1967.

White, Dorothy Shipley. *Seeds of Discord: De Gaulle, Free France and the Allies*. Syracuse, N.Y.: Syracuse University Press, 1964.

Wilmot, Chester. *Struggle for Europe*. New York: Harper, 1952.

Wilt, Alan F. *The Atlantic Wall: Hitler's Defenses in the West 1941–1944*. Ames, Iowa: The Iowa State University Press, 1975.

Ziemke, Earl F. *Stalingrad to Berlin: The German Defeat in the East*. Washington: U.S. Department of the Army, 1968.

Zink, Harold. *The United States in Germany, 1944–1955*. Princeton, N.J.: D. Van Nostrand Co., 1957.

INDEX

ABOUT THE AUTHOR

STEPHEN E. AMBROSE is currently a professor of history at the University of New Orleans. He was awarded a Ph.D. from the University of Wisconsin and has taught at L.S.U., Johns Hopkins University, and the Naval War College, and was the Dwight D. Eisenhower Professor of War and Peace, Kansas State University. Ambrose was the associate editor of the Eisenhower Papers and has written articles for numerous scholarly journals as well as a biweekly column on foreign and military affairs for the *Baltimore Evening Sun*.

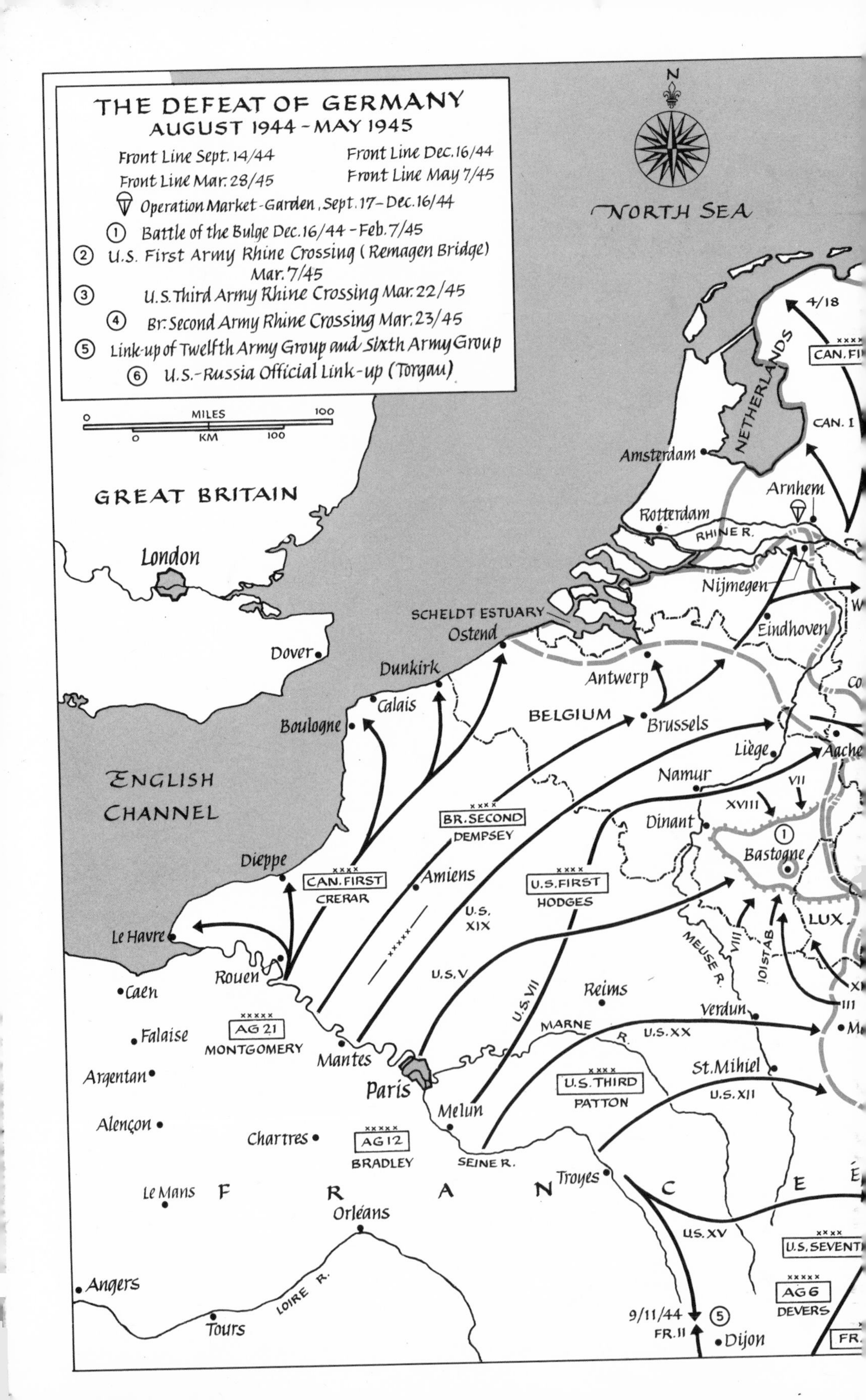

THE DEFEAT OF GERMANY
AUGUST 1944 – MAY 1945
Front Line Sept. 14/44
Front Line Dec. 16/44
Front Line Mar. 28/45
Front Line May 7/45
Operation Market-Garden, Sept. 17–Dec. 16/44
① Battle of the Bulge Dec. 16/44 – Feb. 7/45
② U.S. First Army Rhine Crossing (Remagen Bridge) Mar. 7/45
③ U.S. Third Army Rhine Crossing Mar. 22/45
④ Br. Second Army Rhine Crossing Mar. 23/45
⑤ Link-up of Twelfth Army Group and Sixth Army Group
⑥ U.S.-Russia Official Link-up (Torgau)
MILES
0
100
KM
0
100
N
NORTH SEA
GREAT BRITAIN
London
ENGLISH CHANNEL
Dover
Ostend
SCHELDT ESTUARY
Dunkirk
Calais
Boulogne
Dieppe
Le Havre
Rouen
Caen
Falaise
Argentan
Alençon
Le Mans
Angers
Tours
LOIRE R.
Orléans
Chartres
Mantes
Paris
Melun
SEINE R.
Troyes
Dijon
Reims
MARNE R.
Verdun
St. Mihiel
Amiens
Brussels
Antwerp
BELGIUM
Liège
Namur
Dinant
Bastogne
LUX.
MEUSE R.
Aache
Eindhoven
Nijmegen
Arnhem
RHINE R.
Rotterdam
Amsterdam
NETHERLANDS
4/18
CAN. FI
CAN. I
F R A N C E
AG 21
MONTGOMERY
CAN. FIRST
CRERAR
BR. SECOND
DEMPSEY
U.S. FIRST
HODGES
U.S. XIX
U.S. V
U.S. VII
AG 12
BRADLEY
U.S. THIRD
PATTON
U.S. XX
U.S. XII
U.S. XV
U.S. SEVENT
AG 6
DEVERS
VII
XVIII
VIII
101 STAB
9/11/44
FR. II
FR.